Comparative Economic Systems

Jan S. Prybyla, *Editor*
The Pennsylvania State University

Comparative Economic Systems

APPLETON-CENTURY-CROFTS
EDUCATIONAL DIVISION
New York MEREDITH CORPORATION

Contributors

Adrian A. Basora
Specialist in Latin American economic and political studies

Elliot J. Berg
Professor of Economics, University of Michigan

Morris Bornstein
Professor of Economics, University of Michigan

Michael E. Bradley
Assistant Professor of Economics, The Pensylvania State University

Andrzej Brzeski
Associate Professor of Economics, University of California, Davis

Neil W. Chamberlain
Professor of Business, Columbia University

R. W. Davies
Professor of Soviet Economic Studies, Director, Centre for Russian and East European Studies, University of Birmingham (England)

Peter Donaldson
Visiting Reader in Economics, Osmania University, Hyderabad (India); Lecturer in the Department of Economics, Leicester University (England), 1959-62

Mieczysław Falkowski
Chief, Economic Books Department, Polish Scientific Publishers, Warsaw (Poland)

John Kenneth Galbraith
Paul M. Warburg Professor of Economics, Harvard University

Alvin II. Hansen
Lucius N. Littauer Professor of Political Economy, Emeritus, Harvard University

Karl Jungenfelt
Associate Professor, University of Stockholm (Sweden)

Joungwon Alexander Kim
Assistant Professor of Political Science, Hobart and William Smith Colleges, New York

Kenneth K. Kurihara
Distinguished Professor of Economic Theory, State University of New York, Binghampton

L. Leontiev
Corresponding Member, USSR Academy of Sciences

H. Myint
Professor of Economics at the University of London and the London School of Economics and Political Science

Dwight H. Perkins
Associate Professor of Economics, Associate in Research, East Asian Research Center, Harvard University

Glauco della Porta
Head of the Economic Intelligence Department, Banco di Roma (Italy)

Ralph B. Price
Professor of Economics, Western Maryland College

Jan S. Prybyla
Professor of Economics, The Pennsylvania State University

Milos Samardzija
Professor of Economics, Belgrade University (Yugoslavia)

Karl Schiller

Federal Minister for Economic Affairs, Bonn; Professor of Economics, the University of Hamburg (Germany)

Harry G. Shaffer

Professor of Economics, The University of Kansas

Morris L. Sweet

Senior Planner, Housing and Redevelopment Board, New York City

Raymond Vernon

Professor of Economics, Harvard University

Francesco Vito

Professor of Economics, Universita' Cattolica del Sacro Cuore, Milan (Italy)

D. J. Waller

Research Fellow in Chinese Politics at The School of Oriental and African Studies, University of London

Oleg Zinam

Associate Professor of Economics, University of Cincinnati

Preface

The thesis underlying the present collection of essays is that: (1) a workable way of classifying economic systems is by function and property structure—the function consisting in resource coordination and control through markets or administrative command, the property structure being identified as private or public; (2) operational economic systems are mixtures of the market and command functions, and of private and public property structures, with custom playing a significant role under both headings, especially in the less developed economies; (3) in spite of an apparent functional-structural convergence of the more advanced economies, the gulf that separates market-oriented from command-oriented economies is real and traceable to: a) the basic pluralistic or monolithic assumptions on which controlled market and marketized command systems respectively operate, and b) the pluralistic or monolithic ideologies to which, in spite of many qualifications, each explicitly or implicitly adheres; (4) the developing economies are searching for modernizing blueprints in the market-oriented and command-oriented worlds. The search, while primarily economic, is not without ideological overtones. Growth and development are imperatives, but so is the yearning for national identity, political self-assertion, and social justice interpreted in the light of local traditions and aspirations.

The first corollary is that the study of comparative economic systems defies the rigorous limitations placed on economic inquiry by economic theory *sensu stricto*. It propels economics beyond its self-imposed borders into the important realms of ideology and politics. Since "we are all planners now" (Donaldson), whether the planning be primarily through the market and the agency of private ownership or through administrative command and collective property, political calculation, the interplay of social forces, and the persuasiveness of ideology, fashion the systems within which men carry on the ordinary business of life.

A second corollary is that the field is too vast and the change too rapid for a single economist to adequately handle. The reasonable alternative is to appeal to the talents of men versed in the various disciplines which impinge on comparative economics, to spread one's net far and wide. The present collection makes use of the reflections of economists, political scientists, politicians, urban planners, and students of government in the United States, Germany, Britain, Italy, Sweden, Poland, the Soviet Union, and Yugoslavia. They and their publishers have been most kind in helping to make this joint venture possible. The variety of viewpoints and the frequent disagreement reflect the present state of the discipline. There is, however, a common thread which runs through all the essays: it concerns the role of conscious and spontaneous forces in allocating scarce resources, that of pluralistic and centralistic goals guiding this allocation, the balance between pluralism and centralism, and between market and command, the precise place of the many and the one in shaping the systems within which men earn their daily keep and nations assert their power and influence. It is as much as to say that we are agreed on what the fundamental problems dividing us are, but that our answers are still far apart. The practical usefulness of the study of comparative systems is that it enables us to see the underlying causes of the things that divide us.

I wish to thank the Department of Economics and the Central Fund for Research of The Pennsylvania State University for their understanding and assistance.

J. S. P.

Contents

III

MARKET-ORIENTED ECONOMIES

IV
COMMAND-ORIENTED ECONOMIES

V

THE CONVERGENCE OF MARKET-ORIENTED
AND COMMAND-ORIENTED SYSTEMS

VI

DEVELOPING ECONOMIES IN SEARCH OF SYSTEMS

A Readers' Guide

CRITERIA FOR CLASSIFICATION

In comparing different systems within which men earn a living, this book departs from the familiar classifications of capitalist, socialist, communist, and fascist. Economic systems are instead classified and analyzed according to methods of resource coordination and control (market, administrative command, custom), and type of property relations (private or public). On this basis the major division is between market-oriented and command-oriented economies, the first relying primarily on private property in the means of production, the latter on public property. A third division includes customary economies in search of modernizing systems, the quest being directed toward one or another of the major methods of resource coordination-control and property relations. ("Custom" implies specific rules of conduct inherited from the past—that is, a relatively static, largely nonmonetized economy characterized by modest marketable surpluses.[1]) In short, the book's approach is functional-structural.

MAJOR THEMES

Bearing in mind the functional-structural approach, three main themes dominate the essays in this collection: 1. analytical models of economic systems, 2. ideological models, and 3. operational economies.

1. Analytical models These are hypothetical thought models, simplified versions of existing, or blueprints of possible, economic systems. Their main function is to identify and interrelate the fundamental operational principles of different economic systems and to reveal the assumptions underlying these principles.

The treatment of analytical models is here divided into two parts: Part I.A (Prybyla, Zinam) examines the basic features of the perfectly competitive market model and the absolute command model. These two abstractions represent two possible, extreme (though not very workable) methods of resource coordination and control, each accompanied by a pure type of property structure. Both authors mention the Lange-Taylor model of competitive socialism which combines the functions of the

---

[1] See, for example, George Dalton (Ed.), *Tribal and Peasant Economies: Readings in Economic Anthropology* (American Museum Sourcebooks in Anthropology, Garden City, New York: The Natural History Press, 1967); George Dalton, "Economic Theory and Primitive Society," *American Anthropologist*, 1961, No. 63, pp. 1–25.

perfectly competitive market model with public ownership of the means of production. Reference to the Lange-Taylor model is also made by Falkowski in Part VI.

Part I.B (Chamberlain, Vito) introduces imperfections, qualifications, and modifications into the basic models so as to bring the models nearer to operational reality. The rigid assumptions of the pure models are here relaxed. The qualifications concern, in each case, methods of resource coordination and control and property relations. Thus, account is taken of command elements in market systems and market elements in command economies, the role of public property in economies characterized by private ownership of the means of production, and of private property in economies dominated by the public ownership of the means of production. Part I.B clears the ground for the case studies of market- and command-oriented economies which form the substance of Part III and IV.

A methodological note is perhaps in order. There is, as yet, little agreement on whether market-oriented and command-oriented economies can be analyzed with the same set of conceptual tools. The monist view is that the corpus of Western economic theory can be applied to the analysis of command systems. The dualists argue that Western economic theory developed in a particular setting cannot be used to gain an understanding of command-oriented economies, and that it is of limited use to the study of largely nonmonetized economies dominated by custom. The dualist argument means, in essence, that the comparative study of economic systems calls for a special general theory, which we do not have as yet. There are elements of both approaches discernible in the essays by Prybyla and Zinam, with Zinam leaning toward the second. The monist view also appears to be shared by Myint and Kurihara in Part VI. One thing, however, is clear: command systems have not so far defined themselves analytically—there is no command-authored general theory of command systems, although much constructive work on the subject is presently being done in the Soviet Union and Eastern Europe. The "basic laws of socialism" of the standard Soviet texts are normative ("ismic") statements, ideological guideposts, by themselves not very helpful in providing an insight into the workings of command systems. Much the same is true of customary economies, which until recently have been the almost exclusive province of anthropologists, historians, and civil servants. Since their political emergence as independent entities, customary economies have shown a perhaps not surprising tendency to take stock of themselves in normative rather than analytical terms; the stress is on what should be rather than on what actually goes on; on African socialism (see Berg, Part II), the Islamic social order, and other "ismic" explanations. Faced with this proliferation of ideologies and analytical void, the proponents of market and command solutions respond by trying to tailor their theories to a new and puzzling situation. Their arguments are summed up by Myint, Kurihara, and Falkowski in Part VI.

2. *Ideological models*   Normative explanations of what a given economy is all about are not the exclusive property of emergent countries. Ideological models are blueprints of ideal systems, normative constructs, expressions of what those advocating a given system think it is, hope it will become, and believe other systems to be. As firmly held beliefs, explicitly stated, or as preconceptions implicit in analytical assumptions, ideological models exert an influence which one cannot ignore. In spite of assertions to the effect that advanced economic systems of the market or command types reveal a weakening of ideology, the end of ideology does not seem to be in sight. Galbraith (Part II) argues that ideologies underlie many analytical-looking propositions of market systems, dominate a good deal of the thinking of command economists (Bornstein, Bradley), color the solutions offered by market and command systems for the consideration of the developing countries (Myint, Kurihara, Falkowski), and play an important role in the thinking of those who trace the economic profile of emerging countries (see Price and Berg in Part II). The last point is noteworthy. Developing countries have a compelling need to know where they are going and, although willing to draw on the experience of advanced economies, they are at the same time careful not to copy indiscriminately. They introduce into market and command models elements of their own tradition, and add ideological criteria of their own making to systems of beliefs underlying the market and command solutions. The philosopher's stone is, by and large, growth and development: the big push out of poverty. In this respect, both market and command systems have, in their respective areas, much to show. Over wide stretches of the underdeveloped world, however, market-private property systems are ideologically discredited, while the excesses of command are known only from hearsay. The harsh reality of command is minimized, while the ideological vision and promise of classlessness, prosperity, and social justice tends to be accepted at face value, the more so since it is often related to historically dubious memories of a simpler Golden Age, now lost.

The ideologies implicit in market and command systems and in the developing countries' impatient search for modernizing systems are discussed in Part II. In spite of their close conceptual association with analytical models and operational systems, they are formally kept apart so as to bring out their essentially separate identity. The comparison is thus between different analytical models (Parts I.A and B), different ideological models (Part II), and different operational economies (Parts III–VI). Comparisons of existing economies with models of ideal systems, common enough in the literature of comparative economic systems, can in this way be avoided, should one wish to follow the formal outline of this work. On the other hand, if such a comparison is thought desirable, it can easily be made.

3. *Operational economies*   The treatment of existing economic systems is divided into four parts (Parts III, IV, V, and VI). Part III gives a number of examples of market-oriented economies. These represent different subsystems of the general market-private property orientation, the examples being drawn from the experience of developed countries. The emphasis here is on operational changes in the basic instruments of resource coordination and control (market) and property relations (private). A good deal of attention is consequently given to the role of public planning in a market setting, different concepts of planning, and the various approaches to public and private sectors in market-oriented mixed systems. Different as the various subsystems are, they begin with the same functional and structural assumptions. These assumptions are that pluralism does the job of resource coordination and control through the operation of markets and private property structures, but that this pluralism needs to be supervised, protected or restricted, encouraged or held back. The starting point is pluralism; the operational principle is that pluralism is not always or invariably right or efficient. Quite frequently, pluralism generates its own contradictions (market concentrations), often it spawns booms and recessions, at times it fails to promote the desired rate of growth or the full employment of resources. The assumptions on which it rests may clash with ethical principles held by a given society or they may run counter to national political aspirations. The essays in Part III describe various types of managed pluralism.

Part IV gives some examples of existing command-oriented economies. The Soviet Union and China, being the basic operational models, are given considerable space. The relative bulkiness of Part IV is also due to the fact that command-oriented systems receive little attention in Western textbooks, and that most Western students know about them mostly from hearsay. The overall emphasis is on the operational modifications brought about in the instruments of resource coordination and control (central command planning) and in public property structures, a theme touched on earlier by Vito in Part I.B. Attention focuses on the emerging role of market forces in a command setting and on the different approaches to the concept of public property. Like pluralism, centralism frequently fails to live up to expectations: it generates disproportions and bottlenecks, fails on occasion to take account of alternatives foregone, produces rapid if imbalanced growth, and sometimes comes in conflict with the ethical principles held by those whose daily lives it affects. In Part IV, various attempts to pluralize the monolith are analyzed.

A slight difficulty should perhaps be mentioned at this stage. Used as many of us are to the older divisions of capitalism, socialism, com-

munism, and fascism, the question arises how military dictatorships
(equipped or not with a social mystique) and neo-fascist regimes fit into
the functional-structural picture just traced. The approach outlined here
appears sufficient to cope with this problem. The fundamental question
to be asked is whether a particular system functions and is structured on
the assumption of pluralism or centralism, whether the tools of resource
coordination and control and the forms of property relations operate in a
way which promotes the pluralistic or the monolithic assumption regarding the organization and purpose of economic life. A fascist regime
may, and usually does, resort to markets and private property in the
means of production, but the functions of these markets and the decision-
making power bestowed on individuals by private property are so restricted and modified as to give effect to the centralized philosophy and
preference scale of the leaders. We are dealing here with aspects of
market power, a subject raised by all the authors in Part I and by some
in Part II.

Part V (Shaffer, Prybyla, Leontiev) examines the hypothesis of the
convergence of market and command systems. Are the modifications introduced on both sides in regard to the instruments of resource coordination and control and to the concept of property such as to make the hypothesis of an eventual convergence of the two major systems plausible?
Do all post-industrial, mass consumption systems tend to be very much
alike, or is the most mixed market still very different from the most revisionist command? The questions are of interest to those searching for
solutions to the problem of underdevelopment (Part VI), but they are
also important from the standpoint of methodology. If convergence is not
a myth, then perhaps a single body of analysis applicable to all economic
systems may yet emerge. Unfortunately Part V raises more questions than
it answers. As in other areas of the discipline, there is some, but not
enough, agreement here.

Part VI (Customary Economies in Search of Systems) contains essays on some of the developing countries of Asia and Latin America. At
this point the discipline of comparative economics merges imperceptibly
with development economics. Growth and development seem to be the
overriding objectives of all low income, customary economies. These
objectives involve the choice of new methods of resource coordination
and control and changing patterns of property relations. The developing
countries' search for systems involves more than reference to advanced
analytical models and a study of operational economies of the market
and command types. Ideological models intrude into the calculation—
foreign and domestic "isms" that promise prosperity and efficiency with
social justice. Part VI deals with this issue in two sections. In Section A,
the modified market and revised command solutions to the problem of
underdevelopment are set out by Myint, Kurihara, and Falkowski. Section

B contains a case study of Mexico, an economy that has opted for a combination of market and command. We are dealing here with a fluid situation, a groping for answers.

For too long the study of customary economies has been left to anthropologists, historians, and civil servants. The discipline of comparative economic systems is thus ill prepared to cope with the upsurge of interest in the sort of choice that faces economists and statesmen in developing countries. Part VI is meant to draw attention to this problem. If present trends are any indication of the direction which the choice of systems is taking, it may well be that the final solution will in some manner combine market, command, and custom, and also private and public property with their many shadings, and that the synthesis or convergence discussed in Part V may, perhaps, take place on the way to the post industrial economy.

Comparative economic systems is a young discipline, unsure of itself. There is still much controversy about the central topic and the proper methodology. There is considerable discussion about the exact relationship of this branch of economics to other areas of the discipline and also to politics, law, sociology, and the art of administration. The essays in this collection examine some dimensions of these relationships and hopefully suggest possible areas of agreement. Possibly, the choice and arrangement of the studies and the stress on methods of resource coordination and control and property relations will add fuel to the controversy. The inclusion of developing economies and of ideological models may stir the debate further. It is, the Editor believes, the proper way for an emerging discipline to become conscious of itself.

I
Analytical Models
and Operational Economies

Introduction

Part I is divided into two sections. Section A defines a number of basic concepts, examines various possible approaches to the comparison of economic systems, and outlines two analytical models: the perfectly competitive market model with private property in the means of production, and the absolute command model with public property in the means of production. The existence of economies based on custom is mentioned. The assumptions, conceptual usefulness, and limitations of these models are made explicit in the essays by Prybyla and Zinam.

The authors agree that operational economic systems are not pure and constitute departures from the basic models. Markets are not perfect, neither is administrative command, nor, in spite of the absence of a pure analytical model of custom, are tradition-dominated economies. Similarly, private and public property structures are imperfect: direct ownership by individuals is not always the rule; there are variations in the legal definition of and the restrictions placed on private property rights. Many possible private-public ownership combinations exist, and many ways of influencing the behavior of private owners or the property policies of the public authority also exist. In short, all operational systems are "revisionist" both in regard to the methods of resource coordination and control and to property relations. Some of these imperfections are listed by Zinam in "Expanded Taxonomy by Ownership and Control" (pp. 24–27).

The departures from the basic analytical models raise a methodological question discussed at length by Zinam. Assuming that the pure analytical models are valid in that they bring out the fundamental distinguishing features of economic systems, and also assuming that existing systems are departures from these basic models, is it possible to arrive at a reasonably accurate understanding of operational economic systems by starting from pure models and subsequently relaxing the stringent assumptions of such models? Is the method of "successive approximations" to increasingly realistic models likely to yield a general theory of economic systems? The difficulty, noted by Zinam, is that (a) there exists a body of theory (neoclassical, Keynesian, post-Keynesian) which permits successive approximations in the case of market economies, but there is no economic theory of command, and (b) even the existing corpus of Western economic theory is too narrow to adequately account for the political, social, ideological, and other influences on market economies. Western economists have tried to construct a theory of command, but their efforts have been moderately successful at best. The grafting of Western analytical concepts onto administrative command runs up against immense difficulties of 1. obtaining the necessary information, and 2. integrating the numerous economic, political, social, and administrative elements which must make up such a model.

As a possible answer to the problem, Zinam suggests the method of "specialized holism"—an attempt "to view the whole economy as an intrinsic part of the total social system and to identify the strategic variables and crucial relationships needed for the development of the general theory of comparative economic systems." Zinam's Table 2–4 classifies five such levels of strategic relationships: ideological values, organization, power, preference, and freedom.

For all its potential importance and ultimate practicability, Zinam's specialized holism remains at this stage an interesting suggestion. It should be given careful thought, but it does not, in the present state of knowledge, provide a definitive answer. It does not, in part, because modern economics, like its neoclassical predecessor, seems to have abandoned "the lofty mountains of economy" (Hansen), the broad sweep of great issues, in order to descend to the lower ground and seek out, with the help of increasingly refined tools, minor cracks in a vast, unfinished superstructure.

Section B relaxes some of the rigorous assumptions of the basic market and command models and introduces complications and imperfections into market and command systems and into private and public property. Chamberlain discusses five reasons for the introduction of public intervention into market economies. Francesco Vito looks at command's need for decentralization, a need arising out of the quest for efficiency. It would seem that, in the last analysis, effective decentralization means the multiplication, or at least differentiation, of decision-making sources. This implies the introduction of market rules of the game, and some shift away from monolithic public ownership. Absolute command implies coercion which may produce impressive quantitative growth in priority sectors. Efficiency implies the willing participation of broad segments of people within the command structure, a willingness which will be forthcoming only if the participants are given some effective power in making decisions.

In real life, the confrontation is not between perfect market systems and absolute command models but between regulated markets and planned economies with acquired market mechanisms. The difficulties inherent in grafting market mechanisms onto central command economies seem to be more formidable than those presented by imposing public regulation on markets. Vito believes that the former is bound to encounter serious conceptual and practical problems, and that a satisfactory outcome is "hardly conceivable." As Prybyla and Zinam show, the operational feasibility of the market-command-private-public property combination hinges on whether the starting point of the mix is market or command: the "everybody" or the "one" assumption as to who the decision-makers are to be. The question is raised again in Part IV. It reappears in Part V where the hypothesis of convergence is examined. It pervades Part VI which wrestles with the problem of the choice between market and command as the starting line for the race toward affluence, social justice, and freedom.

Thus the theme of successive approximations is taken up again in Parts III, IV, and V. Part II is, in essence, an excursion into specialized holism. It concentrates on one particularly important level of strategic relationships—ideology.

A. Basic Analytical Models of Economic Systems

1   JAN S. PRYBYLA

Meaning and Classification of Economic Systems: An Outline

The question "what is an economic system?" resolves itself into two sub-questions: what do we mean by "economic," and what does "system" mean?

Economic

The term "economic" may be used to mean the allocation of scarce resources among alternative uses.[1] This definition is convenient because it is flexible and yet precise enough to pinpoint the essence of the problem. First, the definition addresses itself to the problem of the scarcity of goods in relation to human wants, a question central to economic inquiry and one which affects all economies, no matter what their ideological foundation, organizational framework, or stage of economic development. Second, the definition may be used to cover both the allocation of resources at a given point of time and over time (i.e., static and dynamic considerations). These "resources" include labor, which encompasses all types of human effort exerted in the productive process (in its broadest rendering this also covers "entrepreneurship" or the bringing together of scarce productive factors to initiate the productive process); land, by which is meant all nonhuman gifts of nature which enter the productive process; and capital, by which economists mean man-made productive inputs. Third, the definition, the way it stands, says nothing conclusive about the efficiency of resource allocation. The notion of optimum resource use can, however, be introduced without difficulty. Fourth, the definition does not restrict the ends or uses about which it speaks: both private and public ends are covered. Finally, the relationship between resources and uses is one of choice. In fact, the major merit of the definition is that it pinpoints the essence of economics which is choice ex-

[1] See Lionel Robbins, *An Essay on the Nature and Significance of Economic Science* (London, Macmillan, 1932, 1952), p. 16: "Economics is the science which studies human behaviour as a relationship between ends and scarce means which have alternative uses."

9

ercised in a particular area of life. A good part of economic analysis (economic theorizing) has been devoted to an ever more rigorous quantification of the choice involved in production, exchange, and distribution, and to the establishment of relationships among the measurable quantities.

SYSTEM

An economic system may be defined as the sum total of devices which through their interaction give effect to economic choice, i.e., which translate choice from an idea into action. Action in this context means the actual movement of resources toward the intended uses.

Three statements may be made about the devices which go to make up an economic system. The first concerns the origins and characteristics of the devices, the second deals with their functions, and the third with their nature.

Origins and characteristics. Economic devices are based on and expressed in law which embodies the traditions, cultural heritage, intellectual evolution, philosophical outlook, or sometimes quite simply the distribution of political power in the society from which it has emerged and to which it applies. At the present time this law is primarily national.

"Any economic system," writes Mrs. Robinson, "requires a set of rules, an ideology to justify them, and a conscience in the individual which makes him strive to carry them out."[2] Economic systems, in short, are never pure: noneconomic forces are always present and powerful. Economic analysis can tell us a great deal about the mechanics of different economic systems, but the picture will be incomplete at best.

Functions. The devices which go to make up an economic system perform three major functions.[3]

1. They help determine the locus of decision-making power (locus of effective choice). In other words, they help determine *who* among the many potential choice-makers will actually make effective, resource-moving decisions.

2. They coordinate the activities of individual economic units, i.e., they are supposed to work in a way which ensures the internal consistency of the various resource allocating decisions both at a point in time and over time, both as between individual inputs and outputs and as be-

[2] Joan Robinson, *Economic Philosophy* (Chicago, Aldine Publishing Company, 1963), p. 13.
[3] For an alternative listing of functions, see Frank H. Knight, *The Economic Organization* (New York, Harper & Row, Harper Torchbooks, 1965), pp. 7–15.

tween different economic aggregates. In other words, they help determine *how* the decisions will be made.

3. They put into effect the decision-makers' scale of priorities, or help determine *what* decisions will actually be made. In this connection it may be noted that all economic systems, at least in their stated intention, share three major goals; the full and efficient utilization of scarce resources, an equitable distribution of income (the definition of "equity" being relative to time and place), and growth of output over time. The proponents of different economic systems tend to put different emphases on these goals at different times. Thus, for example, a high rate of growth has until recently been the top priority of the Soviet and Eastern European economies. Full and efficient utilization of resources, which need not go hand in hand with the desired rate of growth, appears now to be emerging as an important objective of these systems, supplanting the former preoccupation with maximum statistically measurable gross output growth. Although the manner in which this goal is being pursued differs substantially from the ways used in Eastern Europe, the objective of full and efficient employment of resources has been a high priority of most Western economies, at least since the end of World War II. Preoccupation with total and per capita output growth rates has gained in importance in the nineteen fifties and sixties.

Nature. The devices which make up an economic system may conceptually be divided into methods and tools. These methods and tools together provide answers to the who, how, and what questions inherent in any economic system.

In theory, two extreme methods and tools of resource allocation may be envisioned. These two extremes represent two heuristic models of economic systems. Neither of these models has existed or is ever likely to exist.[4]

The two extreme methods of resource allocation are: markets using prices, and central command using physical units. The two extreme tools of resource allocation are: individual ownership of all the means of production, and public ownership of all the means of production. The combination of method 1 and tool 1 is known as the perfectly competitive market model, while the combination of method 2 and tool 2 is known as the absolute command model, sometimes also called the dictatorial model.

---

[4] Then why study them? A model is a simplified and abstracted representation of reality. Theoretical models of economic systems are simplified—though by no means simple—abstractions of methods and tools which are actually or could be used to allocate resources among alternative uses. They are conceptual devices, blueprints, analytical schemes which provide an insight into the operation of complex real-life economies. By concentrating on the essential features of economic systems, economic models perform the practical service of enabling us to understand, modify, and improve real-life economies.

The Tool of Ownership

Ownership or property means the right, always subject to qualifications, to acquire, keep, use, and dispose of material and nonmaterial wealth. This right may be vested in individuals, business organizations such as partnerships, corporations, and mutual societies constituted by individuals (private property), or in the public authority (public property), or in both at the same time. The term "personal" property refers to the household ownership of consumer goods, as distinguished from "private" ownership of productive assets (means of production). It is with the latter form of property that we are mainly concerned here.

In the perfectly competitive market model the social functions of private property in the means of production are:

1. decentralization of decision-making power by distributing wealth and income among the various members of society (distributive function);

2. conservation of wealth—the assumption being that each individual will take good care of what belongs to him (conservation function);

3. incentive to accumulate wealth *via* the profit motive (growth function);

4. provision of material security for individuals and households to foster individual independence (security function).

The perfect market model assumes that these functions are discharged faultlessly, which, of course, is not the case as soon as we pass from the realm of conceptual models to that of functioning economies. In big private corporations, for example, ownership and control are largely separate functions. Corporation executives (who are salaried officials) tend to respond to other than private property stimuli in their management of the corporations' business, and in their decisions regarding corporate saving and investment. They react to the often conflicting interests of employers, suppliers, consumers, society as a whole, and the corporations' legal owners (stockholders). The dividend interest of the owners not infrequently comes last in the corporate calculus.

As Grossman[5] has correctly pointed out, command economies do not arise spontaneously; they are imposed. Public ownership of all the means of production (the tool of command, but also of market socialism) may be reached in seven ways: through nationalization, confiscation, expropriation, death duties, discriminatory taxation, input discrimination, and moral suasion.

Nationalization is the transfer from private to public hands, with or without compensation and usually without the possibility of recourse to

[5] Gregory Grossman, "Notes for a Theory of the Command Economy," *Soviet Studies,* Vol. XV, No. 2, October 1956, p. 106.

the courts, of certain well-defined property rights in given sectors of the economy. As a general rule, the more strategic or pervasive activities— the economy's "commanding heights"—will be nationalized first. These include the banking system, key heavy industries (e.g., coal, metallurgy, electric power), transport, communications, wholesale domestic commerce, foreign trade, and sometimes land. The nationalization process is broad and impersonal.

Confiscation is the transfer to the central authority of assets, belonging to specifically identified individuals, groups, or social classes as, for example, enemies of the state, collaborators, emigrés, "monopoly capitalists," ethnic minorities, religious orders, and so on. Confiscation implies no compensation and usually there is no recourse to the courts. It is criminal law applied to achieve economic ends.

Expropriation is the *ad hoc* transfer from private to public ownership of property rights in real estate whenever the public authority decides that such a transfer is in the social interest, as for example, the expropriation of land which lies astride a projected highway.

Death duties or inheritance taxes, when confiscatory, that is assessed at 100 percent of the value of individually owned assets, may be used to transfer property from private to public hands within the lifespan of one generation. If applied to the whole private sector, it would result in complete public ownership in the space of that generation. Command economies in the process of formation are not usually so patient, and the method of death duties is not, therefore, the one most commonly used.

Discriminatory taxation against private producers and traders has been used by most command-oriented economies to harass the private sector and to make private enterprise less profitable, or even unprofitable. The method has much political appeal to the central authority bent on pushing forward to as pure a command model as possible because it preserves the appearance, if not the substance, of voluntary surrender. By exercising the economic power already vested in it by nationalization, confiscation, and expropriation, the central authority can make individual producers and traders seem to fall in line by their own (coerced) will. Since they cannot make a living within the central authority's fiscal framework, they will "voluntarily" give up their property rights and join the public sector.

Input discrimination may be practised against the private sector in situations in which the central authority controls all or some of the commanding heights of the economy. To operate as producers, traders, or suppliers of all kinds of services, individual owners of productive assets need inputs in the form of raw and semifinished materials, producer, and final goods. The authority may place obstacles in the way of the flow of these commodities to the private sector and eventually force private entrepreneurs out of business.

Moral suasion means the creation of a climate in which to be the private owner of productive assets and to be in business on one's own becomes socially unacceptable, unethical, and politically unwise. Such a climate may be created by a combination of ideological indoctrination and the very size, extent, and pervasiveness of the state sector in economic, political, social, and cultural life.

It should be noted that nationalization, confiscation, expropriation, death duties, and, on occasion, discriminatory taxation may be and have been used by operational market-oriented systems in support of the public sector. The difference between the use of these weapons in command-oriented and market-oriented systems consists in the intent of the former to eliminate the private sector altogether. The intention of market-oriented economies is to correct or supplement, strengthen rather than eliminate, the market mechanism. The idea in this case is to correct, through the use of public power, important deviations from rational self-interest. This difference in intent says a great deal about the character of the authority wielding the weapons just described, and it is a matter of the utmost practical interest.

THE PERFECTLY COMPETITIVE MARKET MODEL*

The perfectly competitive market model has four basic characteristics:

1. Individual economic units (households and firms) legally own all the means of production.

2. These units autonomously and voluntarily enter into exchange relationships on terms mutually acceptable to the parties to the exchange. More specifically, households sell labor, land, and capital to firms and use the income derived from these sales to buy products produced by the firms. Both the resources of the households and the products of the firms are assumed to be homogeneous in each market, infinitely divisible and mobile. The exchange nexus is known as the market. Markets exist for each individual type of goods and services.[6]

3. In entering into exchange relationships, households and firms decide the levels of their economic activity by reference to scarcity prices which confront them in the various goods and factor markets. These prices are mathematical expressions of the terms on which alternatives are offered to the units. They are coefficients of choice, "the needle which

---

* See Oleg Zinam's paper, below, for a fuller listing of the assumptions underlying this model.

[6] In more technical terms a market may be described as a system of mathematical equations which solves the demand functions of consumers, the transformation functions of producers, and the supply functions of factors of production through the reallocation of production and consumption. See Bela A. Balassa, *The Hungarian Experience in Economic Planning* (New Haven: Yale University Press, 1959).

points out the course to follow where there is no reason to deviate from it."[7] Prices in this model are responsive to the interplay of demand and supply which are the market expressions of effective wants (wants backed by purchasing power) and resource scarcity in monetary terms.

For the buyer, prices are costs which provide both a signal and an incentive to cut back on his use of things that are dear and push forward his use of things that are cheap. For the seller, prices are returns which provide both signal and incentive to make more of the things that are expensive and less of those that are cheap. For the system as a whole, prices settle at the level which clears the market. The prices of productive services, together with the pattern of ownership of resources, determine the distribution of income among persons and families; and the income resource owners represents the costs of producers, while the expenditures of resource owners—as consumers of goods and services—represent the income of producers.[8]

It is assumed that all economic units have a perfect knowledge of the economy, so that price discrepancies will be known and rapidly eliminated. It is also assumed that in both the goods and factors markets the number of economic units is so large that no single economic unit is in a position by itself to influence the prevailing market price.

4. It is claimed for this model that it not only allocates resources in conformity with the preferences of consumers revealed in the consumers' market demand, but that it does this job efficiently. The attempt made by each economic unit to maximize its net returns results in equal returns at the margin for agents of equal capacity. Equal returns at the margin means, in turn, maximum returns for the system as a whole. The system, in other words, is not only a coordinating device concerned with internal consistency, but also an optimizing instrument. The efficiency referred to is static allocative efficiency, a situation in which the production of one commodity cannot be increased without reducing the production of another commodity. In this situation any movement away from the optimum cannot make anyone better off without making someone else worse off. This optimum (Pareto optimum) is not a single point since there are many possible positions which foot the bill. All the optima, therefore, are positions of general equilibrium.[9]

The perfectly competitive model, therefore, implies private property, free exchange, personal responsibility, consistency, and static efficiency. It translates individual demands for specific goods into social decisions about prices and outputs. It is the nonpurposeful achievement by private

[7] H. D. Henderson, "The Price System," *Economic Journal*, December 1948, pp. 467–482.

[8] Procter Thomson, "Government and the Market," in *Federal Expenditure Policy for Economic Growth and Stability* (Washington, D. C.: U. S. Government Printing Office, 1957), pp. 130–152. Also available in Morris Bornstein (ed.), *Comparative Economic Systems—Models and Cases* (Homewood, Illinois: Richard D. Irwin, Inc., 1965), pp. 51–77.

[9] Bela A. Balassa, *op. cit.*

persons of a social purpose. Nonpurposeful means (a) that the price mechanism which serves as an information-gathering device and as a basis for choice is not the result of conscious human design, and (b) that those who make their choices in conformity with market signals are not necessarily aware of the social consequences of their actions.

The Absolute Command Model

The absolute command model has five basic characteristics:

1. All means of production are owned by the central authority.

2. The central authority physically determines the size, assortment, and all other dimensions of output, and enforces its orders perfectly through administrative control.

3. The consumption of all goods and services is determined by the central authority through physical rationing.

4. Labor is assigned by the central authority to prescribed jobs, at predetermined rates of reward in kind. The authority also determines the ratio of labor to leisure.

5. There is, strictly speaking, no need for money. However, money as a unit of account may be used if the authority decides to calculate the allocative efficiency of the system.

The absolute command model, therefore, implies public property, central responsibility, and internal consistency. It translates social decisions about outputs into individual receipts of specific goods.

It will be seen that each of these two hypothetical models answers squarely the question "who will make effective decisions?" In the perfectly competitive market model the answer is everybody, or more precisely, all income recipients. In the absolute command model the answer is one (authority).

How decisions will be made is also answered, if in a more general way. In the first model, choices will be exercised in markets through the monetary demands of consumers acting on information about alternatives supplied to them by scarcity prices. In the absolute command model the authority's choices will be communicated to the mass of executors by administrative order expressed in physical units, and the orders will be enforced by physical controls. The means of direct physical control may include such devices as input-output (or transactions) tables, material balances, direct technical coefficients, and linear programming.

What choices will be made in each case cannot be answered with any certainty. To provide an answer, one must inquire empirically into the character (scale of values) of the choice-makers in each model. All that can safely be said is that in the perfectly competitive market model the consumers' ideas about what should be produced will be translated into action by the market and price mechanisms in response to monetary demands, and that this translation will be allocatively optimal in a static sense. In the absolute command model the choices of the central authority will be enforced by the physical instruments of command. What the actual choice priorities will be will depend on the character of the consumers or of the authority, depending on the model we are dealing with. It should be understood, however, that absolute command does not require any consultation between the central authority and the executors of the authority's commands. The commands reveal the autonomously formulated scale of preferences of the authority and only that. Depending on the character of the authority, it may or may not consult the executors on their wishes. The model, however, precludes economic consultation: there is no way in which the authority, should it so desire, could consult the executors through the absolute command system. That is so because the system is built to serve as a transmission belt for the authority's own preferences—it makes no provision for determining the individual preference scales of consumers. Should the authority decide to base its orders more or less accurately on the preferences of those subject to its command, it will have to resort to noneconomic channels of consultation: political elections, perhaps, although not very likely, or some sociological exercise in public opinion sampling. The authority may also simply claim that the ultimate source of its wisdom is the superior historical insight into the needs of society, which it possesses in consequence of a successful revolution that brought those now in command to power— an insight derived, in part, from intimate knowledge of the laws of history outlined and proved beyond doubt by some founding father. In fact, absolute command, if it ever existed and if it felt compelled to explain the nature of its preferences, would very likely offer just that kind of explanation.

MODELS AND REAL-LIFE SYSTEMS

Absolute command systems do not exist in practice any more than does perfect market competition. Operational economic systems may be looked upon as different states of imperfection derived from the perfectly competitive model on the one hand, and the absolute command model on the other. In real-life economies, the perfect market may be in various degrees revised by command, and absolute command may similarly be revised in various degrees by the market. In this sense we are all revisionists. But whatever the degree of imperfection, the point of departure assumptions of each real-life economy are extremely important.

There are in the world today various economic systems which however imperfect, are fundamentally derived from the assumption of perfect market competition, from the "everybody" answer to the resource allocation question, and there are other economies which, however market-oriented, are fundamentally derived from the assumption of absolute command. At the point of tangency, that is, where the degrees of imperfection are most advanced on both sides, we still run into the qualitative problem of the original assumptions. At this point of tangency or convergence the economist will be tempted to conclude that the difference between the most imperfect market economy and the most revisionist command economy is only one of degree. The political philosopher, however, is likely to be more hesitant. He might argue that a De Gaulle is not the same as a Tito, that the most authoritarian manifestation of individualism is qualitatively different from the most diluted form of authoritarianism. In short, the point of tangency of real-life economic systems is the point at which the economist must appeal to the political scientist and the social philosopher, both of whom unfortunately have no conclusive solutions to offer. This is as much as to say that the point of convergence, the point of transition from the economics of the market to that of command and *vice versa* is a matter of political philosophy, a normative problem on which the economist with his relatively sophisticated positive tools has little to say.*

Appendix: Competitive Socialism

The existence of another conceptual model should be mentioned. This is the Lange-Taylor model of competitive socialism elaborated by the authors in an essay *On the Economic Theory of Socialism*.[10] Like the perfectly competitive market and absolute command, Lange's competitive socialism does not exist in practice. The nearest approach to it is the Yugoslav system, but even here the kinship is twice removed.[11]

* For a fuller discussion of the convergence hypothesis, see the essays by Shaffer, Prybyla, and Leontiev in Part V below.

[10] Oskar Lange and Fred M. Taylor, *On the Economic Theory of Socialism*, edited by Benjamin E. Lippincott (New York: McGraw-Hill Book Company, 1964). An excellent survey of this model may be found in Heinz Köhler, *Welfare and Planning: An Analysis of Capitalism versus Socialism* (New York: John Wiley & Sons, 1966), Chapter 7. See also Abram Bergson, "Market Socialism Revisited" in Association for Comparative Economics, Proceedings of National Meetings, December 27–29, 1966 (Dekalb, Illinois, 1967), pp. 1–26.

[11] On the relation of the Lange-Taylor model to the Yugoslav Economy, see Svetozar Pejovich, *The Market-Planned Economy of Yugoslavia* (Minneapolis: University of Minnesota Press, 1966).

2   OLEG ZINAM

The Economics of Command Economies

Much has been written on the subject of centrally directed economy, but most of the scholars working in this area would probably agree that the efforts to develop a theory of a command-type economy as a counterpart of the neo-classical theory of a market economy, have not been successful. Moreover, the attempts to prove that the neo-classical proposition of competitive equilibrium can be achieved within the framework of a collectivized economy, have also met with many almost insurmountable theoretical difficulties.

One reason for this state of affairs lies in artificial circumscription of the scope, the other in the application of one-sided methods to the problems of comparative economics.

The scope of study has been too narrow. The purely economic framework of neo-classical doctrine has been applied to problems in which some crucial non-economic variables have simply been treated as parameters. A consequence of this is inability to develop a proper theoretical framework for such areas of economic dynamics as growth, development, evolution of thought, comparative economic systems, etc.

As to the methods, the historical, analytical, and functional-structural approaches have not been integrated to permit an adequate taxonomy covering all types of existing systems. The application of the traditional partial equilibrium method, which starts with individual economic unit operating under ideal assumptions, and which subsequently proceeds toward more realistic conditions by relaxing these assumptions and "aggregating" to obtain a total theory of the system, resulted in problems of unmanageable complexities.

This paper is an attempt to arrive at a scope and methods adequate for the development of a tentative general theoretical framework applicable to all types of economic systems and possessing sufficient breadth to encompass command, market, and customary economies. The justification of this paper is the belief that a command counterpart to neo-classical theory can be developed only within a broader theoretical frame-

This paper was presented by the author at the ACE–SEA Joint Seminar in New Orleans, November 1967. Published in the Proceedings of the (Dekalb, Illinois) A C E , November 17, 1967. Abridged by permission of the author and the Association for Comparative Economics.

19

work and that attempts to contribute toward the design of such a frame-work is the first basic step toward an adequate analysis of the command economy.

1. NEED FOR A GENERAL THEORY OF COMPARATIVE ECONOMICS

The title of the paper suggests a widely known classification of economic systems in three broad categories: Market, Command, and so-called Customary economies. This division is fortunate because it is based on the most fundamental functional, structural, and operational properties of economic systems. For the purpose of this study, an economic system will be defined as a complex of social institutions providing incentive and coordination of processes directed toward solving economic problems confronting society. In this context, the criterion for our taxonomy is the method of coordination and control prevailing in the economy. Depending on whether these functions are performed by forces of supply and demand operating in the markets, by directions of a central administration, or by custom or tradition, one is dealing with a market, command, and—in the view of some specialists—customary economies respectively.

To begin with, let us keep in mind that for analytical purposes it is important to distinguish the ideal or pure types from the real economic systems. Every actual economic system is, like an individual, a unique product of its historical past. It always represents some particular combination of features associated with pure forms.[1] The ideal types of economic systems are formulated "by abstracting the significant characteristics"[2] from the actual economies. According to Eucken, these pure models, together with their intermediate forms, build a theoretical apparatus through the application of which "we can successfully understand the framework and structure of the economic system in every period and of every people."[3] This paper is primarily concerned with both the theoretical aspects of the command-economy model and some implications of this model's logic for real economies.

Before turning to this arduous task, one must note some difficult theoretical problems confronting a student of comparative economics at the very beginning of such a study. The functioning of the market economy seems to be adequately covered by the existing orthodox neo-classical

[1] Walter Eucken, "On the Theory of the Centrally Administered Economy," *Comparative Economic Systems,* Morris Bornstein (Editor), Richard D. Irwin, Inc., Homewood, Illinois, 1965, p. 197.

[2] Walter Eucken, *The Foundation of Economics,* University of Chicago Press, 1951, p. 57.

[3] *Ibid.,* p. 223.

theory, at least as far as its static aspect is concerned. For reasons to be stated later, the corresponding theoretical counterpart applicable to a command economy has not yet been developed. Ames, in his attempt to build a model of the Soviet economy, stated that "it would be very convenient if the existing body of economics could be applied to Soviet conditions." He asked the crucial question of whether the theory of the command economy is "so different that all economic analysis must be cast aside."[4] At the very heart of the problem is Eucken's crucial question: "Are the same economic 'laws' valid in the centrally administered economy as in the exchange economy?"[5] Short of reaching a conclusion on this point, it is impossible to tackle Eucken's following questions: "Can we understand the economic phenomena of the twentieth century if we approach them with a single theoretical apparatus created for the analysis of the exchange economy?"[6] Or "is it necessary to work out a special theory of the centrally administered economy. . . ?"[7]

The history of economic thought offers two fundamentally different views on this matter, one referring to the "dualists," the other to the "monists." Wieser, Barone, Pareto and Schumpeter held the monistic view, according to which the general principles of economics are really the same in all social systems in spite of different institutional setups.[8] Eucken himself shares John S. Mill's dualist position, which views commercial and the centrally directed economics as entities of different kinds and, therefore, requiring different economic theories.[9]

The majority of contemporary economists would probably support the monistic approach, among them Heinz Koehler's, according to whom the "basic economic problem, scarcity, must be the same in capitalism and socialism" and "inputs do not suddenly become less scarce by being publicly owned rather than privately owned." "It is also hard to believe," he continues, "that the introduction of socialism suddenly changes human nature, reducing wants to the available means to satisfy them, thereby eliminating scarcity."[10] By contrast, Professor Campbell, in one of his papers on the administered economy, stressed "the need for some abstract, theoretical frame of reference for thinking about planning and

[4] Edward Ames, *Soviet Economic Processes*, Richard D. Irwin, Inc., Homewood, Illinois, 1965, p. 15.

[5] Walter Eucken, "On the Theory of the Centrally Administered Economy," *op. cit.*, p. 159.

[6] *Loc. cit.*

[7] *Loc. cit.*

[8] Barone, *Giornale degli Economisti*, 1908; Pareto, *Manuel d'Economie Politique*, 1927, p. 362, ff., and Schumpeter, *Capitalism, Socialism, and Democracy*, 1942, Chap. 16.

[9] John Stuart Mill, *Logic*, Book 6, Chap. 10, para. 3; also H. Dietzel, *Theoretische Sozialoekonomik*, 1895, p. 85 ff. Walter Eucken, "On the Theory of the Centrally Administered Economy," *op. cit.*, p. 195.

[10] Heinz Koehler, *Welfare and Planning*, John Wiley & Sons, Inc., New York 1966, p. 4.

administration of this kind of economy,"[11] and complained that despite the logical relevance of the neo-classical model of allocation and rationality, the institutional peculiarities of the Soviet economy make them not very operational.[12] He suggests that "perhaps appeal to a higher level of generality will make it possible to see parallels better."[13] This suggestion deserves to be explored. In what is to follow an attempt will be made "to make a framework general enough so that we can consider many disparate ideas and points of view within it."[14]

Could it be that both the dualists' conclusions and the monists' difficulties in applying the orthodox economic tools to the nonmarket economies are primarily due to one single cause, namely too narrow a view of what economic theory is? If the principles of the traditional neo-classical school are considered *the* theory, then nonmarket economies need either completely different economic theories, or economic theory is irrelevant for such economic systems and one must search for some new non-economic socio-political theory to search for regularities in their behavior. The first alternative would admit a possibility of as many economic theories as there are institutional setups, whereas the second would lead to an artificial limitation of the scope of economic science to market economies or to market sectors of mixed economies alone, despite the logical relevance of economic theory to problems involving scarcity of economic goods in command and customary economies. Neither alternative seems to be acceptable. It seems that the economists should reexamine the scope of the traditional neo-classical theory and start a search for a broad theoretical framework for the analysis of all types of economic systems, which will include market, command, and customary economies as special cases. In order to survive, all types of economic systems must perform economic functions. The rules of game for the economic activities are modifying the way in which economic forces operate, but they neither annihilate nor suspend them. An expanded theoretical framework should be capable to explain how the economic functions and processes are modified by changes in the rules of game caused by different constellations of socio-political, ideological, and other institutional forces in given economic systems. This is a tall order and its complexity is a frightening one.

The above discussion leads to an analysis of the scope and methods of such a broadened theoretical framework for the study of comparative economic systems.

How broad should the scope of the theoretical framework be? In gen-

[11] Robert Campbell, "On the Theory of Economic Administration," *Industrialization in Two Systems*, Henry Rosovsky (Editor), John Wiley & Sons, Inc., New York, 1966, p. 186.
[12] *Loc. cit.*
[13] *Loc. cit.*
[14] *Ibid.*, p. 187.

eral it must be both broad enough to include pertinent variables and re-lationships among them, and limited enough to prevent it from becoming too indeterminate for the development of meaningful generalizations. The scope of traditional neo-classical analysis is definitely too narrow for an adequate treatment of such dynamic areas of study as economic develop-ment, comparative economic systems, evolution of economic thought, and welfare economics. The very variables crucial to arriving at generalities in these fields of investigation are kept out of neo-classical analysis by assigning to them the passive role of parameters under *ceteris paribus* assumptions. However, the introduction of a large array of non-economic variables will make the theory too complex and incomprehensible. . . .

The need for broadening the scope of the theory of comparative eco-nomics is reinforced by some practical, historical and strategic considera-tions. First, a centrally administered economy displays such an inextri-cable complex of economic, political and ideological factors, that the ex-clusion of the non-economic variables would render the analysis meaning-less. This is also true for traditional economies. The orthodox theory was able to keep the non-economic variables impounded in a *ceteris paribus* pool due to a virtual separation of economic and political orders at the time it was developed in Britain and in the U.S.[15]

Secondly, separation of economics from other social sciences, espe-cially from political science, is of a comparatively recent origin. The study of comparative economic systems might prove more fruitful within the previous framework of "Political Economy" than within the narrow confinements of the orthodox neo-classical theory.

Thirdly, economists must develop some new method or strategy for developing adequate theoretical structures. If they are fearful of broadening the scope of their discipline or prefer to wait till the soci-ologists, psychologists, anthropologists and political scientists construct for them an acceptable theory of human behavior, then useful investiga-tions in the area of comparative economics will be greatly retarded. . . .

And finally, if economists deliberately circumscribe the scope of their study to purely economic aspects of phenomena, they choose to work under an unreasonable artificial constraint. Limits of scope should be attributable only to intellectual limitations, and not to isolationist taboos. The fear of "overextension" invites a much greater danger of nar-rowness.[16]

15 ". . . Alfred Marshall and W. Stanley Jevons in England, and F. W. Taussig and John Bates Clark in the United States . . . wrote . . . just at the time that the separation of the economic and political orders was greatest, and their theories re-flected this in their preoccupation with strictly economic phenomena . . ." Nathaniel Stone Preston, *Politics, Economics, and Power*, The Macmillan Co., New York, 1967, p. 39.

[16] See Alexander Gerschenkron, "Economic Backwardness in Historical Per-spective," in *Industrialization in Two Systems*, Henry Rosovsky (Editor), John Wiley & Sons, Inc., New York, 1966, p. 1.

Perhaps at this point one might attempt a heroic extrapolation concerning the general direction of development in economic theory. In other words, what next after the Keynesian revolution and the "Neo-classical synthesis" which attempted to close the broad cleavage between microeconomics and macroeconomics? One may ask what is the greatest cleavage in our contemporary economic theory. In very general terms, most of the economists' agonies about scope and method arise in connection with the application of traditional economic principles to such areas of study as economic development, comparative economic systems, welfare economics, and general economic dynamics. Both Historical and Institutionalist schools have long ago recognized the narrowness of the neo-classical framework, and their criticism of it has been justified. As the pure theorists become more inclined to use empirical approaches to the areas they investigate, they increasingly realize that what they are dealing with in their study of economic development, comparative systems, and other areas of dynamics are concrete, unique socio-politico-economic systems, and that the analytical tools they are using are abstract, logical, or eiconic[17] systems or models. Perhaps the realization that the systems approach may provide a unifying general principle around which adequate theoretical frameworks for dealing with dynamic phenomena of economics will lead to a "convergence" and eventual "Grand General Synthesis." . . .

2. INTEGRATION OF METHODS—SUGGESTED TAXONOMY

The selection of an adequate scope must be combined with a decision of what method is the most appropriate for constructing the theoretical framework and for the subsequent inquiry. The method must be closely related to the basic characteristics of the subject matter of investigation. The economic processes in different systems are performed in dissimilar ways because of differences in the functions of incentive and control which, in turn, are caused by the dissimilarities in over-all institutional structures. This necessitates the selection of a functional-structural method as a major tool of analysis. But since the theory must not only have a sound empirical base but also be dynamic, the historical method combined with statistical analysis must be used to supplement the functional-structural approach. Moreover, to study the numerous actual combinations of all possible ways in which the systems perform their

[17] Eiconics is a name coined by Boulding to depict the new science dealing with subjective systems of images. Kenneth E. Boulding, *The Image,* The University of Michigan Press, 1956, pp. 148, 155.

functions, the student needs an adequate typology of economic systems by functions and structures. Viewing it from a slightly different angle, the functional-structural method helps both historical and analytical approaches by providing them with variables and relations common to all systems. This might also provide a basis for taxonomy. In such a manner all three methods—historical, analytical and functional—seem to mutually supplement and reinforce each other.

For the purposes of the present discussion, the economies according to Kloten, are classified on the basis of two fundamental criteria: "the primary one of dominance of either individual or public economic control, and the supplementary one of the order of property."[18] Types of control and the property relationship are crucial institutional characteristics reflecting and, in turn, influencing the distribution of power (economic, political, social, etc.). This distribution of power influences the important matter of whose preferences—of the state, or of individuals—are effective, and to what extent. As to the type of controlling or coordinating mechanisms, Grossman's categories of command, market mechanism,[19] and tradition seem to be adequate for functional-structural analysis.* In regulating economic activities, the market mechanism relies on the automatic and impersonal forces of supply and demand in the markets, the command principle on administrative decisions of the central authority, and tradition on customs and mores of society. Since type of ownership of factors of production is one of the crucial characteristics of the institutional structure, it will be used here as the supplementary criterion for taxonomy. The ownership is either private, collective or mixed.

The following analysis will be primarily concerned with command and market. The traditional society is subjected to specific rules of conduct inherited from the past. However, since the interpretation of these rules is in the hands of those few having power, it leans toward the command pattern. Moreover, tradition is not likely to be a very important factor in industrial societies because industrialism has not been around long enough to create its own traditional pattern.[20] Of course, when the focus of attention is turned on the developing countries, the element of tradition becomes extremely important.† But our focus is on advanced economy. This simplification leaves the market mechanism

[18] N. Kloten, "Zur Typenlehre der Wirtschafts—und Gesellschaftsordnungen," *Ordo VII,* 1955, Bonn, p. 129.

[19] Gregory Grossman, *Economic Systems,* Prentice-Hall, Inc., Englewood Cliffs, New Jersey, 1967, p. 13.

* Cf. Jan S. Prybyla, above p. 3 [Editor's Note].

[20] Gregory Grossman, "Notes for a Theory of the Command Economy," *Comparative Economic Systems,* Morris Bornstein (Editor), Richard D. Irwin, Inc., Homewood, Illinois, 1965, p. 137.

† The subject of traditionalism is discussed in Parts II and VI below [Editor's Note].

and the command principle as basic coordinating principles. Where these two principles may coexist, a third, namely a mixed economy, prevails. Of course, advanced economies are not devoid of some traditional elements.

If we also ignore for a while the mixed type of ownership, the simplified taxonomic model will look something like Table 2–1.

TABLE 2-1. SIMPLIFIED TAXONOMY BY OWNERSHIP AND CONTROL

Ownership of Factors / Control of Economic Activity	Private (P)	Collective (C)
Market M	M/P	M/C
Command K	K/P	K/C

The introduction of mixed types as to ownership and control would lead to an expanded Table 2–2.

TABLE 2-2. EXPANDED TAXONOMY BY OWNERSHIP AND CONTROL

Ownership of Factors / Control of Economic Activity	Private (P)	Mixed (PC)	Collective (C)
Market M	M/P	M/PC	M/C
Mixed MK	MK/P	MK/PC	MK/C
Command K	K/P	K/PC	K/C

To get the pure types of both market and command economies, the M/P and K/C types have to be combined with purely democratic and purely totalitarian political rules, respectively. Purely democratic rules here imply a government responsive to the preferences of individuals. Totalitarianism, in the words of Grossman, refers to "a dictatorial regime which, through a single party and police intimidation, seeks to exercise total control over society and to maximally impose its ideology on the mind of its subjects."[21] If economic type M/P is combined with D (po-

[21] Gregory Grossman, *loc. cit.*, p. 37.

litical purely democratic rule) on the one hand, and the combination K/C with T (political totalitarianism), the extreme, pure types, are obtained. All real economic systems range somewhere between these analytical extremes of M/P/D and K/C/T. Since the core of the neo-classical theory is describing market conditions very close to the M/P/D type, it is of interest to compare the basic assumptions of the perfect market model in the neo-classical theory with the ideal conditions of the K/C/T type, which later was named by Grossman an "absolute command economy."[22]

3. APPLICATION OF THE NEO-CLASSICAL METHOD

Both perfect market and absolute command economies are heuristic devices constructed to help our understanding of reality too complex to be comprehended in its entirety. All real economies are mixtures. Outside of Marx, the concept of an economic system devoid of government has not been taken seriously. The economy cannot survive without some minimum government control securing a social framework designed to make it safe to entrust economic decision-making to individuals. On the other hand, a need for a hierarchical organization of government in a complex command economy of K/C/T type implies some minimum decentralization of discretionary decision-making power. Complete concentration of power at the top of government is unrealistic for advanced economies.

All real economies will be somewhere between these extreme types and will represent some combinations depicted in Tables 2–1 and 2–2. Historical evidence shows, however, that some of these combinations are workable and viable, whereas others are not. A priori, the M/P/D and K/C/T types would seem to suggest potential stability. But some other combinations must be considered to be rather unstable and even highly improbable. According to Eucken, the CM type characterized by "the concentration of economic power brought about by collective ownership of the means of production renders it highly improbable that the all-powerful collective property owners would undertake the experiment of leaving the control of the economic process to competition . . ."[23] Sim-

[22] Gregory Grossman, "Notes for a Theory of the Command Economy," *op. cit.*, pp. 139-140.
[23] Walter Eucken, "On the Theory of the Centrally Administered Economy," *Comparative Economic Systems,* Morris Bornstein (Editor), Richard D. Irwin, Inc., Homewood, Illinois, 1965, p. 196.

ilarly, unstable, improbable, or both, are the combinations of K/P,[24] K/C/D and P/M/T.[25]

Among the *real* mixed types of economies, the Soviet Union (and China) can be placed at one end, and the United States at the other end, of our classification. The former is definitely a less-than-absolute command economy; there are at least four areas in which private market forces are operative (labor market, distribution of consumer goods, part of production and distribution of farm products, and some privately furnished services).[26] The U.S., though a predominantly market economy, also has some areas of economic activity dominated and controlled by the government, and even some cases of government ownership of productive resources.*

But since the primary purpose of this study is the development of a broad theoretical framework, the student of comparative systems may ask himself how to go about such an endeavor. Among many possible ways, the following two seem to be of considerable interest. One can start with ideal, pure, or perfect theoretical systems and then gradually introduce "imperfections." The alternative method, which may be named "specialized holism,"[27] consists of concentrating on limited aspects of the total field, usually on strategic variables and relations.

Following the first method, Table 2–3 summarizes in a simplified way the basic assumptions underlying both perfect market and absolute command economies, side by side.

The list of assumptions is just an approximation, i.e., an example of characteristics one would expect to find in such extreme cases of pure theoretical economic systems. Of crucial importance here is the treatment of government. The government is economically neutral in the case of a perfect competitive market. The whole miracle of equilibrium at optimum allocation of all resources is performed by the "invisible hand."

---

[24] The combination of command principle with private ownership of factors of production is unstable because ownership is basically a bundle of rights, of which control is the most important one. Command principle can cause and did cause in the past an erosion of private ownership.

[25] "Political totalitarianism . . . may well permit institutional laissez faire. This was more or less the case with Jacobins and the Nazis." Peter Wiles, *The Political Economy of Communism*, Harvard University Press, Cambridge, Massachusetts, 1962, p. 14. However, a continued existence of totalitarianism on the political level eventually leads to encroachments of political on economic power, to establishment of a command economy and gradual erosion of property rights.

[26] Gregory Grossman, "Gold and Sword: Money in the Soviet Command Economy," *Industrialization in Two Systems*, Henry Rosovsky (Editor), John Wiley and Sons, Inc., New York, 1966, p. 207, and Robert W. Campbell, *Soviet Economic Power*, Houghton Mifflin Company, 1966, p. 83.

* See Alvin H. Hansen, Part III below [Editor's Note].

[27] "Holism views life in all its manifestations as a single system in process of interaction with the inorganic environment." H. G. Wells, J. S. Huxley, & G. P. Wells, *The Science of Life*, Vol. III, p. 926; also Amos H. Hawley, *Human Ecology, A Theory of Community Structure*, The Ronald Press Co., New York, 1950, p. 9.

The "invisible hand" concept is essentially a micro-economic proposition. It leaves a gap in the macro-economic area, largely because of its identification of general equilibrium with full employment. The Chicago School attempted to close this gap with centrally installed automatic devices designed to stabilize the economy at full levels of employment. In doing so, it has attempted to round out the proposition of entrusting the entire economic process to non-discretionary rules of the game. Conceptually, the formula may be persuasive, but, as Heller has shown, the so-called balanced budget proposition contains many implicit and explicit discretionary elements. Neither do we have such a thing as atomistic competition involving market automatism.

In an absolute command economy, on the other hand, an omniscient monolithic government consciously directs the economy toward the desired goals, leaving to individuals the role of passive compliance with government decisions. Ideologically the laissez faire formula of the "invisible hand" is now replaced by that of the perfect "visible hand."

But the perfect "visible hand" proposition is as unrealistic as its neo-classical perfect "invisible hand" counterpart. The task of planning, controlling, and evaluating the operations of a complex economy is enormously difficult. The number of variables and relationships to be known and the number of economic units to be controlled require a complex administrative structure. This means that the economic operations of a command economy cannot be understood without some theory of the administrative system itself. This theory must explain "the way in which the small number of economic variables on which the leadership has an opinion is proliferated into instructions for hundreds of thousands of economic units."[28] In other words, the crucial question in a command economy is "how does the administrative apparatus translate a set of instructions given it by the highest political authority into a set of instructions upon which individual enterprises base their actions?"[29] The study of administration is further complicated by the fact that governments are run by men "and because all men must be privately motivated to carry out their social functions, the structural relation between the function of government and the motives of those who run it is a crucial determinant of its behavior."[30]*

Under the perfect assumptions stated in Table 2–3, total obedient state enterprises can be considered a part of the government itself. But

[28] Edward Ames, *op. cit.*, p. 247.

[29] *Loc. cit.*

[30] Anthony Downs, *An Economic Theory of Democracy*, Harper & Row Publishers, New York 1957, p. 290.

* Explicit identification of government goals and conceptualization of the alternative ways of achieving those goals is also a problem of market-oriented economies. Hence the interest in cost-benefit analysis referred to by Chamberlain, below p. 51 [Editor's Note].

TABLE 2-3. BASIC ASSUMPTIONS IN EXTREME IDEAL TYPES OF SYSTEMS*

Type of Economic System: Assumptions as to Conditions:	Perfect Market	Absolute Command
Government Role in Economic Activity	Not involved except to provide law & order	Omniscient monolith government making all econ. decisions
Setting of National Goals	None	National goals formulated by government
Central Plan	No central plan; decentralized plans, "invisible hand."	Central plan in physical terms to attain the above goals
Price System	Prices determined by supply & demand in the markets (low of one price).	Prices determined by the central authority.
Mobility of Factors of Production	Perfect mobility in response to market conditions.	No free mobility, except by the order of the government.
Type of Competition	Atomistic competition; large number of independent buyers and sellers.	No competition; all producers employees of the state, all supply and demand physically rationed by government.
Type of Behavior of Economic Units	Economic man behavior; maximization of profit, income & advantage.	Economic units perfectly obedient to the plans and directives of the government.
State of Knowledge	Perfect knowledge of supply and demand conditions in the market.	Perfect knowledge of the plans and directives of the government by all units.
Type of Allocation of Resources	Equilibrium at optimum allocation of all resources (equimarginal principle).	Perfect fulfillment of the plan in all details by all economic units.
Utilization of Resources	Full utilization of resources, full employment.	Full utilization and employment of all resources.
Distribution (functional)	Income shares determined by the equilibrium of supply and demand in factor markets.	Income shares determined by the central plan.
Consumption, Saving and Investment Decisions	Made by private decisions of households and firms.	By central government decisions in accordance with the plan.

TABLE 2-3 (Continued)

Type of Economic System: Assumptions as to Conditions:	Perfect Market	Absolute Command
Held as Constant Under the Ceteris Paribus Condition	Technology, population, institutional setup, system of values, tastes.	Technology, population, institutional setup, system of values, tastes.
Relationship Between the Economic and Political Orders.	Separation of political from economic order.	Complete merger; economic order becomes part of political order, political order dominates.
Effect on Distribution of Political and Economic Power	Economic power separated from political power; economic power decentralized; political power decentralized. Plurality of power centers.	Concentration of all economic and political power in one center; monopoly of all economic and political power in hands of the government.
Whose Preferences Effective?	Individual economic sovereignty: consumer sovereignty, freedom of occupational choice, business freedom. Political sovereignty in hands of the people.	Planners' sovereignty; government's preferences effective; no consumer's, producer's or occupational freedom. Political dictatorship.
Ideological Order	Open system; competing ideologies permitted, legitimate right of dissent protected.	Regime's ideology forced on all constituents; no dissent permitted; closed system.

*Cf. Prybyla, above, pp.14–16 [Editor's Note].

when one moves away from the perfect model toward reality, the distinction between the state and the enterprise it owns becomes a necessity, for two reasons. First, the enterprises seldom produce exactly the amount specified by the plan; they might produce more or less, and the theory must explain why. Secondly, for technical as well as political reasons, the response of enterprises to central directives is far from being uniform and predictable. Both the introduction of government into the pure market model and the recognition of organizational limitations of the state administration in a command economy necessitate a study of the effectiveness of the government's "visible hand." This raises the interesting question: which of the instruments of coordination of economic activities is more mechanical, arbitrary, and blind, the "invisible hand" of the market or the "visible hand" of state bureaucracy?

The market mechanism has been persistently accused of its social blindness,[31] impersonality, and automaticity. But are the market forces really blind? A market, by definition, is a complex system of contacts among buyers and sellers making—in compliance with the rules of the market—independent decisions in order to attain a differential advantage over competitors. The highly decentralized decision-making process involving innumerable decision-making centers resembles anything but a blind mechanical force. It has been dubbed blind and mechanical because of its ability to achieve, as a by-product of profit-making, a balance between supply and demand and a determination of prices at no administrative (governmental) cost to society.

On the other hand, there exists a substantial amount of evidence that governmental bureaucracy in both market and command economies not only frequently failed to attain its objectives but created conditions contrary to intentions. One of the leading economists remarks that "the difference between the actual operation of the market and its ideal operation—great though it undoubtedly is—is . . . nothing compared to difference between the actual effects of government intervention and their intended effects."[32] Another economist, comparing managerial incentives and decision-making in the United States and in the Soviet Union, comes to the interesting conclusion that the Soviet incentive system, though generally inducing a "high level of managerial effort and performance, . . . has the unintended consequence of causing managers to engage in a wide variety of practices that are contrary to the interest of the state."[33] Sociologists call such unintended and unrecognized effects "latent functions," the intended and recognized results "manifest functions."[34] A good approximate measure of relative "blindness" of a social institution would be the extent to which its "latent functions" outweigh its "manifest" ones. Using this criterion, both market and governmental bureaucracy are in a sense relatively "blind". . . .

Furthermore, removal of the assumption of perfect knowledge, introduction of market imperfections like monopoly or oligopoly, obstacles

[31] "All socialist ideas have one thing in common—they do not expect social and economic harmony by a natural or harmonic market systems. To achieve this harmony they find it necessary to transform the existing economic forms into a socially conscious order." H. Ritschl, *Die Grundlagen der Wirtschaftsordnung*, Tuebingen, 1954, p. 278.

[32] Milton Friedman, *Capitalism and Freedom*, The University of Chicago Press, 1965, p. 197.

[33] Joseph S. Berliner, "Managerial Incentive and Decision-making: A Comparison of the United States and the Soviet Union," *The Soviet Economy*, Morris Bornstein & Daniel R. Fusfeld, Richard D. Irwin, Inc., Homewood, Illinois, 1966, p. 140.

[34] Robert K. Morton, *Social Theory and Social Structure*, The Free Press of Glencoe, Illinois, 1949, p. 51.

to mobility of factors of production will serve to make the market-economy model more realistic but not necessarily dynamic. This is also true for analogous changes in the command-economy model. In the latter case, the introduction of collective or cooperative enterprises and limited private markets greatly complicates the model.* But the development of the theories of pure competition, oligopoly, monopolistic competition, and monopoly in a market economy has been much easier than corresponding attempts to build realistic analytical counterparts for the command system, for at least three reasons.

First, it is impossible to construct a simple maximizing behavior model for a command economy. A manager in a command economy has to face a jungle of often conflicting incentives and constraints, and it is not clear what he maximizes or even whether he attempts to maximize anything.[35] In this constant maneuvering between obeying government regulations and directives in the interest of his survival, on the one hand, and the pursuit of economic efficiency, on the other, the manager might be attempting to reconcile a bewildering mass of conflicting and often self-contradictory imperatives which severely constrain his freedom of action.

Second, in a command economy, political, economic and ideological elements are so inextricably intertwined that no attempts to separate economic from non-economic factors promise success.[36] To get meaningful results, one must either analyze the whole package, or give up the effort. . . .

Third, the empirical basis for any theory depends on the availability and quality of information about economic behavior. In command economies this information is extremely scarce and unreliable. Even the indigenous economists would have great difficulties to obtain data on managerial decision-making processes. For outsiders the task seems to be almost hopeless. Moreover, an objective selection and interpretation of data might run contrary to the wishes of the governments, especially if the results might fail to glorify the system. This could be one of the factors contributing to the failure of the indigenous economists to develop even an approximation to a theory of the command economy. . . .

Additional handicaps for indigenous theorists have been as follows. First, tenets of Marxian theology inhibit the freedom of inquiry in eco-

---

* See F. Vito, below, p. 61 [Editor's Note].

[35] This difficulty exists also in the market economy. For a stimulating discussion of maximizing, minimizing, satisfying, and other types of behavior of economic decision-making units see Kenneth E. Boulding et al., *What Is the Nature of Man?* The Christian Education Press, Philadelphia, Penna., 1959, p. 31. However, the theory of maximization of profit is much more plausible as a unifying principle of economic behavior of entrepreneurs in a market economy, especially in a static analysis.

[36] This is also true, though not to such an extent, for a market economy, especially when the focus of the study is on the dynamic aspect of economic behavior.

nomic theory.* Second, totalitarian regimes seldom if ever look for guidance from economic theoreticians; rather, they are guided by "the exigencies of a given situation and, most of all . . . (by) . . . the mechanics of power politics."[37] Third, development of micro-economics has been hampered by the Marxists' denial "that economics is a set of constrained maximum models," and by their refusal "to distinguish between the state and the enterprise it owns."[38] Fourth, for political and perhaps also ideological reasons the indigenous economists never attempted to develop an "explicit . . . model of macro-economic equilibrium, either static or dynamic."[39] Such a macro-economic model would be inseparable from a political theory of the government, and no totalitarian government likes their economists to inquire into such matters as economic and political efficiency of the regime.

It can only be briefly mentioned here that attempts have been made to furnish, within the confines of the neo-classical set of economic laws, a common theoretical construct for the pure or ideal models of free enterprise and socialist economic systems. These attempts are known as the so-called "mathematical" and "competitive" solutions. Both ventures are not only predicated on heroic assumptions but have baffling implications for the role that is to be played by central economic planning, which later appears to be the heart of collectivist systems. Like the neo-classical construct of competitive equilibrium which they seem to emulate, they are essentially static propositions and hence fail to furnish an apparatus for dynamic analysis.

Generally speaking, the usefulness of such intellectual exercises is limited by the fact that existing systems represent, in fact, mixtures of institutional and functional elements associated, respectively, with the concepts of market systems, command systems, and customary economies, regardless of whether they are given the popular labels of capitalism, socialism, fascism, or, as the case may be, simply, underdeveloped economies. It would therefore seem that each "type" of economy offers only limited possibilities of theoretical explanation in terms of "Western" economics and, by the same token, of whatever theoretical abstractions emerge from students or propagandists of collectivism.†

All of this seems to indicate that the method of starting with ideal models and subsequently relaxing the stringent assumptions of such mod-

---

* On this subject see Bornstein and Bradley, below pp. 81–95 [Editor's Note].

[37] Alexander Gerschenkron, *Soviet Economic Growth,* quoted in *Industrialization in Two Systems,* Henry Rosovsky (Editor), John Wiley & Sons, Inc., New York, 1966, p. 157.

[38] Edward Ames, *op. cit.,* p. 111.

[39] *Loc. cit.*

† The applicability of "Western" and "Socialist-Command" economics to the problems raised by customary economies in the process of development is discussed by H. Myint, K. Kurihara, and M. Falkowski, below [Editor's Note].

els in an attempt to build a general theory by "successive approxima-tions" to more and more realistic models runs into a host of almost insu-perable difficulties. Such a frontal ground attack can be facilitated and supported by the daring air reconnaissance of "specialized holism," i.e., by an attempt to view the whole economy as an intrinsic part of the total social system and to identify the strategic variables and crucial relation-ships needed for the development of the general theory of comparative economic systems.

4. Suggested Theoretical Framework

All existing economies are facing the same basic economic problem of scarcity of resources relative to the goals they try to attain. The basic components of an economic system are the decision-making units like households, firms, government agencies, etc. They are responsible for carrying out economic processes of production, exchange, distribution, and consumption. The most important functions of any economic system are to provide these decision-making units with incentive and coordina-tion. How the functions of coordination and incentives are performed depends on the nation's natural resources, technology, and institutional structure.

Society's ideology or value system, political system, and economic organization are institutional structures of crucial importance. They have a decisive effect on the "rules of the game" regulating economic activity and "determine the location of decision-making powers over that econ-omy's use of resources."[40] The type of power structure determines whose preferences are going to be effective.*

The study of comparative economic systems is primarily concerned with the problems of how divergent social systems coordinate and con-trol their economic decision-making processes by their institutional struc-tures, the resulting distribution of economic and political power, and the effect of power on the determination of effective preferences of economic units. Table 2–4 classifies strategic structural relations in two extreme types of economies: command and market. Although no real economic system corresponds to these pure types, a proper understanding of their impli-cations is essential.

How the available natural and human resources are used and how the existing technology is utilized depends on numerous levels of strategic

[40] William N. Loucks, *Comparative Economic Systems,* Harper & Row, Pub-lishers, 1965, p. 7.
   * Cf., Prybyla, above, pp. 10, 16 [Editor's Note].

TABLE 2-4. STRATEGIC VARIABLES AND CRUCIAL RELATIONSHIP ON DIFFERENT LEVELS OF ANALYSIS IN THE COMMAND AND THE MARKET ECONOMICS

Types of Systems / Levels of Analysis	Command Economy — Typical Characteristics	Relationship of Strategic Variables and Crucial Relationships (Command)	Relationship of Strategic Variables and Crucial Relationships (Market)	Market Economy — Typical Characteristics
Ideological Values	Basic Philosophy: 1. Collective first; 2. Only elite knows.			Basic Philosophy: 1. Supremacy of individual over collective; 2. Right to make individual choices.
Ideologies	Closed system. Conditioning of individual preferences. No ideological opposition permitted.			Open, competitive ideological system. Right of dissent.
"V-Level"		$V_g \rightarrow V_i$ Regime dominates values of individuals.	V_g v_i Values held by Government reflect values of individuals.	
Organizational	Merger of polit. & econ. orders. Polit. order dominant. Ownership of factors – collective – C			Separation of political from economic order. Ownership of factors – Private – P
"Z-Level"		$Z_p \rightarrow Z_e$ C/K/T type	$Z_p \leftrightarrow Z_e$ P/M/D type	
Economic Order Z_o	Control of economic activity – command – K	Z_e centralized	Z_e decentralized	Control of economic activity – market – M
Political Order Z_p	Controlled political machinery – totalitarian – T			Competitive political system – democracy – D

TABLE 2-4 (Continued)

Levels of Analysis / Types of Systems	Command Economy — Typical Characteristics	Relationship of Strategic Variables and Crucial Relationships	Market Economy — Typical Characteristics
Power Level Whose Opportunity? *"P-Level!"*	Concentration of all political & econ. power in one center. Complete monopoly of econ. & political power. Closed power system.	Separated $P_p \rightarrow P_e$ (Command) $P_p \not{\ } P_e$ (Market, separated)	Political & econ. power separated. Economic power decentralized by market; political power decentralized by system of checks & balances & competitive political order.
Preference Level Whose Effective Preferences? *"I-Level"*	Government's preferences effective. Individuals' preferences made ineffective by restricting opportunity functions or conditioning.	$I_g \rightarrow I_i$ (Command) $I_i \rightarrow I_g$ (Market)	Individuals' preferences effective. Market forces determine individuals' opportunity functions which limit individuals' preferences. Government preferences reflect individual preferences.
Freedom Level Whose Effective Freedom? *"F-Level"*	Government's freedom to attain planned goals.	$F_g \rightarrow F_i$ (Command) $F_i \rightarrow F_g$ (Market)	Freedom of consumer choice, occupational choice, and of business enterprise. Political freedom and ideological freedom for individuals.

TABLE 2-4 (Continued)

Glossary of symbols:

V_g □ Value system of the government or rulers;

V_i □ Value system of individuals;

Z_p □ Political order;

Z_e □ Economic order;

C/K/T □ Collective/command/totalitarian type of economy;

P/M/D □ Private/market/democratic type of economy;

P_e □ Economic power;

P_p □ Political Power;

I_g □ Government's effective preferences;

I_i □ Individual's effective preferences;

F_g □ Government's effective freedom;

F_i □ Individual's effective freedom;

B system becomes a part of A system & A system dominates B system

A ⟶ B   A is separated from B

Definitions of Terms   (meaning of terms for the purpose of this paper):

Ideology   "a systematic set of beliefs, opinions, and doctrines about social phenomena, primarily economic and political phenomena, which is possessed by individuals, classes, and nations,"[a] and "which can be used to mobilize people for action."[b]

Economic and Political Order   "fix relationship among human beings, establishing rights and duties, both confer positions of power and influence in society."[c]

Power   (Social Power) . . . "ability to cause others to do what we wish, or at least to modify their activity in a direction favorable to our desires"[d] or "capacity to influence the actions of others in a predictable way."[e]

Opportunity or Opportunity Function   "expresses *what is* or *what is possible*" for an individual or an organization; it shows different combinations of desired ends which can be attained with given means"; it is often called a possibility function because "only those combinations which lie within the opportunity function are possible."[f]

Preference or Preference Function   "expresses *what is desired*" by an individual or an organization."[g]   It expresses the scale of preferences of a decision-making unit used in a process of choosing among goals, means, and methods of actions.

Effective Preference   "the degree of capacity to get desired thing plus the will to get it";[h]   or that part of the preference function which lies within the opportunity function, i.e. which is attainable. The attainable part of the preference function.

Effective Freedom   availability of the range of choices among potentially effective preferences.

TABLE 2-4. (Continued)

[a] Talcott Parsons, *The Social System*, The Free Press, Glencoe, Illinois, 1951, and Talcott Parsons, *Essays in Sociological Theory*, The Free Press, Illinois, 1954, pp. 134–135 and pp. 266–268.

[b] Daniel Bell, "Ideology and Soviet Politics," *Slavic Review*, Vol. XXIV, Number 4, Dec. 1965, p. 593.

[c] Nathaniel Stone Preston, *Politics, Economics, and Power*, The Macmillan Company, New York, 1967, p. 4.

[d] *Loc. cit.*

[e] Gregory Grossman, *Economic Systems*, Prentice-Hall, Inc., Englewood Cliffs, New Jersey, 1967, p. 16.

[f] Oleg Zinam, *Interaction of Preference and Opportunity Functions and Long Range Economic Development*, Unpublished doctoral dissertation, University of Cincinnati, 1963, pp. 91, 209. Definitions based on Kenneth E. Boulding, *The Skills of the Economist*, Howard Allen, Inc., Cleveland, 1958, pp. 161–162.

[g] *Loc. cit.*

[h] Alfred Kuhn, *The Study of Society*, Richard D. Irwin, Inc., and Dorsey Press, Inc., Homewood, Illinois, 1963, p. 319.

relationships, only five of which are considered in this discussion. It is fully realized that quantitative and qualitative resource availability, as well as the level of technological development, are crucial variables having an important influence on the structural levels analyzed here. They are kept in the background, however, to limit the scope of this paper. The focus of this part of the present study is the problem of how, given the resources and technology, the differences in institutional structures of a society lead to different methods of incentive, coordination, and control of economic activity and to different patterns of effective preferences.

The ideologies as systems of ideas, concepts, and values are guiding individuals and organizations in the interpretation of the environment, the selection of goals to be attained, as well as in the choice of means and methods appropriate for the attainment of these goals. Together with a complex of physiological, psychological, socio-psychological and other factors, ideologies are forging the preference functions of the general population and their leaders. Among the most important preferences of people shaping the economy are those related to the choice of the institutional structure of the society itself. When coupled with adequate power, these preferences become effective. The effective preferences are active forces guiding economic processes and maintaining or modifying social institutions and the methods of coordination, control, and incentive.

Since ideologies have "the capacity to capture men's minds,"[41] they can be used as instruments by those having power and determination to organize strong revolutionary movements to change the existing social order. . . .

Totalitarianism establishes, as a rule, a closed ideological system. This is necessary for both the protection of the regime and for the attainment of the goals chosen by the dictator. . . .

Democratic societies permit open ideological systems to compete for the allegiance of the minds.

Since the views of the totalitarian regime might greatly conflict with the views of its people, there exists a problem of convergence of governmental preference functions and those of the individuals. In a pure command economy model the government makes its preferences effective either by sheer force or by using the educational system and propaganda to condition people, i.e. to shape their preference functions in such a way as to make them come as close as possible to the regime's preferences. . . .

In contrast to the totalitarian regime's efforts to shape and condition the value systems and preferences of the people, the government in a libertarian system attempts to form its own values and preferences in

[41] Carl J. Friedrich, "Ideology in Politics: A Theoretical Comment," *Slavic Review*, Vol. XXIV, Number 4, Dec. 1965, p. 616.

closest possible conformity with those of its constituents. In the political area this is done by circularity of the hierarchical structure.[42] "The absence of a clearly articulated ideology,"[43] and emergence of a multi-interest pluralist government, is the probable outcome of such attempts.

The study of the value structure must be supplemented by an analysis of the organizational order of a society. To facilitate such an endeavor, the analytical distinction can be made between the economic and the political orders, though in reality they "are seldom, if ever, found existing as wholly separate organizational entities."[44] The economic order "consists of those relationships among men in society that arise out of the production and distribution of goods and services,"[45] the political—"of the relationships in society that arise out of or are concerned with the making of authoritative decisions for or in the name of the whole society."[46]

Nathaniel Stone Preston has stated that in a command economy "the political and economic orders are so conjoined that to discuss one as acting upon the other is, in a sense, a distortion."[47] While, conceptually, the distinction of these two is in order, one can agree that the economic order in such a model is completely dominated by the political order. The principles of a market economy "require a limitation of the impact of the political on the economic order."[48] Here the greatest possible degree of separation of the two orders is accomplished.

The economic organization of the pure market-economy model is characterized by the private ownership of the agents of production and by the impersonal market control of economic activities. No national economic goals are set and the decision-making units are not restrained in their activities as long as they are acting in compliance with the law. In the pure command-economy model the agents of production are collectively owned and the economic activity is coordinated and controlled by the government's administration. The production is directed "in the service of goals established by the leadership" which attempts "to structure the environment of each decision-maker . . . so that he makes choices and engages in actions that will maximize the attainment of the goals of the leaders. . . ."[49] The regime is attempting to achieve an

[42] Kenneth E. Boulding, *The Organizational Revolution*, Harper and Brothers, New York, 1953, p. XXXIII.

[43] R. Joseph Monsen, Jr., *Modern American Capitalism: Ideologies and Issues*, Houghton Mifflin Company, Boston, Mass., 1963, p. VI.

[44] Nathaniel Stone Preston, *op. cit.*, p. 3.

[45] *Loc. cit.*

[46] *Loc. cit.*

[47] *Ibid.*, p. 162.

[48] *Ibid.*, p. 56.

[49] Robert Campbell, "On the Theory of Economic Administration," *op. cit.*, p. 187.

absolute command over the "opportunity" functions of all decision-makers and to change the shapes of their preference functions to make them comply with its preferences.

In this model of the command economy the political order is non-competitive and monolithic, based on only one political party ruled in a dictatorial manner by its leader. However, it is conceivable to reconcile the command economy with "democracy." This situation could arise where the citizens have become so disgusted with private ownership and with any responsibility coupled with independent decision-making that they entrust all ownership and control to a freely elected government. In this extreme and improbable case the immense power concentrated in the hands of the government, is, however, likely to lead to eventual crumbling of political democracy. Or the citizens, realizing the danger of losing their political freedom, might insist on denationalization and return to a market system.

The combination of private ownership and market economy with a libertarian political system is perhaps as stable as the arrangement of the command economy. However, the combination of a market economy with a totalitarian political system "will almost inevitably be changed . . . from allocating goods through the market toward more centrally planned decisions in which the goals of the leaders take precedence over those of the consuming public."[50] And though "it is widely believed that politics and economics are separate and largely unconnected . . . such a view is a delusion," because "there is an intimate connection between economics and politics" and "only certain combinations of political and economic arrangements are possible."[51]

In general, each type of political and economic organization imposes the "rules of the game" on economic activities, provides the legally accepted framework for the resolution of the conflicting preferences, contributes to the preservation or change in value systems and ideologies, and affects the distribution of political and economic power in a society. This last factor is of the utmost importance. The character of organization provides the framework within which the power structure can be altered, and any change in the distribution of power, in turn, provides the opportunities to make changes in the organizational structure. If, as is the case in the command economy, the regime attempts to keep the power structure intact and freezes the political and economic organization, the result is stability in terms of mere rigidity.

In our model of the pure command economy all economic and political power is concentrated in one center. The result is a closed power system in which "concentrated economic and political power has been

[50] R. Joseph Monsen, Jr., *op. cit.*, p. 14.
[51] Milton Friedman, *Capitalism and Freedom,* The University of Chicago Press, 1965, pp. 7–8.

placed in the hands of an identifiable ruling group, and it is exercised by them without the necessity of referring to popular choice."[52] Such concentration of power is immense and its employment might become ruthless. A socio-political system of that kind tends to degenerate into an instrument for maximizing power and wellbeing of the ruling elite. . . .

In the market economy model the economic power is decentralized by the operation of competitive market forces. The political power is also subject to competitive processes as well as to institutional arrangements or checks and balances. Laissez-faire makes economic power independent of political power. Under such conditions the economic power can serve as a check of political power. Too great a dispersion of power, however, harbors a danger for a democratic system of this type because it renders it "incapable of swift and concerted action when the need is great."[53]

Deviations from the perfect model, both in regard to the economic and political setup, introduce the following problems: first, that of "political power relationships generated in economic life" and second, of "economic power that finds its source in politics."[54] For example, "wealth may be used to assist the election of favored candidates or to place elected officials under obligation by the generous provision of campaign funds."[55] Wealth has been used by many as a stepping stone to a political office of power. The middle class used its economic power to attain the control of political power in England at the close of the Mercantilist era. In a totalitarian setting, such a circulation of economic into political power is severely circumscribed.

The relationship between economic and political power is at the very heart of economic dynamics and cannot be ignored by the student of comparative systems. The opportunity functions of individuals and organizations are limited by the amount of political and economic power they control. The possessor of adequate power can make his preference functions effective. In the command economy, the all-powerful government can make the individual's preferences ineffective by restricting his opportunity functions. Such a government establishes its priority of goals and uses its power to make its preference functions effective.

In a libertarian market economy the preferences of individuals are being accommodated to the extent of their possession of purchasing power and their determination to use it to render their preference functions effective. Such a system "gives people what they want instead of what a particular group thinks they ought to want."[56] However, the market is incapable of making such decisions as the allocation of re-

[52] Nathaniel Stone Preston, *op. cit.*, p. 194.
[53] Nathaniel Stone Preston, *op. cit.*, p. 218.
[54] *Ibid.*, p. 2.
[55] *Loc. cit.*
[56] Milton Friedman, *op. cit.*, p. 15.

sources between private and collective goods, changes in the economic organization of the society, national defense, equitable income distribution, etc. Most of these decisions are made indirectly by electing the government and letting it act in the name of the people. While the views and preferences of the government acting in behalf of society as a whole can substantially deviate from those of the individuals, the gulf between these two sets of preferences tends to be much wider in the command economy. But in both cases (and in all intermediate ones) the interaction of the state and individual preferences represents one of the crucial problems of comparative economics.

A decisive question here is: "Whose preferences should be relied upon?" The choice is a difficult one. Should the reliance be placed on the decision of individuals, or on a "paternalistic authority whose decisions overrule consumers' preferences?"[57] The dilemma has been brought in sharp focus by Loucks' statement: "If comprehensive goals are chosen, individual action must conform to them or be relatively circumscribed. . . . If, however, individual action is left 'free' . . . , some sort of aggregative behavior will result, but no planned social goals will be possible."[58]

According to Drewnowski, the pragmatic solution to what seems to be an insolvable dilemma is found in a form of coexistence within the same economy of the state, individual, and dual zones of influence. In the state's influence zone "the scales of values are the preferences of the state" and "no consumers' preferences enter into the picture." In the individuals' influence zone the consumers' preferences rule supreme. And the "state and individual preferences jointly decide the allocation of resources and distribution of goods" in a dual influence zone.[59] The limiting cases in which the individual zone or the state zone each encompass the entire economy are possible only in models of pure market or absolute command economies, respectively. All real systems represent some combination of these zones.

This analysis would not be complete without considering the implications of the various forms of organization for human freedom. Neither economic nor political freedom is possible under a regime completely monopolizing all economic and political power in a society. Historical experience shows that the abolition of the institution of private property and the free market has always been accompanied by severe inroads into the competitive pattern of the political order and into such cherished

[57] Bela A. Balassa, "Success Criteria for Economic Systems," *Comparative Economic Systems*, Morris Bornstein (Editor), Richard D. Irwin, Inc., Homewood, Illinois, 1965, p. 13.

[58] William N. Loucks, *Comparative Economic Systems*, Harper & Row, Publishers, 1965, p. 269.

[59] Jan Drewnowski, "The Economic Theory of Socialism: A Suggestion for Reconsideration," *Journal of Political Economy*, Vol. LXIX, No. 4, August 1961, pp. 341-354.

features as the right of dissent, freedom of conscience, freedom of the press, academic freedom, etc. This is the cost a society pays for conferring upon the state the powers to set up overall goals and to mobilize the nation's resources to attain them.

The organizational setup of plurality of economic and political power-centers in a market economy facilitates and protects freedom of consumer and occupational choice, freedom of enterprise, as well as political and ideological freedoms. However, it necessarily limits the state's ability to set and attain overall goals.

5. A Hypothetical Choice

This leads to a challenging question of what is the optimal mix of economic and political orders—with all the implications of power, preferences, and freedom—for a given economy?

Such a question cannot be answered in the abstract. The choice would greatly depend on the totality of the situation in which a given country finds itself, i.e. the nature and urgency of its goals and problems. At the heart of this choice is the question of the best possible balance of political and economic power. Fundamentally, the choice is between the two basic ways of coordinating the economic activities—command or market. However, this is not a categorical either-or proposition. It may well be a proposition of zoning (Drewnowski). The problem at hand is how to match the organizational needs of the disparate sectors of economic activities with the most appropriate influence zones—individual, state, or dual in order to attain maximum efficiency in working toward given goals while taking into consideration the constraints imposed by the prevailing value system and ideology of society.

Here society faces a trade-off between the urgency of setting overall economic goals, on the one hand, and the imperative to preserve the freedom of individual economic, political, and ideological choice, on the other. To a great extent, and especially in the short run, one desideratum impinges on the other. If, as in the laissez-faire model, individual preferences are given a free sway, overall economic goals cannot possibly be set. If overall goals are to be set (and reached), the individual effective preferences must be curtailed. One important qualification is the effect of centralization of economic and political power on efficiency. Radical centralization, i.e. absence of delegation of decision-making powers inside the administrative hierarchy, especially in an increasingly complex and sophisticated economy, is likely to jeopardize the attainment of planned objectives.

While the problem of a libertarian society is how to reconcile the power of the state with the rights and freedom of individuals, those who do not care about liberty are restrained by the considerations of efficiency alone.[60] In their relentless pursuit of high-priority goals, the predominantly command economies, restrained only by the fear of the loss of productive efficiency or the revolt of their constituents, have, at one time or another, carried the centralization of authority and the restriction of individual freedom beyond the point of diminishing returns. The resulting inefficiency and waste have forced them to ameliorate some of their rigid policies of economic control. Witness the NEP and the present controversy over economic reform in the Soviet Union and the partial liberalization of economic control in the communist dominated countries of Eastern Europe.

6. Concluding Remarks

Two concluding remarks are necessary at this point. First, one corollary of this paper is that those who attempt to make meaningful predictions about any command economy cannot derive them adequately from the sole consideration of purely economic factors. At the very barest minimum, the crucial relationships discussed in this paper have to be taken into account.

Second, this paper is much more about the scope and methods of comparative economics than about the command-economy proper. The only excuse for this is the inability of the present writer to treat general theoretical aspects of a command economy model without an attempt to fit it first, side by side with a market model, into a much broader theoretical framework.

[60] The actions of the regime in a command economy are also subject to restraints set by the party's ideology.

B. Operational Imperfections: Regulated Market and Decentralized Command

3   NEIL W. CHAMBERLAIN

Public Planning in Market Systems

If the question is asked whether market economies are increasingly subjected to public planning, the answer must clearly be in the affirmative. This answer has nothing to do with one's feelings as to the desirability of the evident trend.

I shall try to make my statement as succinct as possible, at the risk of sounding dogmatic. There are at least five reasons for the discernible tendency to increased planning.

1. There are institutional interferences with what we often think of as the "automatic" adjustments of the market. The market, of course, is itself an institutional phenomenon, and there is no logical basis for regarding it as somehow autonomous and overriding. But Western economists have treated the market for so long as their own special Eden that we tend to think of it as "natural" or "original," something which would exist except for the corruption of economic man by institutional serpents bearing sociological apples. Every society has its own special brand of apples, whether they come in the form of monopolistic or oligopolistic business organizations, impediments to labor mobility, discriminatory practices based on race or sex, hierarchical or nationalistic social systems, and so on. It would be pointless to elaborate. In the face of such "imperfections," governments have been moved to intervene.

2. Even if we accept such institutional patterns as a kind of dialectic gloss on the basic language of markets, there is a widespread unwillingness by people to submit even to delayed or modified market adjustments. Such market phenomena as unemployment and grossly disparate incomes are now commonly viewed as undesirable or inequitable, and provision is made for dealing with them on a public basis, or for protecting and even encouraging private means for dealing with them, notably through labor unions, with the result that noise is created in the market mechanism.

3. When the market is viewed as autonomous or natural, the rate of growth and the pace of adjustment which it provides must be accepted as a natural by-product. But even Western societies, conditioned though they have been to such a mode of thought, are no longer willing to ac-

From *Proceedings of National Association for Comparative Economics Meetings,* San Francisco, December 27–29, 1966. Association for Comparative Economics, Northern Illinois University, DeKalb, Illinois, pp. 27–33. Reprinted by permission of the author and the Association for Comparative Economics.

cept this economic theology. We often consider impatience with a low rate of growth to be characteristic of the masses, but this is by no means their exclusive propensity. In England, for example, it was an insurgent Federation of British Industries which pressed on a complacent government the need for a more calculated alternative to the halting economic pace of the 'fifties, leading to the formation of the National Economic Development Council, which, however successful or unsuccessful, was intended to be an experiment in planning.

4. In contemporary society, there is a virtual unanimity of view among political leaders to the effect that collective consumption must be promoted more rapidly than private consumption. Such a persuasion cannot be defended by any economic calculus. It comes down to an affirmation of faith similar to that made by Alvin Hansen in the *Review of Economics and Statistics* some ten years ago when he said, and I paraphrase, "I cannot prove, but I *know*, that the marginal tax dollar will provide more benefit than a marginal dollar of private income." Country after country has explicitly stated its intention to step up the rate of expenditure on education, health, and what we now refer to as "infrastructure." But this involves reliance on government planning rather than the market.

5. Last on my list is the episodic but recurring need for drastic change. Much of a society's economic activity can proceed in incremental steps, as my colleague, Professor Lindblom, has argued. But from time to time a society confronts the need for a more radical readjustment than incrementalism will allow. As Henry Phelps Brown has put the point, "The market seems to be better at tactics than strategy. . . . The need for a strategy of adaptation remains, . . . and imposes tasks of redeployment hardly to be performed by the decentralized decision-taking of the market economy alone."[1] A need to reshape the economic structure of a society involves a choice of direction which the incrementalism of market adjustments does not allow for. Japan believes it is presently in this position, as its government seeks to promote business mergers and consolidations to prepare it for a more aggressive role in international competition. On a somewhat lesser scale, most countries in Western Europe are also encouraging by pressure and inducement the rationalization of certain industries.

These five reasons for the increasing resort to governmental planning in the West can be summarized rather crudely by saying that economic issues have more political content to them than formerly. This formulation may be in error: the political content may always have been there, and what may have changed is the greater systematization of the government's approach to these issues.

[1] Henry Phelps Brown, "The National Economic Development Organization," *Public Administration*, Autumn, 1963, p. 242.

This, of course, necessitates a more explicit identification of government goals and an exploration of alternative ways of realizing them. One consequence in recent years has been to give added impetus to the development of more sophisticated cost-benefit analysis. This is not the place to examine the theoretical acceptability of some of the methods employed. Our only concern at the moment lies in the fact that the recent surge of interest in cost-benefit analysis springs largely from the increased importance of government programs.

This movement towards planning has still left unresolved the question of the respective roles to be played by the public and private sectors. The government could act to achieve its objectives by taking over more and more of the direction and control of business firms, converting a larger share of presently profit-making enterprises into non-profit public units. On the whole, Western governments have eschewed such a policy in favor of leaving discretion with private managers but attempting to influence the exercise of that discretion by inducements and sanctions in a variety of forms. These range from outright subsidies to Japan's technique of "administrative guidance," which involves government compulsion but accompanied by a negotiated consensus as to the output and prices of individual firms in specific industries. The intention, on the whole, is to achieve public objectives through private enterprise.

Even when this preference is expressed, it leaves open the question of whether the private element in public planning can best be preserved through general or particular policies. The liberal solution, characterizing the West generally, has been to opt for general policy measures, on the assumption that private actions can be left uncontrolled within the general constraints of appropriate monetary and fiscal actions.

The issue is not so easily resolved as this formula would suggest, however, for several reasons. For one thing, general policies can be discriminatory too. Because one measure—a tax program or credit availability—applies to all business or consumer activities does not mean that it applies equally. Some are affected more than others, even if unintentionally. The fact that the consequences of such purposive action are unintended does not for that reason make them nondiscriminatory. And conceivably it may be wiser to anticipate the discriminatory effects, and modulate regulatory action to secure results which are intended.

As a second consideration, once a government goes beyond such broad objectives as affecting consumer spending or business investment or the balance of payments and sets up more specific objectives dealing with housing or industrial organization or the fostering of a given industry or education or a moon-project, it must necessarily rely on particular inducements or restraints to achieve the particular results wanted. And the roster of such specific government goals has been lengthening in the Western economies.

A third consideration is that general measures are often blunderbuss type instruments which involve side effects we are unwilling to tolerate. General measures can seldom be used with so fine a touch as to achieve just the effect desired. The consequence is that governments tend to delay action until they are certain it is needed. When finally persuaded of the necessity, the action must be on a massive enough scale to stimulate the behavior wanted, and the effects tend to be harsher and more widespread than is desired, often with a built-in boomerang.

The understandable reluctance to cool off an overheated economy or the wish to stimulate a flagging economy in a hurry may lead a government to avoid the dangers of general fiscal and monetary measures by resorting to some other type of general program—an incomes policy, for example, or an export-import policy. But here we run smack into political issues which can only be resolved by *particular* applications of the "general" program. For a government to insist on some general policy which involves compliance by private units necessarily requires it to police private actions and determine whether they are or are not in conformance. For several years we have witnessed an instance of this here in the United States in the 3.2 percent wage-price guideposts, with our colleagues Walter Heller and Gardner Ackley resorting to varying degrees of persuasion, and presumably implied sanctions, in making particular applications of the general policy. This kind of general measure, once adopted, permits the exercise of private discretion within the policy framework.

The same consideration would be present if monetary policy were based on control of the interest rate directly rather than indirectly through control of the supply of money. To make such a policy effective would require some governmental agency to review the lending behavior of every bank and insurance company. Particular applications can be negotiated, over smaller areas of the economy than those to which general formulas apply, and in ways which achieve the results which are wanted, but the exercise is more involved and runs the risk of political discrimination. In this matter the Western economies have little experience to guide them.

The Western endeavor to preserve as large a measure of freedom of private action as possible, and still achieve public objectives, involves a number of basic philosophical dilemmas which can *only* be resolved by political compromise rather than some guiding principle. I suppose that Soviet-style planners have equivalent problems of social values, but certainly the private-public confrontation etches these more sharply for us than for them. I have time to discuss these only briefly. There are at least five of such conflicts of values.

First, there is the inevitable conflict between the efficient allocation of resources to achieve the objectives posed by any public plan—economizing in the traditional sense—and the autonomy (I would even say profligacy) of the individual spirit. Unless we economize, we fail to achieve as much of our goals as is technically feasible. But such planned allocation sacrifices the spontaneity of individual behavior, with its attendant possibilities for indiscretions, sporting actions, and the free if "irrational" play of individual decision. The issue is not subject to a cleancut choice of plan *or* individualism, but how much of each.

A second dilemma arises when we consider the unit within which the efficient solutions of a plan are to be sought. Even when we recognize that individualism must, in some degree or on some fronts, give way to the collective goals of a larger social unit, we are left with the question, within what unit? It need not be the nation, or only the nation. For some purposes, a business firm or a municipality may be the planning unit. For other purposes, a Common Market or even a United Nations. The significance here is that to talk about "planning" in the abstract makes little sense. Some planning is always going on within some units, whether household, labor union, corporation, or state. We inevitably confront the question of the level of aggregation at which planned objectives are to be formulated and planning mechanisms made effective. The larger the unit, obviously the more individuals who are affected, but the degree of the effect on them goes back to the first conflict we have just noted—the extent to which unit goals, whatever the unit, constrain individual discretion. In the West, we tend to accept firm constraints in small units more readily than we do in large units, even though large units may be necessary for appropriate solutions.

A third philosophical difficulty lies in the development of techniques for facilitating the efficient use of resources in the achievement of the planned objectives of whatever unit we have agreed on. As techniques become more technical, they develop a mystique which makes them comprehensible only to the expert, and the results to which they lead must then be accepted on face value, or rejected out of willfullness or ignorance. This dilemma was neatly demonstrated at the time when the Fourth French Plan was presented to the Assembly. (Belgium provided a parallel case.)

Into the plan which was presented in its massive, documented form, had gone the work of innumerable experts, from industry as well as government, producing what was described as a "coherent" plan, with all the pieces fitting together like a mosaic. What then was the function of the Assembly? It could hardly pick at the particulars of the document without destroying the overall design. It could scarcely reject the work of a vast army of specialists without repudiating the whole process.

We just confront, as did the French assembly, the question of the extent to which we should surrender technical decisions to the experts, in the economic pursuit of agreed-upon social objectives, recognizing that this necessarily leaves large areas in which the judgment—not the technique, but the judgment—of the experts puts its impress. This is so since questions of values run all through our social relationships, including intermediate decisions which somehow get swept up into an over-all design. To what extent do we sacrifice discretion in a multitude of "lesser" matters to realize superior achievement in a few broad areas of social purpose?

A fourth conflict that is presented by the private-public aspects of planning involves the use of representative bodies, such as industry commissions, in the formulation of plan objectives and mechanisms. This process provides a form of self-determination, which is a foundation stone of any democracy. But it also unavoidably intrudes control by the group over its constituent members. Participation in the making of a decision does not lessen the compulsion of the decision, especially when one may not be in accord with the results reached. The use of representative bodies avoids a greater centralization of authority, but the representative commissions created can exert more detailed and widespread compulsions than an official but more remote body. The *instruments* of government, even of democratic government, are compulsive, and the question remains as to the circumstances under which they should be employed, and the extent to which private groups should be delegated public power.

The fifth political compromise which must be faced arises from the tendency of a plan which starts with economic growth as an instrument for achieving specific goals to be converted in time into a struggle for economic growth almost for its own sake, without respect to social objectives, creating an autonomy of economic values. As an economy becomes geared to a rate of increase in GNP, employment and income depend on sustaining that rate year in and year out. Without always being aware of the subtle change which takes place in our thinking, we strive for the rate of increase itself, a symbol without content, ignoring the form in which it finds expression, the utilities and values which are all that give GNP meaning. Of course, it is true that it is only the growth in productive capacity and in national income which makes resource-using goals achievable, but nations as well as individuals tend to fall into a frame of mind in which they pursue those economic activities which give greatest growth, highest productivity increases, without much regard to whether the product has some claim to social priority.

These conflicts of philosophical values which inhere in the public planning process, with its inevitable contrast to private initiative, can only be met by tentative political compromises falling somewhere along a private-public spectrum of values.

It is with respect to where we are now coming down on the private-public spectrum that the convergence thesis seems to have considerable support. The political compromises to which I have referred are unavoidable even in the most privately-oriented economy. Even in earlier years, whether we think of such effusive decades as the gay '90's and the halcyon '20's, we still were making our compromises as to the degree of public control over private behavior. Presumably, however, we came down somewhat closer to the private end of the spectrum than is now the case. Since the depression years of the '30's, but especially since World War II, we have been steadily moving along that spectrum in the direction of the public pole. On the whole, our compromises give more weight to social purpose in contrast to private.

It seems to me most dubious that we shall ever wind up precisely at the same spot on the spectrum as the Soviet-socialist economies. After all, a question of political compromise of necessarily conflicting philosophic values is involved, both with respect to ends and means, and I see no reason to believe that either voluntarily or through some economic determinism Western and Soviet philosophies will become identical. But that they will approach each other somewhat more closely than is now the case seems to me more than likely.

4   FRANCESCO VITO

DECENTRALIZATION IN A COLLECTIVIST PLANNED ECONOMY

1. COLLECTIVIST PLANNING AND REGULATED MARKET ECONOMY

The expression Planned Economy covers a variety of meanings. For the sake of simplicity let us assume as a starting point the following definition: by Planned Economy we understand a type of economic policy aiming at influencing the economic system in such a way as to achieve results with regards to production and distribution of goods and services which differ from those of the market economy. This aim can be pursued in two different ways:

(a) by *abolishing* the market mechanism i.e. establishing public ownership of all means of production and giving to a central planning authority the power to impose from above the decisions regarding the rate of increase of national income, the shares of investment and consumption in national income, the allocation of investment outlays between sectors and branches, the distribution of the consumption fund between groups, etc. This is the collectivist or totalitarian type of planning;

(b) by simply *modifying* through a series of different measures and devices the results of the market mechanism, whose essential features i.e. private ownership of the means of production (however limited in its use by public regulation), free choice of occupation and consumption, are fundamentally preserved. The institutional framework in this case is that of a market economy. But its functioning is conditioned and modified by State intervention. It is a type of economic policy which does not limit itself to occasional measures in the fields of taxation, money, tariffs, transports, etc. All these and similar forms of intervention are coordinated and harmonized into a coherent system of economic policy with the purpose of achieving objectives which the interplay of individual decision and efforts alone is unable to arrive at. That is why this type of policy deserves the name of economic planning. However, since it does not destroy the market mechanism, it must be clearly distinguished from the

From *Economia Internazionale*, Vol. XVIII, 2, 1965, pp. 197–206. Reprinted by permission of the author and *Economia Internazionale*.

collectivist or totalitarian planning. For want of a better expression one may speak in this case of a "regulated market economy."

2. THE CASE FOR DECENTRALIZATION

Obviously the countries engaged in collectivist economic planning are seriously confronted with problems of decentralization. Delays in action and waste of resources are inevitable in a system where decision about allocation of means of production among different uses, sectors and branches as well as distribution of intermediate and consumption goods are concentrated in a single authority. Moreover the danger of inefficiency increases with the growing diversity of disposable resources consequent upon technical innovations.

It is also to be expected that as soon as some standard of material welfare is secured in society there will be felt the need of drawing a larger number of people into active participation in shaping the development of the economy. All those elements point toward decentralization. But here the problem arises: to what extent is decentralization compatible with collectivist economic planning? After all, this type of planned economy is by definition a centralistic form of organization. Can it be really decentralized? The question deserves to be investigated carefully. That is what I propose to do, however briefly, in this paper.

3. IS COLLECTIVIST PLANNING COMPATIBLE WITH DECENTRALIZATION?

The great controversy on economic calculation in a collectivist planned economy began some years ago when a collection of reprints was edited by Prof. Hayek under the title: "Collectivist Economic Planning"[1] including the essay first published in 1908 by the Italian economist E. Barone, entitled: "The Ministry of Production in a Collectivist State." The main criticism made against collectivist planning by Barone can be summarized as follows: if the planning authority (the Ministry of Production) wants to act rationally it is bound to accomplish the very same task which is brought about by the market mechanism, i.e. it is confronted with the solution of the same system of equations corresponding to the

---

[1] A French edition was published later: *L'Economie dirigée en régime collectiviste*, Paris, Librairie de Médicis, 1939.

general economic equilibrium which is practically achieved automatically in a market economy. Is that possible? First of all it would be necessary to obtain millions of statistical figures indicating supply of resources, state of technology and scale of preferences. Secondly, there would arise the so-called "problem of the equations," consisting in the solution of innumerable simultaneous equations in order to arrive at a system of accounting prices on which the economic calculation can be based.

The obvious conclusion to be derived from the preceding criticism is that a collectivist economy cannot function according to rational principles.

And yet, the proponents of collectivism object that this view may have been true some decades ago; nowadays such a negative attitude cannot be maintained any longer. The progress which has recently been made in computation techniques now permits difficulties once considered as insuperable to be overcome.

4. Decentralization in an Administrative Sense

It is well known that the collection and circulation of information and its use for purposes of forecasting play an important role in a market economy. But the importance is much greater in any type of planned economy, particularly in a collectivist planned economy, where the planning authority is confronted with the ambitious task of determining the general direction of economic development. Modern information techniques no doubt greatly facilitate the tremendous work of collecting and transmitting a huge mass of statistical data so that it can be processed and transmitted readily to the decision-making authority. That means that many people and agencies collaborate in this work according to rules susceptible to scientific determination. In fact a "theory of teams" has been elaborated which can be applied both to the members of an enterprise and to the administration of an economic plan (Marschak).

In so far as collection, verification and analysis of information is based on team work one can safely say that the planning organization permits a certain degree of decentralization for the purpose of reducing waste and increasing efficiency.

It should be noted that collection of data is not accomplished once and for all. According to the theory, the planning authority lays down accounting prices and then manipulates them in such a way as to maintain equilibrium between supply and demand for each product at the current accounting price. Therefore there must be a continuous information flow from the various quarters of the economy to the planning authority indicating changes in demand and supply. On the basis of this information manipulations of accounting prices are undertaken until the equilibrium situation is reached. That makes even more evident the usefulness of decentralizing the collection of statistical material.

However, it is important to realize that the decentralized process in this case concerns the preparation of the plan and not the content of the plan itself. Or it may concern also the communication of the planning decisions to the executive organs, once the decisions themselves have been centrally adopted. In other words the decentralization concerns the supply of material for central decisions or the procedures for transmission of orders to be executed, or both. It is therefore a decentralization in a purely administrative sense as distinguished from a decentralization in an economic sense, which of course relates to the planning decisions themselves, which will be discussed later in this paper.

5. DECENTRALIZATION IN A TECHNICAL SENSE

This is not all. As has been stated previously, the planning authority is confronted not only with the problem of information but also with the so-called "problem of the equations." One point of criticism raised against collectivist economy has been concentrated for a long time on the practical difficulty of calculating millions of equations in order to arrive at the accounting prices. But now, owing to the possibility of employing electronic brains, this difficulty can be overcome. Given the supply of goods, the state of technology and the scale of preferences, it now becomes easier, thanks to modern mathematical programming techniques, to reach the solutions corresponding to the most appropriate allocation of resources.

Now, the introduction of this highly advanced technical device means at the same time enlarging the number of people and agencies participating in the computing job. Just as in the case of information, as illustrated above, here again we find that the solution of the mathematical programming problem becomes a team work. This implies a further progress toward decentralization. However, even in this case, what is being decentralized does not refer to the very process of planning decisions, i.e., the economic content of the plan, but simply to the planning techniques. It is a decentralization in a purely technical sense.

6. DECENTRALIZATION IN THE ECONOMIC SENSE

Decentralization in the economic sense goes beyond the administrative and the technical aspects of planning. It is not concerned with raising the standard of administrative and technical efficiency of the planning organisation through better flow of information and a more advanced calculation method, but with the much more profound and substantial problem of multiplying or at least differentiating the sources of decision-making. This can be advocated, and in fact has been advocated, by proponents of the collectivist economy on the ground that only in this way is it possible to let a larger number of people participate in shaping the development of the economy and also to facilitate the manifestation of the creative abilities of the members of society.

In order to accomplish this result they propose to substitute a decentralized model to the centralistic one corresponding strictly speaking to collectivist planning.[2] The characteristics of the centralistic model are as follows: (a) one-level-decision-taking; (b) strictly hierarchical structure and predominance of the vertical links between central level and enterprises; (c) communications from the top to the bottom in the form of orders.

The decentralized model rests essentially on the splitting up of the power of decision-making between different agencies. One of its basic features is: (a) the multiplicity of levels of decision-making. In order to simplify matters only two levels of decision-making are considered: the level of the central authority and the level of the enterprise. To the first belong decisions which determine the general direction of the economic development, the rate of increase of national income, the shares of investment and consumption, the allocation of investment outlays between sections and branches, the distribution of the consumption-fund between social groups, etc. Decision on the following matters are left with the enterprises: the size and the structure of outputs of a given branch or production unit; the sources of supplies and direction of sales; the form and the methods of remuneration, etc.

Other features of the decentralized model are: (a) plans on different levels are independently formulated: the central plan on the basis of the aims and standards of the headquarters, the plans of the enterprises on the basis of their rules of the game; (b) the links between different levels are achieved not by orders but by indirect means, i.e., the determination of market magnitudes which serve as parameters of decisions taken by the enterprises. The market mechanism plays an important role in this model, according to its supporters. They even go so far as to define the decentralized model as a "model of functioning of a planned economy with built-in-market mechanism."

But this combination of collectivist planning and market system is hardly conceivable.

Let us confine our criticism of it to essentials.

[2] I am following here the suggestion made by Prof. Brus in his paper on "Problems of Decentralization in a Socialist Planned Economy," first presented at the I.P.S.A. Round Table, Oxford, September 1963.

7. The Conflict between Planning Authority and Enterprise

In so far as the enterprises are allowed to make autonomous decisions, they may disregard the central decisions and consequently endanger the implementation of the plan. To say that the enterprises are expected to remain within the realm of their competence as indicated above or that they have to take the market magnitudes as determined by the central authority as parameters of their own decisions does not really help us to get rid of the difficulties. An autonomous choice among several alternatives as to the structure of inputs and outputs, the product-mix, the methods of remuneration, etc. may bring about changes in the quantitative and qualitative use of factors of production which do not conform to the accounting prices laid down by the higher authority and do not correspond to the objectives of the plan. Obviously this consideration stems from the concept of interdependency of all economic magnitudes on which the general equilibrium idea (Walras and Pareto) is based.

In the light of this concept it becomes apparent that those who propose to combine collectivist planning with multiplicity of levels of decisions are confronted with an inescapable dilemma: either allowance is made for manifestation of creative ability by the enterprises and for a larger participation of people in determining the general direction of the economic development, which make for autonomous decisions at lower echelons: but this may doom the plan to failure; or it is assumed that the plan satisfies in the best way the welfare of the community: and then no interference in its implementation can be admitted by allowing autonomous decisions at lower levels.

This point can be further elucidated by another remark. It is really difficult to conceive of a collectivist economy, i.e., of an economy in which all means of production are in public ownership, which could be combined with a built-in-market mechanism. Suppose the enterprises intend to change the structure of inputs and outputs because they believe they can raise productivity in this way. Are they allowed to do so if there is a possibility that they may be wrong in their estimation? The answer depends on the attitude one takes regarding risk-taking in cases where ownership and control are separated. At any rate one is bound to admit that to the extent that the enterprises are somehow limited in their deciding power the market mechanism must inevitably loose its effectiveness.

8. Choice of Consumption in a Collectivist Economy

Finally it remains to indicate what the place of consumption and occupation choice in a collectivist economy is. It is understood that the decisions by the planning authority on general economic development, production targets, etc. are taken on the basis of the scale of the individual preferences as estimated by the authority itself. Then the initial decisions as to amount of production, prices, etc. are modified in order to take into account successive changes in supply and demand. Of course allowance must be made for the inevitable imperfection of the estimation of the scale of preferences as well as for the time lag consequent on the period required for collecting information. But this is not the major issue. Individual preferences can manifest themselves and be registered, however approximately, by the planning authority only in relation to goods and services which are really offered to the consumer. A situation of this type is conceivable as long as the dimension of the national product does not allow more than the satisfaction of elementary needs. But as soon as the income, and also the resources disposable for consumption increase, people may want to consume goods and services which previously did not exist on the market. How can the preferences in this case manifest themselves? One may think of the procedure of placing a variety of goods on the market at prices covering costs, observing how the demand reacts to it and then letting prices vary until demand equals supply. But there are several objections to this procedure, the most important being: a. it is a very costly method indeed because factors of production employed in order to bring to the market goods which do not find a sufficient demand would be wasted; b. it is always limited by the number of goods which can simultaneously be offered for sale as compared with those which could potentially be produced and demanded. Hence the range of choice by the consumers is always restricted to the possibilities conceded by the planning authority.

9. Choice of Occupation in a Collectivist Economy

The freedom of choice of occupation is an indispensable element of the market mechanism. It is a condition of the functioning of this mechanism and at the same time it is conditioned by the mechanism itself. But it is difficult to preserve this freedom in a collectivist economy. Once the production patterns have been established by the planning authority there is small room for a free choice of occupation on the part of newcomers and for a change of occupation of the workers already employed. Should the choice of occupation be different from that corresponding to the plan, then a different structure of inputs and outputs would result and consequently the objectives of the plan might not materialize.

If the preceding considerations are correct one may express doubts on the validity of the so-called decentralized model of a collectivist planned economy. This type of economy requires that the economic decisions be taken at one and single level, i.e., at the level of the high authority, and that other agencies as well as workers and consumers carry out those decisions or conform to them. There is no place for autonomous decisions either on the part of enterprises or on that of workers and consumers. Any concession in that direction might endanger the working of the plan.

10. Summary and Conclusion

When discussing the issue "Centralization versus Decentralization in a planned economy" it is convenient to adopt some essential distinctions.

First of all one must distinguish between a collectivist planned economy and a regulated market economy. The main features of the first are public ownership of all means of production and the existence of one single source of individual income, i.e., work in public enterprises or institutions. The other system is characterized on the one hand by private ownership of the means of production in a substantial section of the economy and freedom of choice of occupation and consumption; on the other hand by extensive public intervention aiming at a modification of the results of the market forces in order to achieve social ends which could not be reached through the simple interplay of individual decisions.

The other distinction which should be borne in mind relates to decentralization. One can conceive of three kinds of decentralization: a. administrative; b. technical; c. economic. The collectivist economy can usefully adopt the first two kinds of decentralization in order to eliminate or reduce waste and increase operational efficiency. For instance, the planning authority can promote collaboration between agencies operating at lower levels in the task of collecting and transmitting information and in this way the administrative efficiency of the planning operations can be improved. Similarly, the technical efficiency of planning can be increased by ensuring the cooperation of several agencies in the task of the solution of the innumerable simultaneous equations which is required in order to arrive at a system of accounting prices.

Nothing of that kind can be said in favour of economic decentralization. The working of a built-in market mechanism is not compatible with a collectivist economy. It would imply a multiplicity of levels of decision-making; but then there would be a variety of interpretations of current data and forecasting suspectible to lead to different and perhaps conflicting decisions. Furthermore it would imply freedom of choice of occupation and consumption, which again may put serious obstacles to the functioning of the plan.

It is undoubtedly true that the idea of drawing a larger group of people into participation in shaping the economic development and that of facilitating the manifestation of the creative ability of the members of the community can never be put into effect unless a multiplicity of sources of decisions and the free choice of occupation and consumption be established. But the crucial point is that in order to satisfy those prerequisites it would be necessary to abandon the cornerstone of the collectivist economy: i.e., public ownership of all means of production and work in public enterprises and institutions as the only source of individual income.

Of course in economic matters as well as in all fields of human activity some ways of compromising between opposed principles can in practice be found. One thing should be clear however: to the extent that a collectivist planned economy does succeed in the attempt to enlarge participation and stimulate creative abilities, to that extent it moves consciously or unconsciously toward a different type of economy, namely that of the regulated market economy. Consequently the institutional framework sooner or later must accordingly be changed. Economic and social objectives of a pluralistic character, like a large participation of citizens and an increasing manifestation of creative ability can hardly be attained in a collectivist organized society. The achievement of economic and social goals is always conditioned by the existing institutional framework, and not vice versa.[3]

[3] This conclusion is opposed to the view recently expressed by a Russian author, V. V. Novozhilov, in his work on measurement of production expenses and their results in a collectivist economy: a French translation has been published in the volume: *Rationalité et calcul économique en U.R.S.S.*, Paris, I.S.E.A., 1964. Novozhilov maintains that "in spite of differences in their institutional framework and the differences between the objectives pursued by the various economic systems, the theoretical solution of the problem of the economic optimum is independent of the systems."

Suggested Reading

I. General

Boulding, Kenneth E., "The Relations of Economic, Political, and Social Systems," *Social and Economic Studies*, Vol. II, No. 4 (1965), pp. 351–362.

Schweitzer, Arthur, "The Scope of Comparative Economics," in Association for Comparative Economics, 1964 National Program, *Papers and Discussion*, Presented on Problems and Methods of Teaching Comparative Economics (DeKalb, Illinois, 1965), pp. 1–8. See also the discussion of this paper by Fred M. Gottheil, *ibid.*, pp. 9–10. [Mimeographed.]

Tangri, S. S., "Economic Systems and Economic Efficiency," *Asian Economic Review*, November 1967.

II. Market Model

Cirillo, R., "Capitalism, Private Property, and Freedom," *Review of Social Economy*, Vol. 24, No. 2 (September 1966), pp. 157–166.

Demsetz, Harold, "Some Aspects of Property Rights," *The Journal of Law and Economics*, Vol. IX (October 1966), pp. 61–70.

Macesich, George, "The Price System, Planning, and Economic Development," Chapter 4 of *Yugoslavia: The Theory and Practice of Development Planning* (Charlottesville, The University of Virginia Press, 1964), pp. 34–49.

Macfie, A. L., "The Moral Justification of Free Enterprise," *Scottish Journal of Political Economy*, Vol. XVI, No. 1 (February 1967), pp. 1–11.

Wallich, Henry C., *The Cost of Freedom: A New Look at Capitalism* (New York, Harper & Row, 1960).

III. Command Model

Beckwith, Burnham P., *The Economic Theory of a Socialist Economy* (Stanford, Calif., Stanford University Press, 1949).

Feiwel, G. R., "Towards a Model of Soviet Planning," *Economia Internazionale*, November 1967.

Grossman, Gregory, "Notes for a Theory of the Command Economy," *Soviet Studies*, Vol. XV, No. 2 (October 1963), pp. 101–123.

Gutmann, G., "The Distribution Problem in Centrally Planned Economy: A Study in Model Theory," *Weltwirtschaftliches Archiv*, March 1968, pp. 41–69.

Konnik, I., "Plan and Market in a Socialist Economy," *Problems of Economics*, Vol. IX, No. 8 (December 1966), pp. 24–35.

IV. The Lange Model

Bergson, Abram, "Market Socialism Revisited," in Association for Comparative Economics, *Proceedings of National Meetings,* December 27–29, 1966 (De-Kalb, Illinois, 1967), pp. 1–26.

V. Public Planning in Market Systems

Balassa, Bela, "Planning in an Open Economy," *Inter Economics* (March 1967), pp. 75–80.

Bator, Francis M., *The Question of Government Spending: Public Needs and Private Wants* (New York, Collier Books, London, Collier-Macmillan, 1962).

Chamberlain, Neil W., *Private and Public Planning* (New York, McGraw-Hill, 1965).

Heilbroner, Robert L., and Bernstein, Peter L., *A Primer on Government Spending* (New York, Vintage Books, 1963).

Jewkes, J., *Public and Private Enterprise* (London, Routledge, 1965).

Johnson, Harry G., "Planning and the Objectives of a Free Enterprise Economy," Chapter 4 of *The Canadian Quandary: Economic Problems and Policies* (Toronto, McGraw-Hill, 1963), pp. 33–45.

Köhler, Heinz, *Scarcity Challenged: An Introduction to Economics* (New York, Holt, Rinehart and Winston, 1968).

Kirschen, E. S. (ed.), *Economic Policy in Our Time,* 3 volumes (Chicago, Rand McNally, 1964).

Leon, Paolo, *Structural Change and Growth in Capitalism* (Baltimore, Johns Hopkins, 1967).

Podbielski, G., *Some Aspects of Economic Planning in Western European Industrial Countries* (London, Woolwich Polytechnic, Woolwich Economic Papers, No. 12, 1967).

Sirkin, Gerald, *The Visible Hand: A Critique of Economic Planning* (New York, McGraw-Hill, 1968).

VI. Customary Economies

Dalton, George (ed.), *Tribal and Peasant Economies: Readings in Economic Anthropology* (Garden City, N.Y., The Natural History Press, 1967).

Shaffer, H. G. and Prybyla, J. S. (eds.), *From Underdevelopment to Affluence* (New York, Appleton-Century-Crofts, 1968).

Shah, Manubhai, "The Role of Private Sector," *Eastern Economist,* July 21, 1967, pp. 106–108, 111–112.

VII. Market Forces in Command Systems

See Readings List at the end of Part IV.

II
Ideologies
and Economic Systems

Introduction

Ideologies are systems of ideas which justify or attack a given social, economic, or political order. They are normative constructs: explicitly held beliefs, or value judgments implicit in analytical systems. When ideological interest turns to methods and tools of resource allocation, the result is what some have termed "economic theology." Economic theology of one kind or another has always been with us: as qualitative political economy it antedates quantitative economics. For all its apparent precision, quantitative economics is by no means free of ideology. Ideology is concealed in the analytical tool kit of the economist: in the concepts of utility, national income, competition, consumer sovereignty, preference functions, the marginal propensities to save and consume, and in those of labor power, socially necessary labor time, surplus value, and the Law of Planned, Proportional Development of the National Economy. It colors our thinking when we believe ourselves to be analytically rigorous. One of the aims of Part II is to identify, as far as this is possible, some of the ideological elements in analytical concepts.

Value structures, however, are also of interest in so far as they represent one level of the crucial relationships in (an as yet tentative and incomplete) general theory of comparative economic systems. Looked at this way, a study of ideologies can help us gain a better understanding of individual and state preference functions and of their interaction.

Methodologically, therefore, Part II performs two functions:

1. It clarifies the concept of successive approximations by identifying some of the major ideological elements implicit in successive analytical models of economic systems.

2. It advances the search for a general theory of comparative economic systems by discussing at length one level of significant relationships in the economy seen as an intrinsic part of the total social system.

Part II rejects the contention that ideological models are irrelevant to the study of different economic systems. As Price and Berg show, ideologies are extremely pertinent to the study of customary economies in the process of change. The search for new ways of organizing economic activity is not exclusively a search for the most effective means of rapid growth and modernization. It is that, but it is also a quest for social justice, variously understood, and for national power and prestige. The criteria according to which advanced economic models are evaluated in the developing countries, are not solely those of static and dynamic efficiency, internal consistency, and optimum growth. Memories of real or imagined colonial wrongs, and aspirations for an ethically, socially, and politically better future, play an important, and at times determining, part. This theme is taken up again in Part VI.

Ideologies proceed from rigid theses, not subject to inquiry. On this basis they explain all phenomena of life, nature, and society, and formu-, late the only correct guidelines for political, economic, and social action. Ideologies may be basic, in which case they dominate the minds of leaders and followers, or they may be synthetic, in which case they are used by the leaders—with or without conviction—to enlist obedience among their followers. Sometimes they are reduced to mere slogans. As Bornstein notes, ideologies may perform directing, authenticating, or masking functions. They are capable of inspiring commitment to various forms of change or of strengthening resistance to change. They may be used as goals or as *ex post* justifications of particular policies. Not infrequently, they have served to mask the true nature of given courses of action. But whatever the use to which they have been put, ideologies are part of the most diverse operational economic systems and of the purest of analytical models.

Because every ideology claims to formulate the only correct guideline for action, the coexistence of ideologies is strained and potentially explosive. Because ideologies infiltrate economic theory and policy, antagonism and conflict are introduced into competitive economic coexistence. In choosing among different solutions to the problem of underdevelopment, customary economies are, in fact, engaged in ideological choice which is not made any easier by the introduction of indigenous ideological strains.

5   JOHN KENNETH GALBRAITH

IDEOLOGY AND THE AMERICAN ECONOMY

The late Lord Keynes, in what promises to be one of the more widely quoted passages from his pen, observed that "the ideas of economists and political philosophers, both when they are right and when they are wrong, are more powerful than is commonly understood. . . . Practical men, who believe themselves to be quite exempt from any intellectual influences, are usually the slaves of some defunct economist." Ideas underlie the uneasiness described in the last chapter. However it would be wrong to suppose they are the sole explanation. Something must also be attributed to mere reaction to change. The well-to-do and the wealthy man will normally be mistrustful of change. This has been so, in the past, in nearly all times and places. It is a simple matter of arithmetic that change *may* be costly to the man who has something; it cannot be so to the man who has nothing. There is always, accordingly, a high correlation between conservatism and personal well-being.

Generalizing more broadly, as the United States proceeds to higher levels of well-being, there is certain to be a steady retreat from social experiment. Indeed, were it not dangerous to extend a trend derived from only one brief decade of prosperity, one could argue that this rejection of social experiment is already far advanced. As this is written, American liberals have made scarcely a new proposal for reform in twenty years. It is not evident that they have had any important new ideas. Reputations for liberalism or radicalism continue to depend almost exclusively on a desire to finish the unfinished social legislation of the New Deal. It was adversity that nurtured this program; with prosperity social invention came promptly to an end. On domestic matters, liberal organizations have not for years had anything that might be called a program. Rather they have had a file. Little is ever added. Platform-making consists, in effect, in emptying out the drawers. The Midwest and Great Plains, which once provided Congress with its most disturbing radicals, now returns its staunchest conservatives including also its most determined reactionaries. The political destiny of the United States does not rest with those who seek or who are suspected of wishing to repeal laws, withdraw services

From John Kenneth Galbraith, *American Capitalism. The Concept of Countervailing Power*, Second Edition, Revised (Boston, Mass.: Houghton Mifflin Company, 1956), and Hamish Hamilton, Ltd., London. Reprinted by permission of the publishers.

and undo what has been done. This also is change and unwelcomed. But, given peace and prosperity, it no longer rests with those who advocate major social experiment. In a country where well-being is general, the astute politician will be the one who stalwartly promises to defend the *status quo*.[1]

II

The ideas which are the deeper cause of insecurity are the common heritage of liberals and conservatives alike. These derive from a theory of capitalism which has deeply shaped the attitudes of both. This is the system of classical economics which was constructed in the latter part of the eighteenth and during the nineteenth century, primarily in England. Those who would make its acceptance a test of sound Americanism should know that, to a singular degree, it is an alien doctrine. Its principal early architects were Englishmen and Scots. American economists, although they added some important amendments and reproduced it in countless textbooks, contributed comparatively little to the structure itself. Until fairly recent times Americans have not shown high originality in economic theory, and the habit of looking abroad for authority is still strong. It was the classical system, as imported from nineteenth-century England, that became the explicit and remains the implicit interpretation of American capitalism.

The bearing of this system on the insecurity stressed in the last chapter becomes evident, even in cursory view, when it is examined in relation to the world it is presumed to interpret. Given this system or, more accurately, an economy constructed to its specifications where there is stout observance of its rules of behavior, all of the worries of the preceding chapter dissolve. It described an economic system of high social efficiency—that is to say, one in which all incentives encouraged the employment of men, capital and natural resources in producing most efficiently what people most wanted. There could be no misuse of private power

---

[1] I sense, for example, that the unexpected strength of the Democrats in 1948 lay not with Mr. Truman's promise of any great forward steps in economic policy but in his evident willingness to defend what existed including the measures enacted in the New Deal years. The Republican Party, by contrast, was handicapped by the suspicion—which numerous of its spokesmen and supporters reinforced rather than dispelled—that it harbored a deep nostalgia for the past and might seek change in that direction. In 1952, by contrast, General Eisenhower, with rather more capacity to inspire confidence than Mr. Dewey, managed to persuade the public that there would be no important backward change.

In the United Kingdom the Conservatives have also capitalized on the defence of the *status quo* and there, as in the United States, ideas on the left have been severely blighted by prosperity.

because no one had power to misuse. An innocuous role was assigned to government because there was little that was useful that a government could do. There was no place in the theory for severe depression or inflation. The system worked. This was the promise, but it was made only to a society with the proper economic institutions and the proper respect for the rules of behavior which the classical system required. In the contemporary United States few of the preconditions for the system can seriously be supposed to exist. Nor do we pretend to live by its rules. Accordingly, we are forced to assume that we stand constantly in danger of reaping the terrible reward of our neglect and our disobedience. The dangers and even the disasters we risk are no less fearsome because we do not know their precise shape or why they do not come.

III

The first requirement of the classical system, as everyone is aware, is competition. In the design of the system this was fundamental and, if it was prsent in a sufficiently rigorous form, it was also enough. In practice, another condition, more properly an assertion, was added in the form of Say's Law of Markets. This held that the act of producing goods provided the purchasing power, neither too much nor too little, for buying them. Thus there was invariable equivalence between the value of what was produced and the purchasing power available to buy that production. It will be evident, even from the most casual reflection, that this comforting doctrine went far to preclude either a serious depression or a violent inflation.

The kind of competition that was necessary for this system was rigorous or, rather, there was a tendency to specify an increasingly rigorous form of competition with the passage of time. The classical economists—Adam Smith, Ricardo and Mill—were not especially self-conscious in their use of the term. Competition was the rivalry of the merchants of the town or of the cotton manufacturers or pit proprietors of nineteenth-century England. Adam Smith contented himself with distinguishing competition from monopoly by its consequences: "The price of monopoly is upon every occasion the highest which can be got. . . . The price of free competition, on the contrary, is the lowest which can be taken, not upon every occasion indeed, but for any considerable time together."[2] But toward the end of the nineteenth century writers began to make explicit what had previously been implied: namely, that competition re-

[2] *Wealth of Nations* (London: P. F. Collier & Sons, 1902 ed.), vol. I, pp. 116–17.

quired that there be a considerable number of sellers in any trade or
industry in informed communication with each other. In more recent
times this has been crystallized into the notion of many sellers doing
business with many buyers. Each is well informed as to the prices at
which others are selling and buying—there is a going price of which
everyone is aware. Most important of all, no buyer or seller is large
enough to control or exercise an appreciable influence on the common
price. In the language of the most distinguished modern exponent of the
classical system as an economic and political goal, "The price system will
fulfill [its] function only if competition prevails, that is, *if the individual
producer has to adapt himself to price changes and cannot control them.*"[3]
The rigor of this definition of competition must be stressed especially to
the business reader, for it has been the source of an endless amount of
misunderstanding between businessmen and economists. After spending
the day contemplating the sales force, advertising agency, engineers, and
research men of his rivals the businessman is likely to go home feeling
considerably harassed by competition. Yet if it happens that he has measurable control over his prices he obviously falls short of being competitive in the foregoing sense. No one should be surprised if he feels some
annoyance toward scholars who appropriate words in common English
usage and, for their own purposes, give them what seems to be an in-
ordinately restricted meaning.

Yet the notion of a market for an industry in which no producer or
buyer has *any* influence on price is not as improbable as appears at first
glance. There is no wheat or cotton grower in the United States whose
contribution to the wheat or cotton market is appreciable in relation to
the total supply. In January, 1949, a Missouri cotton planter made what
was believed to be the largest sale of cotton in the history of the Memphis
spot market. But the 9400 bales he sold for $1,400,000 was an almost in-
finitesimal fraction of the 1949 supply. This planter could have gone to
heaven with his cotton instead of to Memphis and there would have been
no noticeable tremor on any earthly market.

So it is with most other agricultural products. In the nineteenth century, when the classical system was taking form, agriculture contributed
a considerably larger share of the national product than at present. Moreover the burgeoning cotton industry, coal-mining and metal and metalworking industries of England of the day were all shared by numerous
producers. The production of each was small in relation to that of all.
None could much influence the common price. Finally, in England this
was the time of free trade. Sellers were exposed to prices that were
made in the markets of the world at large. The kind of competition that
was implicit in the pioneering designs of the classical economists of the

---

[3] F. A. Hayek, *The Road to Serfdom* (Chicago: University of Chicago Press,
1944), p. 49. The italics are mine.

nineteenth century was not unrealistic. It described a world that then existed; those who formulated the theory did not, as some have since supposed, misjudge reality. They were practical men.

This did not remain the case. Economists, as noted, in seeking to give precision to their language, added rigor to the notion of competition. They also began to require of competition a meaning which would cause it, in turn, to produce the economic and social consequences which earlier economists had associated with it. The definition of competition was gradually accommodated to the requirements of a model economic society; it became not the definition that described reality but the one that produced ideal results. The preoccupation ceased to be with interpreting reality and came to be with building a model economic society. The definition of competition was, in effect, accommodated to the requirements of that model. Its nexus with the competition of the real world, which in turn was in process of change, was no longer maintained.

By the early decades of the present century the task of constructing this model of a capitalist society regulated by competition was virtually complete. It was an intellectual achievement of a high order. As a device, in theory, for ordering the economic relations between men it was very nearly perfect. Socialist theorists—Enrico Barone, the great Italian scholar, and Oskar Lange, the equally notable Polish economist—used the theoretical performance of the competitive model as the goal of a socialist state. Few of the original architects of the competitive model would have defended it as a description of the world as it is—or was. For some the competitive model was a first approximation to reality—it departed from real life only to the extent that there was monopoly in industry or over natural resources, including land, or that government or custom interposed barriers to competition. For others it was the goal toward which capitalism might be expected to move or toward which it might be guided or a standard by which it might be appraised. For yet others the construction and refinement of the competitive model was a challenging intellectual exercise.

The birth, development and subsequent career of an idea is something like that of a human. The parents have measurable control over the first two stages but not the third. Once constructed, the competitive model passed into the textbooks and the classrooms. In the absence of any alternative interpretation of economic life, it became the system of virtually all who undertook to teach economics. It was and remains the economics of those who essay to popularize the subject—to instruct in one lesson. The qualifications, and especially the warnings that there had been an abstraction from reality, were lost or neglected. To this day the abstraction, largely undiluted and unqualified, is the principal residuum of the considerable time and expense that goes into the effort to teach economics to Americans.

Man cannot live without an economic theology—without some rationalization of the abstract and seemingly inchoate arrangements which provide him with his livelihood. For this purpose the competitive or classical model had many advantages. It was comprehensive and internally consistent. By asserting that it was a description of reality the conservative could use it as the justification of the existing order. For the reformer it could be a goal, a beacon to mark the path of needed change. Both could be united in the central faith at least so long as nothing happened to strain unduly their capacity for belief.

It is now necessary to examine the performance of the model in more detail.

IV

The notion of efficiency as applied to an economic system is many-sided. It can be viewed merely as a matter of getting the most for the least; this is the commonplace engineering view of efficiency. There is also the problem of getting the particular things that are wanted by the community in the particular amounts in which they are wanted. In addition, if an economy is to be efficient some reasonably full use must be made of the available, or at least of the willing, labor supply. There must be some satisfactory allocation of resources between present and future production—between what is produced for consumption and what is invested in new plant and processes to enlarge future consumption. There must also be appropriate incentive to change; the adoption of new and more efficient methods of production must be encouraged.

Finally—a somewhat different requirement and one that went long unrecognized—there must be adequate provision for the research and technological development which brings new methods and (though one is permitted to deplore them if necessary) new products into existence. All this makes a large bill of requirements.

The peculiar fascination of the competitive model was that, given its particular form of competition—that of many sellers, none of whom was large enough to influence the price—all the requirements for efficiency, with the exception of the very last, were met. No producer—no more than the Kansas wheat grower of fact—could gain additional revenue for himself by raising or otherwise manipulating his price. This opportunity was denied to him by the kind of competition which was assumed, the competition of producers no one of whom was large enough in relation to all to influence the common price. He could gain an advantage only by reducing costs. Were there even a few ambitious men in the business he would have to do so to survive, for if he neglected his opportunities others would seize them. If there are already many in a business it can be assumed that there is no serious bar to others entering it. Given an opportunity for improving efficiency of production, those who seized it, and the imitators they would attract from within and without, would expand production and lower prices. The rest, to survive at these lower prices, would have to conform to the best and most efficient practices. In such a manner a Darwinian struggle for business survival concentrated all energies on the reduction of costs and prices.

In this model, producer effort and consumer wants were also effectively related by the price that no producer and no consumer controlled or influenced. The price that would just compensate some producer for added labor, or justify some other cost, was also the one which it was just worth the while of some consumer to pay for the product in question. Any diminution in consumer desire for the item would be impersonally communicated through lower price to producers. By no longer paying for marginal labor or other productive resources the consumer would free these resources for other employment on more wanted products. Thus energies were also efficiently concentrated on producing what was most desired.

In the competitive model these changes did not raise the threat of unemployment. When the taste of the consumer waned for one product it waxed for another; the higher price for the second product communicated to the producers in that industry the information that they could profitably expand their production and employment. They took in the slack that had been created in the first industry. Even had the consumer decided to save, the saving was for investment—for another kind of expenditure. In any case it was always open to the worker in this system to insure his own employment. Any particular employer was restrained from expanding employment only because the outlay for the added employment was not covered by the resulting increase in income at the going price. The worker seeking employment had it within his own power to alter this delicate balance by offering to work for a lower wage. By doing so he could always make it worth the while of an employer to give him a job. A union, by restraining such wage-cutting, could obviously do damage in this delicately adjusted Elysium. But unions were not a part of the system.

V

There was never full agreement among the architects of the model on the manner in which labor and the other productive resources of the community were allotted as between consumption and investment—between current use and the production of plant, equipment, utilities and public works which would yield their return only over a period of time in the future. However, despite sectarian disputes on details, there was something close to a consensus on the nature of the underlying process. Here as elsewhere competition rendered efficient service. The competition of those who sought the prospective return from plant, machinery, utility or other investment established a price, in the form of the rate of interest, for those who were willing to save from current consumption and thereby make these investments possible. A high return from additional investment would bid up the price for savings. This would lead to more savings and less current consumption. Resources would thus be freed for investment. By the same process the community's desire for goods for current consumption would be balanced against the prospect of having more and different goods as the result of investment.

If it is assumed that immediate consumption is man's normal preference, and that he will only save if he is paid to do so, it is wholly unnatural to suppose that anyone would first deprive himself of consumer's goods and then, by not turning over his savings for investment, deprive himself also of the reward for his thrift. Accordingly, whether a man consumed or saved, his income was in either case spent. But even the stubborn hoarder—and no one was quite so scorned by the nineteenth-century builders of the competitive model—did no irreparable damage. By getting income and neither spending it nor allowing others to do so, those who hoarded withheld some demand from the market. The only effect of this was that the impersonally determined prices for goods fell as supply exceeded demand. Others then found their current income buying more than before. Their spending offset the additions to the misers' hoards.

Here was the basis of the notion that there could never be an excess of savings—that the aggregate of demand for all goods must always equal their supply. This was Say's Law—the claim upon immortality of Jean Baptiste Say, the French interpreter of Adam Smith. Few ideas have ever gripped the minds of economists so firmly as Say's Law; for well over a hundred years it enjoyed the standing of an article of faith. Whether a man accepted or rejected Say's Law was, until well into the nineteen-thirties, the test of whether he was qualified for the company of reputable scholars or should be dismissed as a monetary crank.

Say's Law reinforced the conclusion that, in the competitive model, there would always be full use of willing labor. As a result, to the extent that the model was taken to be an approximation to reality, no serious consideration could be given to the possibility or fact of a bad depression. A depression must involve some interruption in the flow of spending—some general reduction in demand for goods below the capacity of the economy to supply them. What is being spent at any given time for consumers' goods is obviously being spent. Interruptions between the receipt of income and its ultimate disposal must be sought for in that part of income that is saved. But Say's Law arrested any search for trouble in this area by declaring that savings or their equivalent must also be spent. A decrease in expenditures by consumers would only mean an increase in saving and investment expenditure. Under such circumstances it was impossible to suppose that a general and progressive reduction in spending—without which, as a moment's thought will suggest, there could be no depression—could get under way.

There was some room in this system for rhythmic cycles of good business and bad. So long as the principal effect of such movements was on profits and the rate of economic growth, rather than on employment, no serious collision with Say's Law occurred. And, in fact, the business cycle became the object of a good deal of statistical study, especially in the United States. Much data could be gathered, and many charts could be drawn without trespassing on Say. But until the mid-thirties, in both England and the United States, the notion of the grave depression was not only foreign to the accepted system of economics but its admission was largely barred to analysis. Unemployment, which was sufficiently a fact so that it could not be ignored, was generally associated with the activities of unions. Unions prevented the worker from getting himself employed by preventing him from reducing the wage at which he offered to work. He was thus restrained from making it worth the while of an employer to hire him. This was not the dogma of mossbacks; it was the only important avenue to an explanation left by Say and the competitive model. As late as 1930, Sir William Beveridge, a modern symbol of progressive ideas, firmly asserted that the effect, at least potentially, "of high wages policy in causing unemployment is not denied by any competent authority."[4]

Say's Law and the resulting sterility of the interpretations of business fluctuations help explain the rather passive role played by economists in the very early years of the Great Depression. Many scholars of reputation either said nothing or vigorously but unhelpfully condemned unbalanced budgets or relief to farmers, businessmen, banks and the unemployed.[5] Politics, in all cases, dictated another and more positive

[4] He subsequently continued: "As a matter of theory, the continuance in any country of a substantial volume of unemployment which cannot be explained by specific maladjustments of place, quality and time, is in itself proof that the price being asked for labour as wages is too high for the conditions of the market; demand for and supply of labour are not finding their appropriate price for meeting." William Beveridge, *Unemployment* (New York: Longmans, Green & Co., 1930), pp. 362–71.

[5] Especially in the field of monetary policy the initiative passed to men who were not beholden to Say's Law because they had not worked in the main stream of economic theory. This was true, for example, of the late Professor George F. Warren of Cornell, the author of the famous gold-buying policy, and of Messrs Foster and Catchings, whose work received wide attention at this time. These were also the years when Major Douglas achieved immortality with his revelation on social credit.

course of action—and the judgments of politicians, not of economists, as viewed in retrospect, reflected the course of wisdom. Fortunately the economists were soon to be rehabilitated by the intellectual repeal of Say's Law.

To return to the competitive model. Clearly it either solved the operating problems of the economy, including the great questions of social efficiency, or, as in the case of the severe depression, it excluded the problem from consideration. Efficiency in its various forms was assured by the pressure on the individual firm to produce cheaply and to keep abreast of others in progress, and by the role of an impersonally determined price in passing gains along to consumers and in passing their demands back to producers. The same price structure, abetted by flexible wages and a theory which identified the act of saving with the fact of investment, went far to preclude unemployment. Say's Law canonized the doubtful points. The reader will already be able to understand the depths of the nostalgia for such a mechanism, however rigorous its specifications. It is also possible to understand how the conviction that its requirements were being ignored, or the admission that the model could never be achieved in practice, could leave a community, which had long used this system as a reference point in interpreting its economy, with a sense of profound disquiet.

6   MORRIS BORNSTEIN

IDEOLOGY AND THE SOVIET ECONOMY

. . . I shall argue that, although the Marxian ideology has exerted some influence (in part, harmful) on the economy, the main role of ideology has been to justify and legitimize the strategy and tactics of Soviet economic development. Thus, the evidence in the economic sphere appears to me to support the 'post-hoc rationalization' explanation much more than the 'ideological determinism' explanation of the connection between ideology and action.

I. THE INFLUENCE OF IDEOLOGY ON THE ECONOMY

There are several reasons, as Joseph Berliner has pointed out, why one might even question *a priori* whether Marxian economic theory could be expected to exert much influence on the Soviet economy. First. Marxian theory is supposedly a set of *objective social laws* which operate regardless of human will—and thus can hardly serve as a basis for a political party or government to make specific decisions on economic policy. Second, Marxian theory presupposes a relatively high level of economic development. Third, and most obvious, the economic theories of Marx and Engels primarily seek to explain (mid-nineteenth century) capitalism, rather than its predicted successors, socialism and communism.[1]

However, although Marx and Engels, understandably, never attempted to define in detail the organization and operation of the post-revolutionary society, they did refer to a number of its features at various places in their writings, most conspicuously in *The Communist Manifesto* and *A Critique of the Gotha Programme*. Diligent searchers of the vast Marxian literature have assembled quotations to document, among others, such elements of the post-capitalist economy as 1. nationalization of the means of production and exchange, 2. planning in place of the 'anarchy' of the market, 3. valuation of goods according to their labour content, 4. abolition of money, 5. liability of all to labour, and 6. distribution ac-

Abridged from *Soviet Studies*, Vol. XVIII, No. 1 (July 1966), pp. 74–80. By permission of the author, *Soviet Studies*, and Basil Blackwell, Publisher, Oxford.
[1] 'Marxism and the Soviet Economy', *Problems of Communism*, vol. XVIII, no. 5 (September–October 1964), p. 2.

cording to contribution in socialism, according to need in communism.[2]

Nevertheless, these prescripts are rather general, and some pertain only to the final historical stage of full communism, rather than to the preceding and intermediate stage of socialism. Hence, they could provide little concrete guidance to the administrators of the Soviet economy. Specifically, Marx and Engels offer no advice on such important questions as the internal organization of production units and their coordination on a national (and international) scale, or the methods of allocating scarce resources to achieve the socially optimal output of goods and services.[3] Thus, Marxism's contribution to the economic theory of socialism—and to Soviet economic policy and practice—has been very limited.

Indeed, the main features of Soviet economic development can fairly easily be explained without any reference to the Marxian ideology. Rather, one need simply point to the desire of a totalitarian regime to mobilize the economy for rapid development and to maintain and enhance its internal and external power. These two goals of the Communist leadership are sufficient to explain both the general policies and the specific institutional arrangements which have characterized Soviet economic development.[4]

In assessing the influence of ideology on the economy, one should, however, also recognize how ideology has adversely affected the Soviet economy, hampering its growth and the attainment of the goals just noted. Perhaps the most striking example of such adverse influence is the ideological commitment to the labour theory of value. On the basis of this theory, official Soviet economics long denied the contribution to production of non-labour factors such as capital and land, ignored the role of demand and scarcity in determining value, and opposed marginal calculations in general.

As a result, industrial transfer prices based on average labour cost (plus a nominal 'surplus product' markup) have been unable to perform an allocative role in the state sector, where producer goods are instead distributed by the cumbersome and inefficient *snabsbyt* apparatus—the very essence of the 'command economy'. Scarce capital was misallocated, and advocates of capital charges were severely attacked on ideological grounds. And mathematical economics and econometrics were strongly

[2] See, for example, P. J. D. Wiles, *The Political Economy of Communism* (Oxford, Basil Blackwell, 1962), ch. 3 and pp. 331–4.

[3] On Marxism's neglect of 'scarcity economics', see P. J. D. Wiles, 'Scarcity, Marxism, and Gosplan', *Oxford Economic Papers*, N.S., vol. 5, no. 3 (October 1953), pp. 286–316; Ronald L. Meek, 'Some Thoughts on Marxism, Scarcity, and Gosplan', *ibid.* vol. 7, no. 3 (October 1955), pp. 281–99 and Wiles, 'Some Thoughts on Marxism, Scarcity, and Gosplan: A Comment', *ibid.* vol. 8, no. 1 (February 1956), pp. 108–12.

[4] Cf. Berliner, *op. cit.*, pp. 6–7, and Alexander Gerschenkron, 'Comments', in Abram Bergson (ed.), *Soviet Economic Growth: Conditions and Perspectives* (Evanston, Illinois: Row, Peterson and Company, 1953), p. 26.

opposed by traditionalist Soviet economists who (correctly) saw in these new techniques a marginalist threat to orthodox Marxian economics in general and to the labour theory of value in particular. The mathematical models of Novozhilov, Kantorovich, Nemchinov and others specifically identify the contributions of land and capital, as well as labour, and stress the need for scarcity evaluations (i.e., prices) of a marginalist character for both products and factors of production.[5]

The conflict of these ideas with the labour theory of value is not only very clear but also profoundly significant in its implications, because the labour theory of value is a cornerstone of the entire Marxian system. The doctrine of labour as the sole value-forming factor is the basis of the theory of surplus value, and thus of the Marxian critique of capitalism both in ethical terms and in regard to the efficiency of an atomistic, free-enterprise market mechanism. The labour theory of value underlies both the Marxian condemnation of capitalism and the assertion of the superiority of socialism. This in turn explains both why Marxist ideologists are alarmed at any challenge to the labour theory of value and why the 'new' Soviet economists go to such lengths to argue (usually not convincingly) that their ideas are consistent with the Marxian labour theory of value. This central Marxian doctrine must be affirmed because of its importance in the ideological struggle against capitalism, rather than because of its contribution to the operation of a socialist economy. The affirmation of the doctrine has, in fact, delayed long-needed improvements in Soviet economic planning.[6]

In summary, Marxian ideology appears to have had little positive impact in shaping the Soviet economy, while it has hampered the search for more efficient ways of allocating scarce resources to achieve the goals of the party leadership.

II. THE INFLUENCE OF ECONOMIC DEVELOPMENT ON IDEOLOGY

What, in contrast, has been the impact of Soviet economic development upon the ideology? On the one hand, it has generated the so-called

[5] These matters are discussed at length in Morris Bornstein, 'The Soviet Price Reform Discussion', *Quarterly Journal of Economics*, vol. LXXVIII, no. 1 (February 1964), pp. 15–48; Gregory Grossman, 'Scarce Capital and Soviet Doctrine', *ibid.* vol. LXVII, no. 3 (August 1953), pp. 311–43; and Robert W. Campbell, 'Marx, Kantorovich, and Novozhilov: *Stoimost'* versus Reality', *Slavic Review*, vol. XX, no. 3 (October 1961), pp. 402–18.

[6] Cf. Alfred Zauberman, 'Revisionism in Soviet Economics', in Leopold Labedz (ed.), *Revisionism: Essays on the History of Marxist Ideas* (London: George Allen & Unwin Ltd., 1962), pp. 277–8.

economic laws of socialism'. On the other, it has compelled modifications in the ideology.

According to the latest edition of the standard Soviet political economy textbook, *Politicheskaya ekonomiya*,[7] the economic laws of socialism are objective laws in the sense that they 'emerge and act independently of the will of men. . . . They cannot be created, transformed or abolished by the will of men' (p. 434). A brief statement of the five principal 'laws' is sufficient to show that they are not laws in the sense indicated, but rather are, at best, goals not yet achieved in the Soviet economy.

1. *The Basic Economic Law of Socialism* is characterized by 'the steady expansion and improvement of production on the basis of advanced technique and socialist collaboration, with the aim of the fullest satisfaction of the steadily increasing requirements and the many-sided development of the members of society' (p. 437).

2. The *Law of Planned, Proportional Development of the National Economy* requires that 'the development of all branches of the economy be subordinated to a unified planned direction by society, so that proportionality among all parts and elements of the economy be preserved' (p. 453).

3. The *Law of Value* 'stipulates the necessity of production and sale of commodities on the basis of socially necessary labour outlays. Prices of commodities are established in accordance with socially necessary labour outlays' (p. 510).

4. The *Law of Distribution According to Work* 'stipulates the necessity of distributing products in direct dependence on the quantity and quality of work of each worker, equal pay for equal work regardless of sex, age, race, and nationality of the citizens of the socialist society. The payment of labour both in industry and in agriculture should be organized on the basis of this law' (p. 571).

5. The *Law of Socialist Accumulation* 'stipulates the systematic use of part of net income for continuous expansion of production and increase of national wealth for the purpose of increasing the people's welfare' (p. 642).

Upon examination, these 'laws' prove to be neither objective conditions inexorably imposed by forces beyond human control, nor even accurate descriptions of the corresponding aspects of the Soviet economy. Rather, they are simply statements of goals with which the CPSU seeks to identify itself. They perform a legitimizing rather than a guiding function. By labelling desirable objectives as 'laws', the party seeks to persuade both itself and the Soviet populace (as well as foreign Communist and non-Communist opinion) that these goals have been, or are being,

[7] *Politicheskaya ekonomiya: uchebnik*, 4th ed. (Moscow: Gospolitizdat, 1962). This discussion follows Berliner, *op. cit.*, pp. 4–6.

achieved, and that conditions are different from what they in fact are: that production is being steadily expanded to enhance the welfare of the Soviet population; that planned economic development is smooth and balanced; that prices have a sound theoretical foundation; that income distribution is fair, etc.

These are, no doubt, features of how a Communist economy (in the stage of socialism) *should* be operating—and so it *must* be operating under the leadership of the party. The constant reaffirmation of these 'economic laws' therefore is an effort to justify and legitimize in ideological terms the economic policies and measures adopted by the regime. The very fact that these statements are *not* descriptive of Soviet reality requires that, for ideological purposes, they should be invested with the designation of objective, irrevocable 'laws'. The 'economic laws of socialism' thus claim what the Soviet economy has so far failed to attain, although they may represent the party's goals and promises for the future, as well as its justification for past actions. In the terminology of D. D. Comey, the 'economic laws of socialism' perform an 'authenticating', and perhaps a 'masking', rather than a 'directive', function.[8]

In addition to contributing, in this special way, some elements to the ideology, Soviet economic development has influenced the ideology by forcing changes in it. Since the denunciation of Stalin in 1956, and especially in the last few years, a number of important principles of economic ideology have been successfully challenged, and others are now under fire. Interest charges on capital and rents on scarce natural resources are included in the economic reforms announced by Kosygin in September 1965.[9] The growing acceptance of marginalist mathematical techniques is indicated by the award of Lenin Prizes in April 1965 to Novozhilov, Kantorovich and Nemchinov. The dispute over mathematical methods no longer concerns their use as such so much as their implications for some long established doctrines. One of these is the proposition that the output of Industry A (the means of production) must grow

[8] Comey classifies ideology as 'directive' when it serves as a guide for choosing and implementing policy; as 'masking' when ideological statements are made to deflect attention from current realities; and as 'authenticating' when policies or measures are justified by citing ideological doctrines and even 'classics' of Marx, Engels and Lenin. The large volume and great scope of their writings can provide a plausible citation for almost any action. See David Dinsmore Comey, 'Marxist-Leninist Ideology and Soviet Policy', *Studies in Soviet Thought*, vol. II, no. 4 (December 1962), pp. 315–16.

[9] However, the information available so far does not suggest that the current industrial price reform is aiming at scarcity prices. It appears that the new prices are still to be based on average branch *sebestoimost'* plus a (larger) profit markup, out of which capital charges (fixed for 1966 at 6% of fixed and working capital) and rents will be paid. See V. Sitnin (President of the State Committee on Prices), 'Vazhnyi rychag ekonomicheskogo rukovodstva', *Ekonomicheskaya gazeta*, no. 1, 1966, pp. 12–13; and 'Metodicheskie ukazaniya po perevodu otdel'nykh promyshlennykh predpriyatii na novuyu sistemu planirovaniya i ekonomicheskogo stimulirovaniya v 1966 godu', *ibid*. no. 6, 1966, p. 35.

faster than the output of Industry B (the means of consumption). Another is the supremacy of planners' (i.e., party) sovereignty over consumers' sovereignty in determining the rate and direction of economic growth.[10]

Several factors explain this 'erosion of ideology' in the economic sphere. One is the progress and changed circumstances of the Soviet economy. The old Stalinist 'command economy' methods of the 1930s and 1940s are not suitable for the contemporary tasks of modernizing, diversifying and expanding an already (unevenly) developed economy. In particular, the slowdown in economic growth after 1958 has convinced the Soviet leadership that major economic reforms are needed, even if they conflict in some respects with received doctrine.

At the same time, successive Soviet regimes have been progressively more flexible and less doctrinaire in their approach to economic questions. Just as Khrushchev was more pragmatic than Stalin, so Kosygin has shown a greater awareness of the realities of the Soviet economy than Khrushchev did. To some degree, this might be explained simply as the response of the current leader to the objective circumstances: growing economic and social problems demanded greater flexibility and innovation. But it is also possible to identify a subjective element in the personalities and backgrounds of different Soviet leaders. Stalin isolated himself from the economic, and other, realities of Soviet life. Khrushchev was clearly more aware of conditions at home and abroad, although he was not always able to cope with them despite his often bold efforts to do so. Kosygin's background and personality, in contrast, lead him to a sober appraisal of economic problems and to a technical, rather than an ideological, approach to their solution.[11]

Finally, economic ideology is more easily revised than, say, Marxist-Leninist teachings on social relations or politics. As already noted, Marx had little to say on the conduct of a socialist economy, and ideology has had not a directive but an authenticating function in the economic sphere. As Soviet economics progresses from qualitative political economy to the quantitative approach of mathematical programming, econometrics and cybernetics, it acquires more of the technical, apolitical character which the physical sciences have enjoyed in the USSR.[12] Eco-

[10] Cf. John M. Montias, 'Moscow University Conference on Mathematical Economics', The ASTE Bulletin, vol. V, no. 3 (Fall 1963), pp. 9–13.

[11] Zauberman holds that Stalin himself may be considered 'the first major revisionist' because he perceived the clash between the needs of the economy and the accepted teaching on the law of value, encouraged revisionist thinking on the subject in the 1940s, and eventually himself revised the doctrine to a limited extent. See Zauberman, op. cit., pp. 272, 280.

[12] For a discussion of how the party ideologists first attacked cybernetics, then recognized its utility, and finally explained its compatibility with dialectical materialism, see Maxim W. Mikulak, 'Cybernetics and Marxism-Leninism', Slavic Review, vol. XXIV, no. 3 (September 1965), pp. 450–65.

nomics is now recognized as dealing with problems of efficient resource allocation, while in the Stalin era it was confined to narrow managerial or technical questions, such as factory management and cost accounting, and, according to Stalin himself, specifically excluded economic planning.[13]

III. Conclusions

This appraisal of the relationship between ideology and the Soviet economy suggests the following conclusions:

1. The party's dependence on ideology in the economic sphere has been rather weak, and insofar as ideology has influenced the Soviet economy, it has been a hindrance more than a help.

2. Ideological flexibility in the economic sphere has progressively increased from Stalin to Khrushchev to Kosygin, under the pressure of changing objective circumstances and as a result of differences in the personality and background of these leaders.

3. In the economic sphere the party has used ideology much more to 'authenticate' and 'mask' its actions than to guide them.

In the last decade ideology's influence on the economy has weakened under overwhelming pressures for economic reforms which entail serious challenges not only to ideological doctrines but also to the role of the party and of the middle-level bureaucracy in the conduct of economic affairs. On the one hand, the mathematical economists propose to replace political or subjective decision-making by objective economic calculations involving rigorous analytical models, extensive information and electronic computers. On the other hand, the Liberman school seeks to substitute market forces for administrative commands.

Even so, the party finds ideology useful in explaining and justifying economic reform to itself, to the economic bureaucracy, to the masses, and to foreign Communist parties. Ideological explanations of the current reform measures seek to affirm their legitimacy by declaring their consistency with both Marxian doctrine and past practice. They deny Chinese charges of revisionism: of the adoption of bourgeois economic theories and capitalist practice. In ideological language, the party asserts, both to itself and to the economic intelligentsia, that despite, or through, the reforms the party remains supreme in the economic sphere (and in other aspects of Soviet life). Finally, the ideological apparatus

[13] Joseph Stalin, 'Concerning the Errors of L. D. Yaroshenko: Other Errors of Yaroshenko', *Economic Problems of Socialism in the USSR* (New York: International Publishers, 1952), pp. 55-56.

is supposed to mobilize popular support for economic reforms, while reminding the populace that the expected benefits in the form of greater production and improved living conditions are due to the party's actions.[14]

Thus, as the 'directive' (or inhibiting) influence of ideology in the economic sphere diminishes, the importance of its 'authenticating' and 'masking' functions increases. The more the Soviet economy changes under the pressure of new conditions and new ideas, the more the party needs ideological explanations of continuity, consistency and legitimacy.

[14] See, for example, V. Stepakov, 'Edinstvo ekonomicheskoi politiki, praktiki i propagandy', *Ekonomicheskaya gazeta,* no. 47, 1965, pp. 3–5; and 'Ekonomicheskaya politika i bor'ba za kommunism', *Pravda,* 14 January, 1966, pp. 2–3. (Stepakov is Chief of the Department of Propaganda and Agitation of the CPSU Central Committee.)

7   MICHAEL E. BRADLEY

MARXISM AND SOVIET
AGRICULTURAL PROBLEMS

This paper is based on the general hypothesis that Marxian theoretical concepts have had a heavy impact on Soviet agricultural problems, and that the consistently Marxian orientation of Soviet economic analysts and policy-makers is one of the causes of recurrent difficulties in the Soviet agricultural sector. It is not my position that Marxian theory is the only cause, or even the most important single cause of the disappointing levels of Soviet agricultural performance. I only attempt here to point out the ways in which Marxian theory, and its consistent application by Soviet economic planners and political leaders, has kept the level of Soviet agricultural performance below the maximum attainable within the limits set by climate, soil quality, and current production techniques in the U.S.S.R.

MARX AND LENIN: THE THEORETICAL FOUNDATIONS

Marx was primarily concerned in his theoretical works with the development of antithetical forces in mature, capitalistic, industrial economies, and he tended to treat agriculture only briefly. He considered small-scale private agriculture as a pre-capitalist form of production, and therefore outside the mainstream of his theoretical analysis.

Marx's greatest influence on later Soviet economic thought and policy stems from his emphasis on large-scale production in agriculture and industry, and from his assertion that private agriculture in any form is deficient as a system of commodity production. According to Marx, small-scale agricultural production could not survive because of its inefficiency, which stems from its inability to realize economies of scale through the systematic application of scientific techniques. Under such a system, there could be little accumulation, concentration of capital or specialization. [13, vol. I, pp. 834-836; vol. III, pp. 937-939] Small-scale agriculture, Marx concluded, ". . . is compatible only with a system of

This is a special contribution.

production, and a society, moving within narrow and more or less primitive bounds." [13, vol. I, p. 835]

Concentration of agricultural production, in the Marxian analysis, provides the initial impetus for the evolution of the capitalist system of commodity production. This centralization of production and concentration of the ownership of resources is the source of greater efficiency than could have been achieved by the smaller producers. Marx asserted that large producing units are economically superior to small units, and that the concentration of production under capitalism is the natural consequence of economies of scale in agriculture and industry. [13, vol. I, p. 835]

Although the development of large-scale capitalistic agriculture initially results in improvements in efficiency and the expansion of agricultural production beyond the capabilities of small-scale peasant agriculture, Marx held that it, too, is inherently deficient as a system of production. In agriculture, as well as industry, private property would lead to monopolization, inherent contradiction, and underconsumption which place "fetters" on the further expansion of production. [13, vol. III, p. 945]

Marx asserted that the negation of capitalist agriculture and its replacement by socialist agriculture would not mean a return to individual private holdings and small-scale agricultural production. In his analysis, this would be a "reactionary" outcome, contrary to the "inevitable" laws of socialist development. Socialized production ". . . does not re-establish private property for the producer, but gives him individual property based on the acquisitions of the capitalist era; i.e., on co-operation and possession in common of the land and of the means of production." [13, vol. I, p. 837] The transition to socialism in agriculture, then, meant the transition from large-scale private agriculture to large-scale socialized agriculture.

The role of the peasantry in the overthrow of capitalism is a subordinate one in the Marxian scheme of socialist development, since Marx saw in the peasantry, artisans and small independent producers the elements of a reactionary class that sought not the advance to socialism, but rather the return to the pre-capitalistic system of production. The primary responsibility for the advance to socialism, said Marx, could fall on but one class—the urban proletariat. [14, p. 75] This concept of the relative importance of the peasantry and the proletariat in the development of socialism may explain in part the traditional Soviet neglect of peasant problems, which is one of the roots of current Soviet agricultural problems.

Lenin, in contrast to Marx, could not accurately be described as an economic theorist. The economic problems which he faced following the November Revolution were those of policy, not of theory. [6, pp. 97-124;

3, pp. 9-24; 18, pp. 80-86] Lenin's policy formulations, however, seem firmly grounded in Marxian economic theory. Following Marx, he emphasized the shortcomings of private agriculture and private property in land, and called for the confiscation of the landed estates as a primary task of the revolution. [9, vol. 26, p. 324] In line with Marxian analysis, he clearly favored state ownership and large-scale production in agriculture as well as in industry. [12, vol. I, p. 97]

The influence of Marxian doctrine on Lenin's policy shows clearly in his solution to the problem of critical grain shortages following the Revolution. Lenin saw the choice of alternative solutions as lying between higher grain prices to stimulate production and sales on the one hand, and forced procurement of grain on the other. According to Lenin, higher grain prices might be influential in expanding the supply of marketed grain, but would give material aid to the counterrevolutionary rich peasants, or *kulaks*. [9, vol. 26, pp. 65-67]

All surpluses were to be confiscated and all holders of surpluses prosecuted as price speculators. [9, vol. 26, p. 501] This solution is consistent with the Marxian notion that the peasantry must be subordinated to the interests of the proletariat. Soviet agricultural policy between 1918 and 1921 also established the tradition of resolving immediate economic crises by squeezing the agricultural sector.

The peasantry responded to forced confiscation of grain surpluses by reducing sown acreage and output. Between 1913 and 1920, the combined effect of war and coercion in the agricultural sector was a marked decline in sown area. [6, pp. 103-104] Total gross agricultural production in 1921 was only 60 per cent of the 1913 level, and 31.8 per cent below that of 1917. Total production of field crops fell by 33 per cent between 1917 and 1921. [17, pp. 439-440; 22, p. 79]

In his New Economic Policy (NEP), 1921-1924, Lenin was forced to retreat from his earlier positions on the role of peasantry and the agricultural sector in the ultimate success of the Soviet system. The chief objective of the NEP in the agricultural sector was to encourage greater production and sales of agricultural commodities by reducing coercion, leaving a greater marketable surplus to be sold by the peasantry in agricultural markets, lifting the War Communism restrictions on grain prices, and the encouragement of small-scale producers in light industry to increase the availability of consumer goods for the peasantry. [10, vol. 32, pp. 342-343; 12, vol. I, pp. 206-207] This retreat eased many of the tensions which had arisen as a result of the harsh control of the economy between 1918 and 1921, and enabled the state to regroup its forces for the rapid industrialization campaigns of the 1930's. [2, pp. 265-279]

The new incentives offered to agricultural producers under NEP had a favorable effect on agricultural production, and total agricultural production more than doubled in the period 1921-1927. However, agricultural marketings did not expand as dramatically as total production. [8, p. 232] The terms of trade worsened for the agricultural sector in its transactions with the industrial sector, and this led to significant declines in the volume of marketed agricultural produce. [1, p. 258; 2, pp. 276-278; 6, pp. 149-176] The U.S.S.R. experienced periodic crises in grain marketing from 1925 onward, and it was these crises—accompanied by the pro-industrialization orientation of Soviet planners and political leaders and the prevalence of the Marxian concept of the subordination of the interests of the peasantry to those of the proletariat—which eventually spelled the doom of the NEP. [11, pp. 162-166]

Agriculture under Stalin, 1928–1952

In his address to the Fifteenth Congress of the Communist Party of the Soviet Union in 1927, Stalin emphasized the problems of rapid industrialization and the lagging development of the agricultural sector. He asserted the primacy of rapid industrialization, and stated that any slowing down of industrialization to divert more resources to the agricultural sector ". . . would be the most reactionary, anti-proletarian utopianism . . . Nationalized industry must and will develop at an accelerated rate." [19, vol. 10, p. 312]

Following Marxian doctrine, Stalin emphasized that small-scale private agriculture and the independence of the peasantry were the primary causes of agricultural stagnation. [19, vol. 10, p. 313] In January 1928, he unveiled a two-part program for alleviating grain shortages without resorting to higher purchase prices or increased resource allocations for the agricultural sector. The short-run solution was a stepped-up program of confiscation of grain surpluses and criminal prosecution of price speculators. As a long-run solution, he advocated acceleration of the pace of collectivization of agricultural production. Collectives could be expected to deliver a much higher percentage of their total production to the state at low prices because of their lack of independence to withhold their produce in the face of inadequate price incentives.

Stalin's justification of collectivization rested on the Marxian argument that large-scale collectives were inherently superior to smaller private farms in raising the level of agricultural production. Collectivization also served as a means of subordinating the interests of the peasantry to the state's prime objective of rapid industrialization. While legally defined as cooperatives, it soon became clear that the function of the collectives was the maximization of state procurements while shifting the bulk of the costs of industrialization to the farm membership.

[18, p. 177; 19, vol. 13, p. 193] With collectivization, the state became independent of agricultural markets and incentives in raising the level of agricultural deliveries. The overwhelming portion of state agricultural procurements came as obligatory deliveries from the collectives. The effectiveness of collectivization in raising the level of state grain deliveries and shifting the burdens of uncertainty to the collectives is reflected in the fact that between 1928 and 1937, total grain harvests increased by about 32.7 per cent, while the volume of obligatory deliveries of grain to the state nearly trebled. [1, p. 271] State delivery prices were so low relative to production costs for most commodities that the obligatory deliveries to the state in fact constituted a tax in kind on the collectives rather than a market transaction.

By the time of Stalin's death, the institutional pattern of large-scale collectivized agricultural production had been firmly established in the U.S.S.R. While the collectives had been effective in the extraction of agricultural surpluses, they were not generally successful in raising the level of agricultural production. Centralized control over managerial decision-making at the farm level, low wages, residual distributions to labor, and the instability and unpredictability of delivery quotas resulted in a general atrophication of labor and managerial incentives, and continue to be significant institutional barriers to the improvement of performance levels in Soviet agriculture. Current agricultural difficulties seem to stem, in part, from a failure of the Soviet leadership to recognize that the basic institutional structure of Soviet agriculture—based on Marxian arguments on economies of scale in agriculture and the subordination of the agricultural producer—is not conducive to high levels of production.

SOVIET AGRICULTURAL PROBLEMS AND POLICIES SINCE STALIN

Between 1953 and 1964 Khrushchev attacked the critical problems of Soviet agriculture with a series of sweeping organizational changes and production campaigns which were implemented on a broad scale with missionary zeal. Khrushchev's initial successes in the agricultural sector between 1953 and 1958 were the result of unusually good weather and the recognition by the peasantry that *something* was being done. The consistently disappointing performance of Soviet agriculture after 1959, however, indicated the numerous inconsistencies in agricultural policies and Khrushchev's lack of sophistication in attacking agricultural problems. [16, pp. 10-12]

The current political leadership in the Soviet Union seems to be taking a more realistic and cautious approach to agricultural problems, and current discussions of agricultural reform seem to indicate a somewhat less rigid attachment to orthodox Marxian economics and a greater concern with production and efficiency. [5; 7; 4, pp. 257-267] However, given the prevalence of Marxian doctrine among most policymakers and the institutional structure of Soviet agriculture, it seems highly unlikely that the Soviet Union will ever approach economic optimality in agricultural production. Suppose, for example, that Soviet planners were somehow able to introduce effective proxies for the market in land, a capital market with realistic interest rates, and free agricultural markets; and to decentralize the decision-making process by greater managerial flexibility and the introduction of material incentives for entrepreneurial innovation and risk-bearing. The result would most probably be smaller producing units; more realistic factor returns; more efficient allocation of resources within the agricultural sector, as well as more efficient intersectoral allocation; and uniform prices on agricultural commodities which would encourage greater geographical specialization of production on the basis of economic efficiency.

In spite of the advantages of such a program, the end result would so nearly resemble large-scale private agriculture that, in all probability, it would be ideologically unpalatable for most Soviet political leaders. It is ironic that the Marxian orientation of Soviet agricultural policy and institutional structure has placed the very "fetters on production" in the Soviet agricultural sector which Marx asserted would be eliminated with the advent of large-scale socialist agriculture. Any really effective solution to Soviet agricultural problems, therefore, will require considerably greater bending of Marxian doctrine and more drastic departures from the traditional Soviet approach to agricultural problems.

NOTES

1. Akademiia nauk SSSR, *Institut istorii, Istoriia sovetskogo krest'ianstva i kolkhoznogo stroitel'stva SSSR.* Moscow, 1963.
2. V. N. Bandera, "The New Economic Policy (NEP) as an Economic System," *Journal of Political Economy,* June 1963, 71, 265–279.
3. Alexander Baykov, *The Development of the Soviet Economic System.* New York, 1947.
4. Michael Edward Bradley, "Wage Determination and Incentive Problems in Soviet Agriculture," Unpublished Doctoral Dissertation, Cornell University, 1967.
5. L. I. Brezhnev, "O neotlozhnykh merakh po dal'neishemu razvitiiu sel'skogo khoziaistva SSSR," *Pravda,* March 27, 1965, 2–4.

6. Maurice Dobb, *Soviet Economic Development Since 1917*. New York, 1949.
7. Jerzy F. Karcz, "The New Soviet Agricultural Programme," *Soviet Studies*, October 1965, 17, 129–161.
8. E. I. Kviring, S. P. Sereda, and A. M. Ginsburg, eds., *Promyshlennost' i narodnoe khoziaistvo*. Moscow, 1927.
9. V. I. Lenin, *Collected Works* (4th ed.). Moscow, 1964.
10. ———, *Sochineniia* (4th ed.), Moscow, 1950.
11. M. Lenin, "The Immmediate Background of Soviet Collectivization," *Soviet Studies*, October 1965, 17, 162–197.
12. V. N. Malin and A. V. Korobov, eds., *Direktivy KPSS i Sovetskogo pravitel'stva po khoziaistvennym voprosam, 1917–1957*. Moscow, 1957.
13. Karl Marx, *Capital: A Critique of Political Economy*. Chicago, 1919.
14. ———, and Friedrich Engels, *The Communist Manifesto*. New York, 1964.
15. M. I. Moiseev, *Ekonomicheskie osnovy gosudarstvennykh zagotovok sel'skokhoziaistvennykh produktov*. Moscow, 1955.
16. Nancy Nimitz, *Agriculture under Khrushchev: The Lean Years*. Santa Monica, Cal., 1965.
17. Vladimir P. Timoshenko, *Agricultural Russia and the Wheat Problem*. Stanford, Cal., 1932.
18. J. V. Stalin, *Building Collective Farms*. New York, 1931.
19. ———, *Works*, Moscow, 1955.
20. Tsentral'noe statisticheskoe upravlenie, *Narodnoe kohziaistvo SSSR v 1958 godu: statisticheskii sbornik*. Moscow, 1959.
21. ———, *Sel'skoe khoziaistvo SSSR: statisticheskii sbornik*. Moscow, 1960.

8   RALPH B. PRICE

IDEOLOGY AND INDIAN PLANNING

The Congress Party of India is noted for the strong ideological position of its pre- and post-independence leadership and for its adoption of
the goal of building a "socialist pattern of society." Many of the spokesmen for the party have maintained that this goal best fits the philosophical foundations of Hinduism. This paper considers some of the ideological background of planning, some of the alleged peculiarities of Hinduism, and some of the implications of development policies in the second
and third five-year plans.

I

India began her national period with an ideological commitment
which places her present-day policy makers under special obligation.
Since 1932 the Congress Party has been committed to some idea of socialism. This ideological position was influenced strongly by the charismatic personality of Jawaharlal Nehru who, although by his own admission he understood little of Marxism, was nevertheless convinced that
socialist and communist theories were based on scientific, moral principles which appealed to him.[1] After his trip to Europe and the Soviet
Union in 1927, he wrote and talked about the importance and desirability
of socialism for India. Mohandas K. Gandhi, too, was emotionally antagonistic to the idea of private property and personal gain. While Nehru
believed in a socialism of industrialization, Gandhi preached with
moralistic fervor a socialism which would be based on the idea of a
self-sufficient village that would literally drain the modern cities of their
populations.[2] Gandhi's socialism was based on his interpretation of the

Abridged from *The American Journal of Economics and Sociology,* Vol. 26, No. 1
(January 1967), pp. 47-64. Reprinted by permission of author and *The American
Journal of Economics and Sociology.*

One of several studies undertaken while the writer, on leave as professor of economics, Western Maryland College, held a research fellowship in India under the
auspices of the American Institute of Indian Studies.
    [1] Jawaharlal Nehru, *Autobiography* (Bombay: Allied Publishers, 1962), pp.
591-2.
    [2] See Shriman Narayan, *The Gandhi Plan* (Bombay: Padma Publications Limited,
1944).

Bagavad Gita, that man should serve but not take the fruit thereof.[3] Furthermore, he would have had a near-static society where a man should fulfill his *dharma* to the extent even of following in and being content with the caste job of his father. Nehru's concept of a socialist industrial society was more acceptable to the educated elite of India, who wanted to develop their country into a modern nation; but Gandhi's moral teachings about the supposed degeneracy of capitalism are an important part of his legacy to modern India.

The moralistic approach to the problem of nation-building fit the predilections of the young Nehru, who was impressed by the communists he met at the Brussels Congress of Oppressed Nationalities in 1927. And it was ready-made for men of the elite castes schooled in the precepts of the *Gita,* especially those bright, young, Westernized intellectuals who went to Cambridge, Oxford, and the London School of Economics, where they came in contact with men such as Harold Laski, R. H. Tawney, Graham Wallas, G. D. H. Cole, and others, who, if not Marxists, were militant Fabians in the 1920's and 1930's. Especially during the 1930's and 1940's it appeared to these young men that the private-enterprise, market-guided economy was collapsing, and that the advances in economic theory, such as the work of E. H. Chamberlain and Joan Robinson on imperfect competition and J. M. Keynes on unemployment, were further evidence of the irrelevance of the neoclassical model for economic policy. The Indian intellectuals were not alone in their doubts about the market-guided economy; they had plenty of evidence of disillusionment on the part of some Western intellectuals. This was the period of the five-year plans in the Soviet Union when economic development and a breakthrough to a new society seemed to some to be dramatic. The neoclassical model was not a growth model and had little relevance for India anyhow. In India the market and institutional imperfections were too great for partial-equilibrium theory alone to explain satisfactorily distribution of income and allocation of resources. Classical theory provided a growth model, but that was not what young Indians studied in the colleges of the United Kingdom and in India. Marshall held the top position in the economic syllabus for the undergraduate—and still does in India!

"Capitalism" became a bad word in India, synonymous with imperialism, monopoly, managing-agency system, etc. "Socialism" was good, idealistic, democratic; it became a word which one used to express whatever idea of progress one held, from nationalization of everything to a mixed economy with limited public ownership. Men like A. K. Shah, Shri-

---

[3] "[The *Gita*] teaches us that we have a right to actions only but not to the fruit thereof, and that success and failure are one and the same thing at bottom. It calls upon us to dedicate ourselves, body, mind and soul, to pure duty, and not to become mental voluptuaries at the mercy of all chance desires and undisciplined impulses." *The Harijan,* August 24, 1934.

man Narayan, V. K. R. V. Rao, D. R. Gadgil, and others lectured about the crassness of competition and the "business morality" contrasted with the "character-building" aspects of socialism. Rao expressed a widely shared belief when he said that only through socialist or cooperative organization could the "pride and dignity element in work" be secured.[4] Once independence was won, there was an opportunity to begin building a socialist society. The leadership of India had never had in mind a proletarian revolution; they were Western-educated and committed to a democratic concept of socialism which had been developed in nations mature in technological and industrial development. Yet, they ruled a nation where over 80 per cent of the people were illiterate and lived in a traditional, subsistence agriculture. Furthermore, the modern private industrial sector, while small, made the major contribution to national income, and it was on this group which the Congress Party had depended for financial support during the struggle for independence. Yet to build a socialist State required the control over property in an industrial society. Faced with the reality of power, the Congress Party devised a compromise for the foreseeable future in the Industrial Policy Resolutions of 1948 and 1956 in which three groups of industries were specified.[5] "A" group (munitions, atomic energy, iron and steel, heavy engineering and heavy electrical plant, coal, oil, most mining, aircraft, air transport, railways, shipbuilding, communications, and electrical generation and distribution) included those "the future development of which will be the exclusive responsibility of the state"; "B" group (including some mining, aluminum, machine tools, ferroalloys and tool steels, heavy chemicals, essential drugs, fertilizers, synthetic rubber, and road and sea transport) included those "which will be progressively State-owned and in which the State will therefore generally take the initiative in establishing new undertakings, but in which private enterprise will also be expected to supplement the effort of the State"; and "C" group included the residual, whose "future development will, in general, be left to the initiative and enterprise of the private sector," but "it will always be open to the State to undertake any type of industrial production."

The adoption of this resolution demonstrated how much Nehru, who did so much to shape the form which economic policy took in the post-independence period, had changed his ideas from the pre-independence period of the 1930's and 1940's when he believed that

Reform is an impossible solution of any vital problem at a critical moment when the basic structure has to be changed, and however slow the progress might be later on, the initial step must be a complete break with existing order. . . . In India, only a revolutionary plan can solve the two related questions of

[4] V. K. R. V. Rao, *Essays in Economic Development* (Bombay: Asia Publishing House, 1964), p. 27.
[5] See *India 1964* (New Delhi: Government of India, 1964), pp. 254-5.

land and industry as well as almost every other major problem before the country. . . .[6] I incline more and more to a communist philosophy.[7]

The Congress Party adopted the Avadi resolution in 1954 establishing the "Socialist Pattern of Society" as an object of policy. But when Nehru initiated debate on the Second Plan in the *Lok Sabha,* he stated:

I do not propose to define in precise terms what socialism in this context means, because we try to avoid any doctrinaire thinking, any rigid thinking, because even in my lifetime I have seen the world change so much, and I have seen so many other changes that I do not want to confine my mind to any rigid dogma. But broadly speaking . . . we mean a society in which there is social cohesion, which is without classes, where there is equality of opportunity and the possibility for everyone to live a good life. The essential thing is that there must be wealth and production. There is a good deal of talk about ceilings and it is talk with which one naturally tends to agree because you want to remove disparities. But one has to remember that the primary function of a growing society is to produce more wealth; otherwise it will not grow. And you will have nothing to distribute. We must not imagine that we have grown up because we have satisfied some textbook maxim of a hundred years ago. We talk of nationalization as if it were some kind of magic remedy to every ill. I believe that ultimately all the principal means of production will be owned by the nation, but I do not see why I should do something today which will hamper my progress, my increasing production, simply to satisfy some theoretical belief.[8]

Nevertheless, it is significant that while Nehru showed a surprising ideological mellowness by this statement, there was little evidence on his part of the recognition of the ebb tide of socialism in Europe and the resurgence of the market economy. The Indian conception of socialism remained pretty much that of the socialist parties of Europe in the 1930's and 1940's. . . .

After a survey of the literature on economic policy in India and after discussion with many persons, academic and otherwise, one cannot help but agree with a correspondent of *The Economic Weekly* who said:

At the level of an idea, the socialism of the Nehru era has emerged as a rather weak and hollow reed in which one can blow almost any kind of music. . . . [There has been accomplished] a respectable degree of public ownership . . . in the sphere of basic industry, but amidst the vast ocean of private property in land, buildings, commerce, small industry and a major part of large industry as well, the prevailing tone of social behavior is unmistakably that of acquisitiveness and private profit. What is more, these erstwhile vices are increasingly—and rightly—acclaimed as necessary agents of progress.[[9]]

[6] Jawaharlal Nehru, *op. cit.,* p. 362.

[7] *Ibid.,* p. 591.

[8] "The Socialist Legacy," *The Economic Weekly,* Special Number (India), July, 1964.

[[9]] (Contributed), *The Economic Weekly,* Special Number (India), July, 1964, p. 1225.

Nevertheless, this is not to say that the ideological commitment has been ineffective in molding political climate in India or that it has had no effect on growth. It has been quite effective in producing a government bureaucracy supported by the ruling party, both of which tend to view private enterprise with suspicion and hostility. The commitment has had the strong effect to develop what Wallich[10] has called in his concept of "derived development" a consumption rather than a production approach to development. He defines derived development as development derived from innovations made elsewhere. It is usually accomplished through government, which can more readily borrow than it can originate.

As Wallich points out, this approach has its costs. Origination requires innovation, experimentation, imagination, a willingness to take chances, and a capacity to correct mistakes—things in which governments do not excel. The major task in derived development is organization, something governments can do, for the purpose of borrowing ideas. In a production-oriented society the individual visualizes benefits coming from his own productive efforts. In a consumption-oriented society the tendency is to expect to share in general progress. In the latter type of economy individual saving is lower. Social demand works through political and labor-union channels seeking to get more from the economy than it is capable of producing with a secular tendency toward inflation as the result. Also the major emphasis is placed on government for the solution of economic problems with the consequent lack of an acceptance of individual responsibility—the one thing most needed for the required rate of social change. Finally, because the saving ratio tends to be low in a consumption-oriented society and there is a tendency to allocate considerable investment to social overhead projects due to political pressure, there occurs a relatively high capital/output ratio in the public sector resulting in a growth rate lower than acceptable. The latter phenomenon in India will be examined in the third section of this paper below.

II

Whether Hinduism presents peculiar obstacles to economic development and growth in India is an open question. In 1958 an exchange of opinion on this subject took place in the pages of *Economic Development and*

[10] Henry C. Wallich, "Some Notes Toward a Theory of Derived Development," in Agarwala and Singh, *The Economics of Underdevelopment* (London: Oxford University Press, 1958). See also Martin Bronfenbrenner, "'Hard' Versus 'Soft' Economic Development," *The Economic Weekly*, Annual Number, February, 1963.

Social Change.[11] The conclusion of this discussion, if such there was, was that there are practical values held by the Hindu peasant strong enough to give welcome support to economic reform. Professor Srinivas pointed to how B. G. Tilak's reinterpretation of the *Gita* placed "the weight of Hindu tradition . . . once again behind social and political action."[12] Professor Singer, too, felt that the very ascetic qualities of Hinduism are those needed for the sacrifice necessary for economic development.[13] Other observers have reached similar conclusions; for example, Professor Lewis believes that "it is fair to say that inherent popular apathy is not one of the critical restraints on the development process."[14]

However, there are observers, both Indian and Western, who believe that Hindu values do act in a powerful way to inhibit the social change necessary for development and growth. While they do not deny that practical values by necessity have a place in Indian life, they point to certain aspects of Hindu culture which stifle rational economic behavior. For example, Professor N. V. Sovani,[15] who makes a distinction between economic development and economic growth, holds that development is merely a technical matter resulting in the application of new technology which does not necessarily set in motion self-generating change, and without the latter over-capacity may be easily created. Economic growth, on the other hand, he holds is a dynamic, qualitative change in behavior patterns, institutions, values, etc.; it feeds upon itself and induces people to undertake growth on their own. He maintains that India has experienced mostly economic development to date and very little growth. In emphasizing this point he quotes Mr. Asoka Mehta, Deputy Chairman of the Planning Commission, when he observed that "our [Third Plan] implementation succeeded where it was a question of technical achievement such as power production, but it broke down the moment it became a human problem and the people's cooperation was required."[16]

[11] John Goheen, M. N. Srinivas, D. G. Karve, Milton Singer, "India's Cultural Values and Economic Development: A Discussion," *Economic Development and Social Change*, October, 1958. This discussion was inspired by Milton Singer's "Cultural Values in India's Economic Development," *Annals of the American Academy of Political and Social Science*, May, 1956.

[12] *Ibid.*, p. 6. Professor N. V. Sovani believes that "Tilak's commentary on the *Gita*, however, did not make much headway against the age-old slumber. Hindu Pandits always regarded his thesis as not proved and it hardly percolated to the masses. Though he is remembered today as a great national leader, his book is scarcely remembered and is known only to certain sections of the Indian intellectuals." See his "Non-economic Aspects of India's Economic Development," in R. Braibanti and J. Spengler, eds., *Administration and Economic Development in India* (Durham: Duke University Press, 1963), p. 27.

[13] Milton Singer, "India's Cultural Values and Economic Development: A Discussion," *Economic Development and Cultural Change*, October, 1958, p. 12.

[14] John P. Lewis, *Quiet Crisis in India* (Washington: Brookings Institution, 1962), p. 30.

[15] N. V. Sovani, "A Dilemma for Planning," *Seminar* (India), May, 1964.

[16] *The Times of India*, February 22, 1964.

Sovani believes that apathy is India's major problem. The technical side of planning may be brilliantly accomplished, but if the involvement of people is not enlisted, it bears little fruit. For him the lack of success of planning should be recognized for what it is: a problem which lies deeply embedded in the social structure and *mores* of the society.

Hindu society is characterized by a low basal metabolism. The social structure has a low efficiency for change. It is oriented to maintain a rigid stability, hardly distinguishable from stagnation. The basic type of personality it breeds is apathetic, seeking security in dependence, non-involved, routine loving and fond of empty ritual.

We are . . . non-aligned in personal work commitment and endeavor. We generally seem to act from a sense of duty (*dharma*)—"the pale ash of a burnt-out fire." There is little sense of purpose or involvement. . . . If the causes of our present social and cultural malaise lie so deep, the task of activating the masses would appear to be nothing less than the remaking of the whole nation, a social and cultural change of tremendous magnitude. Economic change is only a part of this wider change. It cannot be brought about successfully while neglecting the other, nor can it, itself, bring about the social and cultural change needed. . . .[17]

According to Sovani, India does not know how to produce this desired change. They might gain something from a study of the experience of other countries, but little of this type of work has been done. Even the developed countries know little about the factors responsible for the Industrial Revolution. These changes were essentially qualitative rather than quantitative, and as a result historians have been unable to isolate the precise causes. But even if they were known precisely, they could not be duplicated in the Indian culture. Whatever the catalytic agent may be, one thing is certain: it must come from within the Indian society itself. It is now clear, according to Sovani, that nationalism has not brought about the social and political integration and regeneration that was hoped for. India does not yet have ways of "bringing about the enthusiastic participation of the people in economic development and bringing about economic growth."[18]

Another native Indian, D. Narain, social psychologist of the University of Bombay, has examined some aspects of the Hindu value system to observe their effect on character.[19] He believes that, in addition to certain aspects of religion and culture which contribute to apathy, childhood in the joint family hampers growth toward maturity. The child cannot identify enough with any particular person to permit him to select desirable character components from each in order to construct an ideal. His sense of security is weak; the family is an impersonal system where the child is

[17] N. V. Sovani, *op. cit.*, pp. 17–18.
[18] *Ibid.*, p. 18.
[19] D. Narain, *Hindu Character* (Bombay: University of Bombay Press, 1957).

never rejected but where he never wholly belongs. As a result there is an absence of a clear-cut personality for identification and imitation which promotes maturity.[20]

Narain also observes that there is so little discipline in such matters as weaning, toilet training, and punishment that they cause a "fixation on the early modes of gratification and prevent maturational development to proceed. Hindus expect to be cared for in their adult life in a manner that is reminiscent of childhood."[21]

The doctrine of *Karma* also adds to passivity and resignation, according to Narain. In this matter he follows the research of Taylor; since life is only a moment of time, the idea of *Karma* tends

to produce a feeling that all the experiences of life are too insignificant to be worried about, except those duties and rites which determine *Karma* and so control the indefinite future. This tends to discourage effort in every sphere except that in which initiative is necessarily replaced by obedience to *Dharma*. . . . By making obedience to *Karma* the essential condition for escape from *Karma*, they effectively remove personal initiative and decision from the field of actions significant for the major purposes of life. By making one's *Karma* the absolute precondition of any future progress, they effectively lower the level of aspiration to the place where the danger of frustration is virtually eliminated, and make resignation and obedience primary ideals of life.[22]

Narain asks the question, "Why should an individual accept a doctrine the import of which is helplessness?" He answers the question by postulating that the Hindu identifies more with mother than father and therefore acquires a helpless orientation.[23]

Finally Narain observes that a Hindu has no rights but elaborate duties. During his lifetime he has to discharge the many debts he owes to others. "Although *artha* and *kama* are permitted as two of the four ideals of life, they are hedged by numerous considerations, proceeding from *dharma and moksha*. . . . Wealth is not to be acquired for personal glory but for the fulfillment of the duties associated with a householder."[24] For Narain, the goal of submergence of self for the good of all is too much to expect of but a few persons; but the effect of such a high ideal is such a frustrating thing that it creates a "mood of such intense resignation that even ordinary improvements are not attempted in despair."[25] Where only a few can succeed with such high ideals, the balance have no idea of even trying. He concludes, "Oddly enough, the two besetting weaknesses of

[20] *Ibid.*, p. 179.
[21] *Ibid.*
[22] W. S. Taylor, "Basic Personality in Orthodox Hindu Culture Patterns," *Journal of Abnormal and Social Psychology*, January, 1948, pp. 5–9. Quoted by Narain.
[23] Narain, *op. cit.*, p. 184.
[24] *Ibid.*, pp. 188–9.
[25] *Ibid.*, p. 189.

Hindu character are, first, an over-severe conscience and, second, an over-indulgent childhood. Unless the conscience relaxes and unless the fixation on infantile stage is prevented, no great change in Hindu character can be expected."[26]

The theses of Sovani and Narain might leave one hopeless in the face of the massiveness of the problems of India, but it will be argued below that such a conclusion is too pessimistic.

III

In view of the ideological commitment of the ruling party in India and some strong cultural barriers to economic development and growth, it is interesting to review some of the implications of planning strategies to date. Real planning got underway with the Second Plan. The strategy of it as well as that of the Third Plan was strongly influenced by P. C. Mahalanobis, physicist-statistician, who prepared a model, or "Plan Frame," for the Second Plan. This model followed generally the Soviet Union's approach of "balanced planning" in terms of resource allocation, *i.e.*, it concentrated on a detailed system of quantitative material balances, and it disregarded comparative advantage.[27] In the Soviet Union priority was given to heavy-industry sectors which were assumed to be essential for growth; production targets were set, and prices, used merely as rationing devices, were not related to cost.

Whatever can be said for an ideological approach to planning, planning of the Mahalanobis type is likely to have limited success in a non-totalitarian society where voluntary involvement of the people must be enlisted. In India there is plenty of evidence that there is a growing supply of active and potential entrepreneurs in both the modern industrial sector as well as in agriculture and that supply curves of output are positively price elastic. India has a private industrial sector which has demonstrated that it is quite capable of dynamic growth when not held in check by licensing, exchange control, and heavy taxation. In agriculture there are thousands of farmers whose progress is checked by land and income ceilings, relative prices of food grains maintained at an artificially low level by the use of P.L. 480 imports from the United States, unavailability of fertilizers, pesticides, and machinery, and rents which absorb over 60 per cent of the gross product in some areas where both the letter and spirit of tenancy laws are evaded. India is a nation of great diversities; and while

[26] *Ibid.*
[27] Hollis B. Chenery, "Comparative Advantage and Development Policy," *American Economic Review*, May, 1961, pp. 42–3. This article is a *tour de force* of recent planning literature.

apathy may be a common trait, there is evidence that, given an improved climate for private initiative with ingenious development strategies, there would not be a crippling scarcity of entrepreneurs. But a vast involvement of the people as individuals in economic change is not implied in the Mahalanobis-type model. As one observer noted:

For most enlightened Indians the sole aim of their five-year plans is social justice and human betterment. No foreign warning of imminent bankruptcy or starvation has yet been enough to deflect them from this single and immaculate objective. But they seem to have thought that they could pull off the economic revolution as a kind of academic exercise, its success guaranteed by scientific principles. Within these limits, they have in fact made outstanding progress. But the elite, while working in the service of the common people, has evidently supposed that it could succeed without their massive and fully organized cooperation.[28]

Development takes place as a result of the reinvestment of savings; therefore investment strategy should, among other things, be such as to maximize savings in some form. There are two ways—the profit maximization and the social-marginal-product-maximization approach—in which this may be done.

Firstly, planning may encourage private investment, in which case relatively capital-intensive investment (depending upon production functions) will likely be undertaken, because even though labor is redundant (zero opportunity cost) the wage paid in industry will be greater than subsistence;[29] and if the propensity to consume on the part of the capitalists is less than that of labor, the profits will be reinvested and development will take place. Alternatively under this approach, the planners may build a relatively capital-intensive public sector themselves in order to reap the profits for reinvestment.

In the second approach planners, following either a policy of encouraging private investment or public ownership, may reject profit maximization as an investment criterion, because in an economy where labor is redundant prices of inputs and values of marginal products measured thereby do not reflect true opportunity costs and the true value of the marginal products.[30] Accounting prices which do reflect the true opportunity costs and the true social value of marginal products would then be used in making investment decisions. In the case of private investment,

[28] Cyril Dunn, "Changing India," *Observer*, London, April 19, 1960. Quoted by Sovani, *op. cit.*, p. 16.

[29] W. Arthur Lewis, "Economic Development with Unlimited Supplies of Labour," *The Manchester School of Economic and Social Studies*, May, 1951.

[30] A considerable body of literature has developed around this concept. For example, see Alfred E. Kahn, "Investment Criteria in Development Programs," *Quarterly Journal of Economics*, February, 1951; Jan Tinbergen, *The Design of Development* (The Johns Hopkins Press, 1958); Hollis B. Chenery, "The Application of Investment Criteria," *Quarterly Journal of Economics*, February, 1953.

subsidies would have to be paid to cover the difference between market and accounting prices in order to encourage undertakings which would otherwise not pay. The maximization of the social marginal product, as this technique is called, would probably result in less capital-intensive techniques being used than would the profit maximization approach. However, it would require an efficient (and ruthless) revenue system in order to increase the rate of aggregate saving, otherwise it would fail. It would be difficult, if not impossible, for a non-totalitarian government to increase revenues from increased income which had come into the hands of low-productivity laborers. Therefore, for most underdeveloped countries development follows the profit-maximization approach, although accounting prices are important for checks on estimates and may be used for a limited number of strategic projects. In any case, the growth of the investible surplus is crucial.[31]

An interesting thing about the Mahalanobis model in the light of what has been said in the above paragraphs was its peculiar assumption that reinvestment did not depend upon the level of saving (profits) but upon the "capacity to manufacture both heavy and light machinery and other capital goods. . . ."[32] One finds little or no treatment of the strategy necessary to provide the all-important surplus in agriculture. Also comparative advantage was ignored: "[The] aim is to make India independent, as quickly as possible, of foreign imports of producers goods so that the accumulation of capital would not be hampered by difficulties in receiving supplies of essential producers goods from other countries."[33] Komoiya[34] has shown that this model neglected demand, the demand for and supply of intermediate products, the balance of payments, and the factor price problems; thus crucial restrictions were overlooked. In another linear programming model Sandee concluded that "up to 1970 more effective ways to employ capital for development exist than highly capital-intensive steel-making."[35]

[31] For a Marxist emphasis on this point see M. Dobb, "Some Problems in the Theory of Growth and Planning," *Kyklos*, Fasc. 2, 1961. See also Gerald Sirkin, "Professor Dobb on Investment Criteria," *Kyklos*, Fasc. 3, 1964, for a critical note.

[32] P. C. Mahalanobis, "The Approach of Operations Research to Planning in India," *Sankya* (India), December, 1955, p. 18.

[33] *Ibid.*, pp. 68–9. This strategy apparently convinced the late Prime Minister Nehru, then *ex officio* chairman of the Planning Commission, of its logic, for he said, "You must go to the root and the base, and build up that root and base on which you will build up the structure of industrial growth. Therefore, it is heavy industries that count, *nothing else counts, excepting as a balancing factor* which is of course important. We want planning for heavy machine-making industries and heavy industries; we want industries that will make heavy machines and we should set about making them as rapidly as possible because it takes time." Quoted in Tarlok Singh, "Jawaharlal Nehru and the Five-Year Plans," *Yojana* (India), June 7, 1964, p. 7. (Emphasis supplied.)

[34] R. Komoiya, "A Note on Professor Mahalanobis' Model of Indian Economic Planning," *Review of Economics and Statistics*, February, 1959.

[35] J. Sandee, *A Long-Term Planning Model for India* (New York: United Nations, 1959).

We must conclude that the Mahalanobis approach is not concerned with efficiency criteria or comparative advantage, that it implies a rigid, inflexible economy which requires complete controls, and that it does not reflect the kind of rapidly growing private industrial sector which is representative of present-day India. Further, it appears that a major objective of this approach was the satisfaction of an ideological principle, as is illustrated by the statement in the "Plan Frame" that "a socialistic pattern of society also implies State ownership or control of the strategic means of production. With rapid development of basic industries, largely in the public sector, the second plan would ensure for the State a significant increase in influence in this sector."[36]

By the use of a Harrod-Domar type equation some of the implications of Indian planning strategy, apart from balance of payments and comparative cost problems, can be observed. In the equation $G = s/k$, G is the rate of growth of output (y), or $\triangle y/y$; s is the aggregate saving ratio including government budgetary deficits financed out of new money, and balance of payments deficits; and k is the capital coefficient or incremental capital (K)/output ratio, or $\triangle K/\triangle y$. If G is to be raised, s must be raised, given k; or k must be lowered, given s. If s is low, then either k or G must be low. If k is raised without raising s, G will be low. Therefore, any failure of the planning strategy to improve the climate for private investment (which has a high marginal propensity to save in India) will begin to lower s, and it may also begin to raise k if overcapacity begins to develop in private industries because of uncertainty. Also, if planning strategy in building the public sector industries is poorly conceived and implemented such that poor balance is achieved, overcapacity is developed, delay and inefficiency is created, political rather than economic decisions account for location of plants, etc., the result will be a raising of k and a lowering of s.

In India, in spite of a strong private industrial sector which could develop more rapidly given adequate incentives, between 1962 and 1965 the usually active capital market was virtually destroyed by restrictive and crippling tax legislation; laws and regulations were changed every few months throughout this period. As a result, a decreasing number of new firms were started and old firms were discouraged from floating new stock issues for expansion. Although foreign firms were being urged to invest in India, it became more and more difficult to raise the rupee capital component of such investment. Thus public policy has led to a lowering of the rate of growth of s in the private sector without raising it in the public sector; and in many instances it has raised k because of overcapacity in both public and private industries due to inadequate demand for inputs. The private sector is frequently being exhorted to be satisfied with low ("reasonable") profits "for the sake of development"—at the same time it is urged to fulfill its investment share of the plan. There is strong political

[36] Mahalanobis, "A Tentative Framework," *Sankya* (India), December, 1955, p. 94.

pressure on some public sector industries such as transport to subsidize passenger travel and to move low-value products at very low rates,[37] lowering s and, by masking real costs in industrial location, raising k. In addition there is strong political pressure to disregard real costs in industrial location in the public sector, raising k.

Public enterprises have paid higher wages and other employee rewards, have overstaffed their plants, and have spent more lavishly than private enterprise on consumer amenities as well as on social overhead, thus raising k and lowering s.[38] Also external, centralized decision-making has led to "periodical increases in the capital cost, extravagance in the investment processes, formulation of defective designs and periodical changes, structural disadvantages relating to site and factor combination . . . and undue adherence to budgeted plans of expenditure."[39] Management officials are deputed from general government administrative services to the public sector enterprises for short periods of a few years. They naturally carry with them the civil service attitudes and incentives of the ministries, which operate on a daily schedule of 11 to 5 with liberal time out for lunch and tea. The managerial problems have been of such magnitude that the vast Hindustan Steel Corporation enterprises have continuously showed losses in spite of rising steel prices and operation at 97 per cent of capacity (1964). In 1964 Hindustan Steel carried inventories of spare parts and raw materials equal to nine months' consumption. Some other public sector operations carried inventories equal to from nine to 30 months' consumption.[40]

In order for some public sector industries to show profits, the government has proposed that prices be raised, without mention of costs being cut to achieve the same end. s may be raised by this procedure, depending upon the elasticity of demand for output, but k will not be lowered. Railway construction continues to get priority over highway transport, which is heavily taxed, even though k of the latter is only about one-fourth of the former. Long delays in both private and public sectors are occasioned by controls, licenses, etc., administered by a slow and ponderous bureaucracy, thus raising k and lowering s.

Industrial trade unions are encouraged as though there were no "un-

[37] The railroads have experienced a falling rate of profit on capital invested over the last ten years, at a time when traffic has been increasing. If interest were charged at the going rate and taxes assessed—Indian railroads pay no taxes whatsoever—they would be running at a loss. See *The Economic Times* (India), Tuesday, January 19, 1965.

[38] V. V. Ramanadham, *The Finances of Public Enterprise* (Bombay: Asia Publishing House, 1963), pp. 62–77.

[39] *Ibid.*, p. 71.

[40] *The Economic Weekly* (India), March 20, 1965, p. 507. See also *ibid.*, p. 69. Ramanadham concludes that the relationship of government to public enterprise is such that "it may never be possible sufficiently to relieve a public enterprise of the institutional forces working on its cost structure to place it on the same footing as a private unit." *Ibid.*, p. 73.

limited labor supply" for development. Strikes, sit-down strikes, and fasts are rampant in the public sector industries. Wages rise faster than productivity; and fringe benefits such as bonuses, dearness allowances, and work rules are bargained with the threat of government intercession to secure a settlement. Bonuses and even company-operated stores selling food at "fair" prices are now becoming mandatory. All of these practices tend to lower s and raise k.

The failure to make the decisions necessary to rationalize agriculture and to put the surplus agricultural labor to work on productive rural public works has been an important factor in the low over-all growth rate. Land reforms have many times been for the benefit of the peasant or landless laborers rather than for economic growth and the good of the nation. At the same time tenancy laws in some areas have been evaded and rents are so exorbitant that they discourage the use of superior inputs. Land taxes and rural income taxes are either relatively low or nonexistent, while the world's highest progressive rates are applicable to urban individuals and to corporations, thus discouraging capital formation, entrepreneurship, and risk-taking. These high tax rates encourage evasion, corruption, and allocation of resources to low-growth investment. To the extent that they are successful, they channel profits and foregone savings into the public sector where there is a lower s and a higher k. Those items of policy which lower s and raise k could be multiplied, but the examples given are sufficient to demonstrate that it should have been no shock to anyone that progress under the Third Plan was unsatisfactory. To the extent that similar policies are continued under the Fourth Plan similar results can be expected.

What has been said here is not intended to convey an impression that no progress has been made under the plans. Some accomplishments since independence have been remarkable. The per capita national income has risen some 20 per cent in the last twelve years,[41] although there has been a distinct leveling off since the late 1950's and the Third Plan shows little improvement at all. National income grew at only 2.5 per cent per year the first two years of the Third Plan and hardly at all the third year, against the 5 per cent per annum projected, but industrial production grew at between 6.5 and 8 per cent per year as against 11 per cent planned.[42] With better harvests in the next two years average growth over the five-year period might be expected to be in the neighborhood of 3.5 per cent, just about the compound rate over the full previous twelve years.[43]

[41] All statistics are calculated from *India 1964* (New Delhi: Government of India, 1964) unless otherwise indicated.

[42] Professor K. N. Raj believes that much of the growth of private, small-scale manufacturing enterprises has gone unrecorded in the official statistics and that therefore the rate of growth of output is closer to 8 than 6.5 per cent. See K. N. Raj, *Indian Economic Growth* (New Delhi: Allied Publishers, 1965), p. 17.

[43] *Ibid.*, p. 2.

Nevertheless population is rising at 2.5 per cent or more a year, and 3.5 per cent leaves little or no room for rising living standards when rising investment plans are considered. Over the planning period there have been significant qualitative improvements in the labor force, in technology, and in the composition of output. A modest beginning in the building of an industrial base has been accomplished. Also significant progress has been made in the private industrial sector. The major limiting factors checking the growth of output have been the choking off of progress in the private sector by government policy, the high capital/output and low saving ratios in the public sector enterprises, and the failure to rationalize agriculture. Without bold policies to deal with these problems, the Fourth Plan may be a greater failure than the Third.

IV

It would be unique if a society where the majority of the population is rural and traditional, holding the values which Hindus do, were not strongly resistant to the secularization and social change necessary for dynamic growth. However, to say that Hinduism is unusually resistant to change is not to say that there are no strategies of economic development adequate to the task of creating the required conditions for economic growth. Nor does it mean that in India there is lacking the required number of persons with strong entrepreneurial characteristics for rapid social change and economic growth.[44] If these persons exist, then Hinduism would not be the major or critical restraint although there might still be required special strategies with strong economic incentives and penalties to encourage self-generative growth.

Assuming that Sovani and Narain are discussing some significant Hindu traits in their appraisal of the role of Hindu values in economic development, we should ask the question as to whether the ideological commitment is appropriate for the promotion of social change and growth in India. While socialism coincides with the Hindu ideal of renunciation of gain and the submergence of the self for the good of all, it may fit it so well that it merely continues the concept of government as the *ma-bap* (mother and father) of all. Whereas, the strategy of development should be such as to cause individuals to make decisions, to become involved in their own future welfare, to become innovators—at least in the sense of adapting borrowed technology from advanced countries to the problems

[44] For a discussion of the values needed for economic progress, see D. D. Mc-Clelland, *The Achieving Society* (New York: D. Van Nostrand, 1961), especially pp. 394–403; and Bert F. Hoselitz, "Entrepreneurial Element in Economic Development," *The Economic Weekly*, Annual Number (India), February, 1963, pp. 163–73.

of production in India—socialist policy may leave them so resigned to their traditional mode of life that even well-organized borrowing of technology (derived development) produces very little growth. In other words, the ideology of the Indian elite may have led the nation to adopt wrong and inadequate strategies in planning.

In order to maximize growth in India, development plans would have to be devoted to the encouragement of the growth of the maximum number of entrepreneurs, to the building of a viable market system, to providing adequate relative price incentives for farmers and to teaching them to react to them, to encouraging private capital formation wherever feasible, and to confining government investment largely to those infrastructure items which facilitate development and growth.[45] Such an approach to planning would be pragmatic rather than doctrinaire, practical rather than ideological, and would utilize the latent entrepreneurial energy in developing a growing, mixed, dynamic system. There are those who claim to see such a pattern still as an emerging possibility in India, but to assess its reality is impossible at this time.

[45] It is significant that not a single member of the Planning Commission is a businessman or has ever had business experience, nor have business consultants been utilized in the planning process.

9 ELLIOT J. BERG

SOCIALISM AND ECONOMIC DEVELOPMENT IN TROPICAL AFRICA

I. INTRODUCTION

It is hard these days to find an African statesman who does not advocate "a socialist path" to economic development. Among intellectuals, trade unionists and other politically aware groups, the enthusiasm for "socialism" is only slightly less widespread. On the ideological level, "socialism" has won the day in most of independent Africa.

That no two African socialists mean quite the same thing when they talk of socialism is by now clear. The gamut of conceptions runs from the very general Ujamaa ("Familyhood" or "Socialism" in Swahili) of Tanganyika's President Nyerere and the vague amalgam of Marxism, Christian socialism, humanitarianism, and "Negritude" of President Senghor of Senegal, to the more structured but heretical Marxism of Guinea's President Touré, which denies the presence of class struggle in Africa. There are also those, mainly university students and leaders of the "left opposition," who are more orthodox in their socialism. They see the emergence in Africa of unacceptable inequalities in income and power, and nascent class conflict. They question the meaningfulness of "African Socialism," and the ideological purity of "African Socialists." They are for socialism in Africa but not "African Socialism."[1]

Reprinted by permission of the publishers from Elliot J. Berg, THE QUARTERLY JOURNAL OF ECONOMICS, *Cambridge, Mass.: Harvard University Press,* Copyright, 1964, by the President and Fellows of Harvard College.

[1] We are mainly concerned in this paper with the general economic content of socialist ideology in Africa, not with description and illustration of particular versions of socialism. We will therefore make few specific references. The main sources from which the description of socialist thought is drawn are: *Africa Report: Special Issue on African Socialism,* Vol. 8 (May 1963); A. Fenner Brockway, *African Socialism* (London: Bodley Head, 1963); Mamadou Dia, *Reflexions sur l'économie de l'Afrique noire* (Paris: Editions Africaines, 1960); Kwame Nkrumah, *Building of a Socialist State* (Accra: Government Printer, April 1961), and *I Speak of Freedom* (New York: Praeger, 1961); Colin Legum, *Pan-Africanism—A Short Political Guide* (New York: Praeger, 1962); Abdoulaye Ly, *Les Masses Africaines et l'actuelle condition humaine* (Paris: Présence Africaine, 1956); J. Nyerere, "Ujamaa," speech at a TANU Conference on Socialism, April, 1962, excerpted in *Africa Report: Special Issue on African Socialism, op. cit.,* p. 24; Leopold Senghor, *African Socialism* (New York: American Society of African Culture, 1959), and "Negritude and African Socialism," in *African*

Despite the diversity of socialist doctrine, most Africans who call themselves socialists do hold in common certain economic attitudes or preconceptions. All of them, first of all, view "capitalism" as an unsuitable system for Africa. It is the economy of the colonizers; capitalism and colonialism are really two sides of the same coin. It is old-fashioned, out of place in the modern world. It is inadequate to meet the pressing development needs of poor countries in general and Africa in particular. Individual enterprise cannot be counted on to mobilize resources on the scale required in Africa, and the market mechanism is a wasteful, highly imperfect regulator of economic activity. Development by the "capitalist," free enterprise route is too slow. There is too little private capital accumulation, too few entrepreneurs. Capitalism is—at least according to President Nkrumah—"too complicated." It would, moreover, maintain and even intensify the hold of foreign capital, and the dominance of agricultural exports in the economy. In the absence of forced draft growth policies, which only the state can undertake, Africa will remain a permanent economic dependency of the outside world.

Even if all this were not true, even if the efficiency of capitalism as a model of growth could be satisfactorily demonstrated, it would still be unacceptable on social and ethical grounds. Capitalism rests on the exploitation of man by man. It leads to intolerable inequality, allowing the strong, the crafty, the well-placed to win a large share of society's goods without making corresponding contributions. It is inhuman, destructive of human dignity. It alienates each man from his brother, and prevents a full flowering of the human personality.

There is little that is specifically African about these ideas. They are general indictments of capitalism as a social and economic system, drawn from the mainstream of European socialism. The *African* quality of African socialist thinking in its economic aspects arises from two main sources. First, some of the universal critiques of capitalist economic organization receive special emphasis: the association of capitalism with colonialism, for example, and the unproductive, parasitic role of the merchant. But most universal and most basic is the general argument that a socialist solution to Africa's development problems is fundamentally in harmony with

Affairs: St. Anthony's Papers, No. 15, 1963, pp. 9–22; P. Sigmund (ed.), *The Ideologies of the Developing Nations,* Introduction and Part III (New York: Praeger, 1963); Sekou Touré, *L'Expérience Guinéenne et l'unité africaine* (Paris: Présence Africaine, 1961); L. Hamon, "La voie africaine du socialisme selon la pensée socialiste sénégalaise," in *Penant,* No. 695 (Janvier–Mars 1963), pp. 13–30; V. I. Potekhin, "Réflexions sur le socialisme Africain," in *Recherches Internationales,* 1960.

A forthcoming volume, *African Socialism,* edited by W. H. Friedland and C. G. Rosberg, announced for publication in June 1964, should provide full case studies of socialist doctrine and policy.

It should be noted that the description and analysis in this paper refer to Africa South of the Sahara. While much of it has applicability to North Africa, conditions there are different in certain fundamental respects from those in countries below the Sahara.

the communal traditions of African society. African village life, the argument runs, is essentially socialistic. Land is held by the community, and
much of the villager's work and play is organized on a group basis. Kinship ties remain strong, and among most African peoples firm class distinctions have not yet developed. Individualism has little place in traditional
society. Even among those who have entered the money economy as cash
crop growers or wage and salary earners, group loyalties remain deep.
This social setting is a natural base for the construction of a socialist form
of society, since Africans are by social instinct and economic circumstances
already socialists. All that is needed is to transform the old socialism, re-
cast it into a new and modern mold.

Much remains vague in this formulation. Little is said about whether
it is to be the village, the kinship group, the cooperative work societies
which are to be harnessed and modernized. Less is said about how it is to
be done. Some African socialists emphasize cooperatives, others communal
cultivation. It is only the general tenor of the argument that is universal
among "African socialists" if not among all socialists in Africa: somehow,
the "communitarian" spirit of the villages must be retained and utilized
to build a specifically African kind of socialist society. It is not an altogether unfamiliar argument. The Populists in Russia at the end of the
nineteenth century were saying many of the same things: by building on
the traditions of village socialism, society can skip a stage of history—the
destructive, individualizing, capitalist stage.

II. Economic Policies: The Socialist
Development Model

While most socialists in Africa share this general world view, it is not
easy to define the meaning of African socialism in terms of concrete economic policies. Statements of socialist intent or doctrine rarely descend to
the blueprint level, so they contain little in the way of specific policy proposals. Between theory and reality, furthermore, there may be a big gap;
in Senegal and Tanganyika, among other places, the air is heavy with talk
of socialism, but not much is done about it. In the area of actual economic
policies, finally, different paths are being followed by African governments, all claiming to be headed in a socialist direction.

Thus socialists in Africa emphasize the need for planning. But so do
nonsocialists; planning of some sort is applauded everywhere these days,
even in strongholds of free enterprise. Socialists are sympathetic to nationalization of private industry, but few of them call for such nationalization
on a wholesale basis, and they differ in their view of timing and the scope

to be allowed to the private sector. All admit the need for private foreign investment, though with varying degrees of enthusiasm. Policies toward land ownership differ. In places like Senegal and Ghana, where individual tenure has made headway among peasant growers of export crops, there is no call for nationalization of the land. In Guinea, Mali, and to a lesser extent Tanganyika, individualization is discouraged. Under the banner of socialism, it seems, almost anyone can march.

But this is not quite true. It is possible to see in almost all socialist doctrine and practice a general policy orientation which gives some definable economic substance to socialist ideology. There is a "socialist road" to development, a "socialist model" of development, though it is a construct, an abstraction from which there are many departures in reality. The elements of this "socialist model" can be seen best in those countries which have most loudly and persistently announced their dedication to the building of a socialist society: Ghana, Guinea, Mali, to a lesser extent Senegal and Tanganyika. But the same elements are present as tendencies elsewhere, and are implicit in most socialist doctrine.

It is first of all clear that in all socialist approaches, the State is to be the driving force in development. Its area of action is to be enlarged. It is not only to undertake new initiatives, but to intensify existing controls over private economic activity.

In most of Africa, government has always been the major element in the economy, even though the public sector commands a smaller proportion of total output than in advanced Western countries. The presence of the state is exercised through its economic controls and regulations, and by its predominance in the money sector; between a quarter and a half of the recorded wage labor force in most of the continent has long been employed by government. And the minimum tasks required in the continent's present stage of development (law and order, physical infrastructure, education, research) imply a very large government role even under the most "liberal" economic policies conceivable. But in the "socialist model" the state has a much greater place—in the creation and operation of industrial and agricultural enterprises, in control of marketing, in price regulation and in general management of the economy.

Related to the predominance of the state is an emphasis on direct economic controls, underlying which is a belief in the efficacy of such controls, combined with a lack of faith in individual profit-seeking and the market mechanism as efficient instruments of resource allocation and mobilization. This is most strikingly evident in socialist policy tendencies in the distribution sector. Government monopoly of all or part of foreign and domestic trade is regarded as particularly desirable. In part this springs from a desire to reduce the influence of big foreign trading firms. But behind it is the conviction that private commerce is inefficient—that prices are too high, profits too great, and the number of traders too large, and that the merchant class is profoundly parasitic, a group of useless exploiters. For all these reasons it is necessary to "democratize the channels of commerce," as President Touré put it—i.e., nationalize trade.

This penchant for state take-over of the trading sector is stimulated by the belief that since trading is a simple matter its nationalization can provide an easy and rich source for development resources. Thus, in both Guinea and Mali, the planned profits of the nationalized trading sector were to provide much of the local contribution to expenditures under the first post-independence development plans—in Mali about one-third of total domestic investment, in Guinea even more.

In agriculture, too, the policy tendencies of African socialists are definable. Agricultural development is not ignored; it comes in for reluctant recognition, reluctant because of the feeling that future price prospects for commodity exports are bleak, that true economic independence can come about in any event only when Africa no longer is dependent on the export of raw materials, and that industrial development is at bottom the only true engine of modernization. But in this socialists are not really different from most others in Africa and elsewhere in the developing countries. Where they part company is in method. The socialist road to agricultural development places little emphasis, or actually discourages, expansion of individual and family production, on the grounds (sometimes explicit, sometimes not) that to do so would involve the creation of a kulak class, a politically retrograde, exploitative rural bourgeoisie.

It is largely for this reason that African socialist thinking runs in terms of mechanization of agriculture, the big project, state farms, and development through conversion and activation of communal cultivation. This is clear, as we will see below, in Guinea, and it is becoming increasingly evident in Ghana, where the main source of planned agricultural expansion is to be in the state farming sector.

III. ORIGINS OF SOCIALIST ATTITUDES

It is worth considering briefly the roots of these attitudes and ideas on economic policy. In part they rest on imported ideology. Much of the distaste with which African elites view "capitalism" reflects the Marxist world view—however modified or heretic in form—which colors the thinking of so many national leaders in Africa. Capitalism is to them simply the projection of colonialism and imperialism, much as Lenin said it was. Related to this are the personal and intellectual relations of African students and political leaders with European socialists, who most steadfastly fought their cause during the years of colonial rule. Development through expansion of the private sector also has political implications which many of the new elites find unpalatable: every foreign private enterprise harbors a latent neocolonial influence; and the emergence or expansion of a rich, energetic African capitalist class raises the specter of potential political opposition. Where there is money, Africans know, power is never very far away.

While all of these are important in explaining the "anticapitalist" spirit abroad in Africa, at least equally fundamental is the image of capitalism and the general economic attitudes inherited from the colonial period. Thus colonialism and capitalism are so closely identified in African thinking not only, or even mainly, because of Marxist-Leninist doctrine, but because most Africans have seen it to be so. Behind them is a half-century of history cluttered with memories of price-fixing arrangements, government-bestowed monopoly privileges, restrictive wage and labor market policies, forced labor—all dependent on an alliance between colonial governments and private (almost exclusively foreign) enterprises, and most of them involving a sacrifice of African interests. It is hardly surprising that "decolonization" and a reduction of the role of private enterprise should seem related.

Moreover, the colonial experience in most of the continent was scarcely designed to encourage an appreciation of the economic potentials of individual initiatives in a relatively free market. Economic policy in colonial Africa was most often paternalist, *dirigiste,* antifree enterprise to the core. More often than not, African peasants were told what to produce, who to sell it to, where, when, at what price. In a number of countries, even the African instinct of survival was discounted; Africans were forced to grow some crops in excess of normal needs, as a guarantee against famine. Wage earners in much of the continent were not until recently thought by colonial officials or employers to be capable of spending their incomes "sensibly," nor were African farmers and traders presumed to be sufficiently alive to price and profit to assure urban food supplies at reasonable prices. Markets had to be "organized," commodity and labor supplies "regularized." Extensive price controls, monopolistic allocation of sales and purchases, regulation of entry into trade, commerce and industry—most of the armory of a benevolent *dirigism* found its way to Africa.

In the early years of the colonial presence this was no doubt inevitable and necessary. Preconditions for the effective functioning of markets had to be established. But it tended to persist, in much of the continent, when its utility was doubtful. That it did so reflected the economic tastes of colonial administrators in charge of economic policy, most of whom had little understanding of and sympathy for the struggles of the market place. They took a dim view of the competitive market, its "disorderliness" and seeming wastefulness; they rarely saw the point of having two sellers (or buyers) where one might do. And they had a particularly low estimate of the merchant, who—as they saw it—grew fat buying cheap and selling dear, exploiting the ignorance and improvidence of the ordinary African. The educational and disciplinary aspects of market decisions were never appreciated. And that the market might in some measure contain corrective tendencies, or reflect underlying forces of supply and demand, these and similar homely notions of the economist were badly received in Africa. When retail prices rose, the instinctive reaction was to damn the traders and look for conspiracy.

These are the habits of thought passed on to independent Africa by its colonial rulers: misunderstanding and mistrust of the market mechanism; an ingrained belief in the ability of government to manipulate economic variables, no matter how contrary the underlying market conditions; an inability to perceive the potential uses of the price system in allocating resources through decentralized decision-making. It is no surprise that so much African thinking on economic development policy runs in terms of state enterprise, direct state controls over production, marketing, and prices, suppression of middlemen, and state-directed activity in general. Aside from the impulses in this direction arising from ideology and from internal political considerations, it represents continuity with the past.

IV. THE GUINEA EXPERIENCE

Consideration of socialist development policies in Africa invites a glance at the experience of the Republic of Guinea.[2] Alone of all the French territories in Africa, this small country of some three million proud and spirited people took its independence when offered it in 1958. Its dynamic political leadership was convinced of the efficacy of the socialist "model" as outlined above and was dedicated to economic transformation along socialist lines.

Its tasks were enormous. Despite their capture of political control, few Guineans had experience in dealing with economic problems, either on the level of the state or the firm; at independence, only a handful held high level technical or administrative posts in government, and almost none knew managerial responsibility in the small private sector. The total stock of university-trained local manpower was probably less than 50 people, the number of high school graduates probably less than 500. In 1957 the high schools of the country produced only 30 graduates. Yet three months after independence almost all French civil servants were gone. Gone too was French economic aid, which had provided most of the development finance during the postwar period, and the protected market in France for coffee and bananas—which accounted for 80 per cent of Guinea's export earnings in 1957.

[2] This account relies heavily on personal observations and unpublished mimeographed documents gathered in Guinea. For further discussion see: J. Charrière, "La Guinée Une expérience de Planification," in *Cahiers Internationaux,* 1960; "Où en est la Guinée?" in *Problèmes d'Outre-Mer,* 1 Juin, 1963, pp. 75–76; and J. Miandre, "L'expérience guinéenne," in *Esprit,* Oct. 1963, pp. 514–32.

The new government attacked its problems with vigor and confidence. One of its first acts, taken three months after independence, was to set up a state trading monopoly limited at first to trade in exports and key imports. This limited role of the state trading organization was soon found to be unsatisfactory; the domestic wholesale and retail trade remained in private hands, so the state had simply imposed itself on the existing "colonial" structure, adding, as it were, another middleman. The scope of state trading was thus extended; it was given a complete monopoly over foreign trade, and over domestic wholesaling.[3] The process was completed in 1960 by the extension of state shops to the retail level.

In mid-1960 a Three Year Plan was initiated; it had been drawn up with the help of French Marxist advisors, and was implemented with the help of 1,000–1,500 communist technicians and over $100 million in credits from the communist countries. The planned investment was large ($140 million, later raised to $155 million), relative to either past investment rates or to GNP.[4] The sectoral allocation of planned expenditure was not much different from that found in most African development plans. But within the sectoral plans, the nature of Guinea's ideological options could be clearly perceived. Agriculture, for example, received 26 per cent of the total plan expenditure, but 90 per cent of this was allocated to the state sector—the main part of it for state-run farms.

The achievements of the plan period, and of the years since independence in general, have in some respects been considerable. The administrative machinery survived the shock of transition to independence. Guinea's government has made massive assaults on the education problem,[5] and if official figures are to be believed the "human investment" program yielded substantial results—at least until 1962.[6]

The achievements of the new state, however, pale before its catastrophic failures in the area of economic policy and planning. In agriculture the state farms apparently never got off the ground, despite the import from the Soviet Union of hundreds of agricultural machines; by 1963 most of the equipment had been abandoned, so far as a visitor could tell,

[3] It was reasoned that the state could "nationalize" importers' profit margins, earn 15 per cent on the sale of imports, and thereby raise 6 billion Guinean francs (about $24 million) in three years, or 60 per cent of the domestic investment component in the Plan.

[4] Estimates of Guinea's GNP vary between $175 and $240 million. The plan was to be financed as follows: current budget surpluses and profits from state trading firms were to provide $40 million over the three year period, free labor (*investissement humain*) $24 million, and foreign aid over $90 million.

[5] The number of primary school pupils enrolled rose from 47,500 in 1958 to 160,000 in 1962, and secondary school attendance grew from 4,600 in 1958 to 10,400 in 1962.

[6] The results claimed for *investissement humain* as of 1961 were: 2,000 buildings constructed, 14,000 acres of collective fields and 150,000 trees planted, and over 8,000 miles of road constructed. Much of this is surely fanciful, the road figure in particular. By 1962, in any event, official as well as popular enthusiasm for "human investment" had sharply declined, as coercive elements appeared and as the usefulness of much of the work became questionable.

and the state farming enterprises quietly laid to rest. Far from meeting the ambitious agricultural goals of the Plan, agricultural output has fallen.[7] Nor has industrial progress been more notable; of the twenty-six plants listed in the Plan, less than a quarter were completed in mid-1963. By 1963 the country faced a severe balance-of-payments crisis. Imported consumer goods were scarce; it was difficult to see how Guinea could meet its debt service payments on loans from Soviet bloc countries, due to begin in that year. And all of this occurred despite an inflow of foreign aid of perhaps $50 million a year, which made Guinea one of the most "aided" countries per capita ($15–20) in the world during these years.

Part of this unhappy record is no doubt attributable to the precipitous withdrawal of the French. Part of it, too, is due to the methods and content of Soviet economic aid.[8] But the major burden of responsibility rests with the Guineans themselves. The state trading venture was an unmitigated disaster, afflicting the whole economy. An inexperienced Guinean management found itself in charge of what was in effect the largest trading firm in Africa. Despite some gallant efforts, the distribution system rapidly fell victim to a massive administrative muddle. Goods were ordered for which there was no demand, or in quantities far beyond normal needs. Desired staples were frequently in short supply because of inadequate inventory policies and irregular deliveries. The old "colonial" evil of the "tied" or "conditional" sale became common enough in state shops to call forth public denunciation by President Touré. Poor inventory control in warehouses resulted in the rotting of perishable items.

Thus Guinean urban consumers came to know shortages, poor quality goods, long queues, and black markets. Consumers of imports in the interior were even more badly served. And the export sector suffered from sparse and unreliable deliveries of pesticides, fertilizers, and other imported inputs.

The absence of consumer imports, or their low quality, combined with low prices fixed for meat and fish, affected the production and marketed

[7] Rice production was to rise from 270,000 tons in 1960 to 315,000 in 1963; actual 1962 output is not known, but imports of rice had risen from $100,000 in 1957 to $6 million in 1962, a rise explainable only in part by the availability of P.L. 480 rice. Banana production of 60,000 tons in 1960 was to rise to 130,000 tons in 1963; actual 1962 output was 44,000 tons. The planned rise in coffee production was from 12,000 tons in 1960 to 16,000 tons (an output which had been achieved in the late 1950's); actual 1962 exports were 8,000 tons. Peanut production did rise from 2,000 tons in 1960 to 6,000 tons in 1962, but planned output in 1963 was 33,000 tons.

[8] The first sugar sent from the Soviet Union was too soft; it melted and spoiled in the tropical heat. Later shipments were too hard; the sugar refused to melt in coffee. The first shipments of cement arrived unexpectedly; thousands of tons were dropped on unready Guinean docks, and were ruined by later rains. In Conakry thousands of toilet units lay in the sun, unused and unusable in a country with little plumbing. Many Eastern bloc vehicles proved ill-adapted to African conditions, and scarcity of maintenance and spare parts led to a frightening mortality rate for them. Soviet projects were ill-planned, and proceeded very slowly.

supply of local foodstuffs and export crops. The flow of meat, fish and rice to urban centers shrank as producers either withheld their output from the market, or diverted their supply to the neighboring countries of Liberia, Sierra Leona and the Ivory Coast. Smuggling became the order of the day, absorbing not only the existing private traders who were hobbled and harassed by official regulations, but new entrants besides. Coffee found its way to the Ivory Coast; Guinea's 1962 export of coffee was half the level of previous years. Diamonds also left the country illegally. Some imports increased fantastically, for reasons that are not clear; imports of cotton prints, for example, rose from 158 million francs in 1959 to 2.3 billion in 1961 and 1.8 billion in 1962. Most of these textiles were almost surely smuggled out of the country to finance either smuggled imports from neighboring countries or capital flight. The propensity to smuggle was aggravated by the drastic depreciation of the Guinean franc in (free and illegal) money markets in neighboring countries.

Troubles were compounded by price policies edicted with cheerful disregard for market forces and in particular without recognition of Guinea's geographical situation. Shortly after independence, for example, President Touré decided, as a symbol of the intentions of the new regime, to sell rice (a gift from the Chinese) at a price well below that prevailing in neighboring countries. In a matter of weeks the rice disappeared from the country, sold across the border at the higher prices prevailing there. Similarly, the government decided that certain basic goods, such as cement, would be sold in the interior either at the same price as in the port city of Conakry, or at a subsidized price. The aim was to favor consumers in the interior, on whom transport costs weighed heavily. But the subsidized items also found their way across the borders, isnce the delivered price in the Guinea interior was substantially lower than across the border.

Despite the obviously faltering performance of the economy, reform has proved difficult. In March 1961 the system of internal distribution was on the verge of complete collapse. Imports were piling up in Conakry, while the interior was without staples. The government was forced to commandeer all available trucks in Conakry to move goods to the interior. Shortly thereafter adaptations were made; the state trading organization was decentralized and a greater role for private traders was announced. But aside from some administrative reshuffling, little basic change occurred. Fundamental reappraisals were hindered by the need to maintain socialist purity, an unwillingness to look coolly at all alternatives. Official economic discussion in fact became increasingly divorced from reality.[9] It was not until the end of 1963, under the pressure of deepening economic

[9] The Economic Report of the 1962 Party Congress, for example, recommended registration of each calf born in the country as a way of controlling smuggling; the formation of self-governed building cooperatives in the construction industry to raise productivity, and detailed work norms for agricultural production.

crisis,[10] that a more basic reform was announced, involving changes in price policies and return of more of the distribution sector to private hands.

The costs of Guinea's false starts cannot be calculated only in terms of wasted resources and foregone growth. Much of the popular enthusiasm for the regime and the dynamism of its leadership has been dissipated. Cynicism and corruption have spread, and signs of disaffection appeared.[11] The moral and political cement binding the state together has been weakened as respect for the law, and for the regime, has diminished.

V. The Inapplicability of the Socialist Model

It is not the business of outsiders—at least outsider economists—to quarrel about the suitability of the goals set out by socialists in Africa. This is their vision of the society they want (however vaguely delineated as yet), and is not open to question by others. What the observer from outside can legitimately consider, however, is the probable effectiveness of the "socialist model" in achieving the goals of economic growth and change which socialists, like most Africans, say they want. For a number of reasons, suggested in the Guinea story, the socialist path to modernization is not likely to bring success in this sense, for the major elements of socialist policy are ill-suited to present African circumstances.

The first and most obvious reason is Africa's scarcity of people equipped by training, experience or education to manage the economy. To an extent unmatched in most of the underdeveloped world, positions of skill and responsibility were until recently in the hands of non-Africans. This was true almost everywhere in the public sector until a decade ago, and remains true throughout the private, nonagricultural sector, with the possible exceptions of Ghana and Nigeria. One main reason for this was the limited availability, until recent years, of upper level education. As late as 1958 there were only about 8,000 Africans graduated from all the academic secondary schools below the Sahara, and only about 10,000 others were studying in universities—more than half of these in Ghana and Nigeria. Educational intake and output have increased markedly since 1958, but in 1962 there were still few African countries where more than 200 Africans received full secondary diplomas. In only a handful of countries will the outflow from universities be more than 250 a year much before 1970.

[10] Late in 1963 there were reports of food riots in a number of urban centers.
[11] In December 1961 discontent among some sections of the Teachers' Union and other intellectuals resulted in an outburst of violence, a charge that a communist plot was being hatched and the closing of secondary schools for several months. Although not due directly to the state of the economy, this was at least in part a reflection of the sense of frustration engendered by economic deterioration.

In these figures lie the most severe indictment of colonial rule. African governments are trying to make up for it with an enormous educational effort. But trained people necessary to man the bureaucracies of the new states will not be available for at least a decade in most of the continent. It is not only the highly-specialized technicians who will be in short supply; all professional and technical manpower will be sparse. And the vital middle levels, now exceedingly shallow, are likely to remain so for even longer, as universities continue to absorb most secondary school graduates. Under these circumstances, to put heavy and exacting new burdens on the state is to invite trouble—waste and inefficiency at the least, economic dislocation on the Guinean scale at the worst. This is the message not only of common sense; it is one of the inescapable lessons of the Guinea experience.

Contrary to President Nkrumah's view, socialism, with the larger state role that it assumes, is not less but much more complicated than a "capitalist" or market system relying heavily on decentralized decision-making in the market. It is in particular much more demanding of trained human resources. Given the pressing scarcity of these resources, it is essential not to use them on tasks that can be performed by others. Where teachers are wanting, and general administration is shoddy, it is dubious wisdom to have trained and able people fixing and enforcing prices, authorizing import licenses or even running industrial enterprises. This is especially pertinent to the extension of the state into the distribution sector. Where private individuals have the proven capacity and experience to perform efficiently, as do traders in most of the continent, the extension of state control, represents a monstrous misallocation of trained manpower, even if government functionaries could do the job as well as the private traders—a most unlikely possibility.

Shortcomings in socialist approaches to agricultural development provide a second major reason for questioning the probable effectiveness of socialist policy. The lackluster record of agricultural development in socialist countries should by itself suggest caution to potential importers of development strategies; socialist achievement in agriculture has almost nowhere been impressive. But there are other reasons, closer to home, to question the efficacy of socialist solutions in agriculture.

The African physical and economic environment, first of all, has shown itself generally uncongenial to mechanization and large-scale farm projects. Most Africans soils are delicate, and little is known about them; the effects of continuous use of fertilizers, plowing and intensive cultivation, for example, have been adequately studied in only a few places. Within small geographic areas African soils tend to vary widely in texture and chemistry, and many operations, such as tree stump removal, do not easily lend themselves to mechanization. Dust, heat and rain, combined with casual handling, sparsity of skilled maintenance men and difficulties with spare parts all take a terrible toll on farm equipment. Machines do not in any case eliminate the need for labor, as Professor Frankel emphasized in his study of the East African groundnut scheme,[12] and unskilled labor tends to be scarce at planting and harvesting time, since most men have farms of their own that require attention.

These and other factors help explain why mechanization and big farm projects in Africa present an almost unbroken record of failure, and sometimes of disaster; Africa, indeed, is the scene of some of the world's most magnificent agricultural white elephants, such as the French-created Office du Niger in Mali, the Gambia poultry scheme of the early postwar years, and the East African groundnut scheme. The Guinea experience outlined above is perhaps even more relevant.

With growing knowledge and changing economic conditions, the prospects for mechanized, large-scale agriculture will no doubt improve; there are some places in Africa where conditions are already more favorable, and in all countries there is room for some effort in this direction. But as a major approach to agricultural development it has little to recommend it. And when it is recalled that mechanized agricultural schemes eat up large amounts of Africa's scarcest resources—foreign exchange and human skill—they become even more questionable.

In addition to the dim prospects for expansion through state farming and mechanization, both of which are central to the economic thinking of most socialists in Africa, another set of considerations limits the applicability of socialist policies in African agriculture. More than any other region, Africa is a continent of subsistence farmers. The majority of Africans are only slightly committed to the money economy; they spend most of their lives in the village, where their main productive activity is the growing of food for their own consumption.

Under these circumstances the key to agricultural modernization and growth is fuller peasant commitment to the money economy; villagers must be induced to use their land, their energies and their time differently from in the past by growing more for the market. This transfer of resources within the village from subsistence production and traditional activities to cash crop production is, in Africa's present stage, the essence of development. It does not by itself guarantee self-sustaining growth, but it is a revolutionary step in the growth process; in the absence of major mineral resources it is an indispensable step.

There are plenty of examples of how an aroused peasantry shifting its energies to cash crops can work great economic transformations. In the space of two decades after the turn of the century, in a country almost without infrastructure and with very little assistance from government,

[12] S. H. Frankel, "The Kongwa Experiment: Lessons of the East African Goundnut Scheme," in *The Economic Impact on Under-developed Societies* (Oxford: Blackwell, 1953), pp. 141–53.

Ghana's peasants made their country the world's greatest cocoa producer. In the Ivory Coast, the creation of a road network and a period of good prices led African farmers to a five-fold expansion of coffee production and a doubling of cocoa output in the fifteen years after World War II. The more recent surge in African export crop production in Kenya offers another example.

If one asks why more such transformations have not occurred, or why some, as in Uganda, seem to be arrested, half-finished, a number of obstacles become apparent: unsuitable soils and climate, including rainfall; expensive or inadequate transport and marketing facilities; lack of knowledge; absence of tools required for small technological changes (plows, for example), and others. Three factors, however, seem of particular significance and generality. The first is neglect of the peasant, the fact that in only a few countries have African villagers in the past received extension services, roads, marketing facilities and other assistance which government might give them. The second is land tenure; the "communal" nature of most land holding, and the difficulties of establishing individual title in some areas affect incentives and the ability of individual farmers to expand sales; in all areas it has limited African access to credit. Finally, rural Africans in most of the continent still have relatively few demands for new goods, and the money income needed to buy them; want levels remain low. It is not, of course, that they would not like more money income; it is that they are not willing to make the changes in ways of life that are required to get more income.

This last point deserves special emphasis, for not only is it open to misinterpretation, but it is uncongenial to much thinking on development, among socialists as well as others. In order for marketed output to claim a larger share of village resources the peasant must be induced to switch from tried and proven activities to new and unknown ones. The peasant and his family must work harder, and give up "leisure" or customary pleasures and activities in the village. In addition to new outlays of effort, all of this involves uncomfortable departures from custom and may involve new risks, a greater dependence on the market, and even outlays of money. It is hard to see why he should make these changes unless he is first convinced that new goods and services are in fact important elements of a better life. His preference for more income as against his present way of life must be increased.

In these conditions, socialist attitudes and approaches lost most of their relevance. The socialist appeal for land redistribution, common in other parts of the underdeveloped world as a means of mobilizing the peasantry (politically, as well as in an economic sense), are devoid of meaning in Sub-Saharan Africa where land is still relatively abundant, and landlordism is a rare problem. Approaches designed to squeeze the peasant into greater production for the market are unpromising. State levies on the agricultural sector, whether by price policies or direct deliveries, can be effective only where agriculture has become monetized and specialized. Peasants still mainly or largely in the subsistence sector cannot be bullied into the market; full retreat back to subsistence production is too easy. The ordinary African village is no Garden of Eden, and life there no idyll; disease is everywhere, famines strikes occasionally, comforts are few. But there is almost everywhere enough to eat, and the village provides the bulk of what most men feel they need. Since life in most African villages is not so oppressive as it is in many other parts of the underdeveloped world, and since many African villagers would find it possible to reduce their demands for goods from outside the village, the result of attempts to squeeze the peasant sector, and consequent peasant dissatisfaction, can easily be "sabotage" in the Veblenian sense—"a conscious withdrawal of efficiency."

The African peasant, then, cannot easily be pushed into the market. He must be pulled into it, encouraged, enticed by positive inducements, among which the most effective is no doubt that most banal of incentives —the possibility of higher real income. To the extent that this is true, it presents socialists in Africa with a fundamental contradiction of the utmost importance. It implies that agricultural transformation is not possible, or is possible only at a much slower rate, without some individualization of land tenure, the emergence of a rural bourgeoisie composed of the more energetic or more fortunate peasants, and the accentuation of rural income inequalities.

Socialists in Africa have not yet come seriously to grips with this set of problems. Their writing, and in a few places their policies, shows more concern with the dangers of individualism and the rise of rural moneyed classes than with the potential output effects of peasant awakening. They emphasize harnessing the communal spirit of the villages, and utilization of the cooperative work groups which perform much labor in traditional agriculture. They tend to rely on appeals to larger social goals—Patriotism, National Construction, the General Good. It is, of course, possible that some considerable mobilization of peasant energies can be brought about in this way, more perhaps in Africa than elsewhere because of the strength of traditional culture there. But it is unlikely by itself to provide the kind of wrench from the past inherent in fuller commitment to the market.

Nor are abstract appeals likely to provide a continuous spur to increased effort. Experience with these methods of rural mobilization is not encouraging, either in Africa or elsewhere. In addition to administrative and technical problems, there exist in all communal efforts powerful propensities to coercion, especially since lower level cadres tend to be overzealous. Unless these communal efforts are genuinely voluntary and devoted to local public works or other projects of immediate and obvious village utility, they may actually have negative effects on the release of peasant energies. Even where coercion is absent or mild, it often turns out that the list of useful projects which can be performed effectively by village communal labor is distressingly short in the absence of administrative aid, so that communal labor campaigns tend to fizzle out. The appearance of coercive elements and administrative and technical difficulties seem to explain the decline of Tanganyika's brief experiment in post-independence "self-help" programs,[13] and Guinea's attempts to utilize "human investment."

Large-scale transformation of the subsistence sector, then, is unlikely to be achieved unless villagers can see some close relation between their greater effort and a better life, and unless they come to believe that consumption of more goods is essential to this better life. To the extent that this is true, it raises serious doubts about the meaningfulness of most socialist prescriptions for agricultural development.

It is here, also, that socialist policies in the distribution sector are especially relevant. State trading companies are poorly designed to engage in the kind of want-creating activity that private merchants in Africa —indigenous and expatriate—have always undertaken. The agent of the state trading firm is unlikely to roam the remote villages with goods of tempting quality and style and, if necessary, with credit as well, in order to whet peasant appetites for money income and cajole them into new lines of production. He is not, in short, likely to be a creator of markets. So in the area where the distribution system has its most vital role to play—maintenance and expansion of the flow of marketed output from the villages through stimulating the demand for goods—a nationalized trading system is most deficient.

A third major pitfall for socialist solutions in Africa has its basis in geography. Africa has the highest ratio of frontiers to total area of any continent. Goods and people have always flowed over these frontiers in the past, usually with few restrictions. Effective controls were scarcely possible, traders roamed at will between countries, and when prices in one country moved out of line with those in neighboring countries, smuggling on a large scale tended to develop.

The most striking examples are to be found in postwar West Africa, where bits and chunks of British colonies, with few import restrictions and relatively low price levels, jutted into the protected, high-price French African land mass. Trade between areas under British and French control existed before the colonial frontiers were established, and resourceful groups of African traders served these areas without regard to frontiers.

The mechanism and extent of smuggling is known only in broad outline, but there is enough evidence to indicate that it is a large-scale phenomenon, involving thousands of people, millions of dollars, and an

[13] Cf. J. Nye, "Tanganyika's Self-Help," in *Transition*, III (Nov. 1963), 35–39.

institutional framework that includes specialized transport, established marketing channels, and free (illegal) foreign exchange markets in border towns and cities, almost all in African hands. Export commodities (cattle, smoked fish, cocoa, coffee, peanuts, diamonds, etc.) are involved, and consumer goods.

In West Africa, until the late 1950's at least, the foundation of the contraband trade was export of cattle and smoked fish from savannah regions in French West Africa (Niger, Mali, Upper Volta, northern Togo and Dahomey) to the British territories. These exports generated sterling, which was used to finance illegal import into the franc areas of textiles, bicycles, spirits, lamps, costume jewelry, cola nuts, matches and a wide range of other goods. A Franc-Sterling Study Mission estimated that total exports from British to French West Africa amounted to 12.2 billion metropolitan francs in 1956, of which 8.5 billion was contraband; British West African imports from French West Africa were estimated at 7.5 billion metropolitan francs, of which 4.5 billion was contraband.[14] French trading firms regarded these estimates as undervalued, but in any event something in the order of 20 per cent of total French African consumer goods imports were smuggled in the mid 1950's, and if only African-consumed goods are considered the proportion would be substantially higher.

Not only consumer goods but export crops too passed over borders, whenever differentials in the prices offered to growers in the French and British areas made it profitable. Thus in some years in the 1950's as much as 60,000 tons of peanuts crossed from Nigeria to French Niger to take account of the subsidized producer prices prevailing in Niger. In 1954–55, it was estimated that 8,000 tons of Ivory Coast cocoa fled to Ghana, when the Ghana Marketing Board maintained its producer price at a high level compared with world (and Ivory Coast) prices. In 1960 the flow of cocoa from Ghana to the Ivory Coast may have been as high as 25,000 tons. And in 1962 an estimated 8,000 tons of export commodities were smuggled from Eastern Nigeria to benefit from higher prices in the Cameroons.[15]

Smuggling has up to now been less prevalent in other parts of the continent, mainly because price structures in southern and central Africa were less dissimilar, and exchange controls less widespread, and trade in East Africa has been relatively free. But recent Congo experience shows how quickly new channels of trade across neighboring frontiers can develop; with domestic inflation, an unrealistic rate of exchange and exchange controls (as well as new and chaotic political arrangements) a significant amount of Congolese production, both of manufactures and raw materials, left the country illegally, at least until the 1963 devaluation of the Congo franc. Its proceeds financed purchases of needed imports and hard currency balances abroad.

[14] Chambre de Commerce de la Côte d'Ivoire, "La Contrebande par Terre en Afrique Occidentale Française," (mimeo., n.d.).
[15] West Africa, June 29, 1963, p. 733.

Suppression of smuggling is exceedingly difficult when conditions for its flowering are present. Frontiers are long. Often the ethnic groups are the same on both sides, which makes general restriction of movement of people hard to enforce. The smugglers are at least as inventive as the government officials trying to control them, and it is usually possible for the smuggler to find some customs officials who are willing to look the other way for a slight consideration. A government determined to crack down on smuggling can, of course, slow the contraband trade. But the expense of effective control is very considerable; even control of smuggling by sea, such as Nigeria is currently attempting, involves purchases of costly patrol boats and helicopters, as well as expansion of the customs staff. And control of smuggling from the sea is infinitely easier than control of the overland trade.

A control that was effective, moreover, might have serious political consequences. Almost everybody seems to benefit from smuggling. Producers of smuggled beef, fish and export crops get higher prices for their products. Consumers get cheaper, better, more varied goods. The level of employment and the wage bill is probably increased, since the ratio of workers and wage payments to sales volume is no doubt greater in the labor-intensive contraband trade than in legal commerce. Where African traders are the main agents of the contraband trade there is also a redistribution of profit income from established (mainly expatriate) trading firms to African traders.

It is, of course, the government that is hurt: its customs revenues decline, its price policies are undermined, income is redistributed from public to private sectors, and respect for the law is diminished. But any government that successfully suppressed smuggling might find itself reaping a political whirlwind, for the list of injured private interests would be imposing.

The smuggler casts a long shadow in Africa. He imposes restraints, actual or potential, on independent economic policies. All of the instruments of direct economic control, as well as price policies generally, will —unless they are in harmony with those prevailing in surrounding countries—threaten to activate or enlarge the current of contraband trade. This will occur, for example, if relatively low prices are paid for locally marketed goods, especially those which are easily transportable, or for export crops; or if austerity policies are introduced, restricting the import of luxury goods and raising their price; or if rate policies on railroads result in internal price distortions; or if exchange controls and restrictions on capital outflows become burdensome. The smuggler even threatens protected local industry with illicit competition.[16]

[16] Gambian imports of matches, for example, amount to 55 boxes per year per capita; most of it is smuggled to Senegal, where the local product is higher priced and of poorer quality. The Federal Minister of Finance of Nigeria publicly estimated at 15 per cent the proportion of Nigerian cigarette consumption produced by smugglers in 1961, and emphasized the threat to the Nigerian tobacco industry.

The Guinea experience is rich with examples. Guinea may be an extreme case, but it is not unique (the Congo provides many parallels), nor is it without relevance to other African areas. It is true that not every part of the continent has frontiers quite so permeable as Guinea's. Nor are there everywhere indigenous traders of such ingenuity and enterprise as Guinea's Dioulas. But comparable groups are found elsewhere, and where they are not, nothing is more calculated to nurture them than the opportunity for quick profit through smuggling.

The difficulty of framing independent economic policies under these circumstances is obvious. This is, of course, true not only for socialist policies, but for all public policies. As conceived in Africa, however, socialist policies involve a greater degree of direct economic control and manipulation of market variables, so the potential restraints implicit in the smuggling phenomenon have more bearing on them. Unless common policies are laid down by geographically-related groups of African states, each of them is at the mercy of policies followed by their neighbors. In this sense, African states have a more limited command over their economies than is probably the case anywhere in the world. Socialism in one country is not possible in Africa.

Manpower scarcity, the inappropriateness of socialist approaches to agricultural development, and the constraints of external market forces on internal economic policies are the main but not the only bases for doubting the effectiveness of the socialist model in Africa. Several others deserve brief mention.

First, the efficient operation of state enterprises in Africa presents numerous difficulties in addition to those arising from trained manpower scarcity. Because of the primacy of politics in the recent history of these countries, public enterprises are subject to particularly intense political pressures of various sorts, all of which reduce their efficiency. The raiding of public corporations for support of political party activity, such as the Coker Commission recently revealed in Western Nigeria, is an extreme example. Political interference is also common in decisions on personnel, price and location policies. Employment policies are especially likely to be subject to external pressure; decisions on how many people are hired, or—more important—fired, and who they are, invite political intervention where unemployment is rife and highly particularistic loyalties persist.

The colonial heritage also raises special obstacles to efficiency, in the kinds of attitudes to work performance which it bequeathed. Under the colonial regime almost all employers and supervisors were white and alien, almost all workers African. Because the gap between the manager and the managed was so great, a sense of common enterprise rarely developed; poor work performance might, in fact, be justified in terms of the national struggle. It was an environment, in any case, uncongenial to the growth of an ethic of hard work and a dedication to ideals of craftsmanship. This has carried over into the independence period, and tends to be notably troublesome in the public sector.

In the public sector it is particularly hard to effect the "decolonization of work habits" necessary for improved work performance. The efficiency consciousness of management and supervisory staff tends to be less than in the private sector, partly because the public enterprise does not ordinarily have to meet the market test, partly because no personal resources are involved, but mostly because enforcement of discipline is harder in public enterprises subject to political restraints.

In addition to the efficiency question, and probably of a lower order of significance, is the fact that at least for some decades African economies will remain export-oriented. Between 25 and 60 per cent of marketed output in African countries is now exported, and this is not likely to change soon. Trading in export markets is a highly specialized and delicate business, demanding quick decisions, high standards of quality control, close attention to timing of deliveries. It does not lend itself to the rougher arrangements possible if production is only for enclosed local markets.

The fact that Marketing Boards throughout the continent have for years adequately performed these functions suggests that foreign commodity trading can be done satisfactorily, so too much weight should not be placed on this argument. However, not all commodities lend themselves easily to state trading. The short, unhappy history of the Ghana Timber Marketing Board, whose policies were responsible in part for a drastic decline in timber exports, is suggestive. Among other difficulties encountered by the Board, foreign buyers complained about the consistency of quality grading.[17]

Finally, the degree to which socialist attitudes and policies are put into effect will influence the rate of inflow of private capital, which though not likely to be large in any case, has vital functions to perform. In addition to the conventional benefits (release of domestic resources for other uses, generation of new resources, increased foreign exchange through import substitution and greater export earnings) there are the general leavening effects that foreign private enterprises have in these societies, through their impact on skill development, and the transmission of ideas and techniques.

VI. Conclusion

Ideology can provide a powerful impetus to economic development. By explaining today's struggles and sacrifices in terms of a vision of a

[17] See *West Africa,* March 17, 1962, p. 296.

better life tomorrow, it can give direction and hope, and inspire new effort. But ideology has its dangers too. It hardens thought. It restricts the search for alternatives, and makes changes of direction difficult. It might even be wrong—in its picture of the world and in its policy prescriptions.

This is the case with socialist ideology in Africa today. For contemporary Africa it is the wrong ideology, in the wrong place, at the wrong time. The state cannot and should not bear the burdens that most African socialists would put upon it. The trained people are lacking, and will not be available for some time. The capacity to control the economy is in any event restricted by African exposure to external market forces. Socialist approaches in agriculture are ill-suited to the special features of Africa's rural environment and are unlikely to effect that mobilization of the peasantry which is essential to continuing growth.

Thus far the predominance of socialist ideology has not had widespread effects on policy, except in a few countries. Guinea rushed along the socialist path after 1958. Ghana has proceeded more slowly, though the pace has picked up. The results are not yet evident, except in Guinea.[18]

The Guinea case is significant precisely because it represents the most extensive experiment in the kinds of policies socialists elsewhere in Africa recommend, and because the difficulties and short-comings of these policies are illuminated with exceptional clarity there. Guinea's troubles also illustrate the blindfold effects of ideology, the extreme reluctance to abandon a patently unsuccessful set of policies when retreat from a hardened ideological position is involved. The economy of Guinea, and particularly its distribution system, has been in obvious disarray since 1960. Full consideration of alternatives was hampered by the continuing hold of economic ideology, and by the political need to repeat the ideological litanies. The 1963 reform, which is intended to return more of the distribution sector to private hands, will probably be more effective. But it is hardly a sign of flexibility or pragmatism—qualities often assigned to socialists in Africa—when it takes three years and movement to the edge of an economic abyss to adjust policies which have so obviously failed.

The fact that present African conditions make improbable the success of the kinds of policies generally called for by socialists in Africa does not leave only a complete laissez-faire alternative. The role of the state will inevitably be large in any development strategy. Planning is needed, in the sense of looking at the economy as a whole, understanding the ramifica-

[18] It is interesting to note, however, that in the *Report of the Territorial Minimum Wages Board* of Tanganyika (Dar-es-Salaam, 1962), the harmful effects of a higher minimum wage on "emergent farmers," the most dynamic elements in African rural society, are discounted on the grounds that these highly individualistic, low-paying farmers have a doubtful place in a socialist society. Encouragement of cooperatives is recommended as more advisable.

tions of particular lines of policy, setting down rationally-defined criteria for the allocation of public expenditures, stimulating the expansion of the private sector and guiding its direction. Nor does it mean that the socialist alternative will not have more promise of success in the future when trained people are more abundant, the agricultural sector monetized, and the state's capacity to control the economic environment more developed.

In reply to all of this African socialists might argue that the prime goals are social—the building of equalitarian and truly independent societies, where individualism is restrained, income inequalities and class lines are minimized, and the influence of the outside world reduced—and that all other goals, including economic growth, are subservient to these. With this there can be little quarrel. Nor could one object if African socialists recognized that these social goals are in some measure incompatible with maximum economic growth in Africa's present circumstances. But they believe that maximum growth can come only through socialist solutions, and this is almost certainly not true.

The prevalance of attitudes and policy inclinations which we have called the "socialist model" is a matter of no small significance for Africa's future. To the extent that these policies are applied they will lead to waste and misdirected effort, to mistakes few African countries can afford. They will increase political instability; by poor performance a state that increases its activities in order to seek legitimacy will instead lose the legitimacy it has. Finally, those most firmly committed to socialist solutions are more often than not the most honest, dedicated and able people on the African scene, reformers, university students, and others inspired by a desire to reconstruct their society and make a better life for all their countrymen. This is the saddest part of it all—that these most admirable men are also those most firmly gripped by the illusion that socialism provides a quick and true path to economic development. Given power, they would lead their countries not forward but backward.

Suggested Reading

I. Ideology—General

La Palambara, Joseph, "Decline of Ideology: A Dissent and an Interpretation," *The American Political Science Review*, Vol. LX, No. 1 (March 1966), pp. 5–16.

Lichtheim, George, *The Concept of Ideology and Other Essays* (New York, Vintage Books, 1967).

Lottich, Kenneth V., "Changing Contemporary Ideologies," *International Review of History and Political Science*, June 1967, pp. 142–156.

Martin-Lipset, Seymour, "Some Further Comments on 'The End of Ideology,'" *The American Political Science Review*, Vol. LX, No. 1 (March 1966), pp. 7–18.

Preston, N. S., *Politics, Economics, and Power: Ideology and Practice Under Capitalism, Socialism, Communism, and Fascism* (New York, Macmillan; London, Collier-Macmillan, 1967).

Roucek, Joseph S., "A History of the Concept of Ideology," *Journal of the History of Ideas*, Vol. 5, No. 4 (October 1944), pp. 479–488.

II. Ideology—Market

Klaasen, A. (ed.), *The Invisible Hand. A Collection of Essays on the Economic Philosophy of Free Enterprise* (Chicago, Henry Regenery, Gateway Editions, 1966).

Macfie, A. L., "The Moral Justification of Free Enterprise," *Scottish Journal of Political Economy*, Vol. XIV, No. 1 (February 1967), pp. 1–11.

Monsen, R. Joseph, Jr., *Modern American Capitalism: Ideologies and Issues* (Boston, Houghton Mifflin, 1966).

Robinson, Joan, *Economic Philosophy* (Chicago, Aldine, 1962).

Stark, J. R., "Normative Elements in Economics," *Review of Social Economy*, March 1968.

Viner, Jacob, "The Intellectual History of Laissez Faire," *The Journal of Law and Economics*, Vol. III, 1960, p. 45.

III. Ideology—Command

Berliner, Joseph S., "Marxism and the Soviet Economy," *Problems of Communism*, Vol. XVIII, No. 5 (September–October 1964), pp. 1–11.

Drachkovitch, Milorad M. (ed.), *Marxist Ideology in the Contemporary World: Its Appeals and Paradoxes* (New York, Praeger, 1967).

Joravsky, David, "Soviet Ideology," *Soviet Studies*, Vol. XVIII, No. 1 (July 1966), pp. 2–19.

Lemberg, Eugen, "The Intellectual Shift in East-Central European Marxism-Leninism," *Modern Age*, Vol. 11, No. 2 (Spring 1967), pp. 131–143.

"Marxism Today," *Survey* (London), No. 62 (January 1967). The whole issue is devoted to this subject.

Meisner, Maurice, *Li Ta-chang and the Origins of Chinese Marxism* (Cambridge, Harvard East Asian Studies, No. 27, 1967).

Schlesinger, Rudolf, "More Observations on Ideology: How a Marxist Concept was turned into its Opposite," *Soviet Studies*, Vol. XIX, No. 1 (July 1967), pp. 87–99.

Sherman, H. J., "Marxist Economics and Soviet Planning," *Soviet Studies*, Vol. XVIII, No. 2 (October 1966), pp. 169–188.

Sowell, Thomas, "Marx's *Capital* After One Hundred Years," *The Canadian Journal of Economics and Political Science*, Vol. XXXIII, No. 1 (February 1967), pp. 50–74.

Ward, Benjamin, "Marxism-Horvatism: A Yugoslav Theory of Socialism," *American Economic Review*, Vol. LVII, No. 3 (June 1967), pp. 509–523.

IV. Ideology—African Socialism

Friedland, H. William, and Rosenberg, Carl G., Jr., *African Socialism* (Stanford, Stanford Paperback, SP 35, 1967).

Gregor, A. James, "African Socialism, Socialism and Fascism: An Appraisal," *The Review of Politics*, Vol. 29, No. 3 (July 1967), pp. 324–353.

Mazrui, Ali A., *Towards a Pax Africana: A Study of Ideology and Ambition* (Chicago, Nature of Human Society Series, 1967).

Nyerere, Mwalimu Julius, "Socialism: An Attitude of Mind," *East African Journal*, Vol. IV, No. 2 (May 1967), pp. 24–30.

Senghor, Leopold S., "The African Road to Socialism," *African Forum*, Winter 1966.

"Socialism: Left, Right, and Centre," *Mizan* (London), March–April 1966. On the Soviet view of African Socialism.

Zartman, I. William, "National Interest and Ideology," in *African Diplomacy*, Vernon McKay, ed. (New York, Praeger, 1966), pp. 25–54.

V. Ideology and Developing Countries

Basi, Raghbir S., "Role of the 'Free Enterprise' Ideology in Less-Developed Countries," *The American Journal of Economics and Sociology*, Vol. 26, No. 2 (April 1967), pp. 173–188.

Blanksten, George I., "Ideology and Nation-Building in the Contemporary World," *International Studies Quarterly*, Vol. 11, No. 1 (March 1967), pp. 3–11.

Charles, E., "The Concept of Neo-Colonialism and its Relation to Rival Economic Systems," *Social and Economic Studies*, Vol. 15, No. 4 (December 1966).

Heimann, Eduard, "Marxism and Underdeveloped Countries," *Social Research*, Vol. XIX (1952), pp. 322–345.

III
Market-Oriented Economies

Introduction

No market economy could ever conform to the stringent assumptions of the perfectly competitive model. All real-life market-oriented economies are, compared to the model, functionally and structurally imperfect. There is much interference with the operation of commodity and resource markets and there are many shadings to property relations. Operational market-oriented economies are imperfectly competitive and/or oligopolistic over wide areas, and they are "mixed" in the sense that a private sector coexists with and is influenced by public policy. Real-life market economies are market-planned economies in which collective property plays a not unimportant role. There is planning by private firms and planning by the public authority. Planning of the public kind arises whenever the market economy shows itself to be less self-sustaining than the theoretical blueprint makes it out to be, when technological advantages could be lost by a limitation on the size of the decision-making units, or when the market fails to register socially significane wants or to turn out indispensable public goods. The market-generated inducement to public planning has already been described by Chamberlain in Part I:B. In respect to social wants the simple market model is an aged delinquent: it has often been lax on growth, full employment, price stability, and the provision of goods and services for the old, the ill, and the underprivileged. It has tended to generate income inequalities and its vision has often been myopic. It has suffered from recurring fits of depression and exuberance which have involved a waste of human and material substance. It has been accused of imperialist expansion (see Parts II and VI), heartlessness, and much else. Its business ethic has been the subject of critical scrutiny and was found wanting in many parts of the world. With all that, it has given millions of people a high standard of living which is the envy of command systems.

The shortcomings of the market system and private property have been taken account of by theory and recognized in policy. Market planning and the interest in macro theory, welfare economics, growth theory, business fluctuations, and cost-benefit analysis express the concern with the market's private and social faults. The principle of public intervention is no longer in doubt, but the extent and methods of such intervention remain the subjects of controversy. All market planning begins with the assumption that markets perform a useful function, even if they do this without the elegance implicit in the simple blueprint. Market planning also recognizes the legitimacy and usefulness of private property, without endowing private property with mystical awe. These two assumptions are important. They are pluralistic assumptions, a way of saying that the ordinary business of life should take as its starting point the "everybody" of the perfectly competitive model, and then adjust for what may have been missed or distorted through aggregation. To proceed from the "everybody" to a recognition of the assumption's social limitations and the market's propensity for self-destruction, is very different from starting with the conviction that the center's command is always right, and that pluralism should be brought in only to make what is right efficient. The original assumption makes all the difference between revisionist market and revisionist command, between, say, the French and the Yugoslav systems. Fascism's assumption was fundamentally one of command, not unlike that of communist command systems. But fascism, earlier than communism, recognized the possibility of using supervised markets and controlled private property to instill internal consistency and efficiency into the bureaucracy of command.

Market planning varies from country to country and over time. The differences turn on (a) the extent of persuasion and force, (b) the precise mix between "self-regulating" market forces and central administrative command, (c) the use of physical versus financial tools of control, and (d) the role of public as compared with private property. Although recognized as valid and necessary, the planning principle may be applied occasionally or more systematically (See Marvin E. Rozen, ed., Comparative Economic Planning, New York, D. C. Heath & Company, 1967). In all instances there is conscious intervention by public authority in the "spontaneous" processes of the market. It should also be added that the kind of market planning described in Part III is performed by a public authority that is duly elected and recallable by those in whose collective name it acts.

The "spontaneity" of the market is, in the last analysis, the result of individual planning within a certain social and political framework. It is not anarchy which somehow works out, courtesy of the law of averages. In essence, the market coordinates millions of individual planning decisions. This coordinating mechanism has been analyzed by microeconomic theory and goes by the shorthand name of economic rationality. Public planning introduces into private planning an element of social perspective, that is all. It tries to achieve what a given society believes at a given time to be right, just, desirable, expedient, and possible in the collective interest. Public planning supplements the market, corrects the market's behavioral pattern, but does not seek to destroy the spontaneous forces of private planning. The delicate problem is how much to plan, how to arrive at a satisfactory balance between private initiative and public intervention, how to reach but not cross the fine line which separates market regulation from market destruction. It is a question of the elusive compromise between private and public action, starting from the assumption that private vices do have a way of turning into public benefits, although this does not happen always or inevitably, or cover the whole spectrum of what a given generation considers to be rightful collective needs.

The goals of market planners are very much the same, whatever the disagreement on how to plan or where to draw the line. There seems to be fairly general agreement that in the course of planning, due process and democratic legality should be observed.

A list of the objectives of market planning would include high employment, price stability, a desirable rate of growth, avoidance of excessive income inequalities, and the improvement in the quality of human resources. These objectives are not necessarily compatible. Their frequent incompatibility gives rise to problems of priority and involves the confrontation and reconciliation of political forces within the community.

The essays in Part III are case studies in the various tools and methods used to achieve the general goals. These range from a preference for general (macroeconomic) to specific and detailed (microeconomic) methods of public intervention. The American approach favors the former, the French approach is biased in favor of the latter. Macro intervention means using monetary and fiscal policy (in that order) to affect aggregate demand, output, and employment. The micro-type intervention is concerned with influencing detailed targets of individual industries, supplemented by global public action in the fields of investment and consumption. The public authority prods industries and firms in the private sector with tax and investment incentives and deterrents, capital controls, and fiscal supervision over the composition and volume of exports and imports. The planning process in this case is more explicit than in the case of macro intervention of the American type. The distinction between the two approaches to market planning must not, however, be overstressed. General planning has tended increasingly to move beyond fiscal and monetary policy into the realm of an incomes policy exemplified in Britain by the Selective Employment Tax and the Early Warning Bill, and by the wage-price guidelines in the United States. In recent years there have been many instances of direct governmental incursions in the United States into the steel, copper, aluminum, and other industries in support of the general incomes policy.

Glauco della Porta's essay on Italian public intervention brings into focus the related problem of property structures. As we shall see again in Part IV, what seems to matter is how private property behaves and how best to influence that behavior. The simplest, at times simplistic way, is to nationalize the allegedly recalcitrant private sector or portions of it. A more complex, but ultimately more effective and less cumbersome way, is to devise general and specific incentives and deterrents so as to evoke the desired behavioral responses. As a significant participant in the market process and part owner of the means of production, the public authority may impose its preferences through the market rather than outside it. It may create a climate within which private decisions are made. This, in general, has been the preferred method used by market planners of all denominations.

10 ALVIN H. HANSEN

THE KEYNESIAN REVOLUTION
IN THE UNITED STATES

I. THE CHALLENGE TO NEO-CLASSICISM

In the early nineteenth century the great economic dualists were Ricardo and Malthus. In our century it was Keynes versus Pigou. In his *Retrospective View of Keynes's General Theory,* Professor Pigou paid high tribute to Keynes.[1] "Nobody before him, so far as I know," said Pigou, "had brought all the relevant factors, real and monetary at once, together in a single formal scheme, through which their interplay could be coherently investigated." Professor Pigou singled out the following paragraph from Chapter 18 of the *General Theory* as the kernel of Keynes's contribution to economic thinking[2]: "Thus we can sometimes regard our ultimate independent variables as consisting of 1. the three fundamental psychological factors, namely, the psychological propensity to consume, the psychological attitude to liquidity and the psychological expectation of future yield from capital assets, 2. the wage-unit as determined by the bargains reached between employers and employed, and 3. the quantity of money as determined by the action of the central bank; so that, if we take as given the factor specified above, these variables determine the national income (or dividend) and the quantity of employment."

Here we have the investment multiplier, the marginal efficiency of investment schedule, the consumption function, the liquidity preference schedule, the quantity of money, and the wage unit (the back-bone of the price level). "This summary statement," said Pigou, "contains . . . Keynes's main and very important contribution to economic analysis."[3] And he added that were he not afraid his audience might feel insulted, he would read it over again.

From *Weltwirtschaftliches Archiv,* Vol. 97, 1966, II, pp. 213–231. Reprinted by permission of author and *Weltwirtschaftliches Archiv.* The original title of the article was "Keynes After Thirty Years (With Special Reference to the United States)."
[1] A. C. Pigou, *Keynes's 'General Theory', A Retrospective View,* London, 1950, p. 65.
[2] *Ibid.,* p. 20.—John Maynard Keynes, *The General Theory of Employment, Interest and Money,* London, 1936, pp. 246sq.
[3] Pigou, *op. cit.,* p. 20.

With the battery of weapons so brilliantly outlined in Chapter 18, and more fully expounded in the volume as a whole, Keynes undertook the herculean task of attempting to demolish not indeed the microeconomics of neo-classicism—this Keynes accepted in full—but rather the neo-classical sophisticated mystique of automatic adjustment of wages and interest rates —the mechanism, it was believed, by which the self-sustaining economy tended to produce full employment.

The great virtue of Keynes's work, as also of the giant classicals— Adam Smith, Ricardo, Malthus, and Mill—was the grand magnificent sweep which it gave us of the overall determining forces at work in the economy. Neo-classicism had descended from the lofty mountain tops of the great classicals to the lower ground in search for petty details in an effort to cement minor cracks in a vast superstructure. Though not altogether without merit, this had directed the attention of economists away from the great issues. Pigou himself characterized the neo-classicism of 1936 as follows[4]: "After Marshall's main work was finished, economic thought on fundamental issues moved little, at all events in this country. We were pedestrians, perhaps a little complacent. Keynes's *Treatise on Money* and later his *General Theory* broke resoundingly that dogmatic slumber. Whether in agreement or disagreement with him discussion and controversy sprang up and spread over the whole world. Economics and economists came alive. The period of tranquillity was ended. A period of active, and, so far as might be, creative thought was born. For this the credit is almost wholly due to Keynes."

The shift in emphasis from analysis of price effects to analysis of income effects stimulated statistical research throughout the world. Econometric studies of the consumption function, the investment multiplier, liquidity preference opened up rich fields for empirical work. The empty boxes were progressively filled, not just hit and miss in the hope that a mere accumulation of facts might turn up something, but within the meaningful pattern of the Keynesian theoretical structure. New analytical insights pointed the way to the areas where empirical research might be rewarding.

The neo-classicism of the early nineteenth century had become a powerful resistant to social and economic reform. Economic analysis could usually be counted upon to show why novel proposals (whether guarantees of bank deposits or social security or other "common-sense" programs) were unworkable and rested on a misunderstanding of an intricate self-regulating mechanism. Confronted with the overwhelming problems of the great depression, neo-classical economics stood helpless. Since the turn of the century it had become largely an escape from reality.

[4] *Idem*, "The Economist", in: *John Maynard Keynes, 1883–1946, Fellow and Bursar*, A Memoir Prep. by the Direction of the Council of King's College, Cambridge, 1949, pp. 21sq.

To this, however, one important qualification must be made. Following the publication of Mitchell's *Business Cycles*[5] in 1913, great interest, both theoretical and statistical, had been aroused in the problem of economic fluctuations. But the contributions of Mitchell and his followers were primarily statistical. The most significant theoretical advances in this area had already appeared in the work of continental writers—Tugan-Baranowski, Spiethoff, Wicksell, Schumpeter, Aftalion.[6]

With respect to business cycle *policy*, the leading innovators were Wicksell, Irving Fisher, and Keynes—the Keynes of the Monetary Reform[7] and the Treatise.[8] These men constituted the "avant garde" of economic thinking—neo-classical rebels, so-to-speak, who ventured to challenge the thesis that the economy had best be left to the automatic functioning of a laissez-faire system. Instead they proposed deliberate control of the monetary mechanism through the Central Bank as a means of ironing out the cycle. Yet this break-away from the rigid neo-classical orthodoxy did not strike deeply at the basic thesis of a self-sustaining economy. Central Bank control of the money supply and the rate of interest spelled no serious government intrusion into the aggregate spending stream. The role of government, properly speaking, was not affected.

A number of bold explorers into the dangerous territory of macroeconomics could possibly be counted in a loose sense as fore-runners of Keynes. All had, however, been laughed out of court. To enter the fray anew took courage. Keynes foresaw quite clearly that his opponents would make an effort to class him with the cranks that had already fallen by the wayside. He therefore deliberately brought this aspect of the matter out into the open by writing a discerning and illuminating chapter on Mandeville, Malthus, Hobson and Gesell. All these had tried their hand at macroeconomics, but all had miserably failed to meet the onslaught of orthodox theory. A good neo-classicist could always show that these rebels just did not understand the intricacies of sophisticated economics. Nobody but a fool or a superman with supreme confidence in his own skill, and in the armor he had donned for the fray, would dare to attack the firmly established orthodoxy. Even so notable a theorist as Aftalion, though respected for his masterly work on business cycles, had been brushed aside by British and American reviewers for his attack on Say's law.

Keynes, supremely confident of his own competence as a good classicist and in his academic credentials, was not a man to fear a good fight. He expected it and was prepared. Time and again one is impressed with the skill with which he anticipated the shafts of his critics. Time and again the answer could already be found in the *General Theory*.

[5] Wesley C. Mitchell, *Business Cycles*, Berkeley, Calif., 1913.
[6] See my *Business Cycles and National Income*, New York, 1951, Chapters 16–18.
[7] John Maynard Keynes, *Monetary Reform*, New York, 1924.
[8] *Idem, A Treatise on Money*, London, 1930, 2 Vols.

That it took the courage of a superb master of his subject is, however, by no means self-evident to the present generation of young economists who wonder what the noise was all about. Keynes's antagonists were sure that he was quite wrong, but the present generation finds it difficult to believe that he said anything new.

II. Early Stages in the Great Debate

On New Year's day, 1935, in a letter to George Bernard Shaw, Keynes wrote[9]: "I believe myself to be writing a book on economic theory which will largely revolutionize—not, I suppose, at once but in the course of the next ten years—the way the world thinks about economic problems."

The progress of the Keynesian revolution over the past three decades can perhaps best be traced by taking account of the changing character of the opposition he aroused. Keynesian doctrines in the first stage had to face complete and total opposition. Then step by step, the critics retreated more or less from ground formerly held. Finally in the third stage they became in effect the "Loyal Opposition." That this last stage has by now been reached in the United States must have been apparent to anyone who attended the recent Washington Celebration of the twentieth anniversary of the Employment Act of 1946. Once this last stage is reached the oft-heard phrase "We are all Keynesians now" begins to have at least some measure of real content and meaning.

Already by 1950 the "loyal opposition" stage had been reached in academic circles.[10] But it took another decade before that stage was reached in the United States in the area of practical politics.

The United Nations Monetary and Financial Conference of forty-four nations at Bretton Woods in July, 1944, marks one milestone in the Keynesian revolution. No one attending that conference could fail to note the breath of fresh air in an intellectual climate permeated with Keynesian thinking. Keynes was the commanding figure, the guiding architect. His great prestige had won over the British Treasury without which there would have been no Bretton Woods.

A new role of government—this was the resounding note that dominated the Conference. Deliberate governmental policy was to supplant the automatic functioning of the economy.

[9] R. F. Harrod, *The Life of John Maynard Keynes*, London, 1951, p. 462.

[10] It should be noted that Pigou never moved beyond the "loyal opposition" stage. In his *Lapses From Full Employment*, London, 1945, he openly admitted (as also in the Memoir paper) that Keynes had won the argument on wage flexibility. In the Preface, p. V, he stated that he no longer favored "attacking the problem of unemployment by manipulating wages rather than by manipulating demand." This represented a big step toward Keynesianism. But he still denied the under-employment equilibrium. He believed that mere *stabilization* of aggregate demand would permit automatic wage adjustment so as to provide full employment.

Shortly before the Bretton Woods Conference the British government had issued (May, 1944) a pioneering White Paper on Employment Policy.[11] Keynes was indeed the Treasury economist, but the White Paper, it must not be forgotten, was a government document, and as such it disclosed cautious restraint. A bolder statement, untrammeled by Treasury traditions, was issued in June, 1944, under the name of Sir William Beveridge,[12] though the volume was in fact a cooperative effort in which a number of brilliant Cambridge University Keynesians had participated. And finally, in October, 1944, six young economists of the Oxford Institute of Statistics issued the Economics of Full Employment—a thoroughgoing Keynesian document.[13]

Immediately after the publication of the *General Theory*, numerous critical articles began to appear in the scientific journals, notably in England and America. Keynes, as editor of the world renowned *Economic Journal*, kept a sharp eye on the debates and wasted little time in answering his critics.

Also in the United States the pot was boiling. A hot debate was initiated by the Hearings in May, 1939, before the Temporary National Economic Committee of the Congress of the United States[14]—the so-called TNEC. The Committee invited me to lead off in the Hearings on Saving and Investment,[15] and I used this occasion to expound the Keynesian analysis of the great depression from which we were still suffering. This analysis was supplemented by statistical materials presented by Laughlin Currie, then Assistant Director of the Division of Research and Statistics of the Board of Governors of the Federal Reserve System.

Keynes's *General Theory* had already in the preceding two years occupied the center of the stage in the Fiscal Policy Seminar (conducted by John H. Williams[16] and myself) at Harvard University. Government

[11] *Employment Policy*, Presented by the Minister of Reconstruction to Parliament by Command of His Majesty, May 1944, Cmd. 6527, London.

[12] William H. Beveridge, *Full Employment in a Free Society*, London, 1944.

[13] *The Economics of Full Employment*, Six Studies in Applied Economics Prep. at The Oxford University Institute of Statistics, Oxford, 1944.

[14] This Committee was authorized and directed to make a full and complete study and investigation with respect to the concentration of economic power in, and financial control over, production and distribution of goods and services. The Committee consisted of six members of Congress and leading officials of the Department of Justice, the Securities Exchange Commission, the Federal Trade Commission, the Department of Labor, the Treasury Department, and the Commerce Department.

[15] See: *Investigation of Concentration of Economic Power*, Hearings Before the Temporary National Economic Committee, Congress of the United States, 77th Congress, 1st Session, Pursuant to Public Resolution No. 113 (75th Congress), Authorizing and Directing a Select Committee to Make a Full and Complete Study and Investigation With Respect to the Concentration of Economic Power in, and Financial Control over, Production and Distribution of Goods and Services, P. 9: *Savings and Investment*, Washington, 1940, pp. 3495 to 3520; 3538–3559; 3837–3859.

[16] Professor Williams, distinguished monetary economist, was consistently an able, liberal-minded critic of Keynesian thinking.

economists not infrequently participated in this seminar, and it became the center from which Keynesian thinking spread to other universities.[17] But it was the Hearings before the TNEC that opened the debate in Washington and before the general public. There emerged vigorous discussion in the public press, in the weekly and monthly magazines (e.g. *Fortune* Magazine, New York) and in the scientific economic journals. The new Keynesian doctrines met sharp opposition.

The British White Paper, alluded to above, represented a major change in official thinking. The Report affirmed the belief that the maintenance of an adequate level of expenditures in goods and services may no longer be realized automatically. At the onslaught of the 1930 depression the British government had, it should be remembered, instituted an economy program. Curtailment, less spending, more saving—these were the pre-Keynesian remedies for depression and unemployment. The White Paper in sharp contrast stated that "the first step in a policy of maintaining general employment must be to prevent total expenditure . . . from falling away."[18]

Clearly all this involved a sharp break with two main principles that had guided governments in the past; first, that government expenditures should be kept down to the barest minimum; and second, that government income and expenditure should be balanced.[19] The government's role was to be that of complete neutrality, leaving the field for the automatic functioning of the economy. These principles, if violated, would, it was believed, destroy confidence. The "confidence argument" remains to this day as an obstacle to progressive reform.[20]

Canada issued two notable documents in April and August 1945—just within Keynes's ten-year forecast.[21] The government declared it was not only prepared to accept large deficits but will "deliberately plan for them

[17] See my *Fiscal Policy and Business Cycles*, New York, 1941, which grew in considerable measure out of these seminar discussions. It became the standard reference book on modern fiscal policy and there evolved around it for several years a lively critical literature.

[18] *Employment Policy, op. cit.*, p. 16.

[19] A budgetary deficit in depression, said the government White Paper (see *Employment Policy, op. cit.*, pp. 24sqq.), must be tolerated in order to help maintain the national income, but it is nonetheless an unwelcome guest. Keynes himself never explored thoroughly the public debt problem. It remained for his disciples to undertake this task—a highly important one. Had the old dogmas about debt burden continued to prevail, Keynesian fiscal policy would have been severely crippled.

[20] Government expenditures were regarded as (a) *ineffective* because funds raised from taxation or by borrowing from the public simply reduced private spending, or (b) *dangerous* because funds borrowed from the banking system were believed to be inflationary and destructive of confidence.

[21] *Employment and Income With Special Reference to The Initial Period of Reconstruction*, Pres. to Parliament by The Minister of Reconstruction, April 1945, Ottawa, 1945, and Dominion-Provincial Conference on Reconstruction, August, 1945.

in periods of threatened unemployment." The "modern governmental budget must be a balance-wheel of the economy."

III. THE U. S. EMPLOYMENT ACT OF 1946

In the United States as elsewhere world shaking events were stirring men's minds. The devastating depression, the expenditures incurred in the Second World War, the sky-rocketing public debt paradoxically parallelled by a vast increase in private and business savings—all this shook orthodox pre-conceptions. Before the war conventional financial wisdom opined that the Federal government could not float more than a 2-billion-dollar bond issue. The war raised the ante. Within five years over 200 billion dollars of U. S. securities had been absorbed. Mental horizons were being widened.

It was in this new milieu of public opinion coupled with the dreadful memory of the great depression and the fear that this could happen again that the Employment Act of 1946 was passed.

President Roosevelt had already outlined an economic bill of rights in his State of the Union message of January, 1944—the right to have "a useful and remunerative job."[22] Governor Dewey, Republican candidate for President, said in his Seattle speech in September, 1944[23]: "If at any time there are not sufficient jobs in private employment to go around, the government can and must create job opportunities because there must be jobs for all in this country of ours." Campaign speeches are, however, no guarantee of governmental responsibility. This required an Act of Congress. The Murray Full Employment Bill of 1945 went all the way. But the Employment Act of 1946 as passed softened the language so as to blunt the assumption of full governmental responsibility for full employment.

The Employment Act did indeed represent a modest step toward counter-cyclical fiscal policy. Still the Congress remained highly conservative, and the influential press was strongly anti-Keynesian. Congress was caught up in a dilemma. War-time expenditures had indeed brought undreamed of prosperity. But in war-time "all bets are off," and one could not believe that such things can go on forever. Peace-time reform measures, even social security, were regarded with suspicion. The New Deal seemed to many to violate the "natural order." How to reconcile the two goals of "fiscal integrity" and full employment remained unresolved.

[22] Franklin D. Roosevelt, *Selected Speeches, Messages, Press Conferences, and Letters*, Ed. With an Introd. by Basil Rauch, "Annual Message to Congress, January 11, 1944", New York and Toronto, 1957, p. 347.

[23] See my *Economic Policy and Full Employment*, New York and London, 1947.

The 1946 Employment Act is studiously vague. It can mean all things to all men. Its real importance is the machinery it set up—The President's Annual Economic Report, the Council of Economic Advisers, and the Joint Economic Committee of the Congress.[24] This institutional setup compelled discussion and debate.

Ever since the Second World War the American economy has done moderately well compared with earlier times. This may, however, have had little to do with the Employment Act or Keynesian economics. The post-war scarcities, the huge defense budget, the government contracts, the new technologies, the rapid population growth, the mass market for consumer durables of all kinds—these spontaneous forces, not government intervention, held the stage.

The post-war re-stocking boom came to a halt in 1948. There followed a period of uncertainty and indecision. Indeed in the sharp recession of 1949 (unemployment rising to 7.6 per cent in February, 1950) instead of a vigorous anti-recession policy, the President and his Council of Economic Advisers continued to be obsessed with the fear of inflation though actually prices had reached a peak in August, 1948, and continued to decline until the Korean war turned the tide. The famous tax cut of 1948 (engineered by Senator Taft, who was certainly no Keynesian) was vigorously opposed both by the President and his economic advisers. In July, 1949, the Council stated with apparent pride that it had not urged anti-cyclical federal spending. Instead the Council (not unlike a later Council under Eisenhower) stressed "its confidence in the internal recuperative forces."[25] At the depth of the recession the Report argued that the public debt should be reduced.

Congressional opinion remained overwhelmingly skeptical about enthroning fiscal policy as a major instrument of economic control. Outside of Congress, bankers, businessmen, and journalists continued their vigorous opposition to Keynesian economics.

The Korean war shifted the problem from depression to inflation. Orthodoxy and Keynesianism under these conditions tend to join hands though there remained sharp differences as to means. It is a pity that during the Korean episode the President's Economic Reports reverted to orthodox slogans about balanced budgets instead of giving the country a sophisticated discussion of the role of fiscal policy as the balance-wheel of the economy.

[24] See *Employment Act of 1946, As Amended, With Related Laws and Rules of the Joint Economic Committee, Congress of the United States*, 89th Congress, 2d Session, February 1966, Washington, 1966, Secs. 3, 4 and 5.

[25] *The Midyear Economic Report of the President to the Congress, July 11, 1949*, Together With a Report: *The Economic Situation at Midyear 1949*, by the Council of Economic Advisers, Washington, 1949.

IV. THE EISENHOWER ADMINISTRATION AND FISCAL POLICY

Enter the Eisenhower Administration in January, 1953. Barely installed, a recession set in. Remembering the Hoover depression many feared the Republican return to power. Eisenhower hastened to re-assure the country. The government, he said, would use all its vast powers to prevent a depression.

The change of administration, after twenty years of Democratic rule, at first threatened the demise of the Employment Act of 1946. Powerful Republican opposition had developed to the entire set-up including the Council of Economic Advisers. President Eisenhower, however, stood firm. Fortunately, Arthur Burns, highly respected and able spokesman for the moderate conservatists, accepted the responsible position of chairman of the Council in this highly critical period.

In two earlier articles (the 1946 Annual Report of the National Bureau of Economic Research; and the Review of Economics and Statistics, November, 1947) Burns[26] had noted that the world had, following the publication of the *General Theory*, "moved swiftly in a Keynesian direction."[27] He cited the epoch making announcement of the British White Paper and noted that also in the United States these ideas were being actively debated. He expressed doubt about the wisdom of these governmental pronouncements, fearful that in the existing state of economic knowledge, the governments might have assumed too great a responsibility. Later, as chairman of the CEA, he remained skeptical and preferred cautious and restrained governmental actions, confident that a vigorous economy would move forward largely on its own steam. Built-in automaticity, he favored. And he did not reject deliberate governmental intervention in the event of a threatened cumulative down-spin. Indeed the Council under his leadership acknowledged[28] that "unless the Government is prepared and willing to use its vast powers to help maintain employment and purchasing power, even a minor readjustment may be converted into a spiralling contraction." The once fashionable theory that a sharp liquidation was good for the economy could not be trusted.

[26] Arthur F. Burns, *Economic Research and the Keynesian Thinking of Our Times,* Twenty-Sixth Annual Report of the National Bureau of Economic Research, New York, 1946.—*Idem,* "Keynesian Economics Once Again," *The Review of Economics and Statistics,* Vol. XXIX, Cambridge, Mass., 1947, pp. 252sqq.

[27] *Idem, Economic Research and the Keynesian Thinking of Our Times, op. cit.,* p. 11.

[28] *Economic Report of the President,* Transmitted by the Congress, January 28, 1954, Washington, 1954, p. 7; also Chapters 4 and 12.

The Council, moreover, accepted fiscal policy as a major policy weapon. The key to governmental planning for economic growth is, it said, the Federal budget. The Council recognized[29] that "automatic stabilizers cannot be counted on to do more than restrain either an upward or a downward tendency of the economy." In view of this limitation "the Government will not hesitate to make greater use of monetary, debt management, and credit policy, . . . or to reduce taxes, or to expand on a large scale the construction of useful public works, or to take any other steps that may be necessary."

The next Economic Report (January, 1955) was equally firm in the declaration[30] that the "Government will shoulder its full responsibility." Both these Reports were written in the closing months of 1953 and 1954 —in short against the background of the 1954 recession. The country was worried. These two Reports constitute the high water mark of Republican acceptance of fiscal policy as a necessary and effective anti-depression weapon.

The Joint Economic Committee enthusiastically welcomed both Reports. The Committee unanimously accepted the view that the Federal government may be called upon to act promptly and vigorously, accepting a deficit as the most appropriate fiscal policy.

Something had clearly happened. The Joint Economic Committee, composed of both Republicans and Democrats, was in a new mood. There was unanimous support for a strong positive fiscal program. The Committee was especially reassured to find an increasing acceptance in the President's Reports of "the theory that the balanced budget, 'hard money,' and reconstruction of the Federal debt structure are not to be regarded as ends in themselves."[31]

But now the tune changed. The President's January, 1956, Report reflected a swing toward orthodoxy. The economy had moved during the year 1955 into high prosperity. Confidence in the self-sustaining economy was revived. Once again the general tone tended to minimize the responsibility of government. Indeed it was argued that the Administration had kept the economy strong and growing by restricting government expenditures. No longer could we find re-assuring statements about compensatory fiscal policy. Both in the State of the Union message and in the Budget message, the balanced budget principle, not the compensatory principle, was set forth as the appropriate criterion for expenditures and tax policy.

The Joint Economic Committee was not slow to notice the new trend

[29] *Ibid.*, pp. 112sq.

[30] *Economic Report of the President,* Transmitted to the Congress, January 20, 1955, Washington, 1955, p. VI.

[31] *Report of the Joint Economic Committee on the January 1955 Economic Report of the President With Supplemental Views and the Economic Outlook for 1955,* Prep. by the Committee Staff, March 14, 1955, Senate, 84th Congress, 1st Session, Report No. 60, Washington, 1955, p. 12.

in the President's thinking. Especially significant is the fact that the Committee firmly re-stated its position that the basic guide to Federal fiscal policy should be the state of the national economy. The President, however, now plumped for the balanced budget. The Democratic members of the Committee bemoaned the fact that while the President's earlier Reports had represented progress in economic thinking, the January, 1956, Report was burdened throughout with strong political overtones. Fiscal orthodoxy was back in the saddle.

The Democratic members of the Committee re-iterated in a firm statement their belief[32] that "fiscal integrity, if it is not to be a hollow phrase, calls for using the Federal Government's fiscal powers deliberately in such a way as to minimize economic fluctuations from the path of steady growth." Referring specifically to the vigorously orthodox position taken by Secretary Humphrey, they noted that "the Secretary of the Treasury apparently does not now accept this generally held principle of fiscal policy."

Then came the severe recession of 1958. The economy shifted into a lower gear. Semi-stagnation and high unemployment rates were defended as necessary to combat inflation and the menacing deficit in the balance-of-payments. A tax cut had indeed been seriously considered in the spring of 1958. But as it turned out, the trough of the recession was reached in April, and the Administration took pride in the fact that a tax cut had apparently not been needed. It was in fact desperately needed to close the gap resulting from the geologic displacement, so to speak, that left the economy throughout 1958–63 some 40 to 50 billions of dollars below its potential capacity.

V. An Intermediate Step Toward Keynesianism

In the meantime an educational process had been going on for some years led by liberal-minded businessmen (mostly moderate Republicans) who had organized in the late forties the Committee for Economic Development, known as the CED. The fiscal policy principles associated with this group amounted to a conservative version of Keynesianism. The Committee had already issued in November, 1947, a basic document on "Taxes and the Budget."[33] It called for a tax structure which would balance the cash budget at "full employment." Expenditures would move on a trend

[32] *Report of the Joint Economic Committee on the January 1956 Economic Report of the President With Supplemental and Minority Views and the Economic Outlook for 1956*, Prep. by the Committee Staff, March 1, 1956, Senate, 84th Congress, 2d Session, Report No. 606, Washington, 1956, p. 32.

[33] *Taxes and the Budget: A Program for Prosperity in a Free Economy*, A Statement on National Policy by The Research and Policy Committee of the Committee for Economic Development, New York, November, 1947.

line (not cyclically) and the tax rate structure also on a trend rate adjusted from time to time so as to balance accounts at full employment. Cyclically, reliance was placed on the built-in stabilizers. And finally a new dimension was added—the principle of marginal budget balancing.

All these formulations made obvious concessions to fiscal orthodoxy —a compromise which served as a useful bridge toward Keynesian thinking. Moderate in character, and couched in part in conventional terms, such a program could and did play an important educational role among men of affairs both in Congress and in business.

A manifesto on marginal budget balancing and built-in stabilizers— the so-called Princeton Manifesto [34]—had, moreover, been issued by leading economists in September, 1949. The substance of this manifesto was competently presented to the Joint Economic Committee, and its recommendations were embodied in the Douglas sub-committee report early in 1950.[35] This clearly helps to explain the advanced fiscal policy pronouncements in the Joint Economic Committee in 1954–55.

The CED program could easily be misinterpreted. Budgetary surpluses, generated by economic growth, were (so it seemed to say) to be eliminated by tax reduction. In fact, however, it is precisely in periods of surging spontaneous expansion that a budgetary surplus may be needed to restrain inflation. The true meaning of the CED program was that taxes should be set low enough so that the tax take would not dissipate the steam needed to produce full employment. If, however, the steam in the boiler exceeded or fell below this amount, taxes should in Keynesian theory be increased or reduced respectively. The CED was not altogether unaware of these matters, but public understanding often lagged behind.

Especially appealing was the emphasis on automaticity. Once installed, the built-in stabilizers and the agreed upon tax structure became a part of the "natural order." No bureaucrat would operate the mechanism. The economy would remain in effect self-sustaining.

This line of reasoning overlooks the fact that the system of built-in stabilizers rests upon a massive government budget—a budget big enough so that the automatically created deficits and surpluses can exert powerful countercyclical movements.

Two world wars in one generation together with a technological revolution with its concomitant upsurge of urbanization and population growth —all this had forced upon governments everywhere in the western world

[34] *Federal Expenditure and Revenue Policies*, Hearing Before the Joint Committee on the Economic Report, Congress of the United States, 81st Congress, 1st Session Pursuant to Sec. 5(A) of Public Law 304, 79th Congress, September 23, 1949, Washington, D.C., 1949.

[35] *Monetary, Credit, and Fiscal Policies*, Report of the Subcommittee on Monetary, Credit, and Fiscal Policies of the Joint Committee on the Economic Report, Congress of the United States, Pursuant to S. Con. Res. 26, Presented by Mr. O'Mahoney, January 23, 1950, Senate, 81st Congress, 2d Session, Document No. 129, Washington, 1950.

massive governmental expenditures. Fiscal policy could no longer remain an academic exercise. Keynesian thinking had arrived, one could say, just in time.

Keynes once complained that governments seemingly cannot be persuaded to spend except for war. Wars do indeed leave behind them the aftermath of enlarged budgets—the so-called "displacement effect." The War of 1812 raised U. S. federal expenditures from 0.6 per cent of aggregate national income before the war to 1.5 per cent after peace was restored; the Civil War to 3.0 per cent; World War I to 4.5 per cent; the great depression to 11.0 per cent; and World War II to 17.0 per cent.[36] U. S. defense expenditures increased from 11.6 billion dollars in 1948 to 50 billion dollars in 1965. In addition, urbanization and industrialization created pressures for increased outlays on social welfare. Federal government transfer payments (social security, grants to state and local governments) increased from 15.7 billion dollars in 1948 to 55.1 billion dollars in 1965. Defense and social welfare expenditures together have lifted the cash budget to a level at which the automatic swings of tax receipts and expenditures (notably the corporate taxes on the one side and the unemployment benefits on the other) exert a strong stabilizing influence upon the economy.[37]

Equipped with a large budget and progressive federal tax system, automatic fiscal policy could now play a large role. This established fact made converts to a half-way Keynesian position. Automatic fiscal policy was welcomed but increases in the budget were deplored. President Eisenhower struggled to hold expenditures down. But the pressure was on. Cash expenditures grew from 70 billion dollars in 1954 to 95 billion dollars in 1960.

The moderate conservatists believed with Pigou that the basic economic problem is simply one of "lapses from full employment." The Keynesian view was that a continuous, sustained fiscal program is needed to insure stable growth at continuing full employment.

The 1961 argument between President Kennedy's Council of Economic Advisers and Arthur Burns about the so-called "gap" between actual and potential GNP illustrates the point. Burns' chief quarrel with the Council was, as he expressed it,[38] that they seemed to lack "faith in the

---

[36] Of course military expenditures *during* the war constituted a far higher per cent of GNP.

[37] The Roosevelt New Deal measures had already laid the groundwork for an effective fiscal policy. New Deal institutional arrangements had opened up responsible and manageable outlets for government spending, including Social Security, Unemployment Insurance, Federal housing programs, the Federal highway system, Rural Electrification, Tennessee Valley Authority, Federal Works Agency, together with the numerous Federal loan and credit institutions.

[38] See his recent book, *The Management of Prosperity*, New York, 1966. He favors a systematic year by year tax reduction program which includes a limited delegation of power to the President to suspend the reductions if conditions justify such action.

capacity of private enterprise to generate full employment." Hence, as he put it, "the Council has—quite logically—been urging active Federal intervention." This Burns believed unnecessary except to prevent a serious cumulative depression.

VI. "THE NEW ECONOMICS"

This brings us to the last stage in the progress of Keynesian thinking in the United States. The inauguration of President Kennedy introduced a new day in public acceptance of modern fiscal policy. A new group of convinced and highly competent Keynesians filled virtually all the important economic posts in Washington, including among others, the Council of Economic Advisers, the Bureau of the Budget, and the Treasury Department. Among the distinguished economists (to name only a few) who played a highly important role in the Kennedy-Johnson Administration were the following: Walter Heller, David Bell, J. K. Galbraith, Paul A. Samuelson, Seymour Harris, Kermit Gordon, Charles Schultze, Gardner Ackley, James Tobin, John P. Lewis, Otto Eckstein, Arthur Okun, James Duesenberry, and Robert Solow. A fruitful close contact was, moreover, maintained with leading economists outside of the government, notably Joseph Pechman and Walter Salant of the Brookings Institution and Gerhard Colm of the National Planning Association. Seymour Harris, as Senior Economic Consultant at the Treasury Department, assembled monthly a group of some twenty (mostly university economists) for the discussion of fiscal and monetary problems confronting the Treasury.

Keynesian ideas were now for the first time in full bloom—twenty-five years after the appearance of the *General Theory*.[39] The Reports of the Council of Economic Advisers, the State of the Union Message and the Budget Message became for the first time genuine Keynesian documents. Lively ideas flooded almost every page. The "full-employment surplus," the "gap," the "fiscal drag," brilliantly illuminated by ingenious diagrams and charts, struck fire. The "new economics" was picked up by the leading newspapers and magazines. A process of public education began. Government documents became textbooks on fiscal policy. President Kennedy himself became, one might say, a professor of economics, as witness his famous Yale Commencement Address in June, 1962.[40]

[39] The growing interest in Keynesian thinking is attested to by the recent appearance in the United States of a paper-back edition of the *General Theory*. Also, the number of foreign language translations of my *Guide to Keynes* (A *Guide to Keynes*, Economics Handbook Series, New York, London and Toronto, 1953) continues to grow especially in recent years. Keynes retains his place in the center of the stage in well-nigh every economic journal or new book on economic policy.

[40] "Commencement Address at Yale University, June 11, 1962", in: *John F. Kennedy*, Containing the Public Messages, Speeches, and Statements of the President, January 1 to December 31, 1962, Public Papers of the Presidents of the United States, Washington, 1963, pp. 470sqq.

Yet as it turned out, the program that was put into effect could properly be called, as Professor Galbraith has pointed out, "conservative Keynesianism" with emphasis on tax reduction rather than on expenditures. Keynesian fiscal policy should aim to achieve three goals: 1. full employment, 2. stable growth with reasonably stable prices, and 3. optimum social priorities. The first two goals can be achieved reasonably well, as far as fiscal policy goes, by manipulating the tax structure. The third goal requires, especially in the United States, enormous increases in federal expenditures to correct the gross imbalance between the private and the public sector.

The spectacular expansionist policies of the Kennedy-Johnson Administration took the form of four tax reductions: 1. the investment tax credit of 1962, 2. the accelerated depreciation guidelines, 3. the famous tax cut of 1964, and 4. the 1965 cut in excises. It was of course notably the tax cut of 1964 that broke new ground by forestalling the historically anticipated recession and boosting the prolonged expansion to a 5.5 per cent growth rate.

A substantial tax cut in the midst of a good recovery and with the Administrative budget still in deficit represents a landmark in public thinking on economic problems. How did it happen?

Businessmen had for years longingly hoped for both a balanced budget and tax reduction. But they had been taught by the Eisenhower Administration that tax reduction must wait until the budget is balanced. Eisenhower had been compelled to accept a peace-time budget deficit of over 12 billion dollars in 1958 and had, moreover, produced a recession in 1960 by deliberately balancing the budget. The "full-employment surplus" and the "fiscal drag" theory appeared to offer an explanation of this conundrum. Under the "new dispensation" businessmen were persuaded to settle for a tax cut without waiting for the balanced budget.[41]

In the Kennedy and Johnson Administration federal cash expenditures increased no faster relative to GNP than under Eisenhower. Under Eisenhower federal cash payments increased from 69.7 billion dollars in 1954 to 95.6 billion dollars in 1959, or an average of 5.2 billion dollars per year. Under Kennedy-Johnson, federal cash payments increased from 94.7 billion dollars in 1960 to 127.9 billion dollars in 1965, an average of 6.6

[41] That the "new economics" has not dispelled the old slogans is abundantly clear from the preamble contained in Section I of the Revenue Act of 1964; "It is the sense of Congress that the tax reduction provided by this Act through stimulation of the economy, will, after a brief transitional period, raise (rather than lower) revenues and that such revenue increases should first be used to eliminate the deficits in the administrative budgets and then to reduce the public debt. To further the objective of obtaining balanced budgets in the near future, Congress by this action, recognizes the importance of taking all reasonable means to restrain Government spending . . ." *Revenue Act of 1964 With Explanation,* Based on the New Law as Approved by the President, February 26, 1964 (P. L. 88–272), Chicago, Illinois, 1964, p. 136 (Sec. 1).

billion dollars per year. But the average GNP for the Eisenhower period was 426 billion dollars and for the Kennedy-Johnson period, 580 billion dollars. In terms of the current GNP the average increase per annum in cash payments was 1.2 per cent of income under Eisenhower and slightly below that under Kennedy-Johnson.

Note, however, that the figures just cited above omitted the fateful year, 1960. Hard pressed by ardent fiscal conservatists, notably Secretary Humphrey, the Eisenhower Administration made the fatal mistake of cutting the Administrative budget by 4 billion dollars in the fiscal year 1960. The Administration budget was indeed at long last balanced at 1.2 billion dollars, but at the cost of the 1960 recession.

VII. The Current Status of Keynesianism in the United States

With this experience behind us, where do we now stand with respect to the Keynesian Revolution? Employing the language used by Keynes himself in his famous letter to Shaw, we could perhaps say that Keynes had indeed "largely" revolutionized the way America thinks about economic problems. But we still have a long way to go. Even with respect to tax policy I suspect that many people look upon the recent tax cut as an episode—a "shot in the arm"—a program that cannot prudently be repeated very often.

Some conservatists, however, have seized upon the "fiscal drag" concept as a powerful weapon, stolen from the Keynesian arsenal, with which to achieve a progressive year by year reduction in federal taxes—a device to capture all the fruits of technological progress for the private sector. Social priorities are thrown to the winds. Government expenditures are to be held, as far as possible, to present or even lower levels.

The great fiscal policy debate in years to come will center not so much on full employment but rather on the burning issue of social priorities. The "Loyal Opposition" has moved an important step forward. The first stage, as noted above, involved acceptance of active fiscal policy, if the economy (a) dipped below the "tolerable bottom" where serious cumulative depression threatens or (b) is pushing up through the "inflation ceiling." In between these two levels the self-sustaining economy was to be given free range to operate on its own, assisted by the built-in stabilizers. The new stage in the progress toward Keynesianism involves the acceptance of active fiscal policy within the area *between* the "tolerable bottom" and the "inflation ceiling" with the proviso, however, that such active fiscal policy take the form of tax reduction—such reduction to be canceled, however, if the economy is heating. The conservatists have learned, perhaps too well, the "new economics" lesson about the "fiscal drag."

There thus remains much unfinished business. Shall irresponsible advertising continue to control people's minds, propelling the economy on to an ever-increasing output of gadgets, or shall we in earnest tackle the problems of the Great Society—air pollution, water pollution, ugly scrap heaps on the roadside, destruction of nature's beauty, slums; and on the positive side, the poverty program, housing, education, medical schools, hospitals, nursing homes, urban renewal, urban transportation, government support of the creative and performing arts. The political battles of the future will of necessity be fought over the size of the government budget.

In addition to the Council of Economic Advisers, we now need a new Act of Congress creating a Council of Social Values[42] to help redress the present unequal emphasis on material things. This act should require the President each year, aided by his Council, to make a report to the Congress and to the people on our cultural goals. This report should set forth the goals for the coming year and should indicate the programs and policies necessary to achieve those goals.

President Eisenhower in his last public address before leaving office warned the nation about another pressing problem—the danger to our economy inherent in our vast military-business complex. To ward off corruption and inefficiency will be no easy task as Secretary McNamara has discovered. The new role of government, not as supplier but as buyer on an undreamed of scale, raises problems about the functioning of the price system unknown to neo-classical economics. Moreover, disarmament—if and when it comes as ardently hoped for—will greatly complicate the management of a peace-time economy.

Fortunately, we shall not allow this problem to take us totally by surprise. The government has already issued (July, 1965) an excellent Report of the Committee on the Economic Impact of Defense and Disarmament under the chairmanship of Gardner Ackley.[43] The Report stays clear of vague complacencies. It is based on good Keynesian economics. The magnitudes are enormous, and the needed adjustments will reach colossal proportions.

VIII. What About Europe?

A final word about the miracle of post-war European prosperity. Is this also a part of the Keynesian Revolution? With the sole exception of

[42] See my *Economic Issues of the 1960's,* Economics Handbook Series, New York, Toronto and London, 1960, pp. 91sq.
[43] *Report of the Committee on the Economic Impact of Defense and Disarmament,* Superintendent of Documents, Washington, D.C., July, 1965, pp. IX, 92.

Sweden (a country that was developing during the Great Depression an active fiscal policy on its own) all European countries were at that time following orthodox reliance upon the self-generating forces of recovery, fearful that active government intervention might destroy the revival of "confidence" upon which they built their hopes.

The impact of Keynesian thinking may well have been greatest in the Anglo-Saxon world. Still in this age of instantaneous communication, new ideas penetrate rapidly throughout the globe. To what extent Keynesian thinking has influenced continental governmental policy I leave to others to say. The post-war European growth miracle is a complex phenomenon. The Marshall aid program with its multiplier effect was itself an injection of governmental active intervention unknown to the pre-war world. Since 1940 the United States has poured over 100 billion dollars into the economies of the free world. The gigantic post-war budgets (inexorably imposed upon all western governments by an increasing industrialization, revolutionary technological developments, and a rapidly growing urbanization) far from being a burden, have powerfully sustained and fed an ever increasing aggregate demand. Technology and capital formation have raised productivity to a level at which the incomes of the masses can afford expensive consumer durables, the purchase of which has in turn opened up large new investment outlets. All this together has produced the post-war European miracle. Keynesian thinking may have played a role not so much possibly, as an activating force but rather in terms of melting away the icy walls of dogmatic resistance to the process of change.

11   KARL SCHILLER

West Germany: Stability and Growth as Objectives of Economic Policy

For many people the combined objectives "stability and growth" confront economic policy with a problem similar to that which faced the seamen of antiquity, who had to sail between Scylla and Charybdis to pass the crucial test. Accordingly, if modern economic policy is to pass the acid test: the ship of the national economy must be steered so that it does not drift either into the vortex of "stabilization at any price" or into the maelstrom of "uncontrolled expansion." And all this while preserving free wage and price formation and without jeopardizing a high level of employment and foreign trade equilibrium.

Yet it must be established from the very outset that both objectives, stability and growth, are a permanent and unavoidable challenge to our modern society. There is no way of getting round them.

The Growth Objective

However, it is worth our while to devote a little thought to this social "must," for stability and growth are by no means values that are recognized unreservedly by all. The prospect of a probable nineteen- to fifty-one-fold increase in the national product over the next hundred years, which my colleague Jöhr set forth two years ago in an article in the "Schweizerische Zeitschrift für Volkswirtschaft und Statistik" is fascinating, but it will certainly not be considered enticing everywhere. True, Jöhr couples this forecast with the prophesy that stability problems will

From "Stability and Growth as Objectives of Economic Policy," *The German Economic Review*, Vol. 5, No. 3 (1967), pp. 177–188. By permission of the Editors of *The German Economic Review*.

This contribution is an English version of an address given by Professor Schiller at the "Schweizerisches Institut für Auslandsforschung" (Swiss Institute for Foreign Research) in Zurich in February 1967. Although meanwhile some of the announced measures have been instituted, the address is reproduced unchanged on account of its programmatic content.

then be of no further importance and inflationary processes will at most be regarded as mere blemishes. But how to find the way into that "Golden Age" and still remain constantly near the path of equilibrium is something that has yet to be discovered. And the question "What do we really need economic growth for?" cannot be ignored; it calls for a clear answer.

As a first answer one might simply draw attention to the elementary urge to strive for a higher standard of living, for a continual improvement of material living conditions. But in the train of this somewhat naive statement follow more complicated considerations: Technological progress, as the precondition for the creation of new processes and products, will continue in future to set free increasing numbers of workers from their former places of work. In order to provide enough jobs for them and the rising generation, the economy must grow "outwards"—to create the necessary new jobs so that employment is ensured. Hence technological progress demands economic growth.

But there is also another point to be considered: The current fund of technological knowledge permits us, for instance, an annual macroeconomic productivity increase of about 4 per cent. At the same time, however, experience has shown us that in countries where the growth rate of the gross national product remains at 2 per cent and less for a fairly long time the increase in productivity also suffers.

Technological progress just simply presupposes a sufficiently high investment rate and macroeconomic growth, so that the technological results found in research departments and laboratories can be taken over into the production plants. For this interdependence of the growth process, technological progress and full employment Samuelson used the alarming though very apt metaphor: Together we are riding a tiger. The danger threatening the rider if the pace slows or the ride comes to an end is easy to picture.

Secondly, however, reasonable growth of the economy is also an essential prerequisite for the fulfilment of the great and growing tasks in modern society. These tasks, whether they are called national health, advancement of science, education, transport, regional planning, municipal engineering, national defence or any other name, are easier to perform when the macroeconomic cake is growing than when the expenditures for those purposes have to be pared from existing slices of cake. As John K. Galbraith emphasized in his theses, in a society heading for the year 2000, precisely when public needs rise more sharply than before, vigorous growth of the entire cake is imperative.

Thirdly, this is similarly true of any envisaged change in the distribution of income and property with a view to greater justice, which can be better and more smoothly achieved in times of prosperity and expansion than in phases of weak growth. Vigorous growth is the best basis for all income-policy action. All social redistribution planners should take this to heart from the very outset.

To cite an example, the social inquiry in the Federal Republic of Germany arrived at the following conclusions: in view of the steep pension gradient lying ahead of us (due to the age structure), the current system of sliding-scale social insurance pensions would collapse in the event of a medium-term fall of the real growth rate of our national product below 3 to 4 per cent.

Finally, the same can be said of economic structural changes. In a dynamic economy they are as a rule perceptibly more violent than in an economy with a curbed rate of growth. But it is equally correct that an expansive economy makes such changes more easily digestible. A striking proof of this is provided by developments in the Federal Republic in the fifties (e.g. in agriculture) as compared with the present difficulties.

A further example is the situation in the German hard coal mining industry. In a nine-year structural crisis and with a policy of postponement, the chance was missed of carrying out structural reorganization in a period of high real growth rates of the gross national product (1964 still 6.8%); now we have to go about this business under far more adverse conditions. And quite generally, we cannot repeat often enough what Peter Sweerts-Sporck wrote in the "Volkswirt" at the end of last year: "In the mass democracy of pluralistic interests of our present age there can be no balancing out of interests and no balancing of the budget without economic growth. In recession, stagnation and deflation the possibilities for social compromise gradually disappear completely; on the other hand, latent radicalism grows, intolerance spreads."

THE STABILITY OBJECTIVE

All that has already been said also applies mutatis mutandis to the stability objective, defined as stability of the price level of consumer goods and measured by the cost of living index. I feel, however, that it is pointless to indulge in abstract argument about the tolerable quantities of price level rises. The stability objective can only mean that it is a matter of bringing down the rate of price increases by way of a medium-term weaning programme for society, that is, by an annual reduction of the inflation rate. In this connection, for the medium run the target figure for movement of the price level of the gross national product in the national accounts could be set at 1 per cent.

The high priority of the stability objective emanates on the one hand from the postulate of social justice. Anomalous rises or falls of the price level always have different effects on the various social groups and hence regularly cause—at least for a short time—a change in distribution to the disadvantage of the weaker groups. An obvious example of how close together economic and political stability lie has been provided by the last few years in the Federal Republic of Germany.

Secondly, stability is also and just as much an important prerequisite for the functional efficiency of the market economy system. Lenin's statement—which has been quoted almost to the point of tedium—that the monetary system would have to be devastated in order to destroy our society has made the vital function of a stable value of money unmistakeably clear even to the general public. It was not without good reason that Walter Eucken listed the postulate of the primacy of monetary policy in second place in his catalogue of the constituent principles; the price mechanism, voluntary savings and the corresponding financing of investment cannot function successfully, if the stability of the value of money deteriorates continually and at an unusual pace.

The Task of Economic Policy

The postulates of stability and growth are unambiguous; the main problem for economic policy begins with the question of its realization with the highest degree of simultaneity possible. The experience of the past two years in the Federal Republic of Germany has shown clearly that the situation with stability and growth is not the same as that of communicating tubes in physics. Suppression of growth itself is still a long way from causing an increase in stability, and conversely more growth is by no means necessarily linked with less stability.

We all know that there are countries with little growth and just as little stability of the price level, and that on the other hand there are countries which have preserved stability despite fast growth. The simple conceptions of the unequivocal association of moderate growth and high stability have meanwhile been refuted. The relationships between the two objectives are more diverse and more complicated than was generally assumed. And an economic policy that sets out to attain both goals simultaneously must take more differentiated action and often apply its instruments in "changing combinations." The beaten track of stop-and-go policy will no longer lead us to our objective. Economic policy in the second half of the 20th century must always be a policy mix.

Such a policy of changing combinations of instruments is now possible only within a synthesis of global control and market economy. The essential macro-decisions in such a system are made by economic and financial policy, but the micro-decisions are left to the market and microeconomic competition.

Monetary Policy

Nowadays the monetary policy of the central bank is generally recognized as an instrument of macroeconomic control, the main emphasis lying without doubt on short-run influencing of the trade cycle. After the Second World War, monetary policy was rediscovered in an extraordinary measure. But meanwhile we have also reached the limits of monetary policy. If, for the moment, we neglect the fact that under free convertibility the central bank is confronted in its monetary and credit policy with a certain set of foreign trade problems, its sphere of action remains limited to controlling the aggregate demand for money. In so far as, say, price increase tendencies have their causes in something other than excessively high demand, monetary policy is condemned to remain largely ineffectual. A contractive monetary policy may then jeopardize growth and full employment, but not achieve stability. From a certain point onwards, far-reaching monetary restrictions may even cause a cost push due to reduced employment of production capacities.

In the other direction, towards stimulation of a new expansion, there is certainly also an area of action for monetary policy. Over and above the immediate quantitative effect of easing monetary and credit policy, above all the signal effect may play a not inconsiderable role. The easing of liquidity restrictions and the lowering of bank rate, if decided on and announced at the right moment and to the right extent, may very well serve as a sign of better future expectations for entrepreneurs and hence also of a strengthened propensity to invest. This psychological effect should not be underestimated, and it is probably one of the factors responsible for the positive opinion of the London "Economist," which wrote on January 14, referring especially to Germany and Japan: "In those countries . . . there is little doubt that an easing of monetary policy is the quickest way forward to re-expansion."

I can only say: I hope the forecast of the "Economist" is right. From our German situation we can only welcome gradual interest "disarmament" and harmonization. But we also know that the easing of monetary restrictions in certain situations may lead only to consolidation of firms' balance sheets, but not always directly to a real expansion of investment. Then, and only then, does modern fiscal policy assume its rights and duties.

Fiscal Policy

Without continual co-ordination with fiscal policy, no economic policy nowadays can find the right course between Scylla and Charybdis.

True, in most countries financial policy has long since grown beyond its original fiscal purpose. The classical "Bedarfsdeckungsfinanz" (finance to cover requirements) has changed—as Gerloff says—into "Ordnungsfinanz" (regulatory finance) or, to use a term employed by Meinhold, financial policy has "mediatized" itself. This is true not only in respect of the increased use of built-in stabilizers, but also of conscious trade cycle and growth policy decisions.

In theory and for the extreme case, fiscal policy had long since been accepted as an instrument of cyclical and growth policy. In mid-1966, however, Fritz Neumark was constrained to remark that though the means of financial policy were acepted as a counter to serious depression, that was not the case with regard to the combatting of a profound stagnation or a recession or the obviation of a boom. I now have the impression that we have recently made a little progress in this direction in Germany.

The decisions of the Federal Government on January 19, 1967, would seem to confirm this. Simultaneously they are an example of how a special situation, necessitates a special policy mix. Following a two-year period of growth losses (growth rate of the real gross national product 1964: 6.8%; 1965: 4.7%; 1966: 2.7%) and ever more marked budget deficits and declining tax revenue, it was necessary to make up a parcel containing both contractive and the now requisite expansive elements; by this means we have made the inconceivable possible:

1. Elimination of a budget deficit in the amount of DM 3,700 mill. in the conventional manner (expenditure cuts of DM 2,600 mill., especially in the sphere of public consumption; revenue increases of DM 1,100 mill.; reduction of tax concessions, etc.).

2. Setting up of a contingent budget of DM 2,500 mill. for additional public investment, financed via the money market.

3. Granting of special depreciation allowances for tax purposes in the amount of 10 or 5 per cent per annum for private investment over a period of 9 months.

The restoration of confidence in the solidity of government financial policy, which had been badly shaken in the past few years, demanded orthodox elimination of the budget deficit. But such action alone would only have speeded up the downhill movement of economic activity and certainly have produced new deficits. So the expansive measures of the investment budget and the special depreciation allowances had to be added. So much for this concrete example of a new combination.

But we also know that fiscal policy in future demands improved institutional and instrumental possibilities.

At the present time it is unanimously agreed that spending policy is an effective weapon. With the help of this policy it is possible to induce above all temporally and economically purposeful impetuses, and also relatively rapidly and exactly acting inhibitive influences. The area of impact of public spending, however, depends decisively on the share of expenditures fixed by statutes. What the statutory earmarking of over 90 per cent of expenditures means as an obstacle to cyclically oriented scheduling of spending has been demonstrated to us in the Federal Republic of Germany by the budget-policy decisions of recent times. So it is in this area that the future tasks of "medium-run financial planning" lie. By such planning, for instance, a basic public investment budget could be made "resistant to cyclical fluctuations," that is, it could be planned for the long run on the basis of growth considerations for infrastructure development. For future growth problems, for the fulfilment of community tasks, public investment will have to play a substantial part in the "allocation of resources." Another variable portion of public investment will have to be matched with current cyclical needs. This would mean, however, that the cyclical variability of public spending as a whole would therefore be limited.

Consequently the question of the leeway for and the effectiveness of taxation policy as an instrument for short-run regulation of demand becomes all the more important. The variation of tax deduction rates for depreciation is, of course, a useful additional instrument, but hardly an effective one on its own. An effective instrument of taxation policy, both in boom and recession situations, is indubitably the variation of the rates for taxes on earnings. For this reason we have included this instrument in our new proposals for an Act for the Promotion of the Stability and Growth of the Economy that have been placed before the Bundestag. As a rule a tax cut will stimulate private consumption and investment spending, just as a tax increase may limit the growth of demand. The difficulties here, however, lie in the correct dosage and dependable determination of the speed of reaction. The shower situation with which we are all familiar and the difficulty of adjusting the water to the right temperature and maintaining it—e. g. despite changes in the water consumption of neighbours—is an exemplary illustration of this task. However, this difficulty does not mean that we have to sacrifice the "pleasure" of a shower because of it.

In political everyday life in the Federal Republic we are now only at the beginning of these new fiscal policy tasks, which demand of all participants a new line of thought and macroeconomic orientation, to which they have not been accustomed hitherto. But it is simply the fate of those who endeavour to find a rational economic and financial policy, that they have to fight time-lags in the public consciousness—social consciousness is always moulded more by the last than by the currently acute situation—and also time-lags in the executive mechanism.

GLOBAL CONTROL IN THE MARKET ECONOMY

Instruments and co-ordination of monetary and fiscal policy that are both better and better adapted to the situation may mean that the Keynesian ideas of the "General Theory" of 1935 are now finally gaining acceptance in Germany. Alvin Hansen recently described the process of reception of Keynesian theory as a three-phase process. The original total opposition was followed by a gradual retreat which, in turn, gave way to the establishment of a "loyal opposition." Whereas the loyal opposition stage was reached in the academic world about 1950, reception in the sphere of practical policy did not take place until about 10 years later in the USA.

Although what then found expression in the reports of the Council of Economic Advisers and the financial policy and budgetary measures that were decided on is ironically labelled "conservative Keynesianism," for continental European conditions at that time it was anything but conservative. In the meantime, however, economic policy in Europe has not stood still. In the Federal Republic at all events, the necessity of a meaningful synthesis between the Freiburg imperative of competition and the Keynesian demand for control of effective aggregate demand is beginning to be understood.

The draft of the Stability Bill of 1966 was a modest start, which has meanwhile—as already mentioned—undergone the requisite transformation into the new draft of an Act for the Promotion of the Stability and Growth of the Economy. In the Federal Republic we are now in the process of developing the partial and ad hoc cyclical and growth policy of the past, which often enough was regrettably not a policy at all, into a system of global control in the sense of a fairly long-run, but simultaneously cyclically flexible "integral economic and financial policy." What is happening in Germany is a progressive synthesis and development of the theories of Keynes and Eucken.

The instruments of a policy geared to growth and stability must not consist of regimentation in individual fields, but rather essentially of global control.

You know the word planning or control, no matter how and in what context it was used, was interpreted for some time—at least in Germany—as a stab in the back of the market economy. I find it all the more gratifying, therefore, that in Bonn recently a witness as trustworthy as Fritz Machlup, in his paper on "Freedom and Planning in the Market Economy," concludes his meditations on global, or what he terms "level" planning with the lapidary but unequivocal sentence: "It hardly requires explanation if we state that level planning is not incompatible with the free market economy."

But the issue is not only the question of the regulatory legitimacy of global control, but what it can and what it should achieve, and what it should look like.

For its decisions and action this policy needs an orientation tableau or comprehensive accounts of the current and foreseeable trend of the macroeconomic circular flow. Of course, the "right" economic policy cannot be derived mechanically from circular flow models. It cannot be contested, however, that a macroeconomic forecast, which must be limited to the large aggregates on account of both the growing number of sources of error when details are taken into account and the regulatory problems involved, is an important and necessary orientation aid for global control via economic policy.

Comprehensive accounts of this nature—which naturally can have nothing more than an indicative character for microeconomic relationships —should perform a twofold function:

1. They should be a source of information for all agencies responsible for economic, financial and social policy and hence also a help in the necessary co-ordination of those agencies, and at the same time

2. also a source of information for the private sector of the economy on the situation of the economy as a whole and its possible paths of development.

This type of comprehensive accounting system differs from the "planification en détail"—which was rightly rejected for the German economy—chiefly in the fact that it is limited to global values of macroeconomic circular flow and that for all involved its character is more that of an orientation guide than a binding rule for detail.

COMPETITION POLICY

In this system, which does not set out to score the parts for every member of the orchestra, but at best indicates a common rhythm, the spontaneity of the market and competition retains its prime function. Competition is and remains the decisive motive force behind the dynamic economic process and economic growth and hence behind stability. No central investment plan, however ingenious it may be and however detailed the calculations and recommendations it contains, can replace the "built-in expansion and stability mechanism" of competition. We have no grounds to depart from the course of competition policy; on the contrary, we have every reason to refurbish vigorously and on modern lines the contours that paled in the late fifties and early sixties.

The wave of enthusiasm for industrial giants now passing over Europe and the ever more clearly defined preference of some circles for mercantilistic ideas and the preservation of a reserve protected from competition must not mislead us to renounce the concept of competition. I certainly have nothing against large units as far as they are demanded in the interests of technological and scientific efficacy, and I also have nothing against the demand for elimination of serious artificial distortions in international competition, but this cannot and must not be allowed to lead to a relapse into a cartel-ridden and monopoly-pervaded economy with privileges and shielded positions in an oligarchically structured society.

A "competition policy with muted trumpets" is not an element of a policy directed towards stability and growth. The attainment of both depends decisively also on the intensity and the functional efficiency of economic competition.

SAFEGUARDS AGAINST FOREIGN INFLUENCES

A policy aiming at stability and growth can be frustrated in an open economy with free movement of goods and money by extraneous disturbances.

So the problem arises of safeguards against foreign influences, a problem that is a dominant theme of recent scientific debate. In the Federal Republic of Germany, particularly the Board of Experts for Assessment of Overall Economic Trends with its expertise thrust its fingers into the wound of the foreign threat to stability. Regardless of whether one agrees in this connection with the thesis of inflationary infection via "direct international price relationships" or whether one regards the danger to domestic economic stability via the "income effect" or the "liquidity effect" as decisive, the problem cannot simply be cast aside. However, we are of the opinion that it will not become acute in 1967.

It would be going beyond the bounds of this address to discuss now and in detail the pros and cons of the various proposals for a solution of this problem. In the Federal Republic we take this question seriously and we shall bring it up for discussion with all due emphasis in the international bodies. We are opposed to any national, unilateral monetary policy. But if it should prove that no common action can be attained on the level of world-wide co-ordination, the Federal Government will seek a solution in the direction of a stable community or a hard currency bloc of countries with similarly oriented economic policies. That hard currency bloc, to which as large a number of countries as possible, especially the Ten, should belong, could effectively counter the danger of a permanent extraneous threat to all internal efforts to achieve stability.

CONCERTED ACTION

Apart from the safeguards against extraneous influences which—as I have already said—will in all probability not constitute an acute danger in the Federal Republic of Germany in 1967, there is another flank still open in the described system of global control. A wages policy oriented to macroeconomic necessities is essential to the achievement of the objective of a "made-to-measure upswing" such as we are now attempting. This is the reason for our attempt at "concerted action," in which endeavours are being made in social consultations with the autonomous organizations of employers and labour to establish macroeconomic orientation data. This concerted action was initiated by the Federal Government, and so far all concerned have already expressed their basic approval.

All the aspects described so far of a policy aiming at stability and growth show that:

The system of global control can be rounded off only by the solution of the co-ordination problem, i. e. by co-ordination on a voluntary basis. The term "concerted action" is therefore much more than a catch-word. It means for the first time: mutual exchange of information among all agencies responsible for the economic process.

Therefore we need concerted action and hence round-table consultations on a large variety of levels.

On the one hand there is the need for co-ordination between central bank policy and government economic and financial policy, but on the other hand there is also the need for co-ordination of the government agencies at various levels. You, in Switzerland, will fully appreciate these problems of the federal system. In the draft of the Act for the Promotion of the Stability and Growth of the Economy we have provided for a special body for the co-ordination of the largely autonomous regional authorities, a so-called trade cycle council which will confer at regular intervals on the necessary cyclical and credit-policy measures in the sphere of government.

But the principal "round-table" institution we are endeavouring to attain consists in the already mentioned consultations with employers and labour within the framework of a comprehensive concerted action programme. Precisely this task demands of the government a very large measure of leadership qualities, for in Germany self-determination in negotiating wages is rightly classified—in no small measure due to the experience of the period from 1933 to 1945—as a highly esteemed right of a peaceful social system. Any attempt to pursue a policy inimical to management and labour is therefore doomed to failure. Furthermore, it is not intended that our concerted action should in any way cover up the social conflicts that are unavoidable in a mature society. But by way of exchange of information and joint establishment of guideposts it is our intention to limit them, to make them rationally recognizable and hence resolvable. I am full of confidence that our present efforts will be crowned with success. In the next few weeks, we shall begin the second round of talks—now in multilateral form—with the employers' associations and trade unions.

To attain stability and growth in an open and free society under the current circumstances is a multiple task extending over many fields and many phases. It demands the rational means and techniques of global accounting and control, and similarly rational information and orientation. In outline it is a policy in keeping with the new, the second phase of our free, market economy system. We are now entering into that phase.

In his "Reden und Schriften" (Speeches and Papers) Franz Böhm said: "Market economy from the left versus market economy from the right—that is far from being the worst thing that could happen in our country. In fact, it is probably the only way . . . that will produce a good market economy."

We are now doing everything in our power to make these prophetic words come true in Germany.

12   PETER DONALDSON

BRITISH PLANNING

'We are all planners now.' But the way in which a Conservative government, pressed by business interests, was suddenly converted to the idea
of planning, is still a little surprising. However, 'planning' can mean very
different things according to what it is expected to achieve and how it is
intended to do so.

Whatever its scope and form, planning involves alteration, in accordance with a central policy, of the pattern of output which would result
from free enterprise. Just how much that pattern is changed depends on
the aims of planning policy. The ends of the private sector may be fully
accepted by the planners who confine themselves to showing private concerns how they can best achieve them. On the other hand, the purpose of
planning may be to modify commercial criteria—by a balancing of economic and non-economic considerations, and the calculation of *social* costs
and benefits. Clearly, the degree to which planning can be equated with
'interference' depends on what the planners are trying to do. The 'weak'
variety may just require the authorities to encourage those conditions in
which basically unconstrained enterprises can do their job most efficiently;
'strong' planning, on the other hand, will involve more direct intervention
from above. . . .

Until very recently most people in Britain have thought of planning as
implying State direction of the economy through a system of controls—
along the lines practised by the two Labour governments during the years
1945 to 1951. During this highly abnormal period the authorities were
faced with the immense problems of reconstructing the economy. Consumers were ready to make good their war-time sacrifices by indulging in a
vast spending spree; industry, on the other hand, was run down, partly
devastated, and mostly still geared to war purposes; the balance of payments had been acutely weakened by the loss of overseas investments, the
acquisition of new liabilities, and the breakdown of traditional patterns of
trade. Demand from consumers for all the things which for so long had
been missing from the shops, demand for new houses to replace bomb
damage, demand for new factories and machines to meet peacetime needs,
demand from overseas countries which had built up substantial credit balances during the war—all this added up to a pressure on resources which

From Peter Donaldson *Guide to the British Economy,* Harmondsworth, England
and Baltimore, Md., Penguin Books, 1965, pp. 183–184, 186–193. Reprinted by permission of Penguin Books, Ltd.

had to be contained if it was not to lead to an explosion of prices or balance of payments disaster.

In these circumstances, the government had no real alternative to maintaining the system of controls on the economy which had been created during the war. The problem of ensuring that enough resources flowed into investment, and that the investment was according to the most pressing social priorities, could only be solved by direct and comprehensive regulation of the economy; instead of being able to enjoy the peace, consumers and producers continued to be harried and frustrated by a complex system of rationing, licensing, and restrictions.

Planning therefore came to connote austerity, the black market, and red tape. In fact, of course, the problems of the immediately post-war years were highly exceptional and necessitated equally extreme policies. The Labour government itself began dismantling the control system as the easing of economic pressures made such comprehensive regulation less necessary; most of what was left was thrown, rather prematurely and indiscriminately, on to the Conservative 'bonfire of controls' after 1951, and, during the following decade, regulation of the economy was largely confined to 'global' fiscal and monetary measures.

And now we are all planners again! However, the present experiment in planning is very different from the control machinery of 1945-50. Influenced by, and partly modelled on the French system, it is indicative rather than imperative, guiding but not directing. It is, in fact, more French than the French.

The National Economic Development Council, immediately rechristened 'Neddy,' began operations in early 1962 with the job of establishing the conditions necessary for maximum economic development compatible with 'soundness' in the economy. If it is to do its work thoroughly, this is a wide enough brief to lead it into consideration of most aspects of the British economy.

The Council itself is made up of some twenty industrialists (representing public as well as private enterprises), trade unionists, and independent members, with the Chancellor of the Exchequer as chairman. Also on the Council is Neddy's Director-General who links the top tier with the Office of a hundred or so technical specialists.*

The initiative in the Council's work lies with its upper tier, and doubts were expressed early on as to whether such an unwieldy group of top people could be anything more than a talking shop. Surprisingly enough, however, the Chancellor's warning against the danger of merely exchanging 'platitudinous generalities' seemed to have some effect, and the parties on the Council appeared genuinely concerned to know how growth rates could be increased. As a result, the Director-General and his lower-tier

---

* There are also nine 'little Neddies' which perform a similar function to the French Modernization Commissions.

experts were not impeded in their efforts to find out, and two major reports were completed within Neddy's first thirteen months.

The first was a blueprint for the growth of the economy over the period 1961–5, and was an attempt to work out the implications for different
sectors of the economy of an annual rate of growth in gross national product averaging 4%. This may not seem a very ambitious target, particularly
when the expected population increase of 0.7% per annum would reduce
the *per capita* rate of growth to only 3.3% However, it is still substantially
higher than any growth-rate previously sustained by the economy.

The conclusion of the experts was that a 4% rate of growth was quite
on the cards, and could be achieved with available man-power providing
that it was fully used. One of the bases of the report was an industrial
inquiry by the Council Office into the impact of faster growth on a cross-
section of seventeen public and private industries. The results were encouraging, showing that these industries would expect to grow at an average of some 4.8% per annum if the economy as a whole was achieving the
4% mark; the rest of the economy would therefore only have to manage
2.5% for the national average to be reached. Only a moderate increase in
investment (5.5%) was called for, and although consumption would have
to rise more slowly (3.5%), the absolute increase in consumption would
be much greater than that of recent years. With regard to the balance of
payments, the Office took as its starting point the need to achieve a surplus
of some £400 million a year—to provide for a substantial overseas investment and a strengthening of Britain's reserve position. Imports were not
expected to rise by more than 4% a year, and on this basis an annual increase of 5% in export earnings would be required. The Office thought that
this was quite possible and refused to be daunted by the fact that imports
subsequently rose a good deal more rapidly; the surplus target was later
cut to £275 million and this, together with one or two other adjustments,
enabled Neddy to keep the required rate of export increase down to the
just conceivable 5.1% a year.

In its second report, in April 1963, the N.E.D.C. embarked on the task
which had been set by the Chancellor—finding out 'what are the obstacles to quicker growth, what can be done to improve efficiency, and
whether the best use is being made of our resources.' Yet again the need
for incomes restraint was restated, this time rather more palatably in a
favorable growth context. If money incomes continued to rise at their past
5 or 6% a year, the plan would be doomed because of the consequent balance of payments difficulties; but, if only there could be restraint, *real*
incomes could shoot up by nearly 40% within a decade. Another prerequisite of faster growth which the Council emphasized was the need for more
labour mobility. In this respect, they suggested a package of policies—the
setting up of a Labour Redundancy Fund, higher unemployment benefits,
increased transferability of pension rights, and more comprehensively

wage-related national insurance contributions. Other things which the report called for included: a close study of the impact of the taxation structure on growth; more technical and managerially oriented education, and a thorough overhaul of the apprenticeship system; and a more dynamic regional policy. All this is very sensible, if not particularly original.

Judged by the behaviour of the economy during the first two years of the Council's plan, the N.E.D.C. certainly appears to have had a favourable impact. Despite the fact that its blueprint was produced a year *after* the start of the planning period, Neddy was able to report, in March 1964, that the economy had been shunted from virtual stagnation on to a growth path sufficient to make up for earlier arrears and was approaching the 4% trend for the whole period. However, most of this progress could be attributed to the fact that the economy started from a position of substantial excess capacity resulting from the last dose of inflation. Much of the rapid rise in output was therefore due to increased use of plant and man-power which had previously been lying idle. The really vital challenge will therefore be faced only during the second half of the planning period when this slack has been taken up. *Sustained* growth will then only be possible if some of the previous obstacles to growth are removed.

In what ways can we expect Neddy-type planning to help in doing this? In its present form, we can distinguish four roles which the Council can play in accelerating economic development:

1. *Investigator* We have stressed several times in this chapter that knowledge of the growth process is very inadequate. It is not difficult to find plausible arguments for the theses that the British economy has not grown faster because of: too little investment, too much investment misdirected, restrictive practices on the part of the workers, restrictive practices on the part of poor quality management, an over-valued pound, fixed exchange rates, insufficient flexibility in the economy, and so on. What we do not know is the relative importance of these various factors, whether some of them are important at all, and whether there are others which have been too much neglected.

Neddy can obviously contribute a good deal by its inquiries into different aspects of the growth process. So far, all that the N.E.D.C. has had time to do is to point out the need for such studies; only when more work has been done in defining the obstacles to growth will we be in a position to set about overcoming them.

2. *Pressure Group* For the first time, we now have an organization which is exclusively concerned with the problems of faster growth. The mere existence of the N.E.D.C. puts an emphasis on the goal of national economic development which makes its achievement more likely. It ensures that whenever discussion of priorities takes place, the case for growth

is fully presented. It can suggest policy alternatives which may never emanate from more hidebound Treasury pundits. Its opinions may help to bolster the weak-hearted and imbue the more cautious elements in government circles with a sense of the importance of keeping the economy moving on its upward path.

3. *Target-Setter*   By setting targets for the economy and showing what could be done, the Council increases the likelihood that it will be done. To suggest a growth-rate which the economy is capable of achieving and to show its implications for different sectors gives a standard by which progress can be judged; it also helps by creating growth-consciousness and buoyant expectations about the future course of the economy. But target-setting, as we shall be emphasizing later, is only useful if it is thought that there is a real possibility that the targets will be reached.

4. *Market Researcher*   To have a picture of how the economy will look if it grows at a certain rate facilitates long-term planning by public and private enterprises and by policy-makers in the government itself. Once an industry realizes that its demand will be increased by simultaneous expansion in the rest of the economy, output can be more boldly pushed to the limits indicated by long-term estimates; on the other hand, certain investments which industries are considering may be shown to be unwarranted, and mistakes which would otherwise have been made can thereby be avoided; seeing in advance the obstacles and bottlenecks which are likely to arise enables measures to deal with them to be prepared well in advance.

To return to a very important point, however, it is vital that the business expectations which Neddy succeeds in creating are in fact fulfilled. Confidence in planning will not be enhanced if firms which expand find that the Neddy programme has failed to work out for the economy as a whole. Indeed, unless there is faith in the Council's estimate of the future rise in demand, enterprises will be very reluctant to expand at all. Unfortunately, this is just what seems to be already happening. In their March 1964 report *The Growth of the Economy* the Council admitted that

several of the industries consulted fear that steady and rapid growth will not be sustained. Unless they can be convinced to the contrary, there may not be sufficient investment to maintain rapid growth after 1966.

Showing the feasibility and implications of a 4% growth-rate can certainly have a stimulating effect in itself. But success of the policy must depend more on changes being made to a system which has failed in the past to produce the results. Neddy, on the other hand, is a purely advisory body with no power to make changes or see that they are made. Purely 'indicative' planning has severe limitations. The French system, for all its emphasis on 'planning by consent,' also involves seeing that the course charted by the planning bodies is in fact followed. Firstly, there is the fact that the government is involved in the planning process and commits itself to its implementation; and secondly, the government has considerable sanctions at its disposal to see that this is done.

In Britain, neither the extent to which the government considers itself committed to the Neddy targets nor the means by which it would hope to achieve them are at all clear. Purely permissive planning is a highly attractive notion, and it would be a pity to forfeit the sense of collective responsibility for growth which it helps to instil. But, even at this stage, it must be seriously doubted whether it can have sufficient impact to achieve its aims. Ineffectiveness will soon rob indicative planning of the general acceptability which is its chief virtue, and it seems probable that future discussion will sooner or later be shifted to the problem, not of whether the planning mechanism should be given teeth, so much as of the form that they should take.*

* Postscript. Since this chapter was written, the economy has once again slipped off the 4% path. The newly-elected Labour government was immediately faced with the familiar problem of how to reconcile sustained domestic expansion with balance of payments stability.

The Council's membership has been increased to twenty-two (to allow stronger government representation) and its chairman is now the new Minister for Economic Affairs whose Department quickly absorbed most of the N.E.D.C. economic experts. The planning initiative will inevitably pass to the new Ministry, leaving Neddy as a discussion group of top people and responsible for overseeing the work of the 'little Neddies'. Whether these changes and the plan for the economy till 1970 which is currently being prepared will mean firmer government commitment to growth and the introduction of positive techniques for achieving it remains to be seen.

13   GLAUCO DELLA PORTA

PLANNING AND GROWTH
UNDER A MIXED ECONOMY:
THE ITALIAN EXPERIENCE

1. FOREWORD[1]

The presence in the Italian economic system of enterprises operated, in mainly indirect forms, by public agencies and, more generally, the formation of a public economic sector definitely distinguishing the Italian economy as a "mixed economy" are the outcome, not of a foreordained ideological scheme but of a series of industry-wide measures, often of an occasional nature, adopted by the government under the pressure of particular situations. In our country these measures, which are in general common to all economies comparable with Italy's have acquired particular importance owing to certain structural deficiencies proper to the Italian economy.

The lack of balance between economic conditions in the north and south of the country, already recognizable at the time of Italy's political unification, subsequently grew even more accentuated as the southern regions remained extraneous to the process of "differentiation" of the country's economic pattern effected above all in the twenty years that preceded the first world war.

In these circumstances industrial development was slowed down by

From Banco di Roma, *Review of Economic Conditions in Italy,* Vol. XIX, No. 6 (November 1965), pp. 443–458. Reprinted by permission of the author and *Review of Economic Conditions in Italy.*

Paper read by the Head of the Economic Intelligence Department of the Banco di Roma at the fourth Conference promoted by the Economic and Social Studies Conference Board of Istanbul and held there from August 23 to September 4 last.

The Economic and Social Studies Conference Board was founded in 1961. Its purpose is to discuss on an open forum basis the principal economic and social development problems of Turkey and thus bring to light some of the issues involved. In order to achieve this end, the Conference Board organizes seminars and conferences, undertakes scholarly research and publishes the results of its various activities.

At the fourth Conference, Turkish experience and various models of international experience in systems of mixed economy were discussed by qualified speakers.

[1] G. Petrilli, *L'IRI nell'economia italiana,* published by Dott. A. Giuffrè, Milan, 1964, page 21 and G. Petrilli, *IRI and Planning,* "Review of the Economic Conditions in Italy", March 1965.

the narrowness of the domestic market while, at the same time, it was this slow rate of development, together with the brisk growth of the population, that contributed to maintain backward conditions in a large part of the country's agriculture. This consolidated the characteristic dual pattern of the Italian economy which, as time passed, was further accentuated by the progress made by the more favoured regions and branches of activity.

This state of affairs, to which must be added a structural deficiency of raw materials, capital and entrepreneurship, accounts for the determinant role played by the State in the country's industrial development, both through customs protectionism and through forms of direct intervention by means of which the State made up for the deficiencies of private enterprise whenever necessary. It is important to bear in mind in this connection that the very formation of a "public sector" of considerable importance was mainly due to the performance of this task of substituting private enterprise in certain circumstances. This in fact was the reason why, in the years of the Great Depression, public bodies took over share holdings in many firms through what were known as "bank salvage" operations.

The conditions under which the reconstruction of the Italian economy took place after the second world war introduced a decisive new element in the working of the system: the opening out of the economy to foreign markets. This element, which made it necessary to align production levels to those of competing industrialized countries, had the advantage of stepping up the exploitation of production factors and of bringing about a rational and revolutionary transformation of the country's economic and social pattern, a progressive widening of the domestic market and the gradual reabsorption of the unemployed and underemployed.

As a result of these changes, the State's direct action in the field of industrial production was also concentrated more and more in key-sectors where large capital investments are required. The State thus acquired a potential capacity to guide and promote a general economic development. In addition it perfected its methods of intervention, taking steps to remedy at least in part the most obvious imbalances with measures taken less and less in a spirit of welfare assistance. We need hardly mention in this connection the far-reaching evolution that has taken place in recent years in the policy for the development of Southern Italy, leading up to a real process of industrialization with the creation of "development areas" in the southern regions and to the large-scale financial commitments of government-controlled firms.

Needless to say the transfer of economic power from private enterprise to the State and from the latter to public enterprises in the past fifteen years did not take place peacefully, with private enterprise deliberately waiving its rights to spheres that until then had belonged to it alone. There was a struggle which still continues and has been particularly fierce in the last four years during which the State has been taking more decisive steps to promote public enterprise in the field of production. This battle is fought by the economic class with all the weapons available: press campaigns to influence public opinion in its favour; political pressure in Parliament and outside; economic pressure on the labour and capital markets; the creation of strong coalitions of enterprises to increase bargaining power in respect of the political class in power and so on. The tenets upon which this struggle is based are the "economic utilization of factors," the "maximation of the national product," and "freedom of the individual," the possibility of solving the problems of economic and social development better and more rapidly with the system of private enterprise only. The political class in power instead bases its defence on two points: social claims and faith in organization and planning. In short the causes accounting for the State's growing intervention in the economy may be summed up in the prominent position given in the scale of values of the community to faith in social and humanitarian principles rather than to faith in individual and liberalist values.[2]

It must be stressed, however, that the Italian system of government holdings is a typical example of the indirect government management of economic activities.

A fundamental feature of the system, which definitely prevails over all other systems, is the fact that the State allots the shares it holds in private companies to public bodies. The latter obtain their powers from the ownership of the shares, just like private shareholders, and use them in compliance with the provisions of private law. This is a newer formula than nationalization by branches of industry. Far better suited than direct management to the requirements of a market economy in respect of profitableness and competition, it allows the State considerable elasticity of action in relation to the general targets set.

Government holdings are, therefore, one of the most typical aspects of the "mixed economy" which, at the present moment, characterizes in varying degrees the principal industrialized countries belonging to the western economic system. In an economy of this kind they are, as we shall see, one of the most suitable instruments for achieving the satisfactory integration of public and private enterprise.

[2] In this connection readers will find it interesting to consult: L. Gualchi, *Motivi della crescente pubblicizzazione dell'attività produttiva in Italia dopo la 2ª Guerra Mondiale,* Centro Italiano di Ricerche e d'Informazione sull'economia delle imprese pubbliche e di pubblico interesse (CIRIEC), quaderno n. 11, provisional text, not on sale.

2. Evolution of Public Enterprise in Italy

2.1. DIFFERENT FORMS OF PUBLIC ENTERPRISE IN THE PRODUCTION SECTOR

In Italy the public firms controlled by the State may be divided into three groups having different origins and features:[3]

(a) firms explicitly nationalized. Most of these are concerns that were nationalized prior to 1914 to ensure the orderly performance of public services and to set up fiscal monopolies: such are the Autonomous Administration of State Monopolies (salt and tobacco), Telephone Services, Post and Telegraph Services and the State Railways Administration. The features distinguishing this group of enterprises are that they are an organic part of the State administration—and must comply with the same rules— and that they are generally financed directly by the State Treasury. The operation of telephone services and of air lines—which however continue to belong to the IRI group—were added to this group in 1957 and the generation and distribution of electricity in 1962. For the latter, however, a special agency—*Ente Nazionale per l'Energia Elettrica* (ENEL)—has been set up which is not a part of the public administration, but a corporation having an independent administration and financing itself with its own resources or by having recourse to the market;

(b) firms taken over by the State following the bank salvage operations performed between the two wars, as well as after the second world war when a number of engineering firms were taken over by the government. These enterprises, which form the largest part of the group headed by IRI (Industrial Reconstruction Institute), established in 1933, are characterized by the fact that they are organized as joint stock companies and financed by the market either through the sale of minority share holdings or through credit;

(c) firms promoted by the State after the second world war to assist in carrying out certain trends of economic policy. The most important of these is ENI (National Hydrocarbon Agency), set up in 1953 to exploit, as sole agent, the hydrocarbon resources in the Po Valley and to compete with private enterprise in prospecting for and exploiting similar resources in the remainder of the national territory. This third form of intervention is also characterized by the fact that the enterprises finance themselves

[3] P. Saraceno, *L'impresa pubblica nell'esperienza italiana*, in "Il controllo dell'-impresa pubblica", Società Editrice Vita e Pensiero, Milan, 1960, page 49 and following.

largely with their own resources as well as by having recourse to the market.

In 1956 the Ministry of Government Holdings was created to coordinate and guide the activity of these groups of government holdings. Every year this Ministry submits a report to Parliament on the trend and programmes of the government-controlled concerns.

2.2. THE "IRI FORMULA"[4]

The IRI formula is undoubtedly the most characteristic expression of the Italian system of government holdings. In this formula we find a typical pyramid structure, at the top of which is the Institute, a chartered corporation, entrusted with the task of translating the general lines of economic policy laid down by the government into investment and production programmes for the enterprises it controls. IRI is therefore responsible for the general financial administration as well as for the guidance and operational control of the whole group. Because of the role entrusted to it, IRI is able to contribute both financially and technically to the solution of problems that cannot be solved by the enterprises themselves, complying with the principles of *multi-sectoral integration* which, as is known, forms one of the principal evolutionary lines of contemporary industrial economy. These very same principles, moreover, justify the presence, in the principal branches of the group's activity, of financial companies whose duty it is to guide, coordinate and control the firms operating in the same branch as well as to perform financing operations similar to those of private holding companies. At the base of the pyramid are the enterprises, which have operational responsibilities and carry out the group's policy.

The fact that IRI is a chartered corporation, whereas the financial companies and controlled enterprises are regulated by the provisions of private law, is sufficient in itself to establish a strict distinction in the "IRI formula" between the responsibilities of the Institute, which must execute the lines of policy laid down by the government, and those of the companies belonging to the group which must operate profitably. IRI is therefore the link required for the realization of efficient government intervention, on economic bases, for the development of the country's production structure.

The "IRI formula" has distinguishing traits also from a financial point of view. First of all it has an endowment fund supplied by the State Treasury which may be compared to the share capital of a private enterprise; then it may also have recourse to the stock market, especially through the issues of debentures, remunerating the capital collected in this way at the normal market rate. Lastly, at the level of the holding and operating com-

---

[4] G. Petrilli, *IRI and Planning, op. cit.*, page 123 and following.

panies, a further important contribution is made by private savings in the form both of minority share holdings and of debentures. In the seventeen years between 1948 and 1964 the requirements of the IRI group amounted to 4,082 billion lire in constant currency (1964 lire). Of this amount 3,680 billions, namely 90.1 per cent, were provided by the firms, the financing companies and IRI through normal market transactions, whereas government intervention in the form of increases in IRI's endowment fund was limited to the remaining 402 billions, equal to 9.9 per cent of the total. The fact that 8.8 per cent—namely very nearly the same percentage as was provided by the government—of the group's financial needs in the seventeen years considered was supplied by outside shareholders is significant. This would obviously not have been possible if the activities carried on by the group had not—though respecting the general directives fixed by the government—been performed *on the whole* in compliance with economic principles guaranteeing the safety and remuneration of the capital supplied by private investers and financing agencies. The "IRI formula" is moreover the empirical result of an historical evolution that has brought about far-reaching changes in the actual meaning of the group's presence in the Italian economy and in the very composition of its holdings.

As far as the group's structure is concerned, it consists of some 130 joint stock companies operating in many different branches producing goods and services: steel and cement, heavy engineering and electronics, shipyards, sea and air transport, telephones, the construction and operation of motorways, radio and TV broadcasting, some minor branches of production (textiles, paper, glass), four important commercial banks, an institute dealing in land credit and another dealing in medium-term credit. As already said, all the enterprises are set up and operate as joint stock companies; they therefore benefit from no particular fiscal or other facilitations and often compete with private companies in the same field both on the Italian and on the international market. The industry-wide holding companies are also set up as joint stock companies and all or the majority of their capital is owned by IRI.

Lastly, it must be stressed that IRI has succeeded in acquiring first rate "issue credit" both on Italian and on foreign stock markets, a fact due more to its size and to its composite nature than to its having a modest government holding behind it. Just as "General Motors" and "American Telephone and Telegraph" are able to finance themselves more easily than other smaller groups, IRI has easier access to the capital market than other smaller groups. This is not a privilege, however, but an advantage that IRI has gained by itself.

In the last analysis, and to conclude, we may say that, just because of its empirical historical evolution, the "IRI formula" is perfectly suited to the development conditions of an "open economy" like Italy's. On the one hand, in fact, it protects the freedom of decision of the public entrepreneur and stimulates competitiveness in a market where competition is ever keener, while on the other hand it adjusts public undertakings to the increasingly large optimum dimensions of entrepreneurial activities, which are dictated by the expediency of extending the latter to several stages of the production cycle, in compliance with criteria of affinity, as well as by the necessity of spreading the financial risk and of achieving the organizational and entrepreneurial integration of different branches of activity.

As can be seen, therefore, the government control of enterprises, as carried out with the "IRI formula," differs as much from the neo-liberalistic attempt to establish conditions of perfect competition exclusively or at least predominantly through legal measures as it does from the traditional Marxist approach based solely on the progressive absorption of the private by the public sector and attributing miracle-working qualities to the mere transfer of ownership. The "IRI formula" provides public enterprise with maximum conditioning capacity in respect of the economic system, both through the manipulation possibilities made available to anticyclical policies and through the "planning" of the activity of the public groups which indirectly "condition" a large part of private operators' choices. Against this background, it is clear that the economic management of the IRI enterprises ensures the maximum multiplying efficiency of government intervention in economic activities and consequently contributes to the growing dynamism of the whole system. It is equally clear that there can in principle be no contrast in this concept between the firms' economic utilization of factors and the pursuance of the public targets for which the whole system of government holdings has been created.

2.3. THE "ENI FORMULA"

ENI (National Hydrocarbon Agency) was set up following a decision taken by the government with regard to the economic policy of hydrocarbons. From a legal, organizational and financial point of view, the "ENI formula" is similar to the "IRI formula."

However its historical evolution has been different and so has the policy pursued, which was dominated by the exceptional personality of its late Chairman, Ing. Mattei. For our purpose, owing also to the fact that this Agency's activity is widely known, it will be sufficient to recall the already mentioned similarity of the two formulas.

2.4. THE "ENEL FORMULA" [5]

The creation of ENEL (National Electric Power Agency) has introduced a new form of organization in the field of public enterprise that is

[5] G. Stefani, "L'evoluzione delle imprese pubbliche in Italia e lo sviluppo economico," "Stato Sociale," n. 3, 1965 and G. Manco, L'ENEL, Collana "CIRIEC," n. 23, Milan, 1964, page 261.

somewhere between the inflexible structure of the autonomous concerns and the "mixed" form of government-controlled enterprises. It adds to and enlarges the sphere of public intervention in the economy. Unlike the IRI and ENI enterprises, this Agency is entrusted with the direct performance of the public function contemplated in its Charter. It is "an autonomous economic public body institutionally and directly carrying on entrepreneurial activity under a legally recognized monopoly system." ENEL provides for "the generation, importation, exportation, transport, transformation, distribution and sale of electricity" and "for its balanced economic development through the coordination and strengthening of the plant or a reduction in costs." It cannot depart from this specific function and undertake other activities on the pretext that they are similar or complementary. ENEL is therefore entrusted with the sole and direct operation of the electric power sector, without share holdings in companies at lower levels and without intermediaries in its relations with the Government and with Parliament. It differs from the autonomous concerns, which are strictly part of the public administration, inasmuch as—though it follows the lines laid down by the special Committee of Ministers and is subject to the supervision of the Ministry of Industry and Commerce—it is not a part of the public administration, has a corporate personality of its own and an autonomous administration, and recruits and replaces its personnel in compliance with the principles in use in private firms. As already mentioned it finances itself with its own resources and through recourse to the market.

3. Public Enterprise and the Economic Development of Southern Italy

So far public enterprise and the "formulas" described above have undergone two principal tests: their capacity to promote the redressal of regional imbalances and therefore to attenuate the dual economic structure between North and South, and their capacity to prevent, or at least correct, imbalances of a cyclical nature. Here we shall only examine the former. If we take past experience as a yardstick, we have to devote our attention mainly to government-controlled enterprises since ENEL has only been set up quite recently. Mention can however be made of two contributions due to the latter: the unification of electricity rates—which previously were nearly always higher in the underdeveloped areas of Southern Italy—and the steps taken to extend the distribution of power to the country. Both these measures are particularly favourable to the underdeveloped areas.

As is known, a process of industrialization is needed to reduce regional imbalances. But this is only possible at the heavy cost of large-scale public intervention of an extraordinary nature, the object of which must be to provide the economic and social infrastructures that are indispensable if economic activities are to be competitive and profitable and if prosperity is to spread. In Italy this task is allotted in particular to the *Cassa per il Mezzogiorno,* however public enterprises have been called upon to make a very considerable contribution to this effort.[6] We shall examine this contribution more from a qualitative than from a quantitative point of view, that is to say from the standpoint of "mixed economy."[7]

In 1957 the government agencies decided to avail themselves of the assistance of government-controlled enterprises in order to step up the development of Southern Italy. In other words, they passed from the stage of preparation of infrastructures and all the other conditions favourable to future industrial development to the stage of intervention, designed to alter the territorial distribution of the Italian industrial apparatus by moving down south—with independent timing and sometimes even prior to the completion of the infrastructures—enterprises capable of having a strong propulsive influence on the industrial economy of Southern Italy. This decision was embodied in Law 634, which made it compulsory for government-controlled firms to make 60 per cent of their investments in new enterprises and 40 per cent of their total investments in the South, obliged the public enterprises to alter both their investment policies—not only territorially but also at branch level—and partly also the organizational, technical and financial patterns adopted for the development of the system. Between 1958—the year following the approval of Law 634—and 1962, the investments of the public enterprises totalled 710 billion lire; in 1963 305 billion lire are estimated to have been invested, namely an amount equal to 43 per cent of the investments made in the five years 1958-62, while over 300 billions are estimated to have been invested in 1964. The changes that occurred in the pattern of the investments by branches of industry and lines of production were briefly the following: investments in services, power excluded, fell from 23 per cent of the total in 1958 to 14 per cent in 1963; those relating to hydrocarbons fell from 18 per cent to 11 per cent, while investments in manufacturing industries rose from 24 per cent to 71 per cent. Important changes also took place inside the manufacturing industry. The large expansion of investments in steelworks and petrochemistry, which rose to 60 per cent of total investments, was accompanied by a noteworthy development of investments in machinery production and sundry manufacturing industries, which accounted for 9 per cent of the total investments as compared with 3 per cent in 1958. The inci-

[6] G. Stefani, *op. cit.,* pages 262–263.
[7] Ministero delle Partecipazioni Statali, *Relazione Programmatica,* Rome, 1964, page 62 and following.

dence of investments in workyards and in the textile industry fell from 4 per cent to about 1 per cent. The shift towards the manufacturing industry grew still more accentuated in 1964, rising according to the provisional figures available to 77 per cent of the total investments; inside the manufacturing industry there was a more marked expansion of investments in sundry manufacturing industries—11 per cent of total investments—while the percentage of investments in the steel and petrochemistry industries fell to 56 per cent.

On the whole the development trends of public enterprises' investments may be summed up as follows: the first stage, in which attention was centred largely on the production of basic services, was followed by a second stage, in which steps were taken to make a breach in the social and economic conditions of the southern regions by means of dual action. On the one hand big plants—steel works and petrochemistry works—were set up that were capable of rapidly transforming the areas concerned and supplying products of prime world importance, in large quantities and at favourable prices, to a wide range of industries in Southern Italy, while at the same time providing investment opportunities for private capital in a number of manufacturing industries. On the other hand medium-sized and medium-small manufacturing plants were set up in particular areas down south where there was the greatest need for propulsive action. These plants were connected with the production cycle of the mining and manufacturing industries already operating locally and capable of forming a rallying point for new private enterprises as well as of breaking through the wall of local environment.

A point that deserves to be stressed is that, in many cases, the growing number of manufacturing enterprises was made possible by joint ventures in which organizational, technical and financial factors were contributed by private enterprises or by foreign groups. The taking up of equal, or more rarely minority, share holdings in productive enterprises therefore acquired growing importance as far as government holdings were concerned. The total impact of public enterprise, through the creation of basic services, and the setting up of industries producing goods of prime industrial importance and manufacturing plants, was of outstanding importance and attracted private investments which increased considerably in recent years, although the investments of public enterprises remained at high levels. This proves the importance of the role played by the latter in the development of Southern Italy.

However the action of the public enterprises is not limited to direct investments only. IRI, for instance, promoted an expansion of the activity of ISAP (Institute for the Development of Productive Activities), whose object is above all to foster the establishment and development of medium and small private firms in Southern Italy by taking up minority holdings and providing technical aid.

4. PUBLIC ENTERPRISE AND NATIONAL ECONOMIC PLANNING[8]

The five-year plan (1965–69) recently submitted to Parliament, after having been examined by the National Council of Economy and Labour, sets several basic targets which may be summed up as follows:

(a) development of the national income at a rate allowing the full employment of the labour force;

(b) stepping up of the rate of development of agricultural production so that it may better satisfy the growing domestic demand and allow exports to be increased;

(c) reduction of the gap between agricultural and non-agricultural incomes to be achieved essentially by increasing agricultural productivity and reducing underemployment in agriculture;

(d) territorial distribution of the new jobs made available in non-agricultural sectors, and particularly in industry, more favourable to the Southern regions;

(e) distribution of resources among the different forms of expenditure that will better satisfy collective needs (schooling, health, scientific research, transport, etc.), which have been accentuated by the economic and social transformations under way, without compressing the expansion of private consumption overmuch.

These targets are to be reached through a planning process carried out in a mixed economy in which both private and public centres of decision exist, each having its own sphere of action. Obviously the plan does not interfere with the various centres' range of action except in as far as coordination and links are necessary for the attainment of the targets. Any public intervention is justified by the necessity of reaching these targets. The clarity and precision with which these targets have been defined leaves each centre no doubt as to the range of its responsibilities and freedom of action in respect of the plan. The range of action and the degree of responsibility of the centres of decision differ according to whether they are:

(a) *Public administrations,* which play an active part in the plan. Their sphere of responsibility is clearly defined by their institutional functions. The problem, as far as they are concerned, is to coordinate their activities in relation to the implementation of the plan;

(b) *Public enterprises and corporations having organizational auton-*

[8] Ministero del Bilancio, *Progetto di Programma di Sviluppo Economico per il quinquennio 1965–1969,* Rome, January 1965, page 13 and page 23 and following.

omy and the enterprises they control; these must make sure that their decisions comply with the targets contemplated by the plan. This calls for a preliminary study of the specific programmes and a study of their results;

(c) *Private enterprises:* as far as these enterprises are concerned, the plan will act through the coordinated exercise of the powers attributed to the public agencies by the laws in force and through policies likely to influence businessmen's decisions. Moreover, the law enacting the procedures for the drafting and approval of the plan grants the planning agencies power—within the framework of the general system of consultation—to obtain information from industrial branch associations concerning the various branches' development programmes and, in particular, to apply to big firms for information concerning their long-term investment programmes. The fact of being acquainted beforehand with the lines of action the big firms intend to pursue will allow the implications of these programmes to be discussed with the persons responsible for their implementation, taking into due consideration both their compatibility with the plan's general objects and reciprocal adjustments with public investments.

The five-year plan also provides for the adjustment of existing institutions and regulations to the plan's requirements. It provides in particular that:

(a) the centres of public enterprise, while preserving their autonomy, shall be strictly engaged in implementing the national economic plan. In this connection the law on planning procedures provides for the unification in the Interministerial Committee for Economic Planning of the directive powers allotted by the legislation in force to the Standing Committee for Government Holdings and to the Interministerial Committee for the National Electric Power Agency. This Committee will be empowered to approve the investment programmes for one or more years submitted by the responsible Minister and the related financial backing of the autonomous administrative bodies in conformity with the provisions of the national economic plan. In order to solve the complex problem of efficiently inserting the financing of the centres of public enterprise into the public finance system, the Committee will express its opinion concerning the bills drafted by the responsible Ministers establishing increases in the endowment funds of the agencies administering public enterprises and, in compliance with the objects of the plan, will inform the Interministerial Credit and Saving Committee which of the various enterprises for which permission to issue debentures has been requested is to be given priority. At an active administrative level, under the terms of Law 589 of 1956, the duties relating to management and control will be performed by the Ministry of Government Holdings. In order to strengthen its powers of control and supervision, the acquisition or sale of government holdings by the administrative agencies will be subject to permission to be granted by the Ministry of Government Holdings;

(b) a reform to take place in the regulations applying to joint stock companies. The main points of this reform should be the following:

1. the amount of shares owned by the companies should become public knowledge;

2. the introduction of standard rules concerning the compilation of profit and loss accounts and directors' and auditors' reports;

3. the obligation for companies subject to the supervisory body mentioned in point 5 below, to draw up a consolidated group balance-sheet in compliance with a standard pattern;

4. expansion of the powers and strengthening of the independence of the auditors to be achieved in particular by having one of their number appointed by a Court of Law;

5. the institution of a supervisory body for joint stock companies whose shares are quoted on the stock exchange or that control other joint stock companies whose shares are listed, as well as for financial joint stock companies operating both in the public interest and in the interest of the minority shareholders. This supervisory body will be set up in the Bank of Italy.

After having been debated at length at the National Council of Economy and Labour, this general division of tasks and these legal reforms were accepted in principle by the General Confederation of Italian Industry, whereas they were rejected by the Italian General Confederation of Labour which is controlled by the Communists.

5. Conclusions

The conclusions that may be drawn from the brief and incomplete picture given above are:

(a) that the system of government holdings came into being and developed empirically and pragmatically and not according to a precise political scheme;

(b) that the "IRI formula," as also the ENI formula which is of a similar nature, has proved particularly suitable and helpful as it allows a high degree of "parity" to be maintained between public and private enterprise and in any case ensures sufficient market control of public enterprises, considerably reducing bureaucratic and political interference in the management of firms;

(c) that there has in practice been most satisfactory cooperation at all levels between public and private capital, particularly in respect of the economic development of Southern Italy. In this connection a fact that deserves to be stressed is the way in which public enterprise first paved the way and then granted assistance to private enterprise, thus helping to render increasingly efficient and flexible "the system of mixed economy" which is predominant in Italy and opening it up progressively to the "rest of the world";

(d) that, now that a planning policy based on consultation between the various categories of economic operators has been adopted, the system of government holdings, grouped according to basic lines of production, seems particularly suitable for determining, together with other forms of intervention, the general trend of economic development, while at the same time respecting the "rules of the game" pertaining to the economic system prevailing in Italy and the western world.

We hope we have succeeded in giving an objective view of the Italian experience of "mixed economy," an experience that may prove helpful in the great political and economic debate being carried on by the democratic forces of most of the developing countries. A general rule may be inferred from this experience, namely that the extent and degree of public intervention is a matter of forms and limits depending directly on the natural and economic-social environment operated in. Our experience also shows that the private ownership of means of production is preserved, even if with certain limitations, and that a fundamental role is allowed to private enterprise, even though it is recognized that the market can no longer be considered to control economic life completely, as its automatism leaves unsolved at least two fundamental problems that all democratic countries are now anxious to solve: the problem of avoiding violent and recurrent economic crises and the problem of developing depressed areas.[9]

In short, despite some conflicts which have at times been bitter, the Italian experience of "mixed economy" may on the whole be considered to have proved a success so far, since it has in any case protected freedom, the most precious possession of all peoples and the indispensable condition for all economic and social progress.

[9] G. Medici, *Appunti di politica economica*, Università degli Studi, Rome, 1963, page 75.

14 KARL JUNGENFELT

THE METHODOLOGY OF SWEDISH LONG-TERM PLANNING

The economic long-term planning that is now being conducted in a number of West European countries has grown up wholly during the post-war period. The origins of this planning activity are partly to be found in the circumstance that, at the end of the war, many of the countries that had been engaged in the war were faced with extremely difficult problems, the rapid and effective solution of which was felt to require a more centralised and coordinated policy. This planning was thus intended to facilitate the reconstruction process, and in some cases (e.g., in England) it went no further. But in other cases, the most well-known example being France, the planning mechanism was developed and efforts were made to mould it into an instrument that could be used to guide development into the desired direction.

Our own economic long-term planning, carried out by the Long-Term Planning Commissions, is partly the result of outside influences: the Marshall Plan required recipient countries to draw up plans covering the uses to which the aid would be put.[1] Long-term planning has subsequently been made into a permanent institution and has gradually been extended through the studies made every fifth year by the Planning Commissions.

Fundamentally, the French and Swedish planning activities have the same goal, i.e., to set out the development tendencies for a free market economy.[2] This form of planning is thus quite different in character from the relatively inflexible long-term programmes of the socialist countries. In the following I shall try to give some idea of the problems involved and methods used in macro-economic planning in an economy of our own type —a free market economy.

The basic problems that long-term plans of this kind are intended to overcome can perhaps be described by reference to the post-war economic development, characterised by lack of balance in many areas. The start

From *Skandinaviska Banken Quarterly Review,* 1964:4, pp. 111–115. Reprinted by permission of the *Skandinaviska Banken Quarterly Review.*

[1] See I. Svennilson and R. Beckman, "Long-Term Planning in Sweden," *Skandinaviska Banken Quarterly Review,* No. 3, 1962. This article also included a general methodological discussion, together with a presentation of the Planning Commission's Report covering the years 1960–65.

[2] This must not conceal the fact that French planning is more "programmatic" than Swedish planning.

was ambitious, with plans for extensive investments. These plans were motivated, at least as far as Sweden was concerned, by two objectives: firstly, to raise the general rate of growth and, secondly, to make up for the lack of investments in certain neglected areas such as roads, houses, etc. The high level of investment made it extremely difficult for the authorities to keep a firm hand on the outer and inner balance. This was very much the case with our own country, but the development in France in the beginning and middle of the 1950s is perhaps a still better example of how excessively ambitious plans can easily give rise to serious imbalance. This lack of balance was a sign that the authorities, in their economic policy, had not managed more than one side of the development programme: investments had reached the required level, but the savings necessary for the attainment of equilibrium—public or private—had not increased to the same extent.

Since savings in this context is the same as "non-consumption," the planning must explicitly deal with consumption, too. It is in this balancing of consumption and investment that we find one of the basic problems of planning: are we prepared to increase investments—and thus abstain from consumption today—so as to ensure a greater increase in our consumption possibilities in the future? In the first place, we must know how our future productive capacity will be influenced by different investment plans—a question on which our factual knowledge is at present extremely limited. In the second place, the "choice" of a rate of growth also entails a balancing and evaluation of the present generation's consumption requirements against those of coming generations. Here, economic theory is unable to offer us any well-established analytical instrument; in fact, it has not even been able to give a satisfactory theoretical formulation to the problems.

In solving this intertemporal problem, it is assumed that the given rate of growth should be attained at the lowest possible cost, i.e., with the smallest possible investments. This means that long-term planning is faced with another problem, i.e., it must aim at the optimum allocation of the resources of the economy. The desired structural development must therefore be studied and, against this background, the resources must be distributed between the different areas of use—between the public and private sectors, and between the component parts of these sectors.

We now come to a third type of problem that must also be taken into account. A problem of this type has already been mentioned: the balance between savings and investments. If the long-term plan in itself is not to lead to changes in the price level, planned savings and planned investments must equal one another in the accepted plan. Even if the objective of an "unchanged price level" is perhaps of a short-term nature, it can in this way guide the development in the long run. A target for the balance of foreign trade has, in principle, the same importance for long-term planning.

There are also other magnitudes that must be brought into balance in a non-contradictory, or a consistent, plan. The labour required for the planned volume of production must be equal to the supply of labour.[3] Natural growth of the working population and the extent of foreign migration are clearly factors that set an upper limit to the growth of the labour force in the economy as a whole.

These balance relationships refer to the whole economy. However, with respect to the distribution of resources within this given total framework, there exist a number of similar problems owing to the general interdependence between the development of the various sectors. If planning is to be consistent, it is necessary, for example, that the forestry sector in the plan should be "allocated" sufficient resources to satisfy the raw material requirements of the forest industries. In recent years, both the French and Swedish plans have taken problems of this nature into account.

PLANNING IN STAGES

There is clearly a very strong interdependence between these three basic problems in that the solution of one problem ties down the solution of the others. In order to get a real grasp of this interdependence, the plan should perhaps be formulated as a strict mathematical model, where the solution to each individual problem is obtained simultaneously. However, it must be said straightaway that this is not practically feasible: we certainly do not have access to such information that would make it possible to describe, in a total model, these complicated relationships in a way that is meaningful for the planning activity.

Both the French and Swedish long-term planners have instead used a planning model which, by means of successive approximations, arrives at a consistent solution to the problems. The method might be referred to as "planning in stages."[4] This means that first of all the basic development trends are set out, trends that can be assumed to be of importance for the individual firm's appraisal of its future development. Examples are the growth of total income, the growth of foreign demand, and perhaps the level of interest rates and the wage development that can be expected during the planning period.

[3] The restriction imposed by the need for balance is really that planned employment may not *exceed* the supply of labour, while full employment is an economic policy target.

[4] It should perhaps be pointed out that this method is not entirely the same as Tinbergen's "planning in stages" method, which seems to be a wider concept. Tinbergen's different stages refer more to the treatment of the basic problems outlined above, and only partly to the successive approximations. (J. Tinbergen, "Planning in Stages", Statsøkonomisk Tidsskrift, 1962, page 1.)

In the light of these perspectives, the plans of the individual economic units are then determined, i.e., their plans in respects to their demand for and supply of productive resources and goods. The methods that have been applied here have varied for different types of sectors. As far as private consumption is concerned, it has been determined—both totally and, to some extent, broken down by a number of product groups—on the basis of the assumed income development. Enquiries have been conducted to ascertain the future demand of individual industrial enterprises for productive resources—labour and investment goods—as well as their planned production. These "micro-plans" have then been aggregated into plans for sectors or industries, at the same time as they are reviewed by experts in the areas concerned.[5] The plans of the public sector have been determined in a similar way. As regards the rest of the economy, use has been made of expert studies which throw light on the future development in respect of the above factors. What is involved here is thus not a direct "fixing" of the plans of the individual units, but rather a "predicting" of the future demand for labour and capital, and the volume of production that can be attained. Similarly, it can be said that the supply of labour is "predicted" on the basis of expected population growth and foreign migration. In the planning process these forecasts are considered to be the aggregated results of the individual entities' plans for production, consumption, investment, and supply of and demand for labour.

However, a basic condition for the fulfillment of these plans is that they must be mutually consistent, so that the planned production on the micro-level gives an income development equivalent to that assumed in the "raw" perspective. The next step is to see how far the total, "aggregated" plan is in harmony with the previously mentioned balance relationships. One of the most important points in this context is, of course, the test associated with the question of stability: does the planned development mean an increase in incomes and thus an increase in consumption and savings, which will make possible the volume of investments planned by the business sector and the public sector? As mentioned earlier, we have the same problems for labour, foreign trade, the interdependence between different sectors, etc.

If we find that we have a gap in the balance relationships, then the aggregated plan is obviously not consistent; all of the units cannot have their plans fulfilled, and the problem will then be to decide which of the possible lines of development the economy should follow. This means that it is not only the final plan that is of interest for the planning activity. The step-by-step corrections that must be made to the original, aggregated plans are of high informative value. For obvious reasons, these have been drawn up on the basis of a "reasonable" appraisal of the future develop-

---

[5] For a more detailed account of the procedure used in determining the plans of the individual economic units, see I. Svennilson and R. Beckman, *ibid.*

ment. If disequilibrium is obtained in one or more of the balance relationships when the plans of the individual units are aggregated, we have put
our finger on the "tender points" in the development. The way in which
the gap is closed is also an important part of the plan, since this determines the direction of economic policy. A gap between savings and investments can thus be closed by measures aimed exclusively at savings or exclusively at investments, or at both savings and investments. The plan
must therefore indicate the economic policy weapons that must be employed if the balanced development is to be attained.

Planning "in stages" thus means that we feel our way forwards to a
final macro-economic plan that fulfills all the balance relationships. The
final product will be just such a plan, which really represents one of many
possible outcomes of the above-mentioned economic model. However, as
the Swedish long-term surveys are neither formally nor in practice raised
to the status of "public plans," there is no guarantee that the economic
policy will be formulated in such a way that the final plan will be realized.
In this respect, the French planning seems to be somewhat more reliable,
due partly to the firmer institutional and organisational planning forms
that have been developed there. A more serious obstacle to the realization
of the plans—and, for obvious reasons, this is the case with all planning
countries—is that the imperfect information on which the planning is based
gives extremely wide margins of uncertainty as regards the relationship
between economic policy and actual outcome.

Planning models of this type thus entail a concentration of interest on
one of the three problems that were earlier described as the basic problems of planning. The primary purpose of planning is to give a picture of
an attainable development. The choice between different possible plans
is hardly made to any great extent against the background of the other
two basic problems. The suggestions in both the French and the Swedish
long-term plans regarding the balance between consumption and investment have, for obvious reasons, become no more than suggestions. As was
mentioned by way of introduction, this problem has not even been given
a satisfactory theoretical formulation. As regards the allocation of productive resources among the various areas of use, the plans are—only to some
extent—intended to give resources the most productive employment. For
example, it is recommended that priority be given to certain public investments—roads, schools, hospitals, etc., where the market mechanism cannot
function. As regards the whole of the private sector, however, we have to
rely on the forces of the market as an effective allocation instrument.

In view of the above, it seems natural that the much-debated problem
regarding the "programme" or "prediction" character of the Swedish long-
term surveys is of limited interest. On certain points a survey of this kind
must be a programme—this is the case with the public sector's programme
for consumption and investments. As far as the private sector is concerned,

on the other hand, the plan looks like a prediction much more than a programme. The presentation of the plan in the form of *a single final* figure
for each individual item, without giving alternative outcomes, can probably be justified to some extent by the volume of work that is thereby
avoided. The most interesting alternative would be a radically "different"
alternative; and this would require an analysis at least as penetrating as
that for the main alternative.

THE PRACTICAL SIGNIFICANCE OF LONG-TERM PLANNING

It is clear that, if this form of "consistent planning" is to be developed
into "optimum planning," greater knowledge is required on both the empirical and theoretical matters. It is perhaps the theoretical deficiencies
that are presently the biggest problem, since all the well-formulated op-
timization criteria that economic theory has to offer seem, from a planning
viewpoint, to be far too abstract. What we need here is a specific planning
theory which gives these criteria an operative meaning and thus makes it
possible for our planners at least approximately to estimate the gains that
can be made through a redistribution of resources. In the second place, we
must find the economic policy instruments that will enable us to turn these
gains to full account.

However, we must not allow these circumstances to conceal the fact
that today's planning furnishes us with very valuable information. Through
its development alternatives it provides us with a framework for our actions, and through the "gap analysis" we learn about the weak points in
the development, etc. In addition, we have the extremely valuable detailed
information on the economic development that is presented in the Swedish
plan. This material must be of importance not only for those responsible
for economic policy, but also for individual enterprises. The latter's possibilities of drawing up relatively effective long-term plans must be considerably improved if society is planning the general economic development.

From the viewpoint of the business enterprises, it is perhaps the
predictions regarding the various commodity markets that are of primary
interest. It is evident that, for enterprises dominating a market, a survey
of the expected development of total demand must be of immense importance. Of course, it is not always the case that plans of this kind contain
specific, detailed forecasts for individual goods. Instead, we have to put
our trust in known relationships between changes in incomes and changes
in demand in order to determine the future demand for an enterprise's
products in the light of the income change indicated in the plan. However,

an enterprise's possibilities of expansion do not only depend on the development of total demand. The competitive situation and the dynamic behaviour of competitors in the given situation are at least equally important. It is possible that information on the existence of a gap, i.e., surplus demand or supply, can give some indication of the future development of the market.

If we consider the market for the factors of production, our interest in the gap analysis is more pronounced—perhaps to the same extent as in the information on the "planned" employment and investment in the enterprise's own sector. An analysis of the saving-investment balance can give valuable information on the development of the credit market. In this way we can, first of all, learn whether the development as a whole will be inflationary or deflationary, but the analysis can also tell us something about the "difficulties" in financing via the capital market and the costs involved, i.e., the level of interest rates, although the conclusions must of necessity be extremely uncertain. The way in which the gap is closed is also of interest, as can be illustrated by an example from the latest Swedish long-term survey. In the original plans there was surplus of demand for labour, which was assumed to be chiefly localised to industry. This surplus was eliminated in the final plan through industrial investments being increased so much that the original production plans could be met with a lower volume of employment. The implications of this procedure seem to be either that the development will be self-correcting in these respects— the increase in investments will then be a consequence of an increase in the relative price of labour, due to the excess demand in the labour market —or that an economic policy with a stimulating effect on investment activity will be pursued. The development since 1960 has in fact shown that industry has, in the main, kept to the higher level of investment planned by the Planning Commission.

A third type of problem met by enterprises in their long-term planning is bound up with the geographical location of industry. Up to now, both the planned development and the gap analysis have been discussed solely in a "whole country" context. In some cases, however, it is obvious that if the plan is to have any real interest for the individual enterprise then it must also contain analyses of the development in different regions. As regards the labour problem, the total balance can conceal appreciable surpluses and deficits in different geographical markets if the productive resources are not highly mobile. It is also obvious that we have other problems of a special type—i.e., regarding transportation, education and training, housing, etc. Unfortunately, the Swedish long-term planners have not yet incorporated regional developments into the overall planning activity—and it is naturally poor consolation to know that the French plans embody such analyses. It is to be hoped that our planners will follow the French example in this respect.

15   MORRIS L. SWEET

Decision Making and French Planning

International interest in the French planning system has been widespread. The structure and operations have been studied by the U.S. and other countries to determine its applicability to their national economies. France is not alone among Western European countries in embarking on a program of national planning, but interest in these countries has been less. Therefore, knowledge of the French impact is desirable.

The scope here is confined to an examination of the decision-making process and the role of various interest groups within the framework of public control. Several fundamental questions are explored:

How can a system of national planning be instituted without a loss of political and economic control to the planners?

Can elected representatives, in a country with a strong executive, be expected to exercise this control?

Background

What circumstances brought about a new approach to planning? In 1945, the condition of French industry was precarious; industrial production had fallen to 40 per cent of the 1938 level, and economic problems were not merely a postwar phenomenon.

Even before the war, France lagged behind most major powers in industrial capacity and productivity. Investment and modernization had long been neglected; the average age of machinery was three times that in Britain; the French worker had only one third the mechanical power available to his British counterpart.[1] Obviously, a formidable task was at hand and the government took a firm hand in guiding the economy.

Development of French planning was facilitated by cooperation between senior civil servants and managers of large business firms. Other groups did not then participate to any great extent, nor have they done so

Reprinted from *Business and Government Review*, University of Missouri (January–February 1967), pp. 21–29, by permission of author and *Business and Government Review*.
[1] F. Ridley and J. Blondel, *Public Administration in France* (New York: Barnes & Noble, Inc., 1965), p. 193.

TABLE 15-1. G.N.P. COMPARISONS (1913 = 100%)

Yr.	France	West Germany	UK	US
30	129	105	112	149
32	115	90	104	121
34	113	103	114	128
36	107	123	122	160
38	109	150	133	163
		(war period)		
48	108	111	149	274
50	130	157	158	297
52	142	190	161	331
54	153	220	175	340
56	170	263	184	373
58	185	287	189	375
60	205	334	207	408
62	229	366	216	443
64	252	403	238	483

Indexes of Gross National Product.
Appendix 3, pp. 248-9.
"Long Term Economic Growth."
Bureau of the Census, Oct. 1966, G.P.O., Washington.

since, but General de Gaulle's intervention and continued stewardship has given planning important impetus.

By protecting the planners in their reorganization efforts and by defying the charges that they were socializing the French economy, the government of the Fifth Republic made its most valuable contribution to France's economic revival. By its support of the young, progressive elements in the professional trade organizations, such as the manufacturer's *Patronat* or the landowners' *Fédération nationale des syndicats d'exploitation agricoles*, the government helped to break their monopolistic power and their traditional resistance to change in the name of the sanctity of all their *droits acquis*. Without de Gaulle's authority this conflict of interests would have been as difficult to settle as the conflict in Algeria.[2]

THE PLANS

The first three plans were primarily concerned with modernization of industry. Emphasis in the Fourth Plan, however, shifted to social and eco-

[2] Vaclav E. Mares, "The French Planning Experiment," *Current History*, Vol. 50 (April 1966), No. 296, p. 225.

nomic development on a broader scale, continued by the Fifth Plan covering 1966 to 1970.

With increasing prosperity, a wider range of alternatives, and the extension of planning to social areas, the decisions took on an increasingly political complexion, more susceptible to conflict.

The emphasis in the Fourth Plan . . . a conscious political decision which owed a good deal to the philosophy of the young civil servants who have been greatly influenced by Galbraith's *Affluent Society*. The Fourth Plan shows something of the influences of 'technocracy' and its tendency towards a *planification moralisante*.[3]

Though the First Plan was drawn up in 1946 under the sponsorship of General de Gaulle's post-liberation Provisional Government, it was not until the Fourth that, apparently by official direction or suggestion, the public gave much attention to planning. Planning became subject to almost daily reference in the press as one of the major accomplishments of national political and economic life and was interpreted in official speeches as a symbol of France's future grandeur. In a May 1961 speech, de Gaulle exhorted the people to regard achievement of Fourth Plan aims as an "ardent obligation" and to make the Plan *la grande affaire de la France*.[4]

THE STRUCTURE

Basic to an understanding of French planning is knowledge of the institutional framework, which in 1946 had to be completely new. At the center of the structure is the *Commissariat du Plan*, or Planning Commission, an autonomous government agency. It was originally attached to the Prime Minister's office as a means of facilitating coordination within the government, yet operating independently of the ministries. Subsequently, it was placed under jurisdiction of the Minister of Finance, partly as a result of his increased influence and partly to reduce the Prime Minister's responsibilities. However, in 1962, the Commission again became answerable directly to the Prime Minister.[5]

PLANNING COMMISSION

The Commission takes the initiative in developing planning policy at the first stages and finally draws up the national plan. The spade work is

[3] Ridley and Blondel, op. cit., p. 201.
[4] Vera Lutz, *French Planning* (Washington: American Enterprise Institute for Public Policy Research, 1965), p. 3.
[5] Ridley and Blondel, op. cit., p. 194.

done by specialized committees involving many individuals outside government. A few civil servants coordinate the work of several thousand individuals concerned only with particular segments.

To meet its responsibilities, the Commission has a large degree of administrative autonomy. The Planning Commissioner has never been considered a subordinate or minor official; he functions at the ministerial level and goes to the Prime Minister for the arbitration of conflicts. The Commissioner's position stems from arrangements made to suit the original incumbent, Jean Monnet. Since the distinction between politicians and administrators in the Fifth Republic has become blurred, the Commissioner can almost be regarded as another nonpolitical minister.

Though the Commissioner has no real executive powers, his influence is considerable. The caliber of the Commissioners has consistently been high as indicated by their subsequent positions. Monnet resigned in 1955 to head the European Coal and Steel Community. His successor was his deputy, Etienne Hirsch, who left in 1959 to become the first president of the European Atomic Energy Community, Euratom. Both Hirsch and his successor, Pierre Massé, were trained as engineers and worked in private enterprise. Massé's interest in economics has been strong as indicated by his 1959 book, *Le Choix des Investissements,* republished in English by Prentice-Hall in 1962 with the title, *Optimal Investment Decisions.*

The importance of the Commission's work should not be measured by the size of its budget or staff. The yearly budget is about $300,000. Of the 100-person staff, half are professionals; the Commissioner, Deputy, Secretary General, and approximately 35 young civil servants with varied technical, legal and economics backgrounds. Only a few are trained economists, but all are committed to the idea "that the state has an active role to play in the direction of the economy."[6] Most economic and statistical studies are done outside the Commission, such as in the economic research unit of the Treasury.

MODERNIZATION COMMITTEES

One unique feature is the Modernization Committees devised by Monnet. Nominations for membership are submitted by the Commission to the Prime Minister. For the Fourth Plan, 27 committees were established; 22 were vertical, dealing with a particular sector of the economy such as the steel industry, agriculture, and school and hospital construction; five were horizontal, concerned with such broad areas as employment, productivity, regional development, scientific research, and finance. The horizontal committees are responsible for synthesizing the information on general problems furnished by the vertical committees. A

[6] Ibid., p. 196.

large number of study groups involve another 2,000 people, including many technical specialists.

Committee membership is drawn largely from three groups: heads of businesses and management organizations; officials of the major trade union confederations; and government officials and experts from interested ministries. The background of the regular membership for the first four plans is shown in Table 15–2.

TABLE 15-2. PLANNING COMMITTEES

From	First	Second	Third	Fourth
		Percentage Distribution		
Labor Union Officials	16%	6%	7%	11%
Farmers, Farm Mgrs.	4	3	3	2
Heads of Enterprises	21	23	17	20
Civil Servants	24	30	29	20
Representatives of Mgmt. Orgns.	12	16	20	24
Other Experts	23	22	24	23
Total	100%	100%	100%	100%
Number	494	604	704	1,006

Source: Ambassade de France, Service de Presse d'Information, France and Economic Planning (New York, April 1963), p. 8.

The Civil Service has extensive influence over work of the committees by providing either the chairmen or vice chairmen, as well as the rapporteurs. The latter have the important task of guiding the work and primary responsibility for interpretation and presenting the conclusions.

HIGH PLANNING COUNCIL

The Council has not played as strong a part in the planning process as was intended when it was established in 1946. Membership then consisted of ministers in addition to representatives of various interest groups. Following the 1961 reorganization, it now has nine representatives of industry, agriculture, and labor, plus 19 members selected for their personal qualifications. Its activities are more effectively performed by the Economic and Social Council to which most of the members also belong.

. . . [The High Planning Council] after having been informed of the various phases in the drafting of the Plan, gives an opinion on the definitive draft proposed by the Commissary-General before the Plan is submitted to the Government and studied by the Economic and Social Council. In addition, it plays a supervisory role in the implementation of the Plan, each year studying the reports on its execution and proposing all appropriate measures to the Government.[7]

ECONOMIC AND SOCIAL COUNCIL

Initially created between the two wars and reestablished in 1946, this body has been categorized as quasi-parliamentary. Title 10 of the 1958 Constitution requires the Council to give an opinion on all plans or programmatic bills of an economic or social nature. Members are selected both by appropriate organizations and by the government to represent broad national interests.

As contrasted to the Fourth, the Fifth Republic uses the Council to a greater extent as a technical adviser with closer ties to the government than to Parliament, and there is a higher proportion of government nominees with specialized backgrounds. The major work of the Council is done in closed sessions by some 15 specialized sections with about 90 experts drawn largely from private enterprise. The Council is consulted at both preliminary and final stages of planning; its opinions are carefully considered.

PLANNING PROCESS

The Fourth Plan (1962–1965) serves to illustrate the development of a plan and the role of the aforementioned groups.

FOURTH PLAN

Early in 1959, the Commission began to study various assumptions on which to base the new plan, which would include goals for economic growth covering the next 15 years. The Economic and Social Council made general recommendations. The Commission advised the government to accept certain recommendations. And in 1960, the government issued directives to the Modernization Committees to prepare the Plan on the recommended basis. Twenty seven committees were involved for a year, their work guided by the Planning Commission. The Commission intervened to resolve conflicts and, as a last resort, the government was asked to settle intractable disputes.

[7] Ambassade de France, Service de Presse d'Information, *France and Economic Planning* (New York: April 1963), p. 8.

The Commission synthesized work of the various committees, after which the actual drafting of the Plan began. In 1961, the Commission presented its report, which was discussed by the High Planning Council and a month later by the Economic and Social Council. The Plan was then submitted to Parliament for ratification in the form of a nine line bill to which were attached three volumes containing 580 pages.

EXECUTION

Even after adoption a plan is not sufficiently binding. Without formal mechanism to assure execution, it can only serve as a voluntary guide for private enterprise. Even in the public sector, government departments disregard planning policy. In 1963, Renault, a nationalized enterprise, resisted government direction with respect to regional location policy by its plans to construct a new plant at Le Havre.[8] However, the government is not completely powerless and has indirect methods of gaining cooperation from individual firms.

Tariff protection can be granted to a firm's own product—or misdirected to others. The invaluable state loans for expansion—particularly desirable in periods when inflation has been confidently expected to transform the loan into a partial gift—cannot go to all companies. The advantages of having the production of one's own firm incorporated into the National Plan are not to be laughed off as minor; valuable tax and other concessions result from it. Nor is the French state a minor customer for French industry. . . .[9]

Insofar as private enterprise is concerned, planning has not been a restrictive force. "French experience has shown that planning is compatible not merely with the spirit of western democracy but also with a relatively conservative attitude to economic affairs."[10]

Decision Making

It is in the area of decision making, in relation to public participation and control, that a fundamental question has relevance to other democratic countries—the impact of national planning outside the economic sphere.

[8] Andrew Shonfield, *Modern Capitalism* (London: Oxford University Press, 1965), p. 140.
[9] David Granick, *The European Executive* (Garden City: Doubleday and Company, Inc., 1962), p. 77.
[10] Ridley and Blondel, op. cit., p. 204.

. . . the participation of the general public or at least their awareness that the Plan exists and has its importance, is needed to offset the dangers with which the Plan inevitably threatens the political life of the country.[11]

POLITICAL PARTICIPATION

Can Parliament act effectively as public representative and protector? Since its decision making power in the Fifth Republic is constricted, its voice in the planning process is likewise weak. The fundamental choices have been those of the Executive. The role of Parliament in the first three Plans was minimal. The Fourth Plan was examined by Parliament with practically no effort to make changes.

Surprisingly planners, with the support of the Executive, have sought to bring Parliament further into planning deliberations by designing preparation of the Fifth Plan so as to involve the Assembly and Senate at an earlier stage. Instead of being presented with a few simple alternatives on rates of growth—after the broad pattern of production and distribution has been determined—Parliament is asked at the beginning to approve fundamental decisions. After the various consultant bodies have developed the plan, it is again reviewed by Parliament. The Executive is still left with an enormous area of autonomous decision-making power.

The question arises as to why the approval of this largely ineffectual body should be sought. Apparently this move had more significance than merely giving Parliament token recognition.

Was it merely quixotry which led the (planners) to insist that they must have more parliamentary intervention—as if they were trying to assert that at a time when France was ruled by an authoritarian Government resting on the referendum, economic planning would provide a model of how to subject policy to the normal democratic process?[12]

To effectuate certain economic policies, popular support may be necessary. Agreement of various interest groups which are represented in Parliament can be a means of avoiding or minimizing conflict. A more specific reason could be the struggle Massé was having at that time with powerful groups within the Administration, especially in the Ministry of Finance, where there was hostility to the concept of planning.[13] In a contest for a popular consensus, parliamentary approval must be considered a key factor.

[11] Pierre Bauchet, *Economic Planning: The French Experience* (New York: Frederick A. Praeger, 1964), p. 250.
[12] Shonfield, op. cit., p. 143.
[13] Ibid., f. n. 36.

CONTROL OF BUREAUCRACY

The growth of contemporary planning demands consideration to the basic problem of who in government is capable of evaluating the work of the specialist bureaucracy. The traditional lines of authority and organizational patterns no longer suffice in a political sense. Even the Soviet Union has had to contend with the issue of how to control the technocrats.

(in France) A small number of technicians constitute the planning corps, a concentration of knowledge authorities whose technical-economic manipulations are beyond the comprehension of politicians and ministries. The former make recommendations as to policy which are influential on the latter, even though the basis for the recommendation is only vaguely understood.[14]

The difficulties encountered by political figures with generalist backgrounds in directing the specialist bureaucracy are depicted by attempts of the National Assembly to review the Fourth Plan.

For hours its members laid bare their frustration at being presented with a technical and complicated document, into the devising of which had gone so much ingenuity, skill and compromise, with a request for their endorsement.

When economic policy is subjected to the judgment of a great many experts whose efforts are devoted to the articulation of a master design, interlocked in all its parts, what effective role is left to the inexpert critic?[15]

Suggestions have been made that the relationship between economic planning and traditional legislative bodies be reexamined. If planning bodies, now supposedly only advisory, function effectively, they are bound to limit legislative power. One proposal calls for a bifurcated system of representation in which economic policies originate in one parliamentary chamber with functional representation. The functional groups would include industry, labor, cooperatives and other concerned interest bodies; their representatives would be elected to an economic council with legislative powers in the field of economic planning and all other matters would remain in the traditional Parliament. There would be a dual franchise, one based on universal suffrage and the other on social and economic status. Such a proposal was made by Mendes France.[16]

14 Neil W. Chamberlain, *Private and Public Planning* (New York: McGraw-Hill Book Company, 1965), p. 195.
15 Ibid., pp. 214–215.
16 Niles M. Hansen, "Indicative Planning in France: Model for the Future?" *Quarterly Review of Economics and Business,* Vol. 4 (Winter 1964), No. 4, p. 18 citing Pierre Mendes France, La République moderne (Paris: Gallimard, 1962).

Even though such a system with its overtones of corporatism may not be realized, the likelihood is that, with continued growth of economic planning by government, the Executive's role will be enhanced.

TRADE UNIONS

A repeated comment on French planning has been the weak influence of trade unions; for example, only 11 per cent of the regular members of the Modernization Committees for the Fourth Plan were labor union officials as compared to 44 per cent for heads of enterprises and representatives of management organizations. The lack of union representation could be a reflection of the shortage of qualified officials. Even when union officials serve, their influence is disproportionately less than that of employer representatives due to the ability of industry to supply their agents with background information unavailable to unions.

But the problem is not so much labor's minority position on the Commissions as it is in the three-way split in the labor movement, exclusions from the economic power structure that surrounds the Plan, fear of tying its hands in wage bargaining, cultural inferiority which may amount to an unwarranted complex. . . .[17]

The political weakness of the trade union movement should not be overlooked; fewer than three million of the total labor force of 12 million are members. Furthermore, there is a long tradition of anti-political feeling and participation.[18]

The three way division of the labor movement further fragments it. The Communist CGT (*Confédération Générale du Travail*) did not participate in preparation of the Second or Third Plans but had a minor part in the Fourth and condemned the planning system as organized support for monopoly capitalism.

Though the Catholic CFTC (*Confédération Française des Travailleurs Chrétiens*) has cooperated with the planning hierarchy, in 1959 it issued the *Declerq* report, which demanded a greater voice for labor. In discussing the Modernization Committees, the report stated: "It seems that everything happens as if the procedure was arranged beforehand in such a way that a certain number of decisions are taken by direct agreement between the employers' representatives and the civil servants."[19]

[17] Robert W. Faulhaber, "Ethical Aspects of Current French Economic Policies," "The French System of Planning," *Review of Social Economy*, Vol. 23 (March 1965), No. 1, p. 65.
[18] Samuel H. Beer and others, *Patterns of Government* (New York: Random House, 1958), p. 253.
[19] Malcolm MacLennan, *French Planning: Some Lessons for Britain*, Vol. 29 (London: PEP Planning, Sept. 9, 1963), No. 475, p. 349.

BUSINESS

There has been no lack of participation by certain segments of business. A businessman speaking largely for industrialists stated ". . . that business management realize very clearly that it has responsibilities for the conditions under which economic development takes place. I believe that it would be a dangerous limitation for management to take the stand that its responsibility is bounded by the framework of the particular business."[20]

The importance attached to planning by private industry is illustrated by the publication (for the information of its staff) by Shell-Berre Corporation of a widely circulated pamphlet, *Qu'est-ce que le IVème Plan?*

Business does not speak with one voice. Small firms with minimum opportunity for participation can be expected to feel skeptical about the benefits. ". . . there is no doubt that the activity of planning, as it is practiced in France, has reinforced the systematic influence exerted by large-scale business on economic policy."[21]

BUSINESS AND THE BUREAUCRACY

A major factor in the enormous influence of large business is the similarity in ideology of government officials and business managers. For example, practically all the giant firms are managed by graduates of the three leading engineering schools—which are also attended by high civil service and military officials.

Many business leaders spend one or two decades in government service before going into industry at the vice presidential or presidential level. In the Fifth Republic, civil servants from the *grandes écoles* have replaced the ministers of the Third and Fourth who were politicians without loyalty to the *grandes écoles*.[22] Staff of the Commission complain on occasion that civil servants, who come from the *ministère de tutelle* of a particular trade or industry, too often act as if they were representing these sectional interests. Whichever way it is, there is no doubt that planning activity has reinforced the systematic influence on economic policy.[23]

[20] Paul Huvelin, "What Business Leaders Think of the Plan," The European Committee for Economic and Social Progress (CEPES), *French and Other National Economic Plans for Growth*, Report from an international conference on French planning, Paris, June 4 and 5, 1962 (New York: Committee for Economic Development, June 1963), p. 52.

[21] Shonfield, *op. cit.*, p. 139.

[22] Granick, *op. cit.*, p. 78.

[23] Shonfield, *op. cit.*, p. 139.

If the success of planning is due to the business-civil service combination,[24] are the French paying a high price for economic growth? Should not the relevance for other countries be viewed closely from the standpoint of political as well as economic impact?

Conclusions

An examination of French planning brings to the fore a fundamental and pervasive problem of how to provide for public control over economic planning without impairing effectiveness of planning systems. Existing Western political institutions were not designed to encompass broad programs of national economic planning. Can these political institutions be made capable of assuming responsibility for safeguarding the public interest in the face of the growth of a specialized bureaucracy?

Economic planning has to be coordinated with, but not allowed to dominate the political apparatus. Changes in Western political institutions are needed which would bring about effective representation of the public interest but not excessively hinder operations of the bureaucracy.

[24] Granick, *op. cit.*, p. 156.

Readers may also find useful material in: Sherman Tingey, "French Economic Planning—Impact upon American Firms Operating in France," *University of Washington Business Review*, April–June 1966. David M. Wood and Sally Angela Shelton, "The Changing French Political Scene—the 1965 Presidential Election," *The Business and Government Review*, November–December 1966, pp. 5–16.

16

FRANCE'S FIFTH PLAN 1966–1970:
TARGETS, INNOVATIONS, AND FORECASTS

THE MAJOR TARGETS

The Fifth Plan applies to the period from January 1, 1966 to December 31, 1970. It took three years to prepare this Plan and define its main objectives on the basis of various projections of the economic situation in 1970, its final year. The Fifth Plan's targets, as adopted by Parliament, are:

Broader expansion at an approximate 5 percent annual rate of increase in gross domestic production.

A 24 percent-25 percent climb in private consumption and a steeper rise—39 percent to 40 percent—for social progress, foreign aid and defense.

Greater emphasis on social targets: 54 percent to 55 percent more funds for schools, hospitals, research and communications; 34 percent to 35 percent more for housing construction; 38 percent to 40 percent more for social allowances; and an average 4.8 percent yearly rise in farm incomes.

More competitiveness in French business, agriculture and industry by improving financing terms and giving incentives for building larger, better-equipped and therefore more profitable units.

More credits and personnel for scientific and technical research to ensure continued progress over the long range.

A new stage for the town and country environment planning program, which includes: continuing farm modernization, intensifying reparceling and reforesting certain areas; industrializing the west and setting up new universities and research centers there; converting the north and east to cope with depleted iron and coal mines, taking corrective measures in depressed areas like the Meuse Valley and the Vosges and expanding tourist facilities in the south; remodeling the Paris region by creating new cities in the outlying area and developing eight balanced "regional metropolises" to take some of the pressure off Paris; building or

Abridged from Ambassade de France, Service de Presse et d'Information, *The Fifth Plan, 1966–1970* (New York: April 1967), pp. 4–10.

modernizing communications networks, implementing a water conservation and pollution control policy and applying the new real estate reforms to halt speculation.

INNOVATIONS IN THE DRAFTING PROCESS

The Fifth Plan will run for five years, instead of four for the three preceding ones, and the added year is expected to broaden its effectiveness. The Plan's drafting was all the more complex due to intensive participation by the new Regional Economic Development Committees, the Economic and Social Council and, especially, Parliament. Whereas Parliament had previously voted only on the final text of the Plan, for the Fifth Plan it was called on to approve the Government's options during the crucial drafting stage. Thus, the Plan was drafted in three main stages.

STAGE ONE: PRELIMINARY FORECASTS (1963)

In stage one, the General Planning Commissariat drew up a chart of the economy for 1970, the final year of the Plan. The chart's purpose was to pinpoint the possibilities for economic expansion in that period and to study any problems of imbalance involved in exploiting them during the Plan. The chart was based on a continuation of the trends that marked the preceding years, but it had to take into account the Government's basic commitments for national defense, basic and applied research and aid to developing countries.

With this provisional data, the planners looked for points where future trends might diverge from past ones, and they changed their chart of the economy accordingly by simple extrapolation. They then broadened their range of possibilities, adjusting some of their original assumptions to take into account specific economic or social goals considered desirable by the Government.

STAGE TWO: SELECTING THE MAJOR OPTIONS (1964)

The preceding plans had gone from stage one directly into the Modernization Committees' detailed draft of the final document to be submitted to Parliament. The Fifth Plan, however, went through a new stage in the drafting process: a Report on the Major Options was drawn up by the Planning Commissariat in the first half of 1964, using data gathered during stage one in 1963, and combining it with that compiled by the Modernization Committees; this report was submitted for approval first to the Economic and Social Council and then to Parliament, which adopted the options by a law of December 22, 1964.

STAGE THREE: SETTING THE TARGETS (1965)

In stage three, the Report's options were translated into a coherent set of targets, based on forecasts for each branch of activity. Public investment programs were outlined from proposals by the Modernization Committees. The General Planning Commissariat, in cooperation with the National Institute of Statistics, made a synthesis of these proposals, from which the first draft plan was pieced together in the first half of 1965. The Government studied the draft and submitted it to the Economic and Social Council, which made some changes and referred it back to the Government. At the beginning of November, it was forwarded to Parliament, where it won final approval on November 19, and was promulgated as a law on November 30, 1965.

TWO INNOVATIONS IN THE PLAN'S CONTENTS

Taking a lesson from the Fourth Plan, the planners made two innovations that bridged an important gap in French planning. Until then, they had simply set the overall targets in volume—so many million tons of steel, so many miles of highway. Difficulties were encountered in implementing the Fourth Plan, not because of any malfunction in the productive machinery, as the figures prove, but because prices, costs and incomes rose too quickly. To prevent this from happening again, the planners built guideposts measured in real terms* and warning signals into the Fifth Plan. [Table 16–1]

GUIDEPOSTS IN REAL TERMS AND THE INCOMES POLICY

Guideposts in real terms for trends in prices, income and flows of funds were added to targets in volume to allow for contingencies that

* I.e., making allowance for possible changes in the purchasing power of the franc.

affect the general price level—for example, wage settlements and import price trends. The guideposts were set in real terms so that increases in the main economic indicators would be consistent with the general price level.

A 1.5 percent guidepost was selected as the most desirable for the annual rise in the general price level. This increase seems most consistent with both the production and social targets. A further refinement in setting the guidepost for the general price level was to specify similar guideposts for its major components—farm prices, public-service rates, rents, etc.

Since the 1.5 percent annual increase in the general price level is considered a desirable ceiling, the goal is to fall short of this rate. Thus, economic goals like balance in foreign trade and realistic public-service rates can be reconciled with a social goal like defending purchasing power.

The basis for the incomes policy is to learn what each Frenchman earns and to take steps to diminish the existing inequalities. The Government will under no circumstances allow excessive claims by any labor group to jeopardize the overall equilibrium; in contrast, it will try to prevent anyone from abusing a dominant position.

Under the incomes policy, the following average annual increases, in real terms, are planned over the next five years:

2.8 percent per capita for wages with no upgrading of skills,

3.3 percent per capita for wages with upgrading of skills,

3.3 percent for gross incomes of individual nonfarm entrepreneurs,

4.8 percent for farm incomes.

THE PLAN'S WARNING SIGNALS

The Fifth Plan contains a new procedure, called the "blinker" method, to spot inflationary or deflationary trends in time. Its warning signals flash when any one of the most important economic indicators crosses a point beyond which variations should not occur.

There are five such signals. The first two are for the general price level and the balance of trade; they signal any inflationary trends. The other three are for gross domestic production and industrial production, productive investment, and employment; they signal a slump or recession. These indicators should remain within certain limits. If one of them oversteps these limits, a warning will be flashed, triggering either corrective measures or an explicit change in one of the Plan's goals.

TABLE 16-1. BALANCE BETWEEN PRODUCTION AND USES IN REAL
TERMS

| Resources and Uses | Billions of $ | | Annual Growth Rate |
	1965*	1970	1970/1965
Resources			
Gross domestic production	73.38	93.63	5.0%
Imports	9.74	13.98	7.5%
Total resources	83.12	107.61	5.3%
Uses			
Net consumption	54.83	69.07	4.7%
Households	51.13	64.07	4.6%
Government	3.30	4.52	6.5%
(Civilian)	(1.52)	(1.92)	4.9%
(Military)	(1.78)	(2.60)	7.8%
Financial institutions	.40	.48	3.7%
Gross fixed capital formation	17.84	22.63	4.9%
Business	10.10	12.87	5.0%
Housing	5.40	6.34	3.3%
Government	2.26	3.31	7.9%
Financial institutions	.08	.11	5.9%
Inventory accumulation	.43	1.21	
Exports	10.02	14.70	7.9%
Total uses	83.12	107.61	5.3%
External account	+.28	+.72	

*Economic Accounts, May 1965.

OTHER INNOVATIONS

WATCHDOG BODIES

Another innovation was the creation, on March 2, 1966, of three interministerial committees: the Administrative, the Public Enterprise and
the Private Enterprise Committees. All three are presided over by the
Premier and include the Director of the General Planning Commissariat,
the Secretary of State for the Budget, the Minister of the Economy and
Finance and any other Ministers concerned. These three committees supervise the Plan's implementation and offer the Government solutions for
any problem that arises in the administrative, public or private sector.

For example, the Private Enterprise Committee's main concern is the
country's industrial expansion. It also takes up problems of environment

planning and mergers and concentrations by private enterprise. With an overall view of the initiatives taken by the private sector and an awareness of any shortages that may occur, the State will then be able to encourage new initiatives, to take them itself where serious weaknesses develop or possibly to discourage branches with no future.

ENVIRONMENT PLANNING BY REGION

A further innovation of the Fifth Plan is that it gives much more emphasis to the problem of regional expansion in the context of the long-range territorial planning program.* Since interregional disparities can act as a brake on expansion, a development plan must aim at balanced expansion between the nation's different regions. For that purpose, the newly created Regional Economic Development Committees were consulted during the Plan's drafting.

During the five years that the Plan is in effect, the town and country environment planning program will give priority to modernizing agriculture, reorganizing the Paris region and building balanced regional metropolises, industrializing the west, and converting and diversifying industry in the north and east.

Implementing the Plan

Every year the Commission for the National Accounts will draw up economic accounts showing the real growth of gross domestic production and its uses and other factors affecting the Plans' major options, particularly those on the balance between gross domestic production, investment and household consumption. These annual economic accounts will enable the Government to estimate the rate required to reach the Plan's targets by its deadline. If necessary, it will use them to look into any measures that could make for better implementation, such as changes in public-service rates or taxes. The Government will also watch the warning signals for possible threats to the achievement of its goals, so that it can impose countermeasures or make adjustments.

In connection with the incomes policy, each year the Government will follow the trend of the main income components, which include savings. After consulting management, labor and social organizations, it will announce the income guideposts for the coming year, giving the

* See the brochure, "France, Town and Country Environment Planning," published by this office in December 1965.

reasons for its choices. In certain specific cases, the Government could propose a guidepost that diverged from the general standards it had set.

When the Government announces the annual incomes guideposts, it may advise a greater effort for the most disadvantaged categories, even if that means doing less for others. Social security and low-income housing are two ways in which the Government can help the least-favored social strata, for in those fields it can take direct action on its own authority; in other cases it can only advise and, at most, urge.

Lastly, the Government has made plans to set up an Incomes Studies Center to investigate the situation in single branches of the economy, or even in single firms. In certain instances, the Center will also look into how the benefits of expansion are being apportioned.

Planning Institutions

GENERAL PLANNING COMMISSARIAT

The General Commissariat is an administrative agency under the authority of the Premier that possesses no power of its own, but prepares the Plan, submits it to the approval of the government authorities, sees to its implementation and assesses the results obtained. Headed by the Commissary General, it has a staff of about 40 planning specialists and 50 executive personnel. On January 22, 1966, M. François Ortoli was appointed Commissary General, replacing M. Pierre Massé who had held that post since 1959.

NATIONAL INSTITUTE FOR STATISTICS AND ECONOMIC STUDIES

The INSEE, as it is known, is an agency within the Ministry of the Economy and Finance that is responsible for drafting medium and long-term projects, making preliminary sketches of the Plan and checking out the studies made by the Modernization Committees. Its Forecasting Department analyzes the data used by the planners to get an idea of long and short-term trends that will be important during the Plan.

ECONOMIC AND SOCIAL COUNCIL

The Economic and Social Council is made up of representatives from all socio-occupational categories and serves as a link between the Modernization Committees and Parliament. Since 1960, the Government has consulted the Council's Investments and Planning Section before the final drafting of the Plan, and the Council has been invited to express an opinion on the final texts prior to their examination by Parliament.

MODERNIZATION COMMITTEES

These 25 Committees are composed of persons who serve without pay and are selected by the Government on the proposal of the Commissary General. The members include management, labor and government officials, and experts from the various Ministries concerned. Twenty of the Committees deal with the production sectors and the public services and the other five with overall problems.

REGIONAL ECONOMIC DEVELOPMENT COMMITTEES

The Regional Economic Development Committees are consultative bodies set up in 1965. They assemble local elected representatives and people from all socio-occupational categories who give their opinions on the Plan's economic and social implications in their region.

Suggested Reading

I. The United States

Ammer, Dean S., "Entering the New Economy," *Harvard Business Review*, September–October 1967, pp. 2–4, 6, 8, 10, 12, 172, 175–176.

Colm, Gerhard, "Economic Planning in the United States," *Weltwirtschaftliches Archiv*, Vol. 92, No. 1 (1964), pp. 31–56.

Ginzberg, Eli, Hiestand, Dale L., and Reubens, Beatrice, *The Pluralistic Economy* (New York, McGraw-Hill, 1965).

Heilbroner, Robert, *The Limits of American Capitalism* (New York, Harper & Row, 1966).

Heller, Walter W., *New Dimensions of Political Economy* (Cambridge, Harvard University Press, 1967).

Redford, E. S., *The Role of Government in the American Economy* (New York, Macmillan, 1966).

Reagan, Michael D., *The Managed Economy* (New York, Oxford, 1967).

Rostow, Eugene V., *Planning for Freedom* (New Haven, Yale University Press, 1959).

Soule, George, *Planning, U.S.A.* (New York, Viking, 1967).

Stevenson, Harold W., and Nelson, J. Russell (eds.), *Profits in the Modern Economy: Selected Papers from a Conference on Understanding Profits* (Minneapolis, The University of Minnesota Press, 1967).

The Future of Capitalism, A Symposium Held Under the Auspices of the National Industrial Conference Board (New York, Macmillan, 1967).

II. Western Germany

Arndt, Hans-Joachim, *West Germany: Politics of Non-Planning* (Syracuse, N.Y., Syracuse University Press, National Planning Series, No. 8, 1966).

Epstein, Klaus, *Germany After Adenauer* (New York, Foreign Policy Association, 1964).

Erhard, Ludwig, *The Economics of Success* (Princeton, N.J., Van Nostrand, 1963).

Pounds, Norman, J. G., *The Economic Pattern of Modern Germany* (London, J. Murray, 1963).

Reuss, Frederick G., *Fiscal Policy for Growth Without Inflation: The German Experiment* (Baltimore, Johns Hopkins, 1963).

III. Britain

Denton, G., Murray, F., and MacClennan, M., *Economic Planning and Policies in Britain, France, and Germany* (London, George Allen & Unwin, 1968).

Dow, J., *The Management of the British Economy* (New York, Cambridge, 1963).

Hackett, J., and Hackett, A. M., *The British Economy: Problems and Prospects* (London, G. Allen, 1967).

Henderson, P. D. (ed.), *Economic Growth in Britain* (London, Weidenfeld & Nicolson, 1966).

Johnson, W., Whyman, J., and Wykes, G. A., *A Short Economic and Social History of Twentieth Century Britain* (London, G. Allen, 1967).

Paish, F. W., "How the Economy Works," *Lloyds Bank Review*, No. 88, April 1968.

Prest, A. R. (ed.), *The United Kingdom Economy: A Manual of Applied Economics* (London, Weidenfeld & Nicolson, 1966).

Robinson, E. A. G., *Economic Planning in the United Kingdom: Some Lessons* (Cambridge, Cambridge, 1967).

Saunders, C. T., "The Development and Problems of Economic Planning in Great Britain," *Weltwirtschaftliches Archiv*, Vol. 92, No. 1 .(1964), pp. 57–90.

IV. Italy

Hennessy, Jossleyn, "Italy Renews Her 'Miracle,'" *Eastern Economist*, Vol. 47 (October 28, 1966), pp. 809–811.

La Palombara, Joseph, *Italy: The Politics of Planning* (Syracuse, N.Y., Syracuse University Press, National Planning Series, No. 7, 1966).

Posner, M. V., and Woolf, S. J., *Italian Public Enterprise* (Cambridge, Harvard University Press, 1967).

Review of Economic Conditions in Italy. Published quarterly by the Banco di Roma, Rome.

Stern, Robert M., *Foreign Trade and Economic Growth in Italy* (New York, Praeger, 1967).

V. Sweden

Fleischer, Frederic, *The New Sweden: The Challenge of a Disciplined Democracy* (New York, David McKay Company, 1967).

"New Paths for Sweden," *The Economist* (October 28, 1967). A special survey following page 412.

Svennilson, Ingvar, "Swedish Long-Term Planning: The Fifth Round," *Skandinaviska Banken Quarterly Review*, No. 2 (1966), pp. 37–42.

VI. France

Balassa, Bela, "Whither French Planning?" *Quarterly Journal of Economics*, Vol. 80, No. 1 (1966), pp. 537–544.

Bauchet, Pierre, *Economic Planning: The French Experience* (New York, Praeger, 1964).

Hackett, John, *Economic Planning in France* (New York, Asia Publishing House, 1965).

Hamilton, R. F., *Affluence and the French Worker in the Fourth Republic* (Princeton, N.J., Princeton University Press, 1967).

Lutz, Vera, *French Planning* (Washington, D.C., American Enterprise Institute, 1965).

Massé, Pierre, "French Methods of Planning," *Journal of Industrial Economics,* Vol. XI, No. 1 (November 1962), pp. 1–17.

Prybyla, Jan S., "The French Economy: Down the Up Staircase and Into the Market," *Current History,* March 1968, pp. 135–142, 180–181.

Shonfield, Andrew, "The Etatist Tradition: France," and "The Development of Planning in France," Chapters V and VIII of *Modern Capitalism: The Changing Balance of Public and Private Power* (New York, Oxford, 1965), pp. 71–87 and 121–150.

VII. Other

de Wolff, P., "Central Economic Planning in the Netherlands," *Weltwirtschaftliches Archiv,* Vol. 92, No. 1 (1964), pp. 181–206.

Shinohara, Miyohei, "Evaluation of Economic Plans in the Japanese Economy," *Weltwirtschaftliches Archiv,* Vol. 92, No. 1 (1964), pp. 208–219.

Silberman, Bernard S., "The Bureaucracy and Economic Development in Japan," *Asian Survey,* Vol. V, No. 11 (November 1965).

IV

Command-Oriented Economies

Introduction

As market-oriented economies are often far removed from the perfect market model, so are command-oriented economies operational departures from the pure command model. Just as there are many types of market economies, so command economies reveal an increasingly complex spectrum of approaches to central planning and public ownership. This has not always been so. With the exception of Yugoslavia, which opted out of the Soviet bloc in 1948, all the communist countries of Eastern Europe had, until about 1956, faithfully copied the Soviet-Stalinist blueprint out of political rather than historical necessity. This blueprint had been authored and applied by Stalin to a vast, underdeveloped country in a given historical period. The main features of the model are drawn by R. W. Davies in the last section of his article "Planning for Rapid Growth in the USSR," and in his "The Soviet Planning Process for Rapid Industrialization." Nominally, the Stalinist model was inspired by Marxist teaching (See Part II) and vaguely by Leninist practice. More fundamentally, it was totalitarianism applied with ruthless determination to the task of rapid, if uneven, economic development in a country which had never known political democracy and whose size and natural endowment made it potentially independent of outside influences. Transplanted to smaller countries, grafted onto very different cultural traditions, and applied to economies much more dependent on foreign trade than Russia had ever been, the model soon showed signs of stress. It was kept intact for some time only by the threat of massive Soviet intervention. China, North Korea, and Cuba had at one time or another tried to apply the Stalinist prescription. It would not be inaccurate to say that the peak of Stalinist command was reached in 1953, the year of Stalin's death. At that time, all command systems, as defined on pp. 16–18 above, (always excepting Yugoslavia) were the same; they all followed the Soviet pattern with only very minor allowances for local conditions.

The peak of Stalinist command was also the end of monolithic command. The model, with its emphasis on rapid, statistically measurable growth of output, its disdain for quality and marginal calculations, and its insistence on obedience to Moscow, became in time embarrassing to the leaders, and, more importantly, unacceptable to the peoples of the various countries saddled with Stalinism. It had even become outdated in the Soviet Union itself. In its obsessive concentration on physical output, its fear of the outside world, and its fascination with administrative means of resource allocation, it began to generate intolerable internal inconsistencies, disproportions, costly waste motion, and popular disaffection. In the Khrushchev–Brezhnev–Kosygin eras, the Soviets shifted their attention from growing at all cost, to a more subtle concern with the cost of growth. They engaged in wide ranging discussions of micro economic issues, addressed themselves to the macro problems of planning, and experimented with various types of incentives for managers, and different types of tools for central planners. The process legitimized by Moscow, was sparked by the Poles after October 1956, and was eagerly taken up by other Eastern Europeans. It was hastened by the defection of China in 1958, and by second thoughts in North Vietnam and Cuba.

Basically, the reform of the rusty Stalinist model concerned the role which markets could play in a command setting. In some cases (Poland, Yugoslavia) it also involved alterations of the structure of property, particularly in agriculture. The Soviet reform proposals and experiments are described in R. W. Davies's "Planning a Mature Economy in the USSR," and in Jan S. Prybyla's "The Soviet Economy: From Libermanism to Liberalism?" Albania's refusal to join the polycentric movement toward revisionism is examined by Jan S. Prybyla in his "Albania: Dependent Command." The movement itself is analyzed in "European Command Systems in Transition," and the articles dealing with Rumania, East Germany, Poland, Czechoslovakia, and Yugoslavia. China's early adherence to the Soviet-Stalinist model and later departures from that model are described by Prybyla, Perkins, and Waller. Revisionist forces in China are strong: they draw their strength from the "Red or Expert" dilemma discussed by D. J. Waller, and have manifested themselves most clearly in the period 1961–1966 (Prybyla), and briefly in 1957 (Perkins). The Cultural Revolution itself is, in many respects, the most acute expression of basic disagreement on developmental policy. Departures from Stalinist command are also noticeable in North Korea, and Cuba (Kim, Basora).

Devolution of decision-making powers from central planners to markets, coupled with the desire to retain strategic powers in the central planning apparatus presents analytical and political difficulties which are far from being resolved. Allocation of resources through markets hinges on the functioning of prices which reflect opportunity costs. Planning goals formulated by the centre may, and frequently do, conflict with market rules of the game. The question is how to combine centrally formulated goals with spontaneously generated market-type performance, a problem which has been met with before in Part III. The solution adopted by market-oriented economies has been to let the markets do their job and to correct market performance for serious departures from socially formulated goals. In other words, the market comes first, the (fiscal, monetary, and other) corrections come second. The difficulty with which command systems are wrestling consists in trying to approach the problem from the other direction. Markets are called upon to bale out command whenever command's goals and methods conflict with efficiency, or internal consistency, or create sectoral disproportions which threaten the goals themselves. The rules of command are imposed on infant markets to an extent which often prevents markets from discharging even the modest functions assigned to them by the planners. In the background there is always the reluctance of the Party to surrender an important segment of total power: the one which deals with the allocation of scarce resources among many possible uses. The inclusion of markets (and in some countries, of private property) in command systems implies always some degree of effective decentralization of decision making power. This appears still to be politically unacceptable to most Communist Parties. Until this essentially extra-economic problem is resolved, the decentralization measures will at best be palliatives, at worst failures.

What appears to be fairly well established is that the Soviet–Stalinist command model is not a universally applicable strategy and tactics of economic development and that it certainly is not suitable for complex, industrialized, advanced economies. The contention that it is applicable to large backward countries is challenged by China's reluctance to apply the model in all its heavy industry obsessive rigidity. Its inapplicability to smaller countries is illustrated by the rush away from Stalinist command methods in Eastern Europe. Czechoslovakia and East Germany have found it to be unsuited to their relatively high level of development. Czechoslovakia's push out of the Soviet model, toward market socialism, was checked in 1968 by the intervention of Soviet arms. In a sense, Part IV shows command economies in search of new systems, a quest which could also be detected, if less spectacularly, in Part III. The theme is taken up again in Part VI.

17

EASTERN EUROPEAN COMMAND
SYSTEMS IN TRANSITION

The Poles started it all. One of the mainsprings of the Polish "spring in October" in 1956 was the determination to have a more liberalised economy. The Russians followed suit—at a distance—groping for greater economic rationality in an endless and rather obtuse debate on the operation of the law of value. Eventually Professor Liberman produced his plan to change the indicators of success and the related system of incentives, which was misleadingly described in the West as taking the road back to capitalism. Nowadays the reforming élan has declined markedly in both Poland and Russia; today Czechoslovakia, Jugoslavia and Hungary are in the forefront of the reformers.

If one ranks European socialist countries by the intensity of their reforming zeal, Jugoslavia, Czechoslovakia and Hungary form Class I. Class II would be the two former front runners, Russia and Poland, and also east Germany. Bulgaria and Rumania qualify for the third class, in that order. (Albania, as usual, is a law unto itself.) Leaving aside Jugoslavia because its politics make it something of a special case, these placings can be correlated broadly with (a) a country's degree of development and sophistication and its dependence on foreign trade; and/or (b) its success, in the more recent past, in applying the traditional communist methods of central planning and control.

Czechoslovakia, economically advanced, has suffered a severe and prolonged crisis since the beginning of the 1960s. Hungary is in the front rank probably because foreign trade accounts for something like 40 per cent of its national income. East Germany's relative conservatism appears anomalous, considering its degree of development; but then its dependence on trade with the West is smaller, and its government is subject to special pressures which make it hard for it to get much out of line with Russia. Rumania, fastest growing country in our classification, alone seems reluctant to embark on radical change.

But whatever the variations, the dogma of the universal validity for socialism of the Soviet-designed economic model is dead—even in the country of its origin. It is now recognised that the workability of any

Reprinted from The Economist of August 19th, 1967. Originally published in The Economist under the title "Towards a Braver, Newer World."

model depends on many factors, including the type of economic environment and the technology of planning itself: what has to be put up with in the era of the abacus is not good enough in the era of electronics. Looking back over the half-century since the Russian Revolution, it can be seen that the old Russian planning system did good service in the primitive, largely self-sufficient country of its origin during the breakthrough phase of accelerated growth. Ironically, it was copied by satellite governments in central and eastern Europe at the very time when its declining efficiency in Russia itself was becoming clear.

The basic problem the Soviet reformers found themselves facing was how to move from the system of direct command from the centre to more indirect means of guidance without affecting the primacy of planning goals. For the Russian reformers—and this fact is fundamental—had no intention of impairing this primacy. At one point Liberman's ideas of profit maximisation seemed to offer a solution. But a closer look made clear what is in fact intuitively obvious: that profit maximisation leads to the most efficient use of resources only if the profit calculation is based on genuine opportunity-cost prices—that is, the prices which would be formed in an ideally free and competitive market. Russian economists appear to have explained to their political leaders that even though in theory it should be possible to compute all such prices from a detailed model of the Soviet economy, in practice it was beyond their resources in spite of all the progress in electronic calculation.

Why then do the Czechs—well known for their sound practical sense, and no doubt as aware as anyone of what is at stake—show less timidity? They seem to believe that the harm the traditional system is doing them in their special conditions is increasing so fast that they must take the plunge. One can see their point. In the first half of the 1960s, the rate of growth of Czechoslovakia's national income dropped to a mere quarter of what it was in the first half of the 1950s. Productivity of investment dropped to only one-sixth of its 1950-55 level. By contrast, our Class II and Class III countries feel that it is more prudent to mark time, to watch the Jugoslavs' efforts to get their system right and the more cautious progress of Czechoslovakia and Hungary before deciding whether they should follow.

Practically all east European countries, whether bold or timid, do share certain aims at the moment. All of them are trying to reduce the number of "imperative" plan targets; to give managers of firms greater freedom in fixing their product-mix and in patterning inputs; to leave them more elbow-room in investment; to put greater emphasis on net returns and therefore on costs, rather than on global output.

All this points in the end to price reform: everywhere the professed purpose is to "activise" the price system—make it an active tool of control and guidance rather than the passive instrument of conventional accountancy. The reformers believe prices should be based on full cost plus margins. One must stress full cost—for there is a striking novelty: the inclusion of a charge on fixed capital. With little concern about the ideological implications, an interest-like levy on productive assets is being employed throughout eastern Europe, with a parallel charge on the other prime factor of production, labour. The purpose is to strengthen discipline in using scarce resources and ensure that capital is not substituted for labour faster than their relative costs would justify at the level of the firm.

Controls on wages, too, are to be relaxed. Basic wages continue to be centrally fixed, but the size of the total wage is to be for the manager to decide. In addition, countries with a strong interest in foreign trade—notably Czechoslovakia and Hungary—are trying to adjust domestic price relations to those prevailing in the world markets, as the Jugoslavs have done. The east Germans have just completed a solid reform of their industrial prices. This looks a tempting short cut to efficiency, but the consequences for economies insulated for decades from capitalist competition does not seem to have been thought out fully.

Otherwise there is no reason why the price reforms as designed should not be carried out quite smoothly. This is true also of integrating the hitherto divorced spheres of inter-industrial and consumer prices. True, the level of factory prices is likely to go up in Czechoslovakia by between a quarter and a half (the rise may be somewhat less in Hungary). But this by itself need not affect consumer prices, and thereby costs of living and wages. Under the traditional system the insulator of the two spheres is the turnover tax, a tax differentiated so as to make the prices charged to the housewife a sort of generalised points-rationing card such as Britain used during the Second World War. In the Russian-designed traditional system, the tax and profit transfers are in substance twins performing the same roles. Hence, changes in factory prices can be absorbed by adjusting the tax.

Self-financing is to become of major importance. The state's own investment activity is supposed to be confined to determining the main structural lines of the economy. Thus centrally controlled investment—which amounted to as much as nine-tenths of all investment only a few years ago—is expected to drop in Hungary to no more than a quarter of the total and to something like one-sixth in Czechoslovakia. The state will have to influence the direction of investment mainly by credit control through the banks and by taxation. This would amount to a drastic relaxation of the state's grip on the economy.

Do the reforms stand a chance of ensuring efficiency? Once again the crucial question is prices—the key instrument on which these countries are in future to rely for steering their economies. Significantly, for the foreseeable future the Czechs propose to keep strong central controls in operation: free fixing of prices will apply to no more than one-fifteenth of total commodity output and only to commodities of lesser importance. The remainder continue to be centrally determined, or—which in practice boils down to more or less the same—to have centrally fixed price ceilings. The chances of securing efficiency in allocating resources through computed full-cost prices are very uncertain. We are back to square one—the impossibility of calculating real opportunity-cost prices which led Russia virtually to abandon Libermanism.

It seems the Hungarians, whose reforms will be introduced next year, are now inclined to face this problem squarely and rely on the market whenever the central computation of scarcity prices is technically not ready to take over. It appears from their announced timetable that after a short transition, as much as four-fifths of the prices in the key area of manufactures are to be formed in the market by the free interplay of competitive forces. The Hungarians seem to believe that they will be able to handle the distorting effects of monopoly power in their system.

This article (like those that follow) is mostly about the difficulties in the way of the reformers, and the inconsistencies of some of the things they are trying to do. (We have not written about the achievements of socialism in such fields as education, health and social welfare, because these are achievements of distribution, whereas the reform has to do with making total production more efficient.) We believe that the reform has to be attempted, and that the attempt is very good news indeed for both East and West. Our point is really that the reformers should and must go farther, and the following article will argue that the process of decentralisation and liberalisation must be allowed to spill over further into political and cultural life too if it is to bear full fruit—even in economics.

It must be stressed repeatedly that the reform, and the further liberalisation we would like to see, imply in themselves no abandonment of socialism. Tight central planning, like the censorship of ideas, is not an intrinsic or essential part of socialism; it was only Stalinist Russia that made it appear so, and eastern Europe is still living out the aftermath. In fact, if and when Czechoslovakia and Hungary complete the reforms on which they are now engaged, the world will for the first time see at work the "market socialism" designed by the Polish economist Oskar Lange in his famous blueprint of the 1930s. Even Lange saw how hard it was to stop there. Shortly before he died, he suggested that "current" economic life might be left entirely to the market, while its dynamic development would still have to be guided by a central long-term plan.

It is patently wrong to talk of capitalistic tendencies in the reform movement (Russia's Libermanism has often been misinterpreted in the West as a drive away from socialism towards capitalism). But in the end it does raise fundamental problems of ideology. What is at issue is this: is the mechanism borrowed from capitalism workable for socialism, without diluting socialism's whole content? The mechanism has been evolved to go with wide private ownership of the means of production, private enterprise, private capital accumulation: consequently, as related to the relatively modest role of the capitalist state. Significantly, at times when the functions of this state had to be drastically expanded—in war, for example—the mechanism had to be at least partly switched off. The aspirations of a socialist state are almost by definition much greater. In particular it assumes much greater responsibility for the shape of the future. In fact, once productive capital formation is socialised, the state can hardly disclaim responsibility for ensuring the economy's growth, and determining the pace and pattern. The mechanism which has proved adequate for capitalism (though it has not avoided a great deal of waste) could well show a chronic tendency to overheat and break down when the socialist state tries to carry out its self-appointed functions in a competitive market.

The proof of this pudding can only be in the eating. Jugoslavia does not provide a conclusive test case. First, the system it is trying has not yet achieved enough consistency. For example, decentralisation has been restricted on the crucial point of pricing; and the Jugoslav reformers have yet to demonstrate that this is really only provisional. Further, the problem of financial control in this system has not yet been solved. But in any case it is doubtful whether a still underdeveloped economy—with a figure for industrial output per caput near the bottom of the European socialist group—could produce a definite test of the model.

18   R. W. DAVIES

PLANNING FOR RAPID GROWTH IN THE U.S.S.R.[1]

THE BACKGROUND

The Soviet planning system emerged in the specific environment of post-revolutionary Russia of the 1920's, in response to the government's objective of rapid industrial growth. Soviet experience can be effectively examined only if this context is understood.

In the first article, we therefore examine

(a) the Soviet environment in the 1920's;

(b) the schemes or models of industrialisation propounded at that time; and

(c) the principal features of planned industrialisation, 1928–1955.

(A) THE ENVIRONMENT

In the mid-1920's, a largely state-owned industrial sector was linked with small-scale peasant family farms through a market which was partly state-controlled and partly privately-controlled. It was a mixed economy, from the point of view both of ownership and of control.

1. THE URBAN SECTOR

(i) Since the 1870's, the tsarist state had fostered the growth of an efficient railway network and of some modern industries (oil and coal,

From *Economics of Planning*, Vol. 5, No. 1–2, 1965, pp. 74–86. Reprinted by permission of the author and *Economics of Planning*.

[1] This is the first of three articles summarising a course on Soviet planning given at the Institute of Social Studies, The Hague, Holland, and at the Centre for Russian and East European Studies, University of Birmingham, England.—The first article deals with the circumstances in which Soviet industrialisation was launched, and summarises the main statistical features of the period of intensive industrialisation. The second article discusses the Soviet planning process during the period of intensive industrialisation. The third article considers the problems of planning a more mature economy. A series of articles on recent Soviet work on the reform of the planning system will complete this outline.

iron and steel, transport engineering and agricultural implements). It supported the new industries by protective tariffs, by its credit and currency policy, by providing facilities for foreign investors and by direct state orders for industrial output (primarily for the railways and the armed forces). Much of this development was financed by foreign loans direct to the state and by direct foreign investment in industry. By 1900, most of the railway system had been nationalised; in the decade before the first world war, there was considerable cartelisation in the new industries, especially in coal and steel. During the first world war, state war industry committees undertook the physical allocation of the output of the major industries: their controls extended to previously highly competitive industries such as cotton textiles.

(ii) At the time of the 1917 Revolution, then, factory industry, employing some three million persons, was to some extent state-sponsored and even state-organised. The Communists were able to use existing instruments of control to administer industry, which was for the most part nationalised during the Civil War (1918–1920).

2. THE RURAL SECTOR

(i) The peasants bound to landowners were liberated from personal serfdom in 1861: the next fifty years saw the economic and political decline of the land-owning nobility and the rise of commercial agriculture. By 1917, there were some specialised commercial estates using relatively capital-intensive techniques. In the villages trade made inroads into traditional communal agricultural patterns: part of the village population was proletarianised, another part became better off or "*kulak*" farmers. The population of the Russian Empire more than doubled between 1861 and 1917, but this population explosion was not accompanied by any fundamental change of techniques: in 1917 most of the peasantry still worked the land in traditional ways—three-field rotation and the strip system, with periodic compulsory redivision of the land by the village commune or *mir*, were normal. Land hunger resulted.

(ii) The agrarian revolution 1917–1918 resulted in the seizure of the estates of landowners and industrialists and the dividing up of land and property among the mass of the peasants. At the same time, greater equality was established within the village, and the economic power of the *kulak* was diminished. The consequences of this social upheaval were highly unfavourable to economic growth. Estate-owner and *kulak* had supplied a substantial part of off-farm sales of agricultural products before the revolution (e. g. some 70 per cent of marketed grain). Their elimination, and the strengthening of the subsistence farmer, had the result that the proportion of total output sold off-farm drastically declined in the

1920's: grain production, for example, reached the pre-war level by 1927, but only about half the prewar quantity was marketed.

3. STATE POLICY

(i) In the mid-1920's, the Soviet government influenced the economy through the following instruments:

(a) nationalised industry and railways—prices and charges were regulated by the government, which also operated some physical controls;

(b) the state budget;

(c) currency and credit—the whole banking system was nationalised;

(d) foreign trade—under the state monopoly, exports could be undertaken and imports obtained only with a specific licence from the central authorities.

(ii) Experience showed that these instruments gave the state a very considerable influence over the short-term situation, but that over a period of more than a few months peasant sales were very elastic: if the state allowed prices of industrial goods sold to the peasant to rise relatively to the prices of agricultural crops, the peasant would cut back his own area and reduce his off-farm sales. But state industry was in a monopolistic or oligopolistic position. If equilibrium were to be maintained on the domestic market, industrial prices therefore needed to be controlled. Bank credits to industry also had to be carefully regulated.

(iii) Nevertheless, by 1926 the state had succeeded in shifting the economy towards the desired rapid expansion of industry:

(a) there had been a substantial reduction in foreign trade turnover due to the decline in off-farm sales and hence in grain exports; however, import controls enabled the amount of industrial equipment imported to equal the prewar level;

(b) terms of trade were to some extent turned against the village and in favour of industry, as compared with 1913;

(c) control of prices and (through the budget) of investment enabled the share of urban building and of the railways in total investment to be reduced, and the proportion of investment in industry to be increased: hence, although total investment was lower than in 1909–1913, investment in industry was by 1926 equal to or higher than pre-war, even though pre-war industrial investment was partly financed by foreign capital.

It can thus be concluded that planning controls by the state were already sufficient in the mid-twenties to enable a modest programme of industrialisation to be initiated.

(B) Proposed Models of Industrialisation

There was considerable scepticism in the mid-1920's about the possibility of permanently following the kind of policy just outlined. Success had depended, it was thought, on the luck of a couple of good harvests; the level of investment was widely believed to be insufficient to enable industry to grow more rapidly than it had before the war (on the latter point, at least, no proper quantitative studies were undertaken). Four possible strategies for development were suggested; they could be followed separately or jointly:

1. FOREIGN INVESTMENT

It was believed by some politicians and economists that rapid expansion would be possible only through substantial investments from abroad, in the form of credits or by the offering of direct "concessions" to foreign firms to build plants under licence in the USSR. But the prevailing opinion in the Communist Party was hostile to extensive dependence on foreign capitalism, and in any case substantial success in the concessions policy was unlikely in view of the hostility to the Soviet government and the suspicions of foreign firms (this was partly because the Soviet government had abrogated the international debts of the previous regime). In the event, Soviet industrialisation was to be supported by foreign credit and investment only to a minor extent; and it is therefore in its methods of handling internal capital that Soviet policy is of most interest to other industrialising countries.

2. RELIANCE ON AGRICULTURAL DEVELOPMENT

An influential group of economists argued that the overall growth rate would be maximised by concentrating investment in agriculture, from which maximum returns could be obtained. Some people in this group frankly favoured a strong private peasantry and were little concerned with the rate of industrial growth (e.g. Kondratiev of "long cycles" fame). Others considered that high agricultural output would enable a high level of exports, and that this in turn would make it possible to import industrial machinery (which could often be purchased abroad at half its internal costs): the optimum path to industrialisation therefore lay through agricultural development (this group included Sokolnikov, in charge of finance for many years).

This approach was firmly rejected by the government. The assumption that agricultural investment could yield maximum returns was challenged (without much solid evidence on either side). It was argued that strengthening of the private peasant would be socially and politically dangerous, as would dependence on the world market for essential equipment. The prevailing view by 1926 was that the USSR must as soon as possible become self-sufficient in all major industrial products.

3. "EXPLOITATION" OF THE PEASANT

Preobrazhensky, Trotsky's principal economic adviser, argued that Soviet Russia must pass through a stage of "primitive socialist accumulation" analogous to the "primitive accumulation" postulated by Marx in his analysis of the history of capitalism. Part of the product or incomes of the small-scale peasant economies must be exploited or "alienated" by the state, through taxation or price policy, and used to expand industry.

At the time, this policy was firmly rejected by the government on the grounds that it would undermine the association between the industrial worker and the peasant on which political stability was grounded.

4. THE "REGIME OF ECONOMY"

The optimistic prevailing opinion among advisers to the Soviet government—which found expression in the first five-year plan as approved in the spring of 1929—was that sufficient savings for industrialisation could be found within industry itself, or at any rate within the state sector. If the productivity of labour rose more rapidly than money wages, the resulting savings could be used both to finance investment (from increased profits) and to reduce industrial prices, so as to improve the terms of trade for the peasant and induce him to increase his off-farm sales. A policy of thrift throughout the state administration would supplement the gain from the productivity : wages gap. Investment in industry would be accompanied by a rising standard of living in town and country.

This policy had partial successes in the mid-1920's. The objection to it was rather that it could not be expected to yield a high rate of savings and a rapid rate of growth.

All these schemes shared certain assumptions about the future of the Soviet economy:

(i) the market relationship between peasant farm and state industry would continue over a long period. Even Preobrazhensky did not wish to raise the rate of "exploitation" to the point at which the peasant would cut back on sales; and did not envisage any coercive action, apart from taxation, even against the *kulak* peasants. This was a very severe constraint on state policy. Preobrazhensky, for example, argued that shortages of industrial goods meant that more industrial output was required, but he was never able to show in practical terms how industrial investment could be financed during the gestation period of new construction projects.

(ii) urban standard of living would rise steadily. While the "agrarianisers" argued that the terms of trade were too favourable to industry and to the industrial worker, even they did not envisage a cut in the real wages of the worker. As the number of industrial workers increased, the higher urban standards would spread to an increasing proportion of the Soviet population (former peasants or unemployed).

(iii) the currency would remain stable or even appreciate in value. In the orthodox financial atmosphere of the 1920's, even mildly inflationary methods of financing new investment were rejected by almost everyone.

The essence of Stalin's solution to the problem of industrialisation was that in practice, though not in theory, he refused to work within these three constraints. This enabled him to combine elements of all the four models of industrialisation into a new synthesis.

(c) The Principal Features of Planned Industrialisation, 1928-1955

By the end of the 1920's the Soviet government had accepted a large range of sub-goals as corollaries to its general policy of industrialisation. These included:

1. A very high rate of industrial growth. The first five-year plan proposed an annual industrial growth-rate of 22–25 per cent, and the annual plan for 1931 even aimed at an increase of 45 per cent in that year.

2. Investment in industry must be so allocated that the output of producer goods would expand more rapidly than that of consumer goods. In particular, resources must be concentrated on "means of production for producing means of production" i.e. on the machine-tools and industrial equipment industries. The case both for high rates of industrial growth and for this concentration on producer goods was put in political and social rather than in economic terms. The Soviet Union must "overtake and surpass" the capitalist countries, and it must for defence reasons be self-sufficient in its main lines of industrial production.

3. In spite of the concentration of effort on the producer goods industries, substantial efforts must be made

(i) to undertake the support of the "social costs" of industrialisation —a large programme of universal and specialised education, health measures, housing, etc.;

(ii) to expand the output of industrial consumer goods;

(iii) to expand the output of agriculture—both foodstuffs and raw materials for industry.

4. Investment must aim at inculcating the latest technology into the economy: it must in particular be allocated at least in part (i) to the construction of new enterprises rather than the expansion of existing ones; and (ii) to the construction of capital-intensive enterprises, even in the labour-abundant Soviet economy. The Soviet case was that large technical changes would in the long-term render irrelevant the present cost equations (including the capital: labour cost ratio)—in order to get to the new set of equations, you could not start at once from what was cheapest given present parameters, but must introduce modern technology in lumps into the existing situation. The new up-to-date enterprises would act as an "example" of modern technology and would enable the training of personnel in the latest skills.

5. Location policy must also be based on long-term needs rather than short-term costs. Iron and steel and engineering industries must be developed beyond the Urals, both because their output would be cheaper in the long run and because this was essential for defence reasons.

The appended tables summarise the principal results of the process as far as points 1–3 are concerned. Such time-series involve complex problems, including weighting, which base-year to choose, degree of double-counting. The figures presented would be broadly acceptable to most Western specialists. The following conclusions may be drawn:

1. A rapid overall rate of growth led to an expansion of the Soviet G.N.P. to between 350 and 600 per cent of 1928 by 1955. Investment (in all sectors taken together) and communal services (mainly health and education) expanded much more rapidly than individual consumption; military expenditure expanded most rapidly of all. Soviet expansion was thus achieved by re-allocating G.N.P. towards investment and communal services, in spite of the expansion of defence expenditure (Tables 18–1 and 18–2).[2]

2. Industry expanded by some 11–16 per cent per annum in 1928–

[2] It will be noticed that in Table 18–2 the proportion of gross investment and defense expenditure to total G.N.P. is much lower in 1937 prices than in 1928 prices. This is because the wholesale prices of machinery, equipment, etc., which constitute a major element in these two items, were relatively much lower in 1937 than in 1928 (owing to the relative reduction in costs which occurred in this sector). For similar reasons, in Table 18–1 G.N.P. expands more rapidly when measured in 1928 prices: in 1928, machinery was relatively highly-priced, and it constitutes a major element in the expansion of G.N.P. between 1928 and 1937. The relatively low price of machinery in the USSR coupled with the fact that it is a high proportion of Soviet G.N.P., also produces the curious result that Soviet G. N. P. is much smaller in relation to that of the USA when the measurement is made in rubles than when it is made in dollars.

TABLE 18-1. G.N.P. (1937 = 100)

(a)	1937 prices	1928	1937	1950	1955
	Household consumption	93	100	130	197
	Communal services	27	100	145	178
	Government administration	41	100	200	142
	Defence	10	100	245	358
	Gross investment	30	100	155	234
	G.N.P.	62	100	150	216
(b)	1928 prices				
	Household consumption	73	100		
	Communal services	24	100		
	Government administration	41	100		
	Defence	7	100		
	Gross investment	21	100		
	G.N.P.	30	100		

1937, and by some 10 per cent per annum between 1950 and 1955 (a further break-down of these figures shows that the expansion of producer goods output was much faster than that of consumer goods). Agricultural output at first declined substantially, and then expanded much more slowly than industry (Table 18–3).

3. International comparisons are necessarily much more tentative. The appropriate comparison is presumably with other countries at a similar stage of development: e.g. Britain in 1780–1830, the USA in 1870–1914,

TABLE 18-2. PERCENTAGE OF G.N.P. TO VARIOUS PURPOSES

(a)	1937 prices	1928	1937	1950	1955
	Household consumption	79.5	52.5	45.7	48.0
	Communal services	4.6	10.5	10.2	8.7
	Government administration	2.1	3.2	4.3	2.1
	Defence	1.3	7.9	12.9	13.1
	Gross investment	12.5	25.9	26.9	28.1
	Total G.N.P.	100.0	100.0	100.0	100.0
(b)	1928 prices				
	Household consumption	64.7	32.5		
	Communal services	5.1	7.7		
	Government administration	2.7	2.5		
	Defence	2.5	13.0		
	Gross investment	25.0	44.3		
	Total G.N.P.	100.0	100.0		

Source Tables 1 and 2: A. Bergson, *The Real National Income of Soviet Russia since 1928* (1961).

TABLE 18-3. OUTPUT OF MAJOR SECTORS OF SOVIET ECONOMY

	1928	1932	1937	1950	1955
Industrial output					
Seton index	100	181	380	733	1210
Nutter index	100	140	279	385	608
Gross agricultural output (1958 prices)					
Johnson-Kahan index	100	79	105	119	148
Communal services (1937 prices)	100	–	370	537	659

Sources Table 3:
   F. Seton, "Soviet Industrial Expansion," *Manchester Statistical Society paper* (January 1957).
   G. W. Nutter, *Growth of Industrial Production in the Soviet Union* (1962).
   D. G. Johnson and A. Kahan in *Comparisons of the United States and Soviet Economies;* Joint Economic Committee of U.S. Congress, Part I (1959).
   A. Bergson, *Op. cit.*

India now? But the USSR had the advantage, at least over Britain, that it could utilise rather than innovate new technology; on the other hand, it had to suffer the expense and devastation of the second world war. We may very cautiously observe:

   (i) The Soviet G.N.P. expanded much more rapidly per annum than the British in 1780–1830, somewhat more rapidly than that of the USA in 1870–1914;

   (ii) Soviet expansion was particularly greater in industry in general and in the producer goods industries in particular;

   (iii) In the Soviet case, individual consumption per head declined or rose very slowly for a few years, and rose slowly afterwards. What happened in Britain is still disputed among the statisticians; in the USA, average consumption per head rose continuously.

   Evidence about sub-goals 4 (type of investment) and 5 (location policy) is not at all precise; special studies are required. The policy of capital-intensive investment in new enterprises was only partially achieved in practice. Short-run pressures for more output and for lower short-run costs diverted resources into the expansion of existing works and into projects yielding immediate results. These pressures also led to what have been described as "labour-intensive variants of capital-intensive projects": when new techniques were introduced in the oil industry, for example, the number of men per drill was much higher than in the United States; and in general capital was used more labour-intensively (less unused capacity, more shifts worked per day). Nevertheless, the policy of introducing new techniques in large lumps (e.g. new iron and steel, vehicle and heavy equipment works) was imposed at least in part. The result of location policy was similar. More was achieved than if the industries concerned had

TABLE 18-4(a). LABOUR AND CAPITAL IN SOVIET AGRICULTURAL
GROWTH

	No. of Persons Employed in Agriculture (Millions)*	Index (1928=100)	Index of Fixed Capital in Agriculture Including Animals (1928=100)**	Index of Fixed Capital in Agriculture Excluding Animals (1928=100)**
1928	69	100	100	100
1940	56	83	123	227
1955	45	65	193	447
1959	?	?	225	612

Sources
   *W. W. Eason in *Comparisons of the United States and Soviet Economies,* Part I.
   **Official Soviet index.

been left to make their own location decisions in the light of known costs, but short-term pressures modified the original plans.

Little analysis of Soviet data has yet been made to determine the contribution of the principal factors of production to growth. Production function analysis is always subject to wide margins of error, and in the Soviet case there are wide confidence limits in the basic data. Table 18–4(a) presents some descriptive data: from this and other work we may conclude:

1. In agriculture, invested capital plus reorganisation plus economies of scale enabled the reduction of the labour force, even though output rose by some 50 per cent between 1928 and 1955. Soviet agriculture has become more capital-intensive, though past under-employment of male and female labour is not reflected in the statistics (which show the numbers of able-bodied available for work).

It should be noted that this shift of labour from the land has not yet gone nearly as far as in the USA, where only 12 per cent of the civilian labour force is employed in agriculture.

2. In industry

(i) much labour became available: urban general unemployment was eliminated, people moved to the towns, villages expanded into towns, and the proportion of female labour in the total increased from 27 per cent in 1928 to 47 per cent in 1959. (The increase in skills and in the proportion of engineers and technicians in the total labour force is not of course reflected in these figures: it was particularly important in the engineering industries.)

(ii) At the same time, capital stock rose much more than equiproportionately.

TABLE 18-4(b). LABOUR AND CAPITAL IN SOVIET INDUSTRIAL GROWTH

	No. of Persons Employed in Industry and Building (Millions) (Annual Average)	Index (1928=100)	Fixed Capital in Industry and Building (1928=100)
1928	4.5	100	100
1940	12.5	279	852
1956	22.1	489	2,305*
1959	25.0	556	3,284

*1955
Source: From official Soviet statistics.

(iii) We are not able to assess accurately the share of capital, labour and the residual "technical progress" in the production function for Soviet industry: the increase in the importance of "technical progress" since the war is striking. Another way of looking at the data in Table 18-4 (b) and (c) is in terms of output per man: 20–40 per cent of the pre-war rise in output was due to increased output per man rather than increased numbers of men; some 56 per cent of the post-war rise was due to increased output per man. The Soviet "capital-intensive" policy finds some reflection here.

TABLE 18-4(c). A ROUGH DISTRIBUTION OF INDUSTRIAL GROWTH
BETWEEN FACTORS OF PRODUCTION

1. Prewar (1928-1937)		
Assuming industrial growth-rate of	12.9% p.a.	15.0% p.a.
Attributable to increment to labour force	3.5%	6.4%
Attributable to increment to capital stock	7.4%	6.5%
Attributable to 'technical progress'	2.0%	2.0%
2. 1950-1955		
Assuming industrial growth-rate of	12.0% p.a.	
Attributable to increment to labour force	3.0%	
Attributable to increment to capital stock	3.0%	
Attributable to 'technical progress'	6-7%	

Source: Based on F. Seton in *American Economic Review*, Vol. XLIX, No. 2 (May 1959).

General Reading

	(i) History of the system
A. Baykov:	*The Development of the Soviet Economic System* (1947).
M. H. Dobb:	*Soviet Economic Development since 1917* (1948).

	(ii) Structure of the system
R. W. Campbell:	*Soviet Economic Power* (1960).
A. Nove:	*The Soviet Economy* (1961).
N. Spulber:	*The Soviet Economy* (1962).

Reading for First Article

	(i) Prerevolutionary industrialisation
T. H. von Laue:	*Sergei Witte and the Industrialization of Russia* (1963).

	(ii) Possible Soviet development paths
R. W. Davies:	"Some Soviet Economic Controllers," in *Soviet Studies*, Vol. XI, Nos. 3 and 4 (January and April 1960), and Vol. XII, No. 1 (July 1960).
A. Erlich:	*The Soviet Industrialisation Debate 1924–1928* (1960).
N. Spulber:	*Soviet Strategy for Economic Growth* (1964).
N. Spulber (Editor):	*Foundations of Soviet Strategy for Economic Growth.* *Selected Soviet Essays 1924–1930* (1964).

	(iii) Statistics of Soviet industrialisation
A. Bergson:	*The Real National Income of Soviet Russia since 1928* (1961).
J. Chapman:	*Real Wages in Soviet Russia since 1928* (1963).
F. Seton:	"Soviet Economic Trends and Prospects—Production Functions in Soviet Industry," in *American Economic Review*, Vol. XLIX, No. 2 (May 1959).
L. A. Neale:	"The Production Function and Industrial Growth in the Soviet Union," *Discussion Papers* of the Centre for Russian and East European Studies, The University, Birmingham 15, England, Series RC/A, No. 1 (1965).

19   R. W. DAVIES

The Soviet Planning Process
For Rapid Industrialisation

A. An Outline of The System

Our first article established that the Soviet government set itself the
objective of a more rapid rate of industrialisation, with a greater investment in capital-consuming industries and processes, than could be
achieved within the framework of the market economy of the 1920's. It
was shown that the main objective was achieved, but with a much slower
increase in living standards (consumer goods, agricultural output) than
had been intended. To enforce its priorities, the Soviet government abandoned the major assumptions of its earlier policy:

1. A market relationship with the peasant was replaced by administrative or coercive control over his output. The centres of economic and
political resistance in the rural commune were destroyed, and hundreds
of thousands of *"kulak"* families were expelled from their home villages.
Twenty-five million individual peasant farms were combined into 250,000
collective farms (*kolkhozy*), one or several to each village. The old boundaries and strips were destroyed, and most land and cattle were pooled and
worked in common. Agricultural machinery was gradually made available
from several thousand state-owned Machine and Tractor Stations (MTS).
The *kolkhoz* was required to supply a substantial part of its output to the
state collection agencies at low fixed prices in the form of compulsory deliveries. These supplies were then used by the state (i) to make available
a minimum amount of foodstuffs to the growing urban population; (ii) for
export. Exports of grain fell from 9 million tons in 1913 to 2 million tons in
1926/7 and 178 thousand tons in 1929: they rose (temporarily) to 4.8 million tons in 1930 and 5.1 million tons in 1931, and this increase was used
to pay for imports of equipment and industrial materials. In the new circumstances, the "right-wing" "Sokol'nikov solution" was thus utilised; but
with a far more drastic exploitation of the output of the peasantry than the
"left-wing" Preobrazhensky had anticipated (for Sokol'nikov and Preobrazhensky, see the first article in this series).

2. Inflation was permitted to develop: the wages of the expanding

From *Economics of Planning*, Vol. 6, No. 1, 1966, pp. 53–67. Reprinted by permission of author and *Economics of Planning*.

industrial and building labour force were partly met by increasing the flow of paper money. Prices began to rise, but the inflation was partly repressed through price control in both the producer goods market and the retail market (private shops and trading agencies were taken over by the state to facilitate this). For several years (1929–1935) a rationing system was introduced in the towns, supplemented by state sales of goods above the ration at high prices. In this way, the available supply of consumer goods and foodstuffs was distributed over the old and the new urban population, and consumption per head in the towns was forced down. This was then an extreme form of the "regime of economy."

3. Within industry, the system of physical controls which had already existed during the 1920's was greatly extended. Prices were fixed, and there was no market for producer goods: instead, materials and equipment were distributed to existing factories and new building sites through a system of priorities, which enabled new key factories to be built and bottlenecks in existing industries to be widened. The plan set targets for the output of major intermediate and final products, and the physical allocation system was designed to see these were reached.

To sum up these first three points: the policy of 1928–1932 enabled a new allocation of G.N.P. to be imposed on the economy. The discussions of the 1920's had assumed that savings would be made by the state within the framework of a dynamic equilibrium on the market between agriculture and industry: this placed a constraint on the proportion of G.N.P. which could be invested, and on the allocation of that investment (investment in consumer goods industries would need to be sufficient to enable the output of consumer goods to increase at the rate required for equilibrium). Now this constraint was removed: urban and rural living standards could be temporarily depressed, and physical controls used to divert resources to the establishment of new capital-intensive industries and techniques which gave no return during the construction period, and were relatively costly in the medium-term. This method of obtaining forced savings through physical controls resembled the war-time planning controls used in capitalist economies to shift resources towards the end-product of the armament and maintenance of the large armed forces. In the Soviet case, the "end-product" was the capital goods industries and the maintenance of the workers employed in building and operating them: but in both cases a shift in the allocation of resources which could not easily be achieved through manipulating the market mechanism was achieved through direct controls.

4. However, the system was not one simply of physical controls. Within a few years, the following features, stable over a long period, supplemented the system so far described:

(i) each peasant household was permitted to work a private plot, and to own its own cow and poultry. After obligations to the state had been met, the separate households and the *kolkhoz* as a unit were permitted to sell their produce on the free market ("collective farm market"), on which prices were reached by supply and demand. Here an important part of all marketed foodstuffs was bought and sold.

(ii) with some important exceptions, the employee was free to change his job. A market for labour existed, if a very imperfect one, and wage-levels were formed partly in response to supply and demand. A corollary of this was that costs controls and profit-and-loss accounting were introduced in industry, to supplement the physical controls.

(iii) rationing of consumer goods was abolished, and an attempt was made to balance supply and demand on the consumer market, as a whole and for individual goods, through fiscal measures, notably a purchase tax (the "turnover tax") differentiated according to commodity.

5. A large variety of unplanned and even illegal activities between firms supplemented and made feasible the rather crude controls of the central plan, and must be considered as part of the logic of the system.

B. The Planning Process

We have so far established that Soviet plan controls may be divided schematically as in Fig. 19–1. Each enterprise receives a set of output targets and input allocations with which to fulfil them; at the same time its monetary expenditures are controlled by financial or costs plans, which are less important to it than its output plan, but which come into operation if the pressure from above for higher output leads the enterprise to increase its money expenditures excessively.

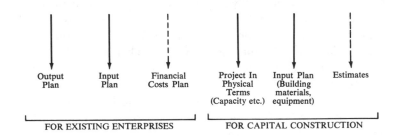

FIG. 19–1. PRINCIPAL PLANNING CONTROLS OVER INDUSTRIAL ACTIVITY

DISAGGREGATION

A key problem for the central planners is to disaggregate their major decisions so that they will be enforced at the plant level; and to aggregate information and proposals so as to be able satisfactorily to take into account the effect of their past and present decisions on different parts of the economy. In Soviet planning, this has normally been dealt with in the following ways:

1. Economic organisation is adapted to handle this problem.

(i) Factories are placed under the control of Ministries or subministries each of which is responsible for a particular group of products (e.g. iron and steel, motor-vehicles). Each Ministry is given very considerable control over its enterprises. The government is therefore to a considerable extent concerned only with handling transfers *between* industries.

(ii) Smaller factories producing low priority items are placed under the control of the government of one of the constituent republics, or under local authorities. In the past, the government tended not to bother with them, and to treat allocations to them as a residual.

(iii) Within the State Planning Committee (Gosplan), which is an advisory body to the government, and within each Ministry or subministry, departmental organisation mirrors the planning arrangements. In the iron and steel industry, for example, there are separate departments of the Ministry responsible for sales of the industry's product, for supplies to the industry, for production plans of iron and steel works, and for capital construction. Within Gosplan, there are separate departments concerned with production, allocation and construction. This is illustrated schematically in Fig. 19–2.

2. The time-horizon is divided so as to disaggregate. Five-year plans set broad rates of growth for G.N.P. by sector of origin and end-use, state

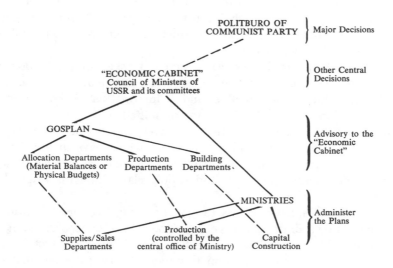

Fig. 19–2. Central Economic Administration

output targets for important intermediate and final products, and list the location and intended capacity of all major construction projects. Annual plans (known as "operative" plans) handle the detailed application of these longer-term plans in a particular year; quarterly and even monthly partial plans handle particular industries or aspects of planning.

3. Planning procedures are designed so as to enable more or less systematic aggregation and disaggregation. We give the procedure for the annual plan as an example:

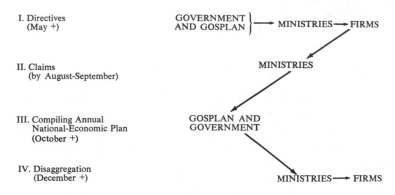

I. Directives
   (May +)

II. Claims
    (by August-September)

III. Compiling Annual
     National-Economic Plan
     (October +)

IV. Disaggregation
    (December +)

FIG. 19–3. PROCEDURE FOR ANNUAL PLANNING

Stage I. Gosplan possesses a mass of data on past performance, and it or the government issues a statement about the principal economic magnitudes to be aimed at for the following year. These directives indicate the main proportions and principal production targets, the proposed investment allocation for each Ministry, and proposals for the growth of output per man-year ("labour productivity," in Soviet terminology) and the reduction of costs.

Stage II. Ministries have already prepared a skeleton production programme and set of claims for materials and equipment; this is now adjusted in the light of the directives and of information received from the firms. The forms on which claims are submitted are approved by Gosplan: the products itemised generally correspond to the nomenclature of the national production and supply plans, which have included up to 5,000 product groups. There are usually substantial differences between the Ministries' output proposals and supply claims and the original directives.

Stage III. Gosplan now has the job of fitting together the Ministry plans and its own draft plans: we enter the "period of coordination and reconciliation" in which the heads of firms and Ministries negotiate with the government in Moscow. From this there emerges the national economic plan, with its constituent production, supplies (allocation) and investment plans. This whole negotiation is conducted in terms of, say, 30 times as many major indicators as were set out in the original directives.

Stage IV. The Ministries now disaggregate the national economic plan to firm level.

4. These aggregation and disaggregation procedures are assisted by two important sets of what might be termed "control coefficients":

(i) *Output targets* (or success indicators). The fulfilment of these has been the main driving motive of the Soviet firm and even Ministry (managerial promotions and salaries tended to be related to success in fulfilment of output targets). Output targets were given for very broad groups of products at the national level, and they were supplemented by the sales departments of each Ministry, whose disaggregation of the planned output target for a product-group is supposed in theory to be binding on the firm. We return to the difficulties involved here later.

(ii) *Norms or consumption standards.* At the shop-floor level, hundreds of thousands of specific consumption standards are used to control the production process and to cut down waste. But at the works' level, discussion already proceeds on the basis of aggregated standards; a further aggregation takes place between works and Ministry. Gosplan uses overall input coefficients to check the claims of Ministries, and many of these are incorporated in the plan: these may be of the form

"x physical units of input of A for y physical units of output of B"

(e.g. tons of crude steel per ton of rolled steel)

or "x physical units of input of A for y value-units of output of B"

(e.g. tons of cement per 1 million rubles' building and erection work).

Different consumption standards will be applied to different processes and even to different plants: these are probably quite reliable as a rough measure of efficiency and of reliability of claims, and a useful device for handling complex production activities centrally.

COORDINATION

The outline so far given of the planning process is unrealistic, for it assumes much smoother control than is possible in practice. Smooth planning has been vitiated by:

1. Uncertainty. Innovations, mistakes and bottlenecks were not predicted with any accuracy; future proportions of coal and oil output, for example, were quite wrongly predicted even after the war.

2. "Tight" planning. The plan was used as an instrument for forcing-up production, and all targets were deliberately strained, all stocks mini-

mised. This reinforced uncertainty and encouraged the emergence of un-expected bottlenecks. (In the early 1930's annual as well as five-year plan targets were sometimes wildly exaggerated.)

Moreover, we have so far been writing as if planning started from a clean sheet with each planning period. In fact, of course, planners work *at the margin.* Of a steel output of 12 million tons, as much as 10 million tons in an annual plan may be irrevocably committed to existing activities. Even in a five-year plan, possible shifts may be small: during the second five-year plan, for example, most capital investment was devoted to completing projects already started during the first plan or earlier.

The "coordination and reconciliation" activities undertaken by Gosplan in drawing up the annual plan are therefore limited by uncertainty, by the consequences of tight planning and by existing commitments. Gosplan has two functions here. Firstly, it seeks to balance programmes by eliminating existing or potential bottlenecks due to the excess of demand over supply. To do this it follows a regular procedure and uses a list of priorities: thus it may cut cement supplies to housing in order to have enough to push through a crash programme to complete a steel foundry needed to produce certain types of steel required by priority industries. Secondly, it tries to inject into departmental programmes the priorities and investment programmes favoured by the government: thus it may increase cement supplies to the constructors of new chemical factories which are regarded as urgent.

In the coordination procedure, a great deal of use has been made by Gosplan of "material balances" or Physical Budgets, showing supplies and requirements for different product-groups or types of equipment. These Physical Budgets were adjusted by the appropriate Gosplan through a fairly crude procedure of rule-of-thumb iteration. These were not input-output tables, for no technical coefficients had been calculated; sometimes a rough allowance was made for indirect outlays (e.g. of steel needed to make more machinery for motor-car factories if the output of motor-cars was increased, as well as direct outlays of steel on the motor-cars themselves). The procedure was therefore slow and inexact. At present, input-output tables and the traditional "material balances" are used side by side.

C. Financial Planning

1. Our account so far has been primarily concerned with physical planning: but as we have seen, a money-flow corresponded to all the physical flows, and some of the money-transactions in the system (e.g.

wage payments, sales on the collective-farm market, sales on the retail market generally) were not accompanied by physical controls. Once the inflationary process had led to the initial re-allocation of G.N.P. in 1928–1930, financial equilibrium was a subsidiary goal of the government. What was required was that money payments to the population (wage payments by the state, payments by the state to *kolkhozy* which were then distributed to their members, etc.) should not exceed the value of the supply of commodities available on the state-controlled market at fixed prices and on the collective-farm market at market prices. As out-payments by the state included the earnings of persons employed in the investment goods industries, in the social services, and in the armed forces, a gap existed between the cost-price of consumer goods (equal to the cost of wages in that sector and the materials, etc. it employed) and the total monetary demand.

This gap needed to be covered by taxation, and could be met in prin-ciple in one or all of three ways:

(i) by direct taxation;

(ii) by allowing the profits of enterprises to rise and then taxing them;

(iii) by an indirect tax: this could be an equiproportional mark-up on all goods, or imposed only on consumer goods.

(i) Direct taxation has been of minor importance: there are no in-comes uncontrolled by the state available to tax, and high income tax on state employees is regarded as undesirable;

(ii) Profits tax has been of some importance, but in the early stages the authorities feared that the monetary pressure on the retail market would lead to very high profits in the consumer goods industries (this pressure was not held back after 1935 by the rationing procedures which still operated in the case of producer goods);

(iii) The misnamed "turnover tax" therefore became the main source of tax: it is a mark-up on the wholesale price of consumer goods and the low delivery price of foodstuffs. The mark-up is differentiated by product for social reasons and to bring about a rough equality between the supply and the demand for each product. It was argued that a high level of tax on producer goods, which were mainly sold to the state, would only re-quire the state to reimburse itself from a still higher tax-rate on consumer goods.

Fig. 19–4 illustrates the principal money flows in the system.

2. Prices in the producer and the consumer goods industries, there-fore, had a common base: they were reached as follows:

(i) costs of production, including wages, the cost of materials, over-heads, a small allowance for depreciation, but no interest charge on capital;

(ii) a small mark-up for profits;

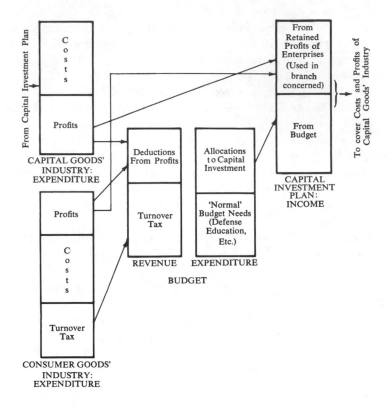

FIG. 19–4. SOVIET FINANCIAL PLANNING: A SIMPLIFIED PICTURE
      (not to scale)

(iii) trade and transport costs.
To these was added in the case of consumer goods
    (iv) turnover tax (differentiated by product)
to reach the retail price.

Profits are partly taxed, partly retained by the firm or industry; a high proportion of profits in excess of the plan is placed at the disposal of the firm in the "Director's Fund" (now the "Enterprise Fund").

It will be noted that the prices of producer goods are unresponsive to supply and demand, and could remain stable for many years. Each industry receives a price for its product equal to average costs for the industry plus a small margin for profit; but the industry itself can pay differential prices, offering high prices to high-cost firms and low prices to low-cost firms. However, prices include no systematic allowance for the varying richness of the capital stock of firms producing similar products. In practice, the rate of profit earned on different products varies enormously, owing to the hit-and-miss way in which prices were fixed.

3. Elaborate arrangements are made to control the flows of

(i) short-term loans (for seasonal stocks, goods in transit, etc.)

(ii) wage issues (we return to this in section (D))

(iii) allocations to investment (mainly financed by the budget) and

(iv) cash

through the State Bank (responsible for working capital) and specialised investment banks (responsible for allocations to fixed capital). All these devices aimed at maintaining the financial equilibrium which was secured through balancing money incomes against money expenditures through the fiscal system. In the end, inflation was repressed over a short period before the war (1935–1937) and in a more systematic way after the war (1948–   ): between 1948 and 1953, retail prices were even substantially reduced.

D. Labour and Labour Controls

1. The following are the principal devices used by the government to control the urban labour force:

(i) Once unemployment had been absorbed (by about 1932), recruitment of labour from the villages to the towns was organised systematically on contract with the collective farms.

(ii) Training and education of semi-skilled, skilled and technical manpower are systematically planned.

(iii) At various stages (particularly in the war and post-war years from 1940 to 1951) scarce grades or types of manpower were restricted in their movement or even subject to allocation.

2. In spite of these measures, labour was highly mobile, particularly in the early 1930's, and both central planners and factory managements utilise money wages to influence the allocation of labour—hence a form of labour market emerged, though recent studies of Soviet production functions have confirmed that it was highly imperfect:

(i) The government approves national scales for different grades and types of labour in different areas, and adjusts these from time to time to take account of demand and supply; there is a high differential for skill.

(ii) There is an elaborate piece-rate and bonus system to encourage higher productivity.

(iii) Management can in practice manipulate bonuses and gradings to attract scarce kinds of labour.

3. Unskilled and even semi-skilled labour are not basically a scarce factor of production (owing to the existence of a large stock of labour in the countryside). There has therefore been a recurrent tendency to substitute labour for capital, as we saw in the first article.

4. The need for labour coupled with the pressure to fulfil the output plan encouraged management to overspend their allocation for wages, and made for an inflationary situation. Control by the State Bank over wage issues is the most important single element in maintaining wage stability.

5. Government control over trade unions has greatly assisted wage policy. The central wage bargaining process was very tenuous from 1929 onwards. At the same time, a policy of cutting the rate for the job as techniques and organisation improved was systematically enforced, so that money wages rose *less* rapidly than output per man.

6. But the government, as well as firmly controlling wage rates, also took responsibility for social conditions. Hours of work were restricted to 7–8 hours daily. Pensions, sickness and maternity benefits, holidays with pay and welfare services (creches, factory clubs, canteens), largely administered through the trade unions, were more generous than was the case in many Western countries at a similar stage of industrialisation. These social benefits (particularly housing tied to the factory) were used to influence the movement of labour (high priority factories tended to have better facilities and housing; benefits were partly dependent on length of service at the particular factory).

STRENGTHS AND WEAKNESSES OF THE SOVIET PLANNING SYSTEM

No adequate "costs-benefit analysis" of the Soviet system or its constituent parts has yet been attempted. Here we simply list some of its principal achievements and failures:

1. ADVANTAGES

(i) The system succeeded in enforcing allocation of a very high proportion of G.N.P. to investment over a long period; within this allocation resources were concentrated on the growth-inducing producer goods industries, which were transformed from high-cost to low-cost industries. In general, it is possible with this kind of mechanism to enforce successfully high priority crash programmes (e. g. the sputniks).

(ii) A high degree of centralisation enabled the planners to inculcate the latest technology, imported from more advanced economies, into the whole economy at a rapid rate: project institutes, such as *Gipromez* (the State Institute for Projects of Iron and Steel Works) were able to plan large-scale technological advance for a whole industry on a national scale.

For many major technological problems, the Soviet system of central-ised research also carries great advantages at a more advanced stage of development (e.g. nuclear research).

(iii) Considerable economies of scale (including economies from standardisation) and economies of effort are possible in nationally-planned industries.

(iv) The output drive from above, characteristic of Soviet planning until recently, provides a powerful instrument for enforcing high capacity working, and for keeping management and men working at a high pace.

2. DISADVANTAGES

(i) The cost of concentrating resources on producer goods industries was very high. Thus the policy adopted towards the peasantry led to a drastic decline in peasant holdings of working livestock, and forced the state in fact to re-allocate unexpected resources to agricultural equipment industry and hence to the high-grade steel industry. It also had a drastic long-term effect on peasant morale.

(ii) When the central planners make a *wrong* technological choice, the cost (because the policy is carried out on a national scale) is propor-tionately heavy; for example, there has been over-investment in the coal industry and under-investment in oil and chemicals.

(iii) When controls are highly centralised, initiative and innovation at the works level are cramped. But decentralisation of a system of ad-ministrative planning is difficult. If the success indicators are not very detailed, managements will produce what it is easier to produce rather than what is wanted. Control of quality through success indicators is very difficult. The sellers' market which was coupled with Soviet administrative planning reinforced these difficulties. At the same time it led to the tend-ency for each industrial Ministry to become a self-contained "Empire," carrying out wasteful backward integration in order to control its sup-plies. If advertising and inflated sales organisations are a high cost of modern capitalism, inflated supplies organisations were (and are) a high cost of Soviet central planning.

To sum up with an example. Central planning enabled the emergence of steel foundries and rolling mills, using home-manufactured equipment, which are technologically as good as those in the United States, and are worked at a much higher capacity. It also produced a situation where Soviet bedsteads were the heaviest in the world (because planned in tons), were produced on too small a scale (because made under several Ministries) and therefore costly, and owing to the sellers' market could be made of iron, when the consumer would have preferred something more modern.

   This is a mere list of factors. Economists need to ask themselves: *how* costly and beneficial were these various factors? How far were the advantages and disadvantages of the system inextricably tied together? Could the Soviet strategy for rapid growth, or some features of it, be employed without the disadvantages? How many of the unsuccessful features were due to the special conditions of Russia (including the difficult external and internal position of the government) and to the inexperience and imperfect knowledge of the people who made the system?

READING FOR SECOND ARTICLE

Comparison of the U.S. and Soviet Economies. Published by the Joint Economic Committee of the U.S. Congress, 3 vols. (1959). (Especially article by H. Levine.)

R. W. Davies, *The Development of the Soviet Budgetary System* (1958).

D. Granick, An Organizational Model of Soviet Industrial Planning: in *Journal of Political Economy*, April 1959.

20   R. W. DAVIES

PLANNING A MATURE ECONOMY IN THE U.S.S.R.

In this article an attempt is made to place the Soviet economic system in the context of traditional economics, and the problems of Soviet-type central planning in a mature economy are discussed.

(A) ECONOMIC THEORY AND THE SOVIET ECONOMY

1. Traditional economic theory contrasts two types of systems: the competitive or market system, with its "ideal type" of perfect competition, and "command economy," or "planning under a dictator." These are treated as two possible alternative methods of allocating resources.

(i) The *market economy* is divided into competing units: a large number of individual consumers bargain with a large number of producers on the market. The goal of the producer is to maximise his profit, the goal of the consumer is to maximise his satisfaction. The resulting demand and supply are equated through price.

The decisions on the consumer market are reflected back into the factor market, where a similar bargaining process settles the distribution of incomes between factors and the distribution of the factors.

As a result, resources in such an economy are allocated "rationally," by which the economist means "in accordance with the desires of the consumers."

(ii) In the *command economy* (often referred to as *"planning under a dictator"*), final demand is determined not by individual consumers but by the decision of the central authority, as "dictator's preferences" or "planners' preferences" replace "consumers' preferences." The central authority also controls the allocation of all factors of production and the distribution of income. The system is completely centralised: its difficulty lies in the ability of the "dictator" to work out the "thousands of equations" involved in transforming his preferences into practical economic decisions.

From *Economics of Planning*, Vol. 6, No. 2, 1966, pp. 138–153. Reprinted by permission of author and *Economics of Planning*.

2. How far does this theory provide an effective framework of analysis for contemporary capitalism and for Soviet planning?

(i) The development of economic analysis in the past forty years has involved a number of realistic modifications of the original theory as applied to modern capitalism:

1. In many cases free entry into industries will be restricted and a state of imperfect competition will exist; at equilibrium, output may be lower and price higher than under perfect competition. However, economies of scale may make for lower costs in a highly organised oligopolistic industry: advantage and disadvantage must be carefully examined;

2. While consumer *choice* exists, advertising, imperfect knowledge, and the power of initiative of the large firm mean that consumer *sovereignty* is quite restricted;

3. The assumption of permanent equilibrium in the system is a microeconomic one. At the level of macro-economics, supply does not create its own demand and hence the possibility of under-employment of factors exists (Keynes). Macro-economic equilibrium requires government intervention;

4. The large government sector requires separate analysis. Nationalised industries produce as monopolies, but often with their "maximum profit" goal constrained; and as consumers they control a large part of the market for certain intermediate goods (e.g. an electricity board purchasing power-station equipment). The defence, education and health departments of central and local governments are also large buyers, and often act as oligopsonies. State fiscal and monetary and tariff policy regulates the market;

5. The view that firms' economic behaviour can be understood solely in terms of aiming at maximum profit in response to market price is an insufficient one. Within the large firm, decisions will be taken administratively (through the hierarchy) or by a cooperative or bargaining process; and much inter-firm behaviour may also be explained in this way. Industry is not an infinite number of atoms responding to price, but a finite number of blocs: the bloc as a whole reacts to price, but also has dealings with other blocs which are to be explained in terms of organisation theory rather than of the price mechanism; and bargaining and administrative processes help to explain economic behaviour within each bloc.

However, even with these modifications the original theory retains much validity:

1. If firms do not always aim at maximising their profits, they are concerned with making a satisfactory level of profits ("satisfising");

2. There is consumer choice, and a market process also operates for intermediate goods and (partly) on the factor market;

3. In spite of the considerable role of the government, a large segment of investment is still determined by the decisions of individual entrepreneurs (or entrepreneurial firms).

(ii) These developments of Western economic theory are of direct relevance to our understanding of the Soviet system:

1. Physical planning is not something unknown in capitalist economies. In the Soviet economy, relationships between firms are regulated by administrative and bargaining processes; in a competitive system they are largely regulated by the market. But analogies to all the administrative and bargaining processes described in the section on "the planning process" in *Economics of Planning*, Vol. 6, No. 1, pp. 55–61 may be found within the capitalist firm, and within the government sector (compare the process for making fiscal estimates in a market economy with the procedures for plan compilation in Soviet industry). The "thousands of equations" of Western economic theory are simplified by the existence of "administrative decentralisation": sub-systems of economic administrators share decision-making with the Council of Ministers; and bargaining and pressure from lower units assist the decision-making process. Moreover, like decisions by private enterpreneurs, planners' decisions are made only "at the margin."

2. Some important economic activity in the USSR is to be explained in terms of a market mechanism, though most Soviet markets are highly imperfect. As we have seen, there is a partial market for labour, a fixed-price market for retail consumer goods, a free market for part of retail food sales, and various unofficial or illegal markets operate in practice.

CONCLUSION

Modern capitalist economies are imperfectly competitive and have important elements of administrative control; the Soviet economy is not entirely "planned from the centre," and imperfect markets exist for certain purposes.

(b) The Soviet Economy as a Special Case of Planned Economy

The Soviet planning system of the 1930's–1950's is not the only possible form of planned economy. In Soviet experience alone, at least two other forms of planning system have existed. In the period of *War Communism* (1918–1920), industry was nationalised and industrial output was allocated physically. Owing to inflation the economy was virtually moneyless; labour was directly controlled, consumer goods were rationed and agricultural output subject to requisition. However, peasants continued to work their own land and no serious attempt was made to socialise agriculture. This system was the closest approach in principle to the "ideal form" of the command economy in the history of the Soviet system. In the period of the *New Economic Policy* (1921–1929), as in present-day Poland, state ownership of industry was combined with private agriculture through a regulated market. The effectiveness of planning was constrained by the existence of the market, but central goals were to some extent enforced.

A considerable variety of forms of central planning is to be found in Eastern Europe.

The systematic study of forms of economic organisation has so far been little developed. One may distinguish two basic ways of classification:

1. OWNERSHIP

A planned economy is unlikely to be one in which all economic activity is nationalised. It will be a "mixed economy," combining private ownership with state ownership, and possibly embracing different forms of state ownership (very varied forms of public ownership have been experienced, incorporating different degrees of state, consumer and workers' control). In this spectrum, the Soviet economy lies considerably towards the "state" end, particularly as far as industry is concerned. Nearly all industrial activity is nationalised, and since 1918 forms of syndicalism or "guild socialism" have been firmly rejected in favour of "one-man management" by administrators appointed by the state and liable to instant dismissal. The argument for this has always been in terms of economic efficiency, and of the need to enforce a central state policy.

2. ALLOCATION OF RESOURCES

Various forms of "market socialism" are in principle conceivable, and have been much discussed among economists (especially in Poland and Yugoslavia). To what extent can a scale of preferences (of planners or individual consumers or a combination of both) be put into effect through a market, on which state firms aim to maximise their profits in simulation of private enterprises? In a variation of this, suggested by Kornai and others, the state would use its regulatory powers only to counter inefficient decisions due to the existence of state monopolies. Prices in "market socialism" might be formed freely, or might be fixed by the planners, but would, of course, need to reflect the chosen preference-scale more or less exactly, as they would indicate to the producer what he should produce, and how he should allocate resources (including investment). In its extreme form, the economic behaviour of "market socialism" ought not to differ from that of a private market economy.

The alternative approach is the one followed by the Soviet government: to allocate resources by direct physical controls, and to allow some degree of decentralisation in decision-making to other controllers at industry, region or plant level.

Planning systems might be classified (a) by the relative strengths in them of the "market principle" and the "physical planning principle"; (b) by the degree to which, within the market sector, the government regulates the market (imposes its preferences); (c) by the degree to which decision-making is decentralised within the physical planning sector.

We have not made any allowance for the *effectiveness* of controls. Should not the degree of planning be measured not only by the all-embracingness of the planners' goals and the detailedness of their controls, but also by the extent to which the planners succeed in fulfilling their goals in the actual allocation of resources? For instance, War Communism was in principle a highly centralised system. But in practice central decisions were usually ineffective; illegal barter and local quasi-markets tended to dominate economic life: what was the "real" economic system? Again, where was there more planning—in industry under War Communism, where detailed orders were not enforced, or in agriculture under the New Economic Policy, where indirect controls succeeded to some extent in moving agriculture in the direction desired by the central government? Further, good planners of course incorporate their knowledge of their objective possibilities into their goals: but is a planner whose goals are very limited, but successfully achieved, as "effective" as, say, the Soviet planners in 1929–1931, who set quite impossible goals but did succeed in re-allocating resources very drastically in the desired direction?

(c) Planning a More Mature Economy

The basic allocation decisions and the planning process in the USSR in 1928–1953 probably had stronger "functional" elements than "dysfunctional" elements in the stage of moving the Soviet economy from a semi-agrarian economy to an industrialised economy. But as the economy matured, the "dysfunctional" elements certainly became more prominent. The changed context may be summarised as follows:

1. Industrial output per head is now above the British level and moving towards the US level for some important producer goods. The economy is vastly more complex than it was in the 1930's.

2. The industrial revolution has been accompanied by major social changes:

(i) in 1928, two-thirds of the population were illiterate; now, nearly everyone can read and write;

(ii) in 1928, some three million persons were employed in industrial labour; it is now (1965) over twenty-five millions;

(iii) in 1928, some 5 per cent of the state-employed labour force (i.e. excluding peasants and collective farmers) had received professional or semi-professional education; the figure now (1965) is about 15 per cent.

3. The technological situation is different: as the economy becomes more mature, the amount of technological borrowing it can do tends to decline, and the amount of innovation required increases. This is reinforced by the long-term trend for labour to become a more scarce factor of production: the economy must increasingly come to rely on higher labor productivity and hence on more capital-intensive production (and/or on technical progress) rather than on increasing the industrial labour-force.

In this new situation, changes in both allocation and organisation are required. It is not easy to demonstrate that industrial efficiency is hampered by a relatively low standard of living (the Soviet average real wage is probably about a quarter that of the United States, but labour productivity may be over half the US level). But in any case political and social pressures have dictated a shift in resources towards consumption. Such a shift requires a much greater output of food; and in agriculture it is very probable that the low return to the peasant for the output of the collective farm has held down productivity. And certainly as the economy has grown, the highly centralised planning structure has become less efficient and less workable.

Here we summarise the principal changes so far made in both respects (1953–1965).

1. ALLOCATION OF RESOURCES

(i) There has been a relative and absolute increase in the resources devoted to consumer goods (manufactures, manufactured foodstuffs). In the 1930's and in 1946–1950, the output of producer goods increased much more rapidly than that of consumer goods; the gap is now much narrower.

(ii) A much higher proportion of total investment has been allocated to urban housing construction.

(iii) In 1953–1958, the prices paid by the state for agricultural products were very substantially increased; according to official figures, the money incomes of collective farms rose from 5 milliard new rubles to 13.2 milliard new rubles between 1953 and 1958. At the same time, the total annual investment in agriculture (state plus collective farm) increased from 2.1 to 5.1 milliard new rubles. This double shift was accompanied by a rapid rise in agricultural output—by some 50 per cent, according to official figures (i.e. a greater increase than in 1928 to 1953).

Between 1958 and 1965 agriculture tended to stagnate (even ignoring the bad harvest of 1963). Recent studies have shown that this stagnation has occurred simultaneously with a falling-off in peasant incomes and in the rate of growth of investment in agriculture. It means likely that agricultural difficulties are at least in part due to the failure of the state to allocate a share of G.N.P. to agriculture adequate enough to enable the goals of the planners to be achieved (organisational weaknesses may also have played a part).

(iv) There has been a significant shift in the distribution of income. The incomes of peasants tended (until 1958) to increase more rapidly than those of the urban population. Within the urban population, there has been a process of levelling-up: the minimum wage has been increased, wage-differentials have been narrowed, social benefits such as pensions have been substantially increased.

(v) Nevertheless, the priorities have not been reversed. It seems certain, however the measurement is done, that a higher proportion of G.N.P. is allocated to net investment than in the U.S., and that a higher proportion of this investment is allocated to the producer goods industries. As a result, the rate of industrial growth has remained high (7–9 per cent a year), though less high than a decade ago.

2. ORGANISATION

Attempts to improve the working of Soviet planning have followed two main lines simultaneously: (i) improvements in central planning; (ii) attempts to decentralise.

(i) Improvements in Central Planning

Central decision-making has undoubtedly tended to be more consistently thought out, and to become more logical and consistent.

Long-term technological decisions have been reconsidered, and a bold policy of technical change has been embarked upon. Thus oil has been given preference to coal, and the transfer of the railways to the diesel has been undertaken; this reverses previous policy. The development and manufacture of pre-fabricated reinforced concrete components and other building materials has been given preference over traditional materials like brick and timber. Plastics are being developed in preference to steel and other metals.

In the discussions about all these changes, most of which had previously been undertaken in capitalist economies in response to market criteria, there has been a great deal of emphasis on economic arguments. The question of the appropriate criteria to use in making investment choices has been predominant here. Thinking has moved in the direction of adopting a single rate of return for the whole economy (the rate of return is, of course, the inverse of the socalled "recoupment period"): the standard formula now used is

$$\frac{I_1 - I_2}{C_2 - C_1} \leq R.P.$$

where I_1 and I_2 are the investment alternatives being compared and C_1 and C_2 are the costs of production in the two alternatives, and $R.P.$ is the maximum permissible period in which the investment may be recouped. (This has tended to vary by industry, from 4–5 years in light industry, i.e. a rate of return of 20–25 per cent, to 16–17 years in electric power, i.e. a rate of return of about 6 per cent.)

The adoption of a standard rate for all industries would require the use of something like a costs-benefit analysis if the social welfare problem is to be taken into account; Soviet thought is moving cautiously in this direction.

A stumbling-bloc to consistent macro-economic decision-making is the inconsistency of the prices in which goods are valued. Investment decisions, and indeed all multi-product decisions, have to be discussed not in physical terms but in value terms. As we have seen, Soviet prices are an inadequate indicator of real costs: they do not include a capital charge (so capital-intensive production is relatively undervalued), they do not vary with the scarcity or abundance of the goods, the rent element for use of natural resources is inconsistent, and the price incorporates a profit mark-up which is more or less arbitrary. Rule-of-thumb adjustments are made by the central planners, but decisions are clumsy and often inaccurate.

A second line of approach to the improvement of central planning has been the attempt to improve knowledge at the centre by use of mathematical methods. Technical coefficients have been worked out so that the consequences of alternative production policies may be taken into account more systematically; national and some regional input-output tables have been constructed (among the largest is the 438 sector matrix for planning purposes of 1964–1965). The central planning of supplies and requirements seems still to be carried out by rule-of-thumb methods, but these are now supplemented by improved information. At the same time various methods of mathematical programming, such as the transportation algorithm, have been used to improve traffic flows (e.g. lorry trans-

port in Moscow, scheduling of Baltic steamers, timber and coal hauls),
bringing savings of about 10 per cent in costs for each problem.

(ii) *Attempts at decentralisation*

Three major attempts have been made since 1953 to devolve some of
the decision-making powers of the central authorities. Both these attempts
have been conducted within the framework of the physical planning system, rather than representing an increase in the market sector of the economy.

1. *1954–1956: "step-by-step" decentralisation.* The Gosplan-Council
of Ministers central organisation attempted to shed some of its powers
by reducing the number of indicators in the national output, supply and
capital investment plans; thus product groups, for which output targets
were laid down, were made more aggregative. The intention was that
each Ministry, possessing more flexibility itself, would devolve some of
its authority to its departments, which in turn would increase the decision-
making powers of economic units.

The reform was on the whole unsuccessful. Ministries failed to pass
down their powers to the factory; instead, they tended to use their increased authority to bind their own "empires" more closely together. At
the same time, the reduction in the number of central output targets
(success indicators) revealed clearly a dilemma inherent in administrative
planning. The enterprise is required to maximise its output in terms of
the output targets. If the targets are broad or loose, it will try to follow
the "easiest" course within the target. If the target is merely for "tons of
nails shorter than 2 inches" the factory will try to produce all $1\frac{9}{10}''$ nails,
because this is easiest. If it is for "numbers of nails", the factory will try
to produce all $\frac{1}{2}''$ nails. But if the plan is set in terms of $\frac{1}{2}''$, $1''$, $1\frac{1}{2}''$ and
$1\frac{9}{10}''$ nails, there will be over-centralisation. If the target is set in terms
of gross value of output, the factory will maximise its use of materials and
semi-fabs and minimise the net value it adds to each product (this has
been dealt with by using a new indicator of "standard cost of work done
to the product", but this has involved further—if smaller difficulties).

2. *1957–1965: regionalisation.* In 1957, industry was "regionalized":
the industrial Ministries were abolished, 104 regions were set up and all
factories in each region were put under the regional economic committee.
However, much of the central machinery was retained, particularly the
sales organisations which control product-mix: and gradually committees
for each industry were re-established, with research organisations attached. What emerged was a mixture of area-by-area and industry-by-
industry control. This probably gave the factory manager greater effective
power, if only because he no longer had one unambiguous boss; it also led
to the break-up of the Ministerial "empires" and a more effective consid-

eration of regional factors in central decision-making. But it also made economic administration very much more complicated.

3. *September 1965– : more authority to the factory*[1]

The reforms introduced by Kosygin contained two main elements. First of all, they abandoned the attempt at regional organisation and returned to control by industrial Ministries; . . . More important, they made the first serious attempt to increase greatly the powers of the factory management. The most important measures are the following:

1. the importance of profits as a success indicator is intended to be greatly increased. Profits retained by factories are to be large and will be related to planned profit (if achieved) rather than actual profit so as to discourage firms from trying to keep their plan low. Bonuses to management and staff will be paid from and related to the amount of profit;

2. various measures are to be adopted to encourage the efficient use of capital investment;

3. the powers of the factory management to determine the way in which it spends the total allocation for wages, are greatly increased; the manager may divide up the total allocations as he wishes between classes of employees—he may for instance reduce the total number of persons employed in order to increase the portion of highly-paid workers;

4. the main global indicator of output is to be "actually marketed production" rather than "gross production"; it is hoped that this will force factories to produce goods for which there is a high demand.

However, the main physical indicators are retained, including both the plan of supplies in physical terms, and the itemisation of production items in physical terms in the national-economic plan; Kosygin merely expressed the hope that the degree of detail would be gradually reduced. The success of the reforms in moving away from administrative planning will depend on the extent to which a linear relationship can be established between the preferences of the planners and the profits earned by the factory; if such a linear relationship exists, and the factory aims at maximising its profits, then the desired pattern of production will be achieved without administrative orders.

But the achievement of such a "linear relationship" requires a radical reform of the price-system. The main suggestions for reform have been: make turnover tax into an equiproportional mark-up on the wholesale price (or value added) of all products; give higher profits for scarce products and negative profits for surplus products; include an interest charge on capital stock. But so far only the last of these proposals appears to be likely to be achieved in the near future. The prices which the planners are to establish have not been worked out in detail, and even the method

---

[1] This account was written in February 1966.

by which they could be reached is unclear. Kosygin has announced an impending price reform, but it seems unlikely to be a radical one.

Three things seem to block a major price reform:

1. fear that an increase in market forces, or the use of profit as a "universal regulator" in a socialist economy, may diminish the control of the centre over the allocation of resources; it is for this reason that proposals permitting a kind of "market socialism" to develop have been firmly rejected;

2. a feeling that profit will not be so powerful an incentive to managers to increase output as output targets in physical terms have been;

3. inability (as yet) to arrive at the actual prices required.

The weakness of the reforms of the planning system we have so far discussed is, then, that they do not tackle the problem of *valuation* systematically or integrally. The reforms are essentially ad hoc. Thus all the proposals for improving the allocation of investment incorporate a required rate of return which is arrived at more or less empirically or even arbitrarily: the choice between investments is not consistently interwoven with long-term production planning. The result is likely to be that the approved pattern of planned investment is not entirely compatible with the approved production targets, so that adjustment by rule-of-thumb will still need to follow. Similarly even the most radical reforms proposed for short and medium-term production and supply planning depend on the availability of a system of prices which systematically reflect the aims or preferences of the planners; prices must favour a production-pattern which not merely widens present bottlenecks but also makes its contribution to the dynamic goals of the planners.

A far-reaching proposal such as Liberman's could worsen the operation of the system rather than assist it, if put into effect without an appropriate set of prices being available. This does not mean that the partial reforms which have been proposed or undertaken would not improve the operation of the present system. Waste and inconsistency have been reduced both by the use of better investment criteria and by the application of linear programming techniques to partial problems.

One general solution—much discussed and partly attempted in Poland and Yugoslavia—is for the required scale of prices to be reached by permitting state enterprises to compete on a market. The central planners would restrict themselves to controlling the general level of investment, and to intervening in order to ensure that the market was as perfect as possible. The principal economic objection to this solution is that it would incorporate into the planned economy most of the disadvantages of modern capitalism, in a situation in which the imperfections of the market would be more considerable than in a privately-owned economy.

An increasingly influential school of Soviet economists holds that with the application of mathematical methods and the use of the computer the major dilemmas of central planning can be solved. Computers make it possible to examine the properties of a very large number of economic variables: with the aid of appropriately designed mathematical models, economic processes can be simulated on the computer so that plan variants can be tested for feasibility and consistency. The core of the method is that objective functions are set up which indicate what is to be maximised or minimised within a system of constraints. The functions yield a system of imputed values (efficiency prices or shadow prices); and these for the problem concerned are the consistent system of prices which, as we have seen, the non-mathematical proposals lacked.

Soviet mathematicians and mathematical economists believe that this technique can be applied to the planning of the entire economy. What is proposed is a "unified and automatised system of national economic planning and management" which would seek to optimise the achievement of goals set by the government. The economy would be divided for planning purposes into a number of blocs or sub-systems (both by area and by sector); for each bloc an appropriate programming model would attempt to optimise sub-goals consistent with and integrated with the overall national goals, which would in turn be incorporated in a macro-model for the economy as a whole. For each bloc, a set of shadow-prices would emerge which would indicate its "best" economic behaviour in the planning period. A measure of decentralisation is inherent in the system: the elements in each sub-system would be free to move so as to optimise their sub-goals within constraints obtained from the larger bloc of which the sub-system formed a part.

A requirement for the efficient working of the new system is the establishment of a consistent computerised system of information flows. All economic information (for instance, all inputs and outputs) will need to be classified by a unified system for the entire economy, so that data may be processed in forms suitable for feeding in to the planning models on which the system is to be based. A chain of computer stations is being established for assembling and processing economic information. (This is a long and arduous business; it is likely to take about ten years.)

For the efficient operation of the system, actual economic forms need to be adapted as far as possible to the solutions found on the computer (inflexibilities in institutions and arrangements constitute constraints on optimisation). In particular, actual prices, it is hoped, will be made to correspond more closely to the shadow-prices obtained from the computations. This does not mean that all prices would necessarily need to be fixed by the state; actual market arrangements in a sub-system could be made consistent with the larger economic models (in principle, a private and uncontrolled sector could be incorporated as a stochastic element in the overall system).

If prices thus correspond to the preferences stated in the models, they would be appropriate for Liberman's proposal that profit should indicate to an economic unit how it should behave. But in the light of Western studies of the behaviour of the private firm, it seems likely that the Soviet firm cannot be expected to behave as though maximising profits were its sole goal; as part of the restructuring of planning, an appropriate system of incentives would be needed to ensure that decisions are executed.

So far we have spoken simply of models which would optimise the achievement of government-fixed goals; we have evaded the problem of the preference functions which would convert those goals into meaningful quantities. At present, the goals of the Soviet government are stated in terms of a long series of targets for investment goods, intermediate goods and final consumption goods. These targets, as we saw in an earlier paper, are reached both for five-year and for annual plans as the result of a long bargaining process, and reflect both the need to overcome expected bottlenecks and the major investment projects and priorities which the government intends to encourage. To optimise the achievement of these targets (as is for example the aim in Hungary) is only to maximise the achievement of a network of decisions reached by a rule-of-thumb process. The alternative is to persuade the politicians to reformulate their goals in more general or more operational terms. A satisfactory outcome will obviously only be achieved as a result of a long and difficult dialogue between the politicians and the mathematically-trained planners. One element in this dialogue must be a discussion on the extent to which the preference functions of the planning models should incorporate the preferences of the individual consumer. Some Soviet and East European economists would be prepared to go a very long way in the direction of consumer sovereignty; others have suggested that zones of state influence, individual influence and mixed influence would need to be determined. One considerable weakness of present Soviet discussions is that they have paid little attention to techniques such as costs-benefit analysis which are needed in order to bring social and other non-economic factors more consistently into the considerations of planners and politicians: the rationale of economic policy-making has not been carefully considered, and hence goals may remain inconsistent or ill-defined.

Conclusion

Few of the techniques of planning we have now been considering were available to the Soviet economist during the period of intensive industrialisation; those which were available were worked out only in elementary form. In any case, the gap between the goals of the politicians and the assumptions of the economists was so great that little dialogue was possible. The politicians, and the politically-minded economists, undertook the elaboration of their own system of planning and their own rule-of-thumb methods of quantifying their goals to make them operational. In doing this, they acquired a rich fund of valuable experience about the problems of development through central planning; the lessons from this experience, both successful and unsuccessful, could save resources in other economies where central planning is being used for development. Unfortunately, it is information about formal mechanisms for planning and financial control which has until now tended to be communicated from the Eastern bloc to the developing countries, rather than a realistic account of problems and achievements. For the developing countries, the further question exists: now that the new techniques for planning are available, can they be coupled with planning for a high rate of growth in conditions of rapid social change? If so, some of the successes of Soviet-type central planning may be achieved at less cost.

READING

P. J. D. Wiles: *The Political Economy of Communism* (1962).

G. Grossman (Editor), *Value and Plan* (1960).

Harry G. Shaffer (Editor). *The Soviet Economy. A Collection of Western and Soviet Views* (1964), Section X contains extracts from useful articles by Campbell, Wassily Leontief, Nemchinov, Kovalev.

A. Zauberman, "The Present State of Planometrics," *Soviet Studies*, Vol. XIV, No. 1, July 1962, p. 62 ff.

A. Zauberman, "The Criterion of Efficiency of Foreign Trade in Soviet-Type Economies," *Economica*, February 1964, p. 5 ff.

M. C. Kaser, "Welfare Criteria in Soviet Planning," in *Soviet Planning* (1964), edited by Jane Degras and Alec Nove.

J. Drewnowski, "The Economic Theory of Socialism," *Journal of Political Economy*, August, 1961.

For current developments in Soviet economic organisation, see *Soviet Studies Information Supplement*, published since January 1964, and available on subscription (10/– per year) from Information Supplement, Institute of Soviet and East European Studies, The University, Glasgow, W. 2., Scotland.

The main regular publications in English in which developments in the application of mathematical methods in centrally planned economies are reported are:

Economics of Planning (formerly Øst-Økonomi), published since 1961: available from the Editor, P. O. box 7030, Oslo, Norway (particularly important are the articles by Cherniak and Modin in Vol. 3, 1963, Nos. 1 and 2)—and

The A.S.T.E. Bulletin (published by the Association for the Study of Soviet-Type Economies): available to libraries on subscription from Professor H. S. Levine, Department of Economics, University of Pennsylvania, Philadelphia 4, Pa., U.S.A.

21   JAN S. PRYBYLA

SOVIET COMMAND:
FROM LIBERMANISM TO LIBERALISM?

THE PROBLEM

In spite of impressive quantitative performance over the years, the
Soviet economy continues to suffer from inefficiency in all but a few priority sectors. Although everyone in the Soviet Union knew about it all
along, the phenomenon was never seriously analyzed, nor was it officially
recognized as a built-in failing of the system. It was, on the contrary,
treated like sin—to be repressed and punished rather than prevented and
cured.

Waste and inefficiency manifest themselves in the Soviet Union in
two forms: the poor quality of many goods and services, and poor planning and management.

Shoddy goods mean rapid obsolescence, antiquated styling, lack of
novelty, narrow range, frequent breakdowns, and inadaptability to the
needs of the job for which the goods are intended. Shoddy service means
delays, inconvenience, poor attention to detail, faulty distribution, seller-
buyer conflict, and lines outside stores. Unsatisfactory goods and services,
in other words, result in a misallocation of material resources, a brain
drain, and psychological wear-and-tear. In a sellers' market (where the
demand for commodities greatly exceeds the supply) there will be, to
use a Soviet expression, little "concrete" evidence of the disease: even
the shoddiest products and the poorest service will be snapped up by
goods-hungry customers and by individual users working against the
norm. In a buyers' market (where the supply of certain goods exceeds
the demand), the "concrete" manifestation of low quality is the piling up
of unsold commodities in stores and warehouses, and consumer resistance
to rude store attendants, clerks and hotel-keepers. Between 1955 and
1963, inventories of non-food consumer goods in wholesale and retail
trade had risen in monetary terms from 12,500 million rubles to 30,600
million rubles. Much of this increase was accounted for by goods rejected
by customers.

From "The Soviet Economy: From Libermanism to Liberalism?" *Bulletin*, Institute for the Study of the USSR, Vol. XIII, No. 7 (July 1966), pp. 19–77. By
permission of the *Bulletin*, Institute for the Study of the USSR.

Unsatisfactory planning and management erupt at all times in a rash of bureaucrats. The bureaucrats fall into two categories: those whose existence is sanctioned by law, and the illegitimate but indispensable *tolkachi,* ZIS-men, or pushers. The legitimate bureaucrats are gainfully employed by the state in planning, accounting, managing, supervising, administering, inspecting, and in a multitude of related tasks. The illegal pushers are hired by socialist enterprises to fill the gaps, unclog the bottlenecks and generally smooth out the unevenness of the plan. Like the private plots of the collective farmers and the kolkhoz market, they are individual initiative called to the rescue of administrative socialism.

Here are a few telling, but not untypical examples. The RSFSR has today more than three million accountants. The Novo-Kramatorsk Machine Factory counted 600 inspectors in a single year. In 1959, the Kazakh Gosplan changed its allocation of rolled steel 538 times, and in 1958 the RSFSR Council of Ministers issued 140 statutory orders to secure additional supplies for the Moscow City Sovnarkhoz—and this after a reform which was supposed to cut down red tape. The late V. S. Nemchinov estimated that if something radical were not done about the quality of Soviet planning and if the growth rates typical of the fifties continued, then by 1980 (the inaugural year of full Communism), the entire adult population of the Soviet Union would have to be employed in economic planning and administration. And where, one might ask, would the pushers then come from? Eight thousand of them invaded the offices of the Dnepropetrovsk Sovnarkhoz in 1959. This sort of thing obviously cannot go on.

The root causes of poor quality were and are the primitive analytical tools used by the overcentralized planners and a system of incentives which until recently took account of and rewarded or punished only one dimension of managerial performance: gross output. The trouble thus lies both at the center and at the periphery of the system.

Let us deal first with the center. Briefly, the planning establishment tries to do too much, from too high up, with too little. The "too little" refers to the crude materials-balances methods used by the planners and to the paucity of reliable information. If economic planning means anything, it is the continuous flow and processing of more or less accurate information. Information there is all right, tons of it, but like the goods which are its end product, its quality leaves much to be desired. Planning information is "good" when it enables the planner to measure accurately the cost of alternative courses of action (plan variants). This the present Soviet system does not do. The Soviet planners are so busy counting and measuring nails down to a fraction of an inch that they have no time left to compile and evaluate more than one or two variants of the overall plan. They are thus rational about the physics of nails but irrational about the need for nails in any given situation. One hesitates to bring up another dreadful thought, namely, that even the "bad" information is worse than it looks because it is falsified many times over on its way up from the enterprises.

What is to be done? Clearly one must tackle both the existing tools and the type of information currently available to the planners. There are better tools in the world than those used by Gosplan. Input-output analysis, linear programming and electronic computers come to mind. The Soviets under the able leadership of men like Kantorovich, Novozhilov, the late V. S. Nemchinov, Dorodnitsyn and others have actually been moving in this direction for some years. High-speed electronic computers are the common denominator. There is, however, a problem here. First of all, there are at the present time about 30,000 computers in the world, most of them in the United States. It is probable that whatever the Soviets decide to do about their planning, they will have to import a fairly large number of computers from abroad. This presents some delicate problems of foreign exchange allocations, but the obstacle is not insuperable. But there is more. If the computers are to be applied to the planning machinery in its present shape, the Soviets will need (and this is a Soviet estimate) something like one million computers working day and night at the rate of 30,000 operations per second. Assuming that the world computer population does not crack under the strain (or the Soviet foreign exchange reserve for that matter), there will still be the problem of setting up an integrated computer network and training large numbers of skilled operators and analysts. The net result may well be quicker bad planning. That is because computers have to be fed information, and it really does not make much sense to process more rapidly the present avalanche of trivia.

So the call has gone out for decentralization. Now, there are two kinds of decentralization. The first is administrative, geographical and "formalistic" from the economist's standpoint. It means dividing among many agencies a job that used to be done by one agency—a sort of socialist putting-out system. The nails are still "planned" as of old, but now in many places. Formalistic decentralization is the centralizers' idea of progress; it has the advantage of being readily comprehended by the Party people whose jobs may be shifted but not eliminated. The concept is, therefore, welcome in Party circles. Khrushchev's sovnarkhoz reform was of this species, and still the pushers kept coming.

The second kind of decentralization is something very different. The underlying idea is to reduce the volume of irrelevant information by allowing the periphery to participate in the decision-making process on a broad front. In this case, the central planners reserve for themselves only a limited number of influential coordinating decisions and leave the rest to enterprise managers. Petty tutelage is minimized (though not totally eliminated), and perhaps only 4,000 integrated computers may be needed. Decentralization through the economic emancipation of the enterprise manager involves a surrender of much decision-making power by the center. It is, therefore, a move toward economic liberalism.

Libermanism, more cautious and in many respects more orthodox, tackles the problem from the other side, i.e., from the enterprise end. From the point of view of the history of Soviet economic thought, the significance of Libermanism was not that it proposed something spectacularly new, but that it was singled out for official recognition, discussed widely on a substantive rather than ideological basis, and applied experimentally though in modified form.

At the enterprise end, the problem of waste and inefficiency is one of incentives. The managerial bonus system (as well as worker incentives) concentrated until 1964 on the gross value of output. This led to all kinds of distortions of managerial behavior, including the almost complete stifling of initiative and innovation, sacrifice of quality for quantity, and the dissimulation of productive capacity by directors anxious to make sure that the quantitative indices sent down from above were attainable with the minimum of risk. In the setting of a highly bonus-conscious society (basic salaries and wages being purposely set at low levels), appeals to socialist consciousness and proletarian duty meant little.

The Liberman Solution

The trouble, Liberman thought, was that the major incentives were not only misguided, but buttressed by a multitude of detailed instructions thought up by administrators at the top, on the basis of administrative art rather than economic science.[1] What Liberman did not say was that socialist economic science did not exist. It had been nipped in the bud by Stalin back in 1928. The centrally-spawned targets (which, while they hampered managerial initiative, usually boiled down to one main incentive) included total quantity, product assortment, product destination, delivery dates, supply sources, sticky purchase and sales prices, the enterprise wages fund, number of workers, grades of skill, labor productivity, planned profit or loss, production costs, capital investment, capital saving, new technology, and many more.

The elements of the now celebrated "Liberman Proposal" were as

[1] See Y. Liberman, "The Plan, Profits, and Bonuses," *Pravda,* September 9, 1962; "The Plan, Profits, and Bonuses," *Ekonomicheskaya gazeta,* November 10, 1962; "Once Again on the Plan, Profits, and Bonuses," *Pravda,* September 20, 1964; "The Plan, Direct Ties, and Profitability," *Pravda,* November 21, 1965.

follows. First, the enterprise managers were to be free to determine most of the details of the plan, including labor productivity, number of workers, wages, production costs, capital investments, savings and new technology. "Shadow indices" for these things were to be worked out by the central planners, but they were not to be communicated to the enterprises. This clearly was meant to meet possible objections from the centralizers. The central planners would, however, still hand down enterprise targets for volume of output according to assortment of products, and delivery schedules. "These," Liberman cautioned, "must be drawn up with the maximum consideration for the direct ties between suppliers and consumers."

Second, the managers would be answerable to the central authorities only for their overall performance measured by a single index, profits, or more exactly, the "profitability rate." The profitability rate was to be calculated as a ratio of profits to the total (fixed and working) capital of the enterprise. Absolute profits were to be calculated on goods actually consumed and not, as in the past, on goods delivered (but often unusable). The central planners were to work out a "profitability norm" for various industrial branches and enterprises within those branches. This profitability norm would have to take into account an enterprise's attempt to introduce new goods (lower norm), and would remain in force for a number of years, the idea being to encourage innovation and avoid punishing an enterprise for good performance by raising norms in the wake of high profitability rates. Bonuses would be scaled to the profitability rates, and to that only. To make managers aim high, Liberman worked out a device for rewarding fulfillment rather than overfulfillment of the profitability rate plan submitted by the enterprise. Since profits were to be computed as a percentage of capital, it was in the manager's interest either to increase his absolute profits by using current inputs of labor and raw materials more efficiently, or to pare down his demand for excess capital. How about managers who tried to increase their profits by inflating the prices of new products? Liberman's answer was that this would be resisted by factory purchasers who needed low prices on the goods they bought so as to make their own profits. In place of the former "formal" (turnover tax) control over industrial prices, there would be control through demand resistance.

All this is quite technical and looks plausible, but what is it trying to achieve and, what is more interesting, would it work? Broadly speaking, what Libermanism is trying to achieve is to make Soviet socialism work better, that is, with less waste motion and inefficiency than hitherto, by releasing grass-roots initiative and resourcefulness, which, it assumes, is still around even after thirty years of Stalinist conformity. It proposes to eliminate much busy work (that is, save the planning principle from being destroyed by its own inner contradictions) and to instill into the executors of the plan some, at least, of the characteristics of the entrepreneur. The end product, it hopes, will be better quality all round, fewer bureaucrats and a minimum of pushers.

Libermanism concentrates on managerial incentives embodied in the profitability rate. In the wide-ranging discussion which followed Liberman's article published in *Pravda* in September 1962, another idea came to the forefront, that of direct contracting between producers and retailers (an idea implicit in Libermanism). The purpose of direct contracting is to cut out the state middleman and thus get rid of the sort of situation that at one time faced the Moscow Likhachev Automobile Plant, which in order to obtain its annual supply of ball bearings from the GPZ factory next door had to furnish 400 pounds of supporting documentation to fourteen planning agencies.

At first glance, it might appear that what Libermanism has done is to substitute one unidimensional target (profit) for another (gross output). This, Liberman argues, is not so, because profit synthesizes many dimensions of managerial behavior. Unfortunately, in the Soviet setting this happens to be untrue. The reason is that Soviet prices—even after the comprehensive reform of 1955—do not even remotely reflect relative resource scarcities. They are not the outcome of seller-buyer bargaining, but simple accounting and control devices used by the central planners to check on plan operation. Industrial and wholesale prices in the Soviet Union are the numerical expressions of leadership ideology, and not too reliable at that. "But we have changed prices many times," pleads Liberman, "and yet we are still not satisfied with them. Why is this?" The answer he gives is politically wise but economically irrelevant: "Because prices are a matter of complete indifference to enterprises." Now if prices were allocating and signaling devices reflecting relative resource scarcities and not transmission belts for administratively determined allocative decisions, they would be of compelling interest to the enterprises. When they are Stalinism, Khrushchevism, or Brezhnev–Kosyginism in Arabic numerals, they are of course "a matter of complete indifference to enterprises" except insofar as they can be manipulated by enterprise accountants to show that what was done was actually what the leadership *via* the central planners' control figures wanted to be done. Economic liberalism is allocative rationality in the former sense. Libermanism goes less than half way. It uses the vocabulary of rationality (profit), but leaves the substance very much as it was. What, to quote but one instance, is the meaning of the profit rate (expressed as a ratio of profit to capital) when there is no price tag on capital? How is the relative scarcity of land measured, when there is no rent? The Soviet mathematical economists are aware of this problem, but they have been strangely silent throughout the great Liberman debate.

The Experiments

"I think," Professor Liberman wrote in November 1962, "that an experiment in a single district would provide documentation and verification, but accomplish nothing more." An experiment in a couple of districts was what the Soviet leaders ordered in July 1964 with a six months' deadline. From an ideological point of view, the decision was significant if only because it showed that pragmatism on a narrow front took over from the traditional dogmatism of the Party die-hards. The two pilot projects were the Bolshevichka clothing plant in Moscow and the Mayak clothing firm in Gorky. Since clothing manufacture is not a priority activity of the workers' state, nobody (with the exception of the Chinese, who promptly rose to the occasion) could accuse the leadership of ideological deviation.

The Bolshevichka and Mayak experiments were Libermanism modified, combining as they did the profit criterion with direct contracting between producers and retailers. However, profitability in this experiment meant profit earned as a percentage of the total cost of production (*sebestoimost*) and not, as in Liberman's proposal, profit as a percentage of total capital investment. Central controls were retained on the prices of established clothing, but enterprise managers were given much freedom to adjust prices to cover additional costs of technical innovations. The prices of new clothing were then written into the producer-retailer contracts. However, this freedom to make price adjustments to cover additional cost was not extended to the profit markup, with the result that innovational clothing (i.e., that wanted by the consumers, bought by them, and showing up in the sales volume) was not permitted to manifest itself in the enterprises' profitability rate—a key idea of Libermanism. The profit margins on new clothing were fixed by the existing price lists. Result: excellent sales during the six months of the experiment for both enterprises and a decline in their profits, both absolutely and as a rate. In short, what was wanted by the consumers was less "profitable" than what was wanted by the planned indicators of profitability.

Were the profitability criterion to be retained under those circumstances, the managers who produced the wanted goods would be punished by having their bonuses whisked away. The criterion was, in fact, kept during the six months of the Bolshevichka-Mayak experiment, but the problem was noted. In the course of 1965, the system was extended to about four hundred enterprises in the light industry and to a large number of retail stores, restaurants and selected food processing plants. A somewhat different experiment in the Ukraine involved three machinery and metalworking plants, a number of coal mines and two light industry plants. The lessons learned in the Bolshevichka-Mayak experiment were applied to that involving the four hundred enterprises. The criterion of managerial success was shifted to the fulfillment of the sales plan on condition that the profit plan was also fulfilled. This was not quite what Liberman had in mind and his role in the experiments is unclear. As we shall see, he was later to be vindicated by another shift in official policy (September 1965), which redefined the profitability rate as a ratio of profits to production capital (rather than profits to production cost).

It must be said in favor of the evaluators of the Bolshevichka-Mayak experiment that they saw through the fog of apparent failure (low profits and profitability rates) to the satisfied smile on the face of the consumers. The Soviet state did not collapse in a fit of atomistic anarchy, which, as the dogmatists see it, is the lot of capitalistic market economies—with which, paradoxically, Soviet producers are urged to catch up. The Party did not disintegrate. There was no commitment to the central planners as to assortment and delivery schedules (the commitment was made instead to retail customers directly), no commitment as to profits, costs of production, labor productivity, number of workers, and the total wage bill. That satisfied the rationalists ("revisionists" as the Chinese call them). But there was commitment to the center with regard to profitability plan (profit divided by cost of production), central approval was needed for price adjustments initiated by managers in response to additional costs stemming from quality improvements stipulated in enterprise contracts, and central control over new investments in fixed and working capital was retained. Basic wage and salary scales continued to be established centrally, and adjustments in prices of inputs written into enterprise contracts had to obtain central approval. That made the centralizers happy. In short, applied neo-Libermanism was a political compromise. The managers, of course, were not too pleased since low profits and profitability rates affected their bonuses, tied as these were to the profitability index. Judging by the accelerated turnover of goods produced by both enterprises, customers seemed to have been quite happy about the whole thing.

THE SEPTEMBER 1965 PLENUM AND AFTER

In his report to the plenary session of the Party Central Committee of September 27, 1965, Kosygin revealed the Soviet government's intention to extend the neo-Liberman system of management incentives and plan indicators to some branches of industry in 1966 and to all industry in

1967–68.[2] At the same time, a thorough price reform was to be initiated and introduced gradually in 1967 and 1968. Khrushchev's regional economic councils were abolished and a number of industrial ministries once again set up. Thus, administrative centralization was to be combined with economic decentralization. This was understood by both the administratively-minded centralizers and the economically-oriented rationalizers, two among a number of contending parties in the post-Stalin Soviet state.

The approach to price reform, it must be said, does not augur well for the rationality of the cumbersome Soviet economic machine. Here is what V. Sitnin, chairman of the USSR State Planning Committee's State Price Committee, has to say about it. "In a number of instances, unsubstantiated prices set without taking objective economic criteria into account have been in effect in our economy. This led to a loss of authenticity of many economic calculations and opened the way for subjective decisions." So far so good. But there is analytical trouble ahead. "It is evidently time," Sitnin writes, "to adopt the practice of setting prices for a definite period. On expiration of the specific time during which this or that product is technically progressive, the prices should be automatically lowered."[3] This is poor thinking on what prices are all about. It is precisely price which should indicate when this or that product is technically progressive and not the other way round. In short, flexibility is to come from the planners (on what basis?) and not from the "objective economic criteria" for which Sitnin earlier makes such an eloquent plea. To make matters worse, the guideline for price setting is to be the "average socially necessary expenditure of production," a pre-1870 brew of Marxist vintage. These average socially necessary expenditures of production are "the average level toward which the production of the majority of enterprises in the branch inevitably gravitates." It sounds incredible, but here it is. The Soviet non-mathematical economists have got as far as Ricardo. In charge of a complex, industrialized, modern economy, they continue to ignore the margin of decisions and reason from average levels, average expenditures and inevitable gravitations.

As far as managerial incentives are concerned, the proposed reforms are cautious and rather hesitant, but they do tend in a promising direction. Compared with the present state of things, the number of indices confirmed for enterprises from above is, indeed, reduced. Compared with Liberman's original proposals and even with the Bolshevichka-Mayak experiment, the picture is less liberal. Nine major indices for managerial behavior are still in the hands of the central planners. These include assignments for volume of output sold (replacing the discredited gross

[2] For the Party-state resolutions on management reforms and Kosygin's report, see *Pravda*, September 28, 1965, and October 10, 1965.

[3] V. Sitnin, "Price Is an Important Tool of Economic Management," *Pravda*, November 12, 1965.

output index), basic assortment, group assignments for "the most important items" (e.g., power, fuels, metals, chemicals, building materials, the more important foodstuffs), profit and profitability rates (expressed in the Liberman manner as a ratio of profit to production assets), the enterprise wages fund (Liberman had hoped that this would be a "shadow index"), payments into and appropriations from the budget, the volume of centralized investments and the putting into operation of production facilities and fixed assets, introduction of new technology, and indices of material and technical supply. So, one may ask, where has all the reform gone?

The answer is that progress toward economic rationality in the Soviet Union is measured in inches. Quite frequently the inches point in the wrong—irrational—direction. This time the trend is unmistakeably correct in a non-ideological sense.

The latest reforms boil down to this. Managerial success is to be measured by what appears to be combined index of profitability and output sold. Managerial bonuses will be tied to this criterion. The size of the incentive fund (a deduction from profits) will depend on the growth of output sales, or on profits and the level of profitability stipulated in the plan. The profitability norms stipulated by the plan will be set for a number of years and overfulfillment of the plan will count for less than the fulfillment of indices stipulated in the plan. This, it is hoped, will induce enterprises to uncover reserves in good time and accept higher plan assignments. The profitability rate is made meaningful by the introduction of a charge on capital (socialist interest), rent payments, or the use of accounting prices. The incentive fund is to be increased according to the share of new types of output and the additional income received by the enterprise from price increments for raising the quality of its products. Direct contractual arrangements are to be made with wholesalers and retail associations rather than directly with individual buyers (this is not original Libermanism). There are a few exceptions. but in general the rule will apply. In a recent gesture of loyalty, Professor Liberman not only concurred, but reversed his previous position. "The establishment of the most rational ties," he wrote, "is not a spontaneous matter, but an extremely important act of long-term planning." And on what principles will that act of long-term planning be based? Administrative art, as in the old days, or inevitable gravitations?

THE OPEN END

What is perhaps most striking about the Soviet economic reforms since 1964 is that they cannot be discussed profitably except in highly technical economic terms. This is new, and it is unusual. Past reforms were mainly administrative and ideological. For the first time since 1920, the Soviets are applying economic remedies to economic ills in a burst of prudence and pragmatism. The scope is still insufficient. The key to the problem is fundamental price reform and, in spite of a new round of tinkering, it does not appear as if the Soviets had yet fathomed the mysteries of rational resource allocation and general equilibrium. The present Soviet leaders still give the impression of being of two minds about the whole thing mainly because price reform means Party reform. They hope that a larger volume of goods will make the changeover less painful, yet the very purpose of the reform is to eliminate waste motion in the process of making more goods. Sheer volume is not a Soviet problem at all. Sooner or later, the "inevitable gravitations" of repressed market forces will make themselves felt more acutely than ever, and when that happens Libermanism will have to plunge into liberalism or die.

Professor Liberman expresses the hope that the central assignments will be treated more as guidelines than as strict and inflexible orders, and that in time the more important among them (e.g., the wages fund and gross output indices for some items) will wither away. This may well be so. It all depends on how those in the political saddle will react to the discomforts of an unwieldy economy.

22   JAN S. PRYBYLA

ALBANIA: DEPENDENT COMMAND

The cause of vassalage is chronic poverty. Persistent economic weakness has to be paid for in political allegiance—to Greeks, Romans, Goths, Byzantines, Serbs, Bulgars, Sicilians, Venetians, Normans, Turks, Italians, Yugoslavs, Soviets and now the Chinese. In a world divided by the rich and powerful, the poor and weak can escape intolerable indebtedness to one power only by finding another protector. From being the political satellites of the capitalist Italians, the present Albanian leaders have managed to steer their country into dependence first on Yugoslavia (1945–48) to which they owed over $80 million after four years, then on the Soviet Union (1949–61), and more recently on China.[1]

BUYING ON TIME

Sino-Albanian trade reflects Albania's unique position as China's beachhead in Europe and her present estrangement from both the Soviet Union and the USSR's political friends. Since 1955 at least, the Albanians have been piling up substantial annual deficits in their trade with Peking. As Table 22–1 shows, this went on right through China's three Great Leap years (1958–60) and gathered momentum after 1960.

The persistent clearing deficits have been financed by Chinese credits, and the amounts of some of these are known. Thus on December 3, 1954, China gave the Albanians a grant-in-aid of $2.5 million and a loan of $12.5 million.[2] In January 1959 a further credit of $13.75 million was

From "Albania's Economic Vassalage," *East Europe*, January 1967, pp. 9–14. Reprinted by permission of *East Europe*.

[1] Albania's relatively brief affair with the USSR is examined in my "The Economic Causes of the Soviet-Albanian Quarrel," *Bulletin of the Institute for the Study of the USSR*, March 1963. A thorough treatment of the political side of this relationship may be found in W. E. Griffith's *Albania and the Sino-Soviet Rift*, Cambridge, Masachusetts: The M.I.T. Press, 1963.

[2] The figures as reported by *Jenmin Jih Pao*, Peking, January 17, 1959 were given in old rubles; the later credit figures for 1961 as reported by the New China News Agency, April 25, 1961, were given in old and new rubles. The grant of $2.5 million had not been used by 1958, and was thereupon applied to 1959–60. It is worth mentioning that a situation similar to that revealed in Table 22–1 prevailed before World War II. From 1934 through 1938, annual Albanian clearing debts ranged from 7.8 million to 13.1 million Albanian francs.

extended for the "purchase of equipment for industrial projects during the period 1961–65"—*i.e.*, during Albania's Third Five Year Plan. This credit was flanked (overshadowed would be a more appropriate term) by Soviet and east European promises of aid for the same period amounting to over $132.5 million. The latter sum was canceled in the spring of 1961, at which time the Soviet Union demanded the immediate repayment of all debts owed to it by Albania even though most of them did not fall due until 1970.[3] Soviet experts were withdrawn from Albania in April and May 1961, and east European advisers packed up and went by August 31. This naturally caused some very bad feelings among the debtors, who had just gone through earthquakes, floods, drought, and collectivization —enough to put them on the verge of mass starvation. Though all the evidence is not in yet (because both the Soviets and the Albanians have elected to say nothing about it), what the Albanians apparently did in the circumstances was simply to default. This is brought out by the drop in Albanian exports to the USSR from $21 million in 1961 to zero a year later, in spite of Soviet demands for about $210 million right away. Given Albania's extremely modest foreign exchange holdings, it is unlikely that settlement was made on that part of the balance of payments account.

In February 1961 China promised the Albanians a loan of $125 million for the purchase of equipment for "twenty-five large industrial plants" during the Albanian Third Five Year Plan (1961–65). Together with the $13.75 million granted earlier, total Chinese aid commitments more than matched the unfulfilled Soviet and east European commitments for the same period. About this time Chinese experts began to arrive in Albania, taking over where the Soviets and the east Europeans had so abruptly left off. Two early technical assistance projects supervised by the Chinese were the rebuilding of Durres harbor (a task originally proposed by the East Germans) and the construction of a nickel processing plant at Pishkashki in central Albania.[4] The Pishkashki project must have caused acute irritation in Prague, because in the days of Albanian-Czechoslovak amity the Prague government had built a plant in Slovakia for the express purpose of treating raw Albanian nickel that was to be sent in payment of Czechoslovak loans.

Another Chinese loan was negotiated in June 1965, presumably covering deliveries during Albania's Fourth Five Year Plan (1966–70). The amount of the new loan has not been officially revealed, but it has been suggested that it is about $214 million.

The Chinese loans thus appear to be, in part at least, the funding of

[3] Cumulative indebtedness to the USSR on clearing account in the period 1951–58 came to $106.5 million. Total Soviet grants and credits to Albania from 1945 through 1960 are estimated at over $250 million. In 1957 the Soviets canceled more than $40 million in Albanian debts to them.

[4] Harry Hamm, *Albania—China's Beachhead in Europe*, New York: Praeger, 1963, pp. 48–49.

Albanian clearing debts, *i.e.*, the conversion of accumulated clearing debts into long-term loans. The announced total of these operations comes to $136.25 million covering the period 1955 through 1965. Albania's cumulative clearing debt to China from 1955 through 1963 (the last year for which official figures are available) comes to $82.7 million (see Table 22–1). The 1964 deficit is estimated at another $38 million. It is possible that Albania's 1965 and 1966 deficits were of very roughly the same order of magnitude as the 1964 debt. If this assumption is correct, total Albanian indebtedness to China amounted to about $159 million at the end of 1965 and now stands at roughly $200 million, all of it taken care of for the time being by loan agreements and the funding procedure.

LEANING TO ONE SIDE

The Albanian debt to China is a political phenomenon for a number of reasons. From the Albanian standpoint there are three main problems, all contributing to give commercial transactions with China an unequivocally political hue: 1. the absolute amount of the debt, 2. Albania's capacity to service the debt, and 3. the possible repercussions of repayment on domestic economic development.

1. The $200 million that Albania now owes China in respect to commodity trade does not include (a) sums owed for the delivery of military materiel and advice, (b) any amounts owed for technical assistance, and (c) shipping costs.

Items (b) and (c) are probably not terribly important for the following reasons. Technical assistance agreements with China usually specify exchange of information which may take care of a substantial portion of the cost of Chinese technical services to Albania, even if the Albanian contribution is purely formal. For instance, the November 1956 technical cooperation protocol specified that in exchange for Albanian advice on social insurance, public health, the construction of small hydroelectric power stations in mountain areas, and the cultivation of tobacco, olive plants and cereal seeds, the Chinese would supply information on the use of by-products of rice, the prevention of alkali deposits in rice fields, and the production of plant seeds. Whatever debts arise in this connection are probably ironed out by the Joint Sino-Albanian Commission for Scientific and Technical Cooperation. Moreover, the services of Chinese technicians are relatively cheap. The salaries of Chinese experts were at one time about half those of the East Germans in equivalent fields of expertise and of equivalent rank. Shipping costs are probably taken care of by the Joint Sino-Albanian Shipping Company set up in 1961, but some indebtedness on this account surely arises for the Albanians, especially in view of the recurrent shipments in non-communist bottoms of Canadian, French and Australian grain to Albania on Chinese order. Since the Albanian merchant marine is very small and China is still quite deficient in this department, wheat switch-deal shipments have to be paid for in hard currencies by the Chinese who can hardly be expected to add ship charter costs to what already is a generous credit line. The Chinese may perhaps be willing to go half way in this matter, but certainly not much farther.

How the delivery of military hardware is handled is anybody's guess, but if standard communist practice is followed it has to be paid for. By now Albania's debt under that heading must be important. The Warsaw Pact shield no longer protects Albania from real or imaginary Yugoslav and Greek threats; since the summer of 1961 Albanian military personnel have not been trained anywhere in the Soviet bloc. Here too the Chinese have had to take over, and doubtless they have supplied more than just the military thought of Mao Tse-tung.

There are probably no interest charges on any of the Chinese loans to Albania. As yet there has been no indication of any Chinese intention to convert the debt into a grant.

The significance of the debt can best be seen by comparing it to China's other foreign-aid commitments and payments. In the period 1956 through 1966 the Chinese promised about $771 million in grants and credits (mostly the latter) to 21 non-communist countries in Asia and Africa. Of this amount, not more than $250 million has actually been disbursed. This is only one-fourth more than what the Albanians have received in a comparable period. The only single country that is likely to have topped the Albanian figure is North Vietnam.

2. It is questionable whether the Albanians will ever be in a position to repay their commercial or other debts to China in economic goods. In the decade 1955–1964 they did not do so, even though there are indications that they tried on one or two occasions. In 1962, for example, Albanian sales to China rose more than three times over the level of the preceding year, while imports from China slightly more than doubled. As far as is known, 1962 was not a year of economic crisis in China but it was one in Albania, where food shortages compelled the Chinese to divert to Albania about 105 thousand metric tons of wheat (worth $6.6 million) which they had earlier purchased in France and Canada for their own use. Again in 1963 the Albanians increased their sales to China by 100 percent over 1962, while imports from China actually declined by one percent notwithstanding another diversion by China of $3.4 million worth of grain purchased in Australia. In 1964 the Chinese (who regularly buy from the "imperialists" between five and six million tons of grain per year) had to help feed Albania once more, this time to the

tune of $10.1 million of Canadian grain.[5] All this means that a significant portion of China's aid to Albania merely keeps the Albanians alive, an activity which the Soviets did not see fit to pursue after 1960. Incidentally, before the farms were collectivized in 1958, the Albanians imported only 57 thousand metric tons of wheat (27 thousand tons in 1955). Now that socialist agriculture is firmly in place, annual wheat imports (on credit) are running at a rate in excess of 140 thousand tons, and the Albanians are fed no better than before.

The Albanians have, in fact, maneuvered themselves into precisely the sort of corner which the Chinese doctrine of self-reliance deplores. The Chinese, after their experience of "leaning to one side" (that is, the Soviet), have since 1961 done their best to lean to all sides on a strictly C.O.D. basis. Leaning to one side as the Albanians are doing (see Table 22–2), has been described by the Chinese as the surest way of courting satellite status, be it in socialist-capitalist or in intra-capitalist relations. Albania now concentrates about 60 percent of its foreign trade on one country (China), and can pay for no more than a quarter to a half of its annual indispensable purchases from that source (see Table 22–3).

The figures in Table 22–3 do not, of course, reflect compensating services which the Albanians may have rendered their creditors over the years, nor for that matter do they take into account the reverse flow of services. Excluding technical advice there is, however, only one economic service which the Albanians could possibly have exported, and that is tourism. Not many Chinese peasants take their vacations in cultural chalets on the Albanian Riviera. For all practical purposes, then, Albania cannot pay for its imports with economic services. The same holds for capital exports, since Albanian gold and foreign exchange holdings must by now be exceedingly modest. It must pay, if at all, in political goods: anti-Soviet propaganda, opposition at inter-party gatherings, the adoption of Mao's thought in politics, economics, education, foreign relations, and so on. From the Chinese standpoint, Albania's importance is as a political nuisance in the Soviets' Balkan hinterland.

ALBANIA'S ECONOMY

3. One price of Chinese aid has been the restructuring of Albania's economy. This boils down to four major demands.

---

[5] How all this squares with Albania's export of technical information to China on such subjects as the cultivation of cereal seeds is one of those proletarian imponderables which are best left alone. Earthquakes caused widespread damage in Albania in 1962. The Chinese Red Cross in March of that year donated 20,000 yuan to aid the victims.

TABLE 22-1. ALBANIA'S TRADE WITH COMMUNIST CHINA (Millions of dollars)*

	1955	1956	1957	1958	1959	1960	1961	1962	1963	1964 (est.)
Imports	1.3	4.1	5.9	1.7	2.4	7.0	19.5	42.1	41.7	66.0
Exports	0	0.7	0.7	0.8	0.8	2.1	2.8	11.7	23.4	28.0
Balance	-1.3	-3.4	-5.2	-0.9	-1.6	-4.9	-16.7	-30.4	-18.3	-38.0
Trade balance with all countries	-30	-20	-24	-50	-51	-32	-23	-24	-23	-38

*Leks have been converted to dollars at the official rate of 50 old leks to one US dollar. Figures for 1964 Chinese-Albanian trade are estimates.

TABLE 22-2. ALBANIA'S TRADE WITH CHINA AS PERCENTAGE OF TOTAL ALBANIAN FOREIGN TRADE (percent)

	1955	1956	1957	1958	1959	1960	1961	1962	1963	1964 (est.)
Total	2.3	8.3	8.0	2.3	2.7	6.9	18.4	50.8	54.7	59.5
Imports	3.0	10.6	11.1	2.1	2.8	8.5	27.1	64.6	58.8	67.3
Exports	0	3.7	2.4	2.7	2.4	4.3	5.7	28.5	48.7	46.6

TABLE 22-3. ALBANIAN IMPORTS FROM CHINA PAID FOR BY ALBANIAN EXPORTS TO CHINA (percent)

1955	1956	1957	1958	1959	1960	1961	1962	1963	1964 (est.)
0	17.7	11.5	48.1	35.1	30.0	14.3	27.8	56.1	42.4

(i) The Albanians must practice internal self-reliance. This means belt-tightening for the people, well beyond the point reached in 1961. "In everything let us depend on our own strength," is the Albanian party's Chinese-inspired slogan—which in spite of ruthless enforcement still leaves an unpaid deficit of about $30 million every year on the country's current trading account.

(ii) The productivity of Albania's agriculture must be raised so as to free China from the moral obligation and financial burden of sending wheat to that country every year. To this end the Chinese have exported about 400 tractors and some 20 thousand tons of chemical fertilizer to Albania every year since 1962, but so far to no apparent effect.[6] China's insistence that the Albanians begin at the beginning, that is, with agriculture (in which they might just possibly have a potential comparative advantage), is consistent with China's own recent domestic emphasis on "agriculture as foundation and industry as the leading factor" in the correct building of socialism.[7] Ironically, this is what Khrushchev used to tell them. Albania, he once said, was "the future orchard of socialism" where bananas and other delicacies would grow for all socialists to enjoy. To the men in Tirana, nurtured in Stalin's industry-oriented school, Khrushchev's gardening talk was unwelcome and downright heretical, and they said so publicly and loudly. The Chinese, on the other hand, appeared at first to go along with the Albanian industrial vision although they had already changed their own economic emphasis.

(iii) The development of agriculture must go hand in hand with rising output in the export industries. In the Albanian case this means oil and mining. Here again, this is also what the Soviets had earlier been saying.[8] During the Albanian Second Five Year Plan they had financed and directed the construction of a power plant, a coal and a copper mine, and iron, nickel, and chrome mines, and had supplied the petroleum-

---

[6] The gain in Chinese tractors has so far been more than offset by the loss of the tractors earlier supplied by the USSR and eastern Europe. Because the Soviets have sent no spare parts since 1961, the 2,000 Soviet-bloc tractors acquired by Albania from 1955 through 1961 are probably by now ready for the scrap heap. For an eyewitness confirmation of this reasoning, see "Visitor to Albania Made Unwelcome," *The New York Times*, October 30, 1966, p. 30.

[7] See Jan S. Prybyla, "Communist China's Strategy of Economic Development: 1961–1966," *Asian Survey*, October 1966. The first (Stalinist) Albanian Five Year Plan (1951–55) was to result in the following changes in sectoral percentage contributions to Albania's G.N.P.:

	1950	1955
Industry	27.5	57.5
Agriculture	72.5	42.5

The target was not reached because it was not reachable.

[8] The Soviets gave the same advice to Fidel Castro after he had run up a $1.5 billion bill with them. After some hesitation he took the advice, rejected Chinese overtures, and reverted to sugar. See Jan S. Prybyla, "Communist China's Economic Relations with Cuba," *Business and Society*, Autumn 1965.

producing industry with about 90 percent of its equipment. China's interest in Albania's extractive industries runs along very much the same lines. It is the interest of a creditor who is patient because patience suits his political calculations, but who is at the same time uneasily aware that he may quite possibly lose his investment. The Chinese are rather humorless in such matters.

(iv) Promotion of the "natural" export industries is to be supplemented by the gradual building up of import-substitute industries. This, again, is not so very different from what Khrushchev had in mind. The Soviets and their allies helped build two refineries that were to cater to Albania's tractor population, a cement works, processing plants for chrome ore, and some other similar projects. The Chinese have, among other things, helped build a ferrous metallurgy plant; a tractor spare parts factory; brick, tile, cement and fiberboard plants; a textile combine; and a hydroelectric power station.

All in all, the Chinese advice has been very much like that of the "revisionist" Soviets, but for the Albanians the degree of dependence has been greater, delivery schedules less certain, and the quality of things received not as good as before. The Albanians export very much the same combination of goods they always did, and import by and large the same product mix as before. The quality of both exports and imports is probably not as good as it used to be. As yet there is no clear indication of a rising ability to pay their way in international markets.

They are, however, expected to pay their way politically. Payment in political goods on a sustained basis is China's second major condition of economic support for Albania. In internal political organization as well as in foreign policy, Albania is urged to follow Peking's line.

Political payment must be accompanied by strict adherence to Mao's interpretation of Marxist-Leninist theory. This third condition of Chinese assistance has been carried out nearly to the letter.

Albania's poverty and smallness force it to rely on outside assistance, an exercise which usually turns into dependence on one power. Now a curious opportunity is opening up. By breaking the Hoxha-Shehu regime, Albania could choose the lesser of two evils: it could go back into the relatively loose and undisciplined Soviet fold instead of persisting in its present course of subservience to China. The Hoxha-Shehu regime, of course, is not about to allow itself to be broken: it wields the weapons of Stalinist terror with great ease and skill.[9]

The major threat to Hoxha actually comes from his supporters, the Chinese. Unless Albania shows some capacity for paying its own way,

[9] Between 1945 and 1956 there were reportedly 80,000 political arrests in Albania (out of a population of about 1.8 million); 16,000 prisoners perished in jail. In 1961 there were 14 concentration camps for political prisoners. See Hamm, op. cit., p. 53.

the Chinese comrades may one day get tired of subsidizing the country; the returns on their investment are obviously diminishing, since everyone knows by now what the Albanian leaders will say next on matters of ideology and foreign policy. Should China herself turn "revisionist," a contingency which cannot be lightly dismissed, the argument in favor of getting rid of anachronistic Albanian Stalinists would be irresistible.

Albania's political future may well depend on her becoming ever so slightly revisionist, on coming to terms with some of the polycentric countries of eastern Europe with which she can trade more naturally. Reconciliation with Rumania could be a first step, and there are indications that some such move is actually being contemplated. The alternative is to remain China's satellite, economically at a dead end, living in fear of some new upheaval in Peking.

23

RUMANIA: HESITANT COMMAND

In Bucharest one may come across a planner who is prepared to learn from American experience; but it would take a very long time to discover one who was ready to admit that Rumania had anything to learn from its communist neighbours. So strong is the Rumanians' determination to establish their country's uniqueness in eastern Europe. This determination is, of course, part of the urge to achieve emancipation from Russian tutelage and control. In the field of foreign relations it has paid off handsomely. With skill and persistence the Rumanians have firmly established their right to follow their own independent line on Germany, the Middle East and anything else; and they have done it to the accompaniment of increasing prestige, and without actually—so far—burning their bridges to Moscow. At home the record is more mixed.

It is part and parcel of the regime's ebullient self-confidence that it has firmly set its sights on giving Rumania a modern, self-sufficient industrial economy as quickly as possible. Helped by the country's rich natural resources—oil, non-ferrous metals, coal, timber and so on—it got off to an excellent start. Industrial production grew at an average annual rate of 14.5 per cent during 1959–65, and last year at 11.5 per cent; during the first half of this year the growth rate was up again to 13.6 per cent.

Yet, in spite of this success story, all is not well with the Rumanian economy, and since the beginning of this year the Rumanians have begun to shed their complacency and admit as much. Mr Ceausescu, the party leader, told a central committee plenum last December that he wished to discuss the efficiency of the economy and he proceeded to do so in pretty uncomplimentary terms: too many enterprises operating at a loss, too much waste, too many rejects, poor labour productivity, over-staffing, delays in starting capital construction and so on. Mr Ceausescu's strictures have been repeated with more or less asperity by the party press and by party leaders at intervals ever since.

But it is not yet clear whether the Rumanians will embark deliberately on an economic reform comparable to those that are being undertaken, or planned, in Russia and elsewhere in eastern Europe. They say that all that is necessary is to carry on the process of adapting, modifying

Reprinted from The Economist of August 19th, 1967. Originally published in The Economist under the title "Rumania: Brinkmanship."

and perfecting the existing system that was initiated at the last party congress two years ago. The ministries are said to be busy studying plans to cut down production costs and so on. They point out, quite fairly, that the growth of the economy has outstripped the supply of trained workers, technicians and managers, and that when this deficiency is overcome, and the inefficient weeded out, things will be much better.

Great store is put on the more efficient and scientific organisation of production, and on developing and spreading the use of computers in industry; the computer age in Rumania is very much in its infancy. Planning techniques too will be improved; and in the drafting of the next plan (1971–75) which is already under way, an attempt is being made to leaven the narrow expertise of the planners by bringing in academic and other economic and industrial experts to help evaluate the ideas and suggestions which individual enterprises are being encouraged to put up. Planning, in other words, is to become a more democratic and a less specialised business.

But there are signs that the Rumanians mean to do more than tinker with the old system. Change is definitely in the air, however much officials, especially the less important and less self-confident ones, may be reluctant to admit it. Important extensions of the rights and powers of enterprises are being discussed and mulled over. Some cautious steps have already been taken. The number of plan targets in the current five-year plan (1966–70) has been cut by comparison with previous plans. And on July 1st some 70 enterprises began for an experimental period, to give their managements considerably increased scope for making independent decisions; they will receive only seven compulsory indicators from the central authorities. They also have authority to expand the existing incentive system in order to reward those responsible for cutting costs and stepping up production. In the past, material incentives have not been considered a very respectable part of the Rumanian economic set-up —which, no doubt, helps to explain why the theoretically elaborate bonus system has not been at all effective in practice; it is now being re-examined.

The reorganisation of the state farms, which was begun this spring and is due to be completed next year, also represents quite a substantial experiment in decentralisation. Formerly the state farms, which cultivate 20 per cent of the arable land, were a particularly happy hunting ground for bureaucrats in Bucharest. Now, in the words of the central committee's communiqué of March 28th, "the farm shall be an independent unit, with full power over the administration of its assets . . ." and the director of each farm, which will specialise either in arable or livestock farming, will have extensive powers to decide for himself what exactly should be produced and how the farm's resources should be disposed of. Moreover, wages and bonuses are to be deliberately geared to production.

An expanding volume of foreign trade is obviously of crucial importance to the rapid development and modernisation of the economy. So it is not surprising to find it also is being emancipated a little from the insensitive and groping hand of the bureaucrats. One is assured that nothing so rash is contemplated as giving export firms any kind of financial incentive or putting them into direct contact with the foreign markets they are trying to sell to. But a start has been made in improving these contacts and in cutting down the number of intermediaries. Selected foreign trade organisations are being removed from the control of the ministry of foreign trade and put under the appropriate technical ministry. Thus, for example, the trade organisation responsible for selling fruit and vegetables is now directly responsible to the Higher Council of Agriculture (that is, the ministry); it should therefore be that much better placed to make the producer understand what the foreign customer really wants.

Plainly, the limits of experimentation are still pretty narrow. The central planners are firmly determined not to allow control over the disposal of investments to slip even slightly out of their hands. If the nettle of price reform is grasped at all it will almost certainly be only in a rather reluctant and gingerly way. In other words, there will probably be a reform of wholesale prices in order to bring them more nearly into line with costs; but it is very unlikely that retail prices will be freed, even in a very small sector. It seems equally unlikely that unprofitable firms will be allowed to close down, as is now beginning to be the fate of industrial failures in Jugoslavia and Czechoslovakia. Such a thing is still shocking to Rumanians—at least to rank and file officials. Whether in fact they will venture further than allowing some modest decentralising and giving some more attractive incentives remains to be seen. It may be that once they start moving down the slope of reform, they will be compelled either to move a good deal faster or give up completely.

Whatever changes the Rumanians may, willingly or unwillingly, make in the way they run their economy, no changes are contemplated at present in the regime's determination to concentrate on heavy industry in order to create a modern industrial state as quickly as possible. In each of the last three years investment has risen by more than 10 per cent and the lion's share of investment in industry has gone to the heavy sector. (In the period 1960–65, 49.5 per cent of total investment was put into industry; and of this, 43.9 per cent went to heavy industry and 5.6 per cent to the consumer industries.) Although last year achievement fell slightly short of the planners' expectations, factories and plants seem to be going up all over the country. The greatest expectations of all are placed on the petro-chemical industry. According to Mr Ceausescu, giving a pep-talk to a conference of chemical industry workers in Bucharest last month, the industry is developing at a faster rate than any other.

Electricity and other sources of power are being vigorously developed
in order to conserve the country's oil supplies; next year Rumania will
even start to import crude oil.

How About the Consumer?

This article does not attempt to estimate whether the Rumanians
are likely hopelessly to overstrain their resources, technological as well
as financial, so that they land in the same kind of trouble as the Jugoslavs have done, with a number of half-completed and unproductive projects on their hands; nor whether they can really build up their foreign
trade sufficiently quickly and substantially to get all the sophisticated
modern machinery and equipment that they need. But it is obvious that
they have set themselves a formidable task, and it seems fair enough to
suggest that a major factor pushing them towards more whole-hearted
economic reforms may be the gradual realisation that they will not
achieve their aims without some more radical changes in the way they run
the country.

What must most concern the ordinary Rumanian is whether the government's ambitious plans are compatible with maintaining even the modest rise in living standards of recent years. The Rumanian man (or
woman) in the street is better off than he was a few years ago; supplies
of clothes, household goods, food and so on are improving—if sometimes
in fits and starts. But the improvement could be much quicker. Mr Ceausescu made a point of telling the party plenum in December that industry was not meeting consumer needs and that "supplementary resources"
would have to be found so that the planned targets of the consumer industries could be raised. This suggests than any increase in supplies for
the shops will not be at the expense of heavy industry or of export earnings.

No one would expect the Rumanian government to spend a high
proportion of its export earnings on importing cars. All the same, there is
something sadly symbolic about the large padlock which usually adorns
the door of Bucharest's only car showroom during business hours. If you
want to buy a car you have to deposit the entire cost in the bank before
you even get on to the waiting list, where you will probably remain for
at least two years. Obviously this kind of, as it were, voluntary forced
saving is convenient for a government which may feel obliged to increase
material incentives in industry but wants to keep a fairly tight hold on
the amount of its resources going into providing more goods for shop
windows and shelves.

One is tempted to guess that the new regulation on the compulsory buying of flats may also be partly aimed at siphoning off purchasing power. All families with a joint income of 2,000 lei (which is quite an average figure for two people) are now obliged to buy their flat, with a down payment of 30 per cent and the rest in instalments over fifteen years. To own one's own house or flat is a more or less universal ambition; but Rumanian householders are less than enthusiastic because they lack the spare cash either for the initial payment or for the cost of repairs and maintenance. By 1970, 80 per cent of the new flats built in Bucharest will be for sale only. Whether they like it or not, the Rumanians are to be turned into a property-owning democracy. The pity is that so many of them do not.

Mr Ceausescu, however, does not have to worry too much about consumer reactions. For in spite of the relaxation of the past few years, Rumania probably remains the least liberal, and its people the least free-spoken, of all the east European communist regimes—barring Albania, of course. Mr Ceausescu's dressing down of the security services, last month, for abusing "socialist legality" and ignoring citizens' rights, may do something to mend this. But the regime shows little sign of abandoning its rather crude and insensitive paternalism. It tells people to work harder, smoke less and take pride in their country's past greatness and present importance; but it does not allow them a trip to the West and only reluctantly allows them a car or a little more space to live in.

The government can reasonably assume that its increased prestige abroad gives it some popularity at home. And Mr Ceausescu tries hard, with his flower-strewn speaking tours, to narrow the gap between government and people. But the regime seems afraid to provide a safety valve for frustrations and discontents by allowing a significantly more liberal political atmosphere to develop. It tries to buy popularity with an assertive foreign policy. But it is not prepared to buy it with speedy and substantial concessions to consumer needs because this would conflict with its economic priorities.

The question which the regime will have to face sooner or later is whether, in order to achieve its economic goals, it should experiment far more boldly with economic reform than it now seems prepared to do. Can it go on indefinitely teetering on the brink of reform? A strong argument for restraint must be the fear that economic reform would weaken the party's grip and strengthen the pressures in favour of political change. Presumably the final decision will depend on the balance of forces and opinions inside the party leadership.

24

EAST GERMANY: STEPS AWAY
FROM COMMAND

East Germany is a communist-ruled society that in terms of income per head is within striking distance of the rich European capitalist countries; that has a long pre-communist tradition of high technical skill and efficient management; and that is forced to take daily note, by the presence of west Berlin in its heart, of what the capitalist world is doing and achieving. The economic technicians elaborating east Germany's new system are highly competent, lively, friendly people who are ready nowadays to receive an unannounced westerner at short notice, and talk with considerable freedom and frankness; but they are still aggressively socialist. And the westerner's appreciation of their welcome is chilled by their cheerful references to 1961 as the year when things began to go right for them. They talk of the building of the Berlin wall in that year as the base date for their economic happiness, rather as a western industrialist might rejoice in his success in getting a quota slapped on imports from his competitors. Challenged, they counter by asking, "Wouldn't you lock your house if your neighbour was robbing you?" To the western visitor, the wall and its monstrous sequel of bloodshed can never quite appear in that light.

In east Germany, however noticeable the change in atmosphere in the past few years, truth is still an official commodity, and free discussion is not yet. This is not only an obstacle to east-west understanding: we believe it is an obstacle, and a serious one, to the very economic reform that the government is attempting to promote.

The reform has three prongs:

1. The adjustment of all industrial prices, which are strictly controlled, to levels that reflect the true costs of production and, it is hoped, will allow an increasing proportion of products to be sold competitively in capitalist markets.

2. The transfer of most investment decisions from the central planning authorities to the managers of individual firms.

3. Reliance for the first time on credit control through the banks to ensure that the state's overall investment aims are observed, in place of

Reprinted from The Economist of August 19th, 1967. Originally published in The Economist under the title "East Germany: Flowers Beyond the Wall?"

the former direct physical control by the planning commission. The planning commission will in future be responsible only for drawing up projections and targets for broad sectors of the economy.

The essence of the reform is that investment will depend in future, almost as much as in a capitalist free enterprise economy, on a multitude of independent decisions by individual managers and banking officials. Other difficulties apart, it is hard to see how this system can work at all well without the regular provision of financial news and comment on as wide a scale as in western industrial countries, or how management personnel at all levels can be really efficient in home and export markets unless they have full access to the foreign financial press. This would imply the substantial abandoning of newspaper censorship—a major reversal of policy which appears to be quite unacceptable at present.

Until 1963 the economy was held in an inefficient straitjacket by the combination of Stalinist central planning with a totally unrealistic structure of prices based on what the regime had picked out of the ruins of war and not changed since. The planners recall that they were writing about the weaknesses of the old system as long ago as 1958, but say the drain of men and foreign exchange through west Berlin forced them to go on with their rigid planning and control until the wall had stemmed the flow. (It is hard to see why a grossly inefficient system of economic management should be thought the best way of containing the movement of human beings out of a state they disliked.)

A fundamental fact of the new economic system is that 70 per cent of industrial production will be in the hands of 1,500 state-owned "People's Own" firms which are now grouped by category into 85 horizontal trusts, the "Unions of People's Own Firms" (Vereinigungen Volkseigener Betrieben or VVBs). The VVBs are strikingly similar in their principles of operation to modern American free-form management or conglomerate companies like Litton Industries or Ling Temco Vought, with the important difference that their operations are strictly confined to their own product sector.

Beyond that, many features of the new economic system recall French planning methods: for example, the ultimate reliance on state control over credit to try to ensure that planning aims are achieved; and the idea of a controlled but flexible system of prices, with a certain freedom for firms to raise the prices of some products in their range if they make compensating reductions in others.

The government's main structural aims are simple enough. The first twenty years after the war were spent in trying to make a balanced economy out of a fragment of the former German Reich. This process is now nearly finished and has left east Germany with a chronic shortage of labour (caused largely by emigration to the West until the Berlin wall was built in 1961) and a far too diversified industry as the result of filling in the gaps in the country's industrial structure. As for investment, the labour shortage, compounded by shortages in building materials, makes building delays endemic. Furthermore, the railway system is obsolescent, and the country has to finish building up a modern petro-chemicals industry to supply the range of modern fibres and plastics that it needs, and to extend the product range of its steel industry. Energy production must also be rationalised, with a switch away from coal and lignite to oil, natural gas and nuclear power. Unfortunately, east Germany has the lowest level of investment in proportion to national income—20 per cent—of any country in eastern Europe. This is because it was impossible to force too many sacrifices on east German consumers when the attraction of west Germany was so close and compelling. Now that the wall is built and living standards have been substantially improved, it is hoped to raise investment fairly quickly to 25 per cent of national income.

Elsewhere, the work of completing the country's industrial structure is now nearly finished; the accent has switched to quality and specialisation with emphasis on high-value products like numerically controlled machine tools, instruments and electronic equipment.

On fundamental aspects of their new system, such as price determination, the technicians express surprising confidence. They appear to believe that the difference between their full-cost centrally calculated prices and real opportunity-cost prices is unimportant. They think that they will become progressively better at measuring and projecting real demand for goods, despite controlled prices. They do say that it will take ten or twelve years to build up an information and data-processing network that will allow them to adjust prices sensitively and quickly, but they think their system will work well enough in the meantime.

Your correspondent remarked that capitalist industry adjusts much faster to the trend of demand, because any number of new products may be launched on individual initiative and the market quickly chooses which it likes; whereas socialist planning of all important lines of production must be based on a study of past demand reactions to already existing goods. The technicians countered that capitalist competition was wasteful, and quite inappropriate to socialism. They seemed to feel that socialism knew what people wanted—mirroring the views of their political masters, who assert their right to determine what people should think, know and do in the higher spheres of human activity. (Almost unbelievably a charming and intelligent party official, a veteran of the 1917 October revolution, argued that a free press was not needed in a socialist state because, by definition, there *could* be no serious divergence of opinion between honest people under socialism—and this in 1967.) Conceivably, the economic technicians have their private reservations, but they were keeping quiet about them.

The technicians do, of course, recognise that the reform involves huge administrative problems, especially on the banking side. The state industrial bank will be called upon to supplement firms' self-financing capacity, and therefore will have a powerful means of enforcing the central planners' intentions for the overall distribution of investment. A branch of the industrial bank attached to each VVB will keep a check on the performance of member firms, assess the viability of their projects, and advise the regional banks (who will actually disburse the money). The bankers will have to try to keep track of each borrower's cash flow to ensure that a smart manager does not get more investment capital into his hands than the state intends for his sector. With management decentralised and the state price commission trying to adjust its controlled prices with the maximum flexibility and speed, the bankers admit that trying to project and follow cash flows will be an enormous problem. Apparently, they will be able to vary interest rate charges and repayment conditions in a much more penal way than western banking practice allows—yet another example of how, in theory at least, the new system looks like being much harsher from management's point of view than tooth-and-claw capitalist competition.

Will east Germany's reform succeed? . . . the economy has grown at a reasonable rate; investment has been comparatively efficient by east European standards; and consumers have something to be grateful for —and appear to be not too dissatisfied. The question is whether economic performance can be really substantially bettered by the elimination of the grosser inefficiencies of central planning. This writer would argue that, on all western experience, the east Germans must go much further in their liberalisation to get the real dividends. Reflecting on western experience of trying to shape investment decisions by the public manipulation of credit conjures up sad images like the British Aircraft Corporation, or France's lengthy attempts to lick into shape a steel industry which, in the end, is unlikely to be showing very much profit anyway. In western experience, the real growth comes from the firms that got away, defying the nice calculations of averages on which the public planning is based and pulling the rest of the economy after them, willy-nilly, on to new technical and financial ground. Again, workers in east Germany enjoy a job security which is unparalleled in the West. But is this a wise policy in a country facing a chronic labour shortage? If firms were free to pay off men when they did not need them, while their social security and redeployment problems were taken care of by the state wearing a different hat, the effective rate of utilisation of labour could surely be raised substantially. And there are limited opportunities for competition among firms under the VVB system. In western eyes all these look like serious objections.

25   ANDRZEJ BRZESKI

Economic Reform in Poland: The Cautious Avant-Garde

Warsaw's attitude toward economic reform was epitomized in a recent report in the *Economist:*

The un-Polish instinct of its rulers now is caution. . . . Poland is a country that has had its fingers burned too often. Its last political revolution was in 1956, and the will at the top, among the men who brought it about, is to conserve it. Other east European countries profited by Poland's mistakes; it is natural that it should now think of waiting to profit from theirs.[1]

This paper examines the hesitant course and the prospect of Polish economic reform. The emphasis is on the changes in the economic system proper, but one cannot refrain from commenting on the broader context of policies and politics—both are inseparable from the problems of economic reorganization.

The Command Economy and Its Growth

For a short period following World War II, the Polish economy was a mixed concern: state-owned industries coexisted with semi-independent cooperatives and private businesses, central planning and rationing with markets. Planning itself was a peculiar mixture of administrative order and indirect regulation, with monetary and fiscal measures performing essential control functions. Some descriptive work has been done on this,[2] but the improvised and pragmatic economics of the "Polish NEP" has yet to be explored in depth. Perhaps, as the Communists have come to assert, the three-sector system was inherently unstable. Although it worked fairly well during the postwar reconstruction, possibly it would not have been equal to the mammoth tasks of rapid industrialization. These must remain forever open questions. As it happened, soon after the consolidation of Communist power—the merger of the Socialist party (PPS) and the Workers' party (PPR) in 1948—Poland adopted the Soviet model of

From *The Quarterly Review of Economics and Business*, Vol. 7, No. 3 (Autumn 1967), pp. 19–28. Reprinted by permission of the author and the editors of *The Quarterly Review of Economics and Business*.

[1] *The Economist*, Vol. 222, No. 6437 (January 7, 1967), p. 25.

[2] See, for instance, D. S. Douglas, *Transitional Economic Systems: The Polish-Czech Example* (London: Routledge and Kegan, 1953).

economic organization. By about 1950, the transition to a Soviet-type centralized administrative economy was completed, except for the still predominantly private agriculture. And in 1951 collectivization pressures (initiated after Gomułka's downfall) mounted, making Poland a nearly perfect replica of the Stalinist prototype.

There is no need to relate here the details of this kind of system. A vast literature is available on the original example. There also exist several monographs on the Polish adaptation.[3] Succinctly listed, the basic characteristics of a Soviet-type economy are social ownership, hierarchical administrative structure, command planning, tautness, subordination to priorities, commitment to industrialization, and autarkic bias.[4] Most of the allocation under this regime is done through material balances, a crude input-output device. Most prices and wage rates are fixed by decree. By and large, wages and consumer prices reflect relative scarcities; but producers' prices, based on an average-cost-plus formula, have little or no allocative significance. Genuine markets, limited to the sphere escaping central controls (direct food sales by peasants and some handicraft), are uncommon. A large array of physical targets, norms, and supply rations is used to secure an allocation pattern desired by the center. Money and finance are relegated to the position of a parallel (and subsidiary) instrument of controls. Decisions, deriving from a somewhat mechanical disaggregation of overall targets, are passed from the top downward to the firm through administrative channels. To spur technical efficiency, various incentive schemes are geared to prescribed success indicators, especially to gross output targets.[5]

In its heyday, the implantation of the Soviet model in Poland was hailed by its partisans as a historic breakthrough:

a safeguard . . . of harmony between productive forces and social relations of production, through which the nation has liberated immense creative energy.[6]

But in a more detached assessment, years later, Oskar Lange saw it as "a *sui generis* war economy"—an exigency of forced draft industrialization in a backward and hostile social environment.[7] Whatever the case, some of the results expected at the time of adoption of the command economy have materialized.

Official statistics claim for the 15-year period from 1951 through

[3] T. P. Alton, *Polish Postwar Economy* (New York: Columbia University Press, 1955) and J. M. Montias, *Central Planning in Poland* (New Haven: Yale University Press, 1962) are the two most informative works in this respect.

[4] See E. Neuberger, "Central Planning and Its Legacies" (Santa Monica: RAND, 1966), p. 5. (P–3492; mimeographed.)

[5] See Gregory Grossman, "Notes for a Theory of the Command Economy," *Soviet Studies*, Vol. 15, No. 2 (October, 1963), pp. 101–23.

[6] See Bronisław Minc, *Wstęp do nauki planowania gospodarki narodowej* (Warsaw: Polskie Wydawnictwa Gospodarcze, 1950), p. 254.

[7] Quoted from a 1957 Belgrade lecture by Lange; see Alec Nove, *The Soviet Economy: An Introduction* (New York: Praeger, 1961), p. 146.

1965 an average annual rate of growth (Marxian "national income") of 7.1 percent. The corresponding claim for gross industrial output is 11.4 percent. Today, Poland's industry produces 9 million metric tons of steel and a great variety of complicated goods. The volume of foreign trade more than tripled during this period, and the share of engineering in Polish exports increased from 8 percent to 34 percent. These feats of industrialization were accomplished by an extensive use of labor surpluses—a 72 percent increase in employment—and consistently high investment concentrated in heavy industry. The growth has been notoriously uneven. Agriculture, ruthlessly taxed for the benefit of capital accumulation, barely managed to achieve during the period under consideration an increase in output of 2.5 percent a year. During the early 1950's, farm output was actually declining. Consumer goods industries were expanding at a rate considerably below that attained in producer goods—9.5 percent versus 12.9 percent annually. The first developmental plan, for 1950 through 1955, clearly fell short of official propaganda slogans: "The Six-Year Plan—The Plan of Satiety." Nor did the promised affluence arrive in the subsequent period. Still, despite setbacks, the increase in per capita consumption—reportedly averaging 4.9 percent a year for the period as a whole—was not negligible. Much of the consumers' gain was in the form of public services: health, social welfare, and so forth. In particular, the widening of education—mainly in technical and vocational fields—was impressive. All in all, save perhaps for drastically lagging housing, the years of the command economy have been marked by the modernization of Polish society. Comparisons with the pre-war situation are impaired by territorial and demographic changes, but the major accomplishments are incontrovertible, even when one discounts the bias of governmental data.[8] Although in the same period several capitalist countries (and one socialist market economy) attained no less success, and although the *post hoc, ergo propter hoc* reasoning may be fallacious, no evaluation of Poland's command economy should overlook this record.

The Arrested Crisis

Its dynamism notwithstanding, the command economy has some striking shortcomings. Physical planning—especially the supply arrange-

---

[8] Figures in this paragraph were obtained (or estimated) from the official *Rocznik statystyczny 1966*. Independent recomputation of aggregate indexes by Western scholars yields substantially lower rates of growth. See, for example, the estimates of industrial output in M. C. Ernst, "Overstatement of Industrial Growth in Poland," *Quarterly Journal of Economics*, Vol. 79, No. 4 (November, 1965), and in Alfred Zauberman, *Industrial Progress in Poland, Czechoslovakia and East Germany, 1937–1962* (New York: Oxford University Press, 1964), p. 120.

ments—is overly rigid. Serious coordination (consistency) problems arise because of the system's irresponsiveness to immediate circumstances. Excessive centralization of decision-making stifles managerial initiative. Where managerial options exist, the choice is frequently at odds with the manifest needs of the economy because of ill-conceived incentive schemes and/or misleading prices out of line with scarcity as well as cost. As a result, output mix is unsatisfactory and sometimes even nonsensical, and quality of goods is bad. Acute shortages coexist with ever rising inventories. Investment funds, scarce as they must be in a low-income economy, are dissipated and squandered.[9]

In Poland the notorious malfunctions of administrative planning were aggravated by habitual overcommitment of resources. Moreover, planners and managers—many of them appointed for political merit—lacked expertise. So long as the ideological freeze and the political terror lasted, few dared to point out the malaise, though it must have been obvious. But with the first signs of a more relaxed regime, the critics came into the open. The discussion of the law of value, inspired by Stalin's remarks in *The Economic Problems of Socialism*, began in 1953, posing the issue of realistic prices and incentives for self-regulation. In another development, a group of economists, questioning the wisdom of investment planning, initiated the search for the criteria for the selection of capital projects. Others expressed doubts about the dogma of the accelerated growth of heavy industry. For approximately two years, these themes were pursued, seemingly without a challenge to the basic precepts of the established order, just as they were in the Soviet Union during this period. However, upon the collapse of the Stalin myth in early 1956 —and especially after the Poznań uprising in June of that year—the tone of the Polish discussions abruptly changed. The critics took to mass media and, castigating the faults of the "Stalinist model," clamored for total reform: complete freedom for the firm in deciding on outputs and inputs, free market prices, profit-oriented investment, and so forth.[10] Yugoslavia, for years branded as crypto-capitalist, was held out as a worthy example to follow.

In this atmosphere, some actually took to dismantling the system. Peasants dissolved collective farms; within weeks only 1,500 collectives were left of the previous 10,000. In industry, workers' councils like those

[9] Perhaps the most dramatic statement on the shortcomings of Polish central planning came from Oskar Lange; see his "W sprawie doraźnego programu," *Życie Gospodarcze*, 1956, No. 14.

[10] A brief survey of views expressed in these debates can be found in Montias, *op. cit.*, especially Ch. 9. Polish economic journals (mainly *Życie Gospodarcze* and *Myśl Gospodarcza*) as well as the general press (particularly *Po prostu* and *Życie Warszawy*) must be consulted for details and nuances. A good number of contributions had been collected by Książka i Wiedza in *Ekonomiści dyskutują o prawie wartości* (1956), *Dyskusji o prawie wartości ciąg dalszy* (1957), *Dyskusja o polskim modelu gospodarczym* (1957), and *Spór o ceny* (1958).

in Yugoslavia sprang up everywhere, and often state-appointed managers were bodily evicted from the premises of the plants. With centrifugal tendencies at work at the grass roots and with confusion at the top, industrial and financial discipline deteriorated, engendering strong inflationary pressures. The party, paralyzed by internal strife, was quickly losing its grip on the situation; and the public, vehemently anti-Soviet and disappointed in the outcome of the Six-Year Plan, demanded revolutionary change. It seemed, indeed, that nothing short of such a change would do. At the time of Gomułka's reinstatement in October, 1956, the days of the command economy (and of its political superstructure) in Poland appeared to be all but numbered.[11] The new leader himself was apparently open to alternatives, saying

What is immutable in socialism can be reduced to the abolishment of man's exploitation by man. The roads to this goal may, and do, differ, depending on the circumstances of time and place.[12]

And yet, against all odds, the system has survived the crisis. Despite earlier doubts, Gomułka, once firmly in charge of the party, showed himself no more inclined toward a Lange-Lerner (or Tito) kind of socialism than he was toward parliamentary democracy. After the January, 1957, elections, ideological pressures and censorship were applied at a steadily accelerating pace to prevent further spread of criticism. The extreme positions taken in the debate were officially condemned as "bourgeois pipedreams" or "revisionism." Political intervention—if not police action—curtailed sundry unorthodox practices that had proliferated since the fall of 1956. The syndicalist doings of factory workers were among the first targets. Strikes were dealt with promptly and, generally, skillfully. Workers' councils—at first wooed, then persuaded into obedience —were deviously liquidated through incorporation into the "conferences of workers' self-government," a lethargic creation of the *apparat*. It required even less effort to bring the managers back under ministerial tutelage; and the paramount authority of the Planning Commission, visibly on the wane only months before, was restored, though admittedly it did not look quite so awesome as it had before.

To be sure, there still was much talk about the urgency of drastic reforms. The Economic Council—a new advisory body—was specifically charged with the task of drafting the blueprint of a "Polish model of socialism." But despite the fanfare and official encouragement greeting its formation, the council soon found that even relatively moderate recommendations fell on the party's deaf ears. Appropriately, after prolonged

11 This is a "phenomenological insight" of a direct observer-participant which I believe was commonly shared in Poland.

12 See *6 lat temu . . . (Kulisy Polskiego Października)*. Instytut Literacki, 1962, p. 41.

inactivity, the council was quietly disbanded. By virtue of its very composition, that defunct body was incapable of spearheading any drastic reform. Lange proved himself an ambivalent and indecisive chairman, and the few economists endorsing bolder schemes (Bobrowski, Brus, and Popkiewicz) were no match for the archbureaucrats appointed to the council (Blinowski, Jędrychowski, Lesz, Szyr, and Tokarski). Kalecki's reasoned distrust of decentralization and markets was also a conservative force, since it lent prestigious academic support to the opponents of reform.

Some sort of change was of course unavoidable. The public's expectations could not be altogether frustrated. Besides, the centralized administrative economy did have undeniable deficiencies. But such partial measures as were undertaken in the aftermath of Gomułka's accession to power fell short of satisfying either need, for they were marred by half-heartedness and contradictions. The planning bureaucracy lost hardly any ground even on those rare occasions when it acquiesced in nontrivial decentralization. The logic of the prevailing institutions of the central plan worked for that.

Thus, immediately in 1956, a new statute of the firm was enacted—with pledges for managerial independence and promises of considerable reduction in detailed directives from above. Yet according to available evidence, firms remained circumscribed by the full rigor of targets, quotas, and norms. Formally or informally, most such devices had to be retained, inasmuch as they were a necessary complement of "material balances," still at the core of allocation procedures.[13]

The upgrading of the "fund of the enterprise" in 1957—another reform echoing the great debate—did little to uplift the firm's status. Neither boosting the profit share of firms (especially of the intake of year-to-year increment in profit), nor stressing profit as a key "success indicator," nor even allowing profit bonuses (up to 8.5 percent of the annual wage) could detract from the preponderance of administrative order and physical allocation. Managerial independence and profit-seeking could hardly be reconciled with the virtually intact structure of central planning.

Sundry reforms of Polish finances could bring no solution to the crucial problem of eliciting managerial initiative under such conditions. As a result of the overhaul of bank credit in 1958, firms, previously bound by unnecessarily restrictive rules, gained a bit of leeway in arranging their finances. Simultaneously, the bank's nominal discretion to lend or to refuse loans was broadened to prevent abuse of the new freedoms. Apart from a reshuffling of accounts, this had only a marginal impact on either finance or "real" activities. As in the past, financial objectives were readily sacrificed when they conflicted with the imperatives of the physical plan.

[13] See the discussion of "Counterreforms" in Montias, *op. cit.*, Ch. 10.

Industrial reorganization, too, did nothing to expand firms' decision powers. The central administrations (intermediate supervisory organs between the firms and the ministry), perennially accused of excessive meddling in management, were scrapped in 1958. In principle, their replacements—the trusts—were to *represent* constituent firms. In fact, like their predecessors, the trusts functioned as an extension of ministerial bureaucracy and were, if anything, even more restrictive than the abolished administrations.[14]

Not surprisingly, the remarkable resistance to change was also noticeable in pricing. Input prices—long debated and no doubt the crux of any meaningful management reform—were revised in 1960, but along traditional lines.[15] The discredited principle of average-cost-plus pricing was preserved, contrary to the recommendation of the Economic Council. No provisions were made for price flexibility—prices, as before, were to be set by the center, though not necessarily at the very top. By raising the level of prices of producers' goods 26 percent, the government was able to wipe out subsidies to most industries (no allowance was made, however, for the cost of capital and land). But since the average-cost-plus formula applied to the entire production within a ministry, high-cost firms continued in the red. So did whole industries, after a while, because of rising wages. Not even the most boastful Warsaw officials would claim that the 1960 reform succeeded in eliminating irrationality in pricing. With "material balances" and "command" planning at the heart of the economy, this was perhaps of little concern.

Thus, the edifice of the command economy that appeared to be on the verge of a breakdown a decade ago has been preserved with merely minor modifications. In this respect, the conservative course taken under Gomułka has proved "successful." The upheaval of de-Stalinization resulted, however, in one major change: farms are mostly private; their spontaneous decollectivization has been accepted as a *fait accompli*. This is because Gomułka, now as in 1949, prefers the carrot to the stick as the means of tackling Poland's agricultural problem. Accordingly, a brisk rise in peasants' income and the encouragement of private farm investment have been distinguishing marks of his rule. Housing, badly neglected during the take-off period, has received special attention too, but otherwise the allocation pattern, as reflected in the rate and distribution of investment, has stayed pretty much the same since the inception of the command economy. This may be partly due to actual constraints of the nation's resources and foreign trade opportunities, but primarily it is a

---

[14] See the discussion of trusts conducted in 1965 by *Życie Gospodarcze*. Note that the term "trust" used here stems from the Polish "association" (*Zjednoczenie*).

[15] A summary of the price reform can be found in H. Machowski, "Grundsätze und Entwicklung der Staatlichen Industriepreisbildung in Polen nach 1945," *Konjunkturpolitik*, Vol. 12, No. 5–6 (1966), pp. 381 ff.

matter of rigid priorities. Here, too, the resistance to change has met with "success."

AT LAST, *the* REFORM?

Warsaw's demonstrated conservatism in things economic is in contrast with recent trends in other East European countries. Paraphrasing Marx, one might describe this part of Europe as "haunted by the spectre of economic reform." Whether because of that or for some different reasons—a question still to be considered here—Gomułka decided to reopen the long-shelved case of fundamental reforms. The announcement to this effect came in 1964 and, according to the usually well-informed *New York Times* correspondent, it came amidst reports of "considerable opposition . . . from some factions in the party."[16]

This time the matter has been placed from the beginning in official hands. The blueprint of the reform—drawn up *in camera* by a commission of party and government experts—is contained in the July, 1965, resolution of the party's central committee.[17] In Communist countries, only the most important policy statements are announced in this solemn fashion.

According to this document the changeover is to be implemented gradually over the period of the current Five-Year Plan. The essential proposals can be grouped under several headings.

(1) PLANNING:

(a) Directive targets for industry are to be narrowed, especially those pertaining to physical output, employment, and wages; export and import quotas are to be set in foreign exchange totals only.

(b) Total production targets are to be expressed in measures other than the value of gross output, but only gradually and on an industry-specific basis. The alternative indicators mentioned are standard labor input, gross turnover (gross output *plus* semifinished products), and, for homogeneous production, natural or conventional units of physical output.

(c) Planning on all levels is to provide for contingency reserves in the form of uncommitted investment funds, wage funds, raw materials, marketable goods, foreign exchange, and eventually, industrial capacities.

---

[16] *New York Times,* December 5, 1965.
[17] See *Nowe Drogi,* Vol. 19, No. 8 (1965). Analytical summaries of the reform proposals can be found in L. Smolinski, "Reform in Poland," *Problems of Communism,* Vol. 15, No. 4 (July–August, 1966), and T. P. Alton, "Polish Industrial Planning," *Journal of International Affairs,* Vol. 20, No. 1 (1966), pp. 94 ff.

(2) FINANCE:

(a) "Economic accountability" (*khozrashchet*) is to be strengthened by extended self-financing. A hierarchical system of specialized funds within each industry (trust) will emphasize the "accountability" of the industry as a whole as well as that of each firm. The funds—earmarked for various purposes, such as development, technical and economic progress, capital repairs, and risk insurance—are to provide the means for self-financing through redistribution of a part of the surplus according to the specific needs of each industry.

(b) Interest charges are to discourage squandering and inefficient use of capital. The rates, differentiated for various industries, apply to the value of net assets (presumably initial cost plus capital repairs minus depreciation); but at a later state, the possibility of the gross-asset basis is considered. The introduction of interest charges is to be gradual. Initially they are to be restricted to industries of relatively high efficiency so as not to necessitate upward price revisions.

(c) Bank loans for fixed investment are to be made available for approved projects. However, smaller items can also be financed from firms' accumulated profits and depreciation. By contrast, "priority projects" (presumably large outlays on new plant) will continue to be paid for with budgetary grants.

(3) INCENTIVES:

(a) "Rentability" (the ratio of profit to cost of marketed output) or, in selected cases, "profitability" (the ratio of profit to assets) is to become the main synthetic success indicator determining the firm's and the trust's share in profits and, through this, bonus payments. Total accumulation (profit plus turnover tax) is to serve as a criterion of performance only in exceptional cases.

(b) Although "rentability" (or "profitability") is to directly affect the firm's share in profits (fund of the enterprise) and the bonus of top management, sectional management as well as that of workers should be judged by more appropriate criteria. These must be concrete and flexible.

Various other items mentioned in the 1965 reform blueprint are of less interest. Some, not excluding a part of the foregoing, look familiar to one who has followed the many reorganizations and campaigns of the past. Many are mere exhortations about the advantages of "better planning," "more efficient management," "proper division of responsibilities," and the like. Much is cast in very general, indeed vague, terms.

Symptomatically, the architects of the new "model" carefully avoid any clear commitment to measures increasing the independence of the firm. Authoritative writers, participating in earlier discussions, put strong emphasis on the trust as the mainstay of the future system.[18] The firm, according to this view, has no grasp of industry-wide problems, not to mention macroeconomics; the trust is likely to make better decisions when choices are open. Moreover, the argument goes, it is easier to set correct parameters for efficient decentralized decision-making by the trusts than it would be in the case of firms. Allegedly, this could be accomplished even without a producer price reform. (The price reform is scheduled for 1967–68, an optimistically short time in comparison with the five years spent on the preparation of the rather unsatisfactory 1960 reform.) Whatever the substance of this argument, the ambitions of firms' managers clearly came to naught this time, too. Instead of independently managing their firms, they have been advised to influence the policies of the trusts through "active participation" in the latter's councils (*Kollegium*).

This emphasis on the Polish version of Ulbricht's *VVB* should not obscure the fact that the future position of trusts vis-à-vis ministers is by no means clearly defined in the blueprint. Avowedly, they will be assured of considerable elbowroom, but the proposals are somewhat indefinite as to details. The *kto-kovo* battle between the ministerial bureaucracy and the trusts is still to be fought out in practice.

The principal source of doubt about the trust's prospect of functioning as a genuine economic entity rather than, as in the past, a new central administration "with less authority, but more red tape,"[19] lies in another ambiguity of the blueprint. Despite the envisioned reduction of physical targets, the principle of central planning is emphatically reaffirmed. This is not a matter of semantics. Reform or no reform, Warsaw's bureaucracy has no desire to exchange direct controls for an "invisible hand" of one kind or another. The advocates of parametrically regulated markets are denounced as antisocialist and utopian.[20] The reform, it is said, must in no way disturb the *direct* central controls over "the distribution of national income, the allocation of investment funds, the total output of industries, the basic material balances, the wage fund, the price proportions, etc."[21] With all that, there does not seem to be much room left for the trusts to maneuver. And what exactly can be the relevance of the newly introduced, presumably "main" financial success indicators is not clear either, since they are described as "insufficient for evaluation

[18] Especially see J. Pajestka, "Funkcje ekonomiczne przedsiębiorstw i Zjednoczeń —strategia reformy," *Życie Gospodarcze*, 1966, No. 15.

[19] See J. Olszewski, "Zjednoczenie? Centralny zarząd administracji? Koncern socjalistyczny?" *Życie Gospodarcze*, 1965, No. 6.

[20] See Jędrychowski's speech in *Nowe Drogi*, Vol. 19, No. 8 (1965), p. 68.

[21] See *Nowe Drogi*, Vol. 19, No. 7 (1965), p. 5. Note the catchall word "etc."

of the performance of trusts and firms." Should performance actually be judged according to "complex criteria, which would take into account . . . the contribution to satisfaction of social needs expressed in the demand by the public, export requirements and so forth,"[22] the gates for conflicting multiple incentives and bureaucratic intervention are open as wide as ever.

Once again the Poles seem to be building a halfway house. Worse yet, they are trying to put it together from incongruous components. The blueprint of the reform is intentionally conservative, and its interpretation by the central planners is even more so.[23] Nonetheless, some of the provisions—for instance, the changes in industrial financing instituted in 1966[24]—present a serious challenge to central controls of the bureaucratic type. Whether such forces can gradually erode from within the elements of "command" of the "new model" cannot be foretold, for that depends on a multitude of internal and external factors—economic as well as other. Conceivably, a reverse trend may eventually dominate. The planning bureaucracy has certainly secured enough of a foothold to attempt a rollback. In any case, it is highly probable, one might even say certain, that the evolution of the system will meander along a course different from the one plotted today. Farsightedly, the blueprint—eclectic and ambiguous—allows more than one interpretation. Nowadays, the Poles *are* cautious. Shouldn't they be?

A Few Generalizations

There is, of course, no simple answer to this query. The economic terms on which large-scale organizational alternatives are given cannot be validated. Each reorganization is conducted once and for all, under unique circumstances. Although organization of the economy does affect the performance, the direction and magnitude of the impact is uncertain before, and sometimes after, the measures are decreed. Even in smaller and much simpler entities—such as capitalist firms—the complexity and the length of the organizational cause-effect loops make "experience . . .

[22] This again is from Jędrychowski's speech closing the central committee debate on the blueprint; *Nowe Drogi*, Vol. 19, No. 8 (1965), p. 78. Note the "and so forth" —another catchall.

[23] Other writers share this view; see Michael Gamarnikow, "The Reforms: A Survey," *East Europe*, Vol. 15, No. 1 (January, 1966), pp. 17–19, and G. Grossman, "Economic Reforms: A Balance Sheet," *Problems of Communism*, Vol. 15, No. 6 (November–December, 1966), especially p. 48.

[24] See J. Albrecht, "Problemy finansowe nowego pięciolecia," *Nowe Drogi*, Vol. 11, No. 2 (1957).

an inadequate and unreliable teacher."[25] In mapping out reorganization of socioeconomic systems, the trial-and-error method holds even less promise. "Holistic experiments," as Popper puts it, "can be called 'experiments' only in the sense in which this term is synonymous with *an action whose outcome is uncertain.*"[26] The unpredictability of results in large-scale rearrangements of institutions is exemplified by the failure of the *sovnarkhoz* and the disappointments of the Czech reorganization of 1958. For us in the West the most instructive lesson should have followed from the successful industrial growth of the Soviet Union. In 1931 few Western economists conceded the viability of Stalin's economy. Many predicted an imminent catastrophe which, after all, never came.

There is no reason why the Polish leaders' conservatism could not be interpreted in similar categories. With all its deficiencies, the centrally planned economy *is* a going concern. The economic effects of a wholesale reform are, however, predictable. A regime that feels secure—either because of popular support or because of complete absence of organized opposition—may take the risk of experimentation. Stalin, Tito, Novotny, Kadar, and Ulbricht may all have been in this position at the time of the reforms, but Gomułka was not. In 1956–57 he was in control of the *apparat,* but the masses were in a mood for revolution. More recently, the party itself has been torn by violent factional struggles,[27] and besides, there is always the Church.[28] Not to rock the boat may seem the best policy in such circumstances.

Furthermore, there may be special economic factors in the Polish conservatism, so much at variance with the Czech and Hungarian attitudes. The East European drive toward basic economic reforms has been correctly traced to 1. the complexity of industrial economies, 2. the exhaustion of the labor surplus that fed extensive growth, 3. an increasing dependence on foreign trade, and 4. a general retardation of growth.[29] With respect to each of these, the Poles are in a situation somewhat different from that of the more eager reformers.

Why then the reform at all right now? Partly, perhaps, to meet the domestic demands of the society at large and of the young Turks within the party. The advancement of the cause of economic reform elsewhere in Eastern Europe makes outright resistance politically cumbersome. And partly in the hope, however feeble, of achieving *some* efficiency gains.

[25] See J. W. Forrester, *The Changing Face of Industry—The Role of Industrial Dynamics,* Report to Management No. 11 (Los Angeles: University of Southern California, 1964), p. 6.

[26] See K. R. Popper, *The Poverty of Historicism* (New York: Harper, 1964), p. 85.

[27] See the March, 1965, issue of *East Europe.*

[28] See Alexander Bregman, "Gomułka's Long Hot Spring," *East Europe,* Vol. 15, No. 8 (August, 1966).

[29] See the article by Grossman cited in note 23.

Political economy rather than pure economics provides the proper perspective on East European reforms—and unfortunately, adds a dimension of intractability to an already complicated problem. The fact that the nation which was in the avant-garde of the reform movement is now lagging is the result of a paradox of power: the present rulers of Poland feel too strong to yield to popular demands for a drastic reorganization of the economy but too weak to maintain the *status quo*.

26

Czechoslovakia:
Command and the Market

Czechoslovakia's new economic system, if it works, promises a pretty large-scale transformation, although it aims at being all things at once—a socialist economy, a planned economy and a market economy. Naturally, public ownership of the means of production and exchange is not in question, and the government is to determine the pace and broad pattern of economic development, both regionally and structurally. More-

Reprinted from The Economist of August 19th, 1967. Originally published in The Economist under the title "Czechoslovakia: What the Reforms Mean."

[*Editor's note*. The Czechoslovak reforms, analyzed in the two articles that follow, tended to move Czechoslovakia away from the rigid and increasingly obsolescent command-type economy and toward market socialism exercised within a framework of indicative planning. The movement was stopped short by the Soviet invasion of Czechoslovakia in late August, 1968. It has been argued in Part I of this volume that effective decentralization of economic decision-making (which the Czechoslovak reforms implied) is a highly political matter for systems in which one political party is assumed to be in possession of all truth and in which that party wields monopoly power over men's lives. The Czechoslovak "plan and market under socialism" was bound to raise, sooner or later, the question of how to understand the guiding role of the Communist Party. Effective decentralization of economic decision-making, unlike administrative decentralization or Liberman's well-intentioned but theoretically deficient tinkering with the command apparatus, tends to subject the central planners' calculus to the test of the marketplace and transforms absolutist Party policy-makers into coordinators and traffic policemen. The Party's truth in such conditions is relativized, its power over a significant area of social life is diffused and shared with others. The Czechoslovak Communist Party faced with "a structure of the national economy which [was], in a way, a veritable merry-go-round: production for production. . . . [a] concept that would eat up whatever there was to devour, and leave the people with crumbs," ("Discussion of the Editors of the daily *Prace* with Professor Ota Sik: Truth in Economy and Politics," *New Trends in Czechoslovak Economics*, May 1968, p. 7.) was, by mid-1968, ready to take the plunge into relative liberalism rather than orthodox Libermanism. The Soviets, however, who still exercise strong influence in Eastern Europe and whose economic reform movement lags behind that of many of its communist neighbors, were not prepared to see Czechoslovakia adopt an economic system that might conceivably have led to social democracy. In a return to Stalinist strong-arm methods, the Soviets arrested the Czech reform movement, at least for the time being. The Czechoslovak situation has been "normalized"—that is, imposed on the Czechs and Slovaks."

In spite of this uncertain normalization, it has been thought useful to leave the following two selections the way they stood before the Soviet invasion. The interest in Czechoslovakia's experiment with market socialism transcends the spectacular, if perhaps transitory, display of power politics by the Soviet Union. It is not at all improbable that in the future the Soviets themselves will be compelled by the logic of history and the illogic of administrative command to revise their views and their economy in the direction taken by the Czechs.]

over, such questions as the distribution of personal income and the rate of increase of the price level will be subject to policy directives. But the details of the production pattern are to be determined by consumer preferences, and profit-conscious producers are to be allowed to compete for custom. True, steps will be taken to achieve major policy objectives, but normally only through the kind of fiscal and credit measures familiar in the West; only if these are considered inadequate will central directives be brought in, and then, it is hoped, only for a transitional period.

Czechoslovakia's surprising enthusiasm for such a liberal transformation of the Stalinist system is in part a reaction to past experience. In the first place, the glaring inefficiencies of the old system had been more apparent in highly-industrialised Czechoslovakia than elsewhere. Second, reserves of non-industrial labour were virtually exhausted by the end of the 1950s—the age and sex composition of the Czechoslovak farm labour force is probably the most awkward in Europe, and many service industries are undermanned by the standards of any western country at a comparable stage of development. Third, a genuine desire to raise living standards made it harder to add to capital stock at the expense of the consumer's current satisfaction. This meant that the rate of future economic growth was increasingly seen to depend heavily on achieving an "intensive" pattern of development, that is, on productivity gains reflecting the more efficient use of capital and labour.

Finally, the more cautious approach to reform tried in 1958 had been discredited by the subsequent poor growth performance of the Czech economy. By 1962 national income had stopped growing; in 1963 it actually fell and recovered to its 1962 level only during 1965. The two tentative earlier reforms were held partly to blame. It was pointed out that decentralisation of investment decisions, for example, unaccompanied by incentives to managers to produce more of what people really wanted, had increased the distortions in the economy. Too much investment went into a rush of new starts on decentralised projects at the expense of basic industry, and there was little technological advance.

What Is Proposed

The original outlines of the "new economic model" as they appeared in 1964 and 1965 have been somewhat modified and some details still remain obscure, but its main features are:

(i) *Targets:* The director of an industrial enterprise will no longer receive annual plan targets or directives. He will decide what to produce, what materials and fuels to use, how much labour to employ and, within limits, how much to pay it: he will pay for his raw materials the prices ruling in the market, or whatever he can negotiate with his suppliers; he will fix prices for his products (possibly subject to some limits or rules for price calculation) or, if he is operating in a highly competitive market, accept the ruling price; he will aim to make as big a profit as possible—and his own remuneration will largely depend on the firm's profits; if he wants to expand capacity or renew equipment he will draw the necessary funds partly from the retained profits of his enterprise and partly from the bank, which will charge interest on its loan and will have to be convinced that the project submitted to it offers the prospect of "adequate" profitability.

(ii) *Wages:* The state will continue to fix basic wages (time rates and piece rates) for different occupations and grades of skill. In effect, these will be minimum wages. Except in firms making losses or just breaking even, actual earnings will include additional amounts which are, in effect, a share in profits. These additional amounts, according to a recent statement, will be "guided by collective agreements between the trade union organisation and the management of the enterprise"; they will also take account of recommendations from a central body concerned with wage trends. There may also be a ceiling on the extent to which any rise in an enterprise's gross income (total receipts less material costs and amortisation) may be assigned to the wage fund, rather than to the investment fund or to reserves.

(iii) *Taxes:* Out of their gross income, as defined above, industrial enterprises now have to pay to the central budget a uniform percentage tax on gross income (i.e. on value added); a 2 per cent charge on stocks; and a 6 per cent tax on the net value of any fixed capital which has not been financed out of either retained profit or bank credit on which interest is still being paid. A turnover tax will be levied at the retail stage. It is planned, eventually, to levy this at a flat percentage rate of the wholesale price on virtually all items, except where social considerations dictate differences (for example, high rates on alcohol).

An ingenious progressive tax may be placed on annual increases in wage funds, with rebates for any reduction in numbers employed, and penalties for any increase. This tax was originally expected to come into operation in 1967; but it now seems that the idea is only under consideration as a possible long-run element in the system. (The British government showed less discretion in introducing its selective employment tax with the same object in mind.)

(iv) *Investment* will still be centrally planned by industrial branch and other sectors of activity, and by region. The National Bank will be given an annual credit plan for fixed investment, with very significant discretionary powers: it will be responsible for allocating credit by sector and region in the light of the national plan and of its knowledge of balances already available to firms in their depreciation and investment (retained profit) funds. Within each sector, it will allocate credit in accordance with the likely effectiveness of the project and may vary repayment terms (and possibly interest rates) from one sector to another in order to retain funds within planned limits. It will not necessarily disburse all credit allocated to a particular sector if insufficient projects satisfy its minimum profitability criteria. Major new projects will still be a matter for central decision, though a centrally-determined industrial project will still be expected to repay its initial credit, with interest, within a stated period.

(v) *Foreign Trade:* Foreign trade corporations will probably remain the only channels through which imports and exports pass; but a significant body of opinion is in favour of allowing producing enterprises (or associations of producers) to engage in trade either directly or in association with trade corporations, and Skoda has already been given this privilege. Trade corporations will work on the basis of an exchange rate that will no longer vary according to the commodity traded; the old system of multiple-pricing subsidies and tax penalties will be abolished. Officials are also trying to devise a way of revising the existing system of import duties (today of little economic significance) so as to constitute a rational tariff structure.

(vi) *Agriculture* appears to be the one major sector for which long-term subsidisation is contemplated. Prices intended to draw forth the desired level of output will be centrally fixed for a fairly long period (5 years) but may be supplemented by premiums possibly differentiated among farms according to their conditions. Direct grants may be given in the early stages to improve particularly backward farms but, in general, investment will be financed from income and from interest-bearing credits. Taxation of farms will include a rent differential.

The changes actually introduced so far constitute only rather short steps towards the new economic model. In 1966, compulsory production targets were set for only 67 products, compared with 1,200 in the previous year; and the number is reported to have been further reduced in 1967, though individual enterprises are tied under old contracts to the delivery of particular products for export. The scope of central allocation of fuels and materials has been somewhat reduced (about 90 items were subject to allocation in 1966), though by no means eliminated. Targets for labour productivity, cost reduction, total wage funds are now things of the past.

PRICE REFORM

It was realised from the beginning, however, that no significant moves towards the new system could be made without a major reform of the price structure, which reflected neither relative production costs nor relative scarcities. At first it was believed that no worthwhile reform could be prepared before 1969; but during 1965 and 1966 central calculations based on a 92 sector input-output table were used to produce indices of average wholesale price levels for each sector. These indices attempted to cover average production costs plus a uniform profit mark-up which is intended to provide a 6 per cent return on capital and a 12 per cent margin over basic wage payments. They were passed on to enterprises, which worked out new prices for particular groups of their products. These were then checked for consistency and eventually new price indices were produced for 25,000 commodity groups. Taking these as a basis, enterprises elaborated still more detailed price lists, which came into effect in January, 1967.* From this point on, further price changes will be regulated as follows:

for the main fuels and materials and basic consumer goods (about two-thirds of all transactions in 1967), central fixing of price ceilings;
for most other products, central fixing of price ranges;
for a small remainder—an estimated 7 per cent of transactions—prices will be determined freely by the market.

This is clearly a cautious beginning, but the aim is gradually to move towards equilibrium prices (that is, prices at which supply and demand would in fact be in balance), by progressive adjustments, while allowing considerable divergences from the average for individual goods. It is hoped that as profit margins on different products then change under the impact of market forces of supply and demand, investment will increasingly be concentrated on the most profitable lines of production and it will prove possible progressively to remove remaining price controls as market equilibrium is reached.

The initial price reform was expected to raise the wholesale price level by 20-25 per cent; but it was calculated that the elimination of subsidies to some branches of production and the new revenue from taxes on enterprises' gross incomes would make it possible to reduce turnover taxes sufficiently to prevent any significant rise in the retail price level in 1967. (In practice, during the first half of 1967 wholesale prices went up by 29-30 per cent, enterprises made unexpectedly large profits and the government was forced to introduce some deflationary measures.)

It is expected that enterprises' depreciation funds plus retained profits will serve to finance about 25 per cent of all fixed investment this year, while 60 per cent will be financed from bank credits and 15 per cent from the central budget. But this last figure does not represent the limit of effective central control over the detailed pattern of investment. As mentioned above, the National Bank will take into account the views of the "branch directorate" as well as "efficiency criteria" in deciding which enterprises should be granted credit for investment projects. Moreover, obligatory investment targets can still be set centrally for projects of key importance, aside from those financed directly by the budget; and all projects above a certain value, however financed, require central approval. Thus the National Bank is being given, at least potentially, enormous power to influence the direction of investment down to the level of

* ECE Economic Survey of Europe in 1966, Chapter II.

the firm—on a western analogy, a far greater power than the French state-controlled credit system wields. The question is how much sophistication the bank will be able to bring to this task in the early years.

Why It May Not Work

The difficulties to be faced in completing the transition to the new economic model—and after—are now becoming increasingly clear. A key to many of them is the reluctance of the authorities to face more than a slow increase in the general price level. This means continuing price control wherever the pressure of demand is tending to push prices up— in the absence of compensating price reductions elsewhere which have been triggered by cost reductions or inadequate demand. An obvious difficulty is that enterprises still enjoying a strong demand for their products have little incentive to pass on cost reductions; and investment of their excess profits to expand capacity, or the entry of new firms into the most profitable lines of production, are likely to produce downward pressures on prices only slowly.

Moreover, monopoly or oligopoly conditions exist in many branches of industry, and here there will be a strong temptation to bid up wages, in the prevailing conditions of labour scarcity, and to pass on only cost increases (not reductions) to the consumer. For many products it is all too easy for the ingenious producer to cheat the price control through changes in quality or specification (as France knows to its cost) and the authorities will be tempted to offset this by trying to exert stronger downward pressures on prices and profit margins.

Hence the pervasiveness of price control today, and the doubts whether it can ever be completely swept away. Hence the continuing allocation of some products in order to limit the pressure of demand; the increasing stress—as compared with the earlier versions of the new reform —on official guidance of wage increases and profit-sharing, and on the role of the trade unions (which can be trusted to support government and party policies) in helping to fix wages in individual firms; and the new hesitation about the alternative contemplated earlier of a progressive tax on increases in enterprises' wage bills, which would clearly contribute, in monopoly conditions, to price increases.

Thus the dilemma exists: if inflation is to be contained without depressing demand and employment to unacceptably low levels, price and wage controls can be only gradually relaxed and may have to be reinforced for some time by some materials allocation and production directives. But the use of such measures inhibits the development of entrepreneurial initiative, which is a vital requirement of the ultimate reform, and it blurs the signals from the market which should influence both current production and, even more importantly, longer-term investment decisions and redeployment of manpower. Moreover, the longer the transition lasts, the greater is the danger that those party members who mistrust the basic concepts of the reform—as heretical or utopian or simply likely to destroy their jobs or face them with responsibilities for which they are untrained—will succeed, perhaps not in putting the clock back, but in limiting the reform to an uneasy amalgam of inefficient directives and distorted "market" incentives.

Czechoslovak economists tend to say that the design of their model was really based on an appreciation of the advantages of perfect competition, but that in fact the typical structure of their industries is monopoly or oligopoly. Until mid-1966, changes in the organisation of industry tended to strengthen monopoly tendencies. All enterprises in industry and construction, apart from local industry (small enterprises under the control of local authorities) were by then grouped into about 100 trusts, vertical and horizontal. Today the horizontal trusts appear to have been rendered virtually powerless. Ministries are again the effective superiors of enterprises lying outside the vertical trusts, and as decentralisation proceeds it will be from ministries to individual enterprises. Still, it is recognised that technical efficiency will require the amalgamation of some enterprises.

Moreover, some watchdog over managers to represent the interests of society (or to fill the role of shareholders in a capitalist economy) is widely regarded as necessary. Workers' councils on the Jugoslav pattern have been officially rejected; ideas currently canvassed include the establishment of an authority over a relatively narrow branch of production (much smaller than that covered by an industrial ministry) which would include among its members representatives of the subordinate enterprises, interested ministries and related research and technical organisations as well as, possibly, the trade union movement. Some such organisational structure might not only provide a disinterested public watchdog. It could also lessen the danger, in the absence of a capital market, of an excessive tendency among managers to plough back profits into their own enterprises.

Some economists have seen the development of a "reserve of import capacity," to be used deliberately to create competitive conditions in the domestic market, as a possible counter to monopoly power; but this must lie in the distant future. At present, the problem is rather to achieve a level of exports sufficient to finance the minimum imports required to avoid serious bottlenecks in the domestic economy; and there is a reluctance to kill off even unprofitable exports until compensating markets for others can be built up.

Finally there remains the major problem of combining the real entrepreneurial responsibility of enterprise directors with effective day-to-day management of the economy by the central government. It is constantly emphasised in discussion in Czechoslovakia that the "rules of the game" for the enterprise must be reasonably stable. Directors, long deprived of any true managerial responsibility, have to regain or acquire confidence and expertise: they must not be discouraged by finding a perfectly rational decision taken today turned into a mistake by a change in the rules tomorrow. Equally, workers in any firm, it is said, cannot be expected to accept a cut in incomes due simply to a change in the conditions created by the government for the enterprise. But manipulation of the economic climate is an essential function of government in any country. The Czechs have indeed reacted to the recent spurt of price inflation and the increase in firms' profits by announcing that from July 1, 1968, any enterprise seeking credit for an investment project must have at least half the necessary finance already available in its bank account. Nevertheless it seems doubtful whether they have yet given enough thought to the elaboration of the information and research services and the flexible tax, credit, and other measures that will in fact be required once the "planned market economy with public ownership" is established—if it ever is.

27 HARRY G. SHAFFER

PROBLEMS AND PROSPECTS
OF CZECHOSLOVAKIA'S
NEW ECONOMIC MODEL
(INCLUDING AN INTERVIEW WITH
PROFESSOR OTA SIK)

INTRODUCTION

Like all the other East European countries which, after the end of
World War II, came to constitute the Soviet bloc of nations, Czechoslovakia patterned her economic system after that of Stalin's Soviet Union.
Once productive industrial property had been nationalized, the Center
began to plan all economic activities of enterprises down to the most
minute detail, prescribing to each productive unit a number of targets to
be met, alloting them the inputs deemed necessary to carry out the
assigned tasks, and rewarding the managers for fulfilling and overful-
filling the goals set by the center, among them first and foremost the
quantitative output goal.

None of the countries that embarked on a Marxist-Leninist course
was less suited for such an economic system than Czechoslovakia. A system of economic planning from the center in which factory directors and
workers are called upon to carry out orders spelled out in detail from
above may have great economic advantages for a crash industrialization
program. This appears to hold true particularly when the country is still
at the beginning stages of industrialization so that relatively few economic decisions have to be made, and when the country's population has
as yet few sophisticated demands and has had little prior experience with
and desire for democratic rights and freedoms. But Czechoslovakia had
had long years of experience with democratic institutions during the
interwar period and she entered the post World War II era as an already

This article is part of a larger study of economic reforms in Eastern Europe to
be published by the author in book form. The article has been published in German
by *Osteuropa*, No. 3, 1968, pp. 208–219 under the title "Das Neue Oenonomische
Modell—Probleme und Aussichten." Reprinted in its English version by permission
of the author and the editors of *Osteuropa*.

developed country.[1] Yet, during the years of postwar reconstruction, the economy performed quite satisfactorily by means of ever more extensive utilization of material and human resources, irrespective of cost. Within fifteen years after the war's end in 1945, national income had risen by 150 per cent and gross-national product by 250 per cent.

By 1960, Czechoslovakia began to run into economic difficulties. Due to the rapid economic expansion, central administration of the country's economy had become more difficult; most available labor reserves had been put to use and many workers had been shifted from agriculture to industry; the international balance of payments had become so unfavourable that imports had to be curtailed; and the incentive structure based on motivation to fulfill the quantitative output plan had led to such "antisocial" actions as the hiding of productive capacity, the hoarding of capital equipment, and the disregard for quality, assortment, and costs. During the early 1960's, Czechoslovakia's economic growth slowed down to a snail's pace, and in 1963 Czechoslovakia became the only industrialized country in the world with not just a slowdown but an actual drop in building construction, industrial output, national income and real wages.[2]

It became ever more apparent that the system of administrative central planning of all the micro aspects of economic activities was ill suited for the efficient performance of an industrialized economy such as that of Czechoslovakia. Under the impact of economic setbacks, a search began for new methods of economic planning and management and for an alteration in the incentive structure that would enhance productive efficiency and increase consumer satisfaction. Upon direction of the Twelfth Congress of the Central Committee of Czechoslovakia's Communist Party, which was held in 1962, work on a "new economic model," as it came to be called, was started. The details of the model were worked out by a group of experts headed by Ota Sik. The fundamental outlines were officially approved by the Party in January, 1965; during the following months, the new economic model was tested in hundreds of enterprises; on January 1, 1966, some of the measures provided for by the model were put into operation; and on January 1, 1967, the entire new system of planning and administration was introduced (although not immediately fully implemented) in all branches of Czechoslovak industry.

Czechoslovakia's new economic model entails a substantial degree of economic decentralization, a corresponding increase in the decision-making power of enterprises, a greatly enhanced role for profit as a

[1] According to official Czechoslovak sources, industry, including building, accounted for 65.7 per cent and agriculture for but 22.1 per cent, of Czechoslovakia's national income in 1948, the year the country embarked on its Marxist-Leninist course. (*Statisticke Prehledy*, No. 2/1964.)

[2] See, for example, *Hospodarske Noviny*, No. 9, 1964, and *Statsticka Rocenka CSSR*, 1964, Prague, 1964.

measuring rod of enterprise efficiency and as the base for incentive premiums, and an extensive utilization of the market forces of demand and supply. More specifically, the new economic model called for a substantial decrease in the number of indicators to be prescribed from above;[3] a change from obligatory indicators to "recommendations" from the center and the replacement of direct methods of central administration (commands) to indirect ones (monetary and fiscal policies such as credit controls); a wholesale price reform, intended to bring wholesale prices up to average costs of production; a gradual enlargement of the sphere of "free" prices;[4] an enhanced voice for enterprises within the concerns and trusts of which they are a part;[5] a rapid diminution of centrally financed investments; the establishment of economic accountability (khozraschot) for each industrial enterprise and greatly increased emphasis on material incentives for workers and managers. In essence, the far reaching economic reforms, as now introduced or at least planned, amount to an attempt to widen the role of the market and of material incentives within the framework of a socialist economy—in other words, to a compromise between central planning on the one hand, and the market and individual initiative on the other.[6] "Economic policy," recently admonished a Czechoslovak economist, "must beware of two extremes: too strict control which would be a brake on the process of creating a market, and, on the other hand, too great liberalization that could open up an inflation spiral, especially under conditions of imperfect equilibrium."[7]

To Czechoslovakia's economists, the rationality of the new economic

[3] As of January 1, 1966, the number of indicators in the field of industrial production was decreased from 1,200 to 67; and since then enterprises have no longer been given obligatory volumes of production nor have targets been set for growth of labor productivity, limits to the wages fund, reduction of production costs, etc. (Miroslav Sokol, "Changes in Economic Management in Czechoslovakia", *Czechoslovak Economic Papers*, 8, 1967, p. 8).

[4] Under the new economic model, there are three types of prices: 1. fixed prices, set at the center, 2. limit prices, permitted to fluctuate freely within maximum and minimum limits set from above, and 3. free prices, permitted to find their own levels on the basis of market demand and supply, or at least of freely negotiated contractual agreements between suppliers and purchasers. On January 1, 1967, only 13% of all prices were free (*Hospodarske Noviny*, Jan. 27, 1967). More specifically, the following distribution between fixed, limit and free prices prevailed in Czechoslovakia in 1966:

	(in per cent)		
	FIXED PRICES	LIMIT PRICES	FREE PRICES
Foodstuffs	92	5	3
Industrial commodities	59	19	22
Services	0	73	27

Source: *Reporter*, Prague, Sept. 30, 1966.

[5] Czechoslovak enterprises are horizontally integrated into trusts and concerns.

[6] It should be pointed out that reforms with the same fundamental purpose (though differing in specifics) have by now been adopted by all the Communist countries of East Europe except Albania.

[7] Sokol, *op. cit.*, p. 14.

model seemed impeccable, and most Western experts agreed. Even the strongly anti-Communist *East Europe* talked about revolutionizing "the very foundations of the Czechoslovak economy" and referred to the system as "economic common sense, rebelling against political programs."[8] But if the new system's advocates thought that there would be smooth sailing, and that economic results of its introduction would be spectacular and immediate, they were mistaken. It soon became evident that the dismantling of an administratively guided system is not all that simple, that old habits are not readily changed, and that it is easier to construct a model than to establish the conditions that make it apply as originally intended. By fall, 1967 there was no longer any doubt: the new economic model was in trouble. Many consumer goods were in short supply; industrial wholesale prices had risen by an average of 29 or 30 per cent instead of the planned 19 per cent;[9] inflationary pressures were mounting on the retail level; the increase in exports amounted to but a fraction of what had been planned; and in a country which until recently has had a pronounced labor shortage[10] at least temporary widespread unemployment began to loom as a distinct possibility on the not too distant horizon.

THE INTERVIEW

Since the economic reforms in the Soviet Union and the Communist countries of East Europe constitute my major research interest, I decided to go to Prague to talk with economists from the Czechoslovak Academy of Sciences and from Charles University who were connected with the preparation or the implementation of the new economic model so that I might gain a better understanding of what had gone wrong and so that I might learn what changes in the methods of implementing the new economic system were being contemplated in light of the experience. Among the many top economists of Czechoslovakia who, in October 1967, gladly gave up their time to answer my questions was Professor Ota Sik, Director of the Economic Institute of the Czechoslovak Academy of Sciences, father of the new economic model, and chief economist in charge

[8] Louis Barcata, "Sik Versus Schweik in Czechoslovakia," *East Europe*, February, 1967, p. 22.

[9] These percentages are weighted averages. Coal and other mining products, for instance, were reported to have risen by 52.5 per cent, industrial chemicals by 46.5 per cent, construction by 40.2 per cent, power by 34.6 per cent, consumer durables and food wholesale prices by 20.2 per cent, pharmaceutical and medical supplies only by 13.9 per cent (*Rude Pravo*, April 4, 1967; see also *Financial Times* April 6, 1967).

[10] See, for instance, Harry G. Shaffer, "The Labor Shortage in Czechoslovakia," *Osteuropa Wirtschaft*, December, 1965, pp. 278–86.

of supervising the economic aspects of its implementation. My questions and Professor Sik's answers are reproduced below.*

HARRY G. SHAFFER (HGS): Professor Sik, there have been reports that Czechoslovakia's economists and planners have been disappointed, so far, by the results of the implementation of the new economic model. It is my understanding that the wholesale price reform in particular has not had the expected effects. Can you tell me what has happened?

OTA SIK (OS): You are quite correct; the price reform did not turn out as anticipated. Prior to the introduction of the reform at the beginning of this year, a very large number of enterprises were unprofitable. These were state-subsidized. The intention of the price reform had been to increase wholesale prices sufficiently so that enterprises *could* operate profitably. I say "could," because the price increases were to be kept to such levels that producing units would be under pressure to cut costs and to operate efficiently if they wanted to make a profit. Only in such a manner could we hope to overcome the gross wastefulness and inefficiency of the past. But what happened was that wholesale prices rose too much. As a result, enterprises began to earn unreasonably high profits; now they have a lot of money to distribute in the form of higher wages and increased investments, but there is no equivalent increase in output of goods. We therefore have a situation today that looks like prosperity to workers and managers; but in reality, there is a shortage of goods, there are strong inflationary pressures, and there is no adequate incentive to induce enterprises to strive for more efficient performance.

HGS: How could this have happened? Why were wholesale prices raised more than necessary?

OS: Let us realize that a price reform such as we attempted is no mean undertaking. There were some one and a half million prices that needed to be adjusted. We reduced this to 27,000 groups of commodities, but that is still a substantial number. Without adequate time to check everything carefully, cost figures submitted from below had to be taken as the basis for price determination. On the other hand, it has become clear since the reform that production costs could be reduced more rapidly than had been supposed. On the other hand, to a certain degree, the figures submitted by some producing units were speculative.

HGS: What do you plan to do about it?

* I wish to express my appreciation to the Czechoslovak economists who granted me interviews; to Dr. Milos Stadnik of the Economic Institute of the Czechoslovak Academy of Sciences, for having made arrangements for the interview with Professor Sik; and to Dr. V. Kralicek, Scientific Secretary of the Institute, for having made arrangements for all the other interviews.

os: We cannot now carry out a second price reform. We are trying to develop gradual pressure on prices either where it is possible through competition, or where it is not quite possible through certain centrally directed simulated market conditions in order to put the enterprises under heavier market pressure.

HGS: Won't this pressure to reduce prices cause hardships for many enterprises?

os: More than that. There will be not only individual enterprises but entire branches that will run into difficulties. Yet, there is no other way. Enterprises will have to be able to manage or they will have to be closed. Inefficient enterprises cost society more than they bring to it; they simply must be shut down. This saves raw materials; workers can be shifted to where they can be comparatively more productive, etc.

HGS: Few Western economists would challenge the wisdom of such action. But can it be done politically in Czechoslovakia today?

os: There is no doubt that such steps are politically difficult. But they MUST be taken. However, the center will have to support temporarily the discharged workers, will have to retrain them if necessary. Workers could for instance be shifted to the building industry or to transportation where additional workers are needed. Just a short time ago, we also had a great shortage of workers in coal mining; as a matter of fact, several thousand Polish coal miners were employed in Czechoslovakia. But under the new economic model, the coal mining industry has become so efficient that we now have a labor surplus there—the first concrete proof of the correctness of our theory.

HGS: The inflationary pressures you have been talking about have at least in part resulted from wage increases outrunning increases in productivity. What do you intend to do about that?

os: This is a recent phenomenon which we have not yet succeeded in overcoming. To do something about it, we'll have to put pressure on enterprises. We'll have to create price conditions where enterprises can no longer sell their products as easily as now, where they will have to start fighting for customers. We'll also have to stop subsidizing them and to make it harder for them to obtain credit. Then they'll become more cost conscious. But since the wholesale price reform has failed, there is not enough pressure now. I wish we could leave it to the forces of competition to obtain these goals. Right now, unfortunately, this is not possible and pressure on prices from above is necessary.

HGS: I understand that the government will sequester a part of the high profits earned by enterprises since the implementation of the price reform. Does this not violate the fundamental principles of the new economic model?

os: Not at all. It will not be done in general, only in exceptional cases. The government is going to do that only in cases where it can be clearly shown that the enterprises obtained their higher profits by giving the government wrong information concerning their costs.

hgs: Still, the central fixing of prices, the governmental appropriation of profits of some enterprises, the supporting, retraining and shifting of workers from unprofitable to profitable enterprises or industries— what will all this do to the new economic model's goal of decentralization and of a relatively free market?

os: The reestablishment of market conditions is our goal, and we will be taking steps in this direction; but for the time being some recentralization will be necessary. We are in a period of hidden inflation with demand outrunning supply. Under such circumstances, drastic anti-inflationary steps will have to be taken.

hgs: In other words, for the moment, you recommend a return to the former centralized methods of planning?

os: Not really. Formerly we had administrative planning, with few economic considerations. It was believed that the only requirement for successful planning was the achievement of equilibrium between production and consumption. Costs were hardly taken into consideration. Administrative planning was not scientifically founded; it was based on a battle between the enterprises and the center. The former tried to get the lowest possible production goals and the highest possible state-allocated supplies; in other words, they tried to get the best deal possible for themselves. The center knew the enterprises were cheating and it attempted to raise production goals and to lower the quantity of inputs allocated. To this kind of situation we must never return. Central guidance, henceforth, must be based on scientifically determined economic considerations.

hgs: How did Czechoslovakia fare under its nearly two decades of administrative planning?

os: Until recent years, plans were fulfilled, but this was accomplished by "extensive" development, in other words by the erection of more factories, the utilization of more workers. Intensive development, meaning modernization and the increase of output with the same inputs of men and material by enhancing efficiency—these were neglected. Most of the industrial growth was at the expense of agriculture which was drained of manpower. Young men, especially, were attracted to the cities until today the average age of Czechoslovakia's agricultural producers is 50, the majority of them being women. Thus, extensive development can no longer continue in the 1960's as it had in the past.

hgs: There has obviously been considerable investment in industry. Would you say, then, that as a whole it has been rather inefficient?

os: Our capital coefficient has gone up so terrifically that nothing like it has happened anywhere in the West. In some countries expensive modernization has of course taken place. But in the West such investment has been labor saving and has resulted in substantially enhanced output. In Czechoslovakia, with average building time for the erection of capital facilities two to three times that of the West, we have increased capital AND labor, and we have not achieved proportionate increases in output. Hence, we cannot talk about efficient progress, but must talk, rather, about the bad effects of administrative planning.

hgs: If I understand you correctly, you advocate the use of market forces when possible, and central planning when considered necessary. Are there distinct areas which are to be reserved for each?

os: From the outset, we have advocated a greater role of the market. It is, however, primarily at the micro-economic level that we want enterprises to be guided by their own cost-revenue relationships, with the market influencing both (costs and revenues) to ever greater degrees. Central planning is to be primarily macro-planning. But even here, we need a change from administrative to economic planning, and from direct commands in the execution of plans to the utilization of economic (fiscal and monetary) tools.

hgs: Could you outline for me, in somewhat greater detail, how economic planning would be carried out under the new economic model?

os: All micro-planning decisions should come from below; the macro plan would be made at the center but would be implemented only by exerting *indirect influences*. The trusts and concerns, on the basis of information supplied from the producing enterprises, would submit proposals based on what they would consider most profitable, and they would also carry out their own investments. Yet, final decisions must be left up to the center. A factory may, for instance, consider the production of a certain commodity the most advantageous to its own interests. But assume that this would involve a substantial increase in the amount of coal needed, which in turn would involve the necessity of opening new coal mines, which would be so expensive as to make the venture undesirable from the point of view of society at large. In this case, the center may oppose the factory's proposal. But, under the new economic model, the center must no longer simply turn down the factory's proposal. Instead, it must exert indirect pressures. Assuming that credit is needed, credit conditions for this venture could, for instance, be made more stringent than for others by, let us say, reducing the repayment period.

hgs: And if an enterprise cannot be deterred by the indirect pressures, what then?

os: If the enterprise finds it profitable to carry out production in spite of the more stringent conditions imposed upon it, it must of course be permitted to follow its original plan. Such profitability would prove that the effort is worth its costs.

HGS: You have been talking about the increasing role of the market under your new economic model. Such a market is of course assumed to function under conditions of relatively unrestrained competition. But you yourself just mentioned your "trusts" and "concerns" and Czechoslovak economists keep writing about monopoly conditions in your country.

OS: There are indeed monopolies in our country, monopolies such as do not exist in the West. Our industries are horizontally integrated into concerns and trusts. All shoe production in Czechoslovakia, for instance, is combined into one trust. In heavy industry, especially, the power of individual enterprises is at present quite restricted.

HGS: How, then, do you propose to establish competitive market conditions?

OS: We must have very strong anti-trust laws. This does not mean, however, that integration should be abolished. As a matter of fact, it would be economically advantageous if vertical integration were introduced also. However, although important functions should be left for the concerns and trusts, the center will have to assist in the establishment of competitive conditions within each industry.

HGS: Let me return, if I may, to price determination under Czechoslovakia's new economic model. If I understand the model correctly, prices are to be based primarily on costs of production which are to include a reasonable return for the efficiently operating enterprise. In this connection I have two questions: First, could you comment on the degree to which demand is to be taken into consideration and, more specifically, do you attempt to estimate income and price elasticity of demand for each product? And, secondly, when Czechoslovak economists talk about costs of production, they usually refer to *average* costs. Does that mean that the marginal cost theories advanced in the West are not accepted in Czechoslovakia?

OS: Elasticity of demand has to be taken into consideration. We are trying to estimate it for a few major items such as bread, meat, and coal. Otherwise, we estimate it not for individual products but for aggregate groups. To compute such elasticities is very difficult without the guidance of an effective market. The center must use a simulated market to arrive at a "correct" price. It must ask itself questions such as: "How would price be changed if we were to permit free importation and market determined prices of this or that commodity?" or "What would be the effect of such market conditions on this or that particular branch of industry?" Once answers have been obtained, the center must implement its decisions not by administrative commands but by indirect pressures, such as the regulation of credit. As to your second question, we are familiar with marginal theory and we do not deny its validity. But in your own competitive models, marginal costs equal average costs in the long run; long run price, therefore, equals average costs. In light industry, competitive forces, permitted to operate freely, could yield correct prices for us also. As regards heavy industry, we will have to depend greatly upon the competition of foreign producers, whenever they are more efficient, to keep prices down.

HGS: Do you mean to advocate importing producers' goods freely whenever they are obtainable more cheaply abroad than in your country? Are you advocating, in other words, unrestrained, international trade?

OS: In principle, yes—but we must not act too hastily. When it comes to price determination, I would want to place my faith in the forces of competition, operating in the market place—and that includes the competition of foreign producers. But right now we do not have sufficient competition, nor is there enough foreign currency for unrestricted imports. Hence, we need more central guidance at the moment than we anticipate needing in the future. At the moment, we are forced to continue subsidization. But producers in heavy industry must be made aware that the time of subsidization is running out. We should give them a definite time limit—let us say three to five years. We should tell them: either you increase your productive efficiency within this time so as to be competitive with producers abroad, or we shall import.

HGS: You are taking a very strong stand against government subsidization. Even in the West we have *some* subsidies. Are you against *all* subsidies?

OS: No. There may be sound reasons for subsidizing certain enterprises or industries. But first of all subsidization should be a rare exception and not the general rule as it has been heretofore in our country. And, secondly, it is essential that the cost of such subsidization be known. After all, the final goal of all our efforts is an increase in living standards; and the more we compromise, the worse off the consumer is likely to be.

HGS: Do you plan to make extensive use of interest and rent under your new economic model?

OS: Yes. We do not contemplate one fixed rate of interest, though. We are planning higher interest rates on fixed capital[11] and lower interest rates on circulating capital.[12] The longer the recoupment period[13] the

---

[11] Machinery and equipment.
[12] Raw material.
[13] The time necessary for a given investment to pay for itself.

higher the interest rate will be. This will be of particular help to light industry. Our banks are now working out the details. As to rent, we have now accepted it in theory; details must still be worked out. We intend to use rent to influence output. When we want to encourage an industry, we'll lower rents and vice versa.

HGS: This is more like a tax. I was talking about differential rent in the Ricardian sense, where rent would be the result of natural advantages and would take up the difference between the better situated enterprise (or, in his example, the more fertile land) and the least productive which it still pays to operate.

OS: No, in this sense we have not contemplated the use of rent in industry yet. Perhaps this will come later.

HGS: And in agriculture? The Soviets, for instance, use a similar concept when they pay lower prices for agricultural output grown in more fertile parts of the Soviet Union.

OS: In agriculture we have been doing something quite similar. Although we pay the same price for wheat, no matter where it is grown in Czechoslovakia, we do have differential taxes.

HGS: Czechoslovak economists during the past few years have emphasized that part of the country's difficulties arise from a lack of incentive which, presumably, is largely the result of the levelling of wages. These economists have called for an "unlevelling" of wages, so as to encourage greater work effort, to make a university education worthwhile in terms of higher incomes, etc. What is your position on the matter and has anything been done to unlevel wages?

OS: The unlevelling of wages is of great importance. The younger generation has lost much of the revolutionary spirit. Without the prospects of higher income, why then should a man try hard? But, as important as the unlevelling of wages is, it must proceed slowly. It is not feasible to reduce the income of some in order to raise the income of others. What has to be done is to raise the incomes of all, but raise those of some faster than those of others. This will take time. Indeed, many of the major goals of the economic reform are still ahead.

HGS: If I may shift to ideology: if such unlevelling of incomes is to proceed, what will it do to the achievement of the final goal of communism in which, presumably, everyone will contribute to the best of his ability and share in the total output in accordance with his needs?

OS: Communism is a long run goal. Even Lenin emphasized that as long as there are not enough goods to satisfy the needs of all, and as long as people must accept jobs they do not like in order to make a living, Communism cannot be achieved. Some men have jobs that they love, that they enjoy for the work itself, irrespective of the financial remuneration. Researchers like you probably fall into that category. Some day, all labor will be like that. But for this day to arrive, mechanization must be much more advanced than it is today, goods must be more plentiful, and work weeks must be shortened. Today, too many men would still choose work other than what they are doing, more interesting work, were it not for financial considerations. That is why so many people, after their day's work in the factory, make things for their own enjoyment at home. We do want to achieve the eventual goal of perfect communism; but we cannot bypass the intermediate stage.

HGS: I understand that Czechoslovakia is seeking foreign investments. Investors from capitalist countries will want to earn a profit. Are you willing to let capitalist entrepreneurs participate in profits and, if so, what does this do to the theory of Marxism-Leninism?

OS: Foreign investors may participate in profits. We must be pragmatic; such foreign capital will help us to develop and to achieve our goals faster. Even Lenin did not hesitate to accept foreign capital.

HGS: Do you anticipate that in the future the development and use of computers will make central planning so efficient that there will no longer be any need for the use of the market?

OS: Computers will undoubtedly be instrumental in improving planning and in making more accurate predictions, but they will *never* be able to replace the market which comes about as the result of the interaction of producers and consumers. The forces which result from conflicting interests cannot be replaced by computers. Computers can rapidly provide answers, logically correct on the basis of information fed into them. But the information itself will be wrong without a regulated market.[14] And if the information is wrong, what can the computer do? How is the computer to know which new products are desired? How is the computer to exert the necessary pressures on producers which the market can exert so effectively?

HGS: Has Czechoslovakia given consideration to the possibility of establishing workers' councils such as exist in Yugoslavia?

OS: We are at present not contemplating workers' councils of the Yugoslav kind; but I should point out that since January 1967 we have had enterprise boards attached to the trusts. These enterprise boards include experts on that particular branch of industry, and representatives of scientific institutes, banks, *and the labor unions.* Directors are obliged to consult these enterprise boards.

HGS: My next question is not really economic in nature; I shall understand if you do not care to answer it. There is a lot of speculation in the West that the implementation of the new economic model will reduce the powers of the Communist Party. Do you agree?

OS: In the past, the Party made many decisions regarding details of pro-

---

[14] By a regulated market, Professor Sik meant a market influenced by overriding decisions made by the center, as explained above.

duction. In these respects, the Party will certainly be losing power. The Party can no longer dictate to directors. But in the macro sense, in the major economic decisions, the power of the Party will remain.

HGS: One final question, and again feel free to refuse to answer it if you so desire: Do you believe that the implementation of the new economic model will have non-economic repercussions in terms of enhanced freedom and democracy in Czechoslovakia?

OS: There is no necessary linear relationship between the economic changes brought about by the new economic model and the political climate in the country. Yet, in my opinion, the new economic model *will* contribute to the advancement of democracy in Czechoslovakia.

HGS: Thank you very much for your most informative answers. Have you ever considered coming to the United States, perhaps on a one-semester or one-year appointment to an American university?

OS: It is my greatest wish to go to the United States, and many of my colleagues have been there or are there right now. But I cannot get away at the moment since my job is no longer purely academic— there is, for instance, a lot of committee work right now, connected with the introduction of the new economic model. Perhaps at some future time!

Concluding Observations

From the outset, the new economic model has had its opponents. There are orthodox Marxist-Leninists who fear that the new system would surrender too much of the socialist principle of central planning; there are party men who have secured a favorable position for themselves in the administrative apparatus and who are likely to lose much of their power if the new decentralization measures are fully implemented; there are factory directors who have held their positions because they were "politically reliable" and because they were good order takers and executors, but who have little of the kind of entrepreneurial ability that will be demanded of managers in the future; there are workers who would rather keep what they have under a system of equalitarian wages than to see their income tied to their and to their enterprises' economic performance; etc. And even if the majority of the Czechoslovak population looked hopefully forward to the new economic model, the apparent shortcomings of its implementation have left many disheartened. At the September Central Committee meeting, Slovak Party leader Alexander Dubcek reported the "existence and growth of distrust and doubt as to whether or not we shall persist on the road embarked upon," and he admonished that the strong optimism with which the introduction of the new economic model was approached "is changing very rapidly into disillusionment and even pessimism."[15]

Whatever the division among the Czechoslovak population, Czechoslovak economists seem agreed on the economic necessity of introducing the reforms and on the benefits to be derived from the utilization of the market mechanism. "The difference among Czechoslovak economists is merely one of degree," Dr. Oldrich Kyn of the Faculty of Political Economy of Charles University commented to me. "I personally do not believe in any Communism without a market," he went on. "The new economic model is Czechoslovakia's only hope," Docent Josef Flek, who directs the Agricultural Section of the Czechoslovak Academy of Sciences' Economic Institute, told me. "The economy will be led by the Plan," he explained further, "but the instrument of fulfillment will be the market." "Either you accept the market mechanism or you don't," remarked Dr. Josef Goldman who heads the Academy's Economic Institute's Section for Research on Business Conditions and Economic Forecasting, "you can't improve on it."

The stand of the economists in favor of a continuation of the new economic model appears to have the full backing of the Party. Party Secretary Drahomir Kolder reaffirmed that the Party Central Committee "stands completely behind the principles and programs of the Reform."[16] Slovak Party leader Alexander Dubcek emphasized that "the old management system will take us nowhere and we must in a concentrated manner introduce the *economic* management system . . ,"[17] and President and First Party Secretary Antonin Novotny stated emphatically that "certain shortcomings that have evolved in the implementation of the new mechanism" do not alter the fact that "the results thus attained prove the correctness of the road embarked upon."[18]

The Czechoslovak economy did progress under the new economic model in 1967: Gross national product, national income, industrial output, labor productivity, real per capita income, living standards—all increased.[19]

---

[15] *Rude Pravo,* Sept. 29, 1967.

[16] *Rude Pravo,* November 9, 1967.

[17] *Rude Pravo,* September 29, 1967. Emphasis mine.

[18] Talk by Novotny as reported by the Hungarian News Agency MTI, October 11, 1967.

[19] Party Secretary Lubomir Strougal, for instance, mentioned in his report to the September Plenum an increase in productivity, better results on farms, and an estimated increase in total output for 1967 over 1966 by approximately six per cent. But, on the other hand, he also pointed out that domestic supplies of consumer goods had fallen by 3 billion korunas below the planned level of 123.8 billion korunas. (Ceteka, September 27, 1967); See also *Economist,* October 13, 1967. Increases in real wages and living standards were claimed by the State Commission for Finance, Prices and Wages at its plenary meeting in December. (Ceteka, December 4, 1967). Retail prices, it should be pointed out, have risen but little. *Prace* of September 27, 1967 reported retail prices during the first quarter of 1967 as 1.1 per cent, and during the second quarter as 1.2 per cent, above the corresponding period of 1966; Czechoslovak Television of November 16, 1967 gave the increase for the first half of 1967 as 1.5 per cent; and there is no indication that retail prices have risen by much more during the rest of the year.

Yet, the shortcomings were so severe and so potentially dangerous that something had to be done without further delay. There seems to be a consensus of opinion among Czechoslovak economists and planners (as also expressed by Professor Sik in the interview above) that in the absence of well-developed competitive market conditions a temporary recentralization in many spheres is necessary. "Central organs now simply cannot let things run their natural course . . . ," stated a recent article in the official Czechoslovak Party organ *Rude Pravo*,[20] "they must take measures to resist the inflationary trends endangering the fate of the whole new system of management." And while the article advocated that such measures be as much as possible "economic" in nature, it emphasized that administrative measures "cannot be wholly excluded . . ."; Party Secretary Lubomir Strougal reported to the September Party Central Committee Plenum on the necessity of "administrative correction;"[21] and Party Secretary Drahomir Kolder explained that although "real market relations have already a strong influence . . . they are far from being able to have an effect to the extent that is necessary," and he argued that therefore "the central bodies must consciously intervene in the management of the economy, even now when the reform is being carried out."[22] As to the long run function of central planning under the new economic model, Dr. Kyn explained it to me as follows:

We hope to combine the market with central planning, but central planning must be something different from Soviet command planning; it should be more like planning in France, perspective planning, aimed at giving each enterprise more information.

The role of the central plan should be 1. to provide a source of information, and, 2. to represent social preferences as to the aims of development.

Via its expenditures on social consumption, via expenditures for education, health, the army, etc., the center will in any case retain a substantial influence on the economy. All else can be left to the market.

But not all Czechoslovak economists assign quite as preeminent a role to the market. Here is how another Czechoslovak economist phrased it:

It is necessary to change the relation between the plan and the market, and to strengthen the function of the market . . .

It is in essence a matter of creating an effective mechanism of central management based partly on the working of the market as a stimulus and criterion for the economy—on the basis of long-term, uniformly established rules—and partly on planning as an instrument for long-term optimizing of economic development and hence the market.[23]

[20] October 3, 1967.
[21] *Economist,* October 13, 1967.
[22] *Rude Pravo,* November 10, 1967.
[23] Sokol, *op. cit.,* pp. 11 and 12.

While most Czechoslovak economists place the primary blame for the economic shortcomings of the last few months on an excessive increase in average wholesale prices with its corollaries of excess demand and inflationary pressures, others point to structural defects in production and pricing which leave some sectors and subsectors undersupplied, while others produce more than they can sell. Josef Goldman, for instance, pointed out to me that great shortages in high quality shoes coexisted with excess supplies of cheap textiles; and Oldrich Kyn explained that the freeing of all retail prices, as desirable as it would be in the future, was now impossible because the pricing structure was so distorted that it would cause great upheavals. That there are indeed structural defects in the Czechoslovak economy is evident from the fact that during the first ten months of 1967 the increasing shortages of some consumer goods and the overall decline of domestic consumer good inventories coincided with a multi-billion koruna increase in total inventories, apparently primarily in the unfinished goods and the producer goods sectors.[24]

The re-emergence of administrative measures and the diminishing emphasis on decentralization—temporary though it may be—is apparent everywhere: Severe penalties were decreed against "those enterprises which this year used the reconstruction of wholesale prices to raise their profits in a speculative way without covering such excessive profits by an adequate increase in production and supplies for the market."[25] A new government decree was issued, effective January 1, 1968, that provided for sanctions in the form of additional taxes against enterprises which "do not fulfill their foreign trade obligations."[26] A "second stage" of the centrally determined wholesale price revision is scheduled for partial introduction on January 1, 1968.[27] The State Commission for Finance, Prices and Wages has prepared a plan whereby at least the upper limits of 81 per cent of all prices, and of 87 per cent of all consumer goods prices, will remain fixed by central bodies.[28] And in 1967 more than fifty per cent of all new investments were "still not in accordance with the new system;"[29] in 1968 invest-

[24] Radio Bratislava, November 13, 1967 gives the overall increase in inventories for the first ten months of 1967 as 6 billion korunas; the West German *Die Welt* of November 30, 1967 gives the increase as "more than ten billion korunas."

[25] Vladimir Janza, Vice Chairman of the State Commission for Finance, Prices and Wages who made the announcement stated that he thought that such government action was "somewhat of a violation of gentlemen's agreements between the center and the enterprises—but it is necessary." (Ceteka, November 9, 1967.) Enterprises were informed by the government that they would not be subject to any penalty if they returned their illgotten gains by September 15, 1967. (Ceteka, August 21, 1967). But by that date, out of an estimated 20 billion korunas of enterprise takings, only 270 million had been declared. (Ceteka, November 9, 1967). By November 15, 1967 this figure had been increased to 700 million korunas. (Radio Bratislava, November 22, 1967).

[26] Radio Prague, December 6, 1967.

[27] Announcement by Vladimir Janza on Radio Prague, November 16, 1967.

[28] *Bratislava Pravda*, November 9, 1967.

[29] *Politika*, Nov. 14, 1967.

ments are likely to be yet more centralized (and even if the new economic model's investment policy is eventually carried out, only 30 per cent of all investments would come out of enterprise funds while most of the rest would be financed by bank credit, thus leaving the center in a very influential position through its control over the state bank).[30]

It seems a reasonable assumption that the present recentralization measures are but temporary, and necessary, emergency measures and do not amount to a retreat from the implementation of the new economic model. Even strongly anti-Communist sources are persuaded that "Party leaders are sincere in their desire to effectuate the reform."[31] Moreover, there is surely great hope in the increasing realization that monopolistic tendencies must be overcome,[32] that at least at this stage of development wage levelling is a deterrent to efficient performance,[33] and that a market can perform its economic functions better the more individual prices, both wholesale and retail, are permitted to find their own level, according to the market forces of supply and demand.[34]

Those who are engaged in the implementation of the new economic model appear quite willing to admit mistakes, to learn from them, to introduce changes where necessary, and to take a step backward in order to be able to take two steps forward in the future. The continuous earnest search for better methods, headed by first rate economists, holds great promise for a more efficient operation of the Czechoslovak economy.

[30] One economist, explaining the financing of capital investments under the new economic model, had this to say on the matter:

A sufficient influence of the center on planning of capital investments must be safeguarded. Furthermore, decisions on the more extensive investments are expressly made for a longer period of time and cannot be subordinated to the immediate market situation . . .

On the other hand, however, . . . enterprises must have an interest in, and be responsible for, the effectiveness of investment . . . For this reason the financing of investments must not be strictly separated from the financing of the enterprise's other needs. (Sokol, op. cit., pp. 16–17).

[31] Harry Trend, "Czechoslovak Economic Problems and Economic Reform," Radio Free Europe Research, November 3, 1967.

[32] Top economists such as Professor Sik (see above) have long taken this position. And the official Czechoslovak news agency Ceteka stated recently that in order to increase the output of goods, there must be "greater competition among enterprises, and the negative influences of the monopolistic organization of production which has hitherto existed must be overcome." (Ceteka, September 27, 1967).

[33] Again, see the interview with Prof. Sik above. A recent news media report warned that "lower and middle echelon functionaries still maintain a favorable attitude toward equal wages," and that "only a few people . . . are able to understand the resulting loss to society when workers do not use their full capacity." (Radio Bratislava, quoted the Slovak Party daily Pravda, October 30, 1967).

[34] "Freely fluctuating market prices have, unfortunately, not been introduced yet," remarked Dr. Kyn to me. "Let us hope," he went on, "that the price reform in 1968 will be the last step in dictating prices from above."

28   MILOS SAMARDZIJA

The Market and Social Planning in the Yugoslav Economy

Significant changes have taken place in the economic organization of contemporary societies since World War II. They have led to changes in the character, place, and role of the market and of social (macroeconomic) planning in various economic systems. In capitalist and socialist societies, the result has been a re-examination of theoretical conceptions on the relationship of macroeconomic planning to the capitalist economy and on the relationship of the market to the socialist economy. The dominant conception in economic theory of the basic contradiction between the market and social planning, which was held by economists of the West as well as economists of socialist countries, was contradicted by the economic and social development of the contemporary world.

For the capitalist world, social planning is no longer a "secret weapon" with which the socialization of economic and social life is carried out. The terms "guided capitalism" and "mixed economy," which are used to define the contemporary stage of development of capitalism, show that the definition of capitalism as a "free enterprise economy" is no longer historically accurate. On the other hand, in the socialist world, the market economy is no longer the "secret weapon" with which capitalism is restored. In theoretical works, "socialist commodity production" is increasingly discussed. Conceptions which identify the socialist economy with a non-market-planned economy are evaluated as dogmatic and conservative.

I.

This world-wide, historical process has had significant influence on the development of Yugoslav society. Yugoslavia was recreated after the liberation of the country in 1945. The leading role in the society was played by social forces whose program of action was the organization of a society of the socialist type. At that time this meant the acceptance of the

From *The Quarterly Review of Economics and Business*, Vol. 7, No. 2, Summer 1967, pp. 37–44. Reprinted by permission of the Editors of *The Quarterly Review of Economics and Business*.

model of social organization of Soviet Russia, as well as the theoretical context which explained this model. A few years (1945–48) were long enough to carry out a new organization of the social system but not to stabilize it. There was no time to eliminate various forms of social resistance, which accompany every social change and reform, because in the middle of 1948 the countries of the Soviet Bloc broke with Yugoslavia.

After the break, Yugoslav society found itself in a complex international and internal political and economic situation. The solution of these problems and the further development of a socialist society could not be carried out through the social and economic forms and measures which corresponded to the system of administrative (state) socialism, according to the assessment of Yugoslavia's leading political group. It was necessary to re-examine the dominant conceptions of socialist theory and on this basis to define a program of social action. Without this re-examination, it was not possible to find solutions for basic tasks, socialist construction, and sustained rapid economic growth under new conditions and on a new basis. There was neither the time nor the experience to work out a complete conception of social organization. It was necessary to start from elementary principles of socialism, from generally accepted principles, and to define long-run goals of social action which were consistent with these principles.

It is a basic principle of Marxist theory on socialist society that the community of working people makes up society. Thus the position and role of man in such a society is determined by his place in society's working organization and by the contribution which his work makes. In Yugoslavia instead of the inherited state organization as a form of social aggregation in socialist society (according to Soviet conceptions, not only political and territorial but also economic aggregation), a new form had to be created. Associations of working people represent the social content of this form of aggregation. The basic form of association of producers is the enterprise, or more broadly, every working organization. Thus the social content of changes in the transitional period of socialist construction is the strengthening of the social significance and role of producers' associations and the weakening and disappearance of forms of state organization.

This theoretical conception was accepted as the basis for the reorganization of Yugoslav society and led to the introduction of workers' self-management in economic enterprises in June, 1950. This was the first decisive measure which started the process of social change whose final goal was the building of a socialist system on the basis of self-management. This process has gone through several phases in which various measures and forms of social organization were applied, and it is not finished today. However, from the first day until now, this system has been characterized by the fact that there was continual development of the social organization whose theoretical conception was defined in 1950.

II.

The first step in Yugoslavia's social transformation was the creation of social and economic autonomy in the enterprise. The material basis for this autonomy was the transfer of production funds (capital) to the management of the collective.

The economic independence of the enterprise required changes in the entire system of social aggregation, as well as in the methods of aggregation which were formed in the previous period. It is known that in the system of state socialism, enterprises are sectorally aggregated in a centrally organized pyramid headed by the central government, with a comprehensive state plan for the national economy which has a directive character as the chief method in the organization of economic life. However, if the institutional basis of the entire system is organized in a different way (by means of workers' self-management), then the forms of social aggregation, the methods, and the content and character of management have to be changed. One cannot speak about autonomous decision-making in enterprises when the decisions for the performance of these organizations are made at the level of the ministry or chief administration in the form of compulsory tasks and directives. One cannot speak of self-management if this form of management is not accompanied by a material basis and does not have independence in decision-making.

Even though the self-management rights of economic enterprises were very limited at the beginning in Yugoslavia, they led to the transformation of the economic system in two directions. On the one hand, the sectoral aggregation of a centralized type, together with the centralized directive state plan, had to be abolished. This was carried out during 1951–52. On the other hand, new social forms for aggregation and management had to be created. These new forms could not be determined arbitrarily. They had to be determined by the material structure of economic life (the level of economic development) and by the social position of working organizations.

The material structure of the Yugoslav economy is characterized by a social division of labor in which specialized productive units have the social form of enterprises. The social condition for the performance of enterprise activity within this material structure is the economic independence (autonomy) of the enterprise: the right of enterprises to make decisions on their activity, which also means decisions on the allocation of factors of production and of produced goods. In all societies, these are social and material conditions for the existence of the market as the specific form of social and economic aggregation of enterprises.

In this respect, the market is not the exclusive form of organization of capitalist societies. The organization of market relations in the context of socialist institutions does not mean the creation of capitalist forms of the market. Whether or not capitalist forms will be adopted in the later development of the socialist economy remains a question of fact.

In 1951 Yugoslavia had to choose between two alternative paths: either self-management and the market mechanism with minimal state intervention or centralized planning and the institutions through which it is carried out. The solution was in favor of the first alternative—self-management and a market. If the new basis of the system is defined in this way, then the problem is how to realize these principles in practice.

Today, a decade and a half after the introduction of these changes, it is possible to analyze the direction and the social content of these processes. In 1951 this could not have been done, since the idea of the capitalist nature of the market and the socialist nature of the central plan represented an axiom of socialist theory. At that time, the Yugoslav social and economic reform was treated as a desertion from the basic principles of socialism—state management and centralized planning—and a return to "capitalistic solutions" of enterprise autonomy and market relations.

In this early phase, the Yugoslav economic system was pregnant with an internal contradiction which manifested itself in a dualism of relations: the socialist state as the owner of social property opposed to the autonomous socialist enterprise as the manager of social property; social planning as the nonmarket form of economic aggregation among enterprises opposed to market forms of aggregation among enterprises. This dualism was treated as an internal crisis of the system which could be resolved by a return to "socialist forms" or by the "restoration" of capitalist forms. It took a long time for socialist theory to accept the view that the autonomy of the enterprise and the market do not automatically signify capitalism. Even today this view has not been completely accepted in socialist theory nor in many views and interpretations of Western economists.

The dualism of the Yugoslav economic system had all the characteristics of social systems which are in the process of transition from one form of organization to another. The dualism is manifested in the fact that the old forms do not disappear immediately but that they change and become deformed during the process, often acquiring a new content, and the new forms do not always appear in a clear and developed form. This was also the case with the relationship between state management and workers' self-management in the Yugoslav economy. The development processes which lead to the creation of a new social organization cannot be explained by their formal similarities. A scientific explanation has to be based on the analysis of the social content of the processes. This will show that new historical forms are developed as a result of this synthesis. Representative bodies with producers' councils within the state apparatus and workers' councils as managers in autonomous enterprises are examples of these new forms in Yugoslavia.

III.

Market relations and forms appeared and developed under specific historical conditions in the Yugolsav context. In other words, they were not pure but were realized in a deformed way, if one compares their realization with theoretical formulations. The reasons for this manifestation of market forms are varied.

First of all, the institutional conditions for a market economy did not exist in a developed form in Yugoslavia. The economic independence of the enterprise, which is one of the most important conditions for the performance of the market mechanism, appeared in a very limited form at first. A that time, it was more a theoretical principle which guided the reorganization of the economy and less a working principle which was actually applied in economic activity. If this principle was to be applied in practice, it was going to be necessary to change the whole system of management and to grant the enterprise autonomy in decisions on production, on distribution of output, on the conditions for the sale of output, and on investment. In addition, it would be necessary to create conditions in which the enterprise could autonomously decide on the forms of its inclusion in sectoral associations, in regional communities, and in the credit system.

It must be pointed out that there were no ready solutions for this and that the only method which could be applied was the method of social experimentation. Thus the process of forming the economic autonomy of the enterprise took a relatively long time and was basically achieved by the measures of the economic reform of 1965. Under these conditions, one could not speak of developed market forms in the Yugoslav economy.

In evaluating the processes by which a market economy was introduced to Yugoslavia, it should not be forgotten that the ideological resistance of socialist theoretical conceptions was a factor which slowed the process. At that time, market forms were treated as unsocialist, and their place in a socialist economic system was seen as a temporary compromise which was indispensable because of the inadequate development of "genuine" socialist relations. Even when the market character of the socialist economy was accepted, the question of the boundaries for market performance was posed. The market mechanism was first accepted as a form of allocation of consumer goods but not of factors of production. The question of market relations in the sector of producers' goods is a problem which has not yet been resolved in socialist theory. This is also the case with the problem of the allocation of labor.

In Yugoslavia, the process of introducing market allocation of material goods included, at the start, consumer goods sectors (by abolishing rationing), raw materials sectors, energy and equipment sectors (by abolishing planned, administrative allocation), and agricultural goods sectors (by abolishing compulsory deliveries). In this way the economic autonomy of the enterprise was affirmed, in principle, in the sphere of current operations. With the change in the system of distribution of income in 1957, the autonomy of the enterprise in determining the personal incomes of working people made possible the introduction of market forms in the allocation of the labor force.

Market allocation was introduced most cautiously, and relatively late, in the sector of investment (capital market). Resistance to decentralization of investment funds was supported by the theoretical conception that only central planning can be an efficient method of allocation of investments, if the main policy goal is accelerated economic development. The introduction of workers' self-management changed the basic conception of the planned economy in such a way that instead of comprehensive planning of the whole national economy, central planning became development planning and concentrated on defining the tasks of investment policy. The institutional basis for the financing of investments was changed. The system of budget grants and subsidies, which was the way that investments were allocated in the administrative period, was transformed into a system of administrative allocation of investment credits. This system, with respect to decision-making, remained monocentric and tied to the state (federal government), even though in form it was implemented by the banking system. It was not possible to realize full autonomy of the enterprise until 1965, because the share of the enterprise in total investment funds was relatively low. The changes in the conditions of distribution of the enterprise's revenues during 1965 raised the enterprise's share in total investments to more than 60 percent. This created the material basis for the enterprise's autonomy with respect to investment, led to reform of the credit system, and prepared the conditions for organizing market allocation of investment funds, that is, a capital market.

One should not lose sight of the fact that the process of developing market relations in the Yugoslav economy depended not only on institutional conditions but also, and perhaps to a greater extent, on conditions related to the level of development. In various situations, market relations were introduced in sectors where material conditions did not provide a basis for them.

In these situations the market mechanism led to such deformations that after a short time the sector had to be put under stronger state control once again. This was evidenced by the constant changes in the lists of products which were under price controls (ceiling prices). The attempt to introduce the market mechanism in the sphere of investment credits also had to be abandoned after a short experiment.

The process of economic development removed obstacles in the material structure of production which blocked the further development of market relations. However, the imbalance created by economic development caused difficulties for the performance of normal market functions. To avoid the negative social and economic effects, it was necessary to reintroduce measures of state intervention, or if these measures already existed, they had to be sharpened. In some periods, imbalances in key sectors led to inflationary pressures, general increase of prices, and economic instability which required state intervention along the entire front (for example, the general price freeze of March, 1965).

Nevertheless, the role of the market has been significantly changed during two decades. Until 1950, the market had the nature of intersectoral (with reference to socialist industry and peasant agriculture as the sectors) and marginal economic aggregation in the context of a centrally organized economy with administrative allocation of factors of production and of goods. Since 1950, the role of the market has been increasing. The allocation of factors of production and of goods has been losing its administrative character and has been increasingly carried out through the market mechanism. The strengthening of the material basis of management and the removal of structural imbalances create the conditions for more complete liberalization of market allocation of goods.

The economic reform of 1965 was a process which speeded up the liberalization of economic management. The high level of enterprise autonomy required the necessary social conditions for full liberalization and for market relations. Administrative elements of control were greatly decreased and transformed in terms of content and in terms of methods of intervention. Intervention on the part of state organs increasingly assumed the character of coordination and general guidance. The goal was to induce appropriate decisions on the part of economic organizations and not to determine them directly. However, the legal regulation of general conditions and of the context of economic activity of the enterprise clearly remained a responsibility of the state, and in particular of central organs. The policy of liberalization included the branches of foreign trade and international payments. Changes in the regime of foreign trade and the introduction of a new exchange rate for the dinar in 1965 were the first steps in this direction. One of the goals of economic policy for the coming period is to create the conditions which will make possible the convertibility of the national currency.

IV.

Changes in the status of working organizations in the Yugoslav economic system had to be accompanied by changes in the forms of social aggregation of enterprises and in the methods used to organize and coordinate their activities at the macroeconomic level. Macroeconomic planning is the most important of these methods.

Centralized, comprehensive planning of the national economy was consistent with a system of state management of economic activities. However, when the institutional context was changed, the system and methodology of social planning had to be changed as well. One must not lose sight of the fact that planning is not an autonomous and isolated economic complex; planning must be consistent with the basic characteristics of the economic system. The conception that in a socialist economy there can only be one type of macroeconomic planning, the Soviet type, is dogmatic and scientifically unacceptable.

The changes which took place in the Yugoslav economy during 1951 and 1952 created a new institutional setting for social planning and had to be accompanied by changes in the system and methodology of planning. The law on the planning system passed in 1951 was the first step in this direction. As a result of the reorganization of the state apparatus for economic management and the introduction of workers' self-management in enterprises, the sectoral aggregation of enterprises based on hierarchic relations was abolished. Political-territorial units—namely, the commune, the republic, and the federation—became the basic forms of social aggregation. Among these, the self-governed commune represented the starting point. This led to decentralization of management and decision-making within political institutions. Sectoral aggregation was given a new form but one which was not particularly influential from the point of view of the economy as a whole. Until two or three years ago, the various forms of sectoral aggregation were not even adequate for effective integration and coordination of the economy. This was particularly evident in the growth of economic localism and particularism, which had their roots in the growth of bureaucratic and centralistic tendencies on lower levels of political organization, especially at the level of the republic.

In an institutional structure in which political and social aggregation was dominant, social plans were approved at various levels of the political system, from the commune to the federation. However, the plans still went from the top down, which gave them a centralistic character. At the enterprise level, independent plans were prepared. However, the method for preparing these plans and the forms by which they were aggregated into social plans were not adequately developed. As a result, the gap which developed in the planning system led to inconsistent relationships and to relative inefficiency of the social plan in organizing economic development. During that period, economic development was largely organized by measures of direct intervention which were not encompassed by the plan, particularly by measures which regulated the distribution of the enterprise's gross income.

Changes in the content of social plans reflected the institutional duality which existed in the Yugoslav economic system. Enterprise autonomy and market relations could not be developed together with comprehensive and directive plans. Social plans became plans for the projection of economic development expressed through highly aggregated flows and growth rates. In other words, they became plans of basic proportions. The first of these basic proportions was the basic distribution of gross material product. This was determined more or less on the basis of linear extrapolations of growth rates realized in the previous period. But the federal social plan also contained a part which was directive in character, namely, that part of the plan which concerned the extent and structure of investment. In the actual planning document, the investment structure was, as a rule, determined on an aggregate basis. Through additional regulatory measures, the central government had full control and decision-making power over investment outlays, both by means of economic policy on distribution and, as a last resort, by means of direct decisions on allocation. Thus, in terms of their content, social plans became development plans, whereas the current activities of the economic system were left to the decentralized decisions of enterprises and to the market mechanism. Social control was limited, and direct intervention on the part of central state organs was exceptional.

The obvious centralism expressed in the decisions on investment created resistance toward the development plans. During four years of the five-year plan for 1957–61, there was a great gap between the planned structure and the realized structure. The development plan for 1961–65 was abandoned after one year. Annual plans, which were passed regularly during that period, did not have a long enough time dimension to be of great service in determining a consistent policy of economic development. The acceptance of the development plan for 1966–70 took a relatively long time; and during the preparations (it was started in 1962 as a development plan for 1964–70), the entire methodology of planning was changed. On the basis of this experience, the outlines for a new law on the planning system were prepared. This law would be consistent with the new institutional context of the economy.

The new methodology for the preparation of social plans starts with the plans of the enterprise as the base. Thus the principle of building from the bottom up has been accepted in the planning system. This means that plans have a new character: they are no longer centralistic and directive. It also means that, in content, the plans coordinate decisions reached at lower levels and thus leave complete decision-making autonomy in the decentralized units. In terms of the time dimension, the plans are only middle-term plans. This is consistent with their content, that is, with decisions through which economic development is coordinated. An active role of the state plan is limited to those sectors in which the market mechanism cannot assure balanced development, either because of their special significance (infrastructure, education) or because of their low level of economic development (underdeveloped regions and underdeveloped industrial sectors).

Thus the decisions of the social plan first of all have the character of coordination and give the general orientation to future economic activity. As for "unstable" sectors, the plans have a strategic rather than a directive character—strategic in the sense that the purpose of decisions on these sectors is to induce activity and development in other sectors. This should contribute to the realization of long-term policy goals of economic development and socialist transformation. In this way the long crisis in the planning system has been resolved. For several years, the methodology for preparing and realizing the goals of development plans was inconsistent with the institutional context of the new economic system: the development plans had been practically a more elastic and more aggregated version of centralized plans.

With the introduction of polycentrism in economic decision-making and the reduction of the content of social plans to coordination and general guidance, the increasing importance of value indicators in planning (monetary, credit, and fiscal policy) has become a basic characteristic of the new type of macroeconomic planning. Value indicators are in principle consistent with an economic system in which economic flows are realized through the market. Thus, in practice, the problem of integrating macroeconomic planning with the market mechanism has been solved in the context of a socialistically organized economy. However, the presentation of a new planning methodology is not the last word. Only with time can the efficiency of the new system be confirmed.

29 JAN S. PRYBYLA

THE DEVELOPMENT OF ECONOMIC THOUGHT
AND POLICY IN COMMUNIST CHINA

In the almost two decades of their tenure of power, China's communists had used no less than five approaches to the problem of economic development, three of them more or less home made. By comparison, the Soviets adhered to a single strategy of development (the Stalinist, administrative command model with steel as the leading sector) from 1928 to about 1955. In their fifty years' history, Russia's communists made use of four distinguishable strategies of development (War Communism, the New Economic Policy, Stalinist command, post-1955 liberalization along Libermanistic lines).

The frequent shifts in strategy by the Chinese are explainable only in part by changes in "objective" economic conditions. Mostly they were responses to domestic and foreign politics: to internal disagreement over the nature of socialist construction and to the monumental quarrel with the Soviet Union.

Briefly, the five strategies employed by China's communists since 1949 were as follows:

1. The strategy of reconstruction and consolidation of political power. This lasted from October 1949 through 1952. From the very outset the approach was clearly transient. Its aims were limited to restoring some measure of orderliness to an economy disrupted by decades of foreign and civil war, ravaged and in the grips of galloping inflation. Rebuilding meant the mobilization of all classes (except "traitors" and "monopoly-comprador" capitalists) for a national purpose. Politically, it meant the application of Mao Tse-tung's concept of "new democracy" which envisaged the collaboration, under communist leadership and supervision, of different political and social groupings in the nation. Economically, it meant a three sector (state, cooperative, private) approach, with the state sector in command of the strategic heights of the economy (heavy industry, banking, wholesale and foreign trade, transport, communications, and so on). In the sensitive area of rural policy, the strategy of reconstruction and consolidation of power involved the distribution of land to the peasants, the setting of limits to private ownership of land and other assets, and the gradual

From *Dalhousie Review*, Autumn 1964, pp. 265–271. Reprinted by permission of the *Dalhousie Review*.

establishment of mutual aid teams as well as other elementary forms of agricultural cooperation. During this period, China roughly doubled its territory by establishing, for the first time in many years, effective central control over such areas as Sinkiang, Inner Mongolia, Manchuria, and Tibet. By harnessing the energies of the whole nation in a vast upsurge of nationalism and socio-economic reform, the task of economic reconstruction and consolidation of political power was successfully carried out, even if it involved the sacrifice of much individual self-assertion and the destruction of many traditional institutions. Toward the end of this period (early 1952) the communists began to exert pressure on the private sector in industry, handicrafts, trade, and agriculture. The "three-anti" and "five-anti" campaigns of 1952 resulted in the quasi-total elimination of the private sector in the first three areas, and an accelerated extension of collective effort in agriculture. The assault on the private sector and on the already emasculated political formations outside the Communist Party, was spurred by the resurgence of private initiative during the Korean War, but it was by no means accidental. The reconstruction strategy was, from the very beginning, meant to prepare the ground for the long range construction of socialism. Although it contained specifically Chinese elements and was theorized in the Maoist concept of "new democracy," it was in many respects modeled on and drew inspiration from the experience of Eastern European countries in the period 1945–1949. There too, a three sector economy, nationalism, and communist-sponsored political alliances, or "fronts," were used to prepare the ground for fundamental changes in the socio-economic and political structure of each country in a subsequent period.

2. The next stage (1953–1957) saw the beginnings of what is usually referred to in communist literature as "socialist construction," that is the radical transformation of the institutional framework and sectoral composition of the economy in a collectivist direction. During this time, which was also the period of the First Five Year Plan, the Chinese communists quickly proceeded to eliminate the remnants of private ownership in retail trade, handicrafts, small industry, and—in 1956—agriculture. Advanced collectivization of agriculture was carried out rapidly and with relative smoothness in the space of one year. This was also the time of Sino-Soviet economic cooperation which, however, was subjected to increasing strains toward the end of the period. The Chinese not only purchased some 65 per cent of their total imports from communist countries (especially the USSR), but received substantial if not overly generous aid from the Soviets. While modest relatively to Soviet capabilities and the USSR's efforts vis-a-vis other, including noncommunist, countries, Soviet economic aid to China was very important in helping the Chinese to build in a short time the infrastructure of heavy industry. Soviet aid to China during this time took the form of long term loans, bilateral trade, and technical assistance.

The latter, especially, was of crucial importance to China, poor as that country was in trained personnel. But the Chinese not only relied on the Soviet Union for machinery, complete plants, blueprints, and technical training and advice. They also imported the Soviet developmental model in its Stalinist version, operating only minor modifications here and there to adapt that model to China's specific conditions. The Soviet "model effect" on China implied high rates of capital formation, emphasis on heavy industry, relative neglect of agricultural investment, and the selective application of advanced technique to priority sectors or subsectors of industry. It was the strategy of unbalanced growth and of the break-through sector (heavy industry), of agricultural neglect, strict limitation of current consumption, and the adoption of Soviet techniques of planning and management. In spite of impressive successes, two factors conspired to make this approach inappropriate for China. In the first place, the strategy began to be seriously questioned by the Soviets shortly after the death of Stalin in 1953. By 1956, with de-Stalinization sweeping the Soviet Union, the Stalinist strategy came in for much criticism and its impact on other communist countries was lessened in consequence. Secondly, China's economic development in 1953 was both structurally different and well behind that of the Soviet Union in 1928, the date when the Stalinist method was first applied in the USSR. In particular China's rate of population growth was much faster than that of the Soviet Union at the time the industrialization process was initiated, and the condition of China's agriculture was much more retarded than that of the Soviet Union in 1928. Consequently the margin of safety between food supplies and mass starvation was narrower in China than it had ever been in the USSR. Protracted neglect of agriculture, which the Stalinist strategy implied, was risky business in an overwhelmingly rural and very underdeveloped country.

3. In 1958 China's impatience with the Soviet model burst into the open in a setting of strained Sino-Soviet political and ideological relations. For the first time the Chinese put into practice their own strategy of development aimed at the rapid transformation of China into an advanced industrial power. The name given to this method was the "Great Leap Forward," and its avowed object was to carry out the Second Five Year Plan (1958–1962) in two years. All caution was thrown to the winds, and politics took command of every sphere of economic endeavor. The essence of the Leap was the total mobilization of China's millions in a round-the-clock effort at economic construction, strict control over consumption, the tackling of many tasks at once ("walking on two legs"), and the introduction of a new organizational form in agriculture, the rural People's Commune. The Commune resulted from the amalgamation of several collective farms. It was vested with local government functions and was made responsible not only for the carrying out of agricultural tasks assigned to it by the central authorities, but also for many labor-intensive projects (e.g.,

road and dyke construction), and numerous so-called subsidiary activities such as iron smelting in home-made backyard furnaces, cloth weaving, handicrafts, tool making and repair, brick manufacture, flour milling, and so on. In spite of inflated official claims to success, the Leap ended in disaster. Part of the blame could be ascribed to three years of bad weather, but the principal reasons were the abandonment of all calculation in the running of the economy, exclusive reliance on political force, and the belief that political will and centrally-inspired enthusiasm could take the place of material incentives and economic calculation, in short a guerrilla warfare approach to economic development. The Leap set the Chinese economy back by several years. In 1960 the Chinese claimed that they had produced 18.45 million tons of steel. This was an inflated figure far removed from reality. The estimate for 1962 production (the Chinese have published no official figures after 1960) was 8 million tons, which probably represented an improvement over the actual state of affairs in 1960. The target for 1962 was 10–12 million tons. This tonnage was estimated to have been reached in 1965. Grain production in the last pre-Leap year was announced as 185 million tons. Estimated output in 1965 was put at 180–200 million tons (the target for 1965 was 250 million tons). More importantly, perhaps, it deepened the rift within the Communist Party between those who saw modernization as a drawn-out process requiring patience, professional expertise, careful planning, the balancing of alternatives, and cooperation with more advanced countries, and those who believed that the thought of Mao Tse-tung which had guided the communist guerrillas from obscurity to power could be applied with equal success to the more elusive task of economic construction. The rift has not been healed to this day. It was essentially a struggle between a radical and a more pragmatic wing of the Party. The Maoist radicals who were in charge of the Great Leap and whose fortunes ebbed with the collapse of the experiment were, paradoxically, the more conservative and dogmatic faction within the leadership. They were revolutionaries wedded to a prescription for success that had put the communists in power, but which had lost much of its relevance once power had been firmly grasped. They stressed the old virtues of asceticism, dogged faith, self-denial, and socialist construction through political insight and the "remolding of the soul." They were suspicious of "experts," wary of too much education, anti-intellectual in their conviction that the answer to all problems—political, economic, social, cultural—was to be found in the pages of Mao's Selected Works. They were unrepentant guerrillas who had never quite made the transition from the caves of Yenan to the more tedious and more complex job of directing the destinies of a nation.

4. The Great Leap Forward resulted in economic retrogression and its failure threatened the very existence of communist power in China. Economic statistics ceased to be published after 1960 except for vague

percentage claims to a continued surge forward. Western estimates suggested that while China's gross national product rose from 71.4 billion yuan in 1952 to a peak of 108 billion yuan in 1958, it then fell to a low of 92.2 billion yuan in 1961. The proponents of the "politics first" approach to economic development appeared by 1960 to have been discredited, even though they were far from beaten. The opposition ("some people," as the official Chinese press obliquely put it), silent since the Hundred Flowers Campaign of 1957, began, after 1960, to quietly implement its own notions of how the economy should be directed. The name given to this policy was "Consolidation Readjustment and Raising Standards." From 1961 until the end of 1965 China's strategy of development revealed a prudence and restraint, a measure of careful calculation and thoughtfulness absent till then. Up to 1963, the strategy aimed at repairing the damage which the economy had suffered in the two years of the Great Leap euphoria. The hallowed tenets of Marxist–Leninist–Stalinist doctrine were reversed, and from a strictly orthodox, that is Marxist–Stalinist, viewpoint the economy was run according to a highly revisionist, but as it turned out, effective pattern. Agriculture became the number one priority, followed by light industry, and finally by heavy industry. The People's Communes were dissolved in all but name, production and accounting authority was vested in the production teams (units smaller than the old collective farms and which roughly corresponded to the former village), emphasis was placed on maximizing the area of high and stable yields rather than on vast land reclamation schemes, simple tool improvement was put ahead of ambitious mechanization, and efforts were exerted to modernize agricultural practice especially as regards the use of chemical fertilizers, pesticides, and insecticides, rational plowing and sowing, harvesting and storage methods. Within the heavy industry sector, agricultural chemicals and implements were given top priority. Emphasis was put on material rewards to spur productivity, the peasants' private allotments (taken from them during the Leap) were restored, and free agricultural markets were once again allowed to operate side by side with planned state procurements. Private allotment production and free market sales proved so successful that by 1963 the Party began to worry about the capitalistic aspects. According to Hong Kong observers, about 80 per cent of the pigs and 95 per cent of the poultry were being raised on private plots as late as 1965. The plots represented about 5 per cent of cultivable area in each former commune. The new policy aimed at reversing the flow of young people from the rural areas into the towns and a campaign was launched to make educated youths return to the farms to help improve agricultural production and supply expert leadership. Particular care was given to scientific and technical education and to the learning of advanced techniques from foreigners no matter what their ideological hue. Foreign trade was diversified geographically, grain was imported from Canada, Australia, France, and Mexico to help feed the population and thus spur productivity, chemical plant and fertilizer were purchased in Western Europe and Japan. A realistic birth control drive was initiated with emphasis on the postponement of marriage. Until 1962 investment in industry, especially heavy industry, was trimmed, uneconomical plants hastily erected during the Great Leap were shut down, and special attention began to be paid to the quality of product in both agriculture and industry. These were the positive aspects of the Chinese New Economic Policy. The result, according to Western calculations, was that by 1965 China's gross national product climbed back to the 1958 level. On a per capita basis, of course, the situation was worse than in 1958 since population in the meantime had risen by over 100 million. The operation was performed quietly in a manner that permitted the proponents of the leaps-and-bounds theory of growth to save face. Yet, the new economic policy, had a hard time making its way. The pragmatism and restraint, the careful weighing of alternatives, were at all times accompanied and challenged by strident cries for political vigilance, by warnings against incipient saboteurs and enemies of socialism who were allegedly lurking everywhere, by a tightening of political control over the countryside, and vituperation against external foes, socialist and capitalist alike. Until 1965 this Jekyl–Hyde feature of the new economic policy puzzled the China watchers accustomed as they were to viewing communist China's leadership as a monolithic comradeship-in-arms that had survived all misfortunes since the early days of the struggle for power. Stress on technical and scientific education, for example, went hand in hand with the assurance that the best learning was to be found in heightened political consciousness, and that the pinnacle of political consciousness was synthesized in the village edition of Mao Tse-tung's thought. While the virtues of being expert were emphasized, the importance of being correctly red—that is versed in the thought of Mao—were loudly proclaimed at one and the same time, even though the two were often contradictory. The production and accounting duties of the production teams were subjected (after 1962) to scrutiny and harassment by judicial investigators dispatched from Peking. Material incentives went uncomfortably hand in hand with calls for moral incentives, self-denial, asceticism, self-sufficiency, and belief in the charismatic force of Mao's guerrilla philosophy. Scientific research, which demands long training and concentration, was constantly set against the allegedly miraculous inventive power of mass research by workers and peasants. Communist cadres in industry and the countryside became, after 1964, the objects of all sorts of investigations and rectification campaigns by poor peasant associations that had been inactive since the early days of the revolution. In short, the work of economic construction was being challenged and disrupted by loud calls for putting politics, Maoist politics that is, in command of science, technology, and economics. The pragmatism of the new course and feverish political elation seemed at the time to come from the same people. As it turned out later, they did not. The new economic policy was merely a stalemate, a compromise between the modernizers and the great leapers, between communist experts and expert communists. This entente was necessary since neither side was strong enough to impose its line fully on the other. After 1964 the policy's survival was in question. It had become complicated by an emerging and ruthless struggle for succession. In so far as one can make out, in spite of all the shouting the pragmatic and rational economic course was still in force early in 1967, but beginning to show severe signs of stress. In spite of widespread purges in 1965–66, the ideas underlying this course are probably entrenched in Party circles at the village, district, plant, and industry levels. As late as 1965 the moderate and relatively realistic approach to the problem of economic development was described by the Chinese as a model for all countries.

5. In mid-1965 Mao Tse-tung's and Lin Piao's Great Cultural Revolution, an enormous, nation-wide revival meeting, got in stride. Its origins were traceable to the failure of the Great Leap Forward in 1959–1960 and the consequent retreat of the ideologues who had thought that economic development was a function of pure political will. Temporarily defeated, those who held Mao's thought to be the panacea for all ills, never quite recognized their error. On the contrary they tended to ascribe the debacle of 1958–1960 to the machinations of revisionist elements within the Party who allegedly were at all times ready to "take the capitalist road." Late in 1964, Chou En-lai stated publicly that "from 1959 to 1962 . . . the class enemies at home launched renewed attacks on socialism and consequently once again a fierce class struggle ensued." The 1961–1966 reforms carried out by the pragmatic opposition were viewed with distrust and irritation by the Leapers. In temporary power exile, the Radicals maintained that class differentiation (between workers and peasants, town and country, physical and mental labor) persisted in China's socialist society, that peaceful evolution threatened to degenerate into Yugoslav and Soviet-type revisionism, and that the masses of young people who had had no first hand experience of the revolution and its trials, risked to grow soft, acquisitive, self-centered, and capitalist. Permanent revolution, even if it only meant long marches to Peking by student groups, the writing of posters, and vigilance, was the answer. As early as 1962 a "Socialist Education" campaign was launched the object of which was to prevent the essentially reformist economic policies from seeping through into the realms of culture and politics. The campaign emphasized the primacy of politics over economics and technology and was reminiscent of the shrill calls to Maoist faith characteristic of the Great Leap years. Ideological and economic revisionism was the main enemy, sympathy for the Soviet Union the major sin. Those who advo-

cated a measure of pragmatism were not only accused of being disloyal to the Party but were charged with dark schemings against the nation. They were described, at first anonymously, later by name, as "traitors, anti-Party, anti-socialist elements, devils with the spirits of snakes and the souls of oxen, bourgeois agents who plotted in coordination with international revisionism and imperialism to destroy socialism and bring back capitalism." By 1964 the Socialist Education campaign had veered against the Party's rural cadres who were accused of corruption and other malpractises, investigated by central judiciary organs, and often forced to publicly confess their alleged trespasses. Poor peasants' association dormant since before 1949 were reactivated for the purpose of on-the-spot supervision of the Party cadres. This was the first concrete indication of the Party's turning against itself and of the growing split within its ranks, a rift which became public in 1965. As it turned out, the majority of local Party officials remained loyal to the anti-Mao-Lin opposition identified with Liu Shao-chi and Teng Hsiao-ping respectively, the Chief of State and General Secretary of the Party. There was, no doubt, some substance to the anti-cadre charges and accusations, but the remedy was worse than the disease. It instilled fear and distrust at the production level and disrupted the process of readjustment and consolidation. The Central Committee Resolution on the Great Cultural Revolution is a document notable for its anti-intellectualism. All schools and universities were closed for a year while curricula were "remolded" so as to better reflect the teachings of Chairman Mao. However Section 12 of the Resolution reveals the apprehension of the Cultural Rebels lest too much revolutionary experience affect the country's scientific and technical standing, as it was surely bound to do. Scientists and technicians who had made valuable contributions, the Section instructs, were to be protected and helped to remold their thinking while working on their assigned tasks. The whole document is a manifesto of the Maoist "politics in command" approach to economic construction, an expression of a factional belief in the innate power of permanent revolutionary upheaval to achieve what patient work and study apparently and allegedly cannot. The Communique of the 11th Plenary Session of the 8th Central Committee further elaborated on this theme. It made explicit mention of the People's Liberation Army as the model of revolutionary fervor to be imitated by all, and repeated the charges often made in the past against Soviet revisionism.

The dichotomy between the communist pragmatists and the radicals was not as clear cut as may appear from this brief summary. There was much equivocation, dissimulation and side-switching. No one was ever quite sure who was friend and who was enemy, real or imagined. The only reality was political turmoil, the substance and essence of the Great Proletarian Cultural Revolution. Those described here as the anti-Mao-Lin opposition were at different times part of the Maoist faction and outside it. They were lauded by some Red Guard character posters, denounced by others. They were, one and all, members of the Party apparatus, deeply involved in the conduct of the economy. Their many simultaneous functions placed them in strategic positions of power from which they could be dislodged only with great difficulty. They remained circumspect in their utterances, appearing to condone the official line, but apparently doing their best to deflect it from the brink of madness. As one Maoist organ put it, these people were "waving red flags to oppose the red flag, and donning the cloak of Marxism–Leninism and Mao Tse-tung's thinking to oppose Marxism–Leninism and Mao Tse-tung's thinking." Po I-po typifies what was involved. Late in 1966 he was denounced in Peking Red Guard posters as one of those "in power, taking the capitalist road." Now, Po I-po was not only Vice-Premier but also Director of the State Council's Industry and Communications Staff Office, Chairman of the State Economic Commission, and Vice-Chairman of the State Planning Commission of which the purged Li Fu-chun was Chairman. The grip of such men on the levers of power was firm and pervasive. Chen Yi who at one time was also abused by wall posters, but who appeared aligned with the Mao–Lin troops, had warned in 1961 against the excessive dominance of politics over science and technology. The first duty of students, he said at the time, was to study and acquire professional skills without which China would be forever backward. Yet in 1966 he supported the closing down of all schools for the duration of the Cultural Revolution and praised Mao Tse-tung's thought as the source of all knowledge.

In an important sense, China's problem centers on the leadership's apparent unwillingness or inability to come to terms with the material rewards of modernization, a capacity to reconcile itself to its own moderate but tangible economic achievements. Communist China glorifies material progress but as certainly it fears the effects of that progress on the Spartan values it ranks high. It yearns after simplicity and the abnegation of the self, virtues that it feels are being threatened by future affluence which it is in the process of creating. It negates its own achievements by conjuring up a conflict between high income and simplicity, material comfort and courage, prosperity and revolutionary spirit. Tensions are manufactured, and packaged revolutionary upheavals served ready-made to the young so as to combat even the most timid suggestion of flagging fervor. Compromise on rather dated principles is exorcised by the old underground formula of "You live, I die; I live, you die." In the process deep rifts are created and the drive toward modernization is stymied. Economic development calls for a judicious combination of pioneering spirit and science. The search for this elusive equilibrium is still on in China.

30 DWIGHT H. PERKINS

MARKET CONTROL AND COMMAND
IN COMMUNIST CHINA: THE EARLY YEARS

Chinese economic policies and institutions have undergone a number of radical changes since the establishment of the Communist regime in 1949. China's economic history from 1949 through 1963 can, as a result, be broken up into five quite distinct periods of development. Certain major characteristics of each period had important influences either directly or indirectly on the Chinese economy and Communist economic policy, including price policy and efficient operation of the market mechanism.

The first two periods are ones in which the Communist regime consolidated its control over the economy. In the first period, which ended in 1952, this consolidation involved recovery from war devastation, stopping of inflation, and breaking the political and economic power of those groups viewed by the regime as most opposed to its long-term interests. The second period was the one in which socialization of the economy and establishment of the mechanisms of planning were largely completed. The third period, which started with the Eighth Party Congress in 1956, was marked by considerable experimentation with relaxation of control both in the economy and in politics. Finally, there are the fourth and fifth periods, the fourth starting in mid-1958 with the crash development program of the "great leap forward" and communization of the countryside, and the fifth, whose precise starting date is difficult to pinpoint owing to a lack of adequate information, a period of agricultural crisis ending with a partial recovery. Although many policies and institutions of each period have carried over into later years, and thus the line of demarcation between them cannot be too sharply drawn, the character of each is distinct enough to justify this division.

As the Red Army moved south through China, the areas it occupied were economically prostrate and prices were spiraling upward. In Shanghai, for example, wholesale prices during the latter half of 1949, when the city was under Communist control, rose on the average of 51 per cent per month.[1] According to Communist statistics, industrial production

[1] Shanghai Price Book, p. 355.

360   COMMAND-ORIENTED ECONOMIES

throughout the country had fallen to nearly half the prewar peak level. Agricultural production also suffered, both from war destruction and from floods, and was certainly well below prewar levels. Even where production was still substantial, a disorganized commercial and transportation network made it difficult to get goods to places where they could be used. The first task of cadres following closely behind or with the army was to put production back on its feet and restore order in the market.

Initially, therefore, the Chinese Communists encouraged free enterprise in all spheres of the economy. It was not long, however, before they began methodically to increase their control over the economy. Whether this process was as systematic at the time as it appears in retrospect is difficult to say. Certainly the unanticipated entry of China into the Korean War in November 1950 accelerated the pace of a number of policies, but it is not easy to tell by how much.

In retrospect, at least, the regime appears to have proceeded along two fronts in expanding its control over the economy. On the one hand, the Communists moved to establish a dominant position in major commodity markets and over prices and the financial system. On the other, they made a concerted attack on the economic, political, and social power of those groups in Chinese society whom they considered most inimical to the long-term interests of Chinese Communism. The history of these latter policies is relatively well known. It involved neutralization or elimination of politically defined classes of "rich peasants" and "landlords" in rural areas during the process of land reform (1949–1952), an attack on private business through the "five anti" movement, beginning in November 1951, and tightening of control over the bureaucracy by means of the "three anti" movement, beginning in August 1951.[2] There were many market- and price-related aspects to the pressure put on private businessmen, such as a profit squeeze. In effect, the state forced private businessmen to sell many products to it at low prices, to increase wages, and to pay large and apparently often arbitrary fines and heavy taxes.[3] These measures, however, are primarily of historical interest, since it is unlikely that the circumstances that recommended them to the Communists will ever be repeated. . . .

Of more interest are the means by which the Communists established

[2] For a more detailed discussion of the "three" and "five anti" movements and how they were designed to "reform" and increase control over the bureaucracy and private industry and commerce, refer, among other sources, to W. W. Rostow, *The Prospects for Communist China* (Cambridge, Mass., and New York, 1954); and T. J. Hughes and D. E. T. Luard, *The Economic Development of Communist China, 1949–1958* (London, 1959). Discussions of the process of land reform are in K. C. Chao, *Agrarian Policy of the Chinese Communist Party* (New Delhi, 1960); Wu Yuan-li, *An Economic Survey of Communist China* (New York, 1956); and C. K. Yang, *A Chinese Village in Early Communist Transition* (Cambridge, Mass., 1959).

[3] See, for example, Hsiao Chi-jung, *Revenue and Disbursement of Communist China* (Hong Kong, 1955), chaps. iv and v.

control over prices and financial affairs, since many policies pursued at that time have been continued with varying degrees of modification up to the present. The principal feature of this initial period's financial policy was the largely successful attempt to channel circulation of money into a relatively few tightly controlled paths. Gold, silver, and foreign exchange were barred from circulation almost immediately after arrival of the Red Army. Later on, handling of all foreign trade was placed in the hands of state-operated companies (March 1950) and trade was conducted in foreign currencies only, thus effectively cutting off the domestic economy from direct access to the international market and turning the *jen min pi,* as the Chinese Communist monetary unit is called, into an isolated currency. At the same time control over domestic circulation of the *jen min pi* was tightened. Authority to issue the *jen min pi* was turned over to the sole control of the People's Bank of China, and private banks were systematically consolidated and socialized between 1949 and 1951, or, what amounts to nearly the same thing from the standpoint of central government control, turned into enterprises under joint public-private control. Only cash itself was left outside of direct central government control. Even here, attempts were made to keep its amount to a minimum by creation of a Soviet-like system of cash control whereby all currency of any significant amount, first of the army and the administrative bureaucracy (March 1950) and later of state enterprises (December 1950), had to be deposited in the People's Bank. In addition, savings deposits by individuals were encouraged by attaching their value to a commodity unit that would not depreciate as prices rose.

Accompanying these attempts was an equally vigorous campaign to balance the government budget through tight control over expenditures and increases in revenue. The "three" and "five anti" campaigns played their part in this movement, the former probably helping to reduce government expenditure and the latter contributing temporarily badly needed funds to the state treasury. Most important, however, was the organization and systemization of the new forms of tax revenue. The principal directive, "Regarding Settlement of the Unification of the Nation's Financial and Economic Work," was passed on March 3, 1950, by the Government Affairs Council.[4] It laid down, among other things, the basic tax structure which, although often revised, still exists today. This system provided the Communist government with an ever-increasing amount of revenue which, with the aid of the extra revenue from the "five anti" campaign, made it possible to balance the budget by 1952 and keep it approximately balanced in every year since except 1956.[5]

[4] For the text of the directive, see *HHYP,* April 15, 1950, pp. 1393–1395.
[5] The Chinese Communists claim that the budget was balanced in 1951, but evidence . . . indicates that there was still a substantial deficit in that year. If one excludes certain items such as revenue from credits and insurance, which the Chinese Communists include in their revenue data, then the budget was also in deficit in 1953, 1954, and 1955.

Even in this period, however, the Communist regime did not rely only on monetary and fiscal controls to stabilize prices. Their most important efforts were directed toward the recovery of production. They also gradually moved toward a position of dominance over the market for certain key commodities and eventually over the greater part of the entire wholesale market. During this period they established the principle of government-determined prices even though they did not immediately attempt to stabilize these prices by government fiat. The culmination of this effort, however, came after 1952. Through 1952, the principal aim of Chinese Communist financial policy had been to gain fundamental control over the nation's finances so as to stabilize prices and to form a base from which to establish more complete control over all areas of the economy. Having thus created financial order, and with the Korean War rapidly approaching a permanent truce, the regime was able to launch a program of planned industrial development in 1953, although planning was still rudimentary and relied heavily on financial controls for its effectiveness.[6] The formal fiscal and monetary structure, however, had reached very nearly its present form by the end of 1952. Subsequent formal changes in the system left the basic structure intact and were designed merely to adapt the structure to changing demands upon it. There were also many informal changes of considerable importance, but these commonly did not involve the formal structure itself so much as the way in which that structure was used.

By the Eighth Party Congress in September 1956, the picture of Communist central-government economic control had changed radically from that at the end of 1952. By 1956 private enterprise in China had ceased to exist except for a few small traders and 3.7 per cent of the farm families.[7] A certain amount of socialization, to be sure, had been occurring for some time. The take-over of the banking system has already been mentioned. Most of the transportation network and nearly half of industry were state-run right from the beginning of the regime. But socialization of industry was not completed until the end of 1955. Similarly agriculture, handicrafts, and commerce were not fully socialized or run by cooperatives until 1956. Putting agriculture and handicrafts, in particular, under cooperative control was pushed through quite rapidly at the end of this period. This transformation of the form of ownership had a profound effect on the function and mode of operation of the Chinese financial system. In particular, basic criteria of success of those making most decisions on what to produce and to whom the produce was to be distributed were fundamentally changed. To some extent this transformation in criteria of success actually took place before the drive

[6] The real first five-year plan was not ready until July 1955, when it was presented to the National People's Congress.
[7] SSB, *Ten Great Years* (Peking, 1960), p. 35.

for socialization. The government had set down strict rules on how profit of private enterprises was to be distributed and had largely taken control over allocation of resources out of the hands of entrepreneurs through monopolization of raw materials and markets. As a result, private firms had to buy from and sell to the state.[8] In agriculture, changes in criteria of success came about more because of the nature of cooperative leadership than from changes in the form of ownership itself. In this sense, the institution of agricultural cooperatives in China was more a transfer of land to state control than it was a matter of setting up cooperatives for their own sake.

In addition to changing criteria of success of China's economic decision makers, socialization marked a temporary high tide in Communist control over the economy. State ownership not only put members of the state or party bureaucracy in charge of almost all economic decision-making units; it also substantially reduced the degree of interdependence between various units, thus giving central policy makers greater freedom of action. The entire rural economy was cut off from direct contact with the urban industrial economy and to some extent from other individual units within the rural sector. This was accomplished by directives requiring most produce to be sold to state or cooperative stores and ensuring that all industrial products would be distributed by these same stores. Until the reopening of the free market in 1956, peasants could not take their produce to the cities, and in most cases were not even allowed to trade with peasants from other cooperatives. Also, the state, by means of strictly enforced agricultural taxes and purchase quotas for major crops, took away the freedom of the cooperatives to decide whether to keep or sell a large part of their production. The state, in addition, had nearly complete control of prices, and turnover and profits taxes meant that retail prices could be changed without influencing agricultural purchase prices. The purchasing power of rural money and the amount of industrial goods to be supplied to agriculture, as a result, could be determined relatively independently of the state's need of farm produce for the cities and for export. The word "relatively" is important here, since the question of the effect of rural incentives on production placed a limit on the state's arbitrariness.

The rural sector, however, was not alone in being isolated. State-controlled commerce and turnover and profits taxes also kept urban and rural consumer preferences from having much influence on the industrial product mix. These same taxes, plus tight bank control over other enter-

[8] Commodities in this category (excluding handicrafts) made up 62 per cent of the total production of private industry in 1953, 79 per cent in 1954, and 82 per cent in 1955; see Yang Chien-pai, *Chieh-fang i-lai wo-kuo kuo-min ching-chi-chung chi-chung chu-yau pi-li kuan-hsi-te pien-hua*. (Changes in several important ratios in our national economy since the liberation; Shanghai, 1957), p. 14.

prise funds, effectively removed investment decisions from individual enterprises and transferred them to central planning authorities. State distribution of a large number of industrial raw materials and of a few consumers' goods allowed the state to operate somewhat independently of market conditions for these materials. It is this isolation of various sectors which, as stated in the previous chapter, makes it possible to deal with these sectors individually. Lack of interdependence cannot be pushed too far, however. Although influences may not always have been direct, consumer preferences still had some effect on the product mix, many of the devices used to separate sectors at times broke down, and factories were not able to operate without food for their workers or agricultural raw materials for their machines, just to name a few examples. Thus, lack of interdependence was only relative even in the middle of 1956, when state control of the economy was most complete.

The history of the first seven years of the Chinese Communist economy was, therefore, a history of gradually tightening central-government control over economic decisions, making it possible for the state to operate somewhat independently of the desires of its individual members and even to some extent of the interdependence that one finds among various sectors of most economies. It was also a period in which the example of the Soviet Union was most clearly in evidence. Many basic economic forms chosen in this period were patterned after their Soviet counterparts, although the timing of their adoption was often quite different. It would not be too great an oversimplification to say that the Soviet Union supplied many of the organizational goals, while China supplied the technique for bringing the various organizations into existence. Even at this early date, however, much of the organization aimed at was being modified to fit conditions in China. This was particularly true in agriculture, where the main policy the Chinese took from the Russians was only the basic decision to collectivize. In industry, lack of experience and of sufficient numbers of skilled personnel dictated a heavier reliance on Soviet methods and Soviet technicians to carry them out than was the case in agriculture.

The Eighth Party Congress of September 1956 marked the beginning of nearly two years of economic liberalization on a limited scale. For a brief period this economic relaxation was accompanied by a political liberalization, the famous "hundred flowers" period, when freedom of speech was briefly encouraged, and which ended so abruptly in July 1957. Some proposals for liberalization brought forward at the congress were put into effect almost immediately, while others were not completed until early 1958, when the economy was already beginning to shift into the "great leap forward." It now seems clear that both the economic and political loosening of central control were meant to have limits. It is probable that one reason for the "hundred flowers" campaign was to use limited public criticism to prevent abuses and to stimulate the ingenuity of lower-level cadres. It was hoped that this would keep them from relying on the powers of their position to force compliance where other methods were more desirable. Objectives of economic liberalization were similarly limited; there was never any intention to return to a market economy. When the reopened free market began to spread beyond intended bounds, a directive was issued clearly stating what was and was not to enter this market. Similarly, directives giving greater power to local government organs and to individual enterprises, most of which were not issued until 1958, were accompanied by an increase in party control within these same units. Thus it appears that the objective of these measures, at least in the economic sphere, was to stimulate and give scope to individual initiative of lower-level cadres while ensuring that this initiative would be directed toward the interests of the state and the party.

Liberalization and decentralization involved a substantial increase in the importance of the role of prices and the market in the Chinese economy. Opening of the free market meant that supply and demand operating through the price mechanism again influenced production of a significant number of commodities. Transfer of authority to lower levels was accompanied by an increase in the relative importance of profits to state industrial and commercial enterprises. Centralized distribution of important commodities was relaxed, and commercial organizations and factories were given greater freedom to select commodities they needed rather than being forced to take whatever was allocated to them. These and many other changes all tended to give market and price controls a more vital role in the economy.

Many economic reforms promulgated during these two years are still in force. In many areas of industrial policy there was no dramatic turnabout comparable to that which took place in the political sphere at the end of the "hundred flowers" period. This was certainly not true in agriculture, however. At the end of 1957 the regime moved to decrease the size of cooperatives and to expand the size of private plots. By the end of September 1958, however, the cooperatives had become organizations over twenty times as large (communes), and private plots and the free market had been abolished.

These organizational changes in agriculture had a profound effect on the economy, but perhaps even more important was the complete change in attitude of the regime toward economic organizations and principles in general. Restraints on lower-level units in the form of planning targets or limited funds were for all practical purposes removed. Heads of factories and communes were given free rein and were told that spectacular achievements were expected. The result was that planning goals were continuously revised upward, and allocation of resources became a matter of who could get hold of the most, regardless of real need. When a firm found itself short of the necessary financing to carry out an enlarged scheme, it merely had to channel funds meant for working capital or other purposes into investment.

Once before, in late 1955 and early 1956, there had been the beginnings of a somewhat similar movement, but at that time strains had manifested themselves fairly quickly—principally in the form of rapidly deteriorating stores of commodities and strong inflationary pressures in those sectors where such pressures could still manifest themselves. Those who had advocated a planned approach to economic development had regained the upper hand, and there had followed a period of retrenchment during which commodity stores were rebuilt and inflationary pressures subsided. This was not the case in 1958 for several reasons. In the first place, there appears to be little reason to doubt that the best agricultural harvest under the Communist regime was that of 1958. In the industrial sector, many projects started during the previous five years were scheduled to be completed in 1958. Thus, even if economic development in that year had been carefully planned, there would still have been rational grounds for stepping up the pace.

Second, many areas where pressures had shown themselves in the past had ceased to exist. With the advent of communes, for example, the free market, the only market on which inflationary pressures could show themselves in the form of price increases, was gone. In addition, the State Statistical Bureau had become little more than an organization for cheering on the "great leap forward" with statistics of limited if any reliability. It is likely that there was a period of several months at least when the central authorities themselves had only the vaguest picture of what was really happening. Finally and most important, those in power had become deeply committed to the belief that the lessons of guerrilla warfare, where *esprit de corps*, a proper ideological outlook, and imaginative independent judgment of those at the scene of action so often proved more important than superior arms, could be applied to development of the Chinese economy. What matter, they felt, that there were imbalances and regulations were flaunted, if the economy kept on surging ahead.

The "great leap," therefore, was not a carefully organized decentralization of authority with certain powers retained in the hands of central planners and the remaining powers turned over to local levels to be used under carefully explained constraints. It was, rather, more like economic anarchy. Under the former situation prices and the market might have played a major role, but under the latter they ceased to have any function at all in areas where decision makers were Communist-trained cadres.

In 1959 and 1960, the pressure of events finally forced the Chinese Communists to abandon the "great leap" and jettison the most important aspects of the communes. Foremost among these events was a series of bad harvests beginning in 1959 and carrying through 1961. This drop in output, which had ramifications throughout the economy, was the result of a combination of bad weather and the effects of the communes. On top of this, the anarchy of the "great leap forward" caused major dislocations in industry and construction. Finally, the Sino-Soviet dispute, which had been building for several years, reached a head with withdrawal in 1960 of practically all Soviet technicians from China.

This combination of disasters led to a gradual reduction in size of the unit controlling agricultural output, reopening of free markets for certain commodities, and a reinstitution of central planning. These moves, however, did not constitute a complete return to the institutions and policies of 1956 or 1957. Many of the formal decentralization measures, some of which were not promulgated until 1958, remain in force. Most important, the cutback in the pace of capital construction in early 1961 was followed by a shift in investment funds to agriculture in recognition of the fundamental importance of a healthy agricultural sector to the whole economy. There also has been a shift in trade away from the Soviet bloc toward developed Western nations.

These measures led to a recovery in agriculture and other sectors of the economy in 1962 and a further recovery in 1963. This moderate success, however, has not bred satisfaction among party cadres with existing relatively conservative institutions. There still is much talk of reforming bourgeois thought as a prelude to another surge forward, but this may be motivated primarily by political considerations, and thus may not constitute a return to more radical institutions and policies in the economy.[9] . . .

[9] Throughout 1964, for example, major ideologically oriented campaigns were in full swing (campaigns to "learn from the People's Liberation Army," "for socialist education," and the like). Even by the end of 1964 however, these campaigns do not appear to have had much effect on the economy in any way comparable to the "great leap forward."

31   JAN S. PRYBYLA

COMMUNIST CHINA'S ECONOMIC SYSTEM 1961–1966

The economic disruption brought about by the ideologically-determined policies of the Great Leap Forward (1958–60), the abrupt withdrawal of Soviet experts (mid-1960), and the natural calamities of the "three bad years" (1959–61) led to a rethinking of communist China's approach to economic development and a revision of key economic policies. By the second half of 1960 it became clear to even the most dogmatically-minded Chinese leaders that ideological faith and centrally-inspired mass enthusiasm were not substitutes for economic calculation. The result was the introduction late in 1960 of a series of new economic policies collectively known as "Readjustment, Consolidation, Filling-Out, and Raising Standards." The methodological guidelines for the new course were gradualness, a modicum of intersectoral balance, an appreciation of the overwhelming rural realities of China's society, and a new understanding of quality as an important dimension of economic growth. However, hand in hand with the policy of prudence, moderation, realism, and restraint, went a renewed assault on the citizens' political consciousness under the name of "Socialist Education." Launched in 1962, the campaign was aimed at preventing the essentially revisionist economic policies from seeping through into the realms of culture and politics and turning into the much-feared Soviet-type revisionism after the disappearance of the present generation of Chinese leaders. Both in its intensity and the shrillness with which it was pursued, the socialist education campaign (culminating in what came to be known as the "Proletarian Cultural Revolution") revealed the anxiety with which China's aging leaders viewed the possible future course of events in the country, and the continued suspicion in which they held the rising generations of technocrats, engineers, and other experts.[1] The campaign is still on. It injects into the new economic course an element of tension and a suggestion of impermanence which may in the end threaten the real achievements made since the abandonment of the Great Leap.

From *Asian Survey* (October 1966), pp. 589–603. Reprinted by permission of *Asian Survey*.

[1] For a clear expression of this anxiety see Edgar Snow's interview with Mao Tse-tung, *The Sunday Times* (London), Feb. 14, 1965, p. 11; and "Mao Tse-tung: A Worried Man at 72?" *China Report* (New Delhi), June 1965, pp. 1–3.

AGRICULTURE AS THE FOUNDATION

In a reversal of the 1953–57 Soviet-type, capital-intensive, heavy industry-oriented planning, and the 1958–60 Great Leap industry-oriented but labor-intensive political drive, the new policy inaugurated in the latter part of 1960 stresses sectoral balance and pays special attention to the hitherto most neglected sector—agriculture. In December 1964 Chou En-lai summed up the general approach to sectoral priorities in the following terms: "The plan for national economic development should be arranged in the order of priority of agriculture, light industry, and heavy industry. The scale of industrial development should correspond to the volume of marketable grain and the industrial raw materials made available by agriculture."[2] After 1960, and until further notice, agriculture was to be the "foundation" and industry the "leading factor" of China's strategy of economic development. The aim was to prevent the recurrence of the natural disasters of the "three bad years" and maximize the area of high and stable yields. The following six points have emerged as the main elements of the new policy of "agriculture as foundation."

The DE FACTO *dissolution of the people's commune as a production and accounting unit:* Since 1962 the institutional structure of Chinese agriculture comprises three levels of ownership: the production team of 20–30 households, the production brigade consisting of several teams, and the rural people's commune (1,620 households, national average 1964). In some cases the production brigade has been eliminated altogether. In contrast to the Great Leap emphasis on "grand-scale collective ownership approaching people's ownership" (i.e., the commune), the new policy stresses the production team which has, in fact, become the basic production as well as income and expenditure distribution unit. In general, land, draft animals, farm tools, and other means of production are owned by the teams, although in a very few cases ownership still vests in the brigades or communes. Production team members are paid either on a piece-rate basis or on the basis of workpoints according to a set scale of workpoints for different types of labor. Production team households were, until

[2] Chou En-lai, "Report on the Work of the Government to the 1st Session, 3rd National People's Congress," Dec. 21–22, 1964, *Peking Review,* Jan. 1, 1965, p. 10. See Liao Lu-yen, "The Whole Party and the Whole People Go In for Agriculture in a Big Way," *Hung-chi,* No. 17, 1960 in *Peking Review,* Sept. 14, 1960, pp. 32–36. The theoretical justification and basic rules for the application of the policy are to be found in an article by Lin Hung, "Actively Develop Diversified Operations, Promote Overall Soaring of Agriculture," *Ching-chi Yen-chiu,* No. 10, Oct. 20, 1965 in *Selections from China Mainland Magazines,* U.S. Consulate General, Hong Kong (hereafter cited as *SCMM*), No. 503, Dec. 20, 1965, pp. 1–20.

mid-1966, allowed to cultivate small garden plots (abolished during the Great Leap), raise pigs, oxen, and poultry, grow tung trees and bamboo, and engage in other sideline occupations (e.g., sericulture, production of wooden farm implements, native paper, essential oils, etc.). The products of this activity could be sold on the free market, but this privilege had apparently been rescinded by June 1966. Because of the "class danger" inherent in both private sideline production and ownership at the team level, efforts are constantly being made to promote team sideline production and strengthen the revolutionary vigilance of rural cadres. After mid-1966, the private plots began to be quietly communized. The production brigade, where it exists, runs enterprises jointly owned by the production teams and organizes cooperation among the teams. The commune, considerably reduced in size since its 1958 heyday, organizes interbrigade cooperation, is in charge of major water and soil conservancy projects, runs repair shops, and constitutes the lowest unit of government in the countryside. The Big Leap Forward attempts to federate all communes within a county and to promote the development of commune industry using "traditional" production methods have been abandoned, and membership in communal mess halls is now voluntary. In short, the post-Leap institutional framework stresses feasibility, material incentives, and local conditions by vesting the smallest unit, the production team, with planning, accounting, and management authority. But the ideological framework of the commune has been left in place.

Emphasis on maximizing the area of high and stable yields in respect to staple crops: The slogan is "diversification of agriculture with grain as the leading link," and the idea behind the slogan is to concentrate on the development of existing high-yield farms rather than push ahead with ambitious land reclamation schemes. While there is plenty of reclaimable wasteland (about 1.1 million square kilometers), the decision has been taken to consolidate what is already under the plough and leave major land reclamation projects to a later date. Consolidation implies four sets of priorities: first, food grain production geared to the development of livestock (especially pigs); second, output of raw materials for industry, particularly cotton; third, production of export crops (oil seeds, rice); and fourth, sideline production on household or team plots involving mainly fruit, vegetables, oxen, poultry, and pigs.

Mechanization and tool improvement: Assuring high and stable yields on the existing farms means raising labor productivity and output per acre. Mechanization of farm operations is one means of achieving this. Since 1961 the approach to the problem has undergone a fundamental change. First, it is now understood that mechanization does not simply mean the serial production of heavy-duty tractors, a mistaken tradition which the Soviets passed on to the Chinese in the years from 1953 through 1957. In so far as tractor production is concerned, the stress now is on variety geared to local topographical conditions and the requirements of the particular job to be done. Second, and more important, the pressure on state funds has led, since 1961, to a policy of making the communes, brigades, and teams responsible for semi-mechanization, that is for the introduction of small but important changes in production methods in the light of local means and conditions. Semi-mechanization involves the replacement of human power with grindstones, flails, simple threshers, huskers, tillers, harrows, multi-share ploughs, sowers, and so on, all of which can be made and repaired on the spot. To help the farms in this task, some 25,000 farm tool workshops have been established in recent years under the Second Ministry of Light Industry. These workshops are in addition to the 1,500 machine tractor stations servicing the more mechanized farms.

Stress on the application of chemical fertilizers, natural manure, pesticides, and insecticides: The new course places agricultural chemicals next only to mechanization and semi-mechanization. Since 1961 the chemical industry has been among China's fastest growing industrial sectors; for one thing, the bulk of industrial imports has been in support of the chemical industry. China's preoccupation with agricultural chemicals is understandable in view of the following data.

Supplies of Fertilizer per Hectare, 1962[3]
(Kilograms per hectare)

Japan	228
Taiwan	110
China	5

According to latest reports, small and medium-sized chemical fertilizer plants are being built all over the country. More prosaically, the Great Leap drive to collect human and animal manure has not been abandoned. In fact, it has come to be one of the techniques of "cultural remolding."[4]

Pushing ahead with water and soil conservancy on a local basis: Probably one of the main practical reasons for retaining the formal structure of the rural people's communes after 1960 was the need to devolve the responsibility for water and soil conservancy projects onto regional authorities, and thus free the state from the burden of financing all but the most "above-norm" projects. One of the major objectives of the new course is to prevent the recurrence of the calamities of the "three bad years." Yet

[3] The Economist Intelligence Unit, *Quarterly Economic Review, China, Hong Kong, North Korea,* No. 44, Dec. 1963, p. 3.

[4] "When the factory [Pu-ling Machine Works] was constructed, it was decided to install latrines instead of water closets to enable the peasants to procure manure locally." Wang Pin, Tsai Tso-hua, Liu Hing-shu, "Concretely Handle the Relationship Between Capital, Industry, and Agriculture in Capital Construction," *Hsin Chien-she,* No. 4, April 20, 1965 in *SCMM,* No. 485, Aug. 16, 1965, p. 31. There is a political advantage to this: it goes by the name of "non-divorcement of the workers from the living standards of the masses." *Ibid.,* p. 34.

both in 1964 and 1965 China suffered from prolonged drought in the north and from floods and typhoons in the south. Drought in north China is also threatening the 1966 harvest in many provinces. In the 1953–56 period the stress was on construction by the state of large reservoirs, each with a capacity in excess of 100 million cubic meters. These were built by the army, penal, and locally conscripted labor with engineering, technical, and supervisory assistance from the Russians. During the Great Leap, accent was shifted to the construction of many small (below 1,000 cubic meters) and medium-sized (100,000 to 1 million cubic meters) reservoirs by the communes.

From 1961 to October 1965 there was some cutback in the building of state-financed large-scale projects, and the communes were directed to repair and rationalize the projects which they had hastily thrown together during the Great Leap. In October 1965 a nationwide water conservancy campaign was launched in the wake of a National Congress on Water Conservancy held in the summer of that year. The essence of the new campaign was to still further shift the responsibility for water and soil conservation from the state to the communes. The task of the commune authorities remains to this day to build secondary irrigation and drainage systems and bring the potential of existing projects into full use. Financing is done entirely by the communes from their own resources, the state apparently intervening only to build a relatively small number of large-scale projects and help finance projects in some outlying regions (e.g., Tibet). Soil conservation is important in the northeast where, since 1951, a grandiose tree-planting campaign has been under way.

Tightening-up of control over the countryside: The moral and physical exhaustion of the masses of peasants which characterized the last months of the Great Leap led to the collapse of such planning as still survived the political euphoria of 1958–59 and to a relaxation of discipline in the people's communes. Around 1964 the central planning and judiciary organs finally got around to checking-up on the financial deals and target reporting of the production teams and the investigation apparently disclosed numerous irregularities in which the rural cadres were implicated. The socialist education campaign inaugurated in 1962 as an antidote to the economic revisionism of the new course, suddenly veered toward the rural technical, administrative, and supervisory cadres who were accused of corruption and extravagance. The practical cause of the rural cadres rectification campaign launched in earnest in September 1964 and still sweeping the countryside, seems to have been the state's failure to supply the countryside with cheap goods with which to absorb the peasants' increased purchasing power derived from free market sales and rising state procurements. A subsidiary cause was the old problem of communication between the center and the provinces, the rural cadres siding with and abetting economic localism. A major point of conflict, mentioned by *Nan-*

fang Jih-pao on December 26, 1964, was the inaccurate allocation of work-points to the peasants by production team officials and falsification of team production accounts which underrated the teams' production performance and resulted in produce hoarding at the team level. This was perhaps inevitable in view of the new policy of devolving capital construction responsibility on the teams, brigades, and communes.

In pursuance of the policy of the "Four Withs," judicial cadres were sent down to the countryside and instructed to investigate abuses of socialist morality by 1. eating, 2. living, 3. working, and 4. discussing together with the poor and lower-middle peasants. The "Four Clearance" movement was intended simultaneously to 1. correct cadre corruption in respect of financial affairs, 2. work-points, 3. accounts, and 4. storage of produce. The "Three Fixes and One Substitution" involved the assignment of rural (as well as industrial and trade) cadres to 1. fixed labor bases, 2. at which they had to report at fixed hours, 3. work for a fixed length of time each day, and—as for the substitution—learn the jobs of regular workers so as to be ready to replace the regular workers whenever necessary. The whole "Fixes and Substitution" program was to be administered and supervised by officials of high rank directly answerable to the center. Peasant associations, dormant since the pre-1949 days, were reactivated for the express purpose of helping the central organs supervise and report on the local rural cadres. In the spring of 1964 a movement of "Comparing, Learning, Overtaking, and Helping" originally applied in industry (end 1963) was extended to the agricultural front. Politically, the objective was to break down local barriers to the flow of technical and innovational information, a problem besetting all command-type economies.

The rural socialist education campaign, while it may have succeeded in uncovering accounting and other malpractices here and there, is quite alien to the spirit of relative rationality which has pervaded the new agricultural policy since 1961. The whole campaign is likely to instill fear and generate distrust at the farm level with adverse effects on production, productivity, and the quality of product. Compared with the 25,000 semi-mechanization stations established in the countryside in the last few years, there are some 19,000 sales stations for Mao Tse-tung's works. These distill the belief that

there is actually no such thing as economic, military, cultural, or other work which is not subordinate to politics . . . Political work takes first place relative to economic work . . . Politics must take command of economics and not *vice-versa* . . . Politics takes first place relative to science and technology. Politics must take command of science and technology and not *vice-versa* . . . Only those who have grasped Mao Tse-tung's thinking and put politics first can become really expert in production, technology, and other spheres of work.[5]

[5] "Politics the Supreme Commander, the Very Soul of Our Work," *Hung-chi* editorial, No. 1, Jan. 1, 1966 in *SCMM*, No. 509, Jan. 31, 1966, pp. 1–4.

In 1965 alone, the Ministry of Culture ordered nine publishing centers in Peking to publish more than 12 million copies of Mao Tse-tung's works suitable for study by the peasants. The application of this village edition of Mao's thinking to the problems of agricultural production and management may prove to be the greatest single threat to the generally moderate and workable policy of "agriculture as the foundation" of socialist construction.

The overall results of the new course in agriculture have been satisfactory in the sense that by 1964 the physical damage wrought by the Great Leap had been, by and large, repaired. In four year (1961–64) total grain output was brought back to the 1957 level, and the same was probably true of cotton, potatoes, and coarse grains. On a *per capita* basis, the picture was, of course, worse than in 1957 because population had in the meantime increased by about 100 million. Hence the need to import food grains on a massive scale.

The vague announcement of the Third Five-Year Plan (1966–70) described the policy of "agriculture as the foundation and industry as the leading factor" as having been "a great success." The course was consequently scheduled to continue, at least through 1966, with grain and cotton production high on the list of priorities.

INDUSTRY AS THE LEADING FACTOR

"All departments and trades should orientate themselves to serve agriculture and the countryside. The department of heavy industry should, in the first place, provide increasing amounts of machinery, chemical fertilizer, insecticides, fuel, electric power, irrigation equipment, and building materials to agriculture and at the same time provide more and more raw and other materials to light industry. To meet these demands it is essential to speed up the development of heavy industry and first and foremost of the basic industries still further." This line enunciated in the latter part of 1960, repeated in 1964 by Chou En-lai, and again during the formal launching of the Third Five-Year Plan in January 1966, has been interpreted in four main ways.

First, in 1961 a moratorium was declared on "the front of capital construction," especially, it would seem, in the manufacturing branches of heavy industry. The drop in the investment rate in 1960–61 was estimated at 67 per cent compared with the previous year.[6] Apart from cutbacks in state-financed water conservancy projects, the steel industry appears to

[6] Yuan-li Wu, *The Economy of Communist China: An Introduction* (New York: Praeger, 1965), p. 103.

have been the sector most affected by the retrenchment. Two reasons are usually advanced for this action: supply bottlenecks created by insufficient development and reckless exploitation of China's raw materials base, and the deterioration of the country's steel-producing machinery, especially of large precision finishing equipment. The investment cutback was paralleled by the closing down of many uneconomical small and medium-sized plants constructed during the Leap, including almost all the backyard furnaces. In 1960, about 30 per cent of the steel made had to be rejected because of poor quality. Since that time quality and variety of output, in steel as elsewhere, have been stressed, but even at the present moment the Chinese are experiencing quality problems in special steels and have resorted to the importation of such products as sheets, plates, pipes, fittings, and tubes. However, the attention given to experimentation and diversification of output since 1961 is indicative of a new and keener understanding of the meaning of industrial growth, at least among some segments of the Chinese leadership.

Following a year of readjustment, the investment rate in industry began to climb once again. Until at least 1964, this rise appears to have benefited mainly light industry which supplies peasants with needed goods and is one of China's most important foreign exchange earners,[7] those branches of heavy industry working directly for agriculture (chemicals, agricultural machinery), and some extractive branches (e.g., coal, petroleum, iron, cement, sulphur and phosphate minerals). In 1965 the investment rate was said to have risen 20 per cent over the previous year. Although an increasing portion of the gain in investment is likely in the future to be directed to new construction, indications are that repair, rationalization, and modernization of existing facilities have thus far absorbed the lion's share of the investment increase. Investment in steel began to rise modestly in 1963 and the upward trend has continued ever since. However, even in 1964 the imbalance between steel capacity and raw materials supply, which was at the root of the 1961 retrenchment, was still worrying the industry.

By 1965 a gradual shift in investment from light to heavy industry, transportation, and communications could be detected, and given the renewed stress on defense, this trend is likely to continue through the current Five-Year Plan. "Detected" is used advisedly, since there is no sure way of determining investment by sectors after 1960. In 1958, state investment in industry accounted for 64.8 per cent of total investment, of which heavy industry took by far the greater share. Compared to this, investment in agriculture (self-financing by collectives apart) was at the most

[7] In 1965 agricultural products accounted for $800 million of Chinese exports ($500 million of which were earned by foodstuffs, mainly rice). Textiles earned $550 million, and miscellaneous manufactured goods $350 million. Light industry was thus China's most important foreign exchange earner, with heavy industry last.

9.9 per cent, and probably less.[8] It is possible that under the new course, direct and indirect (*via* chemicals and farm machinery) investment in agriculture has risen above the 1958 level, both in absolute and proportional terms, but the evidence remains circumstantial. It is, however, clear that the planned growth rates for industry since 1961 have been dictated by what was thought feasible (and, more importantly, what actually was feasible), and were probably achieved.

A second feature of the post-1960 industrial policy with regard to agriculture are the so-called "Three Don'ts" and "Four Musts." The "Three Don'ts" refer to industrial construction in the countryside and reflect the need to conserve arable land and scarce peasant housing. Good fields should not be used for industrial purpose, nor should private homes be demolished or families evicted. The "Four Musts" instruct industrial planners to support such projects as increase the availability of water for agricultural use, extend agricultural electrification, the supply of manure, and pigwash. "The fight for every inch of land is in essence a question of attitude toward the guideline of taking agriculture as the foundation and industry as the leading factor."[9]

Thirdly, educated youths were sent to the countryside, and what appeared to be a massive exodus from the land during the First Five-Year Plan and the Great Leap was now contained. By 1961 industry was evidencing an inability to absorb the masses of unskilled workers flocking to the cities, while the countryside suffered from a lack of technicians and more generally from the unwillingness of educated youth to stay on, or return to the farm. Between 1961 and 1965 about 40 million young people were said to be returned to the countryside. The movement had certainly caused some acute morale problems among the young whose urban ambitions and promising careers were cut short. According to one source, the youth "find it difficult to grasp the complex revolutionary process, and are all too prone to relax into ease and comfortable living. It is, therefore, necessary to strengthen their revolutionary education, temper them in class struggles and in the struggle for production, and teach them how to rough it in simple living conditions. One of the best places to give them this needed education and tempering is in the countryside."[10] The movement

[8] State Statistical Bureau, *Ten Great Years: Statistics of the Economic and Cultural Achievements of the People's Republic of China* (Peking: Foreign Languages Press, 1960), p. 57.
[9] Wang Pin *et al., loc. cit.*, p. 31.
[10] Ching Yun, "Millions of Educated Youth Go to the Countryside," *Peking Review*, July 16, 1965 in *SCMM*, No. 488, 1965, pp. 20–21. According to *Jen-min Jih-pao* of March 20, 1966, evasion of the "educated youth to the countryside" order is rampant. "Some intellectual youths sent to villages to do farm work have been found to have entered rural farm-labor schools for selfish motives. They hoped that with education they could have opportunities of getting assigned to work in government organs or enterprises and become cadres. Their hopes were dashed on the first day they entered Kiangsu Labor University. They were told that they would have to return to the communes where they had come from after completing the prescribed terms of study."

of educated youth to the countryside has strong ideological overtones. The obective is to prevent the re-emergence of China's age-old problem of social alienation of the intellectuals from the laboring masses by making the educated young "engage in the 'dirty work' of shifting muck and manure."[11] The movement is part of the general policy of remolding through menial labor.

Finally, industry as the leading factor needs, in the absence of foreign scientific and technical assistance, a vigorous "Combining of the Three." The program, like the movement of youth to the countryside, is an effort to diffuse information and prevent the emergence of a meritocratic class structure. The "combining" is to be achieved in two ways. In the first place, the political leadership, the workers, and the engineers are to work closely together in a great revolutionary fusion of muscle and intellect. In conformity with Marxist-Leninist teaching, theory and practice are to be combined in labor. There are many variations on this theme: "Three-in-One Movement" for instance, specifies a joint educational effort by college teachers, scientific and research personnel, and workers. Alternatively, it is used in connection with joint work by intellectuals, workers, and members of the People's Liberation Army. "If the intellectuals do not become one with the masses of workers and peasants," Mao has said, "then they will accomplish nothing." Secondly, the "Combining of the Three" means the combined efforts of specialized enterprises. Medium-sized plants are urged to work in planned harmony so as to adequately supply more than one major factory.

Whatever the sociological merits of the movement, it does seem to hamper rather than promote production. In the final analysis, the political participant in the "Three" tends to be more equal than the other two, and not always the best informed. In practise, what it all boils down to is the shifting of scarce engineering personnel in response to ideological criteria and the remolding of obstreperous intellectuals through contact with the harsh realities of the soil, a process which often has little to do with the intellectuals' training or competence. Very often too, the intellectuals and Party professionals break more tools than they make.

SCIENTIFIC AND TECHNICAL EDUCATION

One of the most salient characteristics of the new course has been the preoccupation with scientific and technical education, a matter rendered more urgent by the withdrawal of Soviet experts. More than Maoist Marxism-Leninism, the urge to acquire "modern" knowledge in the

[11] Ching Yun, *loc. cit.*, p. 23.

technical and scientific fields is a constant and fundamental trait of present-day China. Managerial expertise and familiarity with the processes of a planned economy have also, since 1961, come in for more attention, respect, and prestige. As in the Soviet Union, a career in engineering and engineering-oriented management has become one means of climbing the income and social merit ladder. China at the present time suffers acutely from a shortage of well-trained scientific and technical personnel. Since 1960 the numbers of young Chinese trained in the Soviet Union and other socialist countries have been sharply reduced and the economy's need for specialists must henceforth be met at home. The new drive to train large numbers of men and women competent to deal with the increasingly complex processes of a modern society, has taken four main forms.

1. The continued expansion of universities, colleges, technicums, and other institutes of higher learning, in the majority of which students receive instruction which prepares them to handle specific and relatively narrow technical or scientific tasks.

2. The establishment of part-work part-study schools all over the country in which academic courses are combined with work in the fields or the factory. These schools were originally set up by the communes in 1958 and were mainly intended to provide agricultural-type education lasting about three years. At the present time they are usually under the direction of the production brigades or individual industrial enterprises. The syllabus includes political affairs, Chinese, mathematics, and farming techniques (or, alternatively, industrial training), the last taking up about 40 per cent of the syllabus time. In the rural part-time schools the teachers are mostly young people who had completed their secondary education and returned to the villages under the "back to the soil" program. They are paid on the basis of workpoints calculated according to time spent in field labor and on the basis of teaching time rates.

3. Establishment of research and development departments in farms and industrial enterprises and of specialized research institutes under the Academy of Agricultural Sciences, and the proliferation of experimental and demonstration farms. The Academy institutes concentrate on tasks defined in the "Eight-Point Charter for Agriculture" drawn up in 1958 and covering soil amelioration, the proper application of fertilizer, irrigation and water conservancy, popularization of good strains, rational close planting, plant protection, improvement of farm tools, and proper field management. Specialized research of this kind is supplemented by "mass research" and "spare-time research," both politically motivated, but perhaps helpful in the setting of China's present conditions. Mass research is defined as research "by the broad masses of workers and peasants" who are counted upon by the Party to keep a sharp lookout for any signs of wayward tendencies on the part of the specialists. Spare-time research is a commune and industrial enterprise responsibility and is allegedly

conducted by cadres, peasants, and workers in moments of organized reflection in-between work at the lathe and in the field, and political study.[12]

As in other areas, the drive for economic rationality is here accompanied and, more often than not, hampered by the drive for cultural transformation of the Marxist-Maoist Yenan type. What China needs is engineers and agronomists with the competence to tackle engineering and agricultural problems, both of which are eminently non-ideological. What present-day China is trying to get is engineers and agronomists who are correctly Red while being professionally competent. As the post-Stalin Soviets are finding out, there is an element of "antagonistic contradiction" between the two.

4. To selectively learn from the foreigner, be he socialist, fraternal, revisionist, capitalist of the intermediate zone, or imperialist, is the duty of every revolutionary. The Chinese people's latent ability is enormous. For centuries that ability had been frustrated by foreign ideological models (which, incidentally, the foreigners had discarded at home), and by homebred philosophical systems, be they Confucian or Maoist. The pressure is still on, and in the face of it, the Party cannot but be divided. To give in too much, is to breed deviation in the very substance of the caveman-of-Yenan philosophy currently very much in vogue; to resist too much is to fall into dogmatism, which in the long run leads nowhere. Chances are that over the long pull, the drive for extra-ideological modernization, which the Party itself has actively fostered, will prevail, and Maoism will become, what it essentially is, a stage in China's long march toward international equality and domestic prosperity in the twenty-first century.

SELF-RELIANCE

The Soviets are gone, and almost everyone who could possibly help has elected, for one reason or another, not to do so. The outside world's conceptions of the good life differ from those of Mao. The result, backed by centuries of isolation and illusion, is an inward turning upon one's own

[12] "Agricultural Scientific Research Becoming a Mass Movement in China," *New China News Agency* (*NCNA*), Canton news release, March 10, 1964, p. 1. Excluding faculty members of agricultural colleges, China in 1964 was said to have had more than 14,000 agricultural research personnel, *Peking Review*, July 24, 1964, p. 24. "Demonstration Farms Grow," *ibid.*, April 9, 1965, p. 30. Popular editions of scientific and technical manuals are being published and distributed in large numbers. Cf., Mikhail A. Klochko, *Soviet Scientist in Red China* (New York: Praeger, 1964).

resources: self-help and self-reliance, as laudable as they are inadequate. "We advocate regeneration through our own efforts," says Mao. "We hope there will be foreign aid, but we cannot count on it. We rely on our own efforts, on the creative power of the army and the people."[13]

The doctrine of self-reliance, reiterated a hundred times since 1961, is justified on the doctrinal ground that the objective laws governing the development of things are those in which the internal factors play the decisive dialectical role. Nationalistically, "the guideline of self reliance gives full expression to our confidence in the great strength, wisdom, and talents of the people and our confidence in their ability not only to liberate themselves, but also to build a good and happy life with their own hands."[14] Internationally, "it is a manifestation of great-power chauvinism to reduce the economy of another country to that of a dependency in the name of 'economic mutual assistance'. International cooperation must be built on the basis of self-reliance."[15]

The thesis of self-help, which goes deep into Chinese communist history, is being interpreted in two main ways. In the first place, it means belt-tightening and asceticism in the early revolutionary tradition. It means capital formation from as yet meager resources, forced savings, and low consumption for many years to come. "Strict economy is essential to the long-range national construction and necessary for the revolutionary process. It is also very important currently as we have to get prepared for war and famine."[16] Industry and frugality are praised as "proletarian virtues" and their practise is said to represent true "proletarian style."

Secondly, self-reliance does not imply autarchy and fear of foreign economic contacts. On the contrary, as will be seen later, it fits in quite well with diversification of markets and sources of supply, and with selective foreign aid to friendly or neutral countries. "The policy of self-reliance is, of course, not a policy that calls for isolation and rejection of foreign aid. . . . However, such economic cooperation must be founded upon the principle of complete equality, mutual benefit, and comradely mutual assistance. . . . As taught again and again by Comrade Mao Tse-tung, the correct relationship between self-reliance and foreign aid must place primary emphasis on self-reliance and secondary emphasis on foreign aid. . . . [The people] must not look outward, extend their hands, and depend upon other people."[17]

[13] Mao Tse-tung, "We Must Learn to Do Economic Work," *Selected Works*, Vol. III, 2nd ed., 1953 (Peking), p. 1015.
[14] Lu Hsun, "On China's Guideline for Self-Reliance in Socialist Construction," *Ching-chi Yen-chiu*, No. 7, July 20, 1965 in SCMM, No. 488, 1965, p. 2.
[15] Chou En-lai, *ibid.*, p. 11.
[16] "Practise Economy for the Revolution," *Chung-kuo Fu-nu* (Women of China), No. 1, Jan. 1, 1966 in *SCMM*, No. 511, Feb. 14, 1966, p. 13. Women, incidentally, are an important component of China's labor force, especially in light industry and agriculture. In this respect, China's experience is very much unlike India's.
[17] Lu Hsun, *loc. cit.*, p. 3.

FOREIGN TRADE: LEANING TO ALL SIDES

The new course regards foreign trade as a component part of developmental policy. The total volume of trade has risen steadily since 1961 and is presently in excess of $3 billion per year. The importance attached to foreign economic contacts is in contrast to the Soviet hesitation on this score at roughly a similar stage of the Soviet Union's economic development. The common denominator of the new policy is balanced diversity, which has three main implications.

The first was the termination of the 1949–60 policy of "leaning to one side," that is, toward the Soviet Union and other socialist countries. By 1965 China had repaid all debts to the U.S.S.R., some $1.7 billion in all. Soviet exports to China dropped from a high of $950 million in 1959 to $135 million in 1964, and imports from China fell from $1.09 billion to $314 million in the same period. The last loan extended by the Soviets to China was in 1961. Especially noteworthy has been the reduction in Soviet sales of complete plant and industrial equipment. Exports of nuclear materials were cut off in 1960. The Chinese now lean to all sides, but on a strictly cash and barter basis. Western Europe (especially Britain, France, and West Germany) and Japan have taken the place of the Soviet Union as China's major suppliers of industrial equipment, particularly of equipment for the chemical industry. In 1964 about 35 per cent of China's trade was with communist countries, and some 65 per cent with non-communist countries, almost an exact reversal of the 1957 situation. By 1965 China had trade relations with 125 countries and regions (including South Africa, to the great annoyance of most African countries). Forty of these had signed intergovernmental trade agreements with Peking. Since 1950 the Chinese Council for the Promotion of International Trade has held 25 economic exhibitions and participated in 67 international fairs in 40 countries. In the same period, 11 foreign countries held economic exhibitions in China.

Secondly, the pattern of exports and imports has been stabilized, at least through the present Five-Year Plan. Large-scale purchase of grain from abroad have become a familiar feature of the new course, amounting to about 5 million tons per year. The main suppliers are Canada, Australia, Mexico, Argentina, and France. Grain imports represent about 40 per cent of China's annual total imports in value terms, the remainder being accounted for by purchases of chemical fertilizers, jute, cotton, industrial plant and equipment (especially for the chemical industry), spare parts, means of transportation, and communications equipment. An overall balance between exports and imports is being maintained. Hard currency payments are made promptly and scrupulously (supplemented by occasional silver sales) out of earnings from Hong Kong (which currently supplies the Chinese with about half their foreign exchange surplus, or about $700 million), foreign exchange remittances by overseas Chinese, and occasional favorable balances in hard currency areas.

Thirdly, trade with and economic assistance to a number of economically underdeveloped countries in Asia and Africa are being pushed forward, in spite of diplomatic reverses. The pattern of aid which has emerged since 1961 comprises the tying of assistance to the delivery of Chinese goods and services, long-term interest-free loans, and the selection of those aid projects that tend to have the maximum growth impact on the economy of the recipient country. The recipients too, are carefully chosen, as is the political timing of loan and grant offers. Although small compared with the aid efforts of Western industrialized countries and the Soviet Union, China's foreign aid program has been gradually expanded in some of the world's most sensitive areas. In spite of a careful choice of recipients, there have been surprises and reverses (e.g., Ghana, Indonesia), and the total actually given has, since 1961, amounted to only about one-third of the amount promised.

Population Restraint

Prior to 1961 communist China's population policy went through both populationist and anti-populationist cycles, with the former thesis more than holding its own. There was, in 1956, a vigorous and indiscreet birth control campaign which within a few months was dropped as suddenly as it had begun. At least since 1963, another birth restraint campaign has been in force, this one more prudent and more moderate than the 1956 bluster. The common denominator of the new campaign is to approach people as individuals and to avoid the crudity of the 1956 struggle. The elements of this new policy are advocacy of late marriages, the popularization of contraceptive methods, legalized abortion (if advised and permitted by a recognized physician—this is done free of charge), and sterilization. Postponement of marriage, a truly Malthusian moral restraint phenomenon, is the key. Students on state scholarships, for instance, are not allowed to marry before graduation. The press daily extolls the wisdom and revolutionary virtue of not marrying before the age of thirty for men and twenty-five for women. In 1963 clothing rations were raised, but the rise was tied to population control. Those marrying after the age of thirty were to receive an extra ration, while the fourth child in a family was to be allotted no coupons at all. In his interview with Edgar Snow, Chou En-lai made specific reference to the need for learning population control techniques from Japan.[18]

Conclusions

On the whole, China's economic policies since the retreat from the Great Leap have been marked by prudence and restraint and have taken account of the underlying realities of the country's modest level of economic development. It would seem that the actual application of the new policies has been more rational and careful than the words used to describe the policies themselves. On the verbal front there is still much storming against internal and external foes, incipient traitors, revisionists, etc., and the "proletarian cultural revolution" calls on everyone to sharpen proletarian vigilance and revolutionary consciousness by applying all efforts to the study of the works of Mao Tse-tung. So far the new course amounts to a rationalization of past errors, a rectification which bears within itself no guarantee of permanence. It is quite possible that the Party itself has not yet made up its collective mind about the precise shape of future policies, and that there is considerable debate and dispute on this subject in the innermost sanctum of Party leadership. The current Five-Year Plan is certainly no long-term program in its present state. So far it appears to be a year-by-year proposition with the course followed since 1961 dominating the policies of 1966. There can be no doubt that, however unpalatable the new course may be for the more dogmatic among the Party's leaders, however unrevolutionary the gradualness and prudence, the most eloquent argument in favor of the new course is its economic success. The unknown variables of the international situation will certainly have an important say in the shaping of future domestic policies. The Chinese have been quick to learn from their mistakes. Whether they will in the years to come be equally steadfast, yet flexible, in their solutions, remains an open question.

[18] *The New York Times*, Feb. 3, 1964, p. 8.

32   D. J. WALLER

China: Red or Expert?

The current cultural revolution in China serves to remind us that op-position to the Chinese Communist Party (CCP), either to its leaders or the rule of the Party as a whole, is rarely far below the surface. This article will focus on some of the non-institutional and non-constitutional checks to the absolute authority of the Party which have exerted a powerful in-fluence on the course of events since the communist take-over of 1949, as well as analysing the nature of the dissent that is the motive power behind these forces of opposition.

Two groups will be discussed under the heading of checks: 1. the army, and 2. the bureaucracy *and* the intellectuals. It might seem surpris-ing to link the bureaucrats and the intellectuals together in one group, but it must be remembered that the Chinese definition of "intellectual" (liter-ally *chih-shih fen-tzu,* or "knowledgeable elements"), is much broader than that operative in the West, since it includes all those who have completed a Chinese higher middle school education. Many, if not the majority, of these intellectuals are to be found in the ranks of the bureaucracy. Indeed, Liu Shao-ch'i, in his May 1958 report to the Second Session of the Eighth Party Congress, coupled the administrative workers and the mental work-ers together, thereby implying that state administration and management were filled by intellectuals, so that the social stratum of bureaucrats and the social stratum of intellectuals had become increasingly similar.[1]

In the realm of dissent, one dichotomy that has run through Chinese society since 1949 is that between political reliability, on the one hand, and technical knowledge on the other—or, as it is usually known, the con-tradiction between "red" and "expert." The anti-system, anti-Party bias of the experts manifests itself through "the social and professional (motive) of classes and groups which claim that the government discriminates against them and impedes their activities and trades."[2] Two main groups in China through which this dissent is channelled are the army and the bureaucracy, and since it is precisely they who are the checks, it is this channelling of dissent which provides the link between the two concepts.

From *The Political Quarterly,* London, Vol. 38, No. 2 (April–June 1967), pp. 122–131. Reprinted by permission of *The Political Quarterly.*

[1] Franz Schurmann, *Ideology and Organisation in Communist China* (Berkeley: University of California Press, 1966), pp. 97–98.

[2] Ghita Ionescu, "Control and Contestation in some One-Party States", *Government and Opposition,* Vol. I, No. 2 (January 1966), p. 248.

RED VERSUS EXPERT: THE ARMY

The pre-1949 Chinese communist army was characterised by a fusion of political and military leadership.[3] The Chinese revolution has been described as a "militarised mass insurrection," using an "army . . . built around and trained by the small military cadre provided by the revolutionary party."[4] From the early 1930s to 1949 the Party was in effect the army. However, after victory and the establishment of the People's Republic, a natural bifurcation of the two occurred (though far closer links were maintained than in other communist states), and the Party saw the need for creating a new army, run by a body of professional military officers capable of integrating an intricate and technical military establishment with a society moving towards modernisation. Since the majority of the old veteran guerrilla leaders were incapable of this, military academies were set up soon after 1949 to train the new professional élite.

Thus emerged a professional officer corps whose views, interests and backgrounds were diametrically opposed to those of the guerrilla leaders. The young professionals were experts, and believed in the value of their technical knowledge and in the superiority of weapons over politics. The guerrilla veterans, however, were more red than expert, placed their faith in a politically mobilised army, prizing the quality of their men over weapons, and believed in the predominance of political ideology. This was a doctrine derived partly, of course, from the hard fact of the military backwardness of China, but no doubt the experiences of a generation of guerrilla warfare dominated their minds.

In practice, this conflict of red versus expert realised itself in three ways: first, as a conflict within the People's Liberation Army (PLA), since there were two sections of the army involved; secondly, as a conflict between the PLA and the Party, because the experts in the PLA opposed the military policies inaugurated at the top of the Party hierarchy by men who were mainly veteran partisan campaigners with a primarily hypothetical knowledge of modern war; and, finally, as a conflict within the

[3] I am indebted to several scholars who have analysed the People's Liberation Army at length: Ellis Joffe, "The Conflict between Old and New in the Chinese Army," *China Quarterly*, No. 18 (April–June 1964), pp. 118–140; also his book *Party and Army: Professionalism and Political Control in the Chinese Officer Corps, 1949–1964* (Cambridge, Mass.: Harvard University Press, 1965). Also Harold C. Hinton, "Political Aspects of Military Power and Policy in Communist China," in Harry Coles (Ed.), *Total War and Cold War* (Ohio State University Press, 1962), pp. 266–292.

[4] Chalmers Johnson, *Revolution and the Social System* (Stanford, California: Hoover Institution, 1964), p. 63.

Party itself since the majority of both reds and experts were Party members. Of these three manifestations, it was the PLA/Party conflict that was the most important.

The CCP controls the army through the Military Affairs Committee of the CCP Central Committee, the majority, if not all the members of which, are old "Long Marchers." The technical details are left to the Ministry of Defence, under which the general staff function. At the summit of Party control within the PLA itself is the General Political Department, whose directives go to the Party committees attached to all units. The unit's political commissar is usually the secretary of the Party committee or branch and he stands on an equal footing with the military commander. The Director of the unit's Political Department, whom the political commissar outranks, is primarily responsible for political reliability and discipline within the unit.[5] By means of this tightly organised network of controls, the Party implements Mao's maxim that "political power grows out of the barrel of a gun. Our principle is that the Party commands the gun, and the gun must never be allowed to command the Party."[6]

In the years after 1949, the influence of the expert increased in the Party and the PLA, although it was a slow process. The tasks of the army after victory included the carrying out of all kinds of construction work, and the army was indeed used extensively in construction projects, in the agrarian reform movement throughout China and, for example, in Sinkiang to carry out a large-scale irrigation programme (as well as ensuring Han supremacy over the local minorities).[7] Needless to say, the professionals were opposed to the use of their troops in such non-military activities, and by the mid-1950s it was declining.

The presence of many Soviet military experts in China after 1950, and the education of Chinese officers in Soviet military schools, had an influence, which although it cannot be measured accurately, must have been considerable and pervasive. One result was that the Chinese military machine was reorganised along Russian lines, and this also marked the peak of the influence of the expert in China when, in 1955, the old egalitarian army was changed by the introduction of the new "Regulations on the Service of Officers," which inaugurated ranks and insignia, specified a clear demarcation between officers and men and introduced selective conscription into the army.[8]

From the mid-fifties, the Party began to move away from professionalism in the army towards a policy of "politics in command." Party controls over the PLA were tightened, and there was a heightened indoctrination

[5] Hinton, op. cit., pp. 270–272.

[6] "Problems of War and Strategy," in Selected Works, II (Peking, Foreign Languages Press, 1965), p. 224.

[7] Ellis Joffe, "The Communist Party and the Army," Contemporary China, Vol. IV (1959–60), pp. 55–57.

[8] Joffe, China Quarterly, op. cit., p. 121.

of the officer corps. The writings of Mao and the leading role of the Party committees were stressed. With "politics in command," conflict between the red and the expert increased, because the political commissar could now interfere in anything and overrule the decisions of the military commander. The professional officers naturally viewed the commissars as muddle-headed and technically inept in military matters. The "Great Leap Forward" of 1958 greatly exacerbated this conflict, as "politics in command" was the keynote of the Great Leap, and the use of the PLA for economic tasks was stepped up.

The campaign against professionalism from 1955 on must also have been correlated with the emergence of the Sino-Soviet dispute, which in many respects had its origin in 1956 at the 20th Congress of the Communist Party of the Soviet Union. The CCP therefore acted to reduce the influence, and the number, of Soviet advisers in China. (An act which the Russians were to take to its logical conclusion in 1960 by withdrawing them all.) In 1958 was begun the campaign for self-reliance—implying no reliance on the U.S.S.R. At the same time, the "officers to ranks" movement started, with every officer having to spend one month as an ordinary soldier.

The army resistance to these policies culminated in 1959 in the purging of the Minister of Defence P'eng Teh-huai and his replacement by the politically reliable Lin Piao. P'eng was undoubtedly dissatisfied with CCP policy towards the army, and also in the economic field. He was accused of opposing Mao Tse-tung's principles on building the military, and of fostering the "purely military viewpoint"—or in other words, that of the expert. The Chief of Staff Huang K'o-ch'eng was also replaced, this time by the former Minister of Public Security Lo Jui-ch'ing.

From 1959, and the appointment of Lin Piao as Minister of Defence, the evidence is that simultaneously Party control over the army has increased, while combined with steadily increasing stress on "reddening" the PLA and "putting politics in command." The only time that the stress on politics was relaxed was during the years of crisis following the failure of the Great Leap Forward, when food riots and peasant uprisings in various parts of China caused the Party to fear for the loyalty of the PLA.

During these crisis years there were concessions to professionalism, marked by a renewed emphasis on expertise, and the curtailment of the use of the PLA for economic tasks.[9] During this time, however, Party control over the army continued to be strengthened, and once the crisis was passed, the slogan of "politics in command" came to the fore once more, where it has remained until the present time. One example of this was the

[9] *Ibid.* p. 137. During the 1959–62 period there was a considerable revival of pre-1949 plays, classical Chinese painting and calligraphy. The "socialist education campaign" of 1963 onwards was partially directed against this cultural reflowering. (*China News Analysis*, No. 609, April 29, 1966.)

order of June 1, 1965, that all uniforms and insignia were to be the same for all branches of the armed services, and that all external distinctions between officers and men were to be abolished. This re-established the situation of pre-1955 when it was changed under Russian influence. A further example was the January 25, 1966, speech by the Director of the PLA General Political Department Hsiao Hua, who spoke of some people saying that "military affairs and politics are equally important" and that "military affairs and politics should play their roles in turn." The grievances of the military professionals can be perceived in these comments. Hsiao Hua subsequently ordered the promotion of the politically reliable from low ranks, the promotion to be carried out by the political commissars, which must have raised even further the standing of the commissars *vis-à-vis* the military commanders.[10]

RED VERSUS EXPERT: THE BUREAUCRACY

Having discussed the red versus expert conflict in the army at some length, it is now appropriate to deal with the same conflict as exemplified in the case of the second group of the bureaucracy and the intellectuals, and finally to draw a parallel with the current cultural revolution.

The bureaucratic hierarchy can be viewed as a three-tier structure. At the top is the Central Committee of the Party, deciding broad economic policy. In the case of an individual factory, the top level is the Party committee in charge of the enterprise. In the middle are the bureaucrats, the economic managers and administrators; and at the bottom, the workers. The middle level of management, the bureaucracy, can be functionally divided into two—staff and line. In a factory, the line men are the supervisors of each shop or department, and the staff men are the technicians who work out concrete operational details. The staff men are usually highly educated—they are practical men and relatively immune to ideology. On the other hand, the line men tend to be less-well-educated Party cadres, and as the Party pursues a policy of promoting unskilled workers to line supervisory positions, these factors have resulted in staff-line conflict.[11]

In the early years of the communist régime, the Party needed professionals for staff positions in industry and administration, and also political cadres for line leadership. The staff men and the line men, because they were recruited from different social strata, became two opposed groups, with different backgrounds and interests. The professionals were recruited from the educated intellectuals, the supervisory cadres from the labouring

[10] *China News Analysis,* No. 598 (February 4, 1966).
[11] This is a summary of a lengthy discussion by Schurmann, *op. cit.,* pp. 68–73.

masses. The former derived their prestige from education, the latter from political power.[12]

Until 1955, the Party tended to favour the professionals, while at the same time trying to build up a body of personnel who were both technically qualified *and* politically sound—red *and* expert. This is after all what Stalin did in his industrialisation of the U.S.S.R. in the 1930s. However, by the mid-fifties, it seemed that a similar attempt in China had failed, because the educational system, extremely backward compared with that of the U.S.S.R. of the 1930s, was not producing the number of required intellectuals; nor were the existing intellectuals less motivated by self interest and more by loyalty to Party and state; and nor were the working masses producing sufficient educated personnel from among themselves.[13] Even those who came from worker or peasant class backgrounds tended to adopt a bourgeois point of view.

After 1955, the Party shifted emphasis from the professionals to the use of political cadres, a process which was hastened in 1957 by the failure of the "hundred flowers" campaign to encourage the intellectuals to make a more positive contribution to economic and academic life. The CCP thus acted to prevent the crystallisation of an alternative centre of power around the professionals who had technical know-how and could, therefore, by virtue of their expertise, dictate to the Party. The fact that the Party represented, both in theory and practice, the workers and peasants, whereas the experts were drawn largely from the ranks of the bourgeoisie, was a vital factor in the decision.

This resolution to rely more and more on unqualified political cadres in administration after 1955 can also be seen as a resultant of the discord between the staff and line personnel on the one hand, and the Party bosses in Peking on the other. The former were concerned primarily with day-to-day economic tasks, and the job of meeting their production goals, whereas the latter set broad economic policy. The commands from Party centre, however, often called for rapid or impossible expansion, resulting in opposition from the bureaucracy, which by means of its technical knowledge could thwart the will of Peking.

This discord reached a peak during the Great Leap Forward when the Party called for higher and higher production targets. So in order to circumvent the opposition of the bureaucrats, the Party sacked the middle level of administration in large numbers—particularly the staff officials whom they regarded as conservative hindrances—and ordered the line men to leave their supervisory positions and work in close collaboration with the masses.

[12] *Ibid.* p. 171.
[13] The latter phenomenon is well known elsewhere. In England a child from an educated middle-class family will probably, because of parental influences, receive a superior education to a similar child from a working-class background, even if the latter is given equal opportunity.

As Franz Schurmann has described it: "organisationally, the Great Leap Forward can be seen as an attempt to eliminate the middle and join top and bottom directly; leaders and masses were to be in intimate relationship, bypassing the professionals who earlier stood between them."[14] It will be seen that the cultural revolution today represents a similar attempt within the Communist Party itself.

As has been seen in the army, so in the economic sphere, following the failure of the Great Leap, liberalisation set in, as the Party appealed to the professionals to rescue the country from economic crisis. Again, however, this was only a tactical retreat by the Party leadership. Once the crisis was passed, professionals continued to be attacked and dismissed. In 1964, Political Departments on the lines of those functioning in the PLA were set up in banks and enterprises. These were staffed largely by men sent from the army, and gave an indication of the increasing reliance of the CCP on the armed forces, as well as marking a return to earlier days when the PLA played an intimate role in the economic and political life of society.

CONCLUSION: THE CULTURAL REVOLUTION

The discussion so far can be summarised by saying that in the case of both groups of the army and the bureaucracy-intelligentsia, the stress for the last decade has been in favour of the politically red, and that this policy has been consistently adhered to by the Party except for a tactical retreat in the early 1960s. Looked at from this standpoint, the current cultural revolution can be viewed as a continuation of the policy of eliminating the experts from positions of power and influence—though this time, not within the army or the bureaucracy, but within the Party itself.

This analogy must not be taken too far. The Party membership does not easily lend itself to a division between educated administrators and illiterate revolutionaries. Nor can the cultural revolution be seen solely in these terms—its timing was decided by Mao because of his advancing age, and because he believed he had finally fashioned the PLA as his chosen revolutionary instrument. Once the cultural revolution was unleashed, differences over policy at the highest levels of the Party inevitably became inextricably entwined with a struggle for power.

However, bearing these cautionary notes in mind, certain similarities are apparent between the cultural revolution, the elimination of the professionals in the PLA, and the experience of the bureaucracy during the Great Leap.

Two years ago, when Edgar Snow asked Mao what the younger gen-

[14] *Ibid.* p. 71.

eration, bred under easier conditions, would do with China, Mao replied that they would either ensure the continued development of the revolution towards communism, or that they could perform poorly, make peace with imperialism and negate the revolution.[15] Mao apparently feels that without his active intervention the revolution will indeed be negated, and that China will fall into a Soviet-style revisionist mould. This belief is not without foundation. The vast majority of CCP members joined after 1949 and never knew what it was like to fight either the Japanese or the Kuomintang, while a low attrition rate of under 5 per cent. per annum has made the Party a middle-aged organisation. In administration the Party today has become routinised so that it is no longer an active revolutionary instrument, and life is a far cry from the idyllic guerrilla days on Yenan. The army, on the other hand, is young, and has been forged by Lin Piao into a politically mobilised hard core within Chinese society. All sections of this society are exhorted endlessly to "learn from the PLA"; it was the PLA newspaper that initiated the cultural revolution, and the paramilitary Red Guards who were later to be its main force. The task of the cultural revolution is to weed out those at all levels who are opposed to the policy of permanent revolution, and to forge a new Party capable of leading China to the Maoist vision.

This has meant the dismissal or active criticism of many at the highest levels of the Party. One significant feature of these dismissals is that many of those affected, including P'eng Chen (Politburo member and Mayor of Peking), Lo Jui-ch'ing (Chief of Staff), Lu Ting-yi (head of the Central Committee Propaganda Department) and Yang Shang-k'un were members of the Central Committee Secretariat. This naturally weakened the position of the Secretary-General Teng Hsiao-p'ing, who in time also came under attack. The Secretariat has control over the Party regional organisations throughout China and could well act as a focus of opposition for a faction within the top Party leadership, particularly when one remembers that Khrushchev in 1957 survived an attempt to unseat him by mobilising regional support against the Party centre.[16]

But what might well in the long run turn out to be of more fundamental importance is the Party leadership (or a section of it) thrusting aside its middle echelon personnel—in this case the Party committees at regional, provincial and municipal level—to link itself directly, as in 1958, with the revolutionary masses. This at least seems to be the aim, although the Maoists, again as in 1958, may have misjudged the degree of revolutionary fervour in the minds of the people. It does not need to be stressed that the cultural revolution has created, or at least brought to the surface, strong opposition to Mao's policies.

[15] *New Republic* (February 27, 1965), p. 23.
[16] Franz Schurmann, "China's Power Structure," *Diplomat*, XVII, No. 196 (September 1966), p. 90.

The Chinese party-state therefore acts to reduce the level of dissent by eliminating the sin of professionalism throughout China, thereby reducing the number of checks over the Party by such noninstitutionalised means. However, given the desire of the Chinese leadership to create a powerful modern and industrial society, and the need therefore to rely on the professionals and experts, it is unlikely that this attempt will succeed.

In the larger context, it is just this assumption, that the Chinese wish to develop into an affluent industrial society, which must be thrown into doubt. It now seems that Mao Tse-tung and his followers want to forsake affluence, and the decadence and corruption they consider goes with it, to pursue their own utopia of a different kind.

The period from 1949 to 1956 saw China trying to industrialise on the lines of the Soviet model, with the major investment going into heavy industry and large centralised plants. Many commentators argued that the abandonment of this at the end of the First Five Year Plan and the start of the Great Leap Forward was an "irrational" decision, but given the fundamentally agricultural nature of the economy and its inability to support the population adequately, it can be argued that at least one aspect of the Great Leap—to reverse the priorities and invest more in agriculture than in heavy industry—made very good sense, though a decision to stress agriculture at the expense of heavy industry does not necessarily lead to the renunciation of the desire for modernisation, whether on the Western or Soviet model.

The Great Leap was the first attempt to create the "new society" where government would be decentralised into communes and every man would be both a mental and a manual labourer; a peasant one day and a soldier the next. The communes, or the "buds of communism," as they were described at the time, were to usher in the millenium within a remarkably short while, though without the abundance of material goods that traditional Marxism always considered to be a necessary prerequisite. It was the claim that communes would bring China to communism before the U.S.S.R. that led an angry Khrushchev to remark that the Chinese communists "were like a group of hungry people sitting round an empty table in complete equality."

Objective reality in the shape of peasant recalcitrance, transport failures and bad weather forced the temporary postponement in the realisation of the "Maoist vision," which it appears, is a society characterised by a perpetually high level of tension or "struggle," a puritanical way of life, the submersion of the individual in the collective, and the almost religious belief in the ideological transformation of man.

The present cultural revolution indicates that Mao feels the time to be ripe for another attempt, indeed his final attempt, to reach this dream. The outcome of the struggle will decide China's future course of development.

33 JAN S. PRYBYLA

THE ECONOMIC COST
OF THE CULTURAL REVOLUTION

Attempts to estimate the impact of the so-called Cultural Revolution on the economy of Communist China run up against four major obstacles.

First, the Chinese Communists have released no economic statistics other than percentage data since 1960, and since the autumn of 1965 even the latter have become scarce. In August 1967, for example, there was no statistical reporting of any kind from twenty provinces, while percentage claims from regions under the control of Mao's revolutionary committees have been fragmentary (usually relating to particular counties or industrial plants) and highly suspect. It seems quite probable that the "revolutionary rebels" have communicated to Peking only the sort of data that made the power takeover look good. It is also important to note that even the figures published before 1960 are subject to doubt because of the regime's well-known propensity for political exaggeration and the modest state of statistical science and reporting procedures in China. In addition, the Great Leap years may well have resulted in a disorganization of China's statistical services, with the departure of Soviet experts in 1960 and the administrative breakdown after 1965 further aggravating an already unsatisfactory statistical situation.

Secondly, since the outbreak of the Cultural Revolution—but especially since January 1967, when the revolution was extended to factories and farms—there has been very little meaningful economic discussion and analysis in the Chinese press. Slogans such as "grasp the revolution and stimulate production" are not very helpful, whatever light they may throw on the psychology of the ruling faction. There have been scattered calls for putting an end to disruption in factories, exhortations to the peasants and the army for a special effort in connection with spring work in the fields, and appeals for clearing the channels of communication—all accompanied by reports of strikes, clashes, and lax labor discipline. But both the implications of the various appeals and the truthfulness of the reports are difficult to establish with any precision.

Thirdly, such reports on the state of the Chinese economy as reach the

Reprinted from *Problems of Communism*, published by the United States Information Agency, Washington, D.C., Vol. XVII, No. 2, March–April 1968, pp. 1–13. By permission of the Editors.

outside world through Western tourists, reporters, and businessmen, or through refugees, are conflicting, often questionable, and always fragmentary. Eyewitness reports on Communist China, even when sober and unprejudiced, leave one with the uncomfortable feeling that "being there" does not necessarily ensure a thorough grasp of the Chinese situation. Indeed, a review of some of the eyewitness literature that came out just before the Cultural Revolution reveals an extraordinary lack of insight into both current developments and the whole Communist process in China. Few of the modern Marco Polos noticed any signs of the impending apocalyptic upheaval or even hinted at the rifts that were already nearing the surface of the apparently monolithic regime. The problem of obtaining trustworthy reporting out of China has become even more intractable since early 1966, as travelers to the Chinese mainland have been fewer and their chances of gathering reliable information more restricted than ever. This has curbed but by no means stopped the flow of eyewitness accounts.

Fourth and finally, there is the problem of cultural distance, which makes Western evaluations of Chinese behavior difficult. Moreover, China is vast, the population enormous, and the economy varied and still imperfectly integrated. Generalizations about the Chinese, the Chinese Communists, and the Chinese Communist economy must, therefore, be taken with much caution.

THE POINT OF DEPARTURE: 1965

From 1961 to 1965, the economy of Communist China was run along revisionist lines. It was a period of readjustment and consolidation following the setbacks and disruptions of the Great Leap Forward. It must also have been a period of bitter internal controversy about the future course of economic policy. While some of those in authority were organizing countrywide "socialist education" campaigns and "four clean-up" movements, and were urging everyone to learn from the People's Liberation Army and the thought of Mao, others were breaking up the communes into economically more viable units, restoring private plots, stimulating free markets, reshuffling investment priorities, and generally pursuing a pragmatic and reformist course in the management of the economy.[1] In

[1] See Jan S. Prybyla, "Communist China's Strategy of Economic Development, 1961–1966," *Asian Survey*, October 1966, pp. 589–603; Chi-ming Hou, "Communist China's Economic Development Since the Great Leap," in Jan S. Prybyla (ed.), *The Triangle of Power, Conflict, and Accommodation: The United States, the Soviet Union, Communist China*, University Park, Pennsylvania State University, Center for Continuing Liberal Education, 1967, pp. 75–84.

Marxist language, the former were working on the superstructure, the latter on the base of society. This mute struggle between the Great Leapers, consigned after 1960 to the superstructure, and the reformists in charge of the economy, between the revolutionary romantics and the party bureaucrats, between guerrilla communism and revisionist technocracy, had no visibly adverse effects on the economy; on the contrary, such evidence as is available points to a gradual improvement of economic conditions. The relatively pragmatic course of the economic managers was embodied in the third Five-Year Plan scheduled to run from 1966 through 1970. However, only the most general outlines of the plan were made public in January 1966.

Four phases of the Cultural Revolution may be distinguished to date: 1. a "prerevolutionary" phase from mid-1964 to November 1965—the period of the socialist education campaigns and "four clean-up" movements, ending with the publication in Shanghai of a Maoist-inspired attack on the historian and deputy mayor of Peking, Wu Han; 2. the first, or Party and Cultural Purge phase of the Cultural Revolution proper, from November 1965 to the August 1966 Central Committee plenum—covering the purge of Peking party First Secretary P'eng Chen and the Municipal CCP Committee, of party propaganda chief Lu Ting-yi and others; 3. the second, or Red Guard phase from August 1966 to late December of that year—highlighted by the debut of Mrs. Mao (Chiang Ch'ing) in a leading revolutionary role, by monster Red Guard rallies in Peking, and attacks on everything "bourgeois," by the dismissal of T'ao Chu from his recently acquired post as Lu Ting-yi's successor and the self-criticisms of Liu Shao-ch'i and Teng Hsiao-p'ing; 4. the third, or Economic Warfare and Revolutionary Rebels phase, which began on December 26, 1966, with editorials calling on the Red Guards and new Maoist workers' formations (revolutionary rebels) to carry the revolution into factories and farms—a phase that has been marked by strikes, armed clashes between workers and Red Guards, "takeovers" by revolutionary rebels of factories, banks, railroad yards and ports, and a protracted campaign against "economism." It is this last phase, as yet incomplete, which is likely to have the greatest impact on the performance of the economy. Though it will take time for the full impact to be felt, there already are signs that the economy is beginning to experience the effects of the Maoist infiltration.

To sum up, the Cultural Revolution has gradually progressed from the superstructure—that is, the realms of party and government affairs and of cultural activity in the widest sense[2]—toward the economic base of Chinese

[2] "International historical experience of the dictatorship of the proletariat shows that this dictatorship cannot be consolidated nor can the socialist system be consolidated, unless a proletarian cultural revolution is carried out and persistent efforts are made to eradicate bourgeois ideology." (From *Hung Chi* editorial, "Long Live the Great Proletarian Cultural Revolution," published in English in *The Great Socialist Cultural Revolution in China*, No. 4, Peking, Foreign Languages Press, 1966, p. 5.)

society, that is, towards seizure of the economic apparatus. In a sense, it has also moved from form to content, from ideas about policy to the actual formulation of policy. The transition now going on is crucial and may well prove to be the undoing of the utopian, guerrilla faction. The Maoists have little to offer in the way of economic policy that can be interpreted as a forward thrust toward modernization—and modernization is what China needs, and probably desires, above all else. The effectiveness of Mao's thought has so far been tested in realms that elude quantification; it is now on the point of being tested in terms of tons of steel produced, bushels of wheat grown, etc.—in other words, in terms of "concrete" economic variables.

HISTORICAL PARALLELS

It is important to repeat that the economic effects of politico-ideological disturbances take time to work themselves out. What we have at present is evidence of factors which are likely to contribute toward a more general dislocation of the Chinese economy at some time in the future.

Some historical parallels are useful in this connection. The late Naum Jasny has explored the hypothesis of politically-induced business cycles in Stalin's Russia and has found a correlation between politically-motivated drives, on the one hand, and dips in national income, industrial output, freight traffic, and other indicators of economic activity, on the other.[3] More significantly, he has shown that periods of serious economic recession were associated with all-out attacks by the regime on the economic base, as exemplified by the collectivization drive of the early 1930's. It was when Stalin's "culture" directly invaded the farm and factory that the dip in economic activity was greatest. On the other hand, palace revolutions affected the economy much less. Even formidable ones, such as the great purges of the late 1930's, merely produced stagnation in the economic base; and at times, as for instance during the succession struggle following Stalin's death, the decline in economic activity was small.

Although it would be risky to apply Jasny's analysis to post-1949 China without qualifications, his study does reveal a great deal about the relation between the citizens of Communist countries as producers and their regimes as leaders. It may be that the Chinese are even more adept than the Russians at going their own way regardless of disturbances in the superstructure. When, however, as during the Great Leap, the superstructure invades the farm and workshop in an attempt to impose radical

[3] Naum Jasny, *Soviet Industrialization 1928–1952,* Chicago, University of Chicago Press, 1961.

changes on the economic base, the latent antagonistic contradiction shows up sooner or later in production and productivity performance. Communist China may very well be facing just that kind of development at the present juncture of the Cultural Revolution.

It is widely agreed, moreover, that in the period since the Communist seizure of power China, too, has gone through some such sequence of boom and depression as Jasny detected in Stalinist Russia. The upward swing in the Chinese business cycle lasted from about 1950 through mid-1958 (the period of reconstruction and the first Five-Year Plan, and the beginning of the Great Leap). A downswing followed from the latter part of 1958 through 1961 or early 1962. From 1962 till 1966 there were signs of steady recovery to levels somewhat above those of 1957. In 1967 there was some suggestion of renewed stagnation, perhaps foreshadowing another downswing in the Chinese Communist business cycle.

AGRICULTURE

Part of this argument may be quantified, even though the post-1957 figures must necessarily be extrapolations, estimates, and informed guesses. Taking agriculture first, Table 33-I presents crop acreage and output figures for the years 1952, 1957, 1961, 1965, and a total output figure for food grains in 1966. The year 1952 represents the last year before the launching of China's first Five-Year Plan, which was drawn up with the help of Soviet advisers and followed fairly orthodox Stalinist lines. The year 1957 represents the terminal year of that plan and is not far from the peak of the business cycle, as outlined above. 1961 is the first year after the collapse of the Great Leap Forward and is fairly close to the trough of the post-leap depression (it was also a year of natural disasters). 1965 is the last year preceding the Cultural Revolution and reflects the results of the readjustment and consolidation policies pursued after 1961. The year 1966 covers part of the first phase and the whole of the second phase of the Cultural Revolution. Here we are on very slippery ground, with only the barest estimated data to go on. (More will be said later on developments in that year.)

It should be noted that some estimates have placed the total 1965 output of food grains at substantially less than the 200 million metric tons cited here. These estimates point to a figure of 180 million tons for 1965, following a recovery peak of 185 million tons in 1964 (equaling 1957 output). In any case, there was a distinct recovery of agricultural production after 1961, due in part to favorable weather but also, and more importantly, to the implementation of a new strategy of development which placed agriculture first on the list of planned priorities. This meant vesting production and income-distribution functions in the basic units of the communes (the production teams), renewed toleration of household plots and free agricultural markets, and significant increases in the output of chemical fertilizer and agricultural equipment. Instead of ambitious schemes to expand acreage, the new strategy emphasized the improvement of farming practices on existing agricultural land. This revisionist approach to established Communist economic priorities has been assailed in the course of the Cultural Revolution but nevertheless has apparently managed to survive.

Official Chinese sources claim that the 1967 harvest of winter wheat, barley, peas, beans and some other food crops was 10 percent better than in 1966,[4] and a similar improvement has been claimed in the production of oil-bearing rapeseed. When it comes to specific producing areas, however, mention is made only of those in which Mao's "three-way alliances" (composed of Maoist revolutionary rebels, the military, and rehabilitated party cadres) have allegedly "seized power."

It has been argued that the claim of a 10-percent gain in food crops is subject to considerable doubt, if only because in 1967 China contracted for the purchase of $100.8 million worth of Australian wheat, representing the highest level of Chinese wheat purchases from that country to date. (In the second half of 1967, the Australians were scheduled to deliver 1.5 million metric tons of that commodity.) By itself, however, this argument is not overly convincing since it now appears that a portion of the Australian deliveries was, in fact, intended for Egypt. In 1967 the Chinese shipped to Egypt a total of 150,000 tons of wheat (worth $10 million), one-third under regular contracts and the rest as a "solidarity gift"; and China also offered to supply wheat "unconditionally" to the Sudan.[5] Moreover, in view of the estimated 2-percent annual increase in China's population and assuming 200 million tons to have been the maximum conceivable production of food grains in 1966, a 10-percent increase in 1967 would still require substantial food imports to prevent a noticeable decline in living standards. If the actual production figure in 1966 was closer to the 175–80 million tons shown in Table 33–1, the rise in food imports is even more understandable. Indeed, the very ability of China to import large quantities of wheat from abroad tends to argue against an overstatement of the *immediate* adverse impact of the Cultural Revolution on agriculture. This is all the more so since hard-currency remittances from overseas Chinese have apparently been on the decline from their previously estimated annual rate of $100–150 million.

[4] New China News Agency (Peking), July 7, 8, 12, and 31, 1967.
[5] *China Trade and Economic Newsletter* (London), July 1967, pp. 1–2, 3; August 1967, pp. 4, 6.

TABLE 33-1. ESTIMATED CROP ACREAGE AND OUTPUT OF SELECTED CROPS

	1952	1957	1961	1965	1966
Acreage (million hectares)					
Farmland	109.9	111.8	106.7	109.0	
Sown Acreage	147.3	157.2	142.2	156.0	
Food Grain Crops	116.3	120.9	120.0	125.0	
Output (million metric tons)					
Total Food Grains	170.0	185.0	162.0	200.0	175-180
Rice	78.6	86.8	75.0	97.8	
Wheat	20.0	23.7	15.4	20.4	
Miscellaneous Grain	51.3	52.7	47.0	55.0	
Tubers	20.0	21.9	24.5	26.7	
Other Crops					
Soybeans	9.5	10.05	5.5	7.5	
Oilseeds	3.7	3.8	2.3	3.4	
Cotton	1.3	1.64	0.9	1.4	

Sources: Edwin F. Jones, "The Emerging Pattern of China's Economic Revolution," in Joint Economic Committee, United States Congress, *An Economic Profile of Mainland China* (Washington, DC, 1967), Vol. I, Table III, p. 94. Official data are used for 1957 and for oilseed, technical, and green manure crops in 1952. The estimate of overall 1966 food grain production was made by economic intelligence analysts in Hong Kong.

On the other hand, it is becoming increasingly clear that the second and third phases of the Cultural Revolution—the Red Guard phase and especially the Economic Warfare phase—have finally begun to tell, and they may be expected to exert a continuing adverse effect on agriculture unless promptly curbed. The evidence so far is scattered and circumstantial, but it clearly points in the direction of future disruption, with the everpresent possibility that weather problems may compound the effects of political instability. It is known, for example, that fewer water-control and soil-conservancy projects were initiated between September 1966 and April 1967 than over a comparable period in the preceding years. As 1967 progressed, there also were increasing signs of a breakdown in social discipline. Peasants were reported slaughtering large numbers of draught animals as well as pigs and poultry, and they also indulged in an apparently large-scale hacking down of trees, a traditional phenomenon in rural China during periods of administrative disorder. So serious was the latter situation that telephone conferences were held between administrative centers in the provinces in an effort to get the communes to engage in a massive reforestation drive.

Fluctuations in official policy have contributed to the confusion in rural areas. In the autumn of 1966, Red Guards were warned to keep away from the farms and not interfere with harvesting. In January 1967, however, calls went out to spread the revolution to the countryside, and then, in February, this order was reversed and the revolutionary rebels and Red Guards were forbidden to interfere with spring sowing. In March, Premier Chou En-lai tried to convince the peasants, that, notwithstanding Maoist insistence on "politics first" in everything, top priority must be given to farm work, at least during daylight hours.

The peasants reacted in various ways to all these contradictory instructions. Some deserted the communes to travel about the country and "exchange revolutionary experience." Others began parceling out communal property among themselves, roughed up "good" and "bad" cadres alike, neglected tools and machinery, raided food stocks, failed to collect manure for the collective lands, sold livestock, seed and farm implements on the open market and divided the proceeds among themselves, and wrangled over land boundaries. These disturbances may have appeared worse than they actually were because of the publicity given to particularly blatant instances, but there can be no doubt that a general breakdown of labor discipline did take place. Moreover, passive resistance by peasants and workers may have been just as important as the open opposition, although it was the latter that attracted the most attention.[6]

This conclusion is supported by other evidence. In February 1967, People's Liberation Army troops were mobilized on a considerably larger scale than in previous years to take charge of and assist in spring planting, and they were still on the land in September. In addition, army units were ordered to assume control of all wheat stocks in the main ports, suggesting a history of looting. There also were reports of special measures taken to get the traveling peasants, as well as those who were said to be "lying down" on the farms, back to work on the land: cash advances against future deliveries of industrial crops were authorized and brought forward by as much as two months in a number of provinces. (Of course, in the confusion, it was not always clear whether these advances were ordered by genuine Maoist revolutionary rebels and "three-way alliances" which had "seized power," or by anti-Maoists and other proponents of "economism." In the latter event, the advances may merely have had the effect of making the peasants' trips more comfortable and extensive.)

At any rate, it was still necessary in June 1967 for the Maoist authorities to issue regular radio appeals and urgent injunctions to the peasants against the practice of taking off for a nearby town in order to "rebel and take part in violent struggle," as well as against hoarding and bribery. An interesting instance occurred at the Malu People's Commune in Chaiting *hsien,* where 900 participants in a production-brigade meeting adjourned

[6] Hsiao Ai, "Internal Struggle Hurts Peking's Economy," *Chinese Communist Affairs,* April 1967, pp. 12–13; Hans Granqvist, *The Red Guard: A Report on Mao's Revolution,* New York, Praeger, 1967, chapter 9.

to go to the county seat and "rebel" in the party municipal committee. The deputy brigade chief was quoted as telling the peasants that "it is more profitable to rebel in the municipal committee than to engage in production. Each person can get six big pieces of bread a day in addition to the opportunity for sightseeing."[7]

Although spring droughts were reported in Honan, Anhwei, Shantung and Shansi provinces, weather conditions in 1967 appear to have been generally favorable for agriculture, especially in such important wheat-producing areas as Hopei, Kweichow, Kiangsi, and Ninhsia. Moreover, up till September 1967, there had been no evidence of widespread or serious food shortages in China, although it is impossible to say anything definite about the food situation in the more inaccessible provinces. It does seem probable that there has been some area-to-area disruption in food distribution owing to the overloading of transport facilities by traveling Red Guards, revolutionary rebels and counter-rebels, workers, and peasants, as well as to temporary interruptions and dislocations of rail and other traffic, as described later.

INDUSTRY

The impact of the Cultural Revolution on Chinese Communist industry is equally difficult to measure statistically, and any attempt to do so must again rely largely on informed estimates. Table 33–2 presents figures for the production of selected industrial commodities, including chemical fertilizers, in China in 1952, 1957, 1958, 1961, 1965, and 1966. These years are the same as those selected for the previous table on agriculture, except that 1958 has been added because it shows the peak of the business cycle and because estimates for it are both more readily available and more reliable than for agricultural output. Except for the 1952 and 1957 data and some of those for 1958, the figures cited are admittedly estimates based on spotty Chinese reporting and extrapolation. Nevertheless they may be taken as approximations of the general order of magnitude.

The estimated figures for 1966 point to continued improvement in the overall industrial situation in the first full year of the Cultural Revolution. It must be borne in mind, however, that 1966 fell in what were earlier described as the "superstructural" phases of the upheaval, that is, the phases marked primarily by disturbances in the "cultural" and political spheres. These disturbances the Chinese economy seems to have weathered without too much difficulty, but it still remains to be seen what will

[7] Hsiao Ai, loc. cit., pp. 21–22.

TABLE 33-2. ESTIMATES OF PRODUCTION OF SELECTED INDUSTRIAL
ITEMS

	1952	1957	1958	1961	1965	1966
Crude steel						
(million metric tons)	1.4	5.4	8.0	12.0	11.0	12.2
Coal						
(million metric tons)	66.5	130.7	226.4	180.0	210.0	250.0
Crude oil						
(million metric tons)	0.4	1.5	2.3	4.5	8.0	10.0
Electric power						
(billion kilowatt-hours)	7.3	19.3	27.5	31.0	40.0	—
Cement						
(million metric tons)	2.9	6.9	9.3	6.0	9.0	11.8
Cotton cloth						
(billion linear meters)	3.8	5.0	5.7	3.0	3.9	5.9
Chemical fertilizers						
(million metric tons)	0.2	0.8	1.4	1.5	4.6	5.9
Paper						
(million metric tons)	0.5	1.2	1.6	1.0	1.5	2.0

Sources: *Ten Great Years* (Peking, 1960); Arthur G. Ashbrook, "Main Lines of Chinese Communist Economic Policy," in Joint Economic Committee, U.S. Congress, *An Economic Profile of Mainland China* (Washington, DC, 1967), Vol. I, p. 25; Robert Michael Field, "Chinese Communist Industrial Production," *ibid.*, Appendix C, Table 9 (Field's estimates have been accepted for the years 1958, 1961, 1965); Hong Kong estimates for 1966 reported in *The New York Times*, May 23, 1967, p. 6; Field's estimates for crude oil and paper production in 1966.

be the impact of the third phase of the Cultural Revolution, which has extended down to the very economic base of Chinese society.

Paradoxically, the relative underdevelopment of the Chinese economy may also help to explain why the superstructural phases of the Cultural Revolution had no immediate impact on industrial performance in 1966. Underdeveloped economies (North Vietnam comes to mind as a particularly striking example) are seemingly capable of continuing to function in spite of political and administrative disruptions which would paralyze a more advanced economy. The explanation for this lies in the increasing integration that accompanies economic development. Merely a couple of generating switches pulled the wrong way can paralyze large sections of such a complex and integrated economic system as that, say, of the United States; yet even a natural disaster or a man-made political upheaval will not affect an underdeveloped economy as a whole with proportionate intensity because of the largely autonomous nature of the productive process in such an economy. This seems to be true of underdeveloped economies regardless of whether they are of the "planned" or "market" type, since the integrative effects of planning in the one case, and of the market in the other, are still modest in conditions of underdevelopment. As regards Communist China in particular, Peking's boasts of the successful integration of the country's economy "for the first time in modern history" seem grossly exaggerated. Moreover, since the Great Leap period, Chinese policy has stressed decentralization of economic management hand in hand with centralized political control. Consequently, when the latter broke down amidst the chaos caused by the Cultural Revolution, the regional economic units were apparently able to continue functioning independently, at least in the early stages. Even taking all these factors into account, the satisfactory performance of the Chinese economy in 1966 still remains something of a mystery. As pointed out below, however, the situation appears to have altered considerably since the extension of the Cultural Revolution directly to industry and the communes in December 1966/January 1967.

This drastic new move, which opened the third phase of the Cultural Revolution, hit Shanghai first. Work stoppages were reported throughout the city; the railways and port were paralyzed for several weeks; and local anti-Maoist managers and party officials handed out some $13 million of public funds to demonstrating workers up until January 7, 1967, when Maoist "revolutionary rebels" finally gained control of the banks.[8] The general interpretation of the Shanghai events, and of similar disturbances in other Chinese cities, is that when the Cultural Revolution passed from the stage of simply requiring the workers to take part in demonstrations against alleged opponents of Mao to the stage of telling them how to run their workshops according to Mao's ideas and how to finance the Cultural Revolution by their labor, the workers revolted. They reacted violently not only to the high-handed methods of the Red Guards but also to what they rightly considered to be a threat to their livelihood.

Matters got out of hand in other industrial centers as well. According to Peking's Maoist chief, Hsieh Fu-chih, industrial production in the capital declined by seven percent in April 1967 because of fighting and sabotage.[9] Wall posters also reported disturbances in the Taching and Karami oilfields, the coal-producing areas of Shansi and Shantung, and the oil-refining center of Lanchow. In July, the major industrial complex of Wuhan in central China became the scene of serious disturbances during which the district army commander, Chen Tsai-tao, detained two official emissaries (Hsieh Fu-chih and Wang Li) sent by Mao to hasten a local Maoist takeover. Although the emissaries were eventually released and the Maoist "seizure of power" ostensibly accomplished, the disturb-

[8] New China News Agency (Shanghai), Jan. 20, 1967.
[9] The Economist Intelligence Unit, *Quarterly Economic Review: China, North Korea, Hong Kong* (London), July 1967, p. 6. (Hereafter *QER*)

ances cast revealing light on the strength of the local anti-Maoist opposition and the apparent disaffection of segments of the army command. More important from an economic standpoint, they reportedly caused a temporary paralysis of traffic across the Yangtse River Bridge at Wuhan, a vital link in the main rail artery connecting North and South China. Disturbances were also reported in such widely scattered places as Kaifeng (the fertilizer-producing center), Harbin (Heilungkiang), Chengchow, and Canton, but their exact nature and extent remain unclear.

Meanwhile, the Peking regime continued to reveal virtually nothing in the way of statistical information regarding the overall state of the economy. Although there were occasional references to 1967 as the second year of the third Five-Year Plan, not even a general growth rate for industry was published. About the only figures reported in the press were piecemeal claims of production successes in specific localities currently controlled by Maoist administrations. For example, the Maoist authorities in Tsingtao reported a 22-percent increase in local industrial production in the first half of 1967 over the corresponding period of 1966, claiming a significant rise in the output of 58 major products.[10] (Shortly afterward, however, there was a change in the local political situation which may well have altered the economic picture.) Similar claims of local economic gains came from Harbin and Shanghai after the reported takeover of those cities by new Maoist administrations.

The fact that Communist China pushed ahead with its nuclear weapons development program during 1967 (testing a hydrogen bomb in June) suggests that at least the top-priority sectors of the economy connected with national defense escaped the brunt of the Cultural Revolution. It is significant in this connection that, despite the general anti-intellectualism of the campaign, point 12 of the CCP Central Committee's decision of August 8, 1966, on the Cultural Revolution explicitly exempted scientists, technicians, and others engaged in work of national importance from being made the objects of mass "struggle."[11] Nevertheless, even if spared from Red Guard attacks, these favored personnel have no doubt been required to devote considerable time to participating in public demonstrations and "Mao-think" sessions, which can hardly have contributed to their efficiency. It should also be noted that Sinkiang province, the nervecenter of China's nuclear industry, was for a time in 1967 the scene of incidents bordering on open anti-Maoist rebellion, reportedly involving the regional military commander, Wang En-mao. Although the situation had apparently simmered down to a state of uneasy coexistence between Wang and the Maoists by the fall of 1967, the earlier disturbances and the loosening

10 *Jen-min Jih-pao* (Peking), July 3, 1967, p. 4.
11 *Decision of the Central Committee of the Chinese Communist Party Concerning the Great Proletarian Cultural Revolution*, Peking, Foreign Languages Press, 1966, p. 11.

of governmental controls reportedly prompted the exodus of thousands of workers previously sent to Sinkiang from eastern China.

Turning to another vital sector of the economy, there can be little doubt that the travel mania which gripped hundreds of thousands of Red Guards, "revolutionary rebels," workers, and peasants during 1966–67, ostensibly for the purpose of exchanging "revolutionary experience," seriously impeded the functioning of China's transportation system. After December 1966, a good part of this "cultural" tourism appears to have been actually encouraged and financed by anti-Mao forces. The disruption to which it gave rise was attested to by an urgent order of the Szechwan Provincial Production Committee issued on March 8, 1967, which instructed the provincial communications and transportation departments to take stock of all vehicles under their jurisdiction and see to it that vehicles which had been "borrowed" to transport revolutionaries were returned immediately to their districts of registration (preferably loaded) and were repaired at the expense of the local units to which they belonged. Drivers and mechanics were ordered to return to work at once, and local vehicle pools were directed to use their trucks to support agriculture.[12] There had already been reports, during the winter of 1966–67, of numerous delays in the movement of raw materials to factories, of finished products to users, and of export goods to ports of embarkation. Other reports told of army units being called in to clear piled-up stocks of goods from railroad yards and quais, and of bottlenecks which developed on rail lines in Shansi, Kwangtung, Shantung, Kweichow, and Yunnan provinces. On June 1, 1967, the Central Committee issued a call for the restoration of order on the railways following a series of strikes, acts of sabotage, and armed clashes between rival factions.[13]

FOREIGN TRADE

Because of the possibility of obtaining data on China's exports and imports from her trading partners, the effects of the Cultural Revolution on foreign trade are more easily measurable than its effects on domestic industrial and agricultural output. But important as foreign trade is for China's development, it must be remembered that it does not encompass a very significant component of the country's total domestic product.

The general conclusion to be drawn from the evidence is that the

[12] QER, April 1967, p. 8.
[13] Colina MacDougall, "The Economic Cost," Far Eastern Economic Review (Hong Kong), July 27, 1967, p. 198; Alexandra Close, "Mob Rule," ibid., June 22, 1967, p. 645.

Cultural Revolution had no noticeably adverse effect on China's foreign commerce in 1966, but that the beginnings of a slow-down in trade expansion were becoming detectable in the first half of 1967. This is illustrated by the figures given in Table 33–3, which shows the percentage changes in China's exports and imports in 1965, 1966, and 1967, based on monthly trade averages.

TABLE 33-3. TRENDS IN COMMUNIST CHINA'S TRADE WITH SELECTED COUNTRIES

Trading Partner	1965	1966*	1967
Chinese Imports			
Japan (January-April)	+83	+50	−30
West Germany (January-April)	+235	+150	+83
United Kingdom (January-May)	+21	+74	+32
France (January-April)	+26	+118	−16
Italy (January-April)	+128	+123	+84
Other West European (Switzerland, Netherlands, Belgium, Sweden; first 3-5 months of year)	+75	+142	+9
Aggregate of the above	+77	+81	+9
Chinese Exports			
Japan (January-April)	+67	+64	−4
West Germany (January-April)	+58	+31	−1
United Kingdom (January-May)	+11	+49	−9
France (January-April)	+45	+47	−16
Italy (January-April)	+40	+41	+18
Other West European (same as above)	+19	+23	+12
Aggregate of the above	+44	+48	−2
Hong Kong (January-April)	+36	+4	+22
Total including Hong Kong	+41	+28	+7

*Percentage change from previous year, based on monthly trade averages.
Source: The Economist Intelligence Unit, *Quarterly Economic Review: China, North Korea, Hong Kong* (London), July 1967, p. 7. The percentage changes in the 1965 column relate mainly to the first halves of 1964 and 1965.

Although the table shows that China's important export trade to Hong Kong expanded in early 1967 as compared with early 1966, more recent data indicate a significant falling-off in deliveries to the colony after April. The slowdown from April through June was not enough to keep Chinese exports to Hong Kong in the first half of 1967 from registering a gain over the same period of 1966, rising to $231.25 million as compared with $201 million in 1966; however, Chinese shipments to the colony in June 1967 amounted to only $21 million as compared with $40 million in March and

$37 million in July 1966.[14] Admittedly, the situation was clouded by the Communist-instigated disturbances in Hong Kong in the summer of 1967, and it is difficult to assess to what extent the drop in Chinese exports to the British enclave was politically motivated and to what extent it resulted from internal economic dislocation. To some degree, however, the latter could have been a factor.

In spite of their internal troubles, the Chinese have continued through mid-1967 to make offers of aid to various developing countries. Food shipments to Egypt and offers of wheat to the Sudan have already been mentioned. In addition, "indefinite" development aid was offered to Iraq in July 1967, and a gift of $60 million to Jordan. The Chinese have also expressed an interest in financing and constructing the projected $300 million Zambia-Tanzania railroad (the survey for which was paid for earlier by Britain and Canada), but the status of the offer is still vague.

One further observation may be made with respect to China's recent foreign trade. There has been a notable absence, in 1966-67, of large Chinese purchases of capital equipment from abroad, such as characterized the years 1963 through 1965. This may reflect some disorganization of long-range economic planning in China as a result of the Cultural Revolution.

ECONOMIC PLANNING

So far our attention has been focussed mainly on the short-run economic repercussions of the Cultural Revolution. There can be little doubt, however, that the paroxysm China has experienced in the last two years will continue to affect the economy over an extended period, and the longer-term consequences are likely to be of considerable significance for China's drive toward modernization.

By September 1967, it was becoming increasingly clear that the Chinese Communist Party apparatus as it existed at the outset of the Cultural Revolution had been seriously weakened, if not shattered. There was also much circumstantial evidence to suggest that the economic planning apparatus had ceased functioning. Many high officials in charge of economic affairs had come under public attack: Li Hsien-nien, the Minister of Finance; Li Fu-chun, Chairman of the State Planning Commission; Liao Lu-yen, Minister of Agriculture; Tan Chen-lin, Director of the Office of Agriculture; Po Yi-po, Chairman of the State Economic Commission; Chen Yun, a high economic policymaker; Sun Yeh-fang, Director of the

[14] Report by T. D. Sorby, Hong Kong Director of Commerce and Industry, *New York Times,* Aug. 17, 1967, p. 15.

Economics Division of the Chinese Academy of Sciences; and Liu Ning-yi, a top trade-union official. Hundreds of lesser officials of the planning apparatus and the economic administration had likewise been purged or at the least discredited.

Economic planning obviously requires trained personnel and, above all, a degree of stability. Technical, scientific, and economic innovation is quite a different thing from the seizure of political power. Innovational revolutions demand sustained intellectual effort, and this in turn requires that those engaged in it be left in peace, that they be assured of an appropriate status in society, and that their work not be interrupted by constant calls to Maoist prayer. The Cultural Revolution has destroyed all three of these essential elements. If economic planning is still going on in Communist China, it is surely of the hand-to-mouth variety, with much time out for inspirational politics.

Even more ominous for the long-term development of China's economy is the general anti-intellectualism that has characterized the Cultural Revolution. According to *Pravda* (March 11, 1967), a poster on display in a Peking park proclaimed: "We do not need brains! Our heads are armed with the ideas of Mao Tse-tung!" Whether the poster was put up by Red Guards or by some sly Mao opponents, the slogan does succinctly sum up the anti-intellectual spirit of the current upheaval. In their zeal to eradicate all vestiges of the past, all suggestions of revisionism, and all signs of independent thought, the engineers of the Cultural Revolution have made a mockery of culture and set China back many years. The revolution has fostered indiscipline among students, humiliated teachers, simplified curricula to the point of absurdity, and led to book-burnings and the defacement of school property. Worst of all, it spawned millions of officially-sanctioned school dropouts and made the mindless mouthing of an aging idol's sayings a criterion of revolutionary virtue. "The Hung Weiping [Red Guards]," observed *Pravda* (February 21, 1967), "have mastered the lesson that the main enemy of Mao Tse-tung is he who tries to think." For a backward nation trying to become a modern industrial power, such anti-intellectualism can only prove self-defeating in the long run.

Some Tentative Conclusions

On the basis of the evidence available to date, it is possible to draw two sets of tentative conclusions with regard to the economic consequences of the Cultural Revolution. In the short run, the economy as a whole unquestionably showed an extraordinary ability to continue functioning without noticeable impairment, at least through the winter of

1966-67. In the first half of 1967, when the revolution was extended directly to economic activity at the farm and factory level, there were signs of a slowdown in expansion, but no real evidences of breakdown. In the first few months of the second half of 1967, these signs were multiplying, suggesting more than a slowdown in expansion and the possibility, if not the probability, of an actual recession unless prompt steps were taken to restore order, discipline and political stability.

The long-run perspective appears even gloomier. China's drive to catch up with the 20th century is in the process of being stymied by the anti-intellectualism of the Cultural Revolution, by its irreverence for the one thing China needs most—technical and scientific education, conducted in a climate which allows for doubt and experimentation. Although the attack on the intellectuals seems originally to have had the limited objective of uprooting resurgent Mandarinism and the traditional contempt of the educated Chinese for manual labor and for those engaged in it, the end result has been to undermine intellectual endeavor and promote the adulation of stupidity. China's intellectual birthrate, her supply of new talent, is bound to be seriously affected, and this in turn will act as a brake on economic progress for years to come.

Postscript

Since the preceding analysis was originally written last fall, developments in China have wrought no essential change in the picture. The Cultural Revolution has continued on its confused and fluctuating course with no end as yet in sight, although since last October there has been a noticeably increased effort on the part of the regime to curb the overzealousness of the Red Guards, to check feuding and squabbling among rival "revolutionary" groups, to get students back to school and workers back to their jobs. The resumption of regular classroom sessions with minimal academic content and under army supervision seems primarily intended to get the rampaging youngsters off the streets and keep them from disrupting farm and factory work. In places, the energies of the young people have been harnessed to essential tasks, such as loading and unloading on the waterfront. This has made for bitter disappointment among the more headstrong Red Guards, but it is the price the extremists have been forced to pay to keep the economy on an even keel.

With regard to agriculture, the official New China News Agency on November 16-17 scaled down its earlier claims of "unprecedented harvest gains" and described the 1967 harvest as merely "rather good," which in Communist parlance usually means moderate to poor. Still, total 1967 food-crop production, including grain and potatoes, may have reached an estimated 187 million metric tons, which would exceed the 1966 estimate but still fall short of the 1965 figure. Wheat imports, which totalled over 5.6 million tons in all of 1966, amounted to about 2.5 million tons (from Canada and Australia) in the first half of 1967.

Difficulties were apparently encountered in state procurements of food crops as a result of the relaxation of discipline in the countryside, the weakened authority of the party cadres, and the upsurge of "economism" among the peasants. On December 21, Peking Radio charged that "class enemies" were inciting the peasants "to retain farm crops instead of selling them to the state." Earlier, the army organ *Chieh-fang Chün Pao* (October 9) had complained of a resurgence of private-property inclinations among the peasants, warning that such tendencies were "having a corrosive and destructive effect on the new socialist base." These and similar statements suggest that, in spite of the dispatch of army units to the countryside, the Maoists have been less than successful in their efforts to combat the peasants' preoccupation with private plots, free markets, higher wages, more consumer goods, and a larger share of the harvest. At the same time, the peasants have apparently shown little interest in the political struggles organized by the Maoists in Peking and other cities against Liu Shao-ch'i, "China's Khrushchev." On September 16, *Jen-min Jih-pao* remonstrated against the peasants' lack of revolutionary fervor, complaining that when urged to criticize "China's Khrushchev" they pleaded illiteracy, leaving criticism to those able to read and write. According to the paper, their reaction was: "The Chinese Khrushchev is far from us, and his poison does not reach our little riverside hidden in the mountains. Why waste so much energy on criticizing him?"[15]

In the area of trade, Chinese exports to Hong Kong, after the earlier-mentioned abrupt decline of last summer, registered a spectacular recovery in October, rising 266 percent over the September figure, on a value basis. In spite of this recovery, however, total Chinese exports to the colony for 1967 are likely to be below the 1966 level of 484.61 million dollars. China's overall balance of trade in 1967 shows a considerable excess of imports over exports, a situation which, if allowed to continue, will result in a serious drain on the country's foreign-exchange reserves. The British devaluation of the pound will help a little through its impact on receipts from Hong Kong, which will have to pay some $500 million a year more for its imports of food and other commodities from China, but this only eases the situation temporarily without solving China's problem. It is this concern which may have prompted Peking to try and patch up some of its worst quarrels with other foreign customers and suppliers. China's off-again (September), on-again (November) orders for urea and ammonium

[15] Quoted in L. D. Tretiak, "Feeding Revolution," *Far Eastern Economic Review,* Oct. 26, 1967, p. 169.

sulphate from Japan probably reflected domestic storage and distribution problems arising from the dislocations caused by the Cultural Revolution. By cancelling the orders in September and picking them up again in November for delivery in late winter, Peking saved itself the bother of winter storage at its troubled North China ports while scoring some points with Japanese "friendly firms."

All this, as well as the unusual attention given by the Chinese press to transportation and fuel problems, suggests trouble spots, potential dangers, and the need to curb economic fanaticism, but it does not invalidate the general conclusion reached earlier, that there is as yet no convincing evidence of imminent and wholesale economic crisis. The possibility that such a crisis may eventually develop still exists, of course; whether or not it materializes will depend on how successful the forces of moderation prove to be in keeping the Cultural Revolution from impinging any farther than it already has on the economic base of Chinese society.

The formation of "revolutionary committees" at the provincial, municipal, and county levels is no longer being described in the Chinese press as the result of outright Maoist "power seizures." On the contrary, the new administrations that have been formed since last October appear to be the product of compromise settlements or so-called "three-way alliances" joining Maoist revolutionaries, former party apparatchiks, and army representatives. Thus, some old party hands who somehow managed to weather the spring and summer storms are back in office in these makeshift formations.

Parallel with this outward suffusion of the political struggle, the regime claims that economic dislocation has been localized "in certain areas and certain departments," to use Chou En-lai's phrase. "As soon as disorder is turned into order," said Chou, "production can quickly pick up and rise."[16] This is a very big condition, however, for the forces of disorder unleashed by Mao's cultural revival are not easily contained. For the time being, the Great Proletarian Cultural Revolution still appears to be the political agent of another recession in China's socialist economy, perhaps mild by the standards of the Great Leap debacle, yet with serious long-range repercussions on China's progress toward modernization.

[16] Speech at Wuhan on Oct. 9, 1967, quoted in *Far Eastern Economic Review*, Oct. 19, 1967, p. 125.

34   JOUNGWON ALEXANDER KIM

The "Peak of Socialism" in North Korea: The Five and Seven Year Plans

Since the establishment of the "Democratic Peoples' Republic of Korea" (DPRK) in 1948, Communist North Korea has been relatively stable in political terms. Certain major purges have taken place beneath the surface, but the central leadership of Kim Il-sŏng and his old comrades of Manchurian days has remained unchanged. This has permitted the regime to carry out a continuous policy of economic development aiming at self-sufficiency both in industry and in agriculture. The latter goal has, of course, been difficult due to the relatively limited arable land in the mountainous, mineral rich section of Korea north of the 38th parallel.

The government of North Korea, before the Korean War quite literally a "puppet" of the Soviet Union, emerged from the conflict with considerably increased autonomy and a determination to preserve and expand this new measure of independence. Particularly following the death of Stalin in 1953, when the leadership in the USSR became involved in the internal struggle for power, the ties between the Soviet Union and the DPRK were weakened. The Sino-Soviet rift, following the Twentieth Congress of the CPSU was seized upon as a further opportunity to enhance the maneuverability of North Korea within the Communist bloc. This movement toward independence from Moscow can be observed in the purges—first of 1950–51 and then of 1956–58—when prominent members of the party with pro-Soviet leanings, as well as those with pro-Chinese leanings, were purged from party membership and government ranks.

From the North Korean point of view, increased political autonomy is contingent upon their ability to establish an independent economic base, for "Economic independence is the basis of political independence. Economic dependence on foreign forces entails political dependence on those forces. Economic subordination leads to political subordination."[1]

North Korea has done remarkably well in attempting to establish this independent economic foundation. From the beginning, the regime emphasized establishing a "balance" in the economy—that is, to make all sectors of the economy internally interdependent but externally independ-

From *Asian Survey* (May 1965), pp. 255–269. Reprinted by permission of *Asian Survey*.

[1] *Nodong Shinmun* (Workers' News), the official North Korean Workers' Party newspaper, April 11, 1963.

ent. Until 1945, the Korean economy had been integrated into the Japanese, and the "lopsidedness" of the dependence of Korean industry upon Japan for machinery, spare parts, as well as the existence primarily of raw materials industries in Korea, had to be "corrected." A second necessity was to "correct the lopsidedness" of the North Korean economy due to its former dependence upon South Korea for agricultural products, textiles and other consumer goods.

Although this was the declared policy from the very beginning, the regime was limited by the Soviet policy-makers, who were far more interested in re-orienting the North Korean economy to that of the Soviet Union. During the five years from the beginning of the Russian occupation to the outbreak of the Korean War, large amounts of raw materials were exported to the Soviet Union in "exchange" for machinery and other essential equipment.[2]

Following the Korean War, when the Russian hold on North Korea had been loosened, the regime set about reconstructing the industries and capacities for agricultural production destroyed during the war, with technical aid from the USSR, China and other Communist countries. The task of the "Three Year Plan for Postwar Reconstruction" (1954–56) was to restore the economy to the pre-war stage while continuing to "correct the imbalance." By 1956, upon the completion of the plan, the goals were considered essentially met: the economy, it was claimed, had recovered both from its "colonial imbalance" and the wartime devastation.

The Five Year Plan, originally intended to cover the period from 1957–61, was then the first plan aimed at creating a "socialist economy," meaning that during this period all means of production were to come under the direct control and operation of the state.

Outcome and Effects of the Five Year Plan: The Five Year Plan was initiated in North Korea in 1957. As Premier Kim Il-sŏng announced at the Third Congress of the Workers' (Communist) Party in April 1956, the leading role in the Five Year Plan was to be played by heavy industry, whose development was considered a prerequisite for further growth of the economy. This emphasis on heavy industry was a continuation of the policy of the pre-Korean War years and the Three Yean Plan (1954–56), and was also important in terms of "party line"—a demonstration that they were adhering to the "true" guidelines of Marxist-Leninist theory.

Already by the end of 1959, after only three years of the Five Year Plan, North Korea was claiming a "Glorious Victory" for the plan—which was indeed quite near completion of the output goals, and 1960 was declared a "Buffer Year" in which readjustments would be made before en-

[2] An article in *Nodong Shinmun* on September 7, 1964, discloses how the Soviets exploited North Korea by purchasing raw materials from North Korea at prices much lower than world market prices and selling them equipment and materials at prices "much higher than the world market prices."

tering the next long-term plan. With the exception of the output of steel, it seemed probable that, barring a major setback, planned output for the last year of the Five Year Plan could be attained in 1960. Steel production, however, was not likely to meet the planned annual output until 1961. This was, indeed, the year that goal was to be reached, under the original plan. However, since various other industries depended on the production of steel, it was essential for the plan as a whole that steel reach the target as quickly as possible.

For the Five Year Plan, the Korean Workers' Party of North Korea set the following goals for output of major products:

TABLE 34-1.

Product	Measure	1956 Output	Five Year Plan Annual Output Goal
Total Grain Harvest	metric tons	2,873,000	3,700,000
Textiles	meters	77,080,000	154,000,000
Electric Power	billion kwh	5.12	8.5
Coal	metric tons	3,908,000	6,630,000
Steel	metric tons	189,000	620,000
Cement	metric tons	597,000	1,500,000
Chemical Fertilizer	metric tons	195,000	400,000

Source: Official North Korean statistics.[3]

The main problem in increasing production in the steel industry, a difficulty soon to be felt by other industries using minerals, was the shortage of raw materials, due to the lack of an effective policy in locating new mineral resources and developing new methods of extraction. The practice had been to locate sufficient materials for each year's production at the beginning of the year, and then to concentrate on meeting annual production goals.

The method of planning and control was, in fact, creating a serious

[3] These particular commodities have been selected for analyzing the success of the economic plans partly because a series of statistics is available, and partly because they make up such a large percentage of total output in North Korea: most of agricultural production is covered when the total grain harvest is discussed; electric power and coal constitute essentially all of the fuel and power industry; steel is the main product of the metals industry; chemical fertilizer makes up the major portion of the chemical industry; textiles are generally representative of the growth of consumer goods; and cement is the most important product of the building materials industry.

Of course, as the economy has become more complex and production somewhat more varied during the period of the Seven Year Plan (1961–67), these particular products have lost a certain amount of their absolute significance; nevertheless, they are still useful indexes to determine how the economy is developing.

problem of economic imbalance in North Korea. Theoretically, economic plans are constructed by the State Planning Commission which turns them over to the Cabinet for approval. These plans are supposedly based on estimates of each plant manager of the production capacity of his plant, total estimates submitted by the ministries (which supervise the industries), consideration of resources available, over-all budget expenditures, political considerations, and innumerable other factors. In reality, these plans are decisions of the few top policy makers of the Korean Workers' Party and may not be as economically realistic as they pretend to be.

After approval, these plans are turned over to the ministries to be carried out by the factories under their control. Each factory and each manager are then given a production quota. This process of planning can never be perfect, and a mistaken estimate in one major plant by one manager could conceivably throw the whole production schedule of the economy out of balance.

Production schedules must be met through a system of incentives and control. The workers are divided among the various factories and "cooperatives" (collective farms), and within each group or subgroup is to be found a member, or members, of the Korean Workers' Party (KWP) whose duty is to supervise closely the activities of other workers. Through fear of punishment as a result of a bad report from these ever-watchful eyes, as well as through incentives (awards, privileges), the workers are pushed to produce to the limit of their capacity.

This is what happened in 1959: During the first three years of the Five Year Plan, each worker and manager was exhorted and coerced, wheedled and beguiled into producing more and more over his production goal. Such pressure for over-production in one sector required over-production in another to supply it. Increasing disproportions brought mounting frustrations and rivalries among the various ministries in charge of production, as no sector could rely on any other for definite knowledge of what would be supplied and when. Thus, by the end of 1959, the delicate balance between the sectors broke down. Raw materials simply could not be supplied fast enough to keep up with the unplanned demand, and expansion in heavy industry had to be cut back while concentrated efforts were put into the mining industry. Investment in industry in 1960 as compared with that in 1959, shows that an increased emphasis was placed on mining during that year, while investment in other industries was decreased correspondingly.

The main solution, however, related not to investment, but to time. Concentration of effort in the bottleneck sector and a leveling off of production increases in others was the only feasible approach. This was not the sole difficulty which had to be rectified during the "Buffer Year." Pressure to complete revised and re-revised production plans in each sector had brought about a mad scramble during the last days of each annual planning period. Sometimes machines were run continually for several days and nights until they finally broke down or were badly damaged. A pause in heavy industry expansion during 1960 allowed for repairing and replacing of these over-used machines.

One result of the runaway economy, as mentioned previously, was the impossibility of coordinating the various sectors of industry. In April 1960, an attempt to bring about a smoother relationship between industries resulted in the amalgamation of all earlier industry ministries into two Commissions: Heavy Industry and Light Industry.

The Five Year Plan, while apparently achieving original output goals within four years, had created serious strains throughout the economy.

"Socialization" of the economy allows for more direct control: The goals of the Five Year Plan involved more than an increase in the production of major products. The most important task was the completion of "socialism," that is, the elimination of all forms of private enterprise, which had during the previous years coexisted with "socialist" forms of production, and the substitution of direct party control.

Much of this "socialization" had been brought about before the beginning of the Five Year Plan. In 1956, the "socialist sector" of industry contributed 98 per cent of total output; "state and cooperative enterprise" (collective farms) held 68.8 per cent of the total cultivated land.

By 1958, "cooperativization" (collectivization) was completed and the "socialist sector" of industry produced 99.9 per cent of the total industrial output. In 1959, this latter figure became 100 per cent.

The allocation of manpower was altered in North Korea after the Korean War as follows:

TABLE 34-2.

	Jan. 1, 1953	Sept. 1, 1956	Dec. 1, 1959	End of 1960
Total	100.0%	100.0%	100.0%	100.0%
Labor (Industrial workers)	21.2	27.3	37.2	38.3
Office workers	8.5	13.6	13.4	13.7
Cooperative members	–	40.0	45.7	44.4
Private farmers	66.4	16.6	–	–
Miscellaneous	3.9	2.5	3.7	3.3

Source: *Choson Chungang Nyongkum, 1961* (Korean Central Yearbook, 1961), Pyongyang, 1961, p. 321.

In 1953, 66.4 per cent of total manpower was concentrated in agriculture in the form of private farmers. By 1960, this had decreased to 44.4 per cent of total manpower, in the form of "cooperative" members. Thus

22 per cent of all working people had left the rural economy for offices and factories. It is interesting to note that between 1953 and 1956, almost half of the persons leaving the farms went into offices, with the other half going into the industrial labor force. Between 1956 and 1959, however, there was no further increase in the proportion of office workers. It seems likely that until 1958, farmers were enticed to leave the rural areas in exchange for office jobs. Then, with the initiation of the "Chŏllima (Flying Horse) Movement" these rather unproductive office workers (it is questionable what rural labor, fresh from the farm, can accomplish in an office) were shifted into the industrial labor force. The collectivization program was completed in August 1958. Then, in September 1958, one witness tells of a mass rally to initiate the Chŏllima Movement. At that time, he said, office workers "volunteered" to shift 50 per cent of their number into the factories![4]

This Chŏllima Movement marked the completion of "socialism" in North Korea. It was to be the first experiment of the North Korean government in directing the economy now that all the working population was effectively under the control and supervision of the KWP pyramid-like network.

North Korea's Chŏllima Movement vs. Red China's Great Leap Forward: The Chŏllima Movement actually went into effect at the beginning of 1959. Workers were provided with incentives to produce, including awards and public praise. At first, individual "model workers" were awarded Chŏllima awards for top production; however, when this tended to produce antagonism among the workers (often model workers found themselves ostracized because the other workers accused them of forcing everyone to work harder), teams of workers were formed and "model brigades" were given Chŏllima awards. Awards were given in sufficient numbers to form a new class of "Chŏllima Workers" who were granted special privileges. The results of this Chŏllima Movement have been seen above. A forced competition between workers and the increase in industrial labor brought about a large jump in production in many sectors (though the quality of many products was very poor, as the government repeatedly complained), but ended by throwing the economy entirely off balance and into a state where adequate planning was impossible.

Students of Communist China's economy will note many similarities between this Chŏllima Movement and the "Great Leap Forward" which was initiated in Red China shortly before Chŏllima began in North Korea. The results were, indeed, similar. The Chŏllima Movement in Korea, however, had nowhere near the disastrous results of the Great Leap in China. This was due both to inherent differences in the national economies of Red

---

[4] Dongjun Lee (Yi Tongjun), *Hwansanggwa hyŏnshil: naŭi kongsanjuui kwan* (Fantasy and Fact: My Observations of Communism) (Seoul: Orient Press, 1961), p. 218.

China and North Korea and to the fact that North Korea (perhaps with Russian persuasion) was wise enough to leave the movement a year before the Chinese.

The disaster in Communist China was due, ultimately, to a poor harvest caused by droughts and floods. Their extent, however, was greatly affected by a poorly and hastily built irrigation system.[5] In addition, much of rural labor had been diverted into the building of "back-yard furnaces" for steel production, which proved unsuccessful. The major cause of Red China's economic failure was most likely the strong emphasis on heavy industry, to the detriment of agriculture. In mainland China, agriculture holds the predominant position and a poor harvest brings devastating effects to the entire economy.

In North Korea, where the land area is small, and the cultivable land quite limited, a sudden, massive irrigation project was not undertaken. Increased irrigation is considered important, and projects for developing more irrigated land have been in progress since the war. However, a great expansion of cultivable land has not been feasible, considering the mountainous nature of the terrain.

The "back-yard furnaces," too, were never attempted in North Korea, which was building a quite adequate centralized steel industry. The vast distances in mainland China made centralization more difficult than in the small country of North Korea. North Korea did localize much of the consumer goods industries, and this localization was apparently not unsuccessful, as it utilized local materials and much of local labor, including many housewives, whose labor might not otherwise have been employed.

The most significant reason for the avoidance in North Korea of Red China's disaster was the differing proportion of industry and agriculture in the national economy. Whereas the economy of China is still predominantly agricultural, North Korea is at present primarily an industrial state. Her exports of industrial products are great enough to permit importation of sufficient food to ward off famine. Her foreign trade has in fact expanded considerably since the beginning of the Five Year Plan—and her exports include very few agricultural products; they are primarily industrial.

The very strong emphasis on heavy industry which was inappropriate to the Red Chinese economy was thus *not* unsuitable to North Korea's situation. In fact, the division of Korea left North Korea in a position where rapid industrialization was essential to her economy. Before 1945, Korea as a whole had been a predominantly agricultural country. Although some industrialization had been effected in North Korea, even this area was overwhelmingly agricultural, as can be seen by the fact that 74.1 per cent of its working population were still employed in agriculture. And yet, with the division of the country, North Korea was left without sufficient

---

[5] Chu-yuan Cheng, *Communist China's Economy, 1949–1962: Structural Changes and Crisis* (South Orange, N.J.: Seton Hall, 1963), p. 143 ff.

agricultural resources to feed her population. It was necessary to import large amounts of agricultural goods. These agricultural imports had to be paid for with *something*. Obviously, industrialization was the only solution. Unlike mainland China, where agricultural production may be expanded through concentration of investment in irrigation and other projects, the prospects for agricultural expansion in North Korea are very slight.

Another factor in which the two economies greatly contrast is the relation of available manpower to the development of industry. In North Korea, the existing industrial base was developed enough to readily absorb manpower released from the farms by mechanization, and, in fact, the Kim Il-sŏng regime continually complained of an industrial manpower shortage. By 1960, 38.3 per cent of the labor force in North Korea was concentrated in industry.

Thus, while both the Great Leap Forward and the Chŏllima Movement brought about imbalance and strains in the economies of Red China and North Korea, the emphasis on heavy industry had a very different long-term effect on the two countries. Red China has been forced to abandon her Great Leap and her primary emphasis on heavy industry at this point and to concentrate her resources primarily in the development of agriculture. North Korea merely postponed heavy industry expansion for a three-year period while improving her mining and administrative methods.

Rectifying Chŏllima's strains: North Korea's Seven Year Plan (1961–67) can be divided into two periods. The first three years (1961–63) were to involve no heavy industry expansion (this period was extended an extra year, through 1964). During this initial period, emphasis was placed upon reorganizing and expanding the mining industry so as to turn out raw materials more rapidly, and upon solving administrative problems in allocating supplies. The latter part of the plan (1964–67) envisages renewed heavy industry expansion. As the former part of this plan did not require as large an investment in the heavy industry sector as previous plans, investment was to be diverted into light industry, agriculture, and "cultural" investment (health, education, etc., which Communist economists term "non-productive investment").

This temporary change in policy was pictured by the regime as the period in which the standard of living would rise to a comfortable and easy level, and this was used as effective propaganda. Since it was not feasible to expand heavy industry at this time, an increase in consumer goods and "cultural" facilities was to appease the people who had been worked so hard in the name of Chŏllima, to give employment to those diverted from heavy industry, and to give the people a feeling of accomplishment. In this manner, the earlier poor planning could be remedied and the Kim regime could make political gains at the same time.

North Korea's population has not witnessed a complete reversal of policy, and emphasis on heavy industry has not been renounced, nor has the Chŏllima Movement been discarded. The people probably feel that such increases in consumer goods and cultural facilities as have emerged are the direct and intended outgrowth of the successful Five Year Plan.

The Seven Year Plan is remarkable in that the regime is stressing light industry over heavy industry during the first three years. This does not mean, of course, that *primary* investment is in light industry—percentage of investment in light industry increased from 18.4 per cent of total investment in industry in 1959 to 36.3 per cent in 1962, whereas heavy industrial investment decreased correspondingly from 81.6 per cent to 63.7 per cent. The regime has felt this change in emphasis sufficient to require justification in Marxist-Leninist dogma: the justification being that since this is only to be the case for three years out of the seven, the emphasis on heavy industry for the plan as a whole is maintained.

Independent Economy and the Seven Year Plan: Before the announcement of the output goals for the Seven Year Plan, both the USSR and Red China presented plans for giving substantial aid to North Korea for its fulfillment. The Soviet Union, however, did not anticipate the nature of the plans to be announced. Interested in securing raw materials from Korea, the USSR was willing to give aid to develop the mining industries. The plan of the DPRK to develop its own processing plants for materials, rather than directly exporting raw ores, apparently brought down the wrath of "elder brother." Trade figures between North Korea and the Soviet Union for the first three years of the Seven Year Plan indicate that by

TABLE 34-3. USSR-DPRK TRADE (US$ million)

	Soviet Exports	Soviet Imports
1963	82.1	88.1
1962	80.7	88.2
1961	77.0	79.1

Source: Official statistics of the USSR.

striking out in an independent direction, the Kim Il-sŏng regime has been forced to pay for every bit of equipment and material from the USSR, and that no Soviet aid has actually been forthcoming. [Table 34–3]

North Korea has apparently felt that her economic and hence political independence from the Soviet Union was worth the loss of aid. The USSR, however, remains the most important trading partner for North Korea. China cannot supply the industrial equipment and materials which are required for North Korea's economic development. These must come from

Russia and the East European countries unless they are obtained from Japan or the West. It is evident that trade with the Soviet-East European bloc has not decreased despite North Korea's position on the side of China in the Sino-Soviet dispute. It is nevertheless true that North Koreans are eager to diversify their trade relations so as not to remain dependent upon the Soviet Union in this area. Non-Communist trade relations have not yet developed significantly, however, for although North Korea now trades with a large number of countries, the actual total amount of trade with each is quite small. Japan seems to be the only non-Communist country with whom the total trade exceeds $1 million—the North Korea-Japan trade is around $4 million per year.[6] Contrast this with the trade with Soviet Union, and the North Korean dilemma becomes clear.

The outlook for agriculture: One area which was to be stressed during the first three years of "consolidation of heavy industry" under the Seven Year Plan was agriculture. Official North Korean statistics indicate that the planned annual output by the end of the Five Year Plan was reached by 1960. A U.S. State Department report,[7] however, says that North Korea has exaggerated its farm output since 1957, claiming a 50 per cent increase in grain output between 1957 and 1961. This increase, according to the analysis, has not shown up in the observed consumption levels, and is not justified by the claimed production inputs, especially since the regime has showed increased concern over the level of farm output and the inefficient use of greater inputs. Also, the collectivization of agriculture, creating a new method of reporting agricultural production, interfered with the collection of accurate statistical reporting by placing officials in a position in which they were pressured into inflated production claims. Since the preparation of this memorandum, it has been learned that agricultural organization has been improved, but agricultural statistics are no longer available.

The memorandum goes on to analyze the official statistics and to revise them in the light of other evidence as follows:

Although North Korea is able to import agricultural products, it is her hope to become self-sufficient in agriculture, for agricultural imports still accounted for about one-fifth of her total imports in 1961,[8] and agricultural output has apparently not increased measurably since that time. Decrease in agricultural imports would permit an increase of imports of materials necessary to her industrial expansion.

It can be seen that agricultural cooperativization has not permitted a very large increase in grain production, although a substantial amount of

[6] According to V. Wolpert, "Turns in North Korea Trade," *Far Eastern Economic Review* (Feb. 13, 1964), p. 387, it is about £1.5 million. (£1 = US$2.80).

[7] *The Role of Agriculture in North Korea's Development,* U.S. Dept. of State, Research Memorandum, RSB–105, June 21, 1962 (unclassified).

[8] *Chosŏn Chungang Nyongkam, 1962* (Korean Central Yearbook, 1962), Pyongyang, 1962.

TABLE 34-4. GRAIN OUTPUT (In million metric tons)

	Official Claims	Adjusted Total
1956	2.873	2.792
1957	3.201	2.982
1958	3.700	3.240
1959	3.400	2.278
1960	3.803	2.781
1961	4.830	3.378

Source: See footnote 7.

farm mechanization has been accomplished and thus much of rural man-power has been released for employment in other areas of the economy. It does not seem that the prospects for self-sufficiency in agriculture are very bright. Little, if any, expansion of cultivated land area will be possible, and the regime seems unable to increase grain production fast enough to keep up with the population. The population has increased 27 per cent since 1953; grain production, according to the revised statistics, has increased less than 20 per cent. In addition, the land now under cultivation may be decreasing in fertility, as indicated by the above-mentioned memorandum (p. 11):

There is considerable suspicion that the North Korean regime, desperate to increase its food supplies, has followed in its corn measures a policy designed to increase current output at the expense of the long-term fertility of the land. Corn acreage reached 69% of the dry-land area planted to crops in 1958 and rose to 81% in 1961, indicating that on much of the land there have been successive corn crops and no crop rotation.

The 1961 farm plan announced at the beginning of the year provided for a doubling of the fertilizer application per hectare on corn fields, from 150 kgs. to 300 kgs., suggesting that the depletion of soil fertility was becoming a factor of concern to the regime.

Standard of living: Living standards of the North Korean people have not been high at any time, but they have shown indications of improvement over the past few years. Increased emphasis on light industry during 1960 and the first three years of the Seven Year Plan may have brought more consumer goods into circulation. During the same period "investment" in education and culture, housing, public facilities, and commerce and social services received larger percentages of the total state expenditure than they had during the preceding years.

Although indications are that the amount of food produced domestically, added to that imported, means a sufficient amount of food in terms of calorie intake for the population, this does not indicate a healthy food standard. A large percentage of the population must subsist almost exclusively on grain products. Because livestock raising is not very developed, practically the only source of animal protein is fish, and yet much of the fish catch is exported every year to pay for imports of machinery.

As of 1961, the total area of dwelling houses destroyed during the Korean War had not yet been replaced. According to official statistics, 28,000,000 square meters of dwelling houses were destroyed in the war, and only 24,650,000 square meters were built during the period 1953–61. When the population increase over this period is taken into consideration (a 3 to 4 million, or almost 50 per cent, population increase is claimed), living conditions must certainly be low despite recent gains.

Nevertheless, it was pointed out by British businessmen who had visited North Korea in 1958 and who returned again in 1964,[9] that a great deal of progress has been made in that five year period. In Pyongyang's shops, they said, locally built bicycles, electrical household goods, and various consumer goods were on sale. Also, the trolley cars in Pyongyang and the tractors in the countryside were made in North Korea. They felt that considerable improvements had been made.

Prospects for the Seven Year Plan: It might be expected that the North Korean regime had learned a great deal from the difficulties encountered during the Five Year Plan. One might anticipate much more careful planning, an emphasis on setting realistic goals and adhering to them, and a cut-back of the insistence on over-exertion and over-production which brought about a lack of coordination and an excess of strain under the Five Year Plan. On the contrary, though expansion of heavy industry was not planned for the first three years of the Seven Year Plan, the main ills do not seem to have been successfully rectified.

The Chŏllima Movement, a psychological weapon to prod the toiling masses, has been receiving continued and growing stress. In 1960, the number of persons involved in the Chŏllima Movement was 438,000. In 1961, this number increased to 2,810,000, and in 1963, to 3,210,000. In 1960, 21,000 persons received Chŏllima medals. This number was 210,000 in 1961. Chŏllima Work Teams numbered 911, 8,600, and 17,000, in 1960, 1961, and 1963 respectively, and Twice-Chŏllima Teams (apparently those which had received two awards) were 16 in 1960, 81 in 1961, and 179 in 1963. While such incentives are useful to a certain extent, they create trouble when carried so far as to become a type of coercion bringing about the exhaustion of machinery, available supplies, and most of all, workers.

The plans for output under the Seven Year Plan do not seem to have been worked out by careful attention to economic principles. The expected growth rate has apparently been chosen arbitrarily, without consideration for limiting factors which might enter into the possibilities for production

[9] V. Wolpert, *op. cit.,* p. 386.

during a seven year period. Thus the goal for grain production during the Seven Year Plan is especially unrealistic, considering the "law of diminishing returns" in agriculture.

The output goals for the plan are as follows:

TABLE 34-5.

Product	Measure	1960 Output	Five Year Plan Annual Output Goal
Total Grain Harvest	metric tons	3,803,000*	
		2,781,000**	6,600,000
Textiles	meters	189,699,000	500,000,000
Electric Power	billion kwh	9.139	20.0
Coal	metric tons	10,620,000	25,000,000
Steel	metric tons	641,000	2,300,000
Chemical Fertilizer	metric tons	561,000	1,700,000
Cement	metric tons	2,285,000	4,500,000

Source: Official North Korean statistics.
*Claimed output.
**Output as revised by Department of State memorandum.

The lesson of 1959 was apparently taken inversely by the regime. North Korea saw that while the Chŏllima Movement did produce real strains in the economy, it also did increase production considerably. Therefore, they apparently reasoned, if the production goals were set high enough in the first place, there would be no need for revision of the plans, which caused the administrative problems of 1959–60.[10]

Official statistics on production for 1961, 1962, 1963, and 1964, indicate that no product of our series is increasing at a rate sufficient to meet the Seven Year Plan. In 1963 none of the seven major products, with the highly improbable exception of grain (as data are not available) was able to meet the expected growth rate under the Seven Year Plan. None of the published annual plans for the seven major products was met. Textile and steel production dropped below the 1962 level of output. [Table 34–6]

The 1964 figures which are available make an even poorer showing. The increases in cement and steel are small, chemical fertilizer declined,

10 This writer has an interesting theory on how the Seven Year Plans were derived: If for each product we make a graph and plot the 1959 and 1960 outputs, then draw a straight line through these to 1967, we will cross the 1967 line at exactly the output figure projected for 1967. What an easy way to plan an economy! Joungwon Kim, *North Korea's Economic Progress, 1946–1963*, a monograph reproduced by the U.S. Department of State, has graphs of plans and outputs for this series of products through 1963. Also see this monograph for more complete figures and tables.

TABLE 34-6.

Product	Measure	1960	1961	1962	1963	1964	1965	1966	1967
Grain	million metric tons								
7 year plan[1] (a)[2]		3.803	4.115	4.452	4.818	5.212	5.640	6.102	6.600
7 year plan (b)[3]		2.781	3.146	3.560	4.028	4.558	5.157	5.835	6.600
annual plan			4.803	5.000	5.000	n.a. (same as 1963)			
actual (claimed)		3.803	4.830	5.000	n.a.				
Electric Power	billion kilowatt hours								
7 year plan		9.139	10.220	11.429	12.781	14.293	15.984	17.875	20.000
annual plan			n.a.	n.a.	n.a.	10.715			
actual		9.139	10.000	11.445	11.766	n.a.			
Coal	million metric tons								
7 year plan		10.620	12.000	13.560	15.323	17.315	19.566	22.110	25.000
annual plan			n.a.	15.000	15.000	n.a.	20.000		
actual		10.620	11.764	13.200	14.040	n.a.			
Steel	million metric tons								
7 year plan		.641	.769	.923	1.108	1.330	1.596	1.915	2.300
annual plan			n.a.	1.200	1.200	1.167			
actual		.641	.775	1.050	1.020	1.130			
Chemical fertilizer	million metric tons								
7 year plan		.561	.657	.770	.902	1.056	1.237	1.449	1.700
annual plan			n.a.	n.a.	n.a.	.950			
actual		.561	.662	.779	.853	.640			
Textiles	million meters								
7 year plan		189.659	217.823	250.170	287.320	329.987	378.990	435.270	500.000
annual plan				250.000	300.000	300.000			
actual		189.659	n.a.	256.000	227.000	n.a.			
Cement	million metric tons								
7 year plan		2.285	2.517	2.773	3.055	3.365	3.707	4.084	4.500
annual plan			n.a.	n.a.	n.a.	2.780			
actual		2.285	2.270	2.376	2.530	2.610			

[1] Annual amounts figured from rate of increase needed to meet Seven Year Plan.
[2] Claimed 1960 output as starting point.
[3] Revised 1960 output as starting point.

425

and statistics for the other four products were not even released. The 1964 annual plan envisaged a 21 per cent increase in industrial production, but the claimed achievement was 17 per cent.

Each year it has become more obvious that the Seven Year Plan is unrealistic. The 1964 plan for output of electricity was even less than the actual (claimed) output of 1962. The 1964 annual plan for steel was lower than the 1962 and 1963 plans for steel—which were not met. All of the 1964 plans, in fact, were an admission that the expected Seven Year Plan growth rate would not be achieved.

Beginning in the fall of 1962, the North Korean government started to emphasize the importance of strengthening defense—even to the point that at the Fifth Plenum of the Fourth Party Congress, December 10–14, 1962, defense was the primary topic on the agenda and it was suggested that economic plans might have to suffer for the sake of increased defense measures. During 1963 and 1964, hate-America campaigns have been featured by the North Korean press. Photos of bodies of people killed during the Korean War were displayed, and horrible war stories have been continually recounted. This new emphasis on defense may have two causes: it may be a cover-up for plans which cannot be met, or it may represent an actual diversion of resources to defense to make up for decreasing dependence upon the Soviet Union since the Sino-Soviet split. In either case, the anti-American campaign prepares the people for the excuse that the plans are not being met because funds are being diverted into defense expenditures.

Summary: North Korea has tried, with a fair amount of success, to expand its economy while making itself as nearly self-sufficient as possible. The regime is adamant in its desire to be economically independent. North Korea aims at becoming the "industrial Switzerland of Asia," supplying machinery and highly processed steel and other metals to other Communist nations in Asia. However admirable this goal may be, it is not likely to be achieved during the present Seven Year Plan or for a long time thereafter. The goals which North Korea has set for herself within the next few years are far beyond her present capabilities. This is, of course, not to say that North Korea has made little progress. Her development has been considerable when measured by standards other than her own unrealistic plans. It is questionable, however, whether she can continue to grow at a rate anywhere near that of the past ten years.

The obstacles she has come up against are many: 1. the production limits of many products, particularly in agriculture, have very nearly been reached; 2. technological advancement is slow partly due to the fact that the Soviet Union is apparently giving little technical aid (witness the North Korean statements that they must develop and become dependent upon their own "techniques"); 3. it is inevitable, considering the small area and limited resources, that the rapid postwar growth rate must decline without continuous stimulus from larger economic areas; 4. the North Korean attempt to develop her economic independence has undoubtedly forced her to shoulder a much larger portion of her military expenditures than might otherwise have been necessary—diverting her resources away from the push for industrial growth; 5. North Korea has already shown evidence of a manpower shortage, and this can be expected to become more severe, at least temporarily, in the next few years when the Korean War babies begin entering the labor market.

North Korea is an area too small to be economically independent for any extended period of time, yet one which has an intense desire to demonstrate its political independence within the Communist camp. Its greatest hopes lie in reaching out for further trade with the West, which it has begun to do in feeble fashion. The West, however, is not likely to provide a significant amount of trade so long as North Korea remains politically closed. The regime is hampered also by its unwillingness to expand trade to any great degree with Japan, due to its fear of becoming too dependent upon that nation. Perhaps the day will come when the North Korean regime decides that trading openly with both "camps" will be the best way to maintain both its economic and political independence.

35 ADRIAN A. BASORA

CUBA: CASTROIST COMMAND

THE SETTING

A very brief glimpse at pre-Castro Cuba, and at the nature of the revolutionary group which dislodged the Batista government in January 1959, is a necessary background for a study of the Cuban economic experience under communism.

As of the end of 1958, Cuba was by most economic criteria one of the two or three most advanced countries in Latin America. Per capita income stood at several hundred dollars, urban population was on the verge of outbalancing rural, and a substantial majority of the population was listed as literate. More directly relevant to the economic goals of the Castro revolution, however, were Cuba's very wide disparities in income distribution, her high rate of unemployment, her dependence on one crop (sugar) for 80 to 90% of export earnings, and her overwhelming reliance on the U.S. as trade partner and source of capital, technology and managerial skill.

Whatever the real economic benefits to Cuba of her relationship to the U.S., Fidel Castro and many of those closest to him when he came to power found the island's subsidized client status humiliating. They claimed that the relationship was exploitative and economically detrimental. Furthermore, they were sharply critical of many other aspects of the socio-economic situation under Batista: income distribution, unemployment, illiteracy, and sugar dependency were the most prominent targets.

Radical anti-Americanism, and a drive toward elimination of U.S. influence upon Cuba also had a powerful impact on the revolution's economic course, with regard to both foreign trade and internal economic goals. The quest for "total independence" was a major factor in the early Castroite stress on creating import-substitution industries and on developing domestic food production as a means of eliminating Cuba's dependence on the U.S. for supplies. Furthermore, once Cuban-American relations had reached the point of total rupture—more as a result of political than economic considerations—Castro had no place to turn to but the Soviet Union and other communist countries to supply investment goods and in

Reprinted from *ASTE Bulletin*, Summer 1966, by permission of the author and the Association for the Study of Soviet-Type Economies. The paper has been revised and updated by the author.

general to take up the vast trade slack which resulted. The resultant bonds of dependence were of themselves a further factor pushing Cuba toward adoption of economic patterns closely akin to those of the Soviet Union and other communist countries.

THE INFLUENCE OF IDEOLOGY AND MYSTIQUE ON CASTROITE ECONOMICS

After espousing vaguely defined variants of "humanism," democratic reformism, and radical nationalism during his early months in power, Fidel Castro moved rapidly toward verbal commitment to an imported ideology and toward imitation of foreign political and economic patterns. By 1961, Castro was unconditionally calling himself a Marxist-Leninist and attempting to remake most of Cuba's institutions in a communist mold. Despite the Cuban revolutionary's originality, verging on "deviationism," in foreign policy and in revolutionary theory as it impinges upon the international communist movement, Castroism has been fairly orthodox at home. Nevertheless, Fidel Castro's unique personality and political style, and the historical and geopolitical context of the Cuban revolution, probably assure significant variation from the Soviet economic and political model.

Of particular relevance to Cuban economic theory and practice are the extreme romanticism and impatience for quick results which run through the Castroite mystique, and the cardinal Castro-Guevara ideological tenet of peasant-based revolution.[1]

The thesis that Castro's successful insurgency was based essentially upon the peasantry and the rural proletariat—put forward most forcefully by Ernesto "Che" Guevara—had implications for the economic pattern adopted by the Cubans in the early years of the revolution. A commitment to raise rural living standards, to educate the peasantry, and to execute a rapid agrarian reform, prompted many of the regime's early reforms and its redistribution of income and services in favor of the rural sector. The commitment was based on no more complex a theory than that of peasant-based revolution, and the importance of keeping that sector of Cuban society fully behind Castro. The guerrilla leader's prolonged exposure to rural poverty and seasonal unemployment, particularly among the cane workers, may also have been a factor in this, and in the regime's heavy stress on rapid industrialization and on diversification of agriculture away from sugar.

---

[1] Theodore Draper offers the best available treatment of the ideological and experimental background of Castroism, and particularly of its theory of peasant-based revolution. See especially the first two chapters of *Castroism: Theory and Practice* (New York, 1965).

Also implicit in Castroism is a theory of voluntarism and of impatience with existing realities. In the international communist movement, Castro and his backers have become associated with the call for immediate armed struggle and the attempt to create the "objective conditions" for revolutionary success through guerrilla action. Similarly, the Cuban leaders have shown a strong tendency to seek immediate domestic results in the economic sphere by attempting to impose their will, often in disregard of the objective conditions of resource availability.

"Men with an acutely short-range perspective of taking power could not adapt themselves to a patiently long-range economic program in power. In communist terms, they have largely substituted the 'subjective' elements of revolutionary will or 'consciousness' for the 'objective' factor of the 'productive forces' at their disposal. Just as they have maintained that armed struggle would create the objective conditions to justify it, so they have decided that revolutionary 'consciousness' will bring forth 'productive forces' to fulfill it."[2]

Along with this voluntarism (or subjectivism) and impatience, the "bearded ones" brought a heavy dose of romanticism, utopianism, and stubborn dogmatism to their economic tasks. The same optimism and determination that carried Castro and his followers through their early hardships against seemingly impossible odds remained with them when they were confronted with the business of running the economy. In their romantic but economically naive view, it was possible to better the life of the rural and urban poor, to diversify agriculture and industry, to move rapidly towards socialism, to eliminate all dependence on the U.S., and to achieve a 15 per cent annual economic growth rate—all at one and the same time.

These strands of Castroism explain much of the revolution's early socio-economic policy—and most of its economic blunders. Since about 1963, Soviet "guidance", and the lessons derived from economic setbacks and from increasing experience in managing the economy, have led Cuba's leaders toward more realism and greater orthodoxy in economic matters. Ideology and mystique have nevertheless remained important factors in Cuban economic planning.

THE EVOLUTION OF CUBAN ECONOMIC
GOALS AND PRIORITIES

In contrast with the clear and emphatically pursued industrialization targets of Stalinism, the economic aims of Castroism have changed significantly over time and even now remain somewhat more diversified and fluid. In the original flush of their revolutionary élan, Castro, Guevara, and

[2] Draper, p. 219, *op. cit.*

others who helped shape early economic policy espoused a wide and ambitious range of objectives; they proceeded to pursue all of them with utmost haste.[3] Rapid agrarian reform, nationalization of foreign assets, redistribution of income and of other social benefits to favor the lower classes, agricultural diversification, elimination of Cuba's high economic reliance on the U.S., speedy industrialization—all these major objectives were pursued simultaneously during the first two or three years of the revolution. The early implicit assumption was that all of this could be done at little cost to the rest of the economy: only a moderate de-emphasis of sugar production was envisaged, along with a cut in the high living standards of the upper and upper middle classes. Only after the impossibility of rapid progress along all fronts at once became obvious did the Castro régime define a new and clearer set of goals and priorities.

After the disastrous sugar harvests and other economic failures of 1962 and 1963, however, Castro and his advisers were forced to undertake a massive reappraisal of the possible. Beginning in mid-1963 they began to make public references to new emphases and plans and soon began to trace carefully delineated and very different economic development paths for Cuba.[4] Absolute pre-eminence for sugar production—reminiscent of Stalin's all-out stress on heavy industry—was reinstated as a deliberate goal. Castro and other spokesmen admitted that the rate of non-sugar industrial investment would have to be cut back in order to concentrate sufficient resources on sugar, and it soon became clear that the earlier goals of industrialization and increased welfare and private consumption would have to be largely deferred for Cuba to meet the very concrete and ambitious goal of producing 10 million tons of sugar by 1970.[5]

Secondary emphasis was given to cattle and tobacco production, with the eventual goal of developing significant supplementary exports.[6] This made Cuba's development path an even more predominantly agricultural one. There was of course much exhortation to maintain high levels of production in other sectors, but the absolute priority of sugar was made clear from the start. The decision to defer consumption increases, although less openly discussed by the Castro government, has become just as clearly fixed a feature of Cuban development policy.

But even with the new clarity of definition which they gained after 1962, Cuban economic priorities remain less single-minded than were

[3] Draper, op. cit., and René Dumont, in Cuba: Socialisme et Développement (Paris, 1964); each give brief but useful histories of the Cuban economy since 1959.

[4] The most authoritative early statements of the new policy were contained in Fidel Castro's speeches of August 10 and November 1, 1963.

[5] Cuban production had occasionally reached peaks in the 6–7 million ton range, but production under Castro had slid to 4.5 million tons in 1962 and 3.8 million in 1963. For statistics on yearly Cuban sugar production from 1950 to 1963, see Cuba: Agriculture and Planning 1963–1964 (Miami, 1965), page 94. (Hereafter referred to as Agriculture.)

[6] See Fidel Castro's speech of July 26, 1965.

Stalin's. Castro's economic goals remain more diversified than were Stalin's. Room has been left for considerable investment in infrastructure, particularly in education and a significant (even though much reduced) level of investment in industry; and the régime has shown an unwillingness to cut back very far on private consumption (although the unavoidable sharp drops of 1962–63 have probably not been restored). Perhaps the most graphic index of the régime's lesser single-mindedness is the fact that the country's stated investment rate has not gone beyond 15–20 per cent, as compared with Stalinist Russia's rate of 25–30 per cent.

THEORY VS. PRACTICE

The statement of goals and priorities by Cuban leaders, and their theories about the island's optimal path of economic development, are of course only a partial guide to the nature of the Cuban growth pattern. The actual practice of Cuban economic policy—the real allocation of the island's principal productive resources—provides the indispensable counterpart to their words. Fortunately for the analyst, the verbal pattern has increasingly coincided with practice in the last few years, and public economic policy formulations have thus become a relatively useful predictive tool for the future course of Cuban development efforts. The allocation of capital, of labor, of consumption goods, of land and raw materials, and of foreign exchange has undergone a definite shift to reflect the régime's new, and for the most part explicitly stated or clearly implied, priorities.

THE INVESTMENT PATTERN

The allocation of capital is the best single index of actual—rather than theoretical—development priorities. Cuba presently shows a relatively high rate of investment for the economy as a whole, although not much above the rate which prevailed before Castro's takeover. Gross investment is now variously estimated at 18–20 per cent of GNP.[7] The Cubans have clearly committed themselves to seek a rapid rate of growth but, just as clearly, the pace of the effort remains considerably more relaxed than that of the

[7] *Economic Survey of Latin America 1963* (UN, 1965), page 288, puts the rate of investment at nearly 18% yearly during 1961–63; Charles Bettelheim, who has also had access to official Cuban statistics calculates 1962 investment at 19% and 1963 at 20%, but says that the rate has since been slowed down somewhat. See his article in *Economie et Politique* (Paris, July 1965), pages 75–6. The ECLA Bulletin for October 1959 (p. 62, Table 7) placed the 1956–58 rate in the same range (18–20%) although the present government claims that the pre-Castro rate was only 14–15%.

Stalinist model. Not only is the Cuban rate of overall investment considerably lower than that of the USSR during the early five-year plans, but the strain of the Cuban development tempo has been further mitigated by the heavy import subsidy provided by the USSR and other communist countries. The rate of growth which the Cubans can in fact hope to achieve with a given level of investment is diminished, however, by the high depreciation rate of their extensively U.S.-origin pre-1959 capital stock. Maintenance is significantly impeded by the American embargo whereby service and replacement parts are presently denied. For this and other reasons, the Cuban growth rate is probably well below target levels.

The structure of Cuban investment has reflected an increasingly high priority for quick-yield investments rather than deferred growth. By 1963, investment in the (directly) "productive sectors"—agriculture, industry, construction, transport, communications, commerce—reached 70 per cent of total investment. Outlays for infrastructure and related social services, which as late as 1961 had claimed nearly half of all investment, dropped to 30 per cent of the 1963 investment budget.[8] And, even within the categories of productive investment, the stress has shifted strongly in favor of agricultural production, and thus toward investments which should show a relatively rapid payoff. New projects in electric power, heavy industry, and other major enterprises with long gestation periods have been largely deferred beyond 1970.

The percentage of investment devoted directly to sugar and cattle has itself risen notably, and a substantial portion of the remaining expenditures for industry, transport, and power are for productive facilities and infrastructure supportive of agriculture such as fertilizer production, field-to-factory transportation facilities, mechanical harvesting equipment, etc.[9] Although many of the projects begun during Cuba's period of unrealistic stress on industry have been or are soon to be completed, the rate of progress on these has been slow, and few new projects are being considered for the industrial sector until after 1970.

Consumption, Social Welfare, and Defense: The "Non-Productive" Endeavors

As is implicit in the somewhat lower rate of investment and the substantial import subsidy provided by the Soviet Union, the Cuban leadership has devoted a considerably larger share of the gross national product to other than directly productive purposes than did the Russians

[8] Cuban investment in "social services" (education, housing, public health, etc.) dropped from 48.5% of total investment in 1961 to 29.6% in 1963: *Economic Survey of Latin America 1963*, page 288.

[9] Bettelheim, *op. cit.*, page 79.

of the Stalinist period. A large part of this relative surplus has gone for social welfare expenditures and to the maintenance of a standard of living that is still relatively high by communist standards. Although Cuban consumers suffered a sharp reversal, made graphic by the introduction of rationing in 1962–63,[10] consumer welfare probably still compares favorably with that of Stalinist Russia and with other communist societies during comparable periods in their economic development.

The island's lower economic classes (the peasantry, and rural and urban unskilled workers) substantially advanced their consumption between 1959 and 1961, and may on balance still be better off than they were before the revolution. The large number who were before seasonally or regularly unemployed are now consistent consumers on the market. Although private consumption by the skilled laboring classes and by the remnants of the old middle and upper classes has clearly declined since the revolution, it must be remembered that by 1958 these classes were already moderately affluent. Furthermore, given the socialist nature of the new Cuban economy, private consumption has become a less accurate gauge of individual economic welfare than it was in the past.

After 1959 public expenditures for social welfare[11] climbed sharply, at least until 1961. Particular stress was placed on public health and on crash programs for mass education. The lower classes also benefited from lower rents under a law heavily favoring tenants.

It would be difficult to develop any accurate quantitative method of comparison between the Cuba of the 1960's and the Soviet Union under Stalin. Yet it seems incontrovertible that the Cuban peasantry and unskilled laboring classes have not yet suffered the drastic cuts in consumption absorbed by these two sectors of Russian society under Stalin. The price paid by the more "privileged" Cuban classes has of course been substantial, particularly if reference is made to their past levels of consumption. But even here, their fate might seem mild if comparison were possible with the fate of the *kulaks* and the upper classes in Russia. In terms of consumption and social welfare (the latter measured in purely economic terms), Castro has thus far employed a more benign development formula than did Stalin.

The allocation of material resources to defense, which has long enjoyed very high priority in the Soviet Union, also constitutes an important element in Cuban priorities. Although it is difficult to quantify the comparison on the basis of available data,[12] the economic drain of military

[10] Dumont (pro-Castro) estimates the overall decline in living standards during this period at 15–20%; *op. cit.*, page 91.

[11] Much of this expenditure of course also serves the good of human resource development.

[12] By Cuban budget statistics for 1962, only 5 million pesos (of a total 1.6 billion budget) were set aside for "public defense." (*Agriculture*, p. 18). But this figure is grossly incompatible with the régime's claim (probably well-founded) that

expenditures on Cuba is probably substantially less than it was for Russia under Stalin. This appears likely largely because the cost of Cuban armaments seems to have been borne by the Soviet Union, whereas the Russians have long relied almost exclusively on their own defense production. Another factor is that the Cuban armed forces are to a significant extent used for economic ends.[13] Their primary contribution is in the sugar harvest and in other "emergency" tasks, but the armed forces are also designed as an auxiliary educational institution designed to turn out productive workers after three years of obligatory military service. The net economic contributions and costs of the Cuban military establishment would of course be extremely difficult to quantify. Nevertheless it seems plausible that, all things considered, the Cuban allocation of resources to defense has been proportionately less burdensome than in the Soviet Union.

THE ALLOCATION OF MANPOWER

In direct and striking contrast to the implicit theory of Stalinism, the Cuban leadership looks upon labor as a scarce resource. In the view of the country's economic planners, the "general labor shortage", and particularly the deficit in the agricultural sector, has become one of Cuba's most serious economic problems.[14] This is surprising not only as a contrast with the Stalinist model, but in its discrepancy with the experience of most underdeveloped countries.

As of 1958, Cuba was no exception to the general pattern of widespread unemployment and underemployment in the less developed countries. In that year 16 per cent of the labor force was listed as unemployed and an additional 10 per cent as subemployed.[15] By 1962, the new régime listed total subemployment at less than 9 per cent.[16] More recently, there has been repeated reference to labor shortages in agriculture and no mention of unemployment in the cities. In view of this, and of the fact that "volunteer" workers for agriculture are drawn mainly from government offices and factories, one must presume that Cuba has somehow exhausted its supply of employable labor. Thus, whereas Stalinist economic planners could attempt to obtain maximum use of other scarce resources—espe-

the Cuban armed forces are "the most powerful in Latin America." Since reliable statistics on military size and budget are unavailable, the most one can say with confidence is that military expenditures are probably a major factor in the Cuban economy.

[13] Draper, *op. cit.* p. 175 ff., outlines the thesis that compulsory military service had either as its main reason or its principal byproduct the creation of "a cheap, militarized labor corps."

[14] Carlos Romeo, in *Cuba Socialista,* December 1965, pp. 18–19.

[15] *Agriculture,* p. 19.

[16] *Ibid.*

cially of capital goods—by intensive use of manpower, the Cubans are presently attempting to increase the productivity of a deficient labor force by the relatively generous use of capital goods. This is true particularly in agriculture, where the régime is attempting to relieve the labor shortage through mechanization, particularly in sugar harvesting and loading.

There are several reasons for Cuba's dramatic shift from labor redundancy to labor scarcity. According to government statistics, out of the 1962 labor force of 2.4 million, 493,000 were occupied as students or as soldiers.[17] This represented an increase of 300,000 over 1958 in these largely non-productive categories,[18] and we can assume that the number has since mounted, particularly with the introduction of obligatory military service at the end of 1963. The mass exodus of Cuban refugees (over 300,000 since 1959) was a further cause of labor force depletion. It was mainly members of the middle and upper classes who went into exile. Although some of those who left had performed functions that were eliminated with the adoption of socialism, a much greater number were engaged in essential activities. The bulk of the refugees who had been economically active had to be replaced in one form or another.

Decreasing productivity of labor must clearly also be a significant factor underlying the current shortage of workers. For a variety of reasons, Cuban worker productivity fell notably, particularly in the early years of the revolution.[19] Poor management, inadequate technical direction, decreasing material incentives to production,[20] and frequent work stoppages and other types of inefficiency caused by equipment breakdowns (resulting from poor maintenance and an absence of replacement parts), all played a part. A related factor in the general decrease of productivity and the scarcity of manpower was the burgeoning of an inefficient government bureaucracy, a trend which the regime has taken drastic measures to reverse by its longstanding "campaign against bureaucracy".

The Castro government is engaging in a variety of efforts to compensate for the labor shortage, such as extensive mobilization of "volunteer" agricultural workers during harvests,[21] adoption of an incentive-

[17] *Ibid.*

[18] But it must be remembered that students and conscripts perform a sizeable portion of the "volunteer" labor done in Cuba.

[19] See Dumont, Bettelheim, Romeo, *opere citata* for full discussions of the fall in productivity.

[20] Real-wage incentives decreased because of a shrinking supply of consumer goods and because wages were no longer pegged to productivity.

[21] It is interesting to note that, whereas Stalin had to encourage the flow of labor to the cities artificially, the Castro régime has had the opposite problem. According to Labor Ministry statistics, as of 1965, 58% of the labor force was in the cities, as compared to only 49% in 1962. The government has pointed to over-urbanization as a serious problem, and has taken various steps to rebuild or temporarily replenish the agricultural labor force. (See *Cuba Socialista,* September 1965, p. 38, and *passim.*)

wage system, lengthening of the work week, the use of education and foreign technical assistance to improve the output of the labor force, stress on better management, and of course abundant resort to all forms of exhortation.

There has been considerable debate inside Cuba on the question of moral vs. material incentives to induce greater labor productivity. Thus far a strong strain of revolutionary voluntarism has combined with the great difficulty of importing or producing more consumer goods to keep the emphasis on "moral" incentives or exhortation. So far there is little sign that this approach will result in sustained increases in Cuban labor productivity. Thus, to all appearances, Cuba will be relying heavily on an increasing input of power and machines—rather than efficient man-hours—to augment production.

Allocation of Land and Raw Materials

In practice, during the first few years of the revolution, land was treated as a relatively abundant resource. There was some extension of the cultivated area, often to the detriment of valuable pastures and forests. But, because the early emphasis was on industry rather than on agriculture, the régime made little effort to increase Cuba's relatively low yields in sugar cane and other farm products. Indeed, per hectare yields appear to have fallen substantially between 1958 and 1962.[22] Since then, with the new emphasis on agricultural development, the régime has realized that Cuba's land resources have very definite limits, despite the island's rich soils and generally high rainfall. Castro has noted that there is often a net disadvantage in plowing up pastures and forests. Although some net increase of the cultivated area may still be under way, there is a definite move towards more intensive land use. Plans are afoot to accelerate the use of irrigation and fertilizers, and to introduce more advanced techniques in planting, harvesting, animal husbandry, etc. The sugar and cattle industries, as mentioned previously, are to receive prime attention. The goal is to develop a mechanized, high-yield sugar industry which would make it possible to raise production from 6 million tons (achieved in 1965 and 1967) to 10 million tons in 1970, without substantially increasing the planted surfaces.[23]

Cuban cattle-raising is theoretically slated for the same type of development. The government plans to secure large increases in production

[22] See *Agriculture*, p. 67 and ff., for yield statistics and a discussion of the reasons for the decline.

[23] The ten million ton goal was first mentioned in 1963; it has since been repeated incessantly. Castro's speech of July 24, 1965 to the canecutters is one of the fullest treatments available on how the goal is to be achieved.

through artificial insemination, the use of prepared feeds to supplement grazing, and other technologically advanced methods, rather than through the use of extensive grazing. As a supplement to land production, now that land is seen as a relatively scarce resource, the Cubans have also "defined in" the sea by creating a modern fishing industry (with large-scale Russian assistance).

With raw materials, as with land, the Castro government began its economic management on the implicit assumption of relative abundance —this, in a small country with a narrow range of natural resources. By the admission of "Che" Guevara, a prime exponent and principal architect of the régime's early plans for rapid industrialization, investments for industrial capacity were often made without reference to the availability of raw materials. In some cases, this resulted in the creation of plants whose imported production inputs turned out to cost more than it would have cost to purchase the finished product on the world market.[24]

As mentioned earlier, necessity forced a re-evaluation. The slowing of industrial investment has eased what would otherwise have been an impossible strain on foreign exchange to finance growing raw materials imports. Conversely, the new emphasis on agriculture is calculated to maximize the use of Cuba's own principal natural resources: land and climate. Furthermore, the government is attempting to lessen the waste or inefficient use of those raw materials which must be imported: the recent government campaign to slow the rapidly increasing consumption of petroleum products is a case in point. The foreign exchange constraint has forced Cuban planners to take account of Cuba's deficit in many of the raw materials needed for industrialization. Resource-poverty, rather than resource-abundance, is now implicit in Cuban planning.

THE ROLE OF FOREIGN TRADE

Since 1963, Fidel Castro has placed Cuba squarely on a nonautarchic path of economic development. The Cuban plan is the direct opposite of the Stalinist model with regard to foreign trade. Rather than limiting imports to absolute essentials and one-time purchases necessary to relieve bottlenecks, the Cuban government states that it has adopted the principle of "socialist international division of labor".[25] In fact, the main rationale given for the stress on sugar and cattle is the classic free trade

[24] Draper, op. cit., p. 153.
[25] See Cuba Socialista, December 1965 (article already cited) for a pointed and officially-sanctioned treatment of the principle of comparative advantage as the basis for Cuban economic plans.

principle of comparative advantage. By Cuban reasoning, it is now possible to admit to, and even to increase the island's preponderant reliance on foreign trade (elimination of which was one of the régime's early goals) now that there are guaranteed socialist markets for Cuban exports at "fair" prices. Accordingly, Cuba can now produce that for which the island is best suited without putting the economy at the mercy of "U.S. imperialism" or "the vicissitudes of the (capitalist) world market".

By stressing sugar and cattle, Cuba is resigning itself to remaining almost exclusively an agricultural exporter[26] for many years to come. In practice, the Cubans are not only basing their economy very heavily on foreign trade, but they are depending on the development of modern agricultural export industries to provide the economy with both the "leading sector" growth and the foreign exchange earnings necessary to spark the economy as a whole.

Although the structure of Cuban imports may have been shaped less by the theory of comparative advantage than by pragmatic considerations, necessity has imposed an import structure roughly in accord with what theory might have suggested. Because of the island's lack of heavy industry, nearly all new investment has a high import coefficient. And, given the high rate of investment, capital goods and other items related to investment constitute a very high proportion of all imports. Furthermore, of necessity a substantial portion of available foreign exchange must be spent for raw materials or for semi-finished goods needed as inputs to Cuban industrial and agricultural production. Only the small remainder of foreign exchange is available for expenditure on food, consumer goods and other necessities which Cuba might theoretically produce, but does not for reasons of efficiency (or, in effect, of comparative advantage).[27] It is in this area that the efficacy of the development route chosen by the Castro government will either prove or disprove itself. Thus far, despite massive subsidies on the part of the USSR, Cuba remains hard pressed to earn a sufficiency of the "comparatively advantageous" imports which the sugar and other export industries are supposed to finance.

The Cuban vs. the Soviet Development Model

While the stress of this paper has been largely on the differences, there are of course very important similarities between the Soviet and Cuban development paths. Cuba's is a communist economy in the full

[26] In the 1959–65 period sugar already accounted for 80–90% of all exports; see *Panorama Economico Latinoamericano*, Vol. 12, No. 147, p. 13.

[27] *Economic Survey of Latin America 1963*, p. 277.

sense of the word: the state has assumed ownership and direction of the vast majority of the country's productive resources; it has resorted to many of the mass-mobilization techniques of totalitarianism in attempting to assure desired economic performance; there has been heavy stress on developing one area of the economy as a leading sector; consumption and other areas of lesser priority are being deferred as a means of concentrating resources on favored goals. These are some of the more basic and obvious similarities.

But it is the areas of difference which raise some of the most interesting lines of inquiry and explanation. The Castro régime has embarked upon a non-autarchic, agriculture-based development strategy. It has chosen for the present to get along with a lower rate of investment than that which typified Stalinism; this has permitted better maintenance of minimum standards of consumption, welfare, and education. Finally, Cuba has enjoyed an outstandingly high per capita level of foreign economic and military assistance over a period of several years.

The reasons underlying the main economic differences between Castroism and Stalinism seem relatively easy to identify. The extreme differences in size, resource base, climate, and starting economic base clearly provide the main factors of difference. As Cuba's new leaders soon realized, to adopt literally the Stalinist rapid-industrialization/self-sufficiency model, in a country poor in minerals and in energy sources, and whose population was only seven million, would have been economically suicidal. To have attempted to institute the levels of coercion, depressed consumption, and the other hardships which Stalin was willing to inflict on the Russian people in exchange for high-tempo growth would probably have been politically suicidal during the early years of the Cuban revolution. This is particularly true because geopolitics and history placed the Cuban régime in a highly vulnerable situation which made political consolidation the *sine qua non* of all other Castroist goals.

Cuban development thus provides documentation of the thesis that objective material conditions are at least as important as ideology in shaping the actual course of communism. Nevertheless, it is equally true that communist theory, and a small group of willful men, did much to shape an economy that might have evolved very differently in a number of respects. To these factors of ideology and personal convictions should also be added the example and influence of other communist countries. Not only were the Cubans able to copy from the experience of the Soviet Union and other communist states, but, because of their heavy ties of dependence, they have presumably had to show themselves open to a noteworthy degree of economic suasion by their benefactors. The quests for autarchy and self-sufficient capital formation were made less necessary by the existence of other communist states willing to trade with and aid Cuba.

National character and political context also recommend themselves as worthy lines of inquiry. Because of the numerous exogenous factors at work—especially U.S. economic pressures and massive assistance from the Soviet Union—it is still too early to judge the adaptability of the Latin American character to communist political and economic patterns. Thus it would be pure speculation (though an interesting subject for debate) to suggest that the values and character of the Cuban people may be one reason for the Castro régime's inability to push Cuba towards a more dynamic tempo of growth. Furthermore, the political situation which obliges the Soviet Union and its allies to subsidize heavily, the Cuban economy is clearly a factor inducing the Castro government to feel that it can follow a more relaxed path.

It is still too early to make any firm forecasts as to the future course, and the probability of success or failure, of Cuba's economic development plans. If the régime succeeds in fostering a respectable growth rate despite the lighter domestic sacrifices (than under Stalinism) thus far exacted from the Cuban people, then Cuban development may become a model of some attractiveness in Latin America and elsewhere. If, despite massive Soviet bloc assistance, and despite the very real economic and political price many Cubans have had to pay, economic performance remains drab, then the argument will have been strengthened that communism cannot work in Latin America, or that rapid communist development can only be achieved through the heavy sacrifices implicit in the Stalinist model.

Suggested Reading

I. Command Revisionism in Eastern Europe

Gamarnikow, Michael, "The New Role of Private Enterprise," *East Europe*, Vol. 16, No. 8 (August 1967), pp. 2–9.

Mieczkowski, Bogdan, "The Unstable Soviet-Bloc Economies," *East Europe*, Vol. 16, No. 10 (October 1967), pp. 2–7.

Prybyla, Jan S., "Communism: Its Growing Diversity," *The Journal of General Education*, Vol. 18, No. 3 (October 1966), pp. 207–218.

Spulber, Nicolas, *The State and Economic Development in Eastern Europe* (New York, Random House, 1966).

"Those Economic Reforms Behind the Iron Curtain," A *Challenge* Interview with Abram Bergson, John M. Montias, and Arthur Smithies, *Challenge*, The Magazine of Economic Affairs (May–June 1967), pp. 18–23.

"Toward the Computer Age," *East Europe*, Vol. 16, No. 6 (June 1967), pp. 9–12.

Zebot, C. A., "Fifty Years of the October Revolution: Effects of Economic Reforms on Communist Systems," *Review of Social Economy*, March 1968.

II. Soviet Command Revisionism

Balinsky, A., Bergson, A., Hazard, A., and Wiles, P., *Planning and the Market in the USSR: The 1960's* (New Brunswick, N. J., Rutgers University Press, 1967).

Felker, Jeri L., *Soviet Economic Controversies: The Emerging Marketing Concept and Changes in Planning, 1960–1965* (Cambridge, M.I.T., 1966).

Feiwel, George R., *The Soviet Quest for Economic Efficiency: Issues, Controversies, and Reforms* (New York, Praeger, 1967).

Maddison, Angus, "Soviet Economic Performance," *Banca Nazionale del Lavoro Quarterly Review*, Vol. XVIII, No. 72 (March 1965), pp. 3–51.

Meissner, Boris, "The Soviet Union Under Brezhnev and Kosygin," *Modern Age*, Vol. 11, No. 1 (Winter 1966–67), pp. 7–23.

Prybyla, Jan S., "The Economic Problems of Soviet Russia in Transition," *The Indian Journal of Economics*, Vol. XLV, Part III, No. 177 (October 1964), pp. 135–151.

Prybyla, Jan S., "Soviet Economic Growth: Perspectives and Prospects," *The Quarterly Review of Economics and Business*, Vol. 4, No. 1 (Spring 1964), pp. 57–67.

Sharpe, Myron E. (ed.), *The Liberman Discussion: A New Phase in Soviet*

Economic Thought (White Plains, N.Y., International Arts and Sciences Press, 1966).

Sharpe, Myron E. (ed.), *Reform of Soviet Economic Management* (White Plains, N.Y., International Arts and Sciences Press, 1966).

Wiles, P. J. de la F., "The Political and Social Prerequisites for a Soviet-Type Economy," *Economica*, Vol. XXXIV, No. 133 (February 1967), pp. 1–19.

Zaleski, Eugène, *Planning Reforms in the Soviet Union, 1962–1966* (Chapel Hill, The University of North Carolina Press, 1967).

Zauberman, A., "Recent Developments in Soviet Planning Techniques," *Economia Internazionale*, Vol. XX, No. 2 (March 1967), pp. 255–277.

III. Chinese Command Revisionism

An Economic Profile of Mainland China, Joint Economic Committee, Congress of the United States (Washington, D.C., GPO, 1966; New York, Praeger, 1967).

Adams, Ruth (ed.), *Contemporary China* (New York, Vintage Books, 1966).

Barnett, A. Doak, *China After Mao (With Selected Documents)*, (Princeton, N.J., Princeton University Press, 1967).

Cheng, Chu-yuan, *Communist China's Economy, 1949–1962* (South Orange, N.J., Seton Hall University Press, 1963).

Cheng, Chu-yuan, "The Cultural Revolution and China's Economy," *Current History* (September 1967), pp. 148–154, 176–177.

"Chinese Economic Development Since the Revolution," *Science and Society* (Summer 1967), pp. 342–354.

Eckstein, Alexander, *Communist China's Economic Growth and Foreign Trade* (New York, McGraw-Hill, 1966).

Hsiao, Gene T., "The Background and Development of the Proletarian Cultural Revolution," *Asian Survey*, Vol. VII, No. 6 (June 1967), pp. 389–404.

Kosaka, Zentaro, "Visiting China in the Cultural Revolution," *United Asia*, Vol. 19, No. 1 (January–February 1967), pp. 34–40.

Prybyla, Jan S., "Moscow, Mao, and the Cultural Revolution," *International Review of History and Political Science*, December 1967.

Prybyla, Jan S. (ed.), *The Triangle of Power, Conflict, and Accommodation: The United States, the Soviet Union, Communist China* (University Park, Penn., The Pennsylvania State University, Center for Continuing Liberal Education, Slavic and Soviet Language and Area Center, 1967), Part III, pp. 63–94.

Prybyla, Jan S., "Sino-Soviet Economics," *The Quarterly Review*, July 1965, pp. 238–292.

Watson, Andrew, "Of Freaks and Monsters," *Far Eastern Economic Review*, August 24, 1967, pp. 373–376.

Wheelright, E. L., "Impressions of the Chinese Economy," *Outlook* (Australia), I: Vol. II, No. 3 (June 1967), pp. 7–11; II: Vol. II, No. 4 (August 1967), pp. 5–9.

IV. Rumania: Hesitant Command

Fischer-Galati, Stephen, *The New Rumania: From People's Democracy to Socialist Republic* (Cambridge, The M.I.T. Press, 1967).
Montias, John Michael, *Economic Development in Communist Rumania* (Cambridge, M.I.T., 1967).

V. East Germany: Steps Away from Command

Boehme, H., "East German Price Formation Under the New Economic System," *Soviet Studies*, January 1968.
Elliott, James R., and Scaperlanda, Anthony E., "East Germany's Liberman-Type Reforms in Perspective," *Quarterly Review of Economics and Business*, Autumn 1966, pp. 39–52.

VI. Poland: Reformist Command

Gamarnikow, Michael, "Poland: Political Pluralism in a One-Party State," *Problems of Communism*, Vol. XVI, No. 4 (July–August 1967), pp. 58–61.
Pajestka, Józef, "Certain Problems of Economic Planning in Poland," *Weltwirtschaftliches Archiv*, Vol. 92, No. 1 (1964), pp. 163–178.

VII. Czechoslovakia: Command and the Market

Brown, A. H., "Pluralistic Trends in Czechoslovakia," *Soviet Studies*, No. 4 (April 1966), pp. 453–472.
Goldman J., and Flek, J., "Economic Growth in Czechoslovakia," *Economics of Planning*, Vol. 6, No. 2 (1966).
Holesovsky, Vaclav, "Prague's Economic Model," *East Europe*, Vol. 16, No. 2 (February 1967), pp. 13–16.
Shaffer, Harry G., "Czechoslovakia's New Economic Model: Out of Stalinism," *Problems of Communism*, September–October 1965.
Sik, O., *Economic Planning and Management in Czechoslovakia*, 2nd rev. ed. (Prague, Orbis, 1966).
Prasad, S. B., "Prague Goes Pragmatic," *Columbia Journal of World Business*, Vol. II, No. 2 (March–April 1967), pp. 73–78.

VIII. Yugoslavia: Planned Market and Command

Friedmann, Wolfgang, "Freedom and Planning in Yugoslavia's Economic System," *Slavic Review,* December 1966, pp. 630–640.

Henessy, Jossleyn, "Yugoslavia in Transition," *Eastern Economist,* Vol. 47 (November 4, 1966), pp. 853–855.

Pejovich, Svetozar, *The Market-Planned Economy of Yugoslavia* (Minneapolis, University of Minnesota Press, 1966).

Shaffer, Harry G. (ed.), *The Communist World: Marxist and Non-Marxist Views* (New York, Appleton-Century-Crofts, 1967), Section IV, Chapters 7 and 8, pp. 219–288.

Stankovic, Slobodan, "Yugoslavia's Critical Year," *East Europe,* Vol. 16, No. 4 (April 1967), pp. 12–17.

Stojanovic, Rudmira (ed.), *Yugoslav Economists on Problems of a Socialist Economy* (White Plains, N.Y., International Arts and Sciences Press, 1966).

Zupanov, Josip, "The View from Zagreb," *Columbia Journal of World Business,* Vol. II, No. 4 (July–August 1967), pp. 67–72.

IX. Cuba: Castroist Command

A Study on Cuba. The Colonial and Republican Periods. The Socialist Experiment, The Cuban Economic Research Project (University of Miami, Coral Gables, University of Miami Press, 1965).

Alroy, Gil Carl, "The Peasantry in the Cuban Revolution," *The Journal of Politics,* Vol. 29, No. 1 (January 1967), pp. 87–99.

Bernheim, Robert, "Cuba's Permanent Revolution," *Swiss Review of World Affairs,* November 1966, pp. 9–12.

Devtin, Kevin, "The Permanent Revolution of Fidel Castro," *Problems of Communism,* January–February 1968, pp. 1–11.

Draper, Theodore, *Castroism: Theory and Practice* (New York, Praeger, 1965).

Huberman, Leo, and Sweezy, Paul M., *Cuba: Anatomy of a Revolution* (New York, Monthly Review Press, 1961).

Mesa-Lago, Carmelo, *The Labor Sector and Socialist Distribution in Cuba* (New York, Praeger, 1967).

O'Connor, J., "Agrarian Reforms in Cuba, 1959–1963," *Science and Society,* Spring 1968.

Seers, Dudley (ed.), *Cuba: The Economic and Social Revolution* (Chapel Hill, N.C., The University of North Carolina Press, 1964).

Zeitlin, Maurice, and Scheer, Robert, *Cuba: Tragedy in Our Hemisphere* (New York, Grove Press, 1963).

V

The Convergence
of Market-Oriented and
Command-Oriented Systems

Introduction

It is argued in some quarters that market-oriented and command-oriented economies are converging. The argument of convergence has been debated in the West and officially rejected in the Soviet Union. The typical Soviet reaction is summed up by L. Leontiev; the Western discussion is represented by Prybyla's and Shaffer's articles. The Western debate was launched by Jan Tinbergen in a study published in 1961 (see *Suggested Reading* at the end of Part V).

Parts III and IV and some of the analytical argument in Part I do, indeed, seem to suggest a converging movement of economies, the basic analytical models of which are very far apart. Market-oriented economies have, in fact, introduced important elements of command into their resource coordination and control functions, to the point where it is not inappropriate to speak of administered markets and prices. On the other hand, command systems have increasingly resorted to circumscribed markets to help them solve intricate problems of internal consistency and efficiency. (See, for example Czechoslovakia, Part IV.) Developing economies tend to use both central command and decentralized markets in their quest for modernization. The dividing line between private and public property structures has been blurred by the separation of legal ownership and actual possession, in other words, by the distinction between legal title to the means of production and the management of those means. Nominally private corporations in the West, especially those which by reason of their size, payroll, and turnover bear much weight in a market-oriented economy, are generally managed by salaried officials whose ownership share in the enterprises which they administer is nil or marginal. Questions of the public weal may, and in fact do, enter into the profitability calculus of these managers. In command-oriented economies, on the other hand, managers of state-owned enterprises are being given increasingly wide powers of decision-making within a broad and increasingly elastic framework of centrally-determined goals and policies.

The convergence argument is sometimes formulated in somewhat different, if related, terms. Economic development, so goes the argument, brings with it a widening of the range of choice, a much greater than before interrelationship and interdependence of decisions, and a complexity which call for careful marginal calculation, "rational" managerial behavior, and a minimum of ideological exultation in the day-to-day business of running the economy. Development introduces into the picture a technological and scientific element that was lacking before. Those charged with the conduct of the economy, especially the managers in effective possession of the means of production, must be equipped with an intellectual apparatus that emphasizes expertise, a quality, it is argued, in which the normative element is minimal. The exigencies of a highly integrated modern economic system, whatever its ideological label, are such as to impose on the participants in the economic process, roughly the same type of behavior. There is, according to this line of reasoning, little difference between the behavioral patterns of the managers at General Motors and those at the Likachev Automobile Works in Moscow. Specialized management is exercised in the setting of differential income incentives and cost calculations which implicitly or explicitly involve a charge for capital, with the help of mathematical tools and integrated computers. The corollary seems to be that the convergence of economic systems will bring with it a narrowing of differences in other areas of human action. The implication is that there is a close correlation between world economic wellbeing and worldwide peace and understanding. Irascible, exclusive ideological positions tend to be eroded by the ideologically neutral imperatives of the economic base. In short, the argument tends to suggest that conflicting ideologies will wither away under the combined onslaught of economists, econometricians, mathematicians, computer scientists, technicians of all kinds, chemists, physicists, and the like. The new society would be a combination of markets, commands, private and public property, each with many shadings, supplemented by new forms of economic organization. In its most extreme formulation, the convergence argument envisages the eventual coming of an ideology-free technocracy, a mass consumption mathematician's paradise. Some claim to see it happening already. Others, however, are not so sure.

Of the three essays included here, Shaffer's appears to be the most optimistic with regards to the convergence thesis. Leontiev rejects it as a myth thought up by the enemies of socialism. Prybyla has some misgivings about the validity of the argument, especially that part of it which equates economic wellbeing with a more rational society.

Those who question the convergence thesis do so on just about as many grounds as those who support it. They argue that there is about the convergence idea much economic determinism, perhaps too much wishful thinking, not uncommon in times of international stress. There is about convergence a suggestion of utopian perspective, an implicit belief in the ultimate rational perfectibility of man too reminiscent of Godwin, Condorcet, and Fourier to serve as a workable hypothesis for everyday or long-term action. The paradox of convergence, they say, is that it uses the terminology of economic science and resorts to technological arguments in order to expound a belief. Historical examples of highly developed, highly irrational societies (Hitler's Germany, for one) are brought into evidence as is the persistence of exclusive ideologies. Collective affluence may be qualitatively different from affluence based on the private ownership of the means of production. Moreover, the terms used by those who find the convergence argument convincing are, in the view of others, vague and somewhat misleading. There is an important difference between an enterprise's being able to do everything that is not expressly forbidden, and being able to do only that which is expressly allowed by the public authority. There is a world of difference between the public authority's doing only that which it has been expressly empowered to do and having a blank check for doing everything, while delegating such tasks to enterprises as it considers to be opportune. In a market-oriented, private property economy sovereignty rests with the enterprise not the public authority. It is the other way round in a command-oriented system dominated by public ownership of the means of production.[1] In even the most revisionist command economy, there is still no attempt to vest the enterprise with the private right to appropriate the net floating and fixed assets of the enterprise. The famous "profit motive" is not the same in the two types of system: in command-oriented systems the enterprise does not have the right to freely dispose of its profit. The relationship of the enterprise to its owner (the public authority) is, in command-oriented systems, somewhat like the relationship of a branch office to the central office in market-oriented systems. *Ultra vires* suits are not permitted. Even in Yugoslavia an enterprise cannot sue the federal government even though suits against regional governments are known to have been successfully prosecuted.

There is, therefore, a good deal of disagreement on the exact meaning and scope as well as on the validity of the convergence thesis. There appear to be serious conceptual difficulties implicit in the argument. Zinam shows in Part I that a general theory of comparative economic systems is still in its infancy. If and when such a theory is elaborated, it is likely to be more general than economists would wish it to be. Having, over the years, shied away from the impurities of political economy, they may well find themselves ill equipped when called upon to deal with the problem in all its interdisciplinary complexity. The argument of convergence stems from the far from satisfactory approach of successive approximations (see Introduction to Parts I and II). Since the approach is tentative, the convergence idea should perhaps be regarded as worthy of attention but subject to discriminate doubt.

[1] *See* P. J. D. Wiles, "Fifty Years After: What Future for Communism?" *Lloyds Bank Review*, October 1967, pp. 36–48.

36   HARRY G. SHAFFER

Do the U.S. and Soviet Economies Show Signs of Convergence?

Economic science deals with the allocation of scarce resources for the satisfaction of human wants. As to the ways in which this allocation can be organized (other than to leave it to custom and tradition), there is on the one extreme the pure laissez faire system of economic organization which permits the unrestricted forces of the market to exert their influence without (or with a minimum of) governmental intervention and guidance; on the other extreme, there is total, detailed planning of all economic activities by a central authority.

I

Graduate students in economic theory will testify that it takes years of hard work and concentrated study to acquire a thorough understanding of all the intricate theories which underly the laissez faire system of economic organization. But the fundamental ideas of such a system can be readily explained and easily understood.

Searching for the best way to enhance the economic well-being of a nation, Adam Smith, in his *An Inquiry into the Nature and Causes of the Wealth of Nations* (1776), advanced a revolutionary theory: He proposed that the British system of Mercantilism under which absolute monarchs held absolute power and exercised strict control over all economic life be replaced by one in which each individual would be left free to pursue his own economic ends. Under such a system, Smith argued, each individual in the pursuit of his selfish interests would advance the well-being of the nation, not by conscious design but automatically, as if guided by an "invisible hand."

How could the good of society be served if each individual seeks

Reprinted from Jan S. Prybyla (Ed.), *The Triangle of Power, Conflict, and Accommodation: The United States, The Soviet Union, Communist China* (University Park, Pennsylvania: The Pennsylvania State University Center for Continuing Liberal Education, Slavic and Soviet Language and Area Center, 1967) pp. 39–51. By permission.

only his own advantage? The interests of society at large demand that scarce resources be allocated according to a reasonable system of priorities which takes into account the needs and wants of the members of the society. A disciple of the classical school of economics would argue that for such allocation no government decree, no central plan is required. Individual entrepreneurs, if suffered to pursue their own interests, would want to produce commodities that could be sold at profitable prices; these, in turn, would necessarily have to be commodities people want. But if there were a shortage of one or more such commodities, could not the seller charge exorbitant prices, thus earning unreasonable profits by exploiting the consumer? At best only for a very brief period, a classical economist would argue, for others, learning of the high returns, would enter the field and start competing with the established firm, thus exerting a downward effect on price. And if too many entered the field, making it impossible for all firms to continue operating? Then some would go out of business. Which ones? While nowadays there is a tendency to say that the small producers could not survive, Adam Smith and his followers would have contended that it is the inefficient—in other words, the high cost—producers who would be forced to close shop. Hence, automatically, as if guided by an "invisible hand", a self-adjusting demand-supply-price relationship would prevail. For each commodity a market price would establish itself at which the quantity purchasers are willing and able to buy would just equal the quantity sellers are willing and able to sell; and any change in demand or supply would simply reflect itself in a new price-quality "equilibrium" point.

Classical economists have applied this theory to all aspects of economic life. The interest rate, for instance, would, in a perfectly competitive, free market, establish itself at a level at which the amounts of loanable funds lenders were willing to lend out would equal the amounts borrowers were willing to borrow. Wages, to give one more example, would find their level automatically via the competition of employers for qualified workers and the competition of workers for jobs; wage differentials could be explained in terms of demand-supply relationships for the respective jobs; and general unemployment could be deemed impossible by definition since anyone could find a job, were he but willing to accept a low enough wage. One not inclined to accept such a wage would have simply priced himself out of the market, which would make him "unemployable," and not "employed."

When one reads the works of such classical economists as Adam Smith, David Ricardo, Thomas Robert Malthus, or Jeremy Bentham, their arguments sound logical and the entire system very plausible. Yet, there are definite shortcomings, in part attributable to simplified or unrealistic assumptions and in part to limitations which result from the theory's failure to take into account certain problems for which the market by itself can offer no acceptable solution. While an analysis of all the criticisms of a pure laissez faire system must be reserved for books or more extensive articles on the subject, a few of the more frequently advanced ones will be discussed below:

1. The laissez faire model is based on such oversimplified premises as:

(a) Man is an economic man, always trying to buy where he can buy most cheaply and sell where he can get the highest price (the "economic man concept");

(b) labor can and will readily be shifted from one location or one line of endeavor to another, whenever wage differentials make such a move worthwhile (mobility of labor; the same assumption is made for "mobility of capital"); and

(c) every person who enters the market as a seller, a buyer, a producer, or a consumer is fully aware of all prices, opportunities, etc. ("perfect knowledge").

Assumptions such as these simply do not apply to the real world: man is not guided merely by economic considerations; he neither wants to nor can he readily shift his labor or capital (a man who has earned his law degree cannot readily shift to dentistry, no matter how profitable the latter endeavor may have become while he was enrolled in law school); and knowledge is, alas, quite imperfect.

2. According to the theory of a laissez faire economy, competition assures that each man shares in the nation's output according to his contribution to production. In the real world, however, one type of activity is particularly responsive to the market and therefore rewarded above all other: business ability. Not the great scientist or the brilliant teacher, but rather the capable salesman and advertising manager are the ones rewarded by high incomes. And the highest incomes go to those who know when to buy and when to sell stock on the stock exchange, and who have the wherewithal to make their knowledge effective by sizeable transactions. Are they really the ones who make the outstanding contributions to their country's output? And then, extraordinarily high rewards go to individuals endowed with some monopolistic advantages. Bob Hope, for instance, while competing with other entertainers, has a monopoly over his individual talents. As a result, the price of his services is bid up by prospective buyers to heights out of all proportions to what one could reasonably call "contribution to productions." Do not misunderstand me: I enjoy Bob Hope very much, but can we truly say that in an hour or two on television he contributes as much to our country as a President of the United States in an entire year? as a United States Senator in three years? as I do in eight years???

3. Capitalism entails economic waste; in other words, human and

material resources do not yield the optimum output theoretically attainable from their utilization. This, to a great extent, is the result of the necessity for competitive firms to be fully equipped, even if the market cannot absorb all they can turn out. Hence, two or more fully equipped hamburger stands coexist next to each other where one would be adequate to handle the entire business; milk delivery trucks of several competing dairies duplicate one another's routes, each with customers in all parts of the city, resulting in twice the number of trucks and several times the amount of gasoline being used than would otherwise be necessary, etc.

4. The theory leaves one with the impression that producers in a free market economy would automatically produce the things people want, thus yielding the greatest possible good for the greatest number. But is this really so? Suppose you are an economic man, guided by the desire to maximize your profits. Suppose you discover that returns on investments are considerably higher in less developed countries, where capital is scarcer, than in the United States. Suppose that you are willing to take the greater risk associated with such an investment and that you proceed to undertake a market study of one of the underdeveloped countries which is in search of private investments from inhabitants of the more affluent societies. You might discover without too much difficulty that there is a great need for a certain commodity in that country—let us say milk. The evidence is there: undernourished children, rampant starvation, etc. Will you now proceed to buy some pasture land, import dairy cows, and go into the dairy business? The probability is against such a decision because it is not likely that you would be able to sell your milk to the impoverished masses at a price that would yield you a return—or even enable you to break even—on your investment. Had the people the purchasing power to buy the milk, an extensive dairy industry would in all likelihood have been established long ago. So, you look around further and you discover that in that economically backward country in which most of the people live continuously on the edge of starvation, a very small percentage of the population is extremely wealthy—and this small group has developed a taste for, let us say, French champagne. Thus, you decide to import and market champagne in a country in which the overwhelming majority of the population goes to bed hungry every night. This, unfortunately, is not a theory; this, unfortunately, is a fact in most of the underdeveloped countries in which private enterprise operates either with relatively little government interference or under the protective wing of a government representative of the wealthy classes.

5. The theory of a laissez faire economy stands and falls with the assumption of freedom of competition. Competition is to assure that the consumer will not be exploited, and that the efficient—the low-cost—producers will survive adverse times; competition is to assure the op-

timum allocation of productive resources. But in a land of giant corporations and giant labor unions, such as the United States, competition in the economic sense (meaning primarily, so many sellers or so many buyers that none of them, acting by himself, has any influence on price) exists at best on the fringes of the economic system. There would be real competition in farming were it not for government intervention aimed at protecting farmers who, otherwise, would sell on a competitive but buy on a monopolistic market. There is competition in some service trades such as plumbing or television repairing; there is still considerable competition in retailing, although even here the large chain stores and supermarkets have begun to take over. But can one speak of true competition in an industry such as the telephone service industry? There are hundreds if not thousands of independent telephone companies, but one of them— the American Telephone and Telegraph Company and its subsidiaries— handles well over ninety percent of all telephone calls. Can one speak of competition in the steel industry when one company—the United States Steel Corporation—produces some 50,000 different products and has a steel producing capacity greater than that of the entire British empire? In industry after industry—automobiles, aluminum, electric appliances, tires, etc.—a very few companies have the lion's share of the market, frequently finding it to their advantage to reduce output rather than cut prices. And to the extent to which competition is lacking in our economic system, to that extent is the free market inadequate to assure optimum allocation of resources or consumer-directed production. The choice, then (if private ownership of the means of production is to be continued at all) becomes one between control by the government, or by monopolistic or semi-monopolistic firms. And surely we would hesitate to have a private company which has gained exclusive control over the water supply of a town determine the price of water to the consumers, guided exclusively by the capitalist motivation to maximize profits.

6. In many aspects of economic life, the forces of the free market in and of themselves are inadequate for the goals to be accomplished. The "invisible hand" of the free market would not, for instance, enable each American youngster to get at least a minimum of education; it would not "automatically" keep the children of the poor, or even the middle classes, from starving when the breadwinner has died, become seriously ill, gone to jail, or simply left his family; it would not protect the working man from unsafe working conditions, the sick from worthless or even harmful medicines, nor the consumer from deteriorated and potentially injurious foods, etc.

The laissez faire philosophy has also been taken to task for its apparent inability to prevent the recurrence of depressions during periods when the nation's productive capacity is more than adequate to provide at least the necessities for all the inhabitants of the country (to wit, the United States in the early 1930's); for its inability to prevent even long-run unemployment; for its disdain for cooperation and its "immoral" emphasis on the desirability of selfishness; and for numerous other alleged shortcomings. But let the discussion of the criticisms above suffice for our purpose here.

There is little doubt that whatever the merits of pure laissez faire may have been in 1776, the system is inadequate to prevent recurrent inflations and depressions, to assure full utilization of productive resources, and in general, to cope with the needs of the world's economies in the mid-twentieth century. As a result, the governments of all the "capitalist" nations in the world have found it necessary to intervene where the free market does not perform satisfactorily. This necessity increases as industrial societies move ever further away from small-scale industrial enterprises, and as affluence brings in its wake ever-increasing demands for goods and services which private enterprise is ill-equipped to provide, and which are enjoyed collectively (from schools and hospitals, to parking places and fire protection).

Through various monetary controls aimed at influencing the money supply of the country, and through the fiscal policies of taxation, expenditure, and borrowing, our central authorities exert considerable influence over the nation's economy, often fortifying this influence by legislation aimed at correcting some of the shortcomings enumerated above. While Americans will disagree with one another as to the desirable extent of government intervention in economic life, there are few who would want to permit severe unemployment to remain unchecked, who would advocate the sale of the United States Post Office to private interest, or who would favor discontinuation of state support for education, in an era in which a pure laissez faire policy is neither feasible nor defensible.

II

A thorough understanding of the Soviet type of socialist central planning is by no means simple but, as in the case of capitalism, the basic philosophy can be easily explained. Under that economic system, the means of production are taken over by society and are operated by the state, presumably in the interest of society. Thus, in theory, the whole nation becomes one gigantic corporation in which each citizen is an equal shareholder and in which the government acts as the board of directors; conscious planning of all aspects of economic life replaces the "anarchy of production" prevailing in the uncoordinated economy of capitalism; socialist cooperation takes the place of the selfish competition of the previous dog-eat-dog economic system; production is geared not to profits but to society's needs as determined by scientific studies since no one is allowed any longer to make a profit out of another man's labor, the "exploitation of man by man" is ended once and for all; income is distributed among the working people primarily in accordance to what one does, irrespective of what one owns; and whatever profits state-owned and operated enterprises earn belong to the state and are utilized by the state for the advancement of society (assistance to those unable to work or to help themselves, such as the old or the infirm; allocation of some vital services, such as schools or medical services, according to needs; construction of facilities, such as factories and roads, to enhance the country's productive capacity, etc.). This socialist, centrally planned economic system, this "dictatorship of the proletariat," Soviet Marxist-Leninist theory holds, prevails only during a period of transition. By "laying the economic foundation," by education aimed at transforming selfish human beings into "social beings" (by creating "the new Soviet man") society, during this period of transition, is being prepared for its final stage of development, *perfect communism.* In this "final stage" man will be able to realize his greatest potential as a producer and as a social being: in an environment of totally unrestricted freedom, each man will voluntarily and without any individual material reward work to the best of his ability and take from the common stores what he needs. Society, to put it into Marxist-Leninist terminology, will then "inscribe on its banners: 'from each according to his ability, to each according to his needs.'"

Although socialist central planning may sound as if it could readily cure all of man's economic ills, the theory itself has been subjected to extensive critical scrutiny by its opponents, and its practical application presents some grave problems which the Soviets and most of the communist countries of Eastern Europe have come to realize and have started to tackle in recent years. Let us take a quick glance at some of these criticisms and problems:

1. To decide upon all the economic activities of an entire nation, especially one of the size of the Soviet Union, by means of a central, overall plan is so gigantic a task that it staggers the imagination. In spite of all her undeniable economic successes, the Soviet Union has surely failed, so far at least, to approach under her system of centralized economic planning the maximum output achievable with her available resources and state of technology, reminding one of Adam Smith's admonition that "the duty of superintending the industry of private people and of directing it towards the employment most suitable to the interest of society" is a task "for the proper performance of which no human wisdom or knowledge could ever be sufficient."

Centrally planned, socialist economies have been faced with three major categories of economic problems, i.e., a) keeping the planning personnel to a manageable size, b) coordinating the various economic activities, and c) allocating resources and providing incentives to workers and managers so as to maximize efficiency. The difficulties in finding the proper solutions within the framework of a centrally planned and centrally managed socialist economy multiply as the economy becomes larger and more complex.

(a) The great expansion of the Soviet economy during the past two decades has made it necessary to increase correspondingly the bureaucratic planning machinery. So great an economic expansion for the immediate future has been anticipated that the late Nemchinov (until his death one of the Soviet Union's most renowned economists, statisticians, and experts on central planning) warned three years ago that unless the then prevailing planning methods were changed it would, by 1980, take the entire adult population of the Soviet Union to staff the planning apparatus.

(b) To coordinate all economic activities, to bring about the "proportional development of the economy," as the Soviets call it, involves more than a decision regarding resource allocation between industry and agriculture or between consumer and investment goods. It involves a careful allocation of inputs for the planned output of each commodity. Thus, a decision as to the number of tractors to be produced must be correlated with the allocation of the necessary machinery, equipment, factory space, spare parts, labor, etc. The steel necessary for the production of tractors must be allocated. This, in turn, involves the allocation of the raw materials, equipment, and labor necessary to produce or to keep in operation the steel furnaces. Then, the railroad cars needed to ship the steel must be allocated, the necessary crews to keep the railroads in operation must be assigned, the proper educational facilities must be set up for the children of the steel workers in the places in which they live, etc., etc., ad infinitum. And the amount of monetary income placed in the hands of all income earners must be such that after deduction of taxes and of amounts the income receivers put away as savings, it is just adequate to purchase the goods offered for sale at the prices set by the state. (Any failure of such proper relation between incomes earned and consumer goods available must necessarily lead to surpluses or to shortages.)

(c) The "proper" allocation of economic resources is one that would minimize costs and maximize output. Whether to use coal or oil as fuel in the production of a certain commodity, whether to use more machinery and less labor or less machinery and more labor, whether to produce that commodity (let us say chairs) altogether or sacrifice some or all of that output in order to produce something else (let us say tables)—all these decisions, if they are to be economically rational, depend largely upon a pricing structure reflective of relative scarcities. But how can prices be representative of cost and demand conditions, if they are determined arbitrarily by a central authority under an economic setup that fails to give due consideration to the economic value of land or of machinery (i.e., if neither land nor machinery are for sale or lease; if both are allocated free of charge, according to the overall Plan)?

To induce workers and managers to perform according to the Plan, force and the threat of force, non-material incentives, or material incentives may be used.

Force and the threat of force, from the days of slavery to the days of Stalin's slave labor camps, have proven inadequate to exact maximum performance. And if fear of severe punishment does not prompt an unskilled laborer to perform to the best of his ability, it surely would not make a highly trained technician or a competent scientist put his talents to maximum use! Moreover, if the Soviets are to set an example for other countries to follow, if they are to light the way towards a better, and eventually ideal, world community as Marx and Engels and Lenin promised, how can the use of force be defended, especially now that "socialism" has been "solidly established"?

Such *non-material incentives* as the satisfaction derived from the knowledge that one does his best for the cause may have played a major role during the days of the Revolution and of the "Great Patriotic War" (World War II), but much of the revolutionary fervor has waned since. Even honorary titles, badges, citations, and other symbols of recognition, nowadays, play only secondary roles as incentives. In recent years, the "revolution of rising expectations" has made the Soviet citizen evermore interested in immediate direct increases in cash income. The Soviet government, eager to prove to the world that the U.S.S.R. can surpass the wealthiest of the "imperialist" countries in economic accomplishments, realizes that the "new Soviet man" who would always work for the good of society, unselfishly and without special, material reward, is still the exception. Hence, the recent emphasis on material incentives should not come as a surprise.

Material incentives such as cash bonuses have always been used in the Soviet Union to some extent to motivate workers and managers to fulfill and overfulfill the targets which, in an economy administratively planned from the center, are prescribed for each enterprise by the overall Plan. When all aspects of the productive process are planned at the center (in this case in Moscow) there must be many sub-plans, spelled out for each enterprise in detail. Since, until recently, mere physical output was of primary importance, the highest awards have been paid for the fulfillment and overfulfillment of the enterprise's quantitative output plan. Such other plans as the quality plan, the raw material conservation plan, the cost reduction plan, or the increase-in-labor-productivity plan, although by no means unimportant, were not given equal priority so long as there were pronounced shortages of many goods. However, singling out of the quantitative output plan as the primary basis for bonuses has served as an inducement for many actions contrary to the intentions behind the Plan. Not only has it motivated managers and workers to neglect quality and variety, but it has even been inadequate, in many respects, as an incentive to maximize physical output.

To get more easily fulfillable targets, enterprise managers have often tried to hide the true productive capacity of their plants; to fulfill the plan, quality and variety have been sacrificed; as much machinery and equipment as could be obtained has been accumulated by individual enterprises, irrespective of immediate or foreseeable needs, and regardless of the needs of other producers who might be suffering from great shortages of equipment; innovation finally has been spurned since it would interfere with present output (retooling takes time) and, if successful, would merely result in higher output targets, equally difficult to achieve.

2. Apart from the problems connected with economic efficiency, opponents of Marxism-Leninism have denied that true individual freedom and political democracy can exist under completely centralized economic planning. Although free discussion, for instance, can be permitted while a plan is being prepared, once adopted, the plans must be carried out, at penalty of great economic cost to society. (This could be compared with the operation of a large American corporation. Next year's automobile models can be discussed in great detail by the men who run General Motors and suggestions of stockholders, workers and prospective customers may be welcomed and may be given due consideration; but once the styles have been decided upon and the new models have begun to roll off the assembly line, workers cannot be permitted to refuse cooperation with the "plan," although suggestions for changes for the subsequent year may again be entertained.) Thus, critics assert, even a more benevolent regime than that of Stalin cannot help but restrict freedom and democracy if detailed economic planning from the center is to be retained.

3. The eventual advent of a society of abundance and perfect freedom may seem a realistic prospect to the confirmed Marxist-Leninist. To many non-Marxists, however, "perfect communism" is but a Utopia while others, not quite as negative, hold that evidence is as yet inadequate to enable them to evaluate the possibility of bringing it about. But supposing that the economic and educational problems could be solved satisfactorily so that the dream society of the future could be established, there is still the time element: few today, even in the Soviet Union will support Khrushchev's claim that *this generation* of Soviet citizens shall live under communism." If at all, Western scholars believe, such a system could be established only in the long run, over a period of generations.

However, people are generally more concerned about the immediate future than about the long run. ("In the long run, we shall all be dead," cynically commented one British economist.) Hence, whatever intellectual and moral appeal the theory of the "final stage of communism" may have, most "Free World" social scientists consider the promise of its eventual attainment inadequate as a motivating force. To make people voluntarily choose the communist path, they insist, the intermediate stage of development—the "transition from capitalism to communism"—would have to appear more attractive to them than the economic, political, and social system it is to replace. This is not the case, critics of Marxism-Leninism hold, at least not so far as the inhabitants of the relatively affluent, democratic societies of the non-communist world are concerned.

Point 3 (the possibility of achieving perfect communism) is certainly a matter of debate and speculation, and so is Point 2 (the degree of freedom and democracy during the "era of transition from capitalism to communism"). But there is no gainsaying that Soviet leaders, since Stalin's death, have introduced some measures of freedom and democracy. The Soviets, in this respect, may still lag far behind the societies which can trace their political system back to centuries of British experience with and traditions of democratic processes. Yet, the fear, the terror, the extreme police state atmosphere of the Stalin era are things of the past, and the Soviets are no more proud of that past than Americans are of theirs during the cotton-plantation-slavery era. And as to Point 1 (economic problems resulting from the centralization of economic decision making), the Soviet Union and most of the communist countries of Eastern Europe have, in recent years, shown great willingness to deviate from dogmatic positions held in the past and to alter the entire structure of the planning apparatus. In essence, the economic reforms now being introduced amount to the delegation of details of economic decision making to lower echelons in the economy (primarily to enterprise directors in the Soviet Union, to workers' councils in Yugoslavia), and to the utilization of economic tools which, hitherto, have been applied much more widely by market economies. Thus, for example, greater attention is being paid to consumers' demands by introducing a certain degree of flexibility into the pricing structure, and by permitting marketing organizations (for example retail stores) to place orders directly with suppliers; and, yet more important, profit has begun to play an increasing role, both as a measuring rod of efficiency and as the primary criterion for the award of bonuses. Most Soviet and Western economists agree that such utilization of profits is likely to remove many of the present inadequacies of the Soviet system: With profits as the yardstick, enterprise managers and workers will no longer want to produce mere quantity irrespective of quality and assortment, will no longer find it to their advantage to store unnecessary machinery (profits are computed as a percentage of total capital), etc. Even Soviet mathematical economists who are hopeful that the perfection of mathematical techniques and of computers will facilitate central planning have in general not opposed the economic reforms; many of them, such as Novozhilov, Kantorovich, and the late Nemchinov, have given their wholehearted support to Yevsey G. Liberman, the Kharkov economics professor who has spearheaded the drive for the decentralization measures that are now being introduced in the Soviet Union. Moreover, the economic reforms are the outcome of free criticism of long-standing practices, criticism unprecedented in the recent history of communist countries. Finally, the liberalization tendencies in the economic arena appear to be radiating into other spheres, gradually "thawing" the political, social, and cultural rigidity of the past. Although freedom in all these areas is surely not found in all parts of the so-called "Free World," it is, in the minds of most Americans, a fairly regular as well as a highly desirable aspect of the economic system of capitalism.

III

As has been shown, the economic system of capitalism embodies some serious shortcomings. Does this mean, then, that from an economic point of view capitalism has proved a failure? Nonsense! Under it (perhaps because of it, perhaps irrespective of it, perhaps in spite of it—but in any case under it) the Western World has made great strides forward (even Marx, 120 years ago, acknowledged the achievements of capitalism which "has created more massive and more colossal productive forces than have all preceding generations together"), and the United States in particular has reached a standard of living unprecedented in the history of mankind and unequalled in non-capitalist nations. Although the sphere of government in the economic operation of society has increased from decade to decade and from generation to generation, the system is still basically capitalist: government expenditures may amount to many tens of billions of dollars in the United States, but the commodities that the municipal, state, and federal levels of government purchase are produced primarily by private businessmen and private corporations operating for the purpose of making a profit on the market. And the Soviet type of socialism: has it proven a failure? Nonsense! Under a centralized economic system (perhaps because of it, perhaps irrespective of it, perhaps in spite of it—but in any case under it) the Soviet people have lived and labored in peace and in war for half a century, and they have transformed a semi-literate, semi-feudal, and predominantly peasant nation into a society in which education, art, and science flourish, a society which can be classified today among the affluent nations of the world, and which has reached a position of economic and military power second only to that of the United States. Are the Soviets now moving back towards capitalism? Not really. They have adopted certain economic tools and techniques usually associated with a free enterprise system, but they have not given up—and apparently have no intention of giving up—the essential features of socialism, namely public ownership of the means of production, and the overall Plan as the fundamental guiding rod of all economic activity. Even the extension of the use of the profit motive is actually no more than a profit-sharing system under which workers and managers are entitled to participate in the profits which now, as in the past, belong to the state.

Even in Smith's proposal for a laissez-faire economy, government was to provide those essential goods and services which private entrepreneurs would not be willing to provide because they would not find them profitable (for example, the establishment of public playgrounds for children). As far as economic efficiency is concerned, however, a laissez-faire society in which perfect knowledge, perfect mobility, and perfect competition prevail would have much to recommend itself, but nothing like it does or could exist in the real world. A totally centralized economy in which an all-wise, all-good planner provided all the necessary answers with infallible accuracy and always in the interests of the people: such a system, likewise, would have much to recommend itself, but it likewise is unachievable in the real world. In practice, although no human society has ever approached *perfect* laissez faire or *perfect* planning, the economic achievements of the United States and the Soviet Union are evidence that both a highly centralized economic system and a market economy can function adequately; but the undeniable imperfections and shortcomings in both systems prove that there is room for further improvement. Since most of the necessary changes entail an increase in the economic functions of government in the United States and a decrease in the Soviet Union, the two systems appear to be converging, at least as far as some technical aspects of their economic apparatus are concerned. Gradually, in the interest of better economic performance and of their people's economic well-being, the two countries may be edging their way towards a more common meeting ground between the extremes of a perfectly free market and a totally centralized economy. Such "convergence" may make the two systems look similar, but it surely does not prevent either system—nor either country for that matter—from retaining or developing within its own economic and political structure characteristics suited to its own environment, background, stage of development, and overall ideological orientation. There is no reason why the Soviet Union should have to introduce a two-party system or surrender the public ownership of the means of production, nor would the United States need to establish party-sponsored youth organizations or emphasize "socialist realism" in the arts. Yet, if East and West are willing to learn from each other, and if each is willing to incorporate into its own system what is good in the other, and if, moreover, such primarily technical convergence in the economic sphere leads to a better understanding in other areas also—so much the better. In any case, such a movement not merely towards peaceful but perhaps towards cooperative coexistence seems much preferable to another possible meeting ground: that of a worldwide battlefield in a nuclear World War III.

37   JAN S. PRYBYLA

THE CONVERGENCE OF MARKET-ORIENTED
AND COMMAND-ORIENTED SYSTEMS:
A CRITICAL ESTIMATE

In its broadest rendering the thesis of convergence states that the social, economic, and political systems of the West and of the communist world show a trend toward the attenuation or elimination of the basic differences which separate them. According to this view the socio-economic and political systems of Communism and the West tend to converge over time. A corollary is usually drawn to the effect that convergence will lead to a lessening of international tensions and thus remove the danger of mutual nuclear annihilation.* Clearly this is an intriguing view which deserves close scrutiny, critical appraisal, and a more careful formulation than it has so far received.

Unfortunately such a broad statement of the problem, while ultimately the only valid one, is not easily handled. Hence the various components of the problem are usually dealt with separately.[1] Of these, changes in the Western and communist economic systems lend themselves most readily to quantification and tend, therefore, to be most often used both to support and decry the convergence argument. Also on occasion the geographical coverage is limited to the United States and Western Europe on the one hand, and to the Soviet Union and its East European allies on the other. It is in this restricted sense that the convergence thesis is examined here.[2]

From "The Convergence of Western and Communist Economic Systems: A Critical Estimate," *The Russian Review,* Vol. 23, No. 1 (January 1964). Reprinted by permission of *The Russian Review.*

* *Cf.* Shaffer, above, p. 466.

[1] References to the alleged convergence of Western and communist economic systems are usually offshoots of studies concerned with other subjects. Rarely is the problem dealt with *per se*. Two recent examples of such separate treatment are: Jan Tinbergen's "Do Communist and Free Economies Show a Converging Pattern?" (*Soviet Studies,* April, 1961), and the symposium on convergence in the London *Survey* of April, 1963.

[2] "Western Europe" as used in this paper is a political rather than a geographical concept. It means "non-communist Europe" and includes such geographically eastern countries as Greece and Turkey. However, the concept is mainly relevant to the more industrialized countries of non-communist Europe. The term "communist economic systems" is used to describe the whole spectrum of Soviet-inspired, socialist, command economies in Eastern Europe. The term "Western economic systems" covers non-communist economies from Sweden to the United States.

Even within this much narrower compass the difficulties are formidable. There is, first of all, the problem of the diversity of economic systems; there is also the considerable element of conjecture involved in the projection of past and present trends into the future. There is danger in abstracting economic trends in the communist world from communist political evolution, and there are pitfalls awaiting anyone who attempts to disentangle long-range trends from the still inadequate network of Communist data.

Convergence must be carefully distinguished from coexistence. In a sense convergence is the Western counterpart of the essentially Soviet coexistence thesis. Both convergence and coexistence are dynamic approaches to economic phenomena as against the conservative (Chinese and Goldwaterian) positions which maintain that the nature of capitalism and communism never changes. While both convergence and coexistence are based on the assumption of evolutionary change, there is marked disagreement on the nature and direction of change.

The ideological starting point of the coexistence argument is the Marxian theorem of capitalism's inevitable travel down the path of internal contradictions toward eventual transformation into socialism, and the swift progress of socialist economies toward a communist state of abundance and equity. The distinctive feature of the coexistence thesis is the shift of emphasis from the inequities, weaknesses, and final disintegration of capitalism considered *in vacuo* to the *comparative* performance of capitalist and Soviet-type socialist economies. The confrontation contrasts socialist economic stability with capitalist business cycles and unemployment and stresses comparative growth rates, per capita levels of industrial output, and other selected quantitative criteria of economic performance. In short, coexistence—insofar as it is not fraudulent semantics—is convergence through the eventual recognition of the superiority of socialism over capitalism; it is convergence on communist terms. Coexistence is in essence a theological view couched in economic vocabulary: "right" (communism) triumphs over "evil" (capitalism) by virtue of its own inherent strength and powers of attraction without recourse to global war. It is the theology of a more successful society which has much to lose in open conflict, seeking a way out of anachronistic rigidities without loss of the inspirational impetus which ideology furnishes. The fact that the coexistence thesis is better known and easier to spot than the convergence argument reflects in part the traditional need of communist societies to verbalize historical trends.

Convergence, on the other hand, when properly formulated is free of normative affiliation. It analyzes developmental trends in Western and communist economies without the aid or hindrance of a philosophical apparatus that ascribes to history the power of linear programming. It is essentially analytical and pragmatic. It detects the emergence within the two broad types of economic systems of similar arrangements that have less to do with any preconceived normative notions of capitalism and communism than with the effective solution of problems posed by increasingly complex, mathematized, engineering-oriented facts. It traces the growth of a common core of rationality in economics which is neither communist nor capitalist but which rests rather on the need to quantify, to define with precision, and to draw conclusions that are practicable.

Now to examine some of the major tenets of the convergence thesis. The treatment is necessarily brief and its main purpose is to provide for more exhaustive analyses.

It is argued that at least some of the forces which in the past operated in the direction of divergence between the Western and communist economies are currently on the wane, paradoxically by reason of the fact that communist economic systems have by now established a "safe" distance from their parent capitalist stem, that they no longer are or imagine themselves to be "encircled" by hostile, superior powers, that they are going concerns more interested in improving their performance than in stressing those features, however crude, which distinguish them from their mother system. As a result there is less need to experiment with spectacular innovations such as drastic income levelling, job selection and educational policies geared to proletarian origin, disdain for the division of labor as a capitalist prejudice, physical planning and disregard for opportunity costs, commune-type agricultural organization, autarchic proclivities, and so forth. The implication here is that the end of what may be termed *the process of disaffiliation* means a more sophisticated approach to facile doctrinal slogans and a waning of revolutionary fervor. This line of reasoning is usually buttressed with persuasive examples drawn from the current Soviet-Chinese dispute.

A somewhat similar development is allegedly observable in the West. Western attitude to the communist economies is said to have passed through three stages: (i) a stage at which the very practicability of communism as an economic category was seriously questioned; (ii) a stage at which this practicability was admitted on the basis of rather eloquent evidence, but it was doubted whether communist economies could function at all efficiently; (iii) a stage at which (ii) tends to be answered in the affirmative, but the question is *how* efficiently?

The disaffiliation argument deals with comparative attitudes. It concludes that these are becoming ruled more by reason and technological constraint than by fear and emotion. A parallel is sometimes drawn with the gradual erosion of the crusading spirit of Christianity. While the ideal of the one Shepherd and one flock is on the books, it tends to be prompted by means other than those once employed by Richard Coeur de Lion.

The weakness of the disaffiliation argument is that it tries to do too much with a highly volatile raw material. Also, the connection between the completion of the process of breaking away and convergence is rather flimsy. It could conceivably be argued that the very distance traveled by the communist economies and their success in many fields may lead to a hardening of positions into which so much history had gone. Moreover, a number of the policy objectives spelled out in the Program of the Communist Party of the Soviet Union point away from convergence. Certainly, communist experimenting with new forms of economic organization and novel social processes is no less distinctive and revolutionary than in the past. Thus, the loss of revolutionary fervor implied in the disaffiliation argument is questionable. The revolution is continuing although in different forms. It takes place in the yearly transfer of millions of peasants from agriculture to industry, in the training of vast masses of people, in the gradual internalization by the people of a milder but very real totalitarian structure of government, in the emergence of comrades' courts, citizens' militia, and other "public" organizations for the suppression of individualism, in the development of the Soviet "wild East" and the exportation of communist methods and strategies of economic growth in the guise of Soviet, Czech, and East German steel mills and dams. The disaffiliation argument seems to confuse revolutionary nonsense (conspicuous differentiation) with revolutionary content. It is true that the Russians have over the years shed much revolutionary nonsense. But this does not mean a parallel lessening of revolutionary go. The enthusiastic reception reserved for Fidel Castro by the young people of Leningrad elicited from a British observer the comment that

. . . the outburst of youthful enthusiasm is also a reminder for (Khrushchev) as well as for outsiders, that no Soviet leader can quite forget the revolutionary origins and aspirations of his country. They represent an emotional factor that must be reckoned with even in cold calculations.[3]

A more rigorous version of the disaffiliation argument is found in the view that as the communist economies mature, i.e., as they catch up with the more advanced economies of the West in production, productivity, real wages, per capita income, etc., they will be faced with complex problems of growth and allocative efficiency the solutions to which will tend to be more similar to those adopted in the West than the more primitive, largely administrative and political methods used in the past. What is involved here is convergence through the narrowing of the developmental gap and the gradual disappearance of institutions characteristic of the take-off stage. The argument ascribes much of the tension between the communist and Western economic systems to their different levels of development and to the distinctive patterns of behavior characteristic of those levels. It regards Stalinism as a particularly brutal but not unusual stage in the process of economic growth and recalls in this

[3] The Economist, June 1, 1963, p. 889.

connection the far from rosy conditions of early capitalist development. It thinks of Stalin as a socialist super-Scrooge who one day will be followed by smoother organization men not unlike those who today from the Kremlins of Madison Avenue persuade the American consumer that what he gets is really what he wants. For an explanation of the particularly violent and obnoxious aspects of Soviet economic history in the thirties and forties, the argument appeals to Asiatic cultural influences and the disaffiliation view discussed above. When propounded by modern-day Soviet-type socialists such as Professor Oskar Lange,[4] the explanation runs mostly in terms of "historical necessity" although it is admitted that the Poles, at least, think that it might have been a great political mistake.

This *maturity argument* begins with the proposition that in its beginnings a socialist system of the Soviet type is faced with a twofold task: economic breakthrough and a radical socio-political transformation of the framework of society (disaffiliation). The initial thrust out of poverty and the concurrent setting up of a new socio-economic and political order tend to assume disproportionate importance and manifest themselves in severe centralization of planning and management and the politicalization of economics. Experience shows that this initial step succeeds both in deeply transforming the socio-economic structure of society and in chalking up impressive rates of growth. The latter are largely a function of the political regime's concentration on a few high-priority, industrial objectives. The result is a lop-sided, quick growth with vast areas of allocative inefficiency, as analyzed by Naum Jasny in his "Note on Rationality and Efficiency in the Soviet Economy" (*Soviet Studies*, April 1961). As the process continues, the number of priority claimants to resources goes up sharply. The chronic overcommitment of resources raises problems of alternative costs and points to a need for meaningful allocative principles, criteria of planners' preferences that would take into account relative resource scarcities, scarcity as distinct from control pricing, and the circumscribing of political voluntarism in economic decision-making. All this inevitably leads to a close look at some of the more dogmatic, inspirational, but allocatively useless Marxian tenets, and perhaps eventually to the adoption of a less rigid, less metaphysical, more "economic" theory of resource use. The net result seems to be the rise of market socialism of the Yugoslav type in which political dictatorship is combined with advanced decentralization of economic decision-making and the operation of a system of scarcity prices over broad areas of the economy. The reason that Yugoslavia has moved into this position well before the other communist economies is ascribed to the fact that President Tito found it strategically and geographically practicable not to wait for the sluggish evolution of Soviet thought on these matters.

[4] *The Political Economy of Socialism*, The Hague, 1958, pp. 16–28.

It is interesting to recall that the market mechanism (whether or not modified by governmental intervention and oligopolistic industrial structures) fits in well with a variety of political systems. It is by no means the exclusive property of political democracy as currently understood in the West. The market mechanism is a kind of dictator that rewards and punishes those operating within its laws. Western governments are relieved by it of much unpopular and distasteful activity; with justification they are able to shift the blame for a great deal of potentially explosive economic hardship onto the individual's relationship with an impersonal force, the more since this relationship is said to reflect consumer sovereignty. The incorporation of a modified form of the market mechanism into communist economic systems may not only make these economies perform more efficiently, but remove from the political directorate some of the trappings of coercive totalitarianism associated with administrative management of the economy.

There are some indications that portions of the maturity argument are valid and that the abandonment by communist countries of war-economy methods of management and planning may mean convergence. It is interesting to see that what was once regarded as a question of principle (e.g., central determination of the scope of a production plan) is now looked upon as a question of technique. If the switch makes for better technique, it erodes the principle. This is in essence what is meant by the gradual shift in the direction of an economic rationality common to both East and West. The search for theoretical guides to the achievement of an optimum allocation of resources that would maximize output in terms of planned product mix and preference schedules is actively pursued in the communist world at the intellectual level.[5] Until now party-dominated policy has only marginally taken note of the debate. As will be shown below, Western economic theory and policy have during this time been involved in excursions into state planning and into the meshing of long-range growth objectives for the economy as a whole with short-term individual decision-making. The aim is to resolve a latent conflict between the narrowly private enterprise point of view and a social point of view. In this conflict the state tends to assume an increasingly important and determining role. There does seem, therefore, to be a *prima facie* case for the tendency of the two systems to meet somewhere halfway on the related questions of growth, stability, and efficiency.

The thesis of convergence frequently makes use of the *consumption argument*. In its most popular version the argument of consumption states that a fat Russian is a harmless Russian. What is meant is that rising consumption standards in the communist world will not only efface the

[5] "The Quest for Economic Rationality in the Soviet Bloc," *Social Research,* Autumn, 1963.

more glaring and superficial differences between the underfed (in terms of quality), shoddily clad, and underhoused Russian, and the overfed, well-dressed, air-conditioned American, but that high consumption somehow generates a keen interest in self-improvement and is prejudicial to the ascetic, other-minded, future-oriented faith on which communist societies have traditionally been based. There is implicit in this argument a linking of high-consumption economy with what the Russians call "private property mentality," and a subsidiary connection between the latter and a less bitter, more cheerful and eager outlook on the world.

In the decade of the fifties, per capita consumption in the Soviet Union just about doubled. Without any significant shift in resources away from heavy industry and other priority sectors, a 5 per cent annual per capita increase in consumption is feasible in the years to come. As of now, urban living standards in the U.S.S.R. can be broadly compared with those of Japan and Italy (excluding the north), and with the situation in Britain in the late forties and early fifties. There are, of course, many differences of detail. Thus if fashion and variety are ignored, the volume of clothing purchases in Russia and the United States is just about equal. The Americans have about 83 times as many automobiles per head as the Russians, but the Russians are ahead in second best durables such as motor bikes and sewing machines; the Americans have over four times as much housing space per head as the Soviets (and of incomparably better quality), twice as many radio sets and shoes. The Russians are ahead in movie attendance and in starchy foods.

The current Soviet plans foresee a substantial development of the service sector over the next twenty years. Personal services in all communist economies are still underdeveloped in volume and extremely vexing in quality. A persistent sellers' market in most consumer goods and services makes life under communism reminiscent of the darker days of wartime England. However, even in these neglected areas improvement is discernible. In 1955 transport and trade services generated only 27.8 per cent of the Soviet gross national product as compared with 57.8 per cent in the United States (1960), 47.5 per cent in Japan, (1960), and 39.8 per cent in Italy (1960). In spite of improvements in recent years, much remains to be done.

The convergence through consumption argument is summed up by a correspondent of the London *Economist*:

  . . . although the communist system has not brought as big an advance in consumption standards for the Soviet people as it or any other sensible system could have done, the stage of eventual breakthrough to a tolerably affluent urban society—with which the West might find it cosier to live—could be near.[6]

  [6] *The Economist,* June 1, 1963, p. 871.

Few economists in the West would quarrel with the conclusion that communist living standards are on the rise. The validity of the connection which the argument tries to establish between a tolerably affluent urban society and cosier international living may, however, be doubted. Hitler's Germany and prewar Japan were, after all, tolerably affluent societies in the sense of urban consumer welfare. To directly link levels of affluence to political aggressiveness or the lack of it is dangerous and probably inaccurate. All that can safely be said is that there will be some convergence of over-all living standards. However, if the Soviet Party Program is in earnest, the future development of consumption in the U.S.S.R. (and probably in other countries of the communist world as well) will concentrate on communal consumption (free public transportation rather than private automobiles, communal catering rather than the family dinner), while the area of individual consumption will be strictly circumscribed.[7] Affluence may thus take on a qualitatively different meaning under Communism than in the West. It may mean greater opportunities for organized togetherness in goods and services without any appreciable increase in the private enjoyment of goods individually owned. This view is only partly attenuated by the reflections below concerning socialization trends in the West.

So far the thesis of convergence has stressed the communist side of things. The general impression was that the onus of convergence was on the communist systems in terms of attitudes, decentralization, theoretical refinement, and consumer participation. The *argument of socialization* shifts the emphasis to the behavioral patterns of Western economies. It is argued under this heading that one of the most significant trends in Western economies in recent decades has been the steady growth of the governmental sector and the gradual emergence of the state as an active participant, and in some countries the determining factor, in the economic process. This has been visibly so in Western Europe and less obviously but nonetheless significantly so in the United States.

Government spending on goods and services in the United States has risen from 9.4 per cent of the gross national product in 1900 (on the basis of 1962 prices) to 21.2 per cent in 1962. If transfer payments such as interest, subsidies and welfare benefits are added, it can be said that governmental influence is keenly felt in more than one-quarter of the economy. In contrast to Western Europe defense is an important channel through which this influence comes to be exerted in the United States. In 1900 the governmental sector in the United States employed a mere 4.9 per cent of the labor force; by 1962 over 16 per cent of the labor force held government jobs at the federal, state, and local levels. In all

---

[7] See, Jan Prybyla, "The Soviet Theory of Social Consumption Funds During the Transition from Socialism to Communism," *Southwestern Social Science Quarterly,* July, 1962.

Western countries the socially undesirable effects of the market are corrected by heavy progressive taxation and transfer payments. In sum, a free but carefully watched market is in most instances combined with vigorous state measures of social welfare. In Western Europe, moreover, the state is a heavy investor in the economy although the actual technique of investment varies from country to country.

The actual influence of the public sector on the economy in the United States and elsewhere tends to be understated by figures of the kind cited above. In fact, the government in the United States controls the prices of goods and services in at least half the economy. The manner in which this is done is less formal, less institutionalized than in Western Europe, but no less real. Direct administrative control is exercised over the prices of communications and public utilities, transport, energy and over a wide range of the products of agriculture. Occasional governmental pressure is used to correct prices in key industries of the private sector (e.g., steel), and direct influence is exerted through the manipulation of government stockpiles of key raw materials, and through the use of quotas and other devices (e.g., oil, cane sugar). Government contracts in the defense industries spill over into the most remote corners of the economy. The Federal Reserve Board through its open market operations, discount rate policy, and legal reserve requirements affects the credit conditions in the country and indirectly the climate of investment activity. The use of these and other weapons by the government has risen sharply over the years and there is strong pressure for their extension into areas in which the private sector fails to perform functions for which, perhaps, it had never been intended (e.g., social security, health insurance). Unlike some Western European countries such as France, the United States has not yet ventured into direct government planning for economic growth, but in view of the disappointing growth performance of the period 1953-1961 the possibility of a shift in this direction cannot be discounted. The growth of the role of the state in the economy of Western countries is not due exclusively to successive wars. It is as much the result of a growing desire for social equity, opportunity, and security which the regular commercial network very frequently fails to bring about. It is also the result of the recognition of the state's responsibilities for economic stability and long-range growth. An interesting byproduct of these developments is the tendency for power to shift from the legislative to the executive organs of the state. Economic policy requires for effectiveness quick and sometimes daily responses which a deliberative assembly fails to provide.

The argument of convergence through the gradual socialization of the West is not without strength. However, it has to be very carefully formulated. Thus, before asserting that the state sector in the West is gradually coming to wield economic powers not unlike those held by the state in communist countries, it would be wise to examine carefully the nature of the concept of the state in the West and under communism. It remains nevertheless true that, for example, the avoidance of a serious slump in the Western economies over the last two decades for which the state has in no small measure been responsible is a step in the direction of the communist standards of a cycle-less economy.

Two tentative conclusions seem to emerge from this brief discussion of the convergence thesis in its four aspects of disaffiliation, maturity, consumption, and socialization.

Superficially the Western and Communist economic systems do indeed show signs of convergence. A steel mill in Pittsburgh is run in much the same way as a steel mill in Krasnoyarsk. In over-all levels of technology, consumption, scientific achievement, there is convergence. There is also a community of training which is needed to sustain and raise those levels of technology, consumption, and scientific achievement. The more extreme attitudes which for many years differentiated East and West are beginning to give way to more subtle and sophisticated ones. More and more the stress is on processes rather than on disjointed events, on the variety of techniques of running an economy rather than on unchangeable principles. There seems to be in both the Communist and Western camps a willingness to experiment with different techniques so long as the results are satisfactory from the standpoint of resource allocation and welfare.

On the other hand the basic differences between the two systems remain formidable. Many of these fundamental differences are outside the rather narrow confines of economics: they concern the place of the individual in society and the extent to which individual subjective valuations are allowed to influence the course of events. They deal with the nature of the state power and the effectiveness of the channels of communication between the individual citizen and the state. In short, convergence to be fully meaningful must concern itself with much more than economic processes. Such considerations are important in evaluating the growing socialization of the Western economies and the repeated attempts at decentralization and the use of a limited market within the communist world.

Yet even within the narrow scope of economics the developments of the last twenty years do not always point in the direction of convergence. High consumption, for instance, may mean very different things depending on the balance between individual and communal consumption. The same is true of the freedom of occupational choice and of the mechanism by which the bill of goods is made up. In short, economic convergence is not as simple a matter as it is often taken to be, nor is it the ultimately determining factor. The Western and Communist economies show in this respect a number of conflicting trends which do not, as of now, add up to a clear-cut convergence thesis.

38   L. LEONTIEV

Myth About "Rapprochement" of the Two Systems

Ever since the establishment of the Soviet State, the propaganda machine of the monopolies has found itself faced with a dual or, if you like, a binary task: to slur socialism in every way possible and to try to whitewash capitalism at all costs. Time flew by. The historical situation has changed, and with it of course, the forms of anticommunist propaganda. But its end goal remains the same for almost half a century.

One after another bourgeois myths appeared and burst like so many soap bubbles. It was claimed, for instance, that the socialist revolution was nothing but a "miscarriage" of history, that it was doomed to inevitable collapse, that mankind would simply return to capitalism as the only "normal" system. It was said that while socialism was able to destroy the old, it was unable to create anything new. Finally, it was predicted that the five-year plans would fall through as the fantastic, infeasible "schemes" they really were. All these evaluations and forecasts turned out to be wrong.

Similarly efforts to "embellish" capitalism have ended in failure. For while the bourgeois system was depicted as something "eternal and immutable," the victories of socialist revolutions throughout the world have proved the opposite. Capitalist methods of economic management were claimed to be the "only effective" ones, but this myth too was exploded by the successes of socialism in its economic competition with capitalism.

The superiority of the socialist economic system over the capitalist, the growing force of attraction of socialist ideas, compel bourgeois economists to resort to ever new forms and methods of social falsification. For many long years bourgeois political economy extolled capitalism sky-high as the embodiment of mankind's loftiest aspirations, impudently slandering socialism as the personification of all that is evil on earth. Today, however, many of its representatives are making statements about a "rapprochement" of the two systems.

This version is known in bourgeois economic and sociological literature as the theory of "convergence." Its ideological content is scant to say the least, barely enough to be put in a thimble. Socialism, the advocates

From *Reprints from the Soviet Press,* Vol. IV, No. 3 (February 9, 1967), pp. 3–11. (New York, Compass Publications Inc.). The article originally appeared in *Ekonomicheskaya Gazeta,* No. 49, December 1966.

of this theory profess, is growing less and less socialist, while capitalism is becoming less and less capitalist. Both systems are moving increasingly towards each other. The time is not distant when they will meet somewhere halfway. And then, the bourgeois "theoreticians" strive to persuade us, some sort of a "hybrid" system will be established all over the world, combining the "positive" aspects of both systems and at the same time free of "negative" lapses.

The emergence and spreading of the "convergence" theory is significant indeed. It is proof of the bankruptcy of the traditional forms of attacking socialism and defending capitalism. In our day bourgeois apologetics can no longer come out openly. It has to camouflage capitalism, subject it to cosmetic operations. At the same time, the ideological henchmen of the monopolies can no longer present socialism as the "horned devil." Today, they are trying to discredit it by means of more complicated and subtle methods.

One more thing has to be borne in mind. The proponents of "rapprochement" include also well-wishers from among those whom V. I. Lenin once called the "educated Philistines of the West." They cherish the illusion that "rapprochement of the systems" on the socio-economic plane can allegedly facilitate the easing of international tensions in our troubled world. These are contemporary Manilovs—inactive, futile daydreamers—and their fantasies would be completely harmless if they did not, willingly or unwillingly, serve to bolster those who spread the "convergence" theory for purposes which have nothing in common with genuine concern for the improvement of relations between the countries of the two systems.

The "convergence" theory is an outright ideological subversion, intended to confuse the people, to present the processes taking place both in the socialist and in the capitalist economies in a distorted light. Anticommunist propoganda is resorting to everything it can—gross falsification of the facts, slander against socialism, misinformation about the actual state of affairs in the capitalist system.

The monopolistic propaganda machine has concocted still another myth following the complete fiasco of the ones about the "Soviet menace" and "communist aggression," which no longer impress even the most gullible. Now it is spreading the cock-and-bull story about the "failure" of the socialist methods of economic management and claiming that we were compelled to admit the superiority of capitalist methods. Combined with the theories of "people's capitalism," "general welfare state," "unfluctuating economy," "diffusion of profits," this fabrication is called upon to distort the true course of the economic competition between the two systems, to play down the unquestionable superiority of the socialist system over the capitalist. The methods of misinformation used in this effort are rather standard.

"Why were the economic reforms required?" the ideologists of anti-communism ask. Obviously because not everything is running smoothly in the Soviet economic system, they answer, and because, you see, social-ism has been compelled to "learn from capitalism." The myth-makers care very little for the actual facts. They conceal from their audience that the socialist nations, despite all the shortcomings and difficulties of growth, have always developed at a faster pace than the capitalist economic sys-tem could even dream of. It is an indisputable fact, for instance, that in 1965 the countries of the socialist system produced 410 per cent more manufactured goods than in 1950. In the meantime, the developed coun-tries of capitalism increased their industrial output by only 110 per cent.

"What is the essence of the economic reforms in the Soviet Union and the other socialist nations?" the bourgeois "theoreticians" ask. And without so much as batting an eyelash they reply: their essence lies in the "copying" of capitalist principles and methods of economic man-agement, in "drawing nearer" to the capitalist "standards." They endeavor to prove at the same time that the economic methods of planned guid-ance are allegedly incompatible with the socialist system and contradict the Marxian economic theory of socialism. Is this really so?

Our press has quoted a considerable number of statements by bour-geois economists and journalists, who demagogically and without grounds presented the economic reforms in the socialist countries as a "reversion to capitalism," a "departure from Marxism." It is worth mentioning among these "soothsayers" the authors of the report of the Joint Economic Com-mittee of the United States Congress on the "new trends in Soviet econ-omy." The report claims, for instance, that the "Marxian economic theory is being neglected more and more frequently and all the innovations stem from western theory and practice."

The logic of these "specialists," if I may be permitted to call them that, is pure stereotype. Like bulls when a piece of red cloth is waved be-fore them, they are irritated by the fact that we are going over from the gross output factor to the sales indicator, that we are increasing economic incentives and raising the role and significance of bonuses and other forms of material encouragement. "Are not profits and bonuses, prices and markets, capitalist categories?" the bourgeois falsifiers demand.

Not at all, we reply to our "critics." To paraphrase Molière, there are profits and profits, prices and prices. There are the profits that land in the pockets of capitalists, the safes of monopolies, and this is, indeed, a capi-talist category. But there are also profits made at socialist enterprises and used in full, to the last kopeck, for the good of society. These go to make up the Central Net Profit Fund, which serves to expand production and satisfy other requirements of society as a whole; they also go to make up the incentive funds of enterprises. These profits, of course, have nothing in common with capitalism.

The same holds true of bonuses, prices, profitability, payment for production facilities, and the market. It goes without saying that a market operated by capitalist producers, who manufacture goods to make profit is nothing but a capitalist category. But this is by no means true when the market is operated by socialist enterprises.

The capitalist market, irrespective of all the forms of influence exerted upon it by the monopolists and the bourgeois state through economic programming and control, remains the sphere of operation of the spontaneous forces of private enterprise. In the planned socialist economy the market plays a wholly different role. It does not contradict the principles of planned economy, but on the contrary acts as one of the necessary requisites for its efficiency and rationality.

Familiarization with the efforts of bourgeois falsifiers leaves no doubt that the main purpose of their cock-and-bull stories is to present socialism as being incompatible with the principles of commodity production. The anticommunists are striving to create the impression that socialism is essentially a natural economy, that centralized and planned guidance of the national economy violate the economic laws.

But in reality it is socialism that asserts the new, planned type of economic development and lays the beginnings for a cardinally new phenomenon in the history of economics—conscientious use of economic laws in the interests of society.

The decisions of the March and September 1965 Plenary Meetings of the Central Committee and of the Twenty-third CPSU Congress proceed from the need to perfect the principles and methods of centralized, planned guidance of the national economy, along with the expansion of the economic and operational independence of enterprises. The economic reform is called upon to ensure the consolidation of planned principles in the socialist economy and to create the most favorable conditions for promoting the initiative of enterprises. This end is achieved through the streamlining of planning and intensification of the economic stimulation of production by means of such socialist cost-and-value categories as price, profit, bonus, and credit.

The use of commodity-money relations as an element of the planned socialist economy constitutes an inalienable aspect of the system of economic stimulation of production. Under these conditions the enterprises are bound to display greater flexibility and operational efficiency in planning and directing production, and must be able promptly to take into account the changing economic situation. All this means that within the framework of centralized planning an enterprise is given a chance to find the best methods of solving economic tasks under concrete conditions, drawing on the system of socialist cost-and-value relationships.

These principles seem to be within the comprehension of any more or less intelligent person. It is indeed true that he who does not want to see is worse than blind and he who does not want to hear is worse than deaf.

Sometimes, though very rarely, we hear realistic statements in the bourgeois press. Thus, the West German journalist, Walter Gunzel, notes that the "tendency towards decentralization" in the economies of the socialist countries may easily give rise to the supposition in the West that these nations are gradually departing from centralized economic planning. In reality, he admits, "this is not true. . . . It is out of the question that the East will discard the centralized procedure of guaranteeing the basic proportions of economic development."

Whereas one of the aspects of the "convergence" theory is to present economic reforms in the socialist countries as a kind of evolution towards capitalism, its other feature is to "dress up" capitalism "à la socialism." The main tendency, however, is to play down the distinctions between the two systems.

In his book *The Stages of Economic Growth: A Non-Communist Manifesto*, which made a big splash in the bourgeois world, the American economist W. W. Rostow squeezes the entire history of mankind's economic development into five "stages of growth" invented by him. His scheme omits the revolutionary changes of socio-economic structures and class struggle, these genuine moving forces of history. The conclusion is made that distinctions between countries are determined not by the difference in their socio-economic systems but by the fact that they are at different "stages of growth."

We see here a striking example of the unscientific method employed by modern bourgeois political economy. Based on this theoretical foundation, if indeed it can be regarded as such, is the following sequence of reasoning: capitalism, it is claimed, is no longer what it used to be; it is evolving rapidly towards socialism through the even distribution of property, planning, etc. At the same time socialism is supposedly increasingly recognizing the capitalist methods of economic management, taking the market into account, and making broader use of the methods of economic stimulation and material incentive. As a result, it is contended, we observe a "convergence" of the two systems: the distinctions between them are smoothing out, and "common" features are emerging more and more distinctly.

A central place in the contentions of the advocates of the "convergence" theory belongs to the gross distortion of the role played in socio-economic life by the form of ownership of the means of production. The basic distinction in principle between private capitalist and public, socialist ownership is played down and concealed. The case is presented as though the growth of state property and the spreading of joint-stock societies and corporations "erode" the private-ownership foundation of the capitalist economic system in the bourgeois states. On the other hand, the expansion of the economic and operational independence of socialist enterprises is presented as a departure from the principle of undivided domination of public property. Thus a dual falsification of reality is achieved. An utterly distorted picture of the modern world is presented.

The "convergence" of socialism and capitalism is professed also by certain theoreticians and practical state control officials in the capitalist countries. Indulging in wishful thinking, they claim that the goals of economic policy in the West and the East are becoming increasingly "close" and that both "economic systems" are advancing towards an "optimal structure." Stress is being laid here on the technical methods of drawing up plans, on the use of mathematics in the solution of economic problems. A parallel is drawn between the organization of production in the capitalist and the socialist countries, between socialist planning and the control of capitalist economy, since the method of intersectoral balances and linear programming, are used in both.

All such contentions, however, overlook the basic distinctions between the two socio-economic systems, which determine the completely different roles played by the methods of economic management, by the organizational and technical instruments.

It is significant that even many reactionary Western economists refute this version of the "similarity" theory. Thus, the prominent Dutch economist J. Tinbergen, who spoke about the "convergence" of the two systems at a meeting of the West German "Society for the Study of Eastern Europe," was sharply opposed by the West Berlin Professor K. C. Thalheim, who formulated his objections in five points. It is pertinent to quote them here in full, since they are typical for the bourgeois economists who oppose the "convergence" idea.

First, socialization of the means of production remains in force in the socialist countries. This is why there is little point in comparing the status of economic executives in the socialist countries with the role of capitalist managers. Secondly, centralized planning is preserved in the socialist countries while the "economic market" methods are made to serve it. Third, prices are fixed by state bodies. Due to this, prices do not play the role of indicators of "economic insufficiency" and cannot serve as a reliable basis for making decisions concerning capital investment. Fourth, real competition is out of the question, for enterprises arise and disappear "not from the angle of competition." Finally, the economic goals in the socialist countries are determined by "political institutions."

The reactionary West German economist apparently believed that his list of our economic system's "faults" was enough to "smite" socialism dead. But in reality quite in spite of himself he listed several advantages of socialism over capitalism.

Yes, the directors of socialist enterprises have nothing in common with capitalist managers. Centralized planned guidance of the national economy not only remains in force, of course, but is becoming even more effective by getting rid of the administrative straitjacket which restricted the initiative of enterprises. Prices are fixed according to plan and not through destructive competition. And, finally, the goals of the national economy are not determined by the selfish interests of capitalists but by the interests of the people, who are represented by the "political institutions," that is, the Party and the State.

The fact is that capitalism, despite all the changes that have taken place within it, remains a social system based on private ownership of the means of production. The theory of the "dying off" of private property due to the "dispersion" of shares, the growing role of managers, the expansion of state property, is completely unsound. As to capitalist planning, the need of drawing up and elaborating economic programs for a more or less extensive period testifies most eloquently to the fact that the present level of the development of productive forces, the modern stages of scientific and technical progress, call for the smashing of the slave chains of capitalist property. But planning will be very narrowly restricted if this form of property is preserved. It keeps running up against ever new obstacles, giving rise to sharp contradictions and conflicts.

As long as there is capitalist private property, "convergence" is out of the question. The theory of "convergence" remains nothing but a myth both in theory and in practice.

The present stage of economic development of the Soviet Union and the other countries of socialism is distinguished by an exceptionally intense process of improving the methods of economic management, which occurs in connection with tackling the truly grandiose tasks of building up the material and technical foundations of communism in the USSR, by the further confident economic advance of the world socialist system.

The raising of the standards of economic management is done on a solid foundation of Marxist-Leninist theory. It has passed the test of time and has received full confirmation in our magnificent accomplishments. In our day Marxism-Leninism is increasingly revealing its depth, vitality, and unmatched ability to develop in the light of new historical experience.

Suggested Reading

Association for Comparative Economics, *Proceedings of National Meeting*, San Francisco, December 27–29, 1966. Symposium on the Convergence Hypothesis (DeKalb, Illinois, 1967). [Mimeographed]

Balabkins, Nicholas, "Soviet-American Convergence By A.D. 2000? An Analysis of the Trends of Two Social Orders," *Canadian Slavonic Papers*, Vol. 2, 1968, pp. 133–147.

Linnemann, H., Pronk, J. P., and Tinbergen, J., *Convergence of Economic Systems in East and West*, Research on the International Economics of Disarmament and Arms Control, Oslo Conference, August 29–31, 1965 (Rotterdam, Netherlands Economic Institute, 1966). [Mimeographed]

Millar, James R., "On the Merits of the Convergence Hypothesis," *Journal of Economic Issues*, March 1968, pp. 60–68.

Svendsen, Knud Erik, "Are the Two Systems Converging?" *Øst Økonomi*, December 1962, pp. 195–209.

Tinbergen, Jan, "Do Communist and Free Economies Show a Converging Pattern?" *Soviet Studies*, Vol. XII, No. 4 (April 1961), pp. 331–341.

Wiles, Peter, "Will Capitalism and Communism Spontaneously Converge?" *Encounter*, Vol. XX, No. 6 (June 1963), pp. 84–90.

Wiles, Peter, "Fifty Years After: What Future for Communism?" *Lloyds Bank Review*, No. 86 (October 1967), pp. 36–48.

VI

Developing Economies
in Search of Systems

Introduction

The underdeveloped countries of the world are looking for solutions to the many problems besetting them. Of these, material destitution is the most urgent and acute. No wonder, therefore, that modernizing systems which promise rapid growth are eagerly sought after. The impatient desire for growth is accompanied by the hope of building a just society, one that would minimize social tensions and inspire commitment in the people. Hence the quest for analytical blueprints of growth and development is part of a larger search for social equity and political stability. Some perfectly respectable analytical models may be and have been rejected simply because the accompanying ideology had little appeal to the searchers, or because the proposed system was associated in the minds of many with colonial exploitation, real or imagined, substantiated by historical experience or distorted by historical perspective. This has frequently been the lot of solutions based on the functioning of markets and private property structures. Given the magnitude of the problems to be overcome, command systems and public property structures seem to some to promise the needed break-through out of poverty by vesting in an economically enlightened state the means for the crucial push. In Part IV we observed some of the countries which at one time or another had opted, or were made to opt, for command. We have seen that the adoption of command and the rush toward public property turned out to have been merely the beginning of a more complex and subtle search for allocative efficiency, social justice, and national identity. North Korea, Cuba, China, and the economically more advanced countries of Eastern Europe —even the Soviet Union itself—are still groping for answers, for the fine balance of command and market that would give not just statistically measurable growth of output, but growth at minimum cost. Command systems have shown themselves to be strong in the first respect, deficient in the second. All in all, they have succeeded in generating rapid growth of output in certain sectors of the economy, producing in the process imbalances and disproportions within the system. The experience has had a sobering effect on many command-oriented economists: they are often more skeptical about the absolute necessity or inevitability of the totalitarian big push out of poverty, and more conscious of the human cost involved than are third world economists searching for solutions. These nuances and reservations are noticeable in the essay by Falkowski.

The point is frequently lost that the underdeveloped countries' quest for modernizing systems is not limited to the so-called "uncommitted." It goes on in what used to be called the "Soviet bloc," it has caused deep rifts in apparently monolithic China, and much soul-searching in Cuba and North Korea. Part VI, however, is concerned with the options open to those custom-dominated economies which so far have not settled for either the one or the other of the fundamental assumptions underlying resource coordination and control and property relations. These countries are the battleground of contending solutions, both analytical and ideological. The choice, when it is finally made, is likely to determine the balance of power between pluralism and centralism in the world for some time to come. Complicating this confrontation is the pervasive influence of local traditions struggling for survival and recognition. Tradition presents itself in new national colors and argues in the language of native aspirations. The debate is not made any clearer by outdated semantics and the rediscovery by some leaders of nineteenth century European dissenting ideologies, long since jettisoned in their countries of origin.

Part VI approaches this vast and complex problem in two steps. In Section A, economists whose preferences differ argue their respective cases. Myint and Kurihara represent the market orientation approach to development; Falkowski, with many a reservation, a pragmatic command orientation. Myint's argument applies particularly to smaller underdeveloped countries. Falkowski introduces into his thesis numerous qualifications so that in the end there are important areas of agreement between the Myint-Kurihara and Falkowski approaches. Nevertheless, the starting assumptions are sufficiently far apart to present economists and others in the developing countries with a difficult and delicate choice. Section B contains a single case study: that of Mexico, in which an attempt to combine the benefits of markets and private property with command and public property has been made.

A. Market-Oriented and Command-Oriented Advice

39   H. MYINT

Economic Theory and Development Policy[1]

Both economic theory and development economics are getting highly specialised nowadays. A specialist in a branch of economic theory cannot hope to keep up with the highly technical development in other branches of economic theory. Similarly, a specialist in a particular aspect of economic development or on a particular group of underdeveloped countries cannot hope to keep up with the vast outpouring of publications in other fields of development economics. The proliferation and sub-division of development economics is most dramatically shown by the many periodicals which devote themselves entirely to some particular aspect of the subject, such as development finance, development agriculture and so on.

But, it seems to me that precisely because of this trend towards specialisation, there is some need, in the universities at least, for a general practitioner to act as a middleman between different specialised fields of development economics and also between development economics and general economics. Such an economist should try to acquire a good working knowledge at least, of the broad economic dimensions and the basic features of the situation, in a wide range of underdeveloped countries. His aim should be to try to apply the existing economic theory in a more realistic and fruitful way to suit the varying conditions of the different types of underdeveloped countries. An equally important part of his job would be to try to prevent serious misapplications of economic theory, whether of the orthodox type or the newer modern theories, to the underdeveloped countries.

This way of looking at a general development economist as a middleman between the tool-makers and the tool-users brings me face to face with the perennial controversy: how far are the existing tools of economic theory applicable to the underdeveloped countries? There are many distinguished economists[2] who would be impatient with my proposal to start from the existing theoretical framework and try to improve its applicabil-

From *Economica*, Vol. XXIV, No. 134 (May 1967), pp. 117–130. Reprinted by permission of the author and *Economica*.

[1] The text of an inaugural lecture given at the London School of Economics on December 1, 1966.

[2] For example, G. Myrdal, *Economic Theory and Underdeveloped Regions*, 1957; also his *An International Economy*, 1956; D. Seers, "The Limitations of the Special Case", *Bulletin of the Oxford Institute of Economics and Statistics*, May 1963.

ity to the underdeveloped countries in the light of accumulating experience and factual knowledge. They would say that the existing "Western" economic theory is so intimately bound up with the special conditions, problems and preconceptions of the industrially advanced countries that large portions of it have to be abandoned before we can come to grips with the problem of the underdeveloped countries.

These economists have advanced three main types of criticism against the existing economic theory.

First, they question the "realism" of trying to apply the standard models of theoretical analysis meant for the advanced countries to the different economic and institutional setting of the underdeveloped countries. I have no quarrel with this line of criticism. In fact I shall be giving illustrations of other types of lack of realism in applying economic theory to the underdeveloped countries which are not mentioned by the critics. But it seems to me that this is not an argument for abandoning existing economic theory but merely an argument for trying to improve its applicability.

Second, the critics question the "relevance" of the static neo-classical economics concerned with the problem of allocating given resources within an existing economic framework to the problem of promoting economic development in the underdeveloped countries, which is concerned with increasing the amount of available resources, improving techniques and generally with the introduction of a dynamic self-sustaining process of economic change, disrupting the existing framework. Here again I agree that we do not possess a satisfactory dynamic theory for studying development problems. In fact, I would go further and say that the recent developments in the theory of dynamic economics in terms of the growth models are not very relevant and are not meant to be relevant for the underdeveloped countries.[3] But I do not accept the conclusion which the critics have drawn, viz. that the static theory of efficient allocation of given resources is irrelevant for the underdeveloped countries. I shall come back to this point.

Third, the critics maintain that the orthodox economic theory is inextricably bound up with preconceptions and biases in favour of the orthodox economic policies of *laissez-faire*, free trade and conservative fiscal and monetary policies. They believe that these orthodox economic policies are generally inimical to rapid economic growth, which can be promoted only by large-scale government economic planning, widespread protection, import controls and deficit financing of development programmes, if sufficient external aid is not available. Thus they propose that large chunks of existing economic theory, particularly the orthodox neo-classical theory, should be abandoned to pave the way for the adoption of these new development policies.

[3] Cf. Sir John Hicks, *Capital and Growth*, Oxford, 1965, p. 1.

There are two questions here. The first is the general question whether the new policies are always more effective than the orthodox policies in promoting economic development in the underdeveloped countries. The second is the more specific question whether there is an unbreakable ideological link between orthodox economic theory and orthodox economic policies so that if we wish to adopt the new development policies we must necessarily abandon much of the existing theory.

The underdeveloped countries vary widely among themselves and I, therefore, find it difficult to accept the general presumption that the new policies will always be better for their economic development whatever their particular individual situation. Later, I shall give some examples where the orthodox type of economic policies have in fact been more effective in promoting economic development than the new-style development policies. However, I have chosen as the subject of my lecture today, not the general debate on the rival merits of the orthodox and the new development policies but the relation between economic theory and development policy. I have done this partly because I feel that such a general debate without reference to a concrete situation generates more heat than light and partly also because it has been rapidly overtaken by events. Whether we like it or not, it is no longer an open question whether the underdeveloped countries should choose the orthodox or the new type of development policies. One after another, they have already made their choice in favour of the new policies which have now become a part of conventional economic wisdom. Accepting this as one of the facts of life, the more immediately relevant question seems to be the second question, viz. whether large parts of orthodox economic theory have now become obsolete because the underdeveloped countries wish to plan for rapid economic development.

I shall argue that this is not so; that on the contrary, the orthodox economic theory assumes a greater significance in the context of the new "progressive" development policies. I shall show that even if development planning is to be regarded as new and radical policy, the *theory* underlying development planning is, technically speaking, quite orthodox and conventional. Similarly, I shall show that the orthodox theory of international trade can be made to support more liberal and generous trade and aid policies towards the underdeveloped countries, if we choose to use it in this way. What I am saying is not new. It is merely a restatement of the familiar doctrine that economic theory is "ethically neutral" and can be made use of in the more efficient pursuit of the economic objectives to be chosen by the "value judgments" of the policy maker.

However, let us start from a closer look at the question of "realism" in applying existing economic theory to the underdeveloped countries. Some critics speak of "existing theory" as though it were contained in a modern textbook like Samuelson. Properly speaking, it should include the whole corpus of Western economic theory, offering a wide choice of theoretical models, ranging from those of the older economists writing at earlier stages of economic development to the highly complex and abstract models of contemporary economic theory. To my mind, a very important cause of lack of realism arises from the wrong choice of theoretical mōdels to be applied to the underdeveloped countries. In much the same way as the governments of the underdeveloped countries succumb to the lure of the "steel mills" embodying the most advanced and capital-intensive type of Western technology, many development economists have succumbed to the lure of the intellectual "steel mills" represented by the latest and most sophisticated theoretical models. This is where I believe the greatest mischief has been done. This is why I have always maintained that a good development eonomist should also be something of an applied historian of economic thought.

If it is unrealistic to apply highly sophisticated theoretical models meant for the complex economic structures of the advanced countries to the simpler economic structures of the underdeveloped countries, has this been corrected by the new theories of development and underdevelopment which are specially meant for the underdeveloped countries? Looking at these new theories which became popular during the 1950s, such as the "vicious circle", the "take-off" or the "big push", it does not seem to me that these have stood up any better to the test of realism. The weakness of these new theories is that they try to apply to all the underdeveloped countries a composite model of *the* underdeveloped country incorporating in it certain special features of some one or other type of underdeveloped country. The "vicious circle" theory assumes poverty and stagnation caused by severe population pressure on resources; the "take-off" theory assumes the pre-existence of a fairly high level of development in the political, social and institutional framework; the "big push" theory assumes both and also an internal market large enough to support a domestic capital-goods sector. By the time we have incorporated all these special features into a composite model, the number of the underdeveloped countries to which this model might apply becomes severely limited to one or two countries such as India and possibly Pakistan.

The limitations of these new theories of development, particularly the "vicious circle" theory, can be illustrated by looking at the broad dimensions of the economic performance of the underdeveloped countries during the decade 1950–60. During that decade, compared with the 4 per cent. average annual growth rates for the advanced Western countries, the gross domestic product of underdeveloped countries as a group has grown at the average annual rate of 4.4 per cent., giving them a growth in *per capita* incomes of a little over 2 per cent. per annum.[4] This may or may not be very much, but the really interesting thing is that

[4] United Nations, *World Economic Survey*, 1963, Part I, p. 20.

some underdeveloped countries have been growing at a faster rate than the average, say between 5 and 6 per cent., while others have been barely able to keep up with their population increase. Thus instead of the earlier *simpliste* view according to which all underdeveloped countries are caught up in a vicious circle of stagnation and population pressure, we are led to the question why some underdeveloped countries grow faster or slower than others.

When we try to answer this question, we become greatly aware of the differences between the underdeveloped countries, in size, in the degree of population pressure on natural resources, in the conditions of world demand for their exports and in their general level of economic development and political stability. These differences by themselves will explain quite a lot of the differences in the growth rates among different underdeveloped countries. If in addition we want to say something about the influence of development policies, we shall have to choose a fairly uniform group of countries where the basic social and economic differences are small enough for us to isolate the effect of economic policy.

To illustrate, let me take the concrete example of the post-war economic development of Southeast Asia. This will also serve to illustrate the dangers of generalising about development policies, particularly the danger of assuming that the new "progressive" development policies will always promote faster economic growth than the orthodox economic policies.

The five countries I have chosen, Burma, Thailand, the Philippines, Indonesia and Malaya, form a fairly homogeneous group. In contrast to India or China, they are not only much smaller but also do not suffer from any great pressure of population. They do not have to contend with food shortage and have much more elbow room in respect of natural resources to allow for the working of economic incentives. They are also similar in the general level of social and economic development and moreover have common exports such as rice, timber and rubber. Yet the rapid postwar economic development of Thailand, the Philippines and Malaya contrasts sharply with the economic stagnation of Burma and Indonesia. By 1960, both Thailand and the Philippines doubled their prewar gross national product (in real terms) combined with a considerable growth in import-substituting industries, while the gross national product of Burma and Indonesia rose by a bare 11 per cent. above the pre-war level, much slower than their rate of population growth during the same period. Malaya, starting at a somewhat higher *per capita* level than the others, has also enjoyed economic prosperity which compares favourably not only with Burma and Indonesia but also with Ceylon to which her economic structure is similar in many aspects.

These large differences in the rates of economic growth are closely related to the rate of expansion in the exports of the two groups of countries and, since they have common exports sharing the same world market conditions, the differences in their export performance must be traced largely to the domestic economic policies which have affected the supply side of their exports. Here, broadly speaking, the first group of countries with the faster rates of economic growth, viz. Thailand, Malaya and the Philippines, have pursued the more orthodox type of economic policies with a greater reliance on market forces, private enterprise and an outward-looking attitude to foreign trade and enterprise; while Burma and Indonesia lean heavily on economic planning and large-scale state intervention in economic life combined with an inward-looking and even hostile attitude towards foreign trade and enterprise.

More specifically we may note the following. (i) Thailand and the Philippines have very successfully used market incentives to encourage their peasants to bring more land under cultivation and expand production both of export and domestic food crops, while the Burmese peasants have been depressed by the operation of the state agricultural marketing board which has used peasant agriculture simply as a milch cow for government investment in state enterprises in manufacturing industry and social overhead capital. (ii) Thailand and the Philippines have encouraged their domestic entrepreneurs to set up new manufacturing industries through protection and subsidies, while Burma and Indonesia have tried to do this by state enterprises which have failed, amongst other reasons, because of a shortage of entrepreneurial ability among the civil servants. Here it may be noted that all these Southeast Asian countries suffer from the fear of being dominated by the Chinese or the Indian entrepreneurs who are or were prominent in small or medium scale enterprises in light manufacturing industries. Thus one may say that Burma and Indonesia have chosen to substitute Indian and Chinese private enterprise by indigenous state enterprise while Thailand has absorbed the Chinese entrepreneurs into her own business class and the Philippines have successfully substituted Filipino private entrepreneurs for them. This problem has yet to be solved in Malaya. (iii) Malaya, Thailand and the Philippines have offered a stable economic climate to Western enterprises both in the traditional plantation and mining sectors and in the new manufacturing sector and have benefited from a considerable inflow of private foreign capital, while Burma and Indonesia have discouraged fresh inflow of private investment by nationalization and other hostile policies. (iv) Malaya and Thailand have pursued conservative monetary and fiscal policies and their currencies have been strong and stable, and the Philippines tackled her balance-of-payments disequilibrium successfully by devaluation in 1962. In contrast Burma and Indonesia have tried to solve their balance-of-payments problems arising out of deficit financing and domestic inflation through an intensification of inefficient and hurtful import controls, which, combined with pervasive state interference at all levels of economic activity, have throttled most of the promising infant industries.[5]

It is not for me to judge the ultimate rightness or wrongness of the economic nationalism and the anti-Western attitude of Burma and Indonesia contrasted with the more pro-Western attitude of Malaya, Thailand and the Philippines. But at the conventional level at which economists judge development policies, it seems to me that in the case of Southeast Asia at least that the orthodox type of economic policies have resulted in a more rapid rate of economic development during the post-war period than the newer "progressive" development policies. How far is the Southeast Asian experience applicable to other underdeveloped countries outside the region? I think that it may be of some relevance to the other smaller and less densely populated export economies, notably in West Africa. There, also, expansion in the exports of primary products still offers the most promising engine of economic development both as a source of foreign exchange earnings to finance the new import-substituting industries and, even more important as the method of drawing the under-utilised natural resources of the subsistence sector into the money economy. But these conclusions in favour of the orthodox policies are likely to become weaker as we try to extend them to less similar types of country, particularly to large overpopulated countries like India. But conversely it would be equally unrealistic to try to apply the Indian model to the smaller export economies.

Let me now conclude my remarks on the "realism" of applying economic theory to the underdeveloped countries by drawing attention to the dangers of trying to be too different from the standard models of economic analysis. These arise from selecting the "queer cases" in the standard Western models of analysis and in taking it for granted that these exceptions to the standard case must automatically apply to the underdeveloped countries because they are so different from the advanced countries in social values and attitudes and institutional setting. Such for instance is the famous case of the "backward-sloping supply curve" of labour attributed to the underdeveloped countries by many writers, who nevertheless speak also of the "demonstration effect" and "the revolution of rising expectations". Such also is the belief that the people of the underdeveloped countries, being more communally minded, will take more easily to co-operative forms of economic organization, despite the fact that writers on the co-operative movement in the underdeveloped countries frequently complain about the lack of co-operative spirit and the excessive individualism of the people. Yet another example is the generalisation that the people of the underdeveloped countries naturally lack

[5] For a fuller treatment, see my article, "The Inward and the Outward Looking Countries of Southeast Asia and the Economic Future of the Region", Symposium Series II, *Japan's Future in Southeast Asia*, Kyoto University, 1966.

entrepreneurial ability, irrespective of the economic policies followed by their governments. Here, if one were to tell the politicians of the underdeveloped countries that their people are lazy, stupid, lacking in initiative and adaptability, one would be branded as an enemy: but if one were to rephrase these prejudices in another way and say that they lack entrepreneurial capacity, one would be welcomed for giving "scientific" support for economic planning. To take just one more example, there is the hoary belief that peasants in the underdeveloped countries do not respond to economic incentives, while agricultural economists have been accumulating abundant evidence to show that peasants do respond to price changes by switching from one crop to another or by bringing more land under cultivation. The real problem is how to introduce new methods of cultivation which will raise productivity: this is a difficult practical problem, but in principle it is little different from, say, the problem of introducing new methods to raise productivity in British industry.

This is where I think that a closer co-operation between economics and other branches of social studies is likely to prove most useful, both in getting rid of questionable sociological generalisations and also in tackling the more intractable problems of analysing social and economic change.

Let me now turn from the "realism" to the "relevance" of the existing economic theory to the underdeveloped countries. The problem of promoting rapid economic development in these countries may ultimately lie in the realm of social and economic dynamics of the sort we do not at present possess; and there is nothing in my argument to prevent anyone from launching into new dynamic theoretical approaches to the underdeveloped countries. But in the meantime it is dangerously easy to underestimate the significance to the underdeveloped countries of the orthodox static theory of the allocation of given resources. The affluent Western economies with their steady rates of increase in productivity may be able to take a tolerant attitude towards misallocation of resources. But the underdeveloped countries are simply too poor to put up with the preventable wasteful use of their given meagre economic resources. In particular, they can ill afford the well recognised distortions of their price system such as the excessively high levels of wages and low levels of interest rates in their manufacturing and public sectors compared with those in the agricultural sector, and the over-valuation of their currencies at the official rates of exchange. Having to bear the brunt of low earnings and high interest rates discourages the expansion of agricultural output both for export and for domestic consumption and this in turn slows down the overall rate of growth of the economy. Higher wages attract a large number of people from the countryside to the towns but only a small proportion of this influx can be absorbed because of the highly capital-intensive methods adopted in the modern import-substituting industries. This aggravates the problem of urban unemployment and the problem of shanty towns which increases the requirements for investment in housing and social welfare. The scarce supply of capital tends to be wastefully used both in the government prestige projects and in private industry because of the artificially low rates of interest. This is aggravated by the over-valuation of currencies and import controls in favour of capital goods which positively encourage the businessmen who are fortunate enough to obtain licences to buy the most expensive and capital-intensive type of machinery from abroad.

These then are some of the glaring sources of waste which can be reduced by a better allocation of resources. Now I should point out that just because the orthodox neo-classical theory is concerned with the efficient allocation of *given* resources, it does not mean that the theory becomes unimportant in the context of aid policies to increase the volume of resources available to the underdeveloped countries. On the contrary, a country which cannot use its already available resources efficiently is not likely to be able to "absorb" additional resources from aid programmes and use them efficiently. That is to say, a country's absorptive capacity for aid must to a large extent depend on its ability to avoid serious misallocation of resources. A similar conclusion can be drawn about an underdeveloped country's ability to make effective use of its opportunities for international trade. If we find that a country is not making effective use of its already available trading opportunities, because of domestic policies discouraging its export production or raising the cost in the export sector, then we should not expect it to benefit in a dramatic way from the new trading opportunities to be obtained through international negotiations.

This is a part of the reason why I have suggested that orthodox economic theory, instead of becoming obsolete, has assumed a greater significance in the context of the new "progressive" policies for promoting economic development in the underdeveloped countries. Let me illustrate this argument further by examples from development planning theory and from recent discussions about the appropriate trade and aid policies.

I think that a great deal of confusion would have been avoided by clearly distinguishing the *policy* of development planning and the economic *theory* which underlies development planning which is, as we shall see, only an application of the traditional theory of the optimum allocation of the *given* resources. This confusion was introduced during the 1950s when it was the fashion to try to make out the case for development planning mainly by attacking the orthodox equilibrium and optimum theory. At the macroeconomic level, there were theories of deficit financing trying to show how economic development might be accelerated by forced saving and inflation or by making use of "disguised unemployment" for capital formation. More generally, the theories of the "vicious circle", the "big push" or "unbalanced growth" tried to show, in their different ways, the desirability of breaking out of the static equilibrium framework by deliberately introducing imbalances and disequilibria which would start the chain-reaction of cumulative movement towards self-sustained economic growth. Ironically enough, when the underdeveloped countries came to accept the need for development planning and asked how this might be done efficiently, it turned out that the economic theory required for this purpose was basically nothing but the traditional equilibrium and optimum theory.

Thus according to the present day textbooks on development planning,[6] the first task of the planner is to test the feasibility of the plan at the macroeconomic level by making sure that the aggregate amount of resources required to carry out the plan does not exceed the aggregate amount of resources available. That is to say, deficit financing and inflation are to be avoided and this is to be checked at the sectoral level by seeing to it that the projected rate of expansion of the services sector does not exceed the possible rate of expansion in the output of commodities by a certain critical margin. The next task of the planner is to test the consistency of the plan at the sectoral and microeconomic level to make sure that the demand and supply for particular commodities and services are equated to each other and that there is an equilibrium relationship between the different parts of the economy, not only within any given year, but also between one year and another during the whole of the plan period. Finally, if the plan is found to be both feasible and consistent, the task of the planner is to find out whether the plan adopted is an optimum plan in the sense that there is no alternative way of re-allocating the given resources more efficiently to satisfy the given objectives of the plan.

If this standard formulation of development planning is accepted, then there is no fundamental theoretical difference between those who aim to achieve the efficient allocation of the available resources through the market mechanism and those who aim to achieve it through the state mechanism. Both accept the optimum allocation of resources as their theoretical norm and their disagreements are about the *practical* means of fulfilling this norm. In any given situation, they will disagree how far planning should be "indicative" or "imperative", that is to say, how far the task of allocating resources should be left to the decentralised decision-making of the market or to the centralised decision-making of the state. But technically speaking they are using the same type of economic theory, viz, the extension of the orthodox neo-classical theory, in the pursuit of their different practical policies.

[6] See, particularly, W. A. Lewis, *Development Planning*, 1966; A Waterson, *Development Planning: Lessons of Experience*, Oxford, 1966; and W. B. Reddaway, *The Development of the Indian Economy*, 1962.

From a theoretical point of view the great divide is between those who believe on the one hand that economic development of the underdeveloped countries can be promoted in *an orderly manner* by a more efficient allocation of the available resources which is assumed to be steadily expanding between one period and another through good management of domestic savings and external aid, and those who believe, on the other hand, that only sudden disruptive and *disorderly* changes such as social revolutions and technical innovations can bring about economic development. Now this second revolutionary approach to economic development may well be the correct approach for some underdeveloped countries. But it is difficult to see how this can be incorporated into the planning approach. Development planning is by definition an orderly approach: on the other hand, genuinely far-reaching and disruptive social changes cannot be turned on and turned off in a predictable way and incorporated into the planning framework. Those who advocate the necessity of breaking out of the static equilibrium framework by deliberately introducing imbalances and tensions are in effect advocating at the same time the need to break out of the planning framework. Thus one may advocate social revolution now and planning later, but one may not advocate social revolution and planning at the same time without getting into serious contradictions. Further, it should be pointed out that the revolutionary approach to economic development is by no means the monopoly of the critics of the private enterprise system. The case for *laissez-faire* can be made, not on grounds of static allocative efficiency, but on the ground that it imparts a "dynamism" to the economy by stimulating enterprise, innovation and savings. Schumpeter's picture of the disruption of the existing productive framework through a process of "creative destruction" by innovating private entrepreneurs is a well-known illustration of this type of revolutionary approach to economic development.

Let me conclude by illustrating how the orthodox theory of international trade may be used in support of more liberal or generous trade and aid policies towards the underdeveloped countries. There is still a considerable amount of prejudice against the export of primary products in the underdeveloped countries. To some extent this has been overlaid by the more pro-trade views which have gained ground since the United Nations Conference on Trade and Development. The views which are now accepted by most underdeveloped countries must be summarised as follows. (i) While the underdeveloped countries should be allowed to protect their domestic manufacturing industries in any way they think fit, they should have preferential treatment or freer access to the markets of the advanced countries for their exports of primary products, semi-processed products and fully-manufactured products. (ii) More aid should be given to supplement the trade concessions, but there should be less tying of aid to imports from the donor country and also less tying of aid to the specific projects chosen and managed by the donor country.

Now it is possible to find a variety of opinions among the orthodox-minded economists on the question of giving aid to the underdeveloped countries. There are some who are against aid-giving either because they fear that this would lead to a misallocation of the world capital resources or because of the various undesirable political and sociological side effects of aid. For instance, Professor Bauer has recently argued that the material benefits which an underdeveloped country might obtain from aid would be swamped by the deleterious sociological and political effects, such as the development of a beggar mentality and the growth of centralised power which would pauperise the aid-receiving country.[7] On the other hand, not all orthodox economists are against aid-giving. In this connection, I should mention the name of the late Professor Frederic Benham who wrote what I consider to be the best book stating the case for aid-giving.[8] These individual views aside, the standard orthodox economic theory would say something like this on the subject: how much aid the rich countries should give the poor countries should be decided by "value judgments" based on moral and political considerations which are beyond the scope of economic analysis. But once it is agreed that a certain amount of aid, say 1 per cent. of the national income of the rich countries, should be given, economic analysis can be used to show how this given policy objective can be carried out in the most efficient way. By a familiar process of reasoning, orthodox theory would say that this could be most efficiently carried out by free trade for both the aid-givers and the aid-receivers. For the aid-givers, the more efficient allocation of their resources through free trade would enable them to spare the 1 per cent. of their income they are giving away with the least sacrifice. For the aid-receivers, free importation of goods at cheaper prices than could be produced at home would maximise the value of the aid they received. Further, if the aid resources are to be invested, the more efficient choice of investment opportunities under free trade would raise the returns from investment.

Thus from the point of view of orthodox trade theory the one-way free-trade plus aid for which the underdeveloped countries are asking is less efficient than two-way free trade plus the same amount of aid. This is likely to be so even when the need to protect the "infant industries" has been conceded.[9] But if the underdeveloped countries insist on adopting

[7] *Two Views on Aid to the Developing Countries,* by Barbara Ward and P. T. Bauer, Institute of Economic Affairs, Occasional Paper 9, 1966.

[8] F. Benham, *Economic Aid to Underdeveloped Countries,* 1961.

[9] For one thing, the import controls practised by the underdeveloped countries are too indiscriminate and bound up with short-run balance-of-payments considerations to give selective protection to the promising infant industries; for another, the correction of the distortions due to the imperfections of the domestic market may require other forms of government intervention than protection. See my paper (ch. 7) in R. Harrod and D. C. Hague (eds.), *International Trade Theory in a Develop-*

what they consider to be the less advantageous option, then the orthodox trade theory can still say something useful within this restricted framework: and what it has to say is in support of opening the markets of the advanced countries more freely to the products from the underdeveloped countries and in support of the untying of aid.

Take the rather protracted debate about "reciprocity", on the question whether the advanced countries should give trade concessions to the underdeveloped countries without getting back some *quid pro quo*. In support of one-way free trade the champions of the underdeveloped countries usually appeal to moral considerations such as not having the same rule for the lion and the lamb and the need for a double moral standard when dealing with unequal trading partners. The advanced countries, on the other hand, tend to argue that while they do not expect "reciprocity" from the underdeveloped countries, they would like other advanced countries to give similar concessions to the underdeveloped countries before they commit themselves. Professor Harry Johnson[10] has recently reminded us that these arguments, based on the mercantilistic view of trade, have entirely overlooked the point that according to the theory of comparative costs the gains from trade consist in having cheaper imports. By allowing free imports from the underdeveloped countries, the consumers in the advanced countries already would have gained from trade by being able to buy these imports more cheaply: thus there is no need to ask for a further *quid pro quo*.

Basing himself entirely on the orthodox trade theory, Professor Johnson has argued that the United States would gain by a unilateral removal of trade barriers to the products from the underdeveloped countries without waiting for other advanced countries to follow suit. Similarly, he has shown that the official figures for the United States aid to the underdeveloped countries would be very appreciably reduced if the goods and services given under tied aid, notably aid in the form of agricultural surpluses, were revalued at world market prices under free-trade conditions.

These seem to me to be very good illustrations of how orthodox trade theory can be used in support of more liberal trade and aid policies, if we choose to do so. What has given flexibility to the theory is the much-maligned postulate of the "ethical neutrality" of economic theory. The champions of the underdeveloped countries tend to look upon it with great suspicion as a sign of an underdeveloped social conscience on the part of those who adopt it. But I hope that I have shown it to be no more objectionable than the notion of a constrained maximum.

---

ing World, 1963; and H. G. Johnson, "Optimum Trade Intervention in the Presence of Domestic Distortions", in *Trade, Growth and the Balance of Payments*, Economic Essays in Honor of Gottfried Haberler, Amsterdam, 1965.

[10] H. G. Johnson, *U.S. Economic Policy Towards the Less Developed Countries*, Washington, D.C., 1967.

Finally, the question of how far aid should be tied to the specific projects to be chosen and managed by the donor country raises fundamental issues of how far we consider the underdeveloped countries to be competent to run their own affairs without a benevolent supervision from the advanced country. Here we come at last to the "presumptions" and "preconceptions" of the orthodox economists which conflict sharply with those of the planning-minded economists. One important presumption of the liberal orthodox economists which I believe in, is that the underdeveloped countries can best educate themselves for economic development by being allowed to make their own mistakes and learning from them, and that without this painful process of self-education and self-discipline they are not likely to acquire the degree of competence required for economic development. I think this runs contrary to the implicit or explicit philosophy of the present-day administrators of aid. They would like to make up for the underdeveloped countries' lack of "absorptive capacity" for aid by insisting upon tighter planning and supervision of their economic affairs by economic and technical experts from the advanced donor countries. Ultimately, then, we have two philosophies about aid-giving to the underdeveloped countries. The liberal orthodox view is to give an agreed amount of aid to the underdeveloped countries and then leave it to them to use it freely in any way they think fit, to learn from their mistakes and to take the consequences of their action. According to this view the advanced countries can only guarantee the amount of aid but not the rate of economic development of the underdeveloped countries which must to a large extent depend on how they use the aid. One further implication of this view is that, since the underdeveloped countries differ so much in their circumstances and capacity to benefit from mistakes, it would be unrealistic to expect an equally fast rate of economic development for all the underdeveloped countries. The alternative view which pervades thinking at present is that the advanced countries should take the responsibility of guaranteeing a politically-acceptable target rate of economic growth for all underdeveloped countries and, if this cannot be achieved by the latter countries' own efforts, the advanced countries should be prepared not only to increase the total volume of aid but also to increase the planning and supervision of the use of this aid so that the peoples of underdeveloped countries may enjoy economic development in spite of themselves.[11] Obviously the underdeveloped countries cannot insist on freedom to use aid in any way they like and at the same time insist that the advanced countries guarantee a minimum target rate of economic growth for them all. Ultimately they will have to choose the one or the other. I, with my orthodox liberal inclinations, hope that they will choose the former.

[11] For example, contrast I. M. D. Little and J. M. Clifford, *International Aid*, 1965, p. 192, with H. G. Johnson, *op. cit.*, ch. 4.

40   KENNETH K. KURIHARA

MIXED ECONOMIC STATECRAFT
AND DEMOCRATIC SAFEGUARDS

The less developed economies bent upon rapid growth are understandably tempted to adopt the extreme form of centralized economic planning, especially in these times of hyper-susceptibility to the international "demonstration effect" (the higher consumption and production standards of advanced economies). To resist such a temptation is not to discourage the idea of economic planning but to encourage the *democratic* pattern of growth programming in the *long-run* interest of the developing economies concerned. This essay is broadly intended to be an additional contribution to the literature on the state's role in economic development. To be more specific, this essay will discuss the rationale, operational significance, and practical applicability of mixed economic statecraft most closely associated with the name of Keynes, and also suggest the necessary safeguards against the possible abuses of that statecraft in any developing economy that might be inclined to adopt it.

1. KEYNESIAN MIXED STATECRAFT

The anonymity and impersonality of the modern "mixed economy,"[1] so-called, is in itself a great scientific advance over the emotion-laden labels "capitalism" and "socialism." However, since the concept of a mixed economy represents an ingenious combination of the advantages of capitalism and socialism without their disadvantages, it seems useful to begin with an introductory discussion of the disadvantages of extreme statecraft.

On the one side, there is a policy of *laissez-faire* designed to leave individual economic decisions and activities entirely unchecked even when those activities lead to general instability, insecurity and inequity.

From: *Social and Economic Studies,* Vol. 10, No. 2, 1961, pp. 223–228. Reprinted by permission of author and *Social and Economic Studies.*
[1] As far as I am aware, Professor A. H. Hansen was the first to coin this expression. See his *Fiscal Policy and Business Cycle* (W. W. Norton, N.Y.), 1941.

Here economic man is assumed to be so rational, economic calculus so precise, economic machinery so efficient, and private property so sacrosanct that inferentially almost nothing and nobody should be subjected to public control. Here is the one extreme case of statecraft where individual liberty is misconstrued as individual license, where political democracy is undermined by economic anarchy, where private virtues are mistaken for the public good, and where private initiative is misinterpreted as a sufficient as well as necessary condition for economic and social progress. The only notable exception to this rule has been the public control of "big business" in the interest of greater atomistic competition. Even today there are a few economists and policymakers who are interested and concur in the government's function *only* as "the preserver of competition" on the classical assumption that competition is an "all-sufficient" regulator, stabilizer and innovator.

On the other side, there is a policy of authoritarian planning aimed at organizing individual economic units into "classes" for central control at the calculated risks of class wars, partisan strife, personal hatred, and individual injustice. Here central authority is assumed to be so omnipotent, economic man so class-conscious, personal choice so anti-social, and public ownership so indispensable that, by implication, almost everything and everybody should be subjected to public control. Here is the other extreme case of statecraft where economic planning is abused by political totalitarianism, where the national interest is misrepresented by class interests, and where public policy is misinterpreted as the self-sufficing, self-justifying promoter of all economic blessings, social and personal. The only promising exception to this rule is seen in the avowed attempts of some existing authoritarian regimes to "decentralize", presumably in the interests of economic efficiency, individual initiative and consumer choice. Even outside those regimes there are a few economists and policy-makers who contemplate and manipulate the agencies of the state for the authoritarian or autocratic control of economic life on the dogmatic assumption that complete regimentation is the only alternative to complete *laissez-faire*.

It was as offering a better alternative to those extreme types of statecraft that Keynes conceived his *mixed* statecraft, with a specific view to providing technical means to three technical ends, namely: (a) full and stable employment; (b) greater equality in the distribution of wealth and income in so far as it would aid the first aim; and (c) the international homogenization of living standards, especially in the post-war period of reconstruction and development. These are, it is to be stressed, essentially *technical* ends, since their attainment requires rigorous analysis, dispassionate judgment, and clear perception, irrespective of what political attitude or ideological bearing the social scientist may have. Obviously these goals are so great in magnitude and so global in scope that they can be reached only with the aid of the state possessing sufficient resources and the power to use them in the public interest. These technical objects become political issues when they are deemed inconsistent with non-economic goals of society or when they are reached by emotional means. However, apprehensions about the political danger of achieving "full employment at any cost," intimations about the political instability of "an egalitarian society," insinuations about "the road to serfdom," and other misgivings about the consequences of Keynesian statecraft will be found unwarranted when seen in the clear light of Keynes' own democratic premise and technical precaution.[2]

To see the practical usefulness of Keynesian mixed statecraft more readily, it is only necessary to recall the following advantages, as compared with the disadvantages of extreme statecraft indicated above:

First, Keynesian analysis and policy would leave individual economic units perfectly free to pursue their self-interest, thus letting producers maximize their profits, consumers maximize their utility, savers maximize their security or amenity, investors maximize their marginal efficiency of capital, etc. In other words, microeconomic units do not constitute subjects of Keynesian statecraft. Thus the principles of free enterprise, competitive pricing, consumer sovereignty, and private initiative are left intact.

Second, macroeconomic aggregates, such as total saving, total consumption, and total investment constitute the subjects of Keynesian public control, and they cut across economic classes. As such, these aggregates have the effect of declassing "the working class," "the capitalist class," and other emotion-ridden labels. For instance, the Keynesian concept of "the propensity to save," which is a variable subject to public control, does not admit of blame on any one class when it misbehaves relatively to the given inducement to invest so as to reduce effective demand (in the short run) or to retard economic growth (in the long run).[3] For the propensity to save is an impersonal macroeconomic variable which incorporates the saving propensities of individuals and groups of

[2] Keynes, while advocating a "system of State Socialism" to exercise "a guiding influence" on private economic decisions and activities, nevertheless was careful to add such qualifications as "the common will, embodied in the policy of the State" and "whilst preserving efficiency and freedom." (See the concluding chapter in the *General Theory.*)

[3] To be more precise, saving can be said to misbehave in the sense that it falls short of full-employment investment to create an inflationary gap or exceeds full-employment investment to create a deflationary gap—according to the familiar short-run income mechanism of the form $\triangle Y = f (I - S)$, where $\triangle Y$ is an increment (or a decrement) of effective demand, I investment, and S savings. In the long run, on the other hand, it is as causing an inflationary or deflationary divergence from the equilibrium rate of growth that saving can be said to misbehave—when that equilibrium rate is given by $\triangle Y'/Y' = s/b$, where Y' is productive capacity, s the average propensity to save out of full-employment real income, and b the average and marginal capital-output ratio. (For detail see my *The Keynesian Theory of Economic Development,* London, 1959.)

individuals, regardless of what "class" they may represent from a socio-logical or ideological point of view. The same holds valid for all other macroeconomic variables which are to be made subject to public control in a Keynesian mixed economy; these variables simply do not lend them-selves to the fanning of emotions.

Third, macroeconomic variables subject to Keynesian public control are operationally significant in the sense that they are measurable as definite quantities and quantitative relations, thus making scientific con-trol and prediction possible within technical limits. The technical limits here refer to the dynamic nature of human behaviour, the variability of socio-cultural data impinging on economic man's decisions and activi-ties, and the logical necessity of making the simplifying assumptions of constant behaviour patterns for useful prediction. These limits are, of course, characteristic of all *social* sciences. The main point to be stressed here is that the subjects of Keynesian public control permit quantitative manipulation and plausible prediction, thereby lending themselves read-ily to scientific analysis and objective policy.

Fourth, and lastly, the variables subject to Keynesian public control are related to national income and wealth in such a way as to allow *in-direct* monetary and fiscal control mechanisms to operate effectively, thus rendering direct controls (e.g., rationing, priority allocations, price fixing, and import quotas) largely superfluous. For monetary and fiscal policies are capable of influencing the behavior of saving, consumption, invest-ment, and other macroeconomic variables through their influence on na-tional income and wealth. Moreover, the effective use of monetary and fiscal policies would make the doctrinaire espousal of public ownership irrelevant. This does not, however, imply that Keynesian statecraft dog-matically excludes direct controls or public ownership under all circum-stances, for surely experience warrants the complementary use of direct controls and supplementary resort to public ownership under some cir-cumstances (e.g., wartime, underdeveloped economies without much private initiative and capital,[4] trading nations with persistent balance-of-payments difficulties, and advanced economies with strong democratic safeguards).

2. DEMOCRATIC SAFEGUARDS AGAINST ABUSES

The democratic principle was so much of a second nature to Keynes[5] that he apparently considered it redundant to specify democratic safe-guards against the possible abuses of central authority in the economic field. None the less, his digressive remarks here and there are helpful in

[4] Cf. R. J. Alexander, "State vs. Private Enterprise in Latin America," *American Journal of Economics and Sociology,* January 1958.
[5] See R. F. Harrod, *The Life of John Maynard Keynes* (N.Y., 1951).

enumerating the kinds of safeguards which a mixed economy ought to evolve, as follows:

1. The central controls necessary to guide the smooth functioning of a mixed economy should be coupled with a public policy of encouraging "the decentralisation of decisions and of individual responsibility."[6] Such a policy implies a due diversification of central authority at the national, provincial and local levels, collaboration between the public and private sectors, and the co-functioning of the price mechanism and the public-control mechanisms. To the extent that these implications are brought out as a matter of deliberate policy, to that extent will democratic values (e.g., the exercise of personal choice, the variety of life, the love of the common man, and the independence of mind) be helped rather than hindered. To that extent, conversely, totalitarian homogeneity and authoritarian inelasticity will be averted.

2. The necessary central controls should be supplemented by a public policy of fostering the natural evolution of public-spirited, public-relations-conscious, semi-autonomous private enterprises and institutions (e.g., public utilities, banks, schools and churches) as well as of constructing built-in stabilizers and equalizers (e.g., social security programmes, progressive taxation, collective-bargaining legislation, fair-employment-practice legislation, and public housing and schooling). Such a policy would help safeguard a mixed "welfare state" against the abuses of collectivism inasmuch as the need for complete planning and the clamour of sentimental egalitarianism would thereby be mitigated.

3. The necessary central controls should be implemented by the creation and protection of autonomous monetary and fiscal agencies free from partisan political considerations and private lobbies, that is, government agencies armed with permanent control powers as well as with flexible control mechanisms—subject to the ultimate Parliamentary constraint. Here the traditional principle of monetary sovereignty protecting the independence of central bank policy-making must be extended to a fiscal authority entrusted with the task of applying fiscal measures in the interests of economic stability and growth.

4. The state should encourage "the collection and dissemination on a great scale of data relating to the business situation, including the full publicity, by law if necessary, of all business facts which it is useful to know."[7] Such a policy of promoting mass enlightenment on economic affairs would make for more effective democratic voting[8] and policy-mak-

---

[6] *General Theory*, p. 380.

[7] Keynes, *Essays in Persuasion* (London, 1952), p. 318.

[8] An enlightened voting public is presupposed by C. A. R. Crosland when he asserts: "Any Government which tampered seriously with the basic structure of the full-employment Welfare State would meet with a sharp reverse at the polls; and this knowledge acts as rather a strong inducement to politicians not to tamper." (See his *The Future of Socialism*, London, 1956, p. 61.)

ing, while at the same time making against demagogic pleading. Mass education is therefore a powerful long-run safeguard against theoretically unsound policy-making in the economic field as well as in other fields.

5. The state should be willing to "entrust to science the direction of those matters which are properly the concern of science."[9] Applied to economic policy-making, this would mean that the economic problems of national and international importance should be discussed, analyzed and approached for their solution in the spirit of "Bretton Woods" (monetary conferences of international experts at Bretton Woods, N.H., U.S.A.). Apropos, Sir Roy Harrod tells us that "Keynes tended till the end to think of the really important decisions being reached by a small group of intelligent people, like the group that fashioned the Bretton Woods plan."[10] He then raises the pertinent question: "But would not a democratic government having a wide multiplicity of duties tend to get out of control and act in a way of which the intelligent would not approve?"[11] Neither Keynes nor Harrod answers this question, however. One might answer that the possible danger of a democratic government resorting to undemocratic solutions to economic problems is likely to be lessened by its executive branch working closely with its legislative and judiciary branches, as a truly democratic government should, as well as by its policy-makers having the benefit of the vision and precaution of technical advisers in and out of the government service.[12]

[9] Keynes, *Persuasion*, p. 373.
[10] See his *The Life of John Maynard Keynes*, p. 193.
[11] *Ibid.*
[12] It is fitting, in this regard, to cite Kenyes' own defence of experts: "I dare to speak for the much abused so-called experts. I even venture sometimes to prefer them, without intending any disrespect, to politicians. The common love of truth, bred of a scientific habit of mind, is the closest of bonds between the representatives of divers nations." (Speech on the International Monetary Fund before the House of Lords, May 23, 1944.)

41 MIECZYSŁAW FALKOWSKI

SOCIALIST ECONOMISTS
AND THE DEVELOPING COUNTRIES[*]

The position of socialist economists in regard to problems of the developing countries has undergone a remarkable evolution. A series of
studies and scientific debates on the model of economic growth for the
underdeveloped countries, followed by a confrontation with economic
realities in the countries concerned, resulted in a re-examination of some
opinions which had hindered further advance in these studies. It is now
possible to see the outline of a Marxist theory of growth of the developing countries, reflected in a growing number of publications in recent
years.

In the meantime the West has become increasingly interested in
learning the views of economists in the socialist countries. This is mainly
because so many 'third world' countries have decided to set themselves
to building a socialist system (even though this notion seems to embrace
a fairly wide variety of ideas and programmes). Another reason is that
planning, development of the public sector, and some techniques typical
of the economic policy of socialist countries are playing an increasingly
important part in the economic practice of 'third world' countries.

In tackling the problem of 'third world' countries, the research
methods and viewpoints of most economists in the West differ very much
from those in the socialist countries. They produce different explanations
of the causes and sources of economic underdevelopment and they suggest different ways of overcoming it. These divergent views are the product of historical experience of two very different systems, each of them
having waged its own battle to surmount the difficulties inherent in it.
It is only human to feel that one's own experience, one's own political
formulae and ideological and economic models ought to be accepted by
everyone. But one learns soon enough that mechanical transplantation of
ideas serves no purpose. Indeed, there is no way of making the economic
problems of 'third world' countries fit the traditional, well-tested sche-

From *Polish Perspectives* (Warsaw), Vol. X, No. 3, March 1967, pp. 16–28. Reprinted by permission of the author. This article has been revised by the author.
   [*] Abridged version of an article published in *Polish Round Table*, Polish Association of Political Sciences, Yearbook 1966.

mata. The conditions prevailing in the second half of the twentieth century and the available methods of promoting economic growth differ radically from those in the past. This is becoming more and more evident to everybody. Socialist economists, 'third world' economists and many economists in the capitalist countries have given up the concept of traditional patterns of development and are seeking new ways and means to overcome stagnation and bridge the gap between the underdeveloped countries and the advanced parts of the world.

In studying the notion of an underdeveloped country and examining its specific features economists in the socialist countries do not intend to limit themselves to a formal, quantitative analysis enumerating the external characteristics and categorizing the typical features. They reject any static concept and replace it by dynamic analysis and historical explanation. They are less concerned with settling terminological disputes than with investigating the existing phenomena with a view to revealing the mechanism of economic backwardness and, having comprehended it, seeking positive solutions of the problem.

The notion of an underdeveloped country, as Marxist methodology understands it, has many important implications. The difference between the level of development of an advanced and a developing country is not only quantitative. Not only does the latter lag somewhat behind the advanced country. Not only is it in a lower phase of development. Not only is it separated from the advanced country by an evolutionary stage or an interval of time by the end of which, given the proper rate of growth, the existing differences will be evened out and finally disappear. To quote Charles Bettelheim, the underdeveloped countries have also evolved, but in another way. Contrary to the industrialized countries where the evolution consisted in progressive integration of the capitalist forms which gradually drove out the feudal forms of economy, the economy of the underdeveloped countries has been warped, twisted and deformed. It is a non-integrated economy, dependent on foreign markets, and makes no effort to expand its domestic market. In an economy of this type, in the absence of interconnections between various economic sectors which could serve as a connective mechanism, the processes of accumulation and investment are completely distorted.

It is not enough, however, to note the twisted mechanism of development in an underdeveloped country. The student of the problem must proceed to uncover the pattern of functioning of a backward economy in relation to the external factors and the internal hindrances inherent in it.

Economists in the socialist countries concentrate on examining the mechanism which, under the capitalist system, engenders inequality. Contrary to their colleagues in the West, they are looking for the causes of the gap between the 'A' and 'B' worlds (the advanced and the backward countries) not in the differences of environment, climate, geographical situation, natural resources, race, civilization, etc., but in the sphere of development of the productive forces.

Economists in the socialist countries believe that the division of the world into rich and poor countries was caused by the law of unequal development of capitalism as a world system. This is borne out by an analysis of the capitalist system within one country or on a world-wide basis. Capitalism did not develop smoothly and harmoniously; it grew up in bitter competitive struggle between business companies and industries, between individual countries and regions of the world. On an international scale, the victims are the weak countries; reduced to the role of agrarian and raw-material producers they use the most obsolete means of production and are petrified in their stagnant, anachronistic, socio-institutional way of life. They were forced to confine themselves to producing raw materials and farm products because it enabled them to maintain their position given the two important factors—cheap and abundant labour and favourable natural conditions. The advanced countries took the upper hand in all the other fields of production because of unprecedented rises of productivity and reduced costs of production. West European countries made a huge leap forward owing to machine-oriented industrialization, but this was done at the expense of a deformed profile of development of the backward countries. The price was high indeed.

An analysis of the unequal development of the capitalist system is of key importance for two reasons: it uncovers the mechanism which produced the group of underprivileged countries and it helps formulate the theoretical principles of the strategy and tactics aimed at overcoming the backward status of those countries.

The experience of the past leads to another important conclusion—namely that both the mechanism that produced backwardness and the mechanism that helps overcome it have their socio-institutional framework. Any effort to explain the causes of economic stagnation without clarifying the role of the social conditions which reinforce this stagnation, just as any effort to formulate a programme of development of the productive forces without socio-political reforms, is bound to end in failure.

Science never restricts itself to description alone. This is true also in regard to the science of political economy. To reply to the crucial questions asked by life itself, it must discover and generalize the laws governing the phenomena under study and build on this basis the theoretical foundations for the strategy of economic development of the 'B' countries. Judging from the direction of research carried on by socialist economists, the overwhelming majority of them seem to agree that state capitalism will be the fundamental economic formula for the development of 'third world' countries. But at the same time they point out that in the underdeveloped countries the concept of state capitalism has new economic and social connotations. Admittedly, it is similar to the concept of state capitalism in the advanced countries, particularly in regard to the role of the state, the degree of its being engaged in active economic and social policies, etc. But the similarities, important as they are, do not cover the whole issue. The point is not in the different degree of state interventionism but in the qualitatively different nature of the state and its functions, closely related to the ideology and socio-political attitudes of the social forces that assume power. From the economist's point of view the model of state capitalism will mean, in the case of a developing country, much more than a certain degree of state intervention in the sphere of economic relations. Contrary to what once occurred in the now advanced countries, the state will not limit itself to creating a propitious climate and favourable internal and external conditions for development but will assume the role of manager and organizer of the process of development in its entirety. It will consciously shape the economic model of the country, select the trends of investment, determine the priorities; briefly, it will become the biggest entrepreneur in the country. And the result will be a typical controlled economy, the principal part in it being played not by a market mechanism but by a central body engaged in running and planning the economy and using an arsenal of tools devised to serve this end. It is remarkable that in suggesting such a pattern of development for the 'third world' economists in the socialist countries are not guided by any ideological doctrine; they deduce their postulates from the economic conditions, based in particular on the belief that the traditional way of development cannot be reproduced and that the 'classical' mechanism of development is of doubtful use in the case of an underdeveloped country.

A controlled economy with centralized apparatus of economic management, a strong public sector playing the leading part in the national economy, and an elaborate central planning apparatus which determines the allocation of means of production and controls price policy—such is, in general terms, the outline of the economic model suggested by socialist economists for underdeveloped countries. With such vast economic powers at their disposal the leaders will have to proceed to put into effect a series of socio-political and cultural reforms which would produce the institutional guarantees needed in the process of development.

It is worth noting that studies of problems of economic growth in the 'third world' have appeared in the Polish literature on a wide scale. This has stemmed not from abstract theoretical interests, but principally from the need to answer a number of questions about economic practice raised by life itself. The endeavours of Polish economists have been directed to pinning down the specific differences between the economies of the emergent nations and those of the capitalist and socialist countries, to discovering their development laws. Another object has been to adapt the theory of socialist economy to the needs of an underdeveloped country, to show the relevance of such socialist policies as nationalization of foreign capital, industrialization, development of a strong public sector, agrarian reform and so on. Here the writings of Oskar Lange and Michał Kalecki, our two leading economists, have played a crucial role. The path they opened up has since been followed by many economists of a younger generation, and the body of work that has resulted is already fairly substantial.*

Before passing to sum up the conclusions in regard to the set of measures within a state-capitalist pattern of economic management, let us have a look at some general laws ruling the economy as a whole. In trying to build an economic policy it is essential to know and respect these objective laws. An interesting attempt at presenting a model of relevant economic interrelations can be found in the works of Michał Kalecki and Oskar Lange.

The aim of Kalecki's model of growth is to maximize the national income. All the other aggregate values are examined in relation to this aim. In particular, Kalecki investigates the relationship between national income increase and between investment and consumption.

The model demonstrates the strategic variables of growth, especially the rate of investment and capital output ratio, on the one hand, and the rate of increase in employment and productivity on the other. Although it is directly concerned with the socialist economy, the model has cognitive value far exceeding the institutional framework of the socialist system. The variables used in the model are indispensable in economic planning of any type and planning has become by now an inalienable feature of the less developed countries as well. Hence the contradiction, inherent in the process of growth, between the levels of short-term and long-term consumption. An accelerated rate of growth, while setting limitations to short-term consumption, is necessary if the countries concerned intend to achieve a higher level of consumption in the long run. A great many problems arise when it comes to choosing the capital output ratio related to various types of technological progress. In the case of a developing country, considering its large surplus of unemployed manpower, the problem consists in finding, first and foremost, the optimal production techniques. These will not necessarily prove to be highly mechanized

* There is no space here to treat the theoretical problems of a 'mixed' economy in detail. Readers are referred to the works of Oskar Lange and Michał Kalecki (bibliographies can be found in *On Political Economy and Econometrics. Essays in Honour of Oskar Lange,* Warsaw 1964 and *Problems of Economic Dynamics and Planning. Essays in Honour of Michał Kalecki,* Warsaw 1964. Another useful source is *Essays on Planning and Economic Development,* Vol. 1, Warsaw, 1963 and Vol. 2 Warsaw 1965.

techniques. Given the available manpower resources and the volume of investment outlays, the optimum solution might be found in a less mechanized technique which could be the way to safeguarding a relatively high increase in employment and national income.

Market equilibrium is another important problem involved in the process of growth. Wages and salaries paid to workers producing capital goods add directly to the demand for consumer goods. When starting investment programs it is imperative to set in motion all the levers that foster the output of consumer goods, agricultural produce first of all. It is unfortunate that in the developing countries this branch of production shows so little flexibility. This may engender inflationary pressures since in the final analysis inflation is caused by the fact that food supply lags behind the rapidly growing demand for food in the investment sector.

Under the circumstances, the way out ought to be sought in anti-inflationary measures, i.e., imposing new taxes or getting credits from foreign countries. Besides easing inflationary pressures, such measures are intended to counteract the adverse effects of fluctuations in the terms of trade which, as a rule, reveal changes unfavorable for 'third world' countries.

The point of departure in Lange's model is the conception of full employment. As he formulates it, the main problem faced by an underdeveloped economy is how to employ redundant labour under the conditions of shortage of capital. An underdeveloped economy can choose either to increase employment while sticking to less advanced production techniques or introduce new and more effective techniques. Actually, it is not an 'either-or' choice between two extreme solutions; a decision must be made which of the two should prevail in the specific situation. In making economic decisions it is necessary to take into account the available manpower and capital resources and, at the same time, to foresee the short-range and long-range consequences of the decision. Lange's theoretical formula points out the importance of two elements in the process of economic growth. One of them is the population factor, mainly the problem of employment, and the other is the above mentioned choice of production techniques in an economy with large manpower resources.

In discussing the problems of economic policy in a developing country the following points need to be emphasized.

Economists in the socialist countries, contrary to some in the West, do not regard the development of agriculture as the main evolutionary trend and the basis of reconstruction of the national economy in developing countries. They ascribe this role to industrialization—even though the very idea of industrialization has undergone an evolution and the dogmatic, one-sided concept of fostering at any cost the development of heavy industry is no longer in force. They regard the industrialization of developing countries as the main lever of long-term growth; they see in it a solution to the problems of employment and a means to achieve a more favourable position within the international division of labour. But at the same time they insist on accelerating the development of agriculture as the provider of food for the population and the basis of industrial growth of the country. They do not accord absolute priority to agriculture, but neither do they deny its substantial contribution to development as well.

Since the majority of population in the developing countries (in some cases up to 80 per cent) are employed in farming, a realistic strategy of growth cannot afford to disregard the agricultural problem. If it did, it would doom itself to failure.

In trying to integrate the agricultural sector in the strategy of growth it is important to realize the low level of labour productivity in this sector, the high rate of population increase (from two to three per cent annually, which results in the long run in a steep rise in the number of productive population, mostly seeking non-agricultural jobs), and the fact that the agricultural problem, more than any other, is a combination of technical and economic elements along with institutional and socio-political factors.

Consequently, the planner engaged in mapping out agricultural development programmes must provide for stepped-up productivity per acre of arable land so as to raise the overall agricultural produce on the given area. At the same time, in a developing country it is often possible to get an increase in agricultural produce by extending the arable area. Insofar as the first solution is concerned there are large resources for growth in the developing countries; it is hard, however, to put them into effect in view of economic difficulties and institutional barriers.

Instead of resorting to quantitative changes in its farming methods an underdeveloped country with a backward agricultural economy should literally reverse its production techniques; this would involve changes in farm tools, methods of land cultivation, and the general level of agricultural training among farmers. Only if all these tasks are performed simultaneously will it be possible to create the conditions for obtaining increased agricultural produce to cover the growing demands of consumers and provide all the food and raw materials needed in other sectors of the economy.

The role played in the development of agriculture by the institutional factor or, to be more precise, by agrarian reforms in the broad meaning of the word, deserves special emphasis. Reforms are necessary in view of the defective structure of agricultural property, non-profitability of peasant labour, and absence of incentives encouraging investment and stimulating productivity. Although the need of reforms is evident enough to be admitted by the great majority of economists, in actual practice any reform encounters resistance on the part of large landowners, middlemen, leaseholders, usurers—in other words, a whole army thriving on exploitation of peasant misery. Their resistance is sometimes so powerful that it cannot be broken even by state authorities fully aware of the necessity of social reforms. Political and social factors are thus having a decisive impact in this field. This is borne out by the fact that it is virtually impossible to proceed with an agrarian reform even though it would cost far less than any investment project needed in agriculture.

As economists in the socialist countries see it, agrarian reform can have broad implications depending on the specific conditions in the country concerned, the situation of the peasants, and the changes that ought to be carried into practice. The agrarian reform should strive to transform the anachronistic structure of land property, relieve the peasants from the burdens imposed by usurers and middlemen, free them from their obligations to landowners, etc. In some countries, India for instance, what is essential is not so much to redistribute the land but to grant property to those who cultivate it or hold it in tenure, to annul the debts and to overcome the traditional or religious habits that stand in the way of rationalizing the economy. An agrarian reform of this kind, when implemented, would produce the necessary stimuli to increase productivity and step up production and would create the institutional framework conducive to social transformations.

The principal solution in the developing country should be sought, according to socialist economists, in preserving and reinforcing the individual property of small and medium holdings brought to life by the land reform. Large holdings, owned by the state, by co-operatives or by private individuals, should be regarded as an exception. In proceeding with a land reform the state should be determined to accomplish deep social changes with a view to promoting the interests of small and medium holders. This is where an important part could be played by the cooperative movement under various forms, such as credit and loan cooperatives, service cooperatives to supply more effective agricultural tools, or marketing cooperatives to protect the farmer against exploitation by the middleman.

The objective of the land reform is to raise the level of agriculture so as to include it in the general programme of lifting the national economy from the state of stagnation. To be able to pursue its accumulation programme in the village the state has to use wisdom in levying taxes on the peasants. According to economists in the socialist countries, progressive taxation not only safeguards accumulation and fair contribution to investment expenditures by various social groups but it is also an instrument of economic integration in a country artificially divided into disconnected sectors.

After the land reform has been implemented and proved successful there arises the next problem: how to effectively use accumulation for investment purposes. To pursue an effective policy means to prevent waste of funds and ensure reasonable centralization, to establish a hierarchy of the tasks that must be accomplished and use the limited resources available to cover the most pressing needs. Such a centralized investment policy should be combined with measures encouraging the farmers themselves to invest. The desirable result is a combination of public and private investment.

In the belief of economists in the socialist countries the industrialization process is, in the long run, the main driving force of economic development in underdeveloped countries. The importance of industrialization is explained by internal laws of development which call for simultaneous growth of different sectors of the national economy, including agriculture, and by external factors, especially those that tend to modify the international division of labour to the advantage of the underdeveloped countries.

Professor Kalecki has argued that, in the first place, industrialization is necessary because industrial development of productive investment is the determinant in accelerating the rate of growth of national income. Secondly, as an underdeveloped country makes progress in economic growth, there occur changes in the structure of consumption which lead in turn to changes in the structure of production. After a certain level of social development has been achieved it is inconceivable to be able to meet consumers' demands without producing industrial goods. It is equally impossible in the long run, to seek the solution to the problem in imports. The troubles with trade balance in the countries where the economy is sensitive to imports are only too well known. The only way of surmounting the barrier of foreign trade is to replace imports, at least in part, by home-made goods. This might lead after some time to starting production of a diversified range of goods for export, in accordance with the whole pattern of economy and in line with its immediate and future requirements.

Another problem for the developing countries is how to use the existing manpower resources. This is one more variable to be included in the strategy of economic development. Without industrial development there is no way of profitably using the manpower reserve. This is where the problem of selecting appropriate techniques, adapted to the specific conditions and factors of production in an underdeveloped economy, acquires capital importance.

One can hardly agree with those economists to whom, regardless of the specific conditions in the country concerned, industrialization always means building up heavy industry. This is a lopsided concept of industrialization. We concur with those economists in the socialist countries who believe that there is no universal solution, no ready-made recipe for the process of industrialization. The planner must know how to reconcile the elements of short-run and long-run growth. The concrete solution he arrives at will depend on the objective and subjective factors in the given country. In some countries the point of departure might be heavy industry, in some others, light industry or agriculture. In any event, in the course of the development process it will be necessary to put up an industrial basis according to the choice made at the start.

From this point of view what industrialization signifies is not a concentration of economic activities in a selected field but the development of different branches of the economy subordinated to an economic strategy based on the existing factors of production. Industrialization requires harmonious, many-sided development resulting from interdependence of various economic sectors.

This concept of industrialization can be accomplished only in a planned economy comprising an important public sector.

The connotations of the term 'planning' are not a matter of indifference to economists in the socialist countries. As they understand it, it has much more than a purely technical significance. Planning renders it possible to coordinate *ex ante* economic decisions; it supplies an arsenal of tools to sponsor economic expansion in different economic spheres. Marxists consider that planning must be direct and imperative to become an effective economic instrument. This is what planning ought to be in an underdeveloped country, where the economy is typically disintegrated and sharply differentiated. In an underdeveloped country planning cannot be reduced to passivity or confine itself to prognostication, as is the case of some advanced countries. The public sector will prove the most reliable field of such planning in an underdeveloped country.

Different economic sectors, including a private sector, coexist in an underdeveloped economy. The task of the planner is to determine the role of each sector, the private sector in particular. This is an extensive field of activity covering agriculture, services and industries; but, according to Marxist economists, the key position must be controlled by the public sector. This thesis is confirmed by the practice of nationalization of several economic sectors in 'third world' countries. It is generally known that socialist economists differ from western economists in viewing the role of the private sector in the whole economy. The former recognize that the private sector must exist, but believe that its activity should be limited and controlled by the public sector. The latter, while more and more willing to accept the existence of the public sector, insist that it should not predominate. In the practice of developing countries one notices large differences in the range and proportions of these two sectors. Furthermore, the situation in all the countries is continually changing. Economic science has not as yet found a reply to the important question of what the relationship of the two sectors should be. In our belief, it would be desirable for economists in both the socialist countries and the West to proceed to empirical and theoretical research on the problem. One thing seems obvious enough: inclusion of private economic units in the plan is a prerequisite of effective planning.

Economic science in the socialist countries is faced with the urgent task of expanding the scope of research on the underdeveloped economy and critically re-examining the existing scientific concepts in this field.

Although the general direction of research appears to be quite correct, it seems to be sometimes hindered by a tendency to draw too far-going analogies between the underdeveloped and the socialist economy or even identifying one with the other. In further research, economic science in the socialist countries should proceed from real facts, taking as its point of departure the existing model of a mixed economy in an underdeveloped country, with several co-existing sectors—public, cooperative, and private. Naturally, the model must not be regarded as something rigid and static. The interrelation of the three sectors is constantly changing. It would be a mistake, however, to presume that the cooperative or the private sector is necessarily doomed to atrophy in the course of development.

Following the result of theoretical studies and the existing outline of the general theory of growth, economists in the socialist countries can continue research along two main lines—empirical analysis of the functioning of the national economy and analysis of specific theoretical and methodological problems. As far as theoretical studies are concerned it seems advisable to concentrate, first of all, on such issues as the choice of techniques, substitution of capital by manpower in an underdeveloped country, different aspects of technological progress, methodology of short-range and long-range planning, and the problem of development cycles in the light of the impact of business cycles in the advanced capitalist countries upon the developing countries. These are, of course, only a few of the many problems, selected at random.

As regards international economic cooperation, it is important to study the effectiveness of foreign trade of the underdeveloped countries. Economists in the socialist countries should focus on examining the conditions of mutual cooperation between socialist countries and underdeveloped countries; this seems all the more urgent in view of the rapid increase of trade between these two groups. The quantitative aspect of the problem is not the only one that comes into play. With growing development of the socialist and the underdeveloped countries their structure of production will change and, hence, so will the structure of their imports and exports. Studies of the dynamics of these processes, accurate forecasting and prognostication of development trends are of material help in working out the proper foreign trade policy. This is where economic science has made little progress and the efforts made so far have proved insufficient.

I have concentrated on the economic aspect of the process of growth in the developing countries, leaving aside other aspects of underdevelopment—the political, social, cultural, educational, etc. We believe, nevertheless, that in the multitude of problems facing the developing countries today it is the economic problem that deserves special attention. This paper is intended to emphasize not only the importance of the economic problem but also its difficulties and complexities, and to show that there are no ready-made solutions to it. This is not an easy task for economic science; nor does the complicated political situation in this world of ours make the economist's job any easier.

There is one more point to be made in conclusion—namely, that the success of any attempt at overcoming stagnation will depend, first and foremost, on the internal factors within the developing countries, and on their own efforts. Not that we underestimate the importance of external aid, or, more generally, external factors. International cooperation in the field of trade, as well as financial and technological assistance might prove an important contribution to rapid economic growth. But they can never play the decisive part. In our view, the final result will be determined by the activities of the country concerned; it will depend on its economic and technical personnel, the initiative of its people, the help of the population in realizing the envisaged tasks. In the world we live in, the transformation of society must be the product of the society itself, a society consciously striving to attain the goals it has set itself in the programme of socio-economic reforms.

B. A Case Study

42 RAYMOND VERNON

MEXICO: PUBLIC PLANNING AND PRIVATE INITIATIVE

THE PUBLIC SECTOR

A study of any one country offers something less than an adequate basis for generalization. But in any list of countries whose experiences may suggest fruitful hypotheses, the case of Mexico surely ranks high. Ever since economists began to produce the relevant data by which economic growth is measured, they have been aware that Mexico was growing, sometimes at a modest pace, sometimes very rapidly. In the twenty years from 1939 to 1960, the country's physical output of goods and services—calculated about as carefully as such magnitudes are usually calculated in countries with sparse and uncertain statistics—seems to have tripled. Table 42–1 gives us some perspective for gauging this performance by comparing Mexican growth rates with those of a variety of other countries, both developed and otherwise. Mexico's growth rates, as the table shows, have been fairly impressive, both in total output and on a per capita basis. The country has grown faster than any of the Big Three of South America, though not so fast as truly spectacular performers like postwar Japan and Germany.[1]

By 1960, Mexico's per capita annual income had risen to slightly over 300 U.S. dollars, a figure far above the levels characteristically encountered in Africa, Asia, and many parts of Latin America itself.[2] By

Reprinted by permission of the publishers from Raymond Vernon THE DILEMMA OF MEXICO'S DEVELOPMENT *Cambridge, Mass.: Harvard University Press,* Copyright, 1963, by the President and Fellows of Harvard College.

[1] In Mexico, as in most developing countries, each decennial population census probably improves somewhat in coverage over the prior census. It may be, therefore, that the rate of population growth for Mexico is systematically overstated and the increase in per capita income accordingly understated. Compare Ansley J. Coale and Edgar M. Hoover, *Population Growth and Economic Development in Low-Income Countries* (Princeton: Princeton University Press, 1958), app. B, p. 368, where some of the coverage shortcomings of the 1950 population census for Mexico are described.

[2] This kind of figure should not be taken to mean that the average Mexican, in real terms, had only one ninth the living standard of the average United States resident. The official 8-cent rate by which the peso is converted into dollars undervalues the peso in terms of its purchasing power for the consumption needs of the "average" Mexican.

TABLE 42-1. ANNUAL GROWTH RATES OF PHYSICAL OUTPUT OF
GOODS AND SERVICES, TOTAL AND PER CAPITA,
SELECTED COUNTRIES[a] (In per cent)

Country	1938-1954[b]		1950-1959	
	Total	Per capita	Total	Per capita
Mexico	5.7	2.9	5.2	2.3
U.S.A.	4.6	3.2	3.3	1.1
Argentina	3.2	1.1	1.7	c
Brazil	4.8	2.4	4.8	1.9
Canada	5.1	3.3	4.0	0.9
Chile	4.0	2.3	2.4	c
Germany	3.0	1.4	7.4	5.4
Israel	–	–	9.9	2.9
Japan	13.5	11.1	7.9	5.6
Peru	5.1	3.1	4.3	1.4
South Africa	4.5	2.2	5.1	2.6

[a]For some countries, the figures are based on measures of gross national product, for others, gross domestic product, and for still others, national income.

[b]For Mexico, 1939–1954; Japan and South Africa, 1946–1952; Brazil, 1939–1953; Chile, 1940–1952; Peru, 1949–1952.

[c]Less than 0.1 per cent.

Sources: For Mexico, our own estimates based upon various official sources. For other countries, 1938–1954; U.N. Statistical Papers, series H, nos. 8 and 9, table 2. For other countries, 1950–1959: output data, U.N. World Economic Survey, 1959, tables 1-1, 2-9, 3-1; population data, U.N. Demographic Yearbook, passim.

that year, too, Mexico's output had acquired a composition characteristic of a reasonably advanced economy. Output of the manufacturing industries made up about one fifth of the gross national product; if the petroleum and electric power industries are added to manufacturing, this enlarged "industrial" sector accounted for about one quarter of the total. Agricultural output, it is true, still came close to matching that of manufacturing in value; but more than three quarters of it by this time was commercial rather than subsistence agriculture.

The appropriateness of studying Mexico as an instructive case of economic development, however, stems from more subtle indicators of successful progress. Mexico today is a nation, not a collection of loosely-joined localities or an appendage of a foreign power. It has a well-developed public sector, consisting of its government agencies and its government-controlled enterprises, which by now have acquired a sense of continuity and of effective performance. It has a firmly established indigenous private sector producing not only in the traditional agricultural activities but also in the modern areas of industry, banking, and commerce. Indeed, the human and material resources which spark Mexico's growth today are largely indigenous. The men who design the dams, roads, and factories of the country, direct its businesses and financial institutions, plan its educational system, provide its advanced training, and guide its agricultural research are principally Mexican nationals. The funds that finance its capital formation in every major sector of its economic life come predominantly from Mexican sources. Foreign contributions, both in human and material terms, are still important—just how important is the subject of continuous acrimonious debate. Despite the debate, however, no one any longer doubts that Mexico has the internal human and physical resources, the social organization, and even the level of income which most other countries of the underdeveloped world would be content to achieve thirty or forty years hence.

For the scholar who is probing to understand the actual and potential roles of the public and the private sectors in the development process, the Mexican case is attractive on other grounds as well. Both sectors have had vigorous parts to play in the development of the country. In some countries and for some periods, it is easy to describe the performance of one of the two sectors as "dominant"—as both the necessary and the sufficient condition for growth. Egypt since the middle 1950's, for instance, has been dominated by the activities of the public sector. Peru, on the other hand, owes its recent growth principally to activities in the private sphere. But no such obvious statement can be made about Mexico.

The importance of the public sector in Mexico is not apparent on first impact. Table 42–2 indicates that the public sector—when measured in terms of its direct contribution to the nation's gross national product—seems to occupy a minor role in the economy. To be sure, the government owns the petroleum industry, the bulk of the electric power industry, and the railroads; some major steel plants, fertilizer plants, and railroad equipment plants; a number of commercial and industrial banks; organizations engaged in the distribution of foodstuffs and newsprint; and a variety of other institutions. Still, the activities of these enterprises plus those of the governmental institutions proper—which together comprise the public sector as a whole—account for less than one tenth of the gross national product.

The position of the public sector looms somewhat larger when it is measured by its relative importance in the capital formation of Mexico. The rather infirm figures on this subject suggest that in recent years public investment has been running at about 5 per cent of gross national product, while domestic private investment has been about 9 per cent.[3]

---

[3] Mexico's investment figures require qualification on many counts. Here it is enough to say that the figures exclude changes in inventory, since these are not available separately for the public and private sectors. Annual inventory accumulation for both sectors combined has amounted to another 2½ per cent or so of gross national product in recent years.

TABLE 42-2. CONTRIBUTION TO MEXICO'S GROSS NATIONAL PRODUCT
BY PUBLIC AND PRIVATE SECTORS, 1959

	Public sector[a]		Private sector	
Activities	Millions of pesos	Percentage of activity in sector	Millions of pesos	Percentage of activity in sector
Petroleum	4,243	100.0	0	0
Electric power[b]	626	74.8	231	25.2
Transportation	1,222	44.4	1,529	55.6
Mining	134	5.4	2,362	94.6
Manufacture	873	3.6	23,458	96.4
Construction	4	0.2	2,511	99.8
Agriculture	0	0	22,298	100.0
Other[c]	4,469	7.1	58,040	92.9
Total	11,571	9.6	110,429	90.4

[a] Includes most enterprises in the public sector plus federal, state, and local governments.
[b] After 1959, the Mexican government purchased most of the remaining private interests in the electric power industry, rasing the public sector's position to nearly 100 per cent.
[c] Principally trade and services, including services of government agencies.
Sources: Secretaría del Patrimonio Nacional and Banco de México.

The largest part of public investment goes into such overhead items as transportation and communications, electric energy, and petroleum; but a significant part also goes into agriculture and manufacturing. One gains the impression, therefore, of a vigorous—but hardly a dominant—public sector.

The importance of the public sector, of course, cannot be gauged solely by the size of its output or by its contribution to investment. Since the public sector consists not only of enterprises but also of government agencies, there is also the question of the role of public regulation as it affects the country's growth. On this subject impressions are necessarily qualitative and subjective; but there are a number of points on which wide agreement would exist.

In some countries the existence of a national "plan" offers a clue to some of the goals which the public sector has set for itself. In Mexico, little light comes from this quarter. Until very recently, Mexico had no development plan, at least no development plan with articulated quantitative objectives and an articulated strategy of achievement. From time to time, statements of general priorities, labeled as "national plans," were issued by one administration or another. In addition, some of the operating agencies of the government maintained internal projections for use in connection with their own programs. But there were no integrated targets for gross national product, for capital formation, for steel production, and the like. Today, quantitative targets of this sort have begun to be produced inside the Mexican government and to receive the president's stamp of approval. At this writing it is too early to say whether the targets are part of an operating plan, which will include a strategy of achievement and which will command the allegiance of all the branches of government concerned with its execution, or whether they are a sterile quantitative exercise of the sort which the requirements of the Alliance for Progress have made popular in many Latin American capitals.

In any case, one is bound to say that the Mexican government is unequivocally committed to the objective of economic growth. And it does consistently accept the responsibility for at least three major courses of action which bear on national development.

One is the improvement of the education, health, and general well-being of the ordinary citizen. It is true that official performance in the immediate discharge of this responsibility has sometimes been fairly feeble as governments have wrestled with conflicting objectives, such as the desire to hold down taxes and avoid inflationary financing. But no government since the Revolution of 1910 has failed to assert its fealty to these objectives nor to contribute a little toward their achievement.

A second acknowledged responsibility of all governments since the Revolution has been to provide the basic industrial "overhead" facilities, including transport, communication, power, and water. Though motives and emphases have differed from one administration to the next, no administration has failed to make substantial contributions to the building of the nation's infrastructure.

The third cause to which all recent governments of Mexico have adhered has been to encourage import replacement as a matter of high priority. It has been taken as an article of faith that as soon as the domestic demand for a product was large enough to offer some hope of domestic production on a scale appropriate to the technology of the industry, every effort should be made to stimulate the necessary domestic investment and to eliminate imports.

While operating on these lines, Mexico's governments of the last two decades have not shown any particular ideological hostility to the concept of private enterprise. On the contrary, a private investor intent on producing a hitherto imported product could be reasonably well assured that the competition of imports would be suppressed or eliminated; that he would be given some relief from income taxes and from import duties on his materials and machinery; and that he would have access to relatively cheap governmental credits. He could even assume that if some bottleneck existed in the form of inadequate public facilities—inadequate power, for instance, or inadequate transportation—there would be a sympathetic governmental response to his difficulties and a genuine effort to meet his needs.

If the private investor is Mexican, his assurances on all these points are fairly clear and unequivocal; but if he is a foreigner he may run into various difficulties. His risks will not seem obvious from a reading of Mexican law; in fact, on first blush, the law will seem reassuringly non-discriminatory in most respects. Except for some significant restrictions on landowning rights, some limitations on foreign ownership in a few strangely assorted industries, and some flatly discriminatory tax legislation in the field of mining and metal processing, the foreigner's opportunities will appear on a par with those of Mexican nationals. In practice, however, the consummation of any major foreign investment is likely to turn on the granting of a variety of licenses, beginning with the issuance of articles of incorporation and continuing with licenses to import the necessary machinery or raw materials and licenses to permit foreign managerial personnel to work in the country. Therefore, the foreigner who is considering any large direct investment in Mexico is obliged to determine if the contemplated investment is acceptable to the Mexican government. And at this stage, notwithstanding the blandly neutral character of the legal structure, the foreigner is likely to discover that in a considerable number of industries the existence of a large Mexican equity interest in the investment is indispensable to the granting of the necessary licenses.

Though there is no obvious hostility to domestic private investment in official Mexican government policy, neither is there any ideological barrier which restrains the Mexican government from investing in any branch of economic activity when it believes the investment to be in the public interest. For instance, if private investment is not forthcoming speedily or in quantity in some important import-replacing field of production at a stage when such an investment appears feasible, the government may well take a direct hand in that sector. This is what accounts for some of the government enterprises in the steel, fertilizer, and paper industries. Nor is the government strongly inhibited from making *ad hoc* investments in industry, whether or not they contribute to import substitution, when some bottleneck problem arises or some political interest would be served. So we find the government investing heavily in the production of rail cars, in the promotion of a local motion picture industry, and in a dozen other miscellaneous pursuits, most of them representing the uninhibited responses of a government unhampered by any well-articulated limitations on public investment.

The readiness of the government to provide easy credit to favored segments of the private sector explains the existence of numerous public banks and investment institutions, set up to provide loans for activities as diverse as manufacturing, cooperative agriculture, and foreign trade. The existence of this public credit system affords one more crude means of comparing the importance of the public and the private sectors. In recent years, the outstanding credits of private lending institutions have been a little greater in the aggregate than those of the public credit agencies. The private sector has led heavily in the making of short-term loans, and the public institutions have led slightly in long-term ones. Once more, therefore, we come away with the impression of two very active sectors, neither obviously dominated by the other.

Thus the case of Mexico offers attractions to those who are interested in discovering the implications which the relationships between a public sector and a private sector have for the development process. The comparatively advanced state of Mexico's development, the experimental and eclectic character of Mexico's use of the two sectors, the vigor with which both sectors have operated—all these commend the Mexican case for study. . . .

THE PRIVATE SECTOR

Measured in output terms, Mexico is an economy of private enterprise; over nine tenths of its production comes from the private sector.* A few words about the composition of this sector, therefore, are needed to set the stage.

Any description of the structure of Mexico's private sector, as it bears on the problem of economic development, gets us into a good deal of conjecture; but some points are clear. One is that agriculture, when measured in terms of sheer manpower, is the dominant activity of the private sector. Though the output of agriculture is roughly equal to that of private manufacturing activities (as Table 42–2 showed), agriculture nonetheless engages four or five times as much manpower as manufacturing; indeed agriculture accounts for more than half of Mexico's total labor force.

Mexican agriculture, however, is far from a homogenous activity. For one thing, about half of the land under cultivation in the country is held under individual title and the other half is held under collective title. There is a gulf between the two kinds of holdings, both in legal and in operational terms. True, the collectively held land, organized through the collective village or the *ejido,* is almost always worked by individual farmers rather than by the collective group. But the position of the ejidal farmer differs from that of the private landowner principally in two respects: in the inability of the farmer on ejidal land to mortgage the

* When Mexicans use the phrase "el sector privado," they usually mean to exclude agriculture and labor. Here, however, the phrase is applied to all the economic activity outside the public sector.

land, and in the somewhat equivocal character of his rights of continued possession and of inheritance.

Partly as a result of these differences but partly also for other reasons such as location and quality, the agricultural lands owned by individuals channel a larger proportion of their output into commercial outlets than do the ejidal lands; as a rule, the individual lands operate with larger credit resources, more irrigation water, more fertilizer, and more machinery per unit of land or labor than the ejidal lands; and, on the whole, the individual lands yield more per acre, measured in value terms, than do the ejidal lands. Of course, there are numerous exceptions to all these generalizations. The individual proprietors of tiny parcels of land, for instance, are more closely akin to the ejidal farmers in their operating patterns than to the individual proprietors of larger land parcels.[4] But the distinctions are useful nonetheless, and they are reflected in a rather different relationship between the government and the landowning farmers than prevails between the government and the members of the ejidos.

The attitude of the government toward the ejidos is constantly solicitous and paternalistic, at least as far as the outside observer can tell. It would be surprising if it were otherwise. The ejidos in large part are the creatures of the government, constituted or regenerated by one administration or another since the Revolution as a vehicle through which land reform and redistribution are achieved. A special government bank, noted for its disposition not to press too hard on loans in arrears, is the principal source of credit for the ejidal farmer. Special dispensations are made to the ejido in the public provision of water, fertilizer, and machinery. In return, the ejidos form an overtly acquiescent and dutiful part of the PRI, a part which can generally be counted on to support official policy without apparent demurrer.[5]

The seeming preference of the government for the ejido does not mean that the individual landowner, particularly the large landowner, suffers from excessive discrimination at the government's hands. On the contrary, his final performance—as recorded by his inputs of water, fertilizer, and machinery and his outputs of agricultural products—points to the opposite conclusion. But the individual landowner differs from the collective farmer in the means by which he achieves results. To begin with, he feels that he owes nothing to the government for the possession of his lands. On the contrary, any large landowner is always confronted with the threat that some of his property may be expropriated under the discretionary powers of the land reform laws. For many large landhold-

---

[4] Rich materials on the structure of agriculture are to be found in Armando González Santos, *La agricultura* (Mexico, D.F.: Fondo de Cultura Económica, 1957), and Ramón Fernández y Fernández and Ricardo Acosta, *Política agrícola* (Mexico, D.F.: Fondo de Cultura Económica, 1961).

[5] See Carlos Manuel Castillo, "La economía agrícola en la región de El Bajío," in *Problemas agrícolas e industriales de México*, vol. VIII, nos. 3–4 (1956), pp. 160–162.

ers, there is also the nagging worry that some of the extra-legal means by which they hold the oversized parcels may be exposed and that control over some of the land may be lost.

Worried or not, the individual landowner has no hesitation in demanding government credits to match the credits which are granted to the ejidal farmers. In fact, such credits have been funneled through credit unions to the individual farmer in aggregate amounts exceeding those extended to the ejido. Unlike the ejidal farmer, however, the individual landowner also draws heavily upon private domestic banks; and in the north of Mexico, where production is strongly oriented to the export markets, the individual landowner even draws a considerable part of his financing from foreign sources.

In the individual landowner's demand for the things that only the government can provide—notably, in his efforts to obtain roads and irrigation works—he seems to work on a much more aggressive and individualistic basis than do the farmers of the ejido. Many landowners, for instance, elect not to join that sector of the PRI which is reserved to agriculture but instead to exert their influence in the party through the so-called "popular sector," which is much the most aggressive and individualistic of the various party sectors. Others will have nothing to do with the PRI and prefer to exert their influence through direct intervention in the government ministries. Some of these farmers, especially in northern states, react on this pattern out of a long-time hostility to the government party. Some, including those who are farmers only in the sense that they provide the financing for fairly large-scale commercial agriculture, avoid the party simply because it can be more efficient for a businessman of substance to take his problems directly to the officials and technicians concerned.

Outside agriculture, a number of major groups in the private sector serve as the principal organizational structures for the purpose of dealing with the government. The bankers, for instance, use as their main organizational channel an Asociación de Banqueros; the manufacturers, a Confederación de Cámaras Industriales (CONCAMIN); the merchants, a Confederación de Cámaras Nacionales de Comercio (CONCANACO). But this does not mean that each group is a homogeneous package.

Consider the case of Mexico's private banking community. A certain element of homogeneity exists, to be sure. Except for one or two mavericks, for instance, practically every member of the banking community is devoted to two general propositions: that the credit restrictions imposed by the Banco de México are too severe and too particularistic, leaving little room for the exercise either of creativeness or discretion on the part of the private banking fraternity; and that the competition of government banks has been both unfair and destructive of the development of an effective credit mechanism. These are standard affirmations of faith essential to continued good standing in the banking community. But each of the country's major banks, apart from its support of these general positions, appears to have a distinct personality in its relations with the government, developed over many years of operations. The Banco-Nacional de México, the country's leading commercial bank, enjoys the reputation of being a responsible and sympathetic collaborator with recent government administrations. The Banco de Londres y México is generally considered more remote and unbending in its relations with the government. A number of other banks, typically newer and smaller, are commonly thought of as institutions "on the make," concentrating on the use of inside government connections to build their affiliated industrial enterprises. And so it goes. Each of a dozen or so banks is sufficiently large and sufficiently well connected that it need not rely upon the collective strength of the Asociación de Banqueros to press its points effectively before the government.

A certain measure of heterogeneity also exists inside the organizations which represent the nation's industry and commerce. Once again, there are common elements of interest to which a clear majority subscribes; for example, taxes on corporate profits should be kept low; government enterprises should not engage in unfair competition with existing Mexican industry; foreign investment should be restrained in some degree; and machinery and materials used by any particular industry for its operations should be admitted into Mexico without restriction, whereas the end-products of the industry should be protected from foreign competition. But there are also striking differences. First, there is the traditional aloofness of the Monterrey industrial group—a group whose origins go back beyond the 1910 Revolution and whose traditions are those of open hostility to the "socialistic and godless" central governments of the Revolution. Then there is the difference in emphasis between the industries which in general feel their interests best served by a minimum of government activity in the economic sphere and those which still feel the need for government help.

This split over government activity finds its principal expression through the public utterances on the one hand of the manufacturers' CONCAMIN and the merchants' CONCANACO, and on the other hand of the Cámara Nacional de la Industria de Transformación (CNIT), a constituent group of CONCAMIN consisting principally of small manufacturing enterprises. CONCAMIN and CONCANACO tend to be under the control of entities which are capable of generating their own internal sources of credit or of borrowing from private domestic or foreign sources, and which therefore show a predilection for keeping the government's role in economic activity under considerable restraint. CNIT, on the other hand, consists largely of smaller, newer, and on the whole more "indigenous" units, lacking adequate credit and fearful of the competition of foreign capital; hence their preference for extensive government intervention in these areas.

Broad national organizations such as CONCAMIN, CONCANACO, and CNIT are not the only structures through which Mexican business tries to pool its strength. Of considerably more importance in the day-to-day contacts between business and government are the dozen or so major groups which have been created in Mexico through the linking of the country's principal enterprises. A large proportion of the major industrial and banking enterprises of Mexico belong to one or another of these groups.[6] Nonetheless, though the existence of the groups is an important and indisputable fact of Mexican business life, it is not easy to define them precisely. Each group characteristically incorporates a banking institution or two and an assortment of industrial enterprises. Sometimes a dominant personality or principal stockholder is the chief link among them, as in the case of the Antonio Sacristán and Carlos Trouyet groups; sometimes it is a common major source of credit, as in the case of the Banco Nacional de México group; sometimes it is a community of interest blended of credit sources, family connections, or geography, as illustrated by the complex composed of Monterrey and Banco de Londres y México interests or by some of the smaller groups of the provincial cities. Even the public sector can be said to have its group, composed mainly of Nacional Financiera—the government's principal development bank—and the thirteen companies in which it has a controlling interest.

To add to the complexity, many of the groups work with others in an intricate system of alliances. Some groups work more easily with the government-controlled enterprises than do others. Some frequently operate in tandem, as in the case of the Carlos Trouyet and Raúl Bailleres groups. Others have so many interconnections that one may think of them either as separate groups or as parts of a single group, as in the case of the Banco Nacional de México and the Carlos Prieto interests.

Whatever the patterns may be, however, the motivations which have generated the patterns are clear. One such motivation is the need of businessmen for an assured source of credit. The pooling of enterprises means, in effect, that the profits of the slow growers in the group can be made available to those expanding more rapidly. It also means that the collective borrowing power of the whole group is available to any of its members; thus a group can go to foreign sources or to government credit agencies such as Nacional Financiera, and negotiate for credits on a scale which gives it a decided advantage over unconnected firms. Negotiations

[6] This is a statement to be taken on faith rather than statistics. The aggregate sales of manufacturing firms overtly identified with one or another of the known groups does not constitute a very large part of total manufacturing output, according to our estimates. But the identified firms do tend to dominate the list of the country's larger companies; and the affiliated banks of the identified firms tend to control much of Mexico's private credit resources.

are carried on not only for credits but for other purposes; indeed, another major motivation for the creation of the groups has been the general enhancement of bargaining power vis-à-vis the government. The fact that a central core of entrepreneurs could call on the resources of a number of enterprises has meant that proposals to the government could be put together, modified, or expanded to achieve the most favorable possible reception. For example, the ability of the group to command large resources means, as it does in most countries, that the government's contracting agents look more benignly on a bid for public business from some enterprise in the group. If the group is trying to obtain import permits for an oversized drill press or for supplies of stainless steel, its offer to have an affiliate produce some intermediate product for a government-owned plant may create an important friend in court. If an enterprise in the group is faced with the need to use scarce Mexican materials in a manufacturing process in order to qualify for a tax exemption under the law, its ability to command those materials from a related company gives it an important advantage. And so on.

In short, in a manner which suggests the operation of the Galbraithian doctrine of countervailing power, the industries of Mexico have tended to group themselves in a way which permits them to deal more effectively with the Goliath represented by the Mexican government.

One final aspect of the private sector of Mexico's economy needs to be introduced at this point, namely, the influence of foreigners in the economy's operation and control. Most Mexicans are extraordinarily sensitive on the subject, for reasons which will become perfectly clear to the reader as he works his way through the chapters that follow. The existence of that sensitivity makes the facts more than usually difficult to come by. Nevertheless, the situation is clear on a number of points, which we shall summarize here and elaborate in later chapters.

The pervasive influence of United States consumer tastes and United States technology is evident throughout the Mexican economy. United States brand names and United States designs are paraded before the Mexican public through publications, moving pictures, tourism, and a dozen other channels. United States technology flows into the country through the *ad hoc* visits of outside technicians, through formal technical assistance or licensing contracts, and through the channels established between subsidiaries and their parent companies.

Actual foreign control of Mexican private enterprise, however, is far more limited than foreign influence of the sort just discussed. In agriculture, one would not be risking much if he were to surmise that a certain amount of United States capital has been quietly invested in the lands devoted to Mexican export crops—such as cotton, tomatoes, and cattle—in the northern states close to the United States border. But outside these areas, foreign ownership in agriculture is probably of very little importance. In mining, electric power, and transportation, the facts are easier to verify; foreign ownership, which once dominated all these sectors, is being squeezed back to a minority position in mining and has been practically extinguished in the others. Only in manufacturing is foreign ownership and control of much significance. Here, as one scans the list of major Mexican manufacturing companies, there is no question that a significant proportion is controlled by foreign interests, principally United States interests. In terms of output, the United States-controlled manufacturing companies probably account for something on the order of one fifth or one sixth of total Mexican production in the manufacturing sector; but since the foreign-controlled activity tends to be concentrated in well-known nationally distributed products, the general impression is one of even greater foreign dominance. This dominance—its continuation, its expansion, its reduction, or its suppression—is never far from the center of the stage in the interplay between the public and the private sectors.

The Confrontation

In a country whose private sector accounts for more than nine tenths of its output, the question of the interplay with the public sector may not seem of transcendental importance. The importance of the subject is fully appreciated only when we recognize that Mexico's government takes a major hand in rationing the supply of three factors which are perennially scarce at this stage of Mexico's growth, to wit, credits, imports, and public facilities.

The scramble for long-term and short-term credits is one of the critical activities of any entrepreneur in Mexico, a life-and-death matter in any growing enterprise. But the Mexican government's control of such credits is pervasive, selective, and particularistic. The government's interest in credits begins with its desire to reserve a certain part of the available supply for the financing of public investment. Then, it tries to channel what is left into activities of the private economy which it considers of high priority, while choking off the flow to "nonproductive" pursuits. In the "high priority" category, for instance, one would usually find industry and agriculture, and in the "nonproductive" category, the construction of high-cost housing and the financing of commodity inventories. Beyond these objectives—reserving credits to the public sector and channeling the rest to "productive pursuits"—the government has still another objective in sitting astride the flow of credits, namely, that of holding down foreign claims and foreign investment in the Mexican economy. To thread one's way through the resulting system of government roadblocks, regulations, and incentives in the field of credit, therefore, becomes an absorbing problem of management.

In the regulation of imports, the stakes are often just as critical to the existence of the private sector. Though imports account for no more than one fifth of the total goods consumed in the country, there is scarcely a major branch of Mexican industry or agriculture which is not affected directly and significantly by the government's import policy. The government uses its powers in the field of foreign trade with vigor and flexibility. It "closes the border" to any product whenever it believes that the public interest would be served by such action. And it raises or lowers official import duties with unusual frequency indeed, whenever the government sees fit, it exempts selected importers from duties while continuing to apply the duties to other importers.

The motivations behind these measures are neither simple nor invariant. They include the desire to stimulate the domestic production of consumer goods; to force existing Mexican producers toward greater use of Mexican materials and machinery; to conserve scarce foreign exchange; to increase government revenue from customs duties; to raise prices on some products and lower them on others, in order to force an internal redistribution of income; to discourage foreign investors and encourage domestic ones inside the country; and so on. The objectives continually change and clash as the situation of the country and the strategy of the government evolve. Scarce wonder that the representatives of the private sector are always preoccupied with the puzzling question of the government's import policy and looking for a path through the maze.

The parceling out of scarce public facilities is the third critical area in the relations between the public and private sectors. At times, the initiative for securing government action comes from existing enterprises; at other times, the initiative comes from the government in the expectation that the facilities will generate new lines of economic activity. Spectacular illustrations are easy to find. The development of the cotton crop of Mexico has depended almost entirely upon the decisions of the Mexican government on whether to build irrigation works and where to place them. The scale and location of Mexico's industry have been influenced critically by the government's decisions on the structure of Mexico's power rates and on the location of Mexico's power and transportation facilities. Once again, the ability to penetrate the structure of the government's decision-making machinery has been decisive in the fortunes of much of Mexico's private sector.

Of course, much of what has been said so far about the importance of the interrelations between the public and private sectors in Mexico could be said with some measure of validity for any modern nation in the world. If there are differences between Mexico and other nations, they stem largely from two related features of the Mexican government's regulatory activities: first, the relative pervasiveness and vigor of the government's regulatory measures; second, the extraordinary degree of particularity and discrimination in the application of those regulatory powers. Enough has already been said to offer a glimpse of the ubiquitousness of the Mexican government's directive efforts. But a word or two may still be in order on the subject of particularity and discrimination.

No writer can free himself altogether from the taint of ethnocentricity. And a writer from the United States cannot avoid being impressed— perhaps overly impressed—with what appear to be fundamental differences in the approach to government regulation as between the two countries. Most federal law and regulation in the United States operate from the premise that there are objective standards to be applied, indeed guaranteed, on a nondiscriminatory basis to all comers. Of course, the actual performance is sometimes at variance with the ideal, as graft, favoritism, and error creep into the administrative machinery; but the ideal persists as a living, operating norm.

Mexican administration, on the other hand, places less emphasis upon the rights and guarantees of the individual, and more emphasis upon the discretionary rights of the state, acting as the agent of the public interest. Therefore fewer cases are decided automatically by general rule and more are determined by specific *ad hoc* decisions. This, in turn, means that the degree of predictability and uniformity of the government's treatment of its citizens tends to be lower than in, say, the United States. Importer A may find his import duties waived on a particular product, but Importer B may not. Foreigner X may be required to sell a half interest in his firm to Mexican investors, but Foreigner Y may continue to hold the full equity in his operation. The cotton crop of the State of Nuevo León may be assessed an export duty of 22 per cent, but that of the State of Sonora may be taxed only 10 per cent. Price control may be imposed and enforced on one critical drug, but price control of another critical drug may be nonexistent. The differences in treatment may be justifiable under the criteria being used by the government—or they may not. The important point is that the private sector operates in a milieu in which the public sector is in a position to make or break any private firm.

At the same time, the style of Mexican politics and Mexican government operations is such that there is continual personal contact between government officials and businessmen. There is no wide ideological barrier, no explosively sensitive public opinion which demands that contact be only at arm's length. The atmosphere varies, of course, from one government agency to another, and from one presidential regime to the next. But it would be wrong to think of Mexico as a battleground on which the public sector and private enterprise are belligerently arrayed. It is altogether possible for Nacional Financiera to arrange a major financing operation jointly with some powerful private financial group, and for the Compañía Nacional de Subsistencias Populares—the government food-marketing agency—to enter into extensive arrangements with the private food-distribution industry. Frictions, suspicions, and uncertainties exist, to be sure, but they are not so great as to paralyze participation by either sector.

It would be conceivable at this point to frame the obvious syllogism and to close the book: Mexico has developed its own special system of relationships between the public and private sectors; Mexico has grown substantially over the past several decades; therefore the Mexican system of public-private relationships, at the very least, is not inconsistent with satisfactory growth.

But even this timid and tentative conclusion could well be wrong. For the Mexican institutions of today are different in many ways from those that existed twenty years ago and strikingly different from those of the pre-Revolutionary era. As a result, all kinds of alternative propositions suggest themselves. Could it be that the growth of Mexico in the modern era is based upon the impetus generated by its public and private institutional structures of earlier decades, rather than by the present structure? Can the country's modern growth be taking place despite drawbacks in the existing structure, rather than because of that structure? Is the recent slowdown in growth perhaps a reflection of inadequacies in the structure, and a forerunner of greater difficulties in the future? To get the glimmerings of answers to questions such as these, one needs to go at least a century back into Mexican history.

Suggested Reading

I. General

Atwater, Elton, Forster, Kent, and Prybyla, Jan S., *World Tensions: Conflict and Accommodation* (New York, Appleton-Century-Crofts, 1967), especially Chapter 6 ("Economic Underdevelopment and Competing Economic Systems") and Chapter 7 ("Democracy, Communism, and the Conflict of Method").

Ayres, C. E., *The Theory of Economic Progress*, 2nd ed. (New York, Schocken Books, 1962).

Bachmann, Hans, *The External Relations of Less-Developed Countries: A Manual of Economic Policies* (New York, Praeger, 1967).

Bergson, Abram, "The Great Economic Race," *Challenge*, the Magazine of Economic Affairs, March 1963.

Friedman, Milton, "Foreign Economic Aid: Means and Objectives," *The Yale Review*, Summer 1958.

Galbraith, John Kenneth, *Economic Development* (Boston, Houghton Mifflin, 1964), especially Chapter III ("The Choice").

Gross, Bertram M., *Action Under Planning: The Guidance of Economic Development* (New York, McGraw-Hill, 1967).

Millikan, Max F., and Blackmer, Donald L. M. (eds.), *The Emerging Nations: Their Growth and United States Policy* (Boston, Little Brown, 1961), especially Chapter 1 ("The Traditional Society"), Chapter 2 ("The Disruption of Traditional Societies"), Chapter 7 ("The Third Choice").

Muscat, Robert J., "Growth and the Free Market: Case Study in Thailand," *The Malayan Economic Review*, Vol. XI, No. 1 (April 1966).

Myrdal, Gunnar, "A Note on 'Accounting Prices' and the Role of the Price Mechanism in Planning for Development," *The Swedish Journal of Economics*, Vol. 68, No. 3 (September 1966).

Nove, Alec, *The Soviet Economy: An Introduction* (New York, Praeger, 1961), especially the section entitled "A Model for Underdeveloped Countries?" pp. 303–306.

Shaffer, Harry G., and Prybyla, Jan S. (eds.), *From Underdevelopment to Affluence: Western, Soviet, and Chinese Views* (New York, Appleton-Century-Crofts, 1968).

Sinai, I. Robert, *The Challenge of Modernisation: The West's Impact on the Non-Western World* (New York, Norton, 1964).

II. Mexico

Freihalter, William O., *Mexico's Foreign Trade and Economic Development* (New York, Praeger, 1967).

Shafer, Robert Jones, *Mexico: Mutual Adjustment Planning* (Syracuse, N. Y., Syracuse University Press, National Planning Series, No. 4, 1966).

Wilkie, James W., *The Mexican Revolution: Federal Expenditure and Social Change Since 1910* (Berkeley, University of California Press, 1967).

Index